50% OFF Online ACT Prep Course!

Dear Customer,

We consider it an honor and a privilege that you chose our ACT Study Guide. As a way of showing our appreciation and to help us better serve you, we have partnered with Mometrix Test Preparation to offer you **50% off their online ACT Course.** Many ACT courses are needlessly expensive and don't deliver enough value. With their course, you get access to the best ACT prep material, and you only pay half price.

Mometrix has structured their online course to perfectly complement your printed study guide. The ACT Online Course contains **in-depth lessons** that cover all the most important topics, **180+ video reviews** that explain difficult concepts, over **1,500 practice questions** to ensure you feel prepared, and more than **500 digital flashcards**, so you can study while you're on the go.

Online ACT Prep Course

Topics Covered:

- English
  - Foundations of Grammar
  - Agreement and Sentence Structure
  - Topic Development
- Math
  - Algebra
  - Geometry
  - Statistics and Probability
- Reading
  - Key Ideas and Details
  - Craft and Structure
  - Integration of Knowledge and Ideas
- Science
  - Life Science
  - Chemistry
  - Physics
- Writing
  - Overview of Writing

Course Features:

- ACT Study Guide
  - Get content that complements our best-selling study guide.
- Full-Length Practice Tests
  - With over 1,500 practice questions, you can test yourself again and again.
- Mobile Friendly
  - If you need to study on the go, the course is easily accessible from your mobile device.
- Praxis Core Flashcards
  - Their course includes a flashcards mode with over 500 content cards for you to study.

To receive this discount, visit their website: mometrix.com/university/act and add the course to your cart. At the checkout page, enter the discount code: **TPBACT50**

If you have any questions or concerns, please contact them at universityhelp@mometrix.com.

Sincerely,

SCAN HERE

 in partnership with

FREE Test Taking Tips Video/DVD Offer

To better serve you, we created videos covering test taking tips that we want to give you for FREE. **These videos cover world-class tips that will help you succeed on your test.**

We just ask that you send us feedback about this product. Please let us know what you thought about it—whether good, bad, or indifferent.

To get your **FREE videos**, you can use the QR code below or email freevideos@studyguideteam.com with "Free Videos" in the subject line and the following information in the body of the email:

    a. The title of your product

    b. Your product rating on a scale of 1-5, with 5 being the highest

    c. Your feedback about the product

If you have any questions or concerns, please don't hesitate to contact us at info@studyguideteam.com.

Thank you!

ACT Prep Book 2022-2023 with Practice Tests

650+ Exam Questions & ACT Study Guide
[8th Edition]

Joshua Rueda

Interested in buying more than 10 copies of our product? Contact us about bulk discounts:
bulkorders@studyguideteam.com

ISBN 13: 9781637755839
ISBN 10: 163775583X

Table of Contents

Quick Overview -- 1

Test-Taking Strategies --- 2

FREE Videos/DVD OFFER --- 6

Introduction to the ACT --- 7

Study Prep Plan for the ACT --- 9

Math Reference Sheet -- 11

ACT English Test -- 12

What to Expect -- 12

Tips for the English Test -- 12

Production of Writing --- 12

Knowledge of Language --- 18

Conventions of Standard English --- 24

Practice Quiz -- 37

Answer Explanations --- 39

ACT Mathematics Test --- 40

What to Expect -- 40

Tips -- 40

Number and Quantity --- 40

Algebra --- 68

Functions --- 91

Geometry --- 112

Statistics and Probability --- 137

Integrating Essential Skills --- 141

Practice Quiz ----- 153

Answer Explanations ----- 155

ACT Reading Test -----157

What to Expect ----- 157

Tips for the Reading Test ----- 157

Key Ideas and Details ----- 157

Craft and Structure ----- 165

Integration of Knowledge and Ideas ----- 175

Practice Quiz ----- 188

Answer Explanations ----- 190

ACT Science Test -----191

Interpretation of Data ----- 191

Scientific Investigation ----- 198

Evaluation of Models, Inferences, and Experimental Results ----- 205

Types of Passages and Tips ----- 211

Practice Quiz ----- 221

Answer Explanations ----- 224

ACT Writing Test -----225

What to Expect ----- 225

Keys to Good Writing ----- 225

On Test Day ----- 226

Writing Prompt -----229

Writing ----- 229

ACT Practice Test #1 -----230

English ----- 230

Math ----- 251

Reading --- 261

Science --- 272

Writing --- 290

Answer Explanations #1 --292

English --- 292

Math -- 299

Reading --- 308

Science --- 313

ACT Practice Test #2 ---318

English --- 318

Math -- 339

Reading --- 352

Science --- 362

Writing --- 379

Answer Explanations #2 --381

English --- 381

Math -- 389

Reading --- 399

Science --- 404

ACT Practice Test #3 ---409

English --- 409

Math -- 432

Reading --- 445

Science --- 456

Writing --- 483

Answer Explanations #3 --485

//Test Prep Books!!!

English--- 485

Math-- 492

Reading--- 504

Science --- 509

//Test Prep Books!!!

Quick Overview

As you draw closer to taking your exam, effective preparation becomes more and more important. Thankfully, you have this study guide to help you get ready. Use this guide to help keep your studying on track and refer to it often.

This study guide contains several key sections that will help you be successful on your exam. The guide contains tips for what you should do the night before and the day of the test. Also included are test-taking tips. Knowing the right information is not always enough. Many well-prepared test takers struggle with exams. These tips will help equip you to accurately read, assess, and answer test questions.

A large part of the guide is devoted to showing you what content to expect on the exam and to helping you better understand that content. In this guide are practice test questions so that you can see how well you have grasped the content. Then, answer explanations are provided so that you can understand why you missed certain questions.

Don't try to cram the night before you take your exam. This is not a wise strategy for a few reasons. First, your retention of the information will be low. Your time would be better used by reviewing information you already know rather than trying to learn a lot of new information. Second, you will likely become stressed as you try to gain a large amount of knowledge in a short amount of time. Third, you will be depriving yourself of sleep. So be sure to go to bed at a reasonable time the night before. Being well-rested helps you focus and remain calm.

Be sure to eat a substantial breakfast the morning of the exam. If you are taking the exam in the afternoon, be sure to have a good lunch as well. Being hungry is distracting and can make it difficult to focus. You have hopefully spent lots of time preparing for the exam. Don't let an empty stomach get in the way of success!

When travelling to the testing center, leave earlier than needed. That way, you have a buffer in case you experience any delays. This will help you remain calm and will keep you from missing your appointment time at the testing center.

Be sure to pace yourself during the exam. Don't try to rush through the exam. There is no need to risk performing poorly on the exam just so you can leave the testing center early. Allow yourself to use all of the allotted time if needed.

Remain positive while taking the exam even if you feel like you are performing poorly. Thinking about the content you should have mastered will not help you perform better on the exam.

Once the exam is complete, take some time to relax. Even if you feel that you need to take the exam again, you will be well served by some down time before you begin studying again. It's often easier to convince yourself to study if you know that it will come with a reward!

Test-Taking Strategies

1. Predicting the Answer

When you feel confident in your preparation for a multiple-choice test, try predicting the answer before reading the answer choices. This is especially useful on questions that test objective factual knowledge. By predicting the answer before reading the available choices, you eliminate the possibility that you will be distracted or led astray by an incorrect answer choice. You will feel more confident in your selection if you read the question, predict the answer, and then find your prediction among the answer choices. After using this strategy, be sure to still read all of the answer choices carefully and completely. If you feel unprepared, you should not attempt to predict the answers. This would be a waste of time and an opportunity for your mind to wander in the wrong direction.

2. Reading the Whole Question

Too often, test takers scan a multiple-choice question, recognize a few familiar words, and immediately jump to the answer choices. Test authors are aware of this common impatience, and they will sometimes prey upon it. For instance, a test author might subtly turn the question into a negative, or he or she might redirect the focus of the question right at the end. The only way to avoid falling into these traps is to read the entirety of the question carefully before reading the answer choices.

3. Looking for Wrong Answers

Long and complicated multiple-choice questions can be intimidating. One way to simplify a difficult multiple-choice question is to eliminate all of the answer choices that are clearly wrong. In most sets of answers, there will be at least one selection that can be dismissed right away. If the test is administered on paper, the test taker could draw a line through it to indicate that it may be ignored; otherwise, the test taker will have to perform this operation mentally or on scratch paper. In either case, once the obviously incorrect answers have been eliminated, the remaining choices may be considered. Sometimes identifying the clearly wrong answers will give the test taker some information about the correct answer. For instance, if one of the remaining answer choices is a direct opposite of one of the eliminated answer choices, it may well be the correct answer. The opposite of obviously wrong is obviously right! Of course, this is not always the case. Some answers are obviously incorrect simply because they are irrelevant to the question being asked. Still, identifying and eliminating some incorrect answer choices is a good way to simplify a multiple-choice question.

4. Don't Overanalyze

Anxious test takers often overanalyze questions. When you are nervous, your brain will often run wild, causing you to make associations and discover clues that don't actually exist. If you feel that this may be a problem for you, do whatever you can to slow down during the test. Try taking a deep breath or counting to ten. As you read and consider the question, restrict yourself to the particular words used by the author. Avoid thought tangents about what the author *really* meant, or what he or she was *trying* to say. The only things that matter on a multiple-choice test are the words that are actually in the question. You must avoid reading too much into a multiple-choice question, or supposing that the writer meant something other than what he or she wrote.

5. No Need for Panic

It is wise to learn as many strategies as possible before taking a multiple-choice test, but it is likely that you will come across a few questions for which you simply don't know the answer. In this situation, avoid panicking. Because most multiple-choice tests include dozens of questions, the relative value of a single wrong answer is small. As much as possible, you should compartmentalize each question on a multiple-choice test. In other words, you should not allow your feelings about one question to affect your success on the others. When you find a question that you either don't understand or don't know how to answer, just take a deep breath and do your best. Read the entire question slowly and carefully. Try rephrasing the question a couple of different ways. Then, read all of the answer choices carefully. After eliminating obviously wrong answers, make a selection and move on to the next question.

6. Confusing Answer Choices

When working on a difficult multiple-choice question, there may be a tendency to focus on the answer choices that are the easiest to understand. Many people, whether consciously or not, gravitate to the answer choices that require the least concentration, knowledge, and memory. This is a mistake. When you come across an answer choice that is confusing, you should give it extra attention. A question might be confusing because you do not know the subject matter to which it refers. If this is the case, don't eliminate the answer before you have affirmatively settled on another. When you come across an answer choice of this type, set it aside as you look at the remaining choices. If you can confidently assert that one of the other choices is correct, you can leave the confusing answer aside. Otherwise, you will need to take a moment to try to better understand the confusing answer choice. Rephrasing is one way to tease out the sense of a confusing answer choice.

7. Your First Instinct

Many people struggle with multiple-choice tests because they overthink the questions. If you have studied sufficiently for the test, you should be prepared to trust your first instinct once you have carefully and completely read the question and all of the answer choices. There is a great deal of research suggesting that the mind can come to the correct conclusion very quickly once it has obtained all of the relevant information. At times, it may seem to you as if your intuition is working faster even than your reasoning mind. This may in fact be true. The knowledge you obtain while studying may be retrieved from your subconscious before you have a chance to work out the associations that support it. Verify your instinct by working out the reasons that it should be trusted.

8. Key Words

Many test takers struggle with multiple-choice questions because they have poor reading comprehension skills. Quickly reading and understanding a multiple-choice question requires a mixture of skill and experience. To help with this, try jotting down a few key words and phrases on a piece of scrap paper. Doing this concentrates the process of reading and forces the mind to weigh the relative importance of the question's parts. In selecting words and phrases to write down, the test taker thinks about the question more deeply and carefully. This is especially true for multiple-choice questions that are preceded by a long prompt.

9. Subtle Negatives

One of the oldest tricks in the multiple-choice test writer's book is to subtly reverse the meaning of a question with a word like *not* or *except*. If you are not paying attention to each word in the question, you can easily be led astray by this trick. For instance, a common question format is, "Which of the following is...?" Obviously, if the question instead is, "Which of the following is not...?," then the answer will be quite different. Even worse, the test makers are aware of the potential for this mistake and will include one answer choice that would be correct if the question were not negated or reversed. A test taker who misses the reversal will find what he or she believes to be a correct answer and will be so confident that he or she will fail to reread the question and discover the original error. The only way to avoid this is to practice a wide variety of multiple-choice questions and to pay close attention to each and every word.

10. Reading Every Answer Choice

It may seem obvious, but you should always read every one of the answer choices! Too many test takers fall into the habit of scanning the question and assuming that they understand the question because they recognize a few key words. From there, they pick the first answer choice that answers the question they believe they have read. Test takers who read all of the answer choices might discover that one of the latter answer choices is actually *more* correct. Moreover, reading all of the answer choices can remind you of facts related to the question that can help you arrive at the correct answer. Sometimes, a misstatement or incorrect detail in one of the latter answer choices will trigger your memory of the subject and will enable you to find the right answer. Failing to read all of the answer choices is like not reading all of the items on a restaurant menu: you might miss out on the perfect choice.

11. Spot the Hedges

One of the keys to success on multiple-choice tests is paying close attention to every word. This is never truer than with words like almost, most, some, and sometimes. These words are called "hedges" because they indicate that a statement is not totally true or not true in every place and time. An absolute statement will contain no hedges, but in many subjects, the answers are not always straightforward or absolute. There are always exceptions to the rules in these subjects. For this reason, you should favor those multiple-choice questions that contain hedging language. The presence of qualifying words indicates that the author is taking special care with their words, which is certainly important when composing the right answer. After all, there are many ways to be wrong, but there is only one way to be right! For this reason, it is wise to avoid answers that are absolute when taking a multiple-choice test. An absolute answer is one that says things are either all one way or all another. They often include words like *every*, *always*, *best*, and *never*. If you are taking a multiple-choice test in a subject that doesn't lend itself to absolute answers, be on your guard if you see any of these words.

12. Long Answers

In many subject areas, the answers are not simple. As already mentioned, the right answer often requires hedges. Another common feature of the answers to a complex or subjective question are qualifying clauses, which are groups of words that subtly modify the meaning of the sentence. If the question or answer choice describes a rule to which there are exceptions or the subject matter is complicated, ambiguous, or confusing, the correct answer will require many words in order to be expressed clearly and accurately. In essence, you should not be deterred by answer choices that seem

4

excessively long. Oftentimes, the author of the text will not be able to write the correct answer without offering some qualifications and modifications. Your job is to read the answer choices thoroughly and completely and to select the one that most accurately and precisely answers the question.

13. Restating to Understand

Sometimes, a question on a multiple-choice test is difficult not because of what it asks but because of how it is written. If this is the case, restate the question or answer choice in different words. This process serves a couple of important purposes. First, it forces you to concentrate on the core of the question. In order to rephrase the question accurately, you have to understand it well. Rephrasing the question will concentrate your mind on the key words and ideas. Second, it will present the information to your mind in a fresh way. This process may trigger your memory and render some useful scrap of information picked up while studying.

14. True Statements

Sometimes an answer choice will be true in itself, but it does not answer the question. This is one of the main reasons why it is essential to read the question carefully and completely before proceeding to the answer choices. Too often, test takers skip ahead to the answer choices and look for true statements. Having found one of these, they are content to select it without reference to the question above. Obviously, this provides an easy way for test makers to play tricks. The savvy test taker will always read the entire question before turning to the answer choices. Then, having settled on a correct answer choice, he or she will refer to the original question and ensure that the selected answer is relevant. The mistake of choosing a correct-but-irrelevant answer choice is especially common on questions related to specific pieces of objective knowledge. A prepared test taker will have a wealth of factual knowledge at their disposal, and should not be careless in its application.

15. No Patterns

One of the more dangerous ideas that circulates about multiple-choice tests is that the correct answers tend to fall into patterns. These erroneous ideas range from a belief that B and C are the most common right answers, to the idea that an unprepared test-taker should answer "A-B-A-C-A-D-A-B-A." It cannot be emphasized enough that pattern-seeking of this type is exactly the WRONG way to approach a multiple-choice test. To begin with, it is highly unlikely that the test maker will plot the correct answers according to some predetermined pattern. The questions are scrambled and delivered in a random order. Furthermore, even if the test maker was following a pattern in the assignation of correct answers, there is no reason why the test taker would know which pattern he or she was using. Any attempt to discern a pattern in the answer choices is a waste of time and a distraction from the real work of taking the test. A test taker would be much better served by extra preparation before the test than by reliance on a pattern in the answers.

FREE Videos/DVD OFFER

Doing well on your exam requires both knowing the test content and understanding how to use that knowledge to do well on the test. We offer completely FREE test taking tip videos. **These videos cover world-class tips that you can use to succeed on your test.**

To get your **FREE videos**, you can use the QR code below or email freevideos@studyguideteam.com with "Free Videos" in the subject line and the following information in the body of the email:

   a. The title of your product

   b. Your product rating on a scale of 1-5, with 5 being the highest

   c. Your feedback about the product

If you have any questions or concerns, please don't hesitate to contact us at info@studyguideteam.com.

Thanks again!

Introduction to the ACT

Function of the Test

The ACT is one of two national standardized college entrance examinations (the SAT being the other). Most prospective college students take the ACT or the SAT, and it is increasingly common for students to take both. All four-year colleges and universities in the United States accept the ACT for admissions purposes, and some require it. Some of those schools also use ACT subject scores for placement purposes. Sixteen states also require all high school juniors to take the ACT as part of the states' school evaluation efforts.

The vast majority of people taking the ACT are high school juniors and seniors who intend to apply to college. Traditionally, the SAT was more commonly taken than the ACT, particularly among students on the East and West coasts. However, the popularity of the ACT has grown dramatically in recent years and is now commonly taken by students in all fifty states. In fact, starting in 2013, more test takers took the ACT than the SAT. In 2015, 1.92 million students took the ACT. About 28 percent of 2015 high school graduates taking the ACT met the test's college-readiness benchmarks in all four subjects, while 31 percent met none of the benchmarks.

Test Administration

The ACT is offered on six dates throughout the year in the U.S. and Canada, and on five of those same dates in other countries. The registration fee includes score reports for four colleges, with additional reports available for purchase. There is a separate registration fee for the optional writing section.

On test dates, the ACT is administered at test centers throughout the world. The test centers are usually high schools or colleges, with several locations usually available in significant population centers.

Test takers can retake the ACT as frequently as the test is offered, up to a maximum of twelve times; although, individual colleges may have limits on how many retakes they will consider. Starting September 2020, test takers can opt to take individual subsections during a retake attempt rather than needing to retake the entire exam.

The ACT does provide reasonable accommodations to test takers with professionally-documented disabilities.

Test Format

The ACT consists of 215 multiple-choice questions in four subject areas (English, mathematics, reading, and science) and takes about three hours and thirty minutes to complete. It also has an optional writing test, which takes an additional forty minutes.

The English section is 45 minutes long and contains 75 questions on usage, language mechanics, and rhetorical skills. The Mathematics section is 60 minutes long and contains 60 questions on algebra, geometry, and elementary trigonometry. Calculators that meet the ACT's calculator policy are permitted on the Mathematics section. The Reading section is 35 minutes long and contains four written passages with ten questions per passage. The Science section is 35 minutes long and contains 40 questions.

The Writing section is forty minutes long and is always given at the end so that test takers not wishing to take it may leave after completing the other four sections. This section consists of one essay in which students must analyze three different perspectives on a broad social issue. Although the Writing section is optional, some colleges do require it.

Section	Length	Questions
English	45 minutes	75
Mathematics	60 minutes	60
Reading	35 minutes	40
Science	35 minutes	40
Writing (optional)	40 minutes	1 essay

Scoring

Test takers receive a score between 1 and 36 for each of the four subject areas. Those scores are averaged together to give a Composite Score, which is the primary score reported as an "ACT score." The most prestigious schools typically admit students with Composite ACT Scores in the low 30's. Other selective schools typically admit students with scores in the high 20's. Traditional colleges more likely admit students with scores in the low 20's, while community colleges and other more open schools typically accept students with scores in the high teens. In 2015, the average composite score among all test takers (including those not applying to college) was 21.

Before September 2020, any test takers who opted to retake the ACT had to retake the entire exam; moreover, the composite score was calculated from the scores achieved over a single testing session. As of September 2020, test takers can select individual sections to retake. Additionally, a "superscore" will be calculated, and will reflect the test taker's highest scores on each of the subsections from any of their attempts at the test. For example, if the test taker took the test twice and earned a higher score on Math and English during the first administration, and a higher score on Reading, Science, and Writing the second time, the "superscore" would be the sum of these top performances.

8

Study Prep Plan for the ACT

1   **Schedule -** Use one of our study schedules below or come up with one of your own.

2   **Relax -** Test anxiety can hurt even the best students. There are many ways to reduce stress. Find the one that works best for you.

3   **Execute -** Once you have a good plan in place, be sure to stick to it.

One Week Study Schedule

Day 1	ACT English Test
Day 2	Algebra
Day 3	Geometry
Day 4	ACT Reading Test
Day 5	ACT Science Test
Day 6	ACT Practice Test #1
Day 7	Take Your Exam!

Two Week Study Schedule

Day 1	ACT English Test	Day 8	Integration of Knowledge and Ideas
Day 2	ACT Mathematics Test	Day 9	ACT Science Test
Day 3	Algebra	Day 10	Types of Passages and Tips
Day 4	Functions	Day 11	ACT Practice Test #1
Day 5	Geometry	Day 12	ACT Practice Test #2
Day 6	Statistics and Probability	Day 13	ACT Practice Test #3
Day 7	ACT Reading Test	Day 14	Take Your Exam!

One Month Study Schedule					
Day 1	ACT English Test	Day 11	Geometry	Day 21	Evaluation of Models, Inferences, and...
Day 2	Knowledge of Language	Day 12	Surface Area and Volume	Day 22	Types of Passages and Tips
Day 3	Conventions of Standard English	Day 13	Translating Between a Geometric...	Day 23	ACT Writing Test
Day 4	ACT Mathematics Test	Day 14	Statistics and Probability	Day 24	ACT Practice Test #1
Day 5	Adding and Subtracting Positive...	Day 15	Integrating Essential Skills	Day 25	Answer Explanations for Practice Test #1
Day 6	Factorization	Day 16	ACT Reading Test	Day 26	ACT Practice Test #2
Day 7	Algebra	Day 17	Craft and Structure	Day 27	Answer Explanations for Practice Test #2
Day 8	Linear Inequalities in One Variable	Day 18	Integration of Knowledge and Ideas	Day 28	ACT Practice Test #3
Day 9	Functions	Day 19	ACT Science Test	Day 29	Answer Explanations for Practice Test #3
Day 10	Piecewise Functions	Day 20	Scientific Investigation	Day 30	Take Your Exam!

Build your own prep plan by visiting:
testprepbooks.com/prep

Math Reference Sheet

Symbol	Phrase
+	added to, increased by, sum of, more than
-	decreased by, difference between, less than, take away
×	multiplied by, 3 (4, 5 . . .) times as large, product of
÷	divided by, quotient of, half (third, etc.) of
=	is, the same as, results in, as much as
x, t, n, etc.	a variable which is an unknown value or quantity
<	is under, is below, smaller than, beneath
>	is above, is over, bigger than, exceeds
≤	no more than, at most, maximum; less than or equal to
≥	no less than, at least, minimum; greater than or equal to
√	square root of, exponent divided by 2

Geometry	Description
$P = 2l + 2w$	for perimeter of a rectangle
$P = 4 \times s$	for perimeter of a square
$P = a + b + c$	for perimeter of a triangle
$A = \frac{1}{2} \times b \times h = \frac{bh}{2}$	for area of a triangle
$A = b \times h$	for area of a parallelogram
$A = \frac{1}{2} \times h(b_1 + b_2)$	for area of a trapezoid
$A = \frac{1}{2} \times a \times P$	for area of a regular polygon
$C = 2 \times \pi \times r$	for circumference (perimeter) of a circle
$A = \pi \times r^2$	for area of a circle
$c^2 = a^2 + b^2; c = \sqrt{a^2 + b^2}$	for finding the hypotenuse of a right triangle
$SA = 2xy + 2yz + 2xz$	for finding surface area
$V = \frac{1}{3}xyh$	for finding volume of a rectangular pyramid
$V = \frac{4}{3}\pi r^3; \frac{1}{3}\pi r^2 h; \pi r^2 h$	for volume of a sphere; a cone; and a cylinder

Radical Expressions	Description
$\sqrt[n]{a} = a^{\frac{1}{n}}; \sqrt[n]{a^m} = (\sqrt[n]{a})^m = a^{\frac{m}{n}}$	a is the radicand, n is the index, m is the exponent
$\sqrt{x^2} = (x^2)^{\frac{1}{2}} = x$	to convert square root to exponent
$a^m \times a^n = a^{m+n}$	multiplying radicands with exponents
$(a^m)^n = a^{m \times n}$	multiplying exponents
$(a \times b)^m = a^m \times b^m$	parentheses with exponents

Property	Addition	Multiplication
Commutative	$a + b = b + a$	$a \times b = b \times a$
Associative	$(a + b) + c = a + (b + c)$	$(a \times b) \times c = a \times (b \times c)$
Identity	$a + 0 = a; 0 + a = a$	$a \times 1 = a; 1 \times a = a$
Inverse	$a + (-a) = 0$	$a \times \frac{1}{a} = 1; a \neq 0$
Distributive	$a(b + c) = ab + ac$	

Data	Description
Mean	equal to the total of the values of a data set, divided by the number of elements in the data set
Median	middle value in an odd number of ordered values of a data set, or the mean of the two middle values in an even number of ordered values in a data set
Mode	the value that appears most often
Range	the difference between the highest and the lowest values in the set

Graphing	Description
(x, y)	ordered pair, plot points in a graph
$y = mx + b$	slope-intercept form; m represents the slope of the line and b represents the y-intercept
$f(x)$	read as f of x, which means it is a function of x
(x_2, y_2) and (x_2, y_2)	two ordered pairs used to determine the slope of a line
$m = \frac{y_2 - y_1}{x_2 - x_1}$	to find the slope of the line, m, for ordered pairs
$Ax + By = C$	standard form of an equation, also for solving a system of equations through the elimination method
$M = (\frac{x_1 + x_2}{2}, \frac{y_1 + y_2}{2})$	for finding the midpoint of an ordered pair
$y = ax^2 + bx + c$	quadratic function for a parabola
$y = a(x - h)^2 + k$	quadratic function for a parabola with vertex
$y = ab^x; y = a \times b^x$	function for exponential curve
$y = ax^2 + bx + c$	standard form of a quadratic function
$x = \frac{-b}{2a}$	for finding axis of symmetry in a parabola; given quadratic formula in standard form
$f = \sqrt{\frac{\Sigma(x - \bar{x})^2}{n-1}}$	function for standard deviation of the sample; where $\bar{x}$ = sample mean and n = sample size

Proportions and Percentage	Description
$\frac{\text{gallons}}{\text{cost}} = \frac{\text{gallons}}{\text{cost}} : \frac{7 \text{ gallons}}{\$14.70} = \frac{x}{\$20}$	written as equal ratios with a variable representing the missing quantity
$\frac{y_1}{x_1} = \frac{y_2}{x_2}$	for direct proportions
$(y_1)(x_1) = (y_2)(x_2)$	for indirect proportions
$\frac{\text{change}}{\text{original value}} \times 100 = \text{percent change}$	for finding percentage change in value
$\frac{\text{new quantity} - \text{old quantity}}{\text{old quantity}} \times 100$	for calculating the increase or decrease in percentage

11

ACT English Test

What to Expect

The English test contains five passages that are each followed by fifteen multiple-choice questions. Therefore, overall, the section contains 75 questions, which much be answered in the allotted 45 minutes. The passages contain underlined portions (words, phrases, or sentences) that are numbered. The questions that follow the passage will pertain to the correspondingly-numbered underlined portion (for example, question 5 would pertain to the underlined text labeled 5). However, some questions pertain to the passage as a whole or a particular section of it. The answer options will provide alternatives to what is written in the underlined text in the passage; typically, answer Choice *A* will say "NO CHANGE" and should be selected when the initial text is correct as is. The content of the passages vary, but they are designed to be pulled from a variety of disciplines and topics that should interest test takers. Familiarity with the content is not important; instead, the function of the English test is to assess the candidate's editing skills and command of the English language.

Tips for the English Test

- Consider the context. When answering a question, it's important to think about how the underlined portion fits into the sentence, paragraph, and passage at large. In this way, the writing style and tone should be consistent in a given passage. Test takers should consider how the potential choices do or do not fit well within the section of the passage. For this reason, it's important to read the entire paragraph surrounding the underlined portion before jumping in and answering a given question. Failing to do so might result in context mistakes.

- Carefully read the questions to identify what element of writing is being addressed in the question. Verb tense, sentence structure, tone, etc. might all be problematic in a given underlined portion, but the question might prioritize the revision of one aspect over another. With that said, do not choose an answer choice that solves one error but creates a different one. The "correct" choice should be the best option overall.

- Double-check your choice. After selecting your answer, reread the portion of the passage with the new change to ensure it is indeed correct.

Production of Writing

Topic Development

Identifying the Position and Purpose

When it comes to an author's writing, readers should always identify a **position** or **stance**. No matter how objective a text may seem, readers should assume the author has preconceived beliefs. One can reduce the likelihood of accepting an invalid argument by looking for multiple articles on the topic, including those with varying opinions. If several opinions point in the same direction and are backed by reputable peer-reviewed sources, it's more likely that the author has a valid argument. Positions that run contrary to widely held beliefs and existing data should invite scrutiny. There are exceptions to the rule, so readers should be careful consumers of information.

While themes, symbols, and motifs are buried deep within the text and can sometimes be difficult to infer, an author's **purpose** is usually obvious from the beginning. There are four purposes of writing: to inform, to persuade, to describe, and to entertain. **Informative** writing presents facts in an accessible way. **Persuasive** writing appeals to emotions and logic to inspire the reader to adopt a specific stance. Readers should be wary of this type of writing, as it can mask a lack of objectivity with powerful emotion. **Descriptive** writing is designed to paint a picture in the reader's mind, while texts that **entertain** are often narratives designed to engage and delight the reader.

The various writing styles are usually blended, with one purpose dominating the rest. A persuasive text, for example, might begin with a humorous tale to make readers more receptive to the persuasive message, or a recipe in a cookbook designed to inform might be preceded by an entertaining anecdote that makes the recipes more appealing.

Identifying the Purposes of Parts of Texts

Writing can be classified under four passage types: narrative, expository, descriptive (sometimes called technical), and persuasive. Although these types are not mutually exclusive, one form tends to dominate the rest. By recognizing the type of passage being read, readers gain insight into how they should read. A narrative passage intended to entertain can sometimes be read more quickly if the details are discernible. A technical document, on the other hand, might require a close read because skimming the passage might cause the reader to miss salient details.

Narrative, at its core, is the art of storytelling. For a narrative to exist, certain elements must be present. First, it must have characters While many characters are human, characters can be defined as anything that thinks, acts, and talks like a human. For example, many recent movies, such as *Lord of the Rings* and *The Chronicles of Narnia*, include animals, fantastical creatures, and even trees that behave like humans. Narratives also must have a plot or sequence of events. Typically, those events follow a standard plot diagram, but recent trends start **in medias res** or in the middle (nearer the climax). In this instance, foreshadowing and flashbacks often fill in plot details. Finally, along with characters and a plot, there must also be conflict. **Conflict** is usually divided into two types: internal and external. **Internal conflict** indicates the character is in turmoil. One can imagine an angel on one shoulder and the devil on the other, arguing it out. Internal conflicts are presented through the character's thoughts. **External conflicts** are visible. Types of external conflict include person versus person, person versus nature, person versus technology, person versus the supernatural, or person versus fate.

13

Expository texts are detached and to the point, while other types of writing—persuasive, narrative, and descriptive—are livelier. Since expository writing is designed to instruct or inform, it usually involves directions and steps written in second person (the "you" voice) and lacks any persuasive or narrative elements. Sequence words such as *first*, *second*, and *third*, or *in the first place*, *secondly*, and *lastly* are often given to add fluency and cohesion. Common examples of expository writing include instructor's lessons, cookbook recipes, and repair manuals.

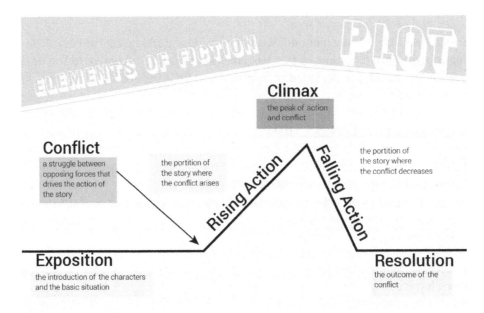

Due to its empirical nature, **technical** writing is filled with steps, charts, graphs, data, and statistics. The goal of technical writing is to advance understanding in a field through the scientific method. Experts such as teachers, doctors, or mechanics use words unique to the profession in which they operate. These words, which often incorporate acronyms, are called **jargon**. Technical writing is a type of expository writing but is not meant to be understood by the general public. Instead, technical writers assume readers have received a formal education in a particular field of study and need no explanation as to what the jargon means. One can imagine a doctor trying to understand a diagnostic reading for a car or a mechanic trying to interpret lab results. Only professionals with proper training will fully comprehend the text.

Persuasive texts are designed to change opinions and attitudes. The topic, stance, and arguments are found in the thesis, which is positioned near the end of the introduction. Later supporting paragraphs offer relevant quotations, paraphrases, and summaries from primary or secondary sources, which are then interpreted, analyzed, and evaluated. The goal of persuasive writers is not to stack quotes but to develop original ideas by using sources as a starting point. Good persuasive writing makes powerful arguments with valid sources and thoughtful analyses. Poor persuasive writing is riddled with bias and logical fallacies. Sometimes logical and illogical arguments are sandwiched together in the same text. Therefore, readers should employ skepticism when reading persuasive arguments.

Determining Whether a Text Has Met Its Intended Goal

Authors typically make it very easy for readers to identify the purpose of a passage: to entertain, inform, or persuade. The author's purpose might be determined through the formatting or organization of the text (such as through headings or a thesis statement), or through the presentation of ideas.

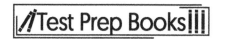

For example, if the author's purpose is to entertain, he or she might use humorous language or share a personal story. The use of personal anecdotes or experiences indicates that the intent is probably to entertain. Description is also often used in writing that seeks to entertain, although some authors choose this as a distinctive purpose. Descriptive writing paints a picture with words, and an author will use various adjectives and adverbs that entail the five senses (sight, sound, touch, smell, and taste) to do this.

If the author's purpose is to inform, the passage will likely contain facts, figures, and studies. The goal in such a passage is to educate readers; therefore, authors typically do this in a very straightforward way. The informative passage uses a clear thesis statement, which usually appears at the end of the introduction. The information will be presented in a fair, balanced manner, without the use of the author's opinion. There may be some elements of entertaining language or even a bias in the way the information is presented, but overall, the informative passage will be a clear presentation of facts.

When the author's intent is to persuade, he or she may employ other types of writing to engage the reader. There may be personal details or humorous language used to draw on the emotions of the reader. The persuasive writer might also include facts and figures to drive a point home. A persuasive passage might also present the point at the beginning, but it will most likely be in the form of a claim.

It's important for readers to be able to identify an author's purpose and determine whether the author has achieved that purpose effectively and consistently.

Evaluating the Relevance of Material in Terms of a Text's Focus

Critical reading strategies are critical for assessing what a text is saying and why the author has written it. The first step of critical reading is to determine why you are reading the text: do you need general information about a topic or are you looking for specific details? Once you determine the purpose, it will be easier to find the relevant material within the text. For example, a text that focuses on the formation of the solar system would not be particularly relevant for a research project delving into lunar eclipses here on Earth. Reading a text should bring up factual and analytical questions.

The factual questions inquire about the content and details of the text. The analytical questions should make readers think about what they learned from the text and draw conclusions about the facts they learned. The relevant material can also be understood by looking at the structure of the text. Headings, subheadings, tables, graphs, and captions can all provide information about the focus of the text. The reader should also look at whether the text is in written to describe cause and effect, a problem and a solution, or in a descriptive pattern as each method can help elucidate the important information. Lastly, the reader should summarize the material in their own words to further enhance comprehension of the text and the main takeaways from the particular text.

Organization, Unity, and Cohesion

Main Ideas and Supporting Details

Topics and main ideas are critical parts of writing. The **topic** is the subject matter of the piece. An example of a topic would be *global warming*.

The **main idea** is what the writer wants to say about that topic. A writer may make the point that global warming is a growing problem that must be addressed in order to save the planet. Therefore, the topic is global warming, and the main idea is that it's *a serious problem needing to be addressed*. The topic can be expressed in a word or two, but the main idea should be a complete thought.

An author will likely identify the topic immediately within the title or the first sentence of the passage. The main idea is usually presented in the introduction. In a single passage, the main idea may be identified in the first or last sentence, but it will most likely be directly stated and easily recognized by the reader. Because it is not always stated immediately in a passage, it's important that readers carefully read the entire passage to identify the main idea.

The main idea should not be confused with the thesis statement. A **thesis statement** is a clear statement of the writer's specific stance and can often be found in the introduction of a nonfiction piece. The thesis is a specific sentence (or two) that offers the direction and focus of the discussion.

In order to illustrate the main idea, a writer will use **supporting details**, which provide evidence or examples to help make a point. Supporting details are typically found in nonfiction pieces that seek to inform or persuade the reader.

For example, in the example of global warming, where the author's main idea is to show the seriousness of this growing problem and the need for change, supporting details would be critical for effectively making that point. Supporting details used here might include *statistics* on an increase in global temperatures and **studies** showing the impact of global warming on the planet. The author could also include **projections** for future climate change in order to illustrate potential lasting effects of global warming.

It's important that readers evaluate the author's supporting details to be sure that they are credible, provide evidence of the author's point, and directly support the main idea. Although shocking statistics grab readers' attention, their use may provide ineffective information in the piece. Details like this are crucial to understanding the passage and evaluating how well the author presents their argument and evidence.

Parts of the Essay

The **introduction** of an essay has to do a few important things:

- Establish the topic of the essay in original wording
- Clarify the significance/importance of the topic or the purpose for writing
- Offer a thesis statement that identifies the writer's own viewpoint on the topic (typically one or two brief sentences as a clear, concise explanation of the main point on the topic)

Body paragraphs reflect the ideas developed in the middle of an essay. Body paragraphs should include the following:

- A **topic sentence** that identifies the sub-point (e.g., a reason why, a way how, a cause or effect)
- A detailed **explanation** of the point, explaining why the writer thinks the point is valid
- Illustrative **examples**, such as personal examples or real-world examples, that support and validate the point (i.e., "prove" the point)
- A **concluding sentence** that connects the examples, reasoning, and analysis of the point being made

The **conclusion,** or final paragraph, should be brief and should reiterate the focus, clarifying why the discussion is significant or important. It is important that writers avoid adding specific details or new ideas to this paragraph. The purpose of the conclusion is to sum up what has been said to bring the discussion to a close.

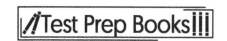

Ensuring a Text Is Logically Organized and Flows Smoothly

A text should be organized in a logical way so that it flows smoothly; ideas should be connected so that readers can follow along. In essence, the text must be coherent. Coherence is simply defined as the quality of being logical and consistent. In order to have coherent sentences, paragraphs, and completed texts, therefore, authors must be logical and consistent in their writing, whatever the document might be. Two words are helpful to understanding coherence: flow and relationship. Transitions are often referred to as being the "glue" to put organized thoughts together. Now, let's look at the topic sentence from which flow and relationship originate.

The topic sentence, usually the first in a paragraph, holds the essential features that will be brought forth in the paragraph. It is also here that authors either grab or lose readers. It may be the only writing that a reader encounters from that writer, so it is a good idea to summarize and represent ideas accurately.

The coherent paragraph has a logical order. It utilizes transitional words and phrases, parallel sentence structure, clear pronoun references, and reasonable repetition of key words and phrases. It is important to use common sense for repetition, consider synonyms for variety, and be consistent in verb tense whenever possible.

When writers have accomplished their paragraph's purpose, they prepare it to receive the next paragraph. While writing, read the paragraph over, edit, examine, evaluate, and make changes accordingly. Possibly, a paragraph has gone on too long. If that occurs, it needs to be broken up into other paragraphs, or the length should be reduced. If a paragraph didn't fully accomplish its purpose, consider revising it.

Within a paragraph, the ideal sentence length—the number of words in a sentence—depends upon the sentence's purpose.

It's okay for a sentence to be brief, and it's fine for a sentence to be lengthy. It's just important to make sure that long sentences do not become run-on sentences or too long to keep up with.

To keep writing interesting, authors should vary sentence lengths, using a mixture of short, medium and long sentences.

Finally, when considering the logical flow and organization of a text, readers should ensure that the author has made appropriate comparisons in their writing. It's easy to make mistakes in sentences that involve comparisons, and those mistakes are difficult to spot. Try to find the error in the following sentence:

Senator Wilson's proposed seat belt legislation was similar to Senator Abernathy.

Can't find it? First, ask what two things are actually being compared. It seems like the writer *wants* to compare two different types of legislation, but the sentence actually compares legislation ("Senator Wilson's proposed seat belt legislation") to a person ("Senator Abernathy"). This is a strange and illogical comparison to make.

So how can the writer correct this mistake? The answer is to make sure that the second half of the sentence logically refers back to the first half. The most obvious way to do this is to repeat words:

> Senator Wilson's proposed seat belt legislation was similar to Senator Abernathy's seat belt legislation.

Now the sentence is logically correct, but it's a little wordy and awkward. A better solution is to eliminate the word-for-word repetition by using suitable replacement words:

> Senator Wilson's proposed seat belt legislation was similar to that of Senator Abernathy.

> Senator Wilson's proposed seat belt legislation was similar to the bill offered by Senator Abernathy.

Here's another similar example:

> More lives in the U.S. are saved by seat belts than Japan.

The writer probably means to compare lives saved by seat belts in the U.S. to lives saved by seat belts in Japan. Unfortunately, the sentence's meaning is garbled by an illogical comparison, and instead refers to U.S. lives saved *by Japan* rather than *in Japan.* To resolve this issue, first repeat the words and phrases needed to make an identical comparison:

> More lives in the U.S. are saved by seat belts than lives in Japan are saved by seat belts.

Then, use a replacement word to clean up the repetitive text:

> More lives in the U.S. are saved by seat belts than in Japan.

Knowledge of Language

Precision

People often think of precision in terms of math, but precise word choice is another key to successful writing. Since language itself is imprecise, it's important for the writer to find the exact word or words to convey the full, intended meaning of a given situation. For example:

> The number of deaths has gone down since seat belt laws started.

There are several problems with this sentence. First, the word *deaths* is too general. From the context, it's assumed that the writer is referring only to deaths caused by car accidents. However, without clarification, the sentence lacks impact and is probably untrue. The phrase *gone down* might be accurate, but a more precise word would provide more information and greater accuracy. Did the numbers show a slow and steady decrease in highway fatalities or a sudden drop? If the latter is true, the writer is missing a chance to make their point more dramatically. Instead of *gone down* the author could substitute *plummeted, fallen drastically,* or *rapidly diminished* to bring the information to life. Also, the phrase *seat belt laws* is unclear. Does it refer to laws requiring cars to include seat belts or to laws requiring drivers and passengers to use them? Finally, *started* is not a strong verb. Words like *enacted* or *adopted* are more direct and make the content more real. When put together, these changes create a far more powerful sentence:

The number of highway fatalities has plummeted since laws requiring seat belt usage were enacted.

However, it's important to note that precise word choice can sometimes be taken too far. If the writer of the sentence above takes precision to an extreme, it might result in the following:

The incidence of high-speed, automobile accident-related fatalities has decreased 75% and continued to remain at historical lows since the initial set of federal legislations requiring seat belt use were enacted in 1992.

This sentence is extremely precise, but it takes so long to achieve that precision that it suffers from a lack of clarity. Precise writing is about finding the right balance between information and flow. This is also an issue of conciseness (discussed in the next section).

The last thing for writers to consider with precision is a word choice that's not only unclear or uninteresting, but also confusing or misleading. For example:

The number of highway fatalities has become hugely lower since laws requiring seat belt use were enacted.

In this case, the reader might be confused by the word *hugely*. Huge means large, but here the writer uses *hugely* in an incorrect and awkward manner. Although most readers can decipher this, doing so disconnects them from the flow of the writing and makes the writer's point less effective.

Concision

"Less is more" is a good rule for writers to follow when composing a sentence. Unfortunately, writers often include extra words and phrases that seem necessary at the time but add nothing to the main idea. This confuses the reader and creates unnecessary repetition. Writing that lacks conciseness is usually guilty of excessive wordiness and redundant phrases. Here's an example containing both of these issues:

When legislators decided to begin creating legislation making it mandatory for automobile drivers and passengers to make use of seat belts while in cars, a large number of them made those laws for reasons that were political reasons.

There are several empty or "fluff" words here that take up too much space. These can be eliminated while still maintaining the writer's meaning. For example:

- *decided to begin* could be shortened to *began*
- making it mandatory for could be shortened to requiring
- *make use of* could be shortened to *use*
- *a large number* could be shortened to *many*

In addition, there are several examples of redundancy that can be eliminated:

- legislators decided to begin creating legislation and made those laws
- automobile drivers and passengers and while in cars
- reasons that were political reasons

These changes are incorporated as follows:

> When legislators began requiring drivers and passengers to use seat belts, many of them did so for political reasons.

There are many general examples of redundant phrases, such as *add an additional, complete and total, time schedule*, and *transportation vehicle*. If asked to identify a redundant phrase on the exam, test takers should look for words that are close together with the same (or similar) meanings.

Consistency in Style and Tone

Style and tone are often thought to be the same thing. Though they're closely related, there are important differences to keep in mind. The easiest way to do this is to remember that **style** creates and affects **tone**. More specifically, style is *how the writer uses words* to create the desired tone for their writing.

Style

Style can include any number of technical writing choices, and some may have to be analyzed on the test. A few examples of style choices include:

- Sentence Construction: When presenting facts, does the writer use shorter sentences to create a quicker sense of the supporting evidence, or does he or she use longer sentences to elaborate and explain the information?

- Technical Language: Does the writer use jargon to demonstrate their expertise in the subject, or do the writer use ordinary language to help the reader understand things in simple terms?

- Formal Language: Does the writer refrain from using contractions such as *won't* or *can't* to create a more formal tone, or does he or she use a colloquial, conversational style to connect to the reader?

- Formatting: Does the writer use a series of shorter paragraphs to help the reader follow a line of argument, or does he or she use longer paragraphs to examine an issue in great detail and demonstrate their knowledge of the topic?

On the exam, test takers should examine the writer's style and how their writing choices affect the way the text comes across.

Tone

Tone refers to the writer's attitude toward the subject matter. Tone is usually explained in terms of a work of fiction. For example, the tone conveys how the writer feels about the characters and the situations in which they're involved. Nonfiction writing is sometimes thought to have no tone at all; however, this is incorrect.

A lot of nonfiction writing has a neutral tone, which is an important one for the writer to use. A neutral tone demonstrates that the writer is presenting a topic impartially and letting the information speak for itself. On the other hand, nonfiction writing can be just as effective and appropriate if the tone isn't neutral. The following short passage provides an example of tone in nonfiction writing:

> Seat belts save more lives than any other automobile safety feature. Many studies show that airbags save lives as well; however, not all cars have airbags. For instance, some older cars don't. Furthermore, air bags aren't entirely reliable. For example, studies show that in 15% of accidents airbags don't deploy as designed, but, on the other hand, seat belt malfunctions are extremely rare. The number of highway fatalities has plummeted since laws requiring seat belt usage were enacted.

In this passage, the writer mostly chooses to retain a neutral tone when presenting information. If instead, the author chose to include their own personal experience of losing a friend or family member in a car accident, the tone would change dramatically. The tone would no longer be neutral and would show that the writer has a personal stake in the content, allowing him or her to interpret the information in a different way. When analyzing tone, the reader should consider what the writer is trying to achieve in the text and how they *create* the tone using style.

Word Parts

By analyzing and understanding Latin, Greek, and Anglo-Saxon word roots, prefixes, and suffixes, one can better understand word meanings. Of course, people can always look words up if a dictionary or thesaurus, if available, but meaning can often be gleaned on the spot if the reader learns to dissect and examine words.

A word can consist of the following combinations:

- root
- root+suffix
- prefix+root
- prefix+root+suffix

For example, if someone was unfamiliar with the word *submarine* they could break the word into its parts.

> prefix+root
>
> sub+marine

It can be determined that *sub* means *below* as in *subway* and *subpar*. Additionally, one can determine that *marine* refers to *the sea* as in *marine life*. Thus, it can be figured that *submarine* refers to something below the water.

Roots

Roots are the basic components of words. Many roots can stand alone as individual words, but others must be combined with a prefix or suffix to be a word. For example, *calc* is a root but it needs a suffix to be an actual word (*calcium*).

Prefixes

A **prefix** is a word, letter, or number that is placed before another. It adjusts or qualifies the root word's meaning. When written alone, prefixes are followed by a dash to indicate that the root word follows. Some of the most common prefixes are the following:

Prefix	Meaning	Example
dis-	not or opposite of	disabled
in-, im-, il-, ir-	not	illiterate
re-	again	return
un-	not	unpredictable
anti-	against	antibacterial
fore-	before	forefront
mis-	wrongly	misunderstand
non-	not	nonsense
over-	more than normal	overabundance
pre-	before	preheat
super-	above	superman

Suffixes

A **suffix** is a letter or group of letters added at the end of a word to form another word. The word created from the root and suffix is either a different tense of the same root (*help+ed=helped*) or a new word (*help+ful=helpful*). When written alone, suffixes are preceded by a dash to indicate that the root word comes before.

Some of the most common suffixes are the following:

Suffix	Meaning	Example
-ed	makes a verb past tense	washed
-ing	makes a verb a present participle verb	washing
-ly	to make characteristic of	lovely
-s, -es	to make more than one	chairs, boxes
-able	can be done	deplorable
-al	having characteristics of	comical
-est	comparative	greatest
-ful	full of	wonderful
-ism	belief in	communism
-less	without	faithless
-ment	action or process	accomplishment
-ness	state of	happiness
-ize, -ise	to render, to make	sterilize, advertise
-cede, -ceed, -sede	go	concede, proceed, supersede

Here are some helpful tips:

- When adding a suffix that starts with a vowel (for example, *-ed*) to a one-syllable root whose vowel has a short sound and ends in a consonant (for example, *stun*), the final consonant of the root (*n*) gets doubled.

  stun+ed=stun*n*ed

- Exception: If the past tense verb ends in *x* such as *box*, the *x* does not get doubled.

  box+ed=boxed

- If adding a suffix that starts with a vowel (*-er*) to a multi-syllable word ending in a consonant (*begin*), the consonant (*n*) is doubled.

  begin+er=begin*n*er

- If a short vowel is followed by two or more consonants in a word such as *i+t+c+h=itch,* the last consonant should not be doubled.

  itch+ed=itched

- If adding a suffix that starts with a vowel (*-ing*) to a word ending in *e* (for example, *name*), that word's final *e* is generally (but not always) dropped.

  name+ing=naming
  exception: manage+able=manag*e*able

- If adding a suffix that starts with a consonant (*-ness*) to a word ending in *e* (*complete*), the *e* generally (but not always) remains.

  complete+ness=completeness
  exception: judge+ment=judgment

- There is great diversity on handling words that end in *y*. For words ending in a vowel+*y*, nothing changes in the original word.

  play+ed=played

- For words ending in a consonant+y, the y is changed to i when adding any suffix except for *–ing*.

  marry+ed=married
  marry+ing=marrying

23

Conventions of Standard English

Sentence Structure and Formation

Sentence Structure

Simple sentence: composed of one independent clause

> Many people watch hummingbirds.

> Note that it has one subject and one verb; however, a simple sentence can have a compound subject and/or a compound verb.

> Adults and children often enjoy watching and photographing hummingbirds.

Compound sentence: composed of two independent clauses

> The wind knocked down lots of trees, but no trees in my yard were affected.

Complex sentence: composed of one independent clause and one dependent clause

> Although the wind knocked down lots of trees, no trees in my yard were affected.

Sentence Fluency

Learning and utilizing the mechanics of structure will encourage effective, professional results, and adding some creativity will elevate one's writing to a higher level.

First, the basic elements of sentences will be reviewed.

A **sentence** is a set of words that make up a grammatical unit. The words must have certain elements and be spoken or written in a specific order to constitute a complete sentence that makes sense.

> 1. A sentence must have a **subject** (a noun or noun phrase). The subject tells whom or what the sentence is addressing (i.e. what it is about).

> 2. A sentence must have an **action** or **state of being** (*a* verb). To reiterate: A verb forms the main part of the predicate of a sentence. This means that it explains what the noun is doing.

> 3. A sentence must convey a complete thought.

When examining writing, readers should be mindful of grammar, structure, spelling, and patterns. Sentences can come in varying sizes and shapes, so the point of grammatical correctness is not to stamp out creativity or diversity in writing. Rather, grammatical correctness ensures that writing will be enjoyable and clear. One of the most common methods successful test takers employ to catch errors is to mouth the words as they read them. Many typos are fixed automatically by the brain, but mouthing the words often circumvents this instinct and helps one read what's actually on the page. Often, grammar errors are caught not by memorization of grammar rules but by the training of one's mind to know whether something *sounds* right or not.

Types of Sentences

There isn't an overabundance of absolutes in grammar, but here is one: every sentence in the English language falls into one of four categories.

Declarative: a simple statement that ends with a period

The price of milk per gallon is the same as the price of gasoline.

Imperative: a command, instruction, or request that ends with a period

Buy milk when you stop to fill up your car with gas.

Interrogative: a question that ends with a question mark

Will you buy the milk?

Exclamatory: a statement or command that expresses emotions like anger, urgency, or surprise and ends with an exclamation mark

Buy the milk now!

Declarative sentences are the most common type, probably because they are comprised of the most general content, without any of the bells and whistles that the other three types contain. They are, simply, declarations or statements of any degree of seriousness, importance, or information.

Imperative sentences often seem to be missing a subject. The subject is there, though; it is just not visible or audible because it is *implied*. For example:

Buy the milk when you fill up your car with gas.

In this sentence, *you* is the implied subject, the one to whom the command is issued. This is sometimes called *the understood you* because it is understood that *you* is the subject of the sentence.

Interrogative sentences—those that ask questions—are defined as such from the idea of the word **interrogation**, the action of questions being asked of suspects by investigators. Although that is serious business, interrogative sentences apply to all kinds of questions.

To exclaim is at the root of **exclamatory** sentences. These are made with strong emotions behind them. The only technical difference between a declarative or imperative sentence and an exclamatory one is the exclamation mark at the end. The example declarative and imperative sentences can both become an exclamatory one simply by putting an exclamation mark at the end of the sentences.

The price of milk per gallon is the same as the price of gasoline!

Buy milk when you stop to fill up your car with gas!

After all, someone might be really excited by the price of gas or milk, or they could be mad at the person that will be buying the milk! However, as stated before, exclamation marks in abundance defeat their own purpose! After a while, they begin to cause fatigue! When used only for their intended purpose, they can have their expected and desired effect.

Transitions

Transitions are the glue used to make organized thoughts adhere to one another. Transitions are the glue that helps put ideas together seamlessly, within sentences and paragraphs, between them, and (in longer documents) even between sections. Transitions may be single words, sentences, or whole paragraphs (as in the prior example). Transitions help readers to digest and understand what to feel about what has gone on and clue readers in on what is going on, what will be, and how they might react to all these factors. Transitions are like good clues left at a crime scene.

Parallel Structure in a Sentence

Parallel structure, also known as **parallelism**, refers to using the same grammatical form within a sentence. This is important in lists and for other components of sentences.

> Incorrect: At the recital, the boys and girls were dancing, singing, and played musical instruments.

> Correct: At the recital, the boys and girls were dancing, singing, and playing musical instruments.

Notice that in the first example, *played* is not in the same verb tense as the other verbs nor is it compatible with the helping verb *were*. To test for parallel structure in lists, try reading each item as if it were the only item in the list.

> The boys and girls were dancing.

> The boys and girls were singing.

> The boys and girls were played musical instruments.

Suddenly, the error in the sentence becomes very clear. Here's another example:

Incorrect: After the accident, I informed the police *that Mrs. Holmes backed* into my car, *that Mrs. Holmes got out* of her car to look at the damage, and *she was driving* off without leaving a note.

Correct: After the accident, I informed the police *that Mrs. Holmes backed* into my car, *that Mrs. Holmes got out* of her car to look at the damage, and *that Mrs. Holmes drove off* without leaving a note.

Correct: After the accident, I informed the police that Mrs. Holmes *backed* into my car, *got out* of her car to look at the damage, and *drove off* without leaving a note.

Note that there are two ways to fix the nonparallel structure of the first sentence. The key to parallelism is consistent structure.

Modifier Placement

Modifiers are words or phrases (often adjectives or nouns) that add detail to, explain, or limit the meaning of other parts of a sentence. Look at the following example:

> A big pine tree is in the yard.

In the sentence, the words *big* (an adjective) and *pine* (a noun) modify *tree* (the head noun).

All related parts of a sentence must be placed together correctly. *Misplaced* and *dangling modifiers* are common writing mistakes. In fact, they're so common that many people are accustomed to seeing them and can decipher an incorrect sentence without much difficulty.

Misplaced Modifiers

Since *modifiers* refer to something else in the sentence (*big* and *pine* refer to *tree* in the example above), they need to be placed close to what they modify. If a modifier is so far away that the reader isn't sure what it's describing, it becomes a *misplaced modifier*. For example:

Seat belts almost saved 5,000 lives in 2009.

It's likely that the writer means that the total number of lives saved by seat belts in 2009 is close to 5,000. However, due to the misplaced modifier (*almost*), the sentence actually says there are 5,000 examples when seat belts *almost saved lives*. In this case, the position of the modifier is actually the difference between life and death (at least in the meaning of the sentence). A clearer way to write the sentence is:

Seat belts saved almost 5,000 lives in 2009.

Now that the modifier is close to the 5,000 lives it references, the sentence's meaning is clearer.

Another common example of a misplaced modifier occurs when the writer uses the modifier to begin a sentence. For example:

Having saved 5,000 lives in 2009, Senator Wilson praised the seat belt legislation.

It seems unlikely that Senator Wilson saved 5,000 lives on her own, but that's what the writer is saying in this sentence. To correct this error, the writer should move the modifier closer to the intended object it modifies. Here are two possible solutions:

Having saved 5,000 lives in 2009, the seat belt legislation was praised by Senator Wilson.

Senator Wilson praised the seat belt legislation, which saved 5,000 lives in 2009.

When choosing a solution for a misplaced modifier, look for an option that places the modifier close to the object or idea it describes.

Dangling Modifiers

A modifier must have a target word or phrase that it's modifying. Without this, it's a *dangling modifier*. Dangling modifiers are usually found at the beginning of sentences:

After passing the new law, there is sure to be an improvement in highway safety.

This sentence doesn't say anything about who is passing the law. Therefore, "After passing the new law" is a dangling modifier because it doesn't modify anything in the sentence. To correct this type of error, determine what the writer intended the modifier to point to:

After passing the new law, legislators are sure to see an improvement in highway safety.

"After passing the new law" now points to *legislators*, which makes the sentence clearer and eliminates the dangling modifier.

Agreement

In English writing, certain words connect to other words. People often learn these connections (or *agreements*) as young children and use the correct combinations without a second thought. However, the questions on the test dealing with agreement probably aren't simple ones.

Subject-Verb Agreement

Which of the following sentences is correct?

A large crowd of protesters was on hand.

A large crowd of protesters were on hand.

Many people would say the second sentence is correct, but they'd be wrong. However, they probably wouldn't be alone. Most people just look at two words: *protesters were*. Together they make sense. They sound right. The problem is that the verb *were* doesn't refer to the word *protesters*. Here, the word *protesters* is part of a prepositional phrase that clarifies the actual subject of the sentence (*crowd*). Take the phrase "of protesters" away and re-examine the sentences:

A large crowd was on hand.

A large crowd were on hand.

Without the prepositional phrase to separate the subject and verb, the answer is obvious. The first sentence is correct. On the test, look for confusing prepositional phrases when answering questions about subject-verb agreement. Take the phrase away, and then recheck the sentence.

Noun Agreement

Nouns that refer to other nouns must also match in number. Take the following example:

John and Emily both served as an intern for Senator Wilson.

Two people are involved in this sentence: John and Emily. Therefore, the word *intern* should be plural to match. Here is how the sentence should read:

John and Emily both served as interns for Senator Wilson.

Shift in Noun-Pronoun Agreement

Pronouns are used to replace nouns so sentences don't have a lot of unnecessary repetition. This repetition can make a sentence seem awkward as in the following example:

Seat belts are important because seat belts save lives, but seat belts can't do so unless seat belts are used.

Replacing some of the nouns (*seat belts*) with a pronoun (*they*) improves the flow of the sentence:

Seat belts are important because they save lives, but they can't do so unless they are used.

A pronoun should agree in number (singular or plural) with the noun that precedes it. Another common writing error is the shift in *noun-pronoun agreement*. Here's an example:

When people are getting in a car, he should always remember to buckle his seatbelt.

The first half of the sentence talks about a plural (*people*), while the second half refers to a singular person (*he* and *his*). These don't agree, so the sentence should be rewritten as:

> When people are getting in a car, they should always remember to buckle their seatbelt.

Fragments and Run-Ons

A *sentence fragment* is a failed attempt to create a complete sentence because it's missing a required noun or verb. Fragments don't function properly because there isn't enough information to understand the writer's intended meaning. For example:

> Seat belt use corresponds to a lower rate of hospital visits, reducing strain on an already overburdened healthcare system. Insurance claims as well.

Look at the last sentence: *Insurance claims as well*. What does this mean? This is a fragment because it has a noun but no verb, and it leaves the reader guessing what the writer means about insurance claims. Many readers can probably infer what the writer means, but this distracts them from the flow of the writer's argument. Choosing a suitable replacement for a sentence fragment may be one of the questions on the test. The fragment is probably related to the surrounding content, so look at the overall point the writer is trying to make and choose the answer that best fits that idea.

Remember that sometimes a fragment can *look* like a complete sentence or have all the nouns and verbs it needs to make sense. Consider the following two examples:

> Seat belt use corresponds to a lower rate of hospital visits.

> Although seat belt use corresponds to a lower rate of hospital visits.

Both examples above have nouns and verbs, but only the first sentence is correct. The second sentence is a fragment, even though it's actually longer. The key is the writer's use of the word *although*. Starting a sentence with *although* turns that part into a *subordinate clause* (more on that next). Keep in mind that one doesn't have to remember that it's called a subordinate clause on the test. Just be able to recognize that the words form an incomplete thought and identify the problem as a sentence fragment.

A *run-on sentence* is, in some ways, the opposite of a fragment. It contains two or more sentences that have been improperly forced together into one. An example of a run-on sentence looks something like this:

> Seat belt use corresponds to a lower rate of hospital visits it also leads to fewer insurance claims.

Here, there are two separate ideas in one sentence. It's difficult for the reader to follow the writer's thinking because there is no transition from one idea to the next. On the test, choose the best way to correct the run-on sentence.

Here are two possibilities for the sentence above:

> Seat belt use corresponds to a lower rate of hospital visits. It also leads to fewer insurance claims.

> Seat belt use corresponds to a lower rate of hospital visits, but it also leads to fewer insurance claims.

29

Both solutions are grammatically correct, so which one is the best choice? That depends on the point that the writer is trying to make. Always read the surrounding text to determine what the writer wants to demonstrate, and choose the option that best supports that thought.

Punctuation

Ellipses

An **ellipsis** (. . .) consists of three handy little dots that can speak volumes on behalf of irrelevant material. Writers use them in place of words, lines, phrases, list content, or paragraphs that might just as easily have been omitted from a passage of writing. This can be done to save space or to focus only on the specifically relevant material.

> Exercise is good for some unexpected reasons. Watkins writes, "Exercise has many benefits such as . . . reducing cancer risk."

In the example above, the ellipsis takes the place of the other benefits of exercise that are more expected.

The ellipsis may also be used to show a pause in sentence flow.

> "I'm wondering . . . how this could happen," Dylan said in a soft voice.

Commas

A **comma** (,) is the punctuation mark that signifies a pause—breath—between parts of a sentence. It denotes a break of flow. As with so many aspects of writing structure, authors will benefit by reading their writing aloud or mouthing the words. This can be particularly helpful if one is uncertain about whether the comma is needed.

In a complex sentence—one that contains a **subordinate (dependent)** clause or clauses—the use of a comma is dictated by where the subordinate clause is located. If the subordinate clause is located before the main clause, a comma is needed between the two clauses.

> Because I don't have enough money, I will not order steak.

Generally, if the subordinate clause is placed after the main clause, no punctuation is needed.

> I did well on my exam because I studied two hours the night before.

Notice how the last clause is dependent because it requires the earlier independent clauses to make sense.

Use a comma on both sides of an interrupting phrase.

> I will pay for the ice cream, *chocolate and vanilla*, and then will eat it all myself.

The words forming the phrase in italics are nonessential (extra) information. To determine if a phrase is nonessential, try reading the sentence without the phrase and see if it's still coherent.

A comma is not necessary in this next sentence because no interruption—nonessential or extra information—has occurred. Read sentences aloud when uncertain.

30

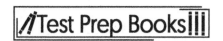

I will pay for his chocolate and vanilla ice cream and then will eat it all myself.

If the nonessential phrase comes at the beginning of a sentence, a comma should only go at the end of the phrase. If the phrase comes at the end of a sentence, a comma should only go at the beginning of the phrase.

Other types of interruptions include the following:

- interjections: Oh no, I am not going.
- abbreviations: Barry Potter, M.D., specializes in heart disorders.
- direct addresses: Yes, Claudia, I am tired and going to bed.
- parenthetical phrases: His wife, lovely as she was, was not helpful.
- transitional phrases: Also, it is not possible.

The second comma in the following sentence is called an Oxford comma.

I will pay for ice cream, syrup, and pop.

It is a comma used after the second-to-last item in a series of three or more items. It comes before the word *or* or *and*. Not everyone uses the Oxford comma; it is optional, but many believe it is needed. The comma functions as a tool to reduce confusion in writing. So, if omitting the Oxford comma would cause confusion, then it's best to include it.

Commas are used in math to mark the place of thousands in numerals, breaking them up so they are easier to read. Other uses for commas are in dates (*March 19, 2016*), letter greetings (*Dear Sally,*), and in between cities and states (*Louisville, KY*).

Semicolons

The **semicolon** (;) might be described as a heavy-handed comma. Take a look at these two examples:

I will pay for the ice cream, but I will not pay for the steak.
I will pay for the ice cream; I will not pay for the steak.

What's the difference? The first example has a comma and a conjunction separating the two independent clauses. The second example does not have a conjunction, but there are two independent clauses in the sentence, so something more than a comma is required. In this case, a semicolon is used.

Two independent clauses can only be joined in a sentence by either a comma and conjunction or a semicolon. If one of those tools is not used, the sentence will be a run-on. Remember that while the clauses are independent, they need to be closely related in order to be contained in one sentence.

Another use for the semicolon is to separate items in a list when the items themselves require commas.

The family lived in Phoenix, Arizona; Oklahoma City, Oklahoma; and Raleigh, North Carolina.

Colons

Colons (:) have many miscellaneous functions. Colons can be used to precede further information or a list. In these cases, a colon should only follow an independent clause.

Humans take in sensory information through five basic senses: sight, hearing, smell, touch, and taste.

31

The meal includes the following components:

- Caesar salad
- spaghetti
- garlic bread
- cake

The family got what they needed: a reliable vehicle.

While a comma is more common, a colon can also proceed a formal quotation.

He said to the crowd: "Let's begin!"

The colon is used after the greeting in a formal letter.

Dear Sir:
To Whom It May Concern:

In the writing of time, the colon separates the minutes from the hour (*4:45 p.m.*). The colon can also be used to indicate a ratio between two numbers (*50:1*).

Hyphens

The **hyphen** (-) is a little hash mark that can be used to join words to show that they are linked.

Hyphenate two words that work together as a single adjective (a compound adjective).

honey-covered biscuits

Some words always require hyphens, even if not serving as an adjective.

merry-go-round

Hyphens always go after certain prefixes like *anti-* & *all-*.

Hyphens should also be used when the absence of the hyphen would cause a strange vowel combination (*semi-engineer*) or confusion. For example, *re-collect* should be used to describe something being gathered twice rather than being written as *recollect*, which means to remember.

Parentheses and Dashes

Parentheses are half-round brackets that look like this: ( ). They set off a word, phrase, or sentence that is an afterthought, explanation, or side note relevant to the surrounding text but not essential. A pair of commas is often used to set off this sort of information, but parentheses are generally used for information that would not fit well within a sentence or that the writer deems not important enough to be structurally part of the sentence.

The picture of the heart (see above) shows the major parts you should memorize.
Mount Everest is one of three mountains in the world that are over 28,000 feet high (K2 and Kanchenjunga are the other two).

See how the sentences above are complete without the parenthetical statements? In the first example, *see above* would not have fit well within the flow of the sentence. The second parenthetical statement could have been a separate sentence, but the writer deemed the information not pertinent to the topic.

The **em-dash** (—) is a mark longer than a hyphen used as a punctuation mark in sentences and to set apart a relevant thought. Even after plucking out the line separated by the dash marks, the sentence will be intact and make sense.

> Looking out the airplane window at the landmarks—Lake Clarke, Thompson Community College, and the bridge—she couldn't help but feel excited to be home.

The dashes use is similar to that of parentheses or a pair of commas. So, what's the difference? Many believe that using dashes makes the clause within them stand out while using parentheses is subtler. It's advised to not use dashes when commas could be used instead.

Quotation Marks

Here are some instances where **quotation marks** should be used:

- o Dialogue for characters in narratives. When characters speak, the first word should always be capitalized, and the punctuation goes inside the quotes. For example:

    > Janie said, "The tree fell on my car during the hurricane."

- o Around titles of songs, short stories, essays, and chapters in books
- o To emphasize a certain word
- o To refer to a word as the word itself

Apostrophes

This punctuation mark, the apostrophe ('), is a versatile little mark. It has a few different functions:

- Quotes: Apostrophes are used when a second quote is needed within a quote.

    > In my letter to my friend, I wrote, "The girl had to get a new purse, and guess what Mary did? She said, 'I'd like to go with you to the store.' I knew Mary would buy it for her."

- Contractions: Another use for an apostrophe in the quote above is a contraction. *I'd* is used for *I would.*

- Possession: An apostrophe followed by the letter *s* shows possession (*Mary's* purse). If the possessive word is plural, the apostrophe generally just follows the word.

    > The trees' leaves are all over the ground.

Usage

Homophones

Homophones are two or more words that have no particular relationship to one another except their identical pronunciations. Homophones make spelling English words fun and challenging. Examples include:

Common Homophones
affect, effect
allot, a lot
barbecue, barbeque
bite, byte
brake, break
capital, capitol
cash, cache
cell, sell
colonel, kernel
do, due, dew
dual, duel
eminent, imminent
flew, flu, flue
gauge, gage
holy, wholly
it's, its
knew, new
libel, liable
principal, principle
their, there, they're
to, too, two
yoke, yolk

Word Confusion

That/Which

The pronouns *that* and *which* are both used to refer to animals, objects, ideas, and events—but they are not interchangeable. The rule is to use the word *that* in essential clauses and phrases that help convey the meaning of the sentence. Use the word *which* in nonessential (less important) clauses. Typically, *which* clauses are enclosed in commas.

> The morning <u>that I fell asleep in class</u> caused me a lot of trouble.

> This morning's coffee, <u>which had too much creamer</u>, woke me up.

Who/Whom

We use the pronouns *who* and *whom* to refer to people. We always use *who* when it is the subject of the sentence or clause. We never use *whom* as the subject; it is always the object of a verb or preposition.

Who hit the baseball for the home run? (subject)

The baseball fell into the glove of whom? (object of the preposition of)

The umpire called whom "out"? (object of the verb called)

To/Too/Two

to: a preposition or infinitive (*to walk, to run, walk to the store, run to the tree*)
too: means also, as well, or very (*She likes cookies, too.; I ate too much.*)
two: a number (*I have two cookies. She walked to the store two times.*)

There/Their/They're

there: an adjective, adverb, or pronoun used to start a sentence or indicate place (*There are four vintage cars over there.*)
their: a possessive pronoun used to indicate belonging (*Their car is the blue and white one.*)
they're: a contraction of the words "they are" (*They're going to enter the vintage car show.*)

Your/You're

your: a possessive pronoun (*Your artwork is terrific.*)
you're: a contraction of the words "you are" (*You're a terrific artist.*)

Its/It's

its: a possessive pronoun (*The elephant had its trunk in the water.*)
it's: a contraction of the words "it is" (*It's an impressive animal.*)

Affect/Effect

affect: as a verb means "to influence" (*How will the earthquake affect your home?*); as a noun means "emotion or mood" (*Her affect was somber.*)
effect: as a verb means "to bring about" (*She will effect a change through philanthropy.*); as a noun means "a result of" (*The effect of the earthquake was devastating.*)

Other mix-ups: Other pairs of words cause mix-ups but are not necessarily homonyms. Here are a few of those:

Bring/Take

bring: when the action is coming toward (*Bring me the money.*)
take: when the action is going away from (*Take her the money.*)

Can/May

can: means "able to" (*The child can ride a bike.*)
may: asks permission (*The child asked if he may ride his bike.*)

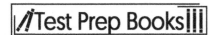

Than/Then

than: a conjunction used for comparison (*I like tacos better than pizza.*)
then: an adverb telling when something happened (*I ate and then slept.*)

Disinterested/Uninterested

disinterested: used to mean "neutral" (*The jury remains disinterested during the trial.*)
uninterested: used to mean "bored" (*I was uninterested during the lecture.*)

Percent/Percentage

percent: used when there is a number involved (*Five percent of us like tacos.*)
percentage: used when there is no number (*That is a low percentage.*)

Fewer/Less

fewer: used for things you can count (*He has fewer playing cards.*)
less: used for things you cannot count, as well as time (*He has less talent. You have less than a minute.*)

Farther/Further

farther: used when discussing distance (*His paper airplane flew farther than mine.*)
further: used to mean "more" (*He needed further information.*)

Lend/Loan

lend: a verb used for borrowing (*Lend me your lawn mower. He will lend it to me.*)
loan: a noun used for something borrowed (*She applied for a student loan.*)

Note

Some people have problems with these:

- regardless/irregardless
- a lot/alot

Irregardless and *alot* are always incorrect. Don't use them.

36

Practice Quiz

Read the following passage and answer Questions 1-5.

Although many Missourians know that Harry S. Truman and Walt Disney hailed from their great state, probably far fewer know that it was also home to the remarkable George Washington Carver. (1) As a child, George was driven to learn, and he loved painting. At the end of the Civil War, Moses Carver, the slave owner who owned George's parents, decided to keep George and his brother and raise them on his farm.

He even went on to study art while in college but was encouraged to pursue botany instead. He spent much of his life helping others (2) by showing them better ways to farm, his ideas improved agricultural productivity in many countries. One of his most notable contributions to the newly emerging class of Black farmers was to teach them the negative effects of agricultural monoculture, i.e. (3) growing the same crops in the same fields year after year, depleting the soil of much needed nutrients and results in a lesser yielding crop.

Carver was an innovator, always thinking of new and better ways to do things, and is most famous for his over three hundred uses for the peanut. Toward the end of his career, (4) Carver returns to his first love of art. Through his artwork, he hoped to inspire people to see the beauty around them and to do great things themselves. (5) Because Carver died, he left his money to help fund ongoing agricultural research. Today, people still visit and study at the George Washington Carver Foundation at Tuskegee Institute.

1. Which of the following would be the best choice for this sentence (reproduced below)?

   (1) As a child, George was driven to learn, and he loved painting.

   a. NO CHANGE
   b. Move to the end of the first paragraph.
   c. Move to the beginning of the first paragraph.
   d. Move to the end of the second paragraph.

2. Which of the following would be the best choice for this sentence (reproduced below)?

   He spent much of his life helping others (2) by showing them better ways to farm, his ideas improved agricultural productivity in many countries.

   a. NO CHANGE
   b. by showing them better ways to farm his ideas improved agricultural productivity
   c. by showing them better ways to farm . . . his ideas improved agricultural productivity
   d. by showing them better ways to farm; his ideas improved agricultural productivity

37

3. Which of the following would be the best choice for this sentence (reproduced below)?

(3) growing the same crops in the same fields year after year, depleting the soil of much needed nutrients and results in a lesser yielding crop.

a. NO CHANGE
b. growing the same crops in the same fields year after year, depleting the soil of much needed nutrients and resulting in a lesser yielding crop.
c. growing the same crops in the same fields year after year, depletes the soil of much needed nutrients and resulting in a lesser yielding crop.
d. grows the same crops in the same fields year after year, depletes the soil of much needed nutrients and resulting in a lesser yielding crop.

4. Which of the following would be the best choice for this sentence (reproduced below)?

Toward the end of his career, (4) Carver returns to his first love of art.

a. NO CHANGE
b. Carver is returning
c. Carver returned
d. Carver was returning

5. Which of the following would be the best choice for this sentence (reproduced below)?

(5) Because Carver died, he left his money to help fund ongoing agricultural research.

a. NO CHANGE
b. Although Carver died,
c. When Carver died,
d. Finally Carver died,

See answers on next page.

Answer Explanations

1. B: The best place for this sentence given all the answer choices is at the end of the first paragraph. Choice *A* is incorrect; the passage is told in chronological order, and leaving the sentence as-is defies that order, since we haven't been introduced to who raised George. Choice *C* is incorrect because this sentence is not an introductory sentence. It does not provide the main topic of the paragraph. Choice *D* is incorrect because again, it defies chronological order. By the end of paragraph two we have already gotten to George as an adult, so this sentence would not make sense here.

2. D: Out of these choices, a semicolon would be the best fit because there is an independent clause on either side of the semicolon, and the two sentences closely relate to each other. Choice *A* is incorrect because putting a comma between two independent clauses (i.e. complete sentences) creates a comma splice. Choice *B* is incorrect; omitting punctuation here creates a run-on sentence. Choice *C* is incorrect because an ellipsis (. . .) is used to designate an omission in the text.

3. B: Choice *B* is the correct answer because it uses "ing" verbs as gerunds. Gerunds are "ing" words that stand in for nouns. The words "growing" and "depleting" are gerunds in this example. Choice *B* also uses the conjunction "and," whereas the other answer choices have comma splices.

4. C: Choice *C* is correct because it keeps with the verb tense in the rest of the passage: past tense. Choice *A* is in present tense, which is incorrect. Choice *B* is present progressive, which means there is a continual action, which is also incorrect. Choice *D* is incorrect because "was returning" is past progressive tense, which means that something was happening continuously at some point in the past.

5. C: The correct choice is the subordinating conjunction, "When." We should look at the clues around the phrase to see what fits best. Carver left his money "when he died." Choice *A*, "Because," could perhaps be correct, but "When" is the more appropriate word to use here. Choice *B* is incorrect; "Although" denotes a contrast, and there is no contrast here. Choice *D* is incorrect because "Finally" indicates something at the very end of a list or series, and there is no series at this point in the text.

ACT Mathematics Test

What to Expect

The Math test contains 60 multiple-choice questions and lasts 60 minutes. Unlike the English and Reading sections, which each contain four answers options, the math questions all have five choices. Certain calculators are permitted, but the questions are all designed to be answerable without the use of a calculator.

Tips

- Use your calculator strategically. Some questions are actually solved faster with reasoning or freehand work. Test takers often rely excessively on their calculators and can get bogged down or miss obvious elements of the question. When a calculator is used, consider substituting numbers for variables to solve equations and test your answer.

- Double-check your work. Any extra time in the section can be used performing the reverse operations or plugging your answer into the problem to ensure it is correct.

- Back-solve when you're stuck. If you can't figure out the answer, try using the provided choices and working backward, selecting the one that works. This strategy may not always work and is time-consuming, but it can be helpful with those questions that you cannot figure out.

- Carefully consider all diagrams and figures. Word problems, data interpretation, and geometry questions, in particular, often include important graphics with valuable information. Examine them carefully.

- Consider the reasonableness of your response in the context of the problem. Careless mistakes are often made when test takers are rushing. By evaluating if your response is reasonable, some of these mistakes can be avoided.

Number and Quantity

Structure of the Number System

The mathematical number system is made up of two general types of numbers: real and complex. **Real numbers** are those that are used in normal settings, while **complex numbers** are those composed of both a real number and an imaginary one. Imaginary numbers are the result of taking the square root of -1, and $\sqrt{-1} = i$.

The real number system is often explained using a Venn diagram similar to the one below. After a number has been labeled as a real number, further classification occurs when considering the other groups in this diagram. If a number is a never-ending, non-repeating decimal, it falls in the irrational category. Otherwise, it is rational. More information on these types of numbers is provided in the previous section. Furthermore, if a number does not have a fractional part, it is classified as an integer, such as -2, 75, or zero. Whole numbers are an even smaller group that only includes positive integers and zero. The last group of natural numbers is made up of only positive integers, such as 2, 56, or 12.

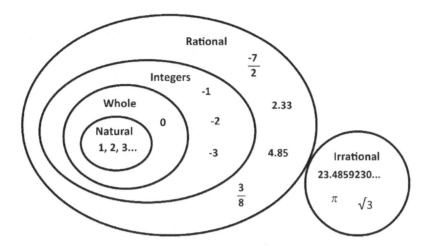

Real numbers can be compared and ordered using the number line. If a number falls to the left on the real number line, it is less than a number on the right. For example, $-2 < 5$ because -2 falls to the left of zero, and 5 falls to the right. Numbers to the left of zero are negative while those to the right are positive.

Complex numbers are made up of the sum of a real number and an imaginary number. Some examples of complex numbers include $6 + 2i$, $5 - 7i$, and $-3 + 12i$. Adding and subtracting complex numbers is similar to collecting like terms. The real numbers are added together, and the imaginary numbers are added together. For example, if the problem asks to simplify the expression $6 + 2i - 3 + 7i$, the 6 and (-3) are combined to make 3, and the $2i$ and $7i$ combine to make $9i$. Multiplying and dividing complex numbers is similar to working with exponents. One rule to remember when multiplying is that $i \times i = -1$. For example, if a problem asks to simplify the expression $4i(3 + 7i)$, the $4i$ should be distributed throughout the 3 and the $7i$. This leaves the final expression $12i - 28$. The 28 is negative because $i \times i$ results in a negative number. The last type of operation to consider with complex numbers is the conjugate. The **conjugate** of a complex number is a technique used to change the complex number into a real number. For example, the conjugate of $4 - 3i$ is $4 + 3i$. Multiplying $(4 - 3i)(4 + 3i)$ results in $16 + 12i - 12i + 9$, which has a final answer of:

$$16 + 9 = 25$$

The order of operations—PEMDAS—simplifies longer expressions with real or imaginary numbers. Each operation is listed in the order of how they should be completed in a problem containing more than one operation. Parenthesis can also mean grouping symbols, such as brackets and absolute value. Then, exponents are calculated. Multiplication and division should be completed from left to right, and addition and subtraction should be completed from left to right.

Simplification of another type of expression occurs when radicals are involved. Root is another word for radical. For example, the following expression is a radical that can be simplified: $\sqrt{24x^2}$. First, the number must be factored out to the highest perfect square. Any perfect square can be taken out of a radical. Twenty-four can be factored into 4 and 6, and 4 can be taken out of the radical. $\sqrt{4} = 2$ can be

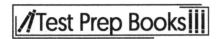
taken out, and 6 stays underneath. If $x > 0$, x can be taken out of the radical because it is a perfect square. The simplified radical is $2x\sqrt{6}$. An approximation can be found using a calculator.

There are also properties of numbers that are true for certain operations. The **commutative** property allows the order of the terms in an expression to change while keeping the same final answer. Both addition and multiplication can be completed in any order and still obtain the same result. However, order does matter in subtraction and division. The **associative** property allows any terms to be "associated" by parenthesis and retain the same final answer. For example:

$$(4 + 3) + 5 = 4 + (3 + 5)$$

Both addition and multiplication are associative; however, subtraction and division do not hold this property. The **distributive** property states that:

$$a(b + c) = ab + ac$$

It is a property that involves both addition and multiplication, and the a is distributed onto each term inside the parentheses.

Rational and Irrational Numbers

All real numbers can be separated into two groups: rational and irrational numbers. **Rational numbers** are any numbers that can be written as a fraction, such as $\frac{1}{3}, \frac{7}{4}$, and -25. Alternatively, **irrational numbers** are those that cannot be written as a fraction, such as numbers with never-ending, non-repeating decimal values. Many irrational numbers result from taking roots, such as $\sqrt{2}$ or $\sqrt{3}$. An irrational number may be written as:

$$34.5684952...$$

The ellipsis (...) represents the line of numbers after the decimal that does not repeat and is never-ending.

When rational and irrational numbers interact, there are different types of number outcomes. For example, when adding or multiplying two rational numbers, the result is a rational number. No matter what two fractions are added or multiplied together, the result can always be written as a fraction. The following expression shows two rational numbers multiplied together:

$$\frac{3}{8} \times \frac{4}{7} = \frac{12}{56}$$

The product of these two fractions is another fraction that can be simplified to $\frac{3}{14}$.

As another interaction, rational numbers added to irrational numbers will always result in irrational numbers. No part of any fraction can be added to a never-ending, non-repeating decimal to make a rational number. The same result is true when multiplying a rational and irrational number. Taking a fractional part of a never-ending, non-repeating decimal will always result in another never-ending, non-repeating decimal. An example of the product of rational and irrational numbers is shown in the following expression: $2\times \sqrt{7}$.

The last type of interaction concerns two irrational numbers, where the sum or product may be rational or irrational depending on the numbers being used. The following expression shows a rational sum from two irrational numbers:

$$\sqrt{3} + \left(6 - \sqrt{3}\right) = 6$$

The product of two irrational numbers can be rational or irrational. A rational result can be seen in the following expression:

$$\sqrt{2} \times \sqrt{8} = \sqrt{2 \times 8} = \sqrt{16} = 4$$

An irrational result can be seen in the following:

$$\sqrt{3} \times \sqrt{2} = \sqrt{6}$$

Integers
An integer is any number that does not have a fractional part. This includes all positive and negative **whole numbers** and zero. Fractions and decimals—which aren't whole numbers—aren't integers.

Prime Numbers
A **prime** number cannot be divided except by 1 and itself. A prime number has no other factors, which means that no other combination of whole numbers can be multiplied to reach that number. For example, the set of prime numbers between 1 and 27 is {2, 3, 5, 7, 11, 13, 17, 19, 23}.

The number 7 is a prime number because its only factors are 1 and 7. In contrast, 12 isn't a prime number, as it can be divided by other numbers like 2, 3, 4, and 6. Because they are composed of multiple factors, numbers like 12 are called **composite** numbers. All numbers greater than 1 that aren't prime numbers are composite numbers.

Even and Odd Numbers
An integer is **even** if one of its factors is 2, while those integers without a factor of 2 are **odd**. No numbers except for integers can have either of these labels. For example, 2, 40, -16, and 108 are all even numbers, while -1, 13, 59, and 77 are all odd numbers since they are integers that cannot be divided by 2 without a remainder. Numbers like 0.4, $\frac{5}{9}$, π, and $\sqrt{7}$ are neither odd nor even because they are not integers.

Order of Rational Numbers

A common question type on the ACT asks test takers to order rational numbers from least to greatest or greatest to least. The numbers will come in a variety of formats, including decimals, percentages, roots, fractions, and whole numbers. These questions test for knowledge of different types of numbers and the ability to determine their respective values.

Whether the question asks to order the numbers from greatest to least or least to greatest, the crux of the question is the same—convert the numbers into a common format. Generally, it's easiest to write the numbers as whole numbers and decimals so they can be placed on a number line. The following examples illustrate this strategy:

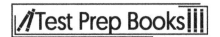

1. Order the following rational numbers from greatest to least:

$$\sqrt{36}, 0.65, 78\%, \frac{3}{4}, 7, 90\%, \frac{5}{2}$$

Of the seven numbers, the whole number (7) and decimal (0.65) are already in an accessible form, so test takers should concentrate on the other five.

First, the square root of 36 equals 6. (If the test asks for the root of a non-perfect root, determine which two whole numbers the root lies between.) Next, the percentages should be converted to decimals. A percentage means "per hundred," so this conversion requires moving the decimal point two places to the left, leaving 0.78 and 0.9. Lastly, the fractions are evaluated:

$$\frac{3}{4} = \frac{75}{100} = 0.75$$

$$\frac{5}{2} = 2\frac{1}{2} = 2.5$$

Now, the only step left is to list the numbers in the requested order:

$$7, \sqrt{36}, \frac{5}{2}, 90\%, 78\%, \frac{3}{4}, 0.65$$

2. Order the following rational numbers from least to greatest:

$$2.5, \sqrt{9}, \text{-10.5}, 0.853, 175\%, \sqrt{4}, \frac{4}{5}$$

$$\sqrt{9} = 3$$

$$175\% = 1.75$$

$$\sqrt{4} = 2$$

$$\frac{4}{5} = 0.8$$

From least to greatest, the answer is: -10.5, $\frac{4}{5}$, 0.853, 175%, $\sqrt{4}$, 2.5, $\sqrt{9}$

Basic Addition, Subtraction, Multiplication, and Division

Gaining more of something is related to addition, while taking something away relates to subtraction. Vocabulary words such as *total, more, less, left,* and *remain* are common when working with these problems. The +sign means *plus.* This shows that addition is happening. The − sign means *minus.* This shows that subtraction is happening. The symbols will be important when you write out equations.

Addition
Addition can also be defined in equation form. For example, $4 + 5 = 9$ shows that $4 + 5$ is the same as 9. Therefore, $9 = 9$, and "four plus five equals nine." When two quantities are being added together, the result is called the **sum**. Therefore, the sum of 4 and 5 is 9. The numbers being added, such as 4 and 5, are known as the **addends.**

44

Subtraction

Subtraction can also be in equation form. For example, $9 - 5 = 4$ shows that $9 - 5$ is the same as 4 and that "9 minus 5 is 4." The result of subtraction is known as a **difference.** The difference of $9 - 5$ is 4. 4 represents the amount that is left once the subtraction is done. The order in which subtraction is completed does matter. For example, $9 - 5$ and $5 - 9$ do not result in the same answer. $5 - 9$ results in a negative number. So, subtraction does not adhere to the commutative or associative property. The order in which subtraction is completed is important.

Multiplication

Multiplication is when we add equal amounts. The answer to a multiplication problem is called a **product.** Products stand for the total number of items within different groups. The symbol for multiplication is× or ·. We say 2×3 or $2 \cdot 3$ means "2 times 3."

As an example, there are three sets of four apples. The goal is to know how many apples there are in total. Three sets of four apples gives:

$$4 + 4 + 4 = 12$$

Also, three times four apples gives $3 \times 4 = 12$. Therefore, for any whole numbers a and b, where a is not equal to zero, $a \times b = b + b + \cdots b$, where b is added a times. Also, $a \times b$ can be thought of as the number of units in a rectangular block consisting of a rows and b columns.

For example, 3×7 is equal to the number of squares in the following rectangle:

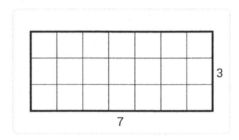

The answer is 21, and there are 21 squares in the rectangle.

When any number is multiplied by one (for example, $8 \times 1 = 8$), the value of original number does not change. Therefore, 1 is the **multiplicative identity**. For any whole number a, $1 \times a = a$. Also, any number multiplied by zero results in zero. Therefore, for any whole number a, $0 \times a = 0$.

Another method of multiplication can be done with the use of an **area model**. An area model is a rectangle that is divided into rows and columns that match up to the number of place values within each number. For example,

$$29 \times 65 = 25 + 4 \text{ and } 66 = 60 + 5$$

The products of those 4 numbers are found within the rectangle and then summed up to get the answer. The entire process is:

$$(60 \times 25) + (5 \times 25) + (60 \times 4) + (5 \times 4)$$

$$1,500 + 240 + 125 + 20 = 1,885$$

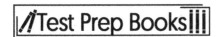

Here is the actual area model:

	25	4
60	60x25 1,500	60x4 240
5	5x25 125	5x4 20

$$
\begin{array}{r}
1,500 \\
240 \\
125 \\
+ \quad 20 \\
\hline
1,885
\end{array}
$$

Division

Division is based on dividing a given number into parts. The simplest problem involves dividing a number into equal parts. For example, if a pack of 20 pencils is to be divided among 10 children, you would have to divide 20 by 10. In this example, each child would receive 2 pencils.

The symbol for division is ÷ or /. The equation above is written as $20 \div 10 = 2$, or 20 / 10=2. This means "20 divided by 10 is equal to 2." Division can be explained as the following: for any whole numbers a and b, where b is not equal to zero, $a \div b = c$ if—and only if—$a = b \times c$. This means, division can be thought of as a multiplication problem with a missing part. For instance, calculating $20 \div 10$ is the same as asking the following: "If there are 20 items in total with 10 in each group, how many are in each group?" Therefore, 20 is equal to ten times what value? This question is the same as asking, "If there are 20 items in total with 2 in each group, how many groups are there?" The answer to each question is 2.

In a division problem, a is known as the **dividend,** b is the **divisor**, and c is the **quotient**. Zero cannot be divided into parts. Therefore, for any nonzero whole number a, $0 \div a = 0$. Also, division by zero is undefined. Dividing an amount into zero parts is not possible.

More difficult division problems involve dividing a number into equal parts, but having some left over. An example is dividing a pack of 20 pencils among 8 friends so that each friend receives the same number of pencils. In this setting, each friend receives 2 pencils, but there are 4 pencils leftover. 20 is the dividend, 8 is the divisor, 2 is the quotient, and 4 is known as the **remainder**. Within this type of division problem, for whole numbers a, b, c, and d, $a \div b = c$ with a remainder of d. This is true if and only if:

$$a = (b \times c) + d$$

When calculating $a \div b$, if there is no remainder, a is said to be *divisible* by b. **Even numbers** are all divisible by the number 2. **Odd numbers** are not divisible by 2. An odd number of items cannot be paired up into groups of 2 without having one item leftover.

Dividing a number by a single digit or two digits can be turned into repeated subtraction problems. An area model can be used throughout the problem that represents multiples of the divisor. For example, the answer to $8580 \div 55$ can be found by subtracting 55 from 8580 one at a time and counting the total number of subtractions necessary. However, a simpler process involves using larger multiples of 55. First, $100 \times 55 = 5,500$ is subtracted from 8,580, and 3,080 is leftover. Next, $50 \times 55 = 2,750$ is subtracted from 3,080 to obtain 380. $5 \times 55 = 275$ is subtracted from 330 to obtain 55, and finally, $1 \times 55 = 55$ is subtracted from 55 to obtain zero. Therefore, there is no remainder, and the answer is:

$$100 + 50 + 5 + 1 = 156$$

Here is a picture of the area model and the repeated subtraction process:

$$8580 \div 55$$

	55
100	5500
50	2750
5	275
1	55

$$
\begin{array}{r}
55 \overline{\smash{)}8580} \\
-5500 \ \text{(100 x 55)} \\
\hline
3080 \\
-2750 \ \text{(50 x 55)} \\
\hline
330 \\
-275 \ \text{(5 x 55)} \\
\hline
55 \\
-55 \ \text{(1 x 55)} \\
\hline
0
\end{array}
$$

If you want to check the answer of a division problem, multiply the answer by the divisor. This will help you check to see if the dividend is obtained. If there is a remainder, the same process is done, but the remainder is added on at the end to try to match the dividend. In the previous example, $156 \times 55 = 8580$ would be the checking procedure. Dividing decimals involves the same repeated subtraction process. The only difference would be that the subtractions would involve numbers that include values in the decimal places. Lining up decimal places is crucial in this type of problem.

Order of Operations

When reviewing calculations consisting of more than one operation, the order in which the operations are performed affects the resulting answer. Consider $5 \times 2 + 7$. Performing multiplication then addition results in an answer of 17 because ($5 \times 2 = 10$; $10 + 7 = 17$). However, if the problem is written $5 \times (2 + 7)$, the order of operations dictates that the operation inside the parenthesis must be performed first. The resulting answer is 45 because ($2 + 7 = 9$, then $5 \times 9 = 45$).

The order in which operations should be performed is remembered using the acronym PEMDAS. PEMDAS stands for parenthesis, exponents, multiplication/division, addition/subtraction. Multiplication and division are performed in the same step, working from left to right with whichever comes first. Addition and subtraction are performed in the same step, working from left to right with whichever comes first.

Consider the following example:

$$8 \div 4 + 8(7 - 7)$$

Performing the operation inside the parenthesis produces $8 \div 4 + 8(0)$ or:

$$8 \div 4 + 8 \times 0$$

There are no exponents, so multiplication and division are performed next from left to right resulting in: $2 + 8 \times 0$, then $2 + 0$. Finally, addition and subtraction are performed to obtain an answer of 2. Now consider the following example:

$$6 \times 3 + 3^2 - 6$$

Parenthesis are not applicable. Exponents are evaluated first, which brings us to:

$$6 \times 3 + 9 - 6$$

Then multiplication/division forms $18 + 9 - 6$. At last, addition/subtraction leads to the final answer of 21.

Properties of Operations

Properties of operations exist that make calculations easier and solve problems for missing values. The following table summarizes commonly used properties of real numbers.

Property	Addition	Multiplication
Commutative	$a + b = b + a$	$a \times b = b \times a$
Associative	$(a + b) + c = a + (b + c)$	$(a \times b) \times c = a \times (b \times c)$
Identity	$a + 0 = a;\ 0 + a = a$	$a \times 1 = a;\ 1 \times a = a$
Inverse	$a + (-a) = 0$	$a \times \dfrac{1}{a} = 1;\ a \neq 0$
Distributive	$a(b + c) = ab + ac$	

The **commutative property of addition** states that the order in which numbers are added does not change the sum. Similarly, the **commutative property of multiplication** states that the order in which numbers are multiplied does not change the product. The **associative property** of addition and multiplication state that the grouping of numbers being added or multiplied does not change the sum or product, respectively. The commutative and associative properties are useful for performing calculations. For example, $(47 + 25) + 3$ is equivalent to $(47 + 3) + 25$, which is easier to calculate.

The **identity property of addition** states that adding zero to any number does not change its value. The **identity property of multiplication** states that multiplying a number by 1 does not change its value. The **inverse property of addition** states that the sum of a number and its opposite equals zero. Opposites are numbers that are the same with different signs (ex. 5 and -5; $-\frac{1}{2}$ and $\frac{1}{2}$). The **inverse property of multiplication** states that the product of a number (other than 0) and its reciprocal equals 1. **Reciprocal numbers** have numerators and denominators that are inverted (ex. $\frac{2}{5}$ and $\frac{5}{2}$). Inverse properties are useful for canceling quantities to find missing values (see algebra content). For example, $a + 7 = 12$ is solved by adding the inverse of 7 (which is -7) to both sides in order to isolate a.

The **distributive property** states that multiplying a sum (or difference) by a number produces the same result as multiplying each value in the sum (or difference) by the number and adding (or subtracting) the products. Consider the following scenario: You are buying three tickets for a baseball game. Each ticket costs $18. You are also charged a fee of $2 per ticket for purchasing the tickets online. The cost is calculated:

$$3 \times 18 + 3 \times 2$$

Using the distributive property, the cost can also be calculated $3(18 + 2)$.

Adding and Subtracting Positive and Negative Numbers

Some problems require adding positive and negative numbers or subtracting positive and negative numbers. Adding a negative number to a positive one can be thought of a reducing or subtracting from the positive number, and the result should be less than the original positive number. For example, adding 8 and -3 is the same is subtracting 3 from 8; the result is 5. This can be visualized by imagining that the positive number (8) represents 8 apples that a student has in her basket. The negative number (-3) indicates the number of apples she is in debt or owes to her friend.

In order to pay off her debt and "settle the score," she essentially is in possession of three fewer apples than in her basket ($8 - 3 = 5$), so she actually has five apples that are hers to keep. Should the negative addend be of higher magnitude than the positive addend (for example $-9 + 3$), the result will be negative, but "less negative" or closer to zero than the large negative number. This is because adding a positive value, even if relatively smaller, to a negative value, reduces the magnitude of the negative in the total. Considering the apple example again, if the girl owed 9 apples to her friend (-9) but she picked 3 (+3) off a tree and gave them to her friend, she now would only owe him six apples (-6), which reduced her debt burden (her negative number of apples) by three.

Subtracting positive and negative numbers works the same way with one key distinction: subtracting a negative number from a negative number yields a "less negative" or more positive result because again, this can be considered as removing or alleviating some debt. For example, if the student with the apples owed 5 apples to her friend, she essentially has -5 applies. If her mom gives that friend 10 apples on behalf of the girl, she now has removed the need to pay back the 5 apples and surpassed neutral (no net apples owed) and now her friend owes *her* five apples (+5).

Stated mathematically:

$$-5 - (-10) = -5 + 10 = +5$$

When subtracting integers and negative rational numbers, one has to change the problem to adding the opposite and then apply the rules of addition.

- Subtracting two positive numbers is the same as adding one positive and one negative number.

  For example, $4.9 - 7.1$ is the same as $4.9 + (-7.1)$. The solution is -2.2 since the absolute value of -7.1 is greater than 4.9. Another example is $8.5 - 6.4$ which is the same as $8.5 + (-6.4)$. The solution is 2.1 since the absolute value of 8.5 is greater than 6.4.

- Subtracting a positive number from a negative number results in negative value.

    For example, $(-12) - 7$ is the same as $(-12) + (-7)$ with a solution of -19.

- Subtracting a negative number from a positive number results in a positive value.

    For example, $12 - (-7)$ is the same as $12 + 7$ with a solution of 19.

- For multiplication and division of integers and rational numbers, if both numbers are positive or both numbers are negative, the result is a positive value.

    For example, $(-1.7) \times (-4)$ has a solution of 6.8 since both numbers are negative values.

- If one number is positive and another number is negative, the result is a negative value.

    For example, $(-15) \div 5$ has a solution of -3 since there is one negative number.

Adding one positive and one negative number requires taking the absolute values and finding the difference between them. Then, the sign of the number that has the higher absolute value for the final solution is used.

Operations with Fractions, Decimals, and Percentages

Fractions

A **fraction** is a part of something that is whole. Items such as apples can be cut into parts to help visualize fractions. If an apple is cut into 2 equal parts, each part represents ½ of the apple. If each half is then cut into two parts, the apple now is cut into quarters. Each piece now represents ¼ of the apple. In this example, each part is equal because they all have the same size. Geometric shapes, such as circles and squares, can also be utilized to help visualize the idea of fractions. For example, a circle can be drawn on the board and divided into 6 equal parts:

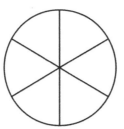

Shading can be used to represent parts of the circle that can be translated into fractions. The top of the fraction, the **numerator,** can represent how many segments are shaded. The bottom of the fraction, the **denominator,** can represent the number of segments that the circle is broken into. A pie is a good analogy to use in this example. If one piece of the circle is shaded, or one piece of pie is cut out, $^1/_6$ of the object is being referred to. An apple, a pie, or a circle can be utilized in order to compare simple fractions. For example, showing that ½ is larger than ¼ and that ¼ is smaller than $^1/_3$ can be

accomplished through shading. A **unit fraction** is a fraction in which the numerator is 1, and the denominator is a positive whole number. It represents one part of a whole—one piece of pie.

Imagine that an apple pie has been baked for a holiday party, and the full pie has eight slices. After the party, there are five slices left. How could the amount of the pie that remains be expressed as a fraction? The numerator is 5 since there are 5 pieces left, and the denominator is 8 since there were eight total slices in the whole pie. Thus, expressed as a fraction, the leftover pie totals $\frac{5}{8}$ of the original amount.

Fractions come in three different varieties: proper fractions, improper fractions, and mixed numbers. **Proper fractions** have a numerator less than the denominator, such as $\frac{3}{8}$, but **improper fractions** have a numerator greater than the denominator, such as $\frac{15}{8}$. **Mixed numbers** combine a whole number with a proper fraction, such as $3\frac{1}{2}$. Any mixed number can be written as an improper fraction by multiplying the integer by the denominator, adding the product to the value of the numerator, and dividing the sum by the original denominator. For example:

$$3\frac{1}{2} = \frac{3 \times 2 + 1}{2} = \frac{7}{2}$$

Whole numbers can also be converted into fractions by placing the whole number as the numerator and making the denominator 1. For example, $3 = \frac{3}{1}$.

The bar in a fraction represents division. Therefore $\frac{6}{5}$ is the same as $6 \div 5$. In order to rewrite it as a mixed number, division is performed to obtain:

$$6 \div 5 = 1 \text{ R } 1$$

The remainder is then converted into fraction form. The actual remainder becomes the numerator of a fraction, and the divisor becomes the denominator. Therefore, 1 R 1 is written as $1\frac{1}{5}$, a mixed number. A mixed number can also decompose into the addition of a whole number and a fraction. For example,

$$1\frac{1}{5} = 1 + \frac{1}{5} \text{ and } 4\frac{5}{6} = 4 + \frac{1}{6} + \frac{1}{6} + \frac{1}{6} + \frac{1}{6} + \frac{1}{6}$$

Every fraction can be built from a combination of unit fractions.

One of the most fundamental concepts of fractions is their ability to be manipulated by multiplication or division. This is possible since $\frac{n}{n} = 1$ for any non-zero integer. As a result, multiplying or dividing by $\frac{n}{n}$ will not alter the original fraction since any number multiplied or divided by 1 doesn't change the value of that number. Fractions of the same value are known as equivalent fractions. For example, $\frac{2}{8}, \frac{25}{100},$ and $\frac{40}{160}$ are equivalent, as they are all equal to $\frac{1}{4}$.

Like fractions, or **equivalent fractions**, are the terms used to describe these fractions that are made up of different numbers but represent the same quantity. For example, the given fractions are $^4/_8$ and $^3/_6$. If a pie was cut into 8 pieces and 4 pieces were removed, half of the pie would remain. Also, if a pie was split into 6 pieces and 3 pieces were eaten, half of the pie would also remain. Therefore, both of the fractions represent half of a pie. These two fractions are referred to as like fractions. **Unlike fractions**

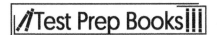

are fractions that are different and do not represent equal quantities. When working with fractions in mathematical expressions, like fractions should be simplified. Both ⁴/₈ and ³/₆ can be simplified into ¹/₂.

Comparing fractions can be completed through the use of a number line. For example, if $\frac{3}{5}$ and $\frac{6}{10}$ need to be compared, each fraction should be plotted on a number line. To plot $\frac{3}{5}$ the area from 0 to 1 should be broken into 5 equal segments, and the fraction represents 3 of them. To plot $\frac{6}{10}$ the area from 0 to 1 should be broken into 10 equal segments, and the fraction represents 6 of them.

It can be seen that $\frac{3}{5} = \frac{6}{10}$

Like fractions are plotted at the same point on a number line. Unit fractions can also be used to compare fractions. For example, if it is known that:

$$\frac{4}{5} > \frac{1}{2}$$

and

$$\frac{1}{2} > \frac{4}{10}$$

Then, it is also known that:

$$\frac{4}{5} > \frac{4}{10}$$

Also, converting improper fractions to mixed numbers can be helpful in comparing fractions because the whole number portion of the number is more visible.

Adding and subtracting mixed numbers and fractions can be completed by decomposing fractions into a sum of whole numbers and unit fractions. For example, the given problem is:

$$5\frac{3}{7} + 2\frac{1}{7}$$

Decomposing into,

$$5 + \frac{1}{7} + \frac{1}{7} + \frac{1}{7} + 2 + \frac{1}{7}$$

This shows that the whole numbers can be added separately from the unit fractions. The answer is:

$$5 + 2 + \frac{1}{7} + \frac{1}{7} + \frac{1}{7} + \frac{1}{7} = 7 + \frac{4}{7} = 7\frac{4}{7}$$

Although many equivalent fractions exist, they are easier to compare and interpret when reduced or simplified. The numerator and denominator of a simple fraction will have no factors in common other than 1. When reducing or simplifying fractions, divide the numerator and denominator by the greatest common factor. A simple strategy is to divide the numerator and denominator by low numbers, like 2, 3, or 5 until arriving at a simple fraction, but the same thing could be achieved by determining the greatest common factor for both the numerator and denominator and dividing each by it. Using the first method is preferable when both the numerator and denominator are even, end in 5, or are obviously a multiple of another number. However, if no numbers seem to work, it will be necessary to factor the numerator and denominator to find the GCF. Let's look at examples:

1) Simplify the fraction $\frac{6}{8}$:

Dividing the numerator and denominator by 2 results in $\frac{3}{4}$, which is a simple fraction.

2) Simplify the fraction $\frac{12}{36}$:

Dividing the numerator and denominator by 2 leaves $\frac{6}{18}$. This isn't a simple fraction, as both the numerator and denominator have factors in common. Dividing each by 3 results in $\frac{2}{6}$, but this can be further simplified by dividing by 2 to get $\frac{1}{3}$. This is the simplest fraction, as the numerator is 1. In cases like this, multiple division operations can be avoided by determining the greatest common factor (12, in this case) between the numerator and denominator.

3) Simplify the fraction $\frac{18}{54}$ by dividing by the greatest common factor:

First, determine the factors for the numerator and denominator. The factors of 18 are 1, 2, 3, 6, 9, and 18. The factors of 54 are 1, 2, 3, 6, 9, 18, 27, and 54. Thus, the greatest common factor is 18. Dividing $\frac{18}{54}$ by 18 leaves $\frac{1}{3}$, which is the simplest fraction. This method takes slightly more work, but it definitively arrives at the simplest fraction.

Adding and Subtracting Fractions
Adding and subtracting fractions that have the same denominators involves adding or subtracting the numerators. The denominator will stay the same. Therefore, the decomposition process can be made simpler, and the fractions do not have to be broken into unit fractions.

For example, the given problem is:

$$4\frac{7}{8} - 2\frac{6}{8}$$

The answer is found by adding the answers to both

$$4 - 2 \text{ and } \frac{7}{8} - \frac{6}{8}$$

$$2 + \frac{1}{8} = 2\frac{1}{8}$$

A common mistake would be to add the denominators so that $\frac{1}{4} + \frac{1}{4} = \frac{1}{8}$ or to add numerators and denominators so that:

$$\frac{1}{4} + \frac{1}{4} = \frac{2}{8}$$

However, conceptually, it is known that two quarters make a half, so neither one of these are correct.

If two fractions have different denominators, equivalent fractions must be used to add or subtract them. The fractions must be converted into fractions that have common denominators. A **least common denominator** or the product of the two denominators can be used as the common denominator. For example, in the problem $\frac{5}{6} + \frac{2}{3}$, either 6, which is the least common denominator, or 18, which is the product of the denominators, can be used. In order to use 6, $\frac{2}{3}$ must be converted to sixths. A number line can be used to show the equivalent fraction is $\frac{4}{6}$. What happens is that $\frac{2}{3}$ is multiplied by a fractional form of 1 to obtain a denominator of 6. Hence:

$$\frac{2}{3} \times \frac{2}{2} = \frac{4}{6}$$

Therefore, the problem is now $\frac{5}{6} + \frac{4}{6} = \frac{9}{6}$, which can be simplified into $\frac{3}{2}$. In order to use 18, both fractions must be converted into having 18 as their denominator. $\frac{5}{6}$ would have to be multiplied by $\frac{3}{3}$, and $\frac{2}{3}$ would need to be multiplied by $\frac{6}{6}$. The addition problem would be $\frac{15}{18} + \frac{12}{18} = \frac{27}{18}$, which reduces into $\frac{3}{2}$.

It is always possible to find a common denominator by multiplying the denominators. However, when the denominators are large numbers, this method is unwieldy, especially if the answer must be provided in its simplest form. Thus, it's beneficial to find the **least common denominator** of the fractions—the least common denominator is incidentally also the **least common multiple**.

Once equivalent fractions have been found with common denominators, simply add or subtract the numerators to arrive at the answer:

1) $\frac{1}{2} + \frac{3}{4} = \frac{2}{4} + \frac{3}{4} = \frac{5}{4}$

2) $\frac{3}{12} + \frac{11}{20} = \frac{15}{60} + \frac{33}{60} = \frac{48}{60} = \frac{4}{5}$

3) $\frac{7}{9} - \frac{4}{15} = \frac{35}{45} - \frac{12}{45} = \frac{23}{45}$

4) $\frac{5}{6} - \frac{7}{18} = \frac{15}{18} - \frac{7}{18} = \frac{8}{18} = \frac{4}{9}$

Multiplying and Dividing Fractions

Of the four basic operations that can be performed on fractions, the one that involves the least amount of work is multiplication. To multiply two fractions, simply multiply the numerators together, multiply the denominators together, and place the products of each as a fraction. Whole numbers and mixed numbers can also be expressed as a fraction, as described above, to multiply with a fraction.

54

Because multiplication is commutative, multiplying a fraction by a whole number is the same as multiplying a whole number by a fraction. The problem involves adding a fraction a specific number of times. The problem $3 \times \frac{1}{4}$ can be translated into adding the unit fraction three times:

$$\frac{1}{4} + \frac{1}{4} + \frac{1}{4} = \frac{3}{4}$$

In the problem $4 \times \frac{2}{5}$, the fraction can be decomposed into $\frac{1}{5} + \frac{1}{5}$ and then added four times to obtain $\frac{8}{5}$. Also, both of these answers can be found by just multiplying the whole number by the numerator of the fraction being multiplied.

The whole numbers can be written in fraction form as:

$$\frac{3}{1} \times \frac{1}{4} = \frac{3}{4}$$

$$\frac{4}{1} \times \frac{2}{5} = \frac{8}{5}$$

Multiplying a fraction times a fraction involves multiplying the numerators together separately and the denominators together separately. For example,

$$\frac{3}{8} \times \frac{2}{3} = \frac{3 \times 2}{8 \times 3} = \frac{6}{24}$$

This can then be reduced to $\frac{1}{4}$

Dividing a fraction by a fraction is actually a multiplication problem. It involves flipping the divisor and then multiplying normally. For example,

$$\frac{22}{5} \div \frac{1}{2} = \frac{22}{5} \times \frac{2}{1} = \frac{44}{5}$$

The same procedure can be implemented for division problems involving fractions and whole numbers. The whole number can be rewritten as a fraction over a denominator of 1, and then division can be completed.

A common denominator approach can also be used in dividing fractions. Considering the same problem, $\frac{22}{5} \div \frac{1}{2}$, a common denominator between the two fractions is 10. $\frac{22}{5}$ would be rewritten as $\frac{22}{5} \times \frac{2}{2} = \frac{44}{10}$, and $\frac{1}{2}$ would be rewritten as:

$$\frac{1}{2} \times \frac{5}{5} = \frac{5}{10}$$

Dividing both numbers straight across results in:

$$\frac{44}{10} \div \frac{5}{10} = \frac{44/5}{10/10} = \frac{44/5}{1} = 44/5$$

55

Many real-world problems will involve the use of fractions. Key words include actual fraction values, such as *half, quarter, third, fourth*, etc. The best approach to solving word problems involving fractions is to draw a picture or diagram that represents the scenario being discussed, while deciding which type of operation is necessary in order to solve the problem. A phrase such as "one fourth of 60 pounds of coal" creates a scenario in which multiplication should be used, and the mathematical form of the phrase is $\frac{1}{4} \times 60$.

Decimals

The **decimal system** is a way of writing out numbers that uses ten different numerals: 0, 1, 2, 3, 4, 5, 6, 7, 8, and 9. This is also called a "base ten" or "base 10" system. Other bases are also used. For example, computers work with a base of 2. This means they only use the numerals 0 and 1.

The **decimal place** denotes how far to the right of the decimal point a numeral is. The first digit to the right of the decimal point is in the **tenths'** place. The next is the **hundredths'** place. The third is the **thousandths'** place.

So, 3.142 has a 1 in the tenths place, a 4 in the hundredths place, and a 2 in the thousandths place.

The **decimal point** is a period used to separate the **ones'** place from the **tenths'** place when writing out a number as a decimal.

A **decimal number** is a number written out with a decimal point instead of as a fraction, for example, 1.25 instead of $\frac{5}{4}$. Depending on the situation, it may be easier to work with fractions, while other times, it may be easier to work with decimal numbers.

A decimal number is **terminating** if it stops at some point. It is called **repeating** if it never stops but repeats over and over. It is important to note that every rational number can be written as a terminating decimal or as a repeating decimal.

Addition with Decimals

To add decimal numbers, each number needs to be lined up by the decimal point in vertical columns. For each number being added, the zeros to the right of the last number need to be filled in so that each of the numbers has the same number of places to the right of the decimal. Then, the columns can be added together. Here is an example of 2.45+1.3+8.891 written in column form:

$$
\begin{array}{r}
2.450 \\
1.300 \\
+\ 8.891 \\
\end{array}
$$

Zeros have been added in the columns so that each number has the same number of places to the right of the decimal.

Added together, the correct answer is 12.641:

$$
\begin{array}{r}
2.450 \\
1.300 \\
+\ 8.891 \\
\hline
12.641 \\
\end{array}
$$

Subtraction with Decimals

Subtracting decimal numbers is the same process as adding decimals. Here is $7.89 - 4.235$ written in column form:

$$
\begin{array}{r}
7.890 \\
- \underline{4.235} \\
3.655
\end{array}
$$

A zero has been added in the column so that each number has the same number of places to the right of the decimal.

Multiplication with Decimals

The simplest way to multiply decimals is to calculate the product as if the decimals are not there, then count the number of decimal places in the original problem. Use that total to place the decimal the same number of places over in your answer, counting from right to left. For example, 0.5×1.25 can be rewritten and multiplied as 5×125, which equals 625. Then the decimal is added three places from the right for 0.625.

The final answer will have the same number of decimal places as the total number of decimal places in the problem. The first number has one decimal place, and the second number has two decimal places. Therefore, the final answer will contain three decimal places:

$$0.5 \times 1.25 = 0.625$$

Division with Decimals

Dividing a decimal by a whole number entails using long division first by ignoring the decimal point. Then, the decimal point is moved the number of places given in the problem.

For example, $6.8 \div 4$ can be rewritten as $68 \div 4$, which is 17. There is one non-zero integer to the right of the decimal point, so the final solution would have one decimal place to the right of the solution. In this case, the solution is 1.7.

Dividing a decimal by another decimal requires changing the divisor to a whole number by moving its decimal point. The decimal place of the dividend should be moved by the same number of places as the divisor. Then, the problem is the same as dividing a decimal by a whole number.

For example, $5.72 \div 1.1$ has a divisor with one decimal point in the denominator. The expression can be rewritten as $57.2 \div 11$ by moving each number one decimal place to the right to eliminate the decimal. The long division can be completed as $572 \div 11$ with a result of 52. Since there is one non-zero integer to the right of the decimal point in the problem, the final solution is 5.2.

In another example, $8 \div 0.16$ has a divisor with two decimal points in the denominator. The expression can be rewritten as $800 \div 16$ by moving each number two decimal places to the right to eliminate the decimal in the divisor. The long division can be completed with a result of 50.

Percentages

Think of percentages as fractions with a denominator of 100. In fact, **percentage** means "per hundred." Problems often require converting numbers from percentages, fractions, and decimals.

The basic percent equation is the following:

$$\frac{is}{of} = \frac{\%}{100}$$

The placement of numbers in the equation depends on what the question asks.

Example 1
Find 40% of 80.

Basically, the problem is asking, "What is 40% of 80?" The 40% is the percent, and 80 is the number to find the percent "of." The equation is:

$$\frac{x}{80} = \frac{40}{100}$$

After cross-multiplying, the problem becomes $100x = 80(40)$. Solving for x produces the answer: $x = 32$.

Example 2
What percent of 90 is 20?

The 20 fills in the "is" portion, while 90 fills in the "of." The question asks for the percent, so that will be x, the unknown. The following equation is set up:

$$\frac{20}{90} = \frac{x}{100}$$

Cross-multiplying yields the equation $90x = 20(100)$. Solving for x gives the answer: 22.2%.

Example 3
30% of what number is 30?

The following equation uses the clues and numbers in the problem:

$$\frac{30}{x} = \frac{30}{100}$$

Cross-multiplying results in the equation $30(100) = 30x$. Solving for x gives the answer: $x = 100$.

Conversions
Decimals and Percentages
Since a percentage is based on "per hundred," decimals and percentages can be converted by multiplying or dividing by 100. Practically speaking, this always involves moving the decimal point two places to the right or left, depending on the conversion. To convert a percentage to a decimal, move the decimal point two places to the left and remove the % sign. To convert a decimal to a percentage, move the decimal point two places to the right and add a "%" sign. Here are some examples:

65%=0.65
0.33=33%
0.215=21.5%
99.99%=0.9999

58

500%=5.00

7.55=755%

Fractions and Percentages

Remember that a percentage is a number per one hundred. So, a percentage can be converted to a fraction by making the number in the percentage the numerator and putting 100 as the denominator:

$$43\% = \frac{43}{100}$$

$$97\% = \frac{97}{100}$$

Note that the percent symbol (%) kind of looks like a 0, a 1, and another 0. So, think of a percentage like 54% as 54 over 100.

To convert a fraction to a percent, follow the same logic. If the fraction happens to have 100 in the denominator, you're in luck. Just take the numerator and add a percent symbol:

$$\frac{28}{100} = 28\%$$

Otherwise, divide the numerator by the denominator to get a decimal:

$$\frac{9}{12} = 0.75$$

Then convert the decimal to a percentage:

$$0.75 = 75\%$$

Another option is to make the denominator equal to 100. Be sure to multiply the numerator and the denominator by the same number. For example:

$$\frac{3}{20} \times \frac{5}{5} = \frac{15}{100}$$

$$\frac{15}{100} = 15\%$$

Changing Fractions to Decimals

To change a fraction into a decimal, divide the denominator into the numerator until there are no remainders. There may be repeating decimals, so rounding is often acceptable. A straight line above the repeating portion denotes that the decimal repeats.

Example: Express $\frac{4}{5}$ as a decimal.

Set up the division problem.

$$5\overline{)4}$$

5 does not go into 4, so place the decimal and add a zero.

$$5\overline{)4.0}$$

59

5 goes into 40 eight times. There is no remainder.

$$
\begin{array}{r}
0.8 \\
5\overline{)4.0} \\
-\ 4.0 \\
\hline
0
\end{array}
$$

The solution is 0.8.

Example: Express $33\frac{1}{3}$ as a decimal.

Since the whole portion of the number is known, set it aside to calculate the decimal from the fraction portion.

Set up the division problem.

$$3\overline{)1}$$

3 does not go into 1, so place the decimal and add zeros. 3 goes into 10 three times.

$$
\begin{array}{r}
0.3 \\
3\overline{)1.0}
\end{array}
$$

This will repeat with a remainder of 1.

$$
\begin{array}{r}
0.333 \\
3\overline{)1.000} \\
-9 \\
\hline
10 \\
-9 \\
\hline
10
\end{array}
$$

So, we will place a line over the 3 to denote the repetition. The solution is written $0.\overline{3}$.

Changing Decimals to Fractions

To change decimals to fractions, place the decimal portion of the number — the numerator — over the respective place value — the denominator — then reduce, if possible.

Example: Express 0.25 as a fraction.

This is read as twenty-five hundredths, so put 25 over 100. Then reduce to find the solution.

$$\frac{25}{100} = \frac{1}{4}$$

Example: Express 0.455 as a fraction

This is read as four hundred fifty-five thousandths, so put 455 over 1,000. Then reduce to find the solution.

$$\frac{455}{1,000} = \frac{91}{200}$$

There are two types of problems that commonly involve percentages. The first is to calculate some percentage of a given quantity, where you convert the percentage to a decimal, and multiply the quantity by that decimal. Secondly, you are given a quantity and told it is a fixed percent of an unknown quantity. In this case, convert to a decimal, then divide the given quantity by that decimal.

Example: What is 30% of 760?

Convert the percent into a useable number. "Of" means to multiply.

$$30\% = 0.30$$

Set up the problem based on the givens, and solve.

$$0.30 \times 760 = 228$$

Example: 8.4 is 20% of what number?

Convert the percent into a useable number.

$$20\% = 0.20$$

The given number is a percent of the answer needed, so divide the given number by this decimal rather than multiplying it.

$$\frac{8.4}{0.20} = 42$$

Factorization

Factors are the numbers multiplied to achieve a product. Thus, every product in a multiplication equation has, at minimum, two factors. Of course, some products will have more than two factors. For the sake of most discussions, assume that factors are positive integers.

To find a number's factors, start with 1 and the number itself. Then divide the number by 2, 3, 4, and so on, seeing if any divisors can divide the number without a remainder, keeping a list of those that do. Stop upon reaching either the number itself or another factor.

Let's find the factors of 45. Start with 1 and 45. Then try to divide 45 by 2, which fails. Now divide 45 by 3. The answer is 15, so 3 and 15 are now factors. Dividing by 4 doesn't work, and dividing by 5 leaves 9. Lastly, dividing 45 by 6, 7, and 8 all don't work. The next integer to try is 9, but this is already known to be a factor, so the factorization is complete. The factors of 45 are 1, 3, 5, 9, 15 and 45.

Prime Factorization
Prime factorization involves an additional step after breaking a number down to its factors: breaking down the factors until they are all prime numbers. A **prime number** is any number that can only be divided by 1 and itself. The prime numbers between 1 and 20 are 2, 3, 5, 7, 11, 13, 17, and 19. As a

61

simple test, numbers that are even or end in 5 are not prime, though there are other numbers that are not prime, but are odd and do not end in 5. For example, 21 is odd and divisible by 1, 3, 7, and 21, so it is not prime.

Let's break 129 down into its prime factors. First, the factors are 3 and 43. Both 3 and 43 are prime numbers, so we're done. But if 43 was not a prime number, then it would also need to be factorized until all of the factors are expressed as prime numbers.

Common Factor
A **common factor** is a factor shared by two numbers. Let's take 45 and 30 and find the common factors:

The factors of 45 are: 1, 3, 5, 9, 15, and 45.
The factors of 30 are: 1, 2, 3, 5, 6, 10, 15, and 30.
Thus, the common factors are 1, 3, 5, and 15.

Greatest Common Factor
The **greatest common factor** is the largest number among the shared, common factors. From the factors of 45 and 30, the common factors are 3, 5, and 15. Therefore, 15 is the greatest common factor, as it's the largest number.

Least Common Multiple
The **least common multiple** is the smallest number that is a multiple of two numbers. Let's try to find the least common multiple of 4 and 9. The multiples of 4 are 4, 8, 12, 16, 20, 24, 28, 32, 36, and so on. For 9, the multiples are 9, 18, 27, 36, 45, 54, etc. Thus, the least common multiple of 4 and 9 is 36 because this is the lowest number where 4 and 9 share multiples.

If two numbers share no factors besides 1 in common, then their least common multiple will be simply their product. If two numbers have common factors, then their least common multiple will be their product divided by their greatest common factor. This can be visualized by the formula $LCM = \frac{x \times y}{GCF}$, where x and y are some integers, and LCM and GCF are their least common multiple and greatest common factor, respectively.

Exponents

An **exponent** is an operation used as shorthand for a number multiplied or divided by itself for a defined number of times.

$$3^7 = 3 \times 3 \times 3 \times 3 \times 3 \times 3 \times 3$$

In this example, the 3 is called the **base**, and the 7 is called the **exponent**. The exponent is typically expressed as a superscript number near the upper right side of the base but can also be identified as the number following a caret symbol (^). This operation is verbally expressed as "3 to the 7th power" or "3 raised to the power of 7." Common exponents are 2 and 3. A base raised to the power of 2 is referred to as having been "squared," while a base raised to the power of 3 is referred to as having been "cubed."

Several special rules apply to exponents. First, the **Zero Power Rule** finds that any number raised to the zero power equals 1. For example, 100^0, 2^0, $(-3)^0$ and 0^0 all equal 1 because the bases are raised to the zero power.

62

Second, exponents can be negative. With negative exponents, the equation is expressed as a fraction, as in the following example:

$$3^{-7} = \frac{1}{3^7} = \frac{1}{3 \times 3 \times 3 \times 3 \times 3 \times 3 \times 3}$$

Third, the **Power Rule** concerns exponents being raised by another exponent. When this occurs, the exponents are multiplied by each other:

$$(x^2)^3 = x^6 = (x^3)^2$$

Fourth, when multiplying two exponents with the same base, the **Product Rule** requires that the base remains the same, and the exponents are added. For example, $a^x \times a^y = a^{x+y}$. Since addition and multiplication are commutative, the two terms being multiplied can be in any order.

$$x^3 x^5 = x^{3+5} = x^8 = x^{5+3} = x^5 x^3$$

Fifth, when dividing two exponents with the same base, the **Quotient Rule** requires that the base remains the same, but the exponents are subtracted. So, $a^x \div a^y = a^{x-y}$. Since subtraction and division are not commutative, the two terms must remain in order.

$$x^5 x^{-3} = x^{5-3} = x^2 = x^5 \div x^3 = \frac{x^5}{x^3}$$

Additionally, 1 raised to any power is still equal to 1, and any number raised to the power of 1 is equal to itself. In other words, $a^1 = a$ and $14^1 = 14$.

Exponents play an important role in scientific notation to present extremely large or small numbers as follows: $a \times 10^b$. To write the number in scientific notation, the decimal is moved until there is only one digit on the left side of the decimal point, indicating that the number a has a value between 1 and 10. The number of times the decimal moves indicates the exponent to which 10 is raised, here represented by b. If the decimal moves to the left, then b is positive, but if the decimal moves to the right, then b is negative. The following examples demonstrate these concepts:

$$3{,}050 = 3.05 \times 10^3$$

$$-777 = -7.77 \times 10^2$$

$$0.000123 = 1.23 \times 10^{-4}$$

$$-0.0525 = -5.25 \times 10^{-2}$$

Roots

The **square root** symbol is expressed as $\sqrt{}$ and is commonly known as the radical. Taking the root of a number is the inverse operation of multiplying that number by itself some number of times. For example, squaring the number 7 is equal to 7×7, or 49. Finding the square root is the opposite of finding an exponent, as the operation seeks a number that when multiplied by itself, equals the number in the square root symbol.

63

For example, $\sqrt{36} = 6$ because 6 multiplied by 6 equals 36. Note, the square root of 36 is also -6 since $-6 \times -6 = 36$. This can be indicated using a **plus/minus** symbol like this: ± 6. However, square roots are often just expressed as a positive number for simplicity, with it being understood that the true value can be either positive or negative.

Perfect squares are numbers with whole number square roots. The list of perfect squares begins with 0, 1, 4, 9, 16, 25, 36, 49, 64, 81, and 100.

Determining the square root of imperfect squares requires a calculator to reach an exact figure. It's possible, however, to approximate the answer by finding the two perfect squares that the number fits between. For example, the square root of 40 is between 6 and 7 since the squares of those numbers are 36 and 49, respectively.

Square roots are the most common root operation. If the radical doesn't have a number to the upper left of the symbol $\sqrt{\ }$, then it's a **square root**. Sometimes a radical includes a number in the upper left, like $\sqrt[3]{27}$, as in the other common root type—the **cube root**. Complicated roots, like the cube root, often require a calculator.

Estimation

Estimation is finding a value that is close to a solution but is not the exact answer. For example, if there are values in the thousands to be multiplied, then each value can be estimated to the nearest thousand and the calculation performed. This value provides an approximate solution that can be determined very quickly.

Rounding is the process of either bumping a number up or leaving it the same, based on a specified place value. First, the place value is specified. Then, the digit to its right is looked at. For example, if rounding to the nearest hundreds place, the digit in the tens place is used. If it is a 0, 1, 2, 3, or 4, the digit being rounded to is left alone. If it is a 5, 6, 7, 8 or 9, the digit being rounded to is increased by one. All other digits before the decimal point are then changed to zeros, and the digits in decimal places are dropped. If a decimal place is being rounded to, all subsequent digits are just dropped. For example, if 845,231.45 was to be rounded to the nearest thousands place, the answer would be 845,000. The 5 would remain the same due to the 2 in the hundreds place. Also, if 4.567 was to be rounded to the nearest tenths place, the answer would be 4.6. The 5 increased to 6 due to the 6 in the hundredths place, and the rest of the decimal is dropped.

Sometimes when performing operations such as multiplying numbers, the result can be estimated by rounding. For example, to estimate the value of 11.2×2.01, each number can be rounded to the nearest integer. This will yield a result of 22.

Rounding numbers helps with estimation because it changes the given number to a simpler, although less accurate, number than the exact given number. Rounding allows for easier calculations, which estimate the results of using the exact given number. The accuracy of the estimate and ease of use depends on the place value to which the number is rounded. Rounding numbers consists of:

- Determining what place value the number is being rounded to
- Examining the digit to the right of the desired place value to decide whether to round up or keep the digit, and
- Replacing all digits to the right of the desired place value with zeros.

To round 746,311 to the nearest ten thousand, the digit in the ten thousands place should be located first. In this case, this digit is 4 (7<u>4</u>6,311). Then, the digit to its right is examined. If this digit is 5 or greater, the number will be rounded up by increasing the digit in the desired place by one. If the digit to the right of the place value being rounded is 4 or less, the number will be kept the same. For the given example, the digit being examined is a 6, which means that the number will be rounded up by increasing the digit to the left by one.

Therefore, the digit 4 is changed to a 5. Finally, to write the rounded number, any digits to the left of the place value being rounded remain the same and any to its right are replaced with zeros. For the given example, rounding 746,311 to the nearest ten thousand will produce 750,000. To round 746,311 to the nearest hundred, the digit to the right of the three in the hundreds place is examined to determine whether to round up or keep the same number. In this case, that digit is a 1, so the number will be kept the same and any digits to its right will be replaced with zeros. The resulting rounded number is 746,300.

Rounding place values to the right of the decimal follows the same procedure, but digits being replaced by zeros can simply be dropped. To round 3.752891 to the nearest thousandth, the desired place value is located (3.75<u>2</u>891) and the digit to the right is examined. In this case, the digit 8 indicates that the number will be rounded up, and the 2 in the thousandths place will increase to a 3. Rounding up and replacing the digits to the right of the thousandths place produces 3.753000 which is equivalent to 3.753. Therefore, the zeros are not necessary, and the rounded number should be written as 3.753.

When rounding up, if the digit to be increased is a 9, the digit to its left is increased by 1 and the digit in the desired place value is changed to a zero. For example, the number 1,598 rounded to the nearest ten is 1,600. Another example shows the number 43.72961 rounded to the nearest thousandth is 43.730 or 43.73.

Vectors

A **vector** can be thought of as an abstract list of numbers or as giving a location in a space. For example, the coordinates (x, y) for points in the Cartesian plane are vectors. Each entry in a vector can be referred to by its location in the list: first, second, third, and so on. The total length of the list is the **dimension** of the vector. A vector is often denoted as such by putting an arrow on top of it, e.g., $\vec{v} = (v_1, v_2, v_3)$.

Adding Vectors Graphically and Algebraically

There are two basic operations for vectors. First, two vectors can be added together. Let:

$$\vec{v} = (v_1, v_2, v_3)$$

$$\vec{w} = (w_1, w_2, w_3)$$

The sum of the two vectors is defined to be:

$$\vec{v} + \vec{w} = (v_1 + w_1, v_2 + w_2, v_3 + w_3)$$

Subtraction of vectors can be defined similarly.

Vector addition can be visualized in the following manner. First, each vector can be visualized as an arrow. Then, the base of one arrow is placed at the tip of the other arrow. The tip of this first arrow now

65

hits some point in space, and there will be an arrow from the origin to this point. This new arrow corresponds to the new vector. In subtraction, the direction of the arrow being subtracted is reversed.

For example, if adding together the vectors $(-2, 3)$ and $(4, 1)$, the new vector will be $(-2 + 4, 3 + 1)$, or $(2, 4)$. Graphically, this may be pictured in the following manner:

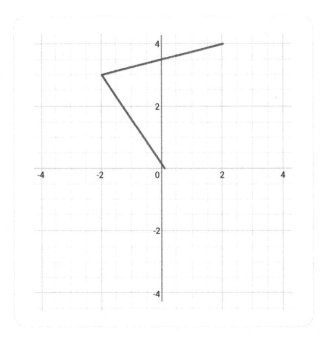

Performing Scalar Multiplications

The second basic operation for vectors is called **scalar multiplication**. Scalar multiplication is multiplying any vector by any real number, which is denoted here as a scalar. Let $\vec{v} = (v_1, v_2, v_3)$, and let a be an arbitrary real number. Then the scalar multiple $a\vec{v} = (av_1, av_2, av_3)$. Graphically, this corresponds to changing the length of the arrow corresponding to the vector by a factor, or scale, of a. That is why the real number is called a **scalar** in this instance.

As an example, let $\vec{v} = (2, -1, 1)$. Then $3\vec{v} = (3 \cdot 2, 3(-1), 3 \cdot 1) = (6, -3, 3)$.

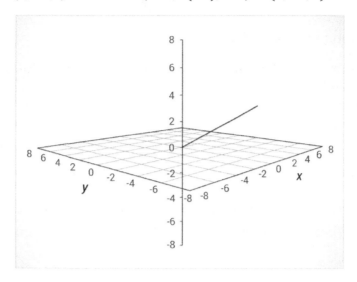

Note that scalar multiplication is **distributive** over vector addition, meaning that $a(\vec{v} + \vec{w}) = a\vec{v} + a\vec{w}$.

Determinants

A **matrix** is a rectangular arrangement of numbers in rows and columns. The **determinant** of a matrix is a special value that can be calculated for any square matrix.

Using the *square* 2×2 *matrix* $\begin{bmatrix} a & b \\ c & d \end{bmatrix}$, the determinant is $ad - bc$.

For example, the determinant of the matrix $\begin{bmatrix} -5 & 1 \\ 3 & 4 \end{bmatrix}$ is:

$$-5(4) - 1(3) = -20 - 3 = -23$$

Using a 3×3 *matrix* $\begin{bmatrix} a & b & c \\ d & e & f \\ g & h & i \end{bmatrix}$, the determinant is:

$$a(ei - fh) - b(di - fg) + c(dh - eg)$$

For example, the determinant of the matrix $\begin{bmatrix} 2 & 0 & 1 \\ -1 & 3 & 2 \\ 2 & -2 & -1 \end{bmatrix}$ is

$$2\big(3(-1) - 2(-2)\big) - 0\big(-1(-1) - 2(2)\big) + 1\big(-1(-2) - 3(2)\big)$$

$$2(-3 + 4) - 0(1 - 4) + 1(2 - 6)$$

$$2(1) - 0(-3) + 1(-4)$$

$$2 - 0 - 4 = -2$$

The pattern continues for larger square matrices.

Algebra

Algebraic Expressions and Equations

An **algebraic expression** is a statement about an unknown quantity expressed in mathematical symbols. A **variable** is used to represent the unknown quantity, usually denoted by a letter. An equation is a statement in which two expressions (at least one containing a variable) are equal to each other. An algebraic expression can be thought of as a mathematical phrase and an equation can be thought of as a mathematical sentence.

Algebraic expressions and equations both contain numbers, variables, and mathematical operations. The following are examples of algebraic expressions: $5x + 3, 7xy - 8(x^2 + y)$, and $\sqrt{a^2 + b^2}$. An expression can be simplified or evaluated for given values of variables. The following are examples of equations: $2x + 3 = 7, a^2 + b^2 = c^2$, and:

$$2x + 5 = 3x - 2$$

An equation contains two sides separated by an equal sign. Equations can be solved to determine the value(s) of the variable for which the statement is true.

Parts of Expressions

Algebraic expressions consist of variables, numbers, and operations. A **term** of an expression is any combination of numbers and/or variables, and terms are separated by addition and subtraction. For example, the expression $5x^2 - 3xy + 4 - 2$ consists of 4 terms: $5x^2, -3xy, 4y$, and -2. Note that each term includes its given sign (+ or −). The **variable** part of a term is a letter that represents an unknown quantity. The **coefficient** of a term is the number by which the variable is multiplied. For the term $4y$, the variable is y, and the coefficient is 4. Terms are identified by the power (or exponent) of its variable.

A number without a variable is referred to as a **constant**. If the variable is to the first power (x^1 or simply x), it is referred to as a linear term. A term with a variable to the second power (x^2) is quadratic, and a term to the third power (x^3) is cubic. Consider the expression:

$$x^3 + 3x - 1$$

The constant is -1. The linear term is $3x$. There is no quadratic term. The cubic term is x^3.

An algebraic expression can also be classified by how many terms exist in the expression. Any like terms should be combined before classifying. A **monomial** is an expression consisting of only one term. Examples of monomials are: $17, 2x$, and $-5ab^2$. A **binomial** is an expression consisting of two terms separated by addition or subtraction. Examples include $2x - 4$ and $-3y^2 + 2y$. A **trinomial** consists of 3 terms. For example, $5x^2 - 2x + 1$ is a trinomial.

Adding and Subtracting Linear Algebraic Expressions

An algebraic expression is simplified by combining like terms. As mentioned, term is a number, variable, or product of a number and variables separated by addition and subtraction. For the algebraic expression $3x^2 - 4x + 5 - 5x^2 + x - 3$, the terms are $3x^2, -4x, 5, -5x^2, x$, and -3. Like terms have the same variables raised to the same powers (exponents). The like terms for the previous example are $3x^2$ and $-5x^2, -4x$ and x, 5 and -3. To combine like terms, the coefficients (numerical factor of the

68

term including sign) are added, and the variables and their powers are kept the same. Note that if a coefficient is not written, it is an implied coefficient of 1 ($x = 1x$). The previous example will simplify to:

$$-2x^2 - 3x + 2$$

When adding or subtracting algebraic expressions, each expression is written in parenthesis. The negative sign is distributed when necessary, and like terms are combined. Consider the following:

$$\text{add } 2a + 5b - 2 \text{ to } a - 2b + 8c - 4$$

The sum is set as follows:

$$(a - 2b + 8c - 4) + (2a + 5b - 2)$$

In front of each set of parentheses is an implied positive one, which, when distributed, does not change any of the terms. Therefore, the parentheses are dropped and like terms are combined:

$$a - 2b + 8c - 4 + 2a + 5b - 2$$

$$3a + 3b + 8c - 6$$

Consider the following problem: Subtract $2a + 5b - 2$ from:

$$a - 2b + 8c - 4$$

The difference is set as follows:

$$(a - 2b + 8c - 4) - (2a + 5b - 2)$$

The implied one in front of the first set of parentheses will not change those four terms. However, distributing the implied -1 in front of the second set of parentheses will change the sign of each of those three terms:

$$a - 2b + 8c - 4 - 2a - 5b + 2$$

Combining like terms yields the simplified expression: $-a - 7b + 8c - 2$.

Distributive Property

The distributive property states that multiplying a sum (or difference) by a number produces the same result as multiplying each value in the sum (or difference) by the number and adding (or subtracting) the products. Using mathematical symbols, the distributive property states:

$$a(b + c) = ab + ac$$

The expression $4(3 + 2)$ is simplified using the order of operations. Simplifying inside the parenthesis first produces 4×5, which equals 20. The expression $4(3 + 2)$ can also be simplified using the distributive property:

$$4(3 + 2)$$

$$4 \times 3 + 4 \times 2$$

$$12 + 8 = 20$$

Consider the following example: $4(3x - 2)$. The expression cannot be simplified inside the parenthesis because $3x$ and -2 are not like terms and therefore cannot be combined. However, the expression can be simplified by using the distributive property and multiplying each term inside of the parenthesis by the term outside of the parenthesis: $12x - 8$. The resulting equivalent expression contains no like terms, so it cannot be further simplified.

Consider the expression:

$$(3x + 2y + 1) - (5x - 3) + 2(3y + 4)$$

Again, there are no like terms, but the distributive property is used to simplify the expression. Note there is an implied one in front of the first set of parentheses and an implied -1 in front of the second set of parentheses.

Distributing the 1, -1, and 2 produces:

$$1(3x) + 1(2y) + 1(1) - 1(5x) - 1(-3) + 2(3y) + 2(4)$$

$$3x + 2y + 1 - 5x + 3 + 6y + 8$$

This expression contains like terms that are combined to produce the simplified expression:

$$-2x + 8y + 12$$

Algebraic expressions are tested to be equivalent by choosing values for the variables and evaluating both expressions. For example, $4(3x - 2)$ and $12x - 8$ are tested by substituting 3 for the variable x and calculating to determine if equivalent values result.

Evaluating Expressions for Given Values

An algebraic expression is a statement written in mathematical symbols, typically including one or more unknown values represented by variables. For example, the expression $2x + 3$ states that an unknown number (x) is multiplied by 2 and added to 3. If given a value for the unknown number, or variable, the value of the expression is determined. For example, if the value of the variable x is 4, the value of the expression 4 is multiplied by 2, and 3 is added. This results in a value of 11 for the expression.

When given an algebraic expression and values for the variable(s), the expression is evaluated to determine its numerical value. To evaluate the expression, the given values for the variables are substituted (or replaced), and the expression is simplified using the order of operations. Parenthesis should be used when substituting. Consider the following: Evaluate $a - 2b + ab$ for $a = 3$ and $b = -1$. To evaluate, any variable a is replaced with 3 and any variable b with -1, producing:

$$(3) - 2(-1) + (3)(-1)$$

Next, the order of operations is used to calculate the value of the expression, which is 2.

Verbal Statements and Algebraic Expressions

As mentioned, an algebraic expression is a statement about unknown quantities expressed in mathematical symbols. The statement *five times a number added to forty* is expressed as $5x + 40$. An

equation is a statement in which two expressions (with at least one containing a variable) are equal to one another. The statement *five times a number added to forty is equal to ten* is expressed as:

$$5x + 40 = 10$$

Real world scenarios can also be expressed mathematically. Suppose a job pays its employees $300 per week and $40 for each sale made. The weekly pay is represented by the expression $40x + 300$ where x is the number of sales made during the week.

Consider the following scenario: Bob had $20 and Tom had $4. After selling 4 ice cream cones to Bob, Tom has as much money as Bob. The cost of an ice cream cone is an unknown quantity and can be represented by a variable (x). The amount of money Bob has after his purchase is four times the cost of an ice cream cone subtracted from his original $20 → $20 - 4x$. The amount of money Tom has after his sale is four times the cost of an ice cream cone added to his original:

$$\$4 \rightarrow 4x + 4$$

After the sale, the amount of money that Bob and Tom have is equal:

$$\rightarrow 20 - 4x = 4x + 4$$

Solving for x yields $x = 2$.

Use of Formulas

Formulas are mathematical expressions that define the value of one quantity, given the value of one or more different quantities. Formulas look like equations because they contain variables, numbers, operators, and an equal sign. All formulas are equations, but not all equations are formulas. A formula must have more than one variable. For example, $2x + 7 = y$ is an equation and a formula (it relates the unknown quantities x and y). However, $2x + 7 = 3$ is an equation but not a formula (it only expresses the value of the unknown quantity x).

Formulas are typically written with one variable alone (or isolated) on one side of the equal sign. This variable can be thought of as the *subject* in that the formula is stating the value of the *subject* in terms of the relationship between the other variables. Consider the distance formula: $distance = rate \times time$ or $d = rt$. The value of the subject variable d (distance) is the product of the variable r and t (rate and time). Given the rate and time, the distance traveled can easily be determined by substituting the values into the formula and evaluating.

The formula $P = 2l + 2w$ expresses how to calculate the perimeter of a rectangle (P) given its length (l) and width (w). To find the perimeter of a rectangle with a length of 3 ft and a width of 2 ft, these values are substituted into the formula for l and w:

$$P = 2(3 \text{ ft}) + 2(2 \text{ ft})$$

Following the order of operations, the perimeter is determined to be 10 ft. When working with formulas such as these, including units is an important step.

Given a formula expressed in terms of one variable, the formula can be manipulated to express the relationship in terms of any other variable. In other words, the formula can be rearranged to change which variable is the **subject.** To solve for a variable of interest by manipulating a formula, the equation

71

may be solved as if all other variables were numbers. The same steps for solving are followed, leaving operations in terms of the variables instead of calculating numerical values. For the formula $P = 2l + 2w$, the perimeter is the subject expressed in terms of the length and width. To write a formula to calculate the width of a rectangle, given its length and perimeter, the previous formula relating the three variables is solved for the variable w. If P and l were numerical values, this is a two-step linear equation solved by subtraction and division. To solve the equation $P = 2l + 2w$ for w, $2l$ is first subtracted from both sides:

$$P - 2l = 2w$$

Then both sides are divided by 2:

$$\frac{P - 2l}{2} = w$$

Word Problems

Word problems can appear daunting, but prepared test takers shouldn't let the verbiage psyche them out. No matter the scenario or specifics, the key to answering them is to translate the words into a math problem. It is critical to keep in mind what the question is asking and what operations could lead to that answer. The following word problem resembles one of the question types most frequently encountered on the exam.

Working with Money

Walter's Coffee Shop sells a variety of drinks and breakfast treats.

Price List	
Hot Coffee	$2.00
Slow Drip Iced Coffee	$3.00
Latte	$4.00
Muffins	$2.00
Crepe	$4.00
Egg Sandwich	$5.00

Costs	
Hot Coffee	$0.25
Slow Drip Iced Coffee	$0.75
Latte	$1.00
Muffins	$1.00
Crepe	$2.00
Egg Sandwich	$3.00

Walter's utilities, rent, and labor costs him $500 per day. Today, Walter sold 200 hot coffees, 100 slow drip iced coffees, 50 lattes, 75 muffins, 45 crepes, and 60 egg sandwiches. What was Walter's total profit today?

To accurately answer this type of question, the first step is to determine the total cost of making his drinks and treats, then determine how much revenue he earned from selling those products. After arriving at these two totals, the profit is measured by deducting the total cost from the total revenue.

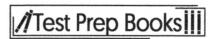

Walter's costs for today:

200 hot coffees	×$0.25	=$50
100 slow drip iced coffees	×$0.75	=$75
50 lattes	×$1.00	=$50
75 muffins	×$1.00	=$75
45 crepes	×$2.00	=$90
60 egg sandwiches	×$3.00	=$180
Utilities, Rent, and Labor		=$500
Total costs		=$1,020

Walter's revenue for today:

200 hot coffees	× $2.00	= $400
100 slow drip iced coffees	× $3.00	= $300
50 lattes	× $4.00	= $200
75 muffins	× $2.00	= $150
45 crepes	× $4.00	= $180
60 egg sandwiches	× $5.00	= $300
Total revenue		= $1,530

$Walter's\ Profit = Revenue - Costs = \$1,530 - \$1,020 = \$510$

This strategy can be applied to other question types. For example, calculating salary after deductions, balancing a checkbook, and calculating a dinner bill are common word problems similar to business planning. In all cases, the most important step is remembering to use the correct operations. When a balance is increased, addition is used. When a balance is decreased, the problem requires subtraction. Common sense and organization are one's greatest assets when answering word problems.

Unit Rate

Unit rate word problems ask test takers to calculate the rate or quantity of something in a different value. For example, a problem might say that a car drove a certain number of miles in a certain number of minutes and then ask how many miles per hour the car was traveling. These questions involve solving proportions. Consider the following examples:

1. Alexandra made $96 during the first 3 hours of her shift as a temporary worker at a law office. She will continue to earn money at this rate until she finishes in 5 more hours. How much does Alexandra make per hour? How much money will Alexandra have made at the end of the day?

73

This problem can be solved in two ways. The first is to set up a proportion, as the rate of pay is constant. The second is to determine her hourly rate, multiply the 5 hours by that rate, and then adding the $96.

To set up a proportion, the money already earned (numerator) is placed over the hours already worked (denominator) on one side of an equation. The other side has x over 8 hours (the total hours worked in the day). It looks like this:

$$\frac{96}{3} = \frac{x}{8}$$

Now, cross-multiply yields $768 = 3x$. To get x, the 768 is divided by 3, which leaves $x = 256$. Alternatively, as x is the numerator of one of the proportions, multiplying by its denominator will reduce the solution by one step. Thus, Alexandra will make $256 at the end of the day. To calculate her hourly rate, the total is divided by 8, giving $32 per hour.

Alternatively, it is possible to figure out the hourly rate by dividing $96 by 3 hours to get $32 per hour. Now her total pay can be figured by multiplying $32 per hour by 8 hours, which comes out to $256.

2. Jonathan is reading a novel. So far, he has read 215 of the 335 total pages. It takes Jonathan 25 minutes to read 10 pages, and the rate is constant. How long does it take Jonathan to read one page? How much longer will it take him to finish the novel? Express the answer in time.

To calculate how long it takes Jonathan to read one page, 25 minutes is divided by 10 pages to determine the page per minute rate. Thus, it takes 2.5 minutes to read one page.

Jonathan must read 120 more pages to complete the novel. (This is calculated by subtracting the pages already read from the total.) Now, his rate per page is multiplied by the number of pages. Thus,

$$120 \times 2.5 = 300$$

Expressed in time, 300 minutes is equal to 5 hours.

3. At a hotel, $\frac{4}{5}$ of the 120 rooms are booked for Saturday. On Sunday, $\frac{3}{4}$ of the rooms are booked. On which day are more of the rooms booked, and by how many more?

The first step is to calculate the number of rooms booked for each day. This is done by multiplying the fraction of the rooms booked by the total number of rooms.

Saturday: $\frac{4}{5} \times 120 = \frac{4}{5} \times \frac{120}{1} = \frac{480}{5} = 96$ rooms

Sunday: $\frac{3}{4} \times 120 = \frac{3}{4} \times \frac{120}{1} = \frac{360}{4} = 90$ rooms

Thus, more rooms were booked on Saturday by 6 rooms.

4. In a veterinary hospital, the veterinarian-to-pet ratio is 1:9. The ratio is always constant. If there are 45 pets in the hospital, how many veterinarians are currently in the veterinary hospital?

A proportion is set up to solve for the number of veterinarians:

$$\frac{1}{9} = \frac{x}{45}$$

Cross-multiplying results in $9x = 45$, which works out to 5 veterinarians.

Alternatively, as there are always 9 times as many pets as veterinarians, it is possible to divide the number of pets (45) by 9. This also arrives at the correct answer of 5 veterinarians.

5. At a general practice law firm, 30% of the lawyers work solely on tort cases. If 9 lawyers work solely on tort cases, how many lawyers work at the firm?

The first step is to solve for the total number of lawyers working at the firm, which will be represented here with x. The problem states that 9 lawyers work solely on torts cases, and they make up 30% of the total lawyers at the firm. Thus, 30% multiplied by the total, x, will equal 9. Written as equation, this is:

$$30\% \times x = 9$$

It's easier to deal with the equation after converting the percentage to a decimal, leaving $0.3x = 9$. Thus, $x = \frac{9}{0.3} = 30$ lawyers working at the firm.

6. Xavier was hospitalized with pneumonia. He was originally given 35mg of antibiotics. Later, after his condition continued to worsen, Xavier's dosage was increased to 60mg. What was the percent increase of the antibiotics? Round the percentage to the nearest tenth.

An increase or decrease in percentage can be calculated by dividing the difference in amounts by the original amount and multiplying by 100. Written as an equation, the formula is:

$$\frac{new\ quantity\ -\ old\ quantity}{old\ quantity} \times 100$$

Here, the question states that the dosage was increased from 35mg to 60mg, so these values are plugged into the formula to find the percentage increase.

$$\frac{60 - 35}{35} \times 100 = \frac{25}{35} \times 100 = .7142 \times 100 = 71.4\%$$

Linear Expressions or Equations in One Variable

Linear expressions and equations are concise mathematical statements that can be written to model a variety of scenarios. Questions found pertaining to this topic will contain one variable only. A variable is an unknown quantity, usually denoted by a letter (x, n, p, etc.). In the case of linear expressions and equations, the power of the variable (its exponent) is 1. A variable without a visible exponent is raised to the first power.

Writing Linear Expressions and Equations

A linear expression is a statement about an unknown quantity expressed in mathematical symbols. The statement "five times a number added to forty" can be expressed as $5x + 40$. A linear equation is a statement in which two expressions (at least one containing a variable) are equal to each other. The statement "five times a number added to forty is equal to ten" can be expressed as:

$$5x + 40 = 10$$

Real-world scenarios can also be expressed mathematically. Consider the following:

> Bob had $20 and Tom had $4. After selling 4 ice cream cones to Bob, Tom has as much money as Bob.

The cost of an ice cream cone is an unknown quantity and can be represented by a variable. The amount of money Bob has after his purchase is four times the cost of an ice cream cone subtracted from his original $20. The amount of money Tom has after his sale is four times the cost of an ice cream cone added to his original $4. This can be expressed as: $20 - 4x = 4x + 4$, where x represents the cost of an ice cream cone.

When expressing a verbal or written statement mathematically, it is key to understand words or phrases that can be represented with symbols. The following are examples:

Symbol	Phrase
$+$	added to, increased by, sum of, more than
$-$	decreased by, difference between, less than, take away
x	multiplied by, 3 (4, 5 . . .) times as large, product of
$\div$	divided by, quotient of, half (third, etc.) of
$=$	is, the same as, results in, as much as
$x, t, n, etc.$	a number, unknown quantity, value of

Solving Linear Equations

When asked to solve a linear equation, one must determine a numerical value for the unknown variable. Given a linear equation involving addition, subtraction, multiplication, and division, isolation of the variable is done by working backward. Addition and subtraction are inverse operations, as are multiplication and division; therefore, they can be used to cancel each other out.

The first steps to solving linear equations are to distribute if necessary and combine any like terms that are on the same side of the equation. Sides of an equation are separated by an=sign. Next, the equation should be manipulated to get the variable on one side. Whatever is done to one side of an equation, must be done to the other side to remain equal. Then, the variable should be isolated by using inverse operations to undo the order of operations backward. Undo addition and subtraction, then undo multiplication and division.

Linear Inequalities in One Variable

Linear inequalities and linear equations are both comparisons of two algebraic expressions. However, unlike equations in which the expressions are equal to each other, linear inequalities compare expressions that are unequal. Linear equations typically have one value for the variable that makes the statement true. Linear inequalities generally have an infinite number of values that make the statement true. Exceptions to these last two statements are covered later on.

Writing Linear Inequalities

Linear inequalities are a concise mathematical way to express the relationship between unequal values. More specifically, they describe in what way the values are unequal. A value could be greater than ($>$); less than ($<$); greater than or equal to ($\geq$); or less than or equal to ($\leq$) another value. The statement "five times a number added to forty is more than sixty-five" can be expressed as:

$$5x + 40 > 65$$

Common words and phrases that express inequalities are:

Symbol	Phrase
$<$	is under, is below, smaller than, beneath
$>$	is above, is over, bigger than, exceeds
$\leq$	no more than, at most, maximum
$\geq$	no less than, at least, minimum

Solving Linear Inequalities

When solving a linear inequality, the solution is the set of all numbers that makes the statement true. The inequality $x + 2 \geq 6$ has a solution set of 4 and every number greater than 4 (4.0001, 5, 12, 107, etc.). Adding 2 to 4 or any number greater than 4 would result in a value that is greater than or equal to 6. Therefore, $x \geq 4$ would be the solution set.

Solution sets for linear inequalities often will be displayed using a number line. If a value is included in the set ($\geq$ or $\leq$), there is a shaded dot placed on that value and an arrow extending in the direction of the solutions. For a variable $>$ or $\geq$ a number, the arrow would point right on the number line (the direction where the numbers increase); and if a variable is $<$ or $\leq$ a number, the arrow would point left (where the numbers decrease). If the value is not included in the set ($>$ or $<$), an open circle on that value would be used with an arrow in the appropriate direction.

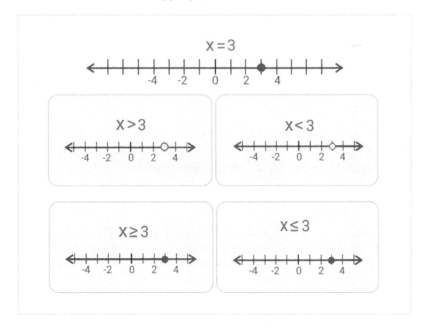

Students may be asked to write a linear inequality given a graph of its solution set. To do so, they should identify whether the value is included (shaded dot or open circle) and the direction in which the arrow is pointing.

In order to algebraically solve a linear inequality, the same steps should be followed as in solving a linear equation (see section on *Solving Linear Equations*). The inequality symbol stays the same for all operations EXCEPT when multiplying or dividing by a negative number. If multiplying or dividing by a negative number while solving an inequality, the relationship reverses (the sign flips). Multiplying or dividing by a positive does not change the relationship, so the sign stays the same. In other words, > switches to < and vice versa. An example is shown below.

Solve $-2(x + 4) \leq 22$ for the value of x.

First, distribute -2 to the binomial by multiplying:

$$-2x - 8 \leq 22$$

Next, add 8 to both sides to isolate the variable:

$$-2x \leq 30$$

Divide both sides by -2 to solve for x:

$$x \geq -15$$

Quadratic Equations

A **quadratic equation** is an equation in the form:

$$ax^2 + bx + c = 0$$

There are several methods to solve such equations. The easiest method will depend on the quadratic equation in question.

Sometimes, it is possible to solve quadratic equations by manually *factoring* them. This means rewriting them in the form:
$$(x + A)(x + B) = 0$$

If this is done, then they can be solved by remembering that when $ab = 0$, either a or b must be equal to zero. Therefore, to have $(x + A)(x + B) = 0$, $(x + A) = 0$ or $(x + B) = 0$ is needed. These equations have the solutions $x = -A$ and $x = -B$, respectively.

In order to factor a quadratic equation, note that:

$$(x + A)(x + B) = x^2 + (A + B)x + AB$$

So, if an equation is in the form $x^2 + bx + c$, two numbers, A and B, need to be found that will add up to give us b, and multiply together to give us c.

As an example, consider solving the equation:

$$-3x^2 + 6x + 9 = 0$$

Start by dividing both sides by -3, leaving:

$$x^2 - 2x - 3 = 0$$

Now, notice that $1 - 3 = -2$, and also that $(1)(-3) = -3$. This means the equation can be factored into:

$$(x + 1)(x - 3) = 0$$

Now, solve $(x + 1) = 0$ and $(x - 3) = 0$ to get $x = -1$ and $x = 3$ as the solutions.

It is useful when trying to factor to remember these three things:

$$x^2 + 2xy + y^2 = (x + y)^2$$

$$x^2 - 2xy + y^2 = (x - y)^2$$

$$\text{and } x^2 - y^2 = (x + y)(x - y).$$

However, factoring by hand is often hard to do. If there are no obvious ways to factor the quadratic equation, solutions can still be found by using the *quadratic formula*.

The quadratic formula is:

$$x = \frac{-b \pm \sqrt{b^2 - 4ac}}{2a}$$

This method will always work, although it sometimes can take longer than factoring by hand, if the factors are easy to guess. Using the standard form $ax^2 + bx + c = 0$, plug the values of a, b, and c from the equation into the formula and solve for x. There will either be two answers, one answer, or no real answer. No real answer comes when the value of the discriminant, the number under the square root, is a negative number. Since there are no real numbers that square to get a negative, the answer will be no real roots.

Here is an example of solving a quadratic equation using the quadratic formula. Suppose the equation to solve is:

$$-2x^2 + 3x + 1 = 0$$

There is no obvious way to factor this, so the quadratic formula is used, with $a = -2, b = 3, c = 1$. After substituting these values into the quadratic formula, it yields this:

$$x = \frac{-3 \pm \sqrt{3^2 - 4(-2)(1)}}{2(-2)}$$

This can be simplified to obtain:

$$\frac{3 \pm \sqrt{9 + 8}}{4}$$

or

$$\frac{3 \pm \sqrt{17}}{4}$$

Challenges can be encountered when asked to find a quadratic equation with specific roots. Given roots A and B, a quadratic function can be constructed with those roots by taking $(x - A)(x - B)$. So, in constructing a quadratic equation with roots $x = -2, 3$, it would result in:

$$(x + 2)(x - 3) = x^2 - x - 6$$

Multiplying this by a constant also could be done without changing the roots.

Rewriting Expressions

Algebraic expressions are made up of numbers, variables, and combinations of the two, using mathematical operations. Expressions can be rewritten based on their factors. For example, the expression $6x + 4$ can be rewritten as $2(3x + 2)$ because 2 is a factor of both $6x$ and 4. More complex expressions can also be rewritten based on their factors. The expression $x^4 - 16$ can be rewritten as $(x^2 - 4)(x^2 + 4)$. This is a different type of factoring, where a difference of squares is factored into a sum and difference of the same two terms. With some expressions, the factoring process is simple and only leads to a different way to represent the expression. With others, factoring and rewriting the expression leads to more information about the given problem.

In the following quadratic equation, factoring the binomial leads to finding the zeros of the function:

$$x^2 - 5x + 6 = y$$

This equations factors into $(x - 3)(x - 2) = y$, where 2 and 3 are found to be the zeros of the function when y is set equal to zero. The zeros of any function are the x-values where the graph of the function on the coordinate plane crosses the x-axis.

Factoring an equation is a simple way to rewrite the equation and find the zeros, but factoring is not possible for every quadratic. Completing the square is one way to find zeros when factoring is not an option. The following equation cannot be factored:

$$x^2 + 10x - 9 = 0$$

The first step in this method is to move the constant to the right side of the equation, making it $x^2 + 10x = 9$. Then, the coefficient of x is divided by 2 and squared. This number is then added to both sides of the equation, to make the equation still true. For this example, $\left(\frac{10}{2}\right)^2 = 25$ is added to both sides of the equation to obtain:

$$x^2 + 10x + 25 = 9 + 25$$

This expression simplifies to $x^2 + 10x + 25 = 34$, which can then be factored into:

$$(x + 5)^2 = 34$$

Solving for x then involves taking the square root of both sides and subtracting 5.

This leads to two zeros of the function:

$$x = \pm\sqrt{34} - 5$$

Depending on the type of answer the question seeks, a calculator may be used to find exact numbers.

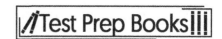
Given a **quadratic equation in standard form**— $ax^2 + bx + c = 0$—the sign of a tells whether the function has a minimum value or a maximum value. If $a > 0$, the graph opens up and has a minimum value. If $a < 0$, the graph opens down and has a maximum value. Depending on the way the quadratic equation is written, multiplication may need to occur before a max/min value is determined.

Exponential expressions can also be rewritten, just as quadratic equations. Properties of exponents must be understood. Multiplying two exponential expressions with the same base involves adding the exponents:

$$a^m a^n = a^{m+n}$$

Dividing two exponential expressions with the same base involves subtracting the exponents:

$$\frac{a^m}{a^n} = a^{m-n}$$

Raising an exponential expression to another exponent includes multiplying the exponents:

$$(a^m)^n = a^{mn}$$

The zero power always gives a value of 1: $a^0 = 1$. Raising either a product or a fraction to a power involves distributing that power:

$$(ab)^m = a^m b^m \text{ and } \left(\frac{a}{b}\right)^m = \frac{a^m}{b^m}$$

Finally, raising a number to a negative exponent is equivalent to the reciprocal including the positive exponent:

$$a^{-m} = \frac{1}{a^m}$$

Polynomials

An expression of the form ax^n, where n is a non-negative integer, is called a **monomial** because it contains one term. A sum of monomials is called a **polynomial.** For example, $-4x^3 + x$ is a polynomial, while $5x^7$ is a monomial. A function equal to a polynomial is called a **polynomial function**.

The monomials in a polynomial are also called the **terms** of the polynomial.

The constants that precede the variables are called **coefficients.**

The highest value of the exponent of x in a polynomial is called the **degree** of the polynomial. So, $-4x^3 + x$ has a degree of 3, while $-2x^5 + x^3 + 4x + 1$ has a degree of 5. When multiplying polynomials, the degree of the result will be the sum of the degrees of the two polynomials being multiplied.

Addition and subtraction operations can be performed on polynomials with like terms. **Like terms** refers to terms that have the same variable and exponent. The two following polynomials can be added together by collecting like terms:

$$(x^2 + 3x - 4) + (4x^2 - 7x + 8)$$

The x^2 terms can be added as:

$$x^2 + 4x^2 = 5x^2$$

The x terms can be added as $3x + -7x = -4x$, and the constants can be added as $-4 + 8 = 4$. The following expression is the result of the addition:

$$5x^2 - 4x + 4$$

When subtracting polynomials, the same steps are followed, only subtracting like terms together.

Multiplication of polynomials can also be performed. Given the two polynomials, $(y^3 - 4)$ and $(x^2 + 8x - 7)$, each term in the first polynomial must be multiplied by each term in the second polynomial. The steps to multiply each term in the given example are as follows:

$$(y^3 \times x^2) + (y^3 \times 8x) + (y^3 \times -7) + (-4 \times x^2) + (-4 \times 8x) + (-4 \times -7)$$

Simplifying each multiplied part, yields:

$$x^2 y^3 + 8xy^3 - 7y^3 - 4x^2 - 32x + 28$$

None of the terms can be combined because there are no like terms in the final expression. Any polynomials can be multiplied by each other by following the same set of steps, then collecting like terms at the end.

FOIL Method

FOIL is a technique for generating polynomials through the multiplication of binomials. A **polynomial** is an expression of multiple variables (for example, x, y, z) in at least three terms involving only the four basic operations and exponents. FOIL is an acronym for First, Outer, Inner, and Last. "First" represents the multiplication of the terms appearing first in the binomials. "Outer" means multiplying the outermost terms. "Inner" means multiplying the terms inside. "Last" means multiplying the last terms of each binomial.

After completing FOIL and solving the operations, **like terms** are combined. To identify like terms, test takers should look for terms with the same variable and the same exponent. For example, in $4x^2 - x^2 + 15x + 2x^2 - 8$, the $4x^2$, $-x^2$, and $2x^2$ are all like terms because they have the variable (x) and exponent (2). Thus, after combining the like terms, the polynomial has been simplified to:

$$5x^2 + 15x - 8$$

The purpose of FOIL is to simplify an equation involving multiple variables and operations. Although it sounds complicated, working through some examples will provide some clarity:

1. Simplify $(x + 10)(x + 4) =$

$$\underset{\text{First}}{(x \times x)} \quad + \quad \underset{\text{Outer}}{(x \times 4)} \quad + \quad \underset{\text{Inner}}{(10 \times x)} \quad + \quad \underset{\text{Last}}{(10 \times 4)}$$

After multiplying these binomials, it's time to solve the operations and combine like terms. Thus, the expression becomes:

$$2x^2 + 4x + 10x + 40 = 2x^2 + 14x + 40$$

2. Simplify $2x\ (4x^3 - 7y^2 + 3x^2 + 4)$

Here, a monomial ($2x$) is multiplied into a polynomial:

$$(4x^3 - 7y^2 + 3x^2 + 4)$$

Using the distributive property, the monomial gets multiplied by each term in the polynomial. This becomes:

$$2x(4x^3) - 2x(7y^2) + 2x(3x^2) + 2x(4)$$

Now, each monomial is simplified, starting with the coefficients:

$$(2 \times 4)(x \times x^3) - (2 \times 7)(x \times y^2) + (2 \times 3)(x \times x^2) + (2 \times 4)(x)$$

When multiplying powers with the same base, their exponents are added. Remember, a variable with no listed exponent has an exponent of 1, and exponents of distinct variables cannot be combined. This produces the answer:

$$8x^{1+3} - 14xy^2 + 6x^{1+2} + 8x = 8x^4 - 14xy^2 + 6x^3 + 8x$$

3. Simplify $(8x^{10}y^2z^4) \div (4x^2y^4z^7)$

The first step is to divide the coefficients of the first two polynomials: $8 \div 4 = 2$. The second step is to divide exponents with the same variable, which requires subtracting the exponents. This results in:

$$2(x^{10-2}y^{2-4}z^{4-7}) = 2x^8y^{-2}z^{-3}$$

However, the most simplified answer should include only positive exponents. Thus, $y^{-2}z^{-3}$ needs to be converted into fractions, respectively $\frac{1}{y^2}$ and $\frac{1}{z^3}$. Since the $2x^8$ has a positive exponent, it is placed in the numerator, and $\frac{1}{y^2}$ and $\frac{1}{z^3}$ are combined into the denominator, leaving $\frac{2x^8}{y^2z^3}$ as the final answer.

Zeros of Polynomials

Finding the **zeros of polynomial functions** is the same process as finding the solutions of polynomial equations. These are the points at which the graph of the function crosses the x-axis. As stated previously, factors can be used to find the zeros of a polynomial function. The degree of the function shows the number of possible zeros. If the highest exponent on the independent variable is 4, then the degree is 4, and the number of possible zeros is 4. If there are complex solutions, the number of roots is less than the degree.

Given the function $y = x^2 + 7x + 6$, y can be set equal to zero, and the polynomial can be factored. The equation turns into $0 = (x + 1)(x + 6)$, where $x = -1$ and $x = -6$ are the zeros. Since this is a quadratic equation, the shape of the graph will be a parabola. Knowing that zeros represent the points where the parabola crosses the x-axis, the maximum or minimum point is the only other piece needed to sketch a rough graph of the function. By looking at the function in standard form, the coefficient of x

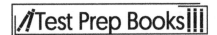
is positive; therefore, the parabola opens up. Using the zeros and the minimum, the following rough sketch of the graph can be constructed:

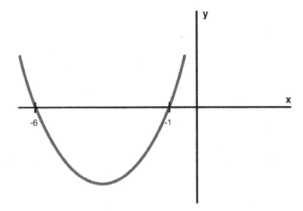

Rational Expressions and Equations

A **rational expression** is a fraction where the numerator and denominator are both polynomials. Some examples of rational expressions include the following: $\frac{4x^3y^5}{3z^4}$, $\frac{4x^3+3x}{x^2}$, and $\frac{x^2+7x+10}{x+2}$. Since these refer to expressions and not equations, they can be simplified but not solved. Using the rules in the previous *Exponents* and *Roots* sections, some rational expressions with monomials can be simplified. Other rational expressions such as the last example, $\frac{x^2+7x+10}{x+2}$, require more steps to be simplified. First, the polynomial on top can be factored from $x^2 + 7x + 10$ into $(x + 5)(x + 2)$. Then the common factors can be canceled and the expression can be simplified to $(x + 5)$.

The following problem is an example of using rational expressions:

Reggie wants to lay sod in his rectangular backyard. The length of the yard is given by the expression $4x + 2$, and the width is unknown. The area of the yard is $20x + 10$. Reggie needs to find the width of the yard. Knowing that the area of a rectangle is length multiplied by width, an expression can be written to find the width: $\frac{20x+10}{4x+2}$, area divided by length. Simplifying this expression by factoring out 10 on the top and 2 on the bottom leads to this expression:

$$\frac{10(2x + 1)}{2(2x + 1)}$$

Canceling out the $2x + 1$ results in $\frac{10}{2} = 5$. The width of the yard is found to be 5 by simplifying the rational expression.

A **rational equation** can be as simple as an equation with a ratio of polynomials, $\frac{p(x)}{q(x)}$, set equal to a value, where $p(x)$ and $q(x)$ are both polynomials. A rational equation has an equal sign, which is different from expressions. This leads to solutions, or numbers that make the equation true.

It is possible to solve rational equations by trying to get all of the x terms out of the denominator and then isolating them on one side of the equation. For example, to solve the equation $\frac{3x+2}{2x+3} = 4$, both sides get multiplied by $(2x + 3)$. This will cancel on the left side to yield:

$$3x + 2 = 4(2x + 3)$$

Then:

$$3x + 2 = 8x + 12$$

Now, subtract $8x$ from both sides, which yields:

$$-5x + 2 = 12$$

Subtracting 2 from both sides results in $-5x = 10$. Finally, both sides get divided by -5 to obtain $x = -2$.

Sometimes, when solving rational equations, it can be easier to try to simplify the rational expression by factoring the numerator and denominator first, then cancelling out common factors. For example, to solve $\frac{2x^2-8x+6}{x^2-3x+2} = 1$, the first step is to factor:

$$2x^2 - 8x + 6$$

$$2(x^2 - 4x + 3)$$

$$2(x - 1)(x - 3)$$

Then, factor $x^2 - 3x + 2$ into $(x - 1)(x - 2)$. This turns the original equation into:

$$\frac{2(x - 1)(x - 3)}{(x - 1)(x - 2)} = 1$$

The common factor of $(x - 1)$ can be canceled, leaving $\frac{2(x-3)}{x-2} = 1$. Now the same method used in the previous example can be followed. Multiplying both sides by $x - 2$ and performing the multiplication on the left yields $2x - 6 = x - 2$, which can be simplified to $x = 4$.

Matrices

Matrices can be used to represent linear equations, solve systems of equations, and manipulate data to simulate change. Matrices consist of numerical entries in both rows and columns. The following matrix A is a 3×4 matrix because it has three rows and four columns:

$$A = \begin{bmatrix} 3 & 2 & -5 & 3 \\ 3 & 6 & 2 & -5 \\ -1 & 3 & 7 & 0 \end{bmatrix}$$

Matrices can be added or subtracted only if they have the same dimensions. For example, the following matrices can be added by adding corresponding matrix entries:

$$\begin{bmatrix} 3 & 4 \\ 2 & -6 \end{bmatrix} + \begin{bmatrix} -1 & 4 \\ 4 & 2 \end{bmatrix} = \begin{bmatrix} 2 & 8 \\ 6 & -4 \end{bmatrix}$$

Multiplication can also be used to manipulate matrices. **Scalar multiplication** involves multiplying a matrix by a constant. Each matrix entry needs to be multiplied by the constant. The following example shows a 3 × 2 matrix being multiplied by the constant 6:

$$6 \times \begin{bmatrix} 3 & 4 \\ 2 & -6 \\ 1 & 0 \end{bmatrix} = \begin{bmatrix} 18 & 24 \\ 12 & -36 \\ 6 & 0 \end{bmatrix}$$

Matrix multiplication of two matrices involves finding multiple dot products. The **dot product** of a row and column is the sum of the products of each corresponding row and column entry. In the following example, a 2 × 2 matrix is multiplied by a 2 × 2 matrix. The dot product of the first row and column is:

$$(2 \times 1) + (1 \times 2) = (2) + (2) = 4$$

$$\begin{bmatrix} 2 & 1 \\ 3 & 5 \end{bmatrix} \times \begin{bmatrix} 1 & 4 \\ 2 & 0 \end{bmatrix} = \begin{bmatrix} 4 & 8 \\ 13 & 12 \end{bmatrix}$$

The same process is followed to find the other three values in the solution matrix. Matrices can only be multiplied if the number of columns in the first matrix equals the number of rows in the second matrix. The previous example is also an example of square matrix multiplication because they are both square matrices. A **square matrix** has the same number of rows and columns. For square matrices, the order in which they are multiplied does matter. Therefore, matrix multiplication does not satisfy the commutative property. It does, however, satisfy the associative and distributive properties.

Another transformation of matrices can be found by using the **identity matrix**—also referred to as the **"I" matrix**. The identity matrix is similar to the number one in normal multiplication. The identity matrix is a square matrix with ones in the diagonal spots and zeros everywhere else. The identity matrix is also the result of multiplying a matrix by its inverse. This process is similar to multiplying a number by its reciprocal.

The **zero matrix** is also a matrix acting as an additive identity. The zero matrix consists of zeros in every entry. It does not change the values of a matrix when using addition.

The **inverse of a matrix** is useful for solving complex systems of equations. Not all matrices have an inverse, but this can be checked by finding the **determinant** of the matrix. If the determinant of the matrix is 0, it is not inversible. Additionally, only square matrices are inversible. To find the determinant of any matrix, each value of the first row is multiplied by the determinant of submatrix consisting of all except the row and column for that value. The results of multiplication are alternatingly subtracted and added for 3 × 3 or larger matrices. The determinant of a matrix can be represented with straight bars (such as $|A|$) or the function $\det(A)$, where A is a matrix.

Using the **square 2 × 2 matrix**, the determinant is: $|A| = \begin{vmatrix} a & b \\ c & d \end{vmatrix} = ad - bc$

The absolute value of the determinant of matrix A is equal to the area of a parallelogram with vertices $(0, 0)$, (a, b), (c, d), and $(a + b, c + d)$.

For example, the determinant of the matrix $\begin{bmatrix} -5 & 1 \\ 3 & 4 \end{bmatrix}$ is:

$$-5(4) - 1(3) = -20 - 3 = -23$$

86

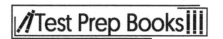

Using a **3 × 3 matrix** $\begin{bmatrix} a & b & c \\ d & e & f \\ g & h & i \end{bmatrix}$, the determinant is $a(ei - fh) - b(di - fg) + c(dh - eg)$.

For example, the determinant of the matrix $A = \begin{bmatrix} 2 & 0 & 1 \\ -1 & 3 & 2 \\ 2 & -2 & -1 \end{bmatrix}$ is:

$$|A| = 2\big(3(-1) - 2(-2)\big) - 0\big(-1(-1) - 2(2)\big) + 1\big(-1(-2) - 3(2)\big)$$

$$|A| = 2(-3 + 4) - 0(1 - 4) + 1(2 - 6)$$

$$|A| = 2(1) - 0(-3) + 1(-4)$$

$$|A| = 2 - 0 - 4 = -2$$

The pattern continues for larger square matrices. For a matrix with real values, this can then be simplified to a real number. If the determinant is non-zero, the square matrix can be inversed.

One way to find an inverse matrix is to use the **matrix of minors**. A **minor** is the determinant of the submatrix found by excluding the row and column of that minor. The matrix formed by all the minors would be M. To use the previous example, the minor of the first row and column is:

$$M_a = ei - fh = 3(-1) - 2(-2) = -3 + 4 = 1$$

When dealing with larger matrices it can be inconvenient to letter the items in a matrix. Another way to refer to them is by the numbers of rows and columns in the matrix. The position of any given value in some matrix A is at row i and column j is thus $A_{i,j}$. Using the previous example, $ie - fh$ was the minor of the first matrix item, which would be $M_{1,1} = A_{2,2}A_{3,3} - A_{2,3}A_{3,2}$. The following matrix shows all the minors:

$$M = \begin{bmatrix} 1 & -3 & -4 \\ 2 & -4 & -4 \\ -3 & 5 & 6 \end{bmatrix}$$

The next step to finding the inverse is to find the **cofactor matrix** from the matrix of minors. This is simply negating every other item in the matrix, in a checkerboard-like pattern. This is done the same for matrices of all sizes. The cofactors of M are:

$$\begin{bmatrix} 1 & 3 & -4 \\ -2 & -4 & 4 \\ -3 & -5 & 6 \end{bmatrix}$$

The last steps to finding the inverse are to transpose the matrix of cofactors and divide it by the determinant of the original matrix, $|A|$. **Transposing** a matrix means turning the rows into columns and vice versa. For example, the third item of the first row would become the third item of the first column. This turns the previous cofactor matrix into an **adjoint matrix**:

$$\begin{bmatrix} 1 & -2 & -3 \\ 3 & -4 & -5 \\ -4 & 4 & 6 \end{bmatrix}$$

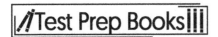

Dividing the transposed matrix by the determinant of our original matrix gives the inverse of matrix A:

$$A^{-1} = \frac{1}{|A|} \times \begin{bmatrix} 1 & -2 & -3 \\ 3 & -4 & -5 \\ -4 & 4 & 6 \end{bmatrix} = \frac{1}{-2} \times \begin{bmatrix} 1 & -2 & -3 \\ 3 & -4 & -5 \\ -4 & 4 & 6 \end{bmatrix} = \begin{bmatrix} -\frac{1}{2} & 1 & \frac{3}{2} \\ \frac{3}{2} & 2 & \frac{5}{2} \\ 2 & -2 & -3 \end{bmatrix}$$

Given a system of linear equations, a matrix can be used to represent the entire system. Operations can then be performed on the matrix to solve the system. The following system offers an example:

$$x + y + z = 4$$

$$y + 3z = -2$$

$$2x + y - 2z = 12$$

There are three variables and three equations. The coefficients in the equations can be used to form a 3×3 matrix:

$$\begin{bmatrix} 1 & 1 & 1 \\ 0 & 1 & 3 \\ 2 & 1 & -2 \end{bmatrix}$$

The number of rows equals the number of equations, and the number of columns equals the number of variables. The numbers on the right side of the equations can be turned into a 3×1 matrix. That matrix is shown here:

$$\begin{bmatrix} 4 \\ -2 \\ 12 \end{bmatrix}$$

Such a matrix can also be referred to as a **vector**. The variables are represented in a matrix of their own:

$$\begin{bmatrix} x \\ y \\ z \end{bmatrix}$$

The system can be represented by the following matrix equation:

$$\begin{bmatrix} 1 & 1 & 1 \\ 0 & 1 & 3 \\ 2 & 1 & -2 \end{bmatrix} \begin{bmatrix} x \\ y \\ z \end{bmatrix} = \begin{bmatrix} 4 \\ -2 \\ 12 \end{bmatrix}$$

Simply, this is written as $AX = B$. By using the inverse of a matrix, the solution can be found: $X = A^{-1}B$. Once the inverse of A is found, it is then multiplied by B to find the solution to the system: $x = 12$, $y = -8$, and $z = 2$.

Systems of Equations

A **system of equations** is a group of equations that have the same variables or unknowns. These equations can be linear, but they are not always so. Finding a solution to a system of equations means finding the values of the variables that satisfy each equation. For a linear system of two equations and two variables, there could be a single solution, no solution, or infinitely many solutions.

A single solution occurs when there is one value for x and y that satisfies the system. This would be shown on the graph where the lines cross at exactly one point. When there is no solution, the lines are parallel and do not ever cross. With infinitely many solutions, the equations may look different, but they are the same line. One equation will be a multiple of the other, and on the graph, they lie on top of each other.

The **process of elimination** can be used to solve a system of equations. For example, the following equations make up a system:

$$x + 3y = 10 \text{ and } 2x - 5y = 9$$

Immediately adding these equations does not eliminate a variable, but it is possible to change the first equation by multiplying the whole equation by -2. This changes the first equation to:

$$-2x - 6y = -20$$

The equations can be then added to obtain $-11y = -11$. Solving for y yields $y = 1$. To find the rest of the solution, 1 can be substituted in for y in either original equation to find the value of $x = 7$. The solution to the system is $(7, 1)$ because it makes both equations true, and it is the point in which the lines intersect. If the system is **dependent**—having infinitely many solutions—then both variables will cancel out when the elimination method is used, resulting in an equation that is true for many values of x and y. Since the system is dependent, both equations can be simplified to the same equation or line.

A system can also be solved using **substitution.** This involves solving one equation for a variable and then plugging that solved equation into the other equation in the system. For example, $x - y = -2$ and $3x + 2y = 9$ can be solved using substitution. The first equation can be solved for x, where $x = -2 + y$. Then it can be plugged into the other equation:

$$3(-2 + y) + 2y = 9$$

Solving for y yields $-6 + 3y + 2y = 9$, where $y = 3$. If $y = 3$, then $x = 1$. This solution can be checked by plugging in these values for the variables in each equation to see if it makes a true statement.

Finally, a solution to a system of equations can be found graphically. The solution to a linear system is the point or points where the lines cross. The values of x and y represent the coordinates (x, y) where the lines intersect. Using the same system of equations as above, they can be solved for y to put them in slope-intercept form, $y = mx + b$.

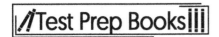
These equations become $y = x + 2$ and $y = -\frac{3}{2}x + 4.5$. This system with the solution is shown below:

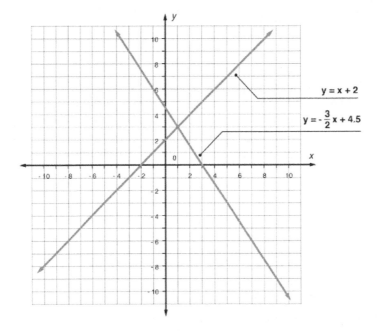

A system of equations may also be made up of a linear and a quadratic equation. These systems may have one solution, two solutions, or no solutions. The graph of these systems involves one straight line and one parabola. Algebraically, these systems can be solved by solving the linear equation for one variable and plugging that answer in to the quadratic equation. If possible, the equation can then be solved to find part of the answer. The graphing method is commonly used for these types of systems. On a graph, these two lines can be found to intersect at one point, at two points across the parabola, or at no points.

Finding solutions to systems of equations is essentially finding what values of the variables make both equations true. It is finding the input value that yields the same output value in both equations. For functions $g(x)$ and $f(x)$, the equation $g(x) = f(x)$ means the output values are being set equal to each other. Solving for the value of x means finding the x-coordinate that gives the same output in both functions. For example, $f(x) = x + 2$ and $g(x) = -3x + 10$ is a system of equations. Setting $f(x) = g(x)$ yields the equation:

$$x + 2 = -3x + 10$$

Solving for x, gives the x-coordinate $x = 2$ where the two lines cross. This value can also be found by using a table or a graph. On a table, both equations can be given the same inputs, and the outputs can be recorded to find the point(s) where the lines cross. Any method of solving finds the same solution, but some methods are more appropriate for some systems of equations than others.

Systems of **linear inequalities** are like systems of equations, but the solutions are different. Since inequalities have infinitely many solutions, their systems also have infinitely many solutions. Finding the solutions of inequalities involves graphs. A system of two equations and two inequalities is linear; thus, the lines can be graphed using slope-intercept form. If the inequality has an equals sign, the line is solid. If the inequality only has a greater than or less than symbol, the line on the graph is dotted. Dashed lines indicate that points lying on the line are not included in the solution. After the lines are graphed, a region is shaded on one side of the line. This side is found by determining if a point — known as a **test**

90

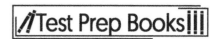
point — lying on one side of the line produces a true inequality. If it does, that side of the graph is shaded. If the point produces a false inequality, the line is shaded on the opposite side from the point. The graph of a system of inequalities involves shading the intersection of the two shaded regions.

Functions

Functions

A **function** is defined as a relationship between inputs and outputs where there is only one output value for a given input. As an example, the following function is in function notation:

$$f(x) = 3x - 4$$

The $f(x)$ represents the output value for an input of x. If $x = 2$, the equation becomes:

$$f(2) = 3(2) - 4$$

$$6 - 4 = 2$$

The input of 2 yields an output of 2, forming the ordered pair $(2, 2)$. The following set of ordered pairs corresponds to the given function: $(2, 2)$, $(0, -4)$, $(-2, -10)$. The set of all possible inputs of a function is its **domain**, and all possible outputs is called the **range**. By definition, each member of the domain is paired with only one member of the range.

Functions can also be defined recursively. In this form, they are not defined explicitly in terms of variables. Instead, they are defined using previously-evaluated function outputs, starting with either $f(0)$ or $f(1)$. An example of a recursively-defined function is:

$$f(1) = 2$$

$$f(n) = 2f(n - 1) + 2n$$

$$n > 1$$

The domain of this function is the set of all integers.

A function $f(x)$ is a mathematical object which takes one number, x, as an input and gives a number in return. The input is called the **independent variable**. If the variable is set equal to the output, as in $y = f(x)$, then this is called the **dependent variable**. To indicate the dependent value a function, y, gives for a specific independent variable, x, the notation $y = f(x)$ is used.

The **domain** of a function is the set of values that the independent variable is allowed to take. Unless otherwise specified, the domain is any value for which the function is well defined. The **range** of the function is the set of possible outputs for the function.

In many cases, a function can be defined by giving an equation. For instance, $f(x) = x^2$ indicates that given a value for x, the output of f is found by squaring x.

Not all equations in x and y can be written in the form $y = f(x)$. An equation can be written in such a form if it satisfies the **vertical line test**: no vertical line meets the graph of the equation at more than a

single point. In this case, y is said to be a *function of x*. If a vertical line meets the graph in two places, then this equation cannot be written in the form $y = f(x)$.

The graph of a function $f(x)$ is the graph of the equation $y = f(x)$. Thus, it is the set of all pairs (x, y) where $y = f(x)$. In other words, it is all pairs $(x, f(x))$. The x-intercepts are called the **zeros** of the function. The y-intercept is given by $f(0)$.

If, for a given function f, the only way to get $f(a) = f(b)$ is for $a = b$, then f is *one-to-one*. Often, even if a function is not one-to-one on its entire domain, it is one-to-one by considering a restricted portion of the domain.

A function $f(x) = k$ for some number k is called a **constant function**. The graph of a constant function is a horizontal line.

The function $f(x) = x$ is called the **identity function**. The graph of the identity function is the diagonal line pointing to the upper right at 45 degrees, $y = x$.

A function is called **monotone** if it is either always increasing or always decreasing. For example, the functions $f(x) = 3x$ and $f(x) = -x^5$ are monotone.

An **even function** looks the same when flipped over the y-axis: $f(x) = f(-x)$. The following image shows a graphic representation of an even function.

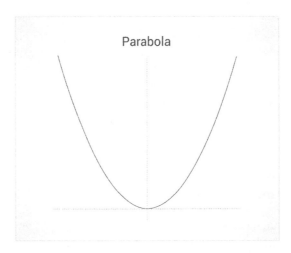

Parabola

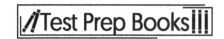
An **odd function** looks the same when flipped over the y-axis and then flipped over the x-axis: $f(x) = -f(-x)$. The following image shows an example of an odd function.

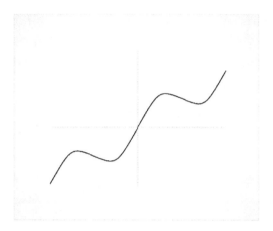

Domain and Range

The domain and range of a function can be found visually by its plot on the coordinate plane. In the function $f(x) = x^2 - 3$, for example, the domain is all real numbers because the parabola stretches as far left and as far right as it can go, with no restrictions. This means that any input value from the real number system will yield an answer in the real number system. For the range, the inequality $y \geq -3$ would be used to describe the possible output values because the parabola has a minimum at $y = -3$. This means there will not be any real output values less than -3 because -3 is the lowest value it reaches on the y-axis.

These same answers for domain and range can be found by observing a table. The table below shows that from input values $x = -1$ to $x = 1$, the output results in a minimum of -3. On each side of $x = 0$, the numbers increase, showing that the range is all real numbers greater than or equal to -3.

x (domain/input)	y (range/output)
-2	1
-1	-2
0	-3
-1	-2
2	1

Function Behavior

Different types of functions behave in different ways. A function is defined to be increasing over a subset of its domain if for all $x_1 \geq x_2$ in that interval, $f(x_1) \geq f(x_2)$. Also, a function is decreasing over an interval if for all $x_1 \geq x_2$ in that interval, $f(x_1) \leq f(x_2)$. A point in which a function changes from increasing to decreasing can also be labeled as the **maximum value** of a function if it is the largest point the graph reaches on the y-axis. A point in which a function changes from decreasing to increasing can be labeled as the minimum value of a function if it is the smallest point the graph reaches on the y-axis. Maximum values are also known as **extreme values**. The graph of a continuous function does not have any breaks or jumps in the graph. This description is not true of all functions. A radical function, for example, $f(x) = \sqrt{x}$, has a restriction for the domain and range because there are no real negative inputs or outputs for this function. The domain can be stated as $x \geq 0$, and the range is $y \geq 0$.

93

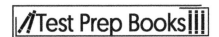

Logarithmic and exponential functions also have different behavior than other functions. These two types of functions are inverses of each other. The **inverse** of a function can be found by switching the place of x and y, and solving for y. When this is done for the exponential equation, $y = 2^x$, the function $y = \log_2 x$ is found. The general form of a **logarithmic function** is $y = \log_b x$, which says b raised to the y power equals x.

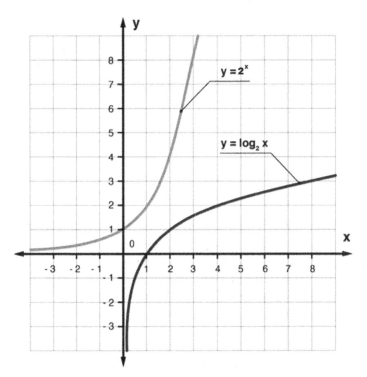

The thick black line on the graph above represents the logarithmic function $y = \log_2 x$. This curve passes through the point $(1, 0)$, just as all log functions do, because any value $b^0 = 1$. The graph of this logarithmic function starts very close to zero but does not touch the y-axis. The output value will never be zero by the definition of logarithms. The thinner gray line seen above represents the exponential function $y = 2^x$. The behavior of this function is opposite the logarithmic function because the graph of an inverse function is the graph of the original function flipped over the line $y = x$. The curve passes through the point $(0, 1)$ because any number raised to the zero power is one. This curve also gets very close to the x-axis but never touches it because an exponential expression never has an output of zero. The x-axis on this graph is called a horizontal asymptote. An **asymptote** is a line that represents a boundary for a function. It shows a value that the function will get close to, but never reach.

Functions can also be described as being even, odd, or neither. If $f(-x) = f(x)$, the function is even. For example, the function $f(x) = x^2 - 2$ is even. Plugging in $x = 2$ yields an output of $y = 2$. After changing the input to $x = -2$, the output is still $y = 2$. The output is the same for opposite inputs. Another way to observe an even function is by the symmetry of the graph. If the graph is symmetrical about the axis, then the function is even. If the graph is symmetric about the origin, then the function is odd. Algebraically, if $f(-x) = -f(x)$, the function is odd.

Also, a function can be described as **periodic** if it repeats itself in regular intervals. Common periodic functions are trigonometric functions. For example, $y = \sin x$ is a periodic function with period 2π because it repeats itself every 2π units along the x-axis.

Linear Functions

A function is called **linear** if it can take the form of the equation $f(x) = ax + b$, or $y = ax + b$, for any two numbers a and b. A linear equation forms a straight line when graphed on the coordinate plane. An example of a linear function is shown below on the graph.

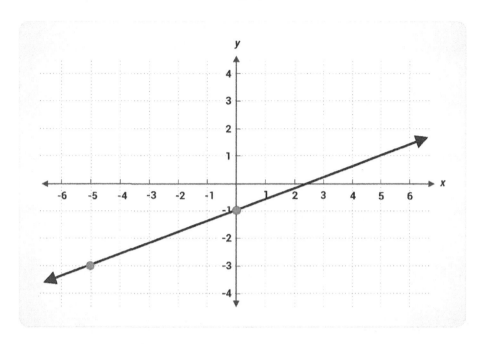

This is a graph of the following function:

$$y = \frac{2}{5}x - 1$$

A table of values that satisfies this function is shown below.

x	y
-5	-3
0	-1
5	1
10	3

These points can be found on the graph using the form (x, y).

To graph relations and functions, the Cartesian plane is used. This means to think of the plane as being given a grid of squares, with one direction being the x-axis and the other direction the y-axis. Generally, the independent variable is placed along the horizontal axis, and the dependent variable is placed along the vertical axis. Any point on the plane can be specified by saying how far to go along the x-axis and how far along the y-axis with a pair of numbers (x, y). Specific values for these pairs can be given names such as $C = (-1, 3)$. Negative values mean to move left or down; positive values mean to move right or

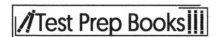
up. The point where the axes cross one another is called the **origin.** The origin has coordinates $(0, 0)$ and is usually called O when given a specific label. An illustration of the Cartesian plane, along with the plotted points $(2, 1)$ and $(-1, -1)$, is below.

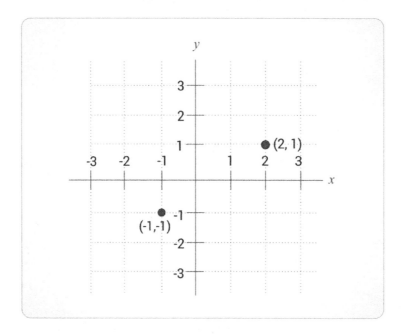

Relations also can be graphed by marking each point whose coordinates satisfy the relation. If the relation is a function, then there is only one value of y for any given value of x. This leads to the **vertical line test**: if a relation is graphed, then the relation is a function if any possible vertical line drawn anywhere along the graph would only touch the graph of the relation in no more than one place. Conversely, when graphing a function, then any possible vertical line drawn will not touch the graph of the function at any point or will touch the function at just one point. This test is made from the definition of a function, where each x-value must be mapped to one and only one y-value.

When graphing a linear function, note that the ratio of the change of the y coordinate to the change in the x-coordinate is constant between any two points on the resulting line, no matter which two points are chosen. In other words, in a pair of points on a line, (x_1, y_1) and (x_2, y_2), with $x_1 \neq x_2$ so that the two points are distinct, then the ratio $\frac{y_2 - y_1}{x_2 - x_1}$ will be the same, regardless of which particular pair of points are chosen. This ratio, $\frac{y_2 - y_1}{x_2 - x_1}$, is called the *slope* of the line and is frequently denoted with the letter m. If slope m is positive, then the line goes upward when moving to the right, while if slope m is negative, then the line goes downward when moving to the right. If the slope is 0, then the line is called horizontal, and the y coordinate is constant along the entire line. In lines where the x-coordinate is constant along the entire line, y is not actually a function of x. For such lines, the slope is not defined. These lines are called vertical lines.

Linear functions may take forms other than $y = ax + b$. The most common forms of linear equations are explained below:

1. Standard Form: $Ax + By = C$, in which the slope is given by $m = \frac{-A}{B}$, and the y-intercept is given by $\frac{C}{B}$.

2. Slope-Intercept Form: $y = mx + b$, where the slope is m and the y-intercept is b.

3. Point-Slope Form: $y - y_1 = m(x - x_1)$, where the slope is m and (x_1, y_1) is any point on the chosen line.

4. Two-Point Form: $\frac{y - y_1}{x - x_1} = \frac{y_2 - y_1}{x_2 - x_1}$, where (x_1, y_1) and (x_2, y_2) are any two distinct points on the chosen line. Note that the slope is given by:

$$m = \frac{y_2 - y_1}{x_2 - x_1}$$

5. Intercept Form: $\frac{x}{x_1} + \frac{y}{y_1} = 1$, in which x_1 is the x-intercept and y_1 is the y-intercept.

These five ways to write linear equations are all useful in different circumstances. Depending on the given information, it may be easier to write one of the forms over another.

If $y = mx$, y is directly proportional to x. In this case, changing x by a factor changes y by that same factor. If $y = \frac{m}{x}$, y is inversely proportional to x. For example, if x is increased by a factor of 3, then y will be decreased by the same factor, 3.

The **midpoint** between two points, (x_1, y_1) and (x_2, y_2), is given by taking the average of the x-coordinates and the average of the y-coordinates:

$$\left(\frac{x_1 + x_2}{2}, \frac{y_1 + y_2}{2} \right)$$

The **distance** between two points, (x_1, y_1) and (x_2, y_2), is given by the **Pythagorean formula**:

$$\sqrt{(x_2 - x_1)^2 + (y_2 - y_1)^2}$$

To find the perpendicular distance between a line $Ax + By = C$ and a point (x_1, y_1) not on the line, we need to use the formula:

$$\frac{|Ax_1 + By_1 + C|}{\sqrt{A^2 + B^2}}$$

Quadratic Functions

A polynomial of degree 2 is called **quadratic**. Every quadratic function can be written in the form:

$$ax^2 + bx + c$$

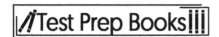
The graph of a quadratic function, $y = ax^2 + bx + c$, is called a **parabola.** Parabolas are vaguely U-shaped.

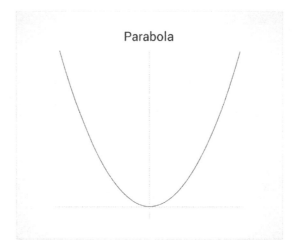

Parabola

Whether the parabola opens upward or downward depends on the sign of a. If a is positive, then the parabola will open upward. If a is negative, then the parabola will open downward. The value of a will also affect how wide the parabola is. If the absolute value of a is large, then the parabola will be fairly skinny. If the absolute value of a is small, then the parabola will be quite wide.

Changes to the value of b affect the parabola in different ways, depending on the sign of a. For positive values of a, increasing b will move the parabola to the left, and decreasing b will move the parabola to the right. On the other hand, if a is negative, the effects will be the opposite: increasing b will move the parabola to the right, while decreasing b will move the parabola to the left.

Changes to the value of c move the parabola vertically. The larger that c is, the higher the parabola gets. This does not depend on the value of a.

The quantity $D = b^2 - 4ac$ is called the **discriminant** of the parabola. When the discriminant is positive, then the parabola has two real zeros, or x-intercepts. However, if the discriminant is negative, then there are no real zeros, and the parabola will not cross the x-axis. The highest or lowest point of the parabola is called the **vertex.** If the discriminant is zero, then the parabola's highest or lowest point is on the x-axis, and it will have a single real zero. The x-coordinate of the vertex can be found using the equation $x = -\frac{b}{2a}$. Plug this x-value into the equation and find the y-coordinate.

A quadratic equation is often used to model the path of an object thrown into the air. The x-value can represent the time in the air, while the y-value can represent the height of the object. In this case, the maximum height of the object would be the y-value found when the x-value is $-\frac{b}{2a}$.

Quadratic equations can be used to model real-world area problems. For example, a farmer may have a rectangular field that he needs to sow with seed. The field has length $x + 8$ and width $2x$. The formula for area should be used: $A = lw$. Therefore:

$$A = (x + 8) \times 2x = 2x^2 + 16x$$

98

The possible values for the length and width can be shown in a table, with input x and output A. If the equation was graphed, the possible area values can be seen on the y-axis for given x-values.

Exponential Functions

An **exponential function** is a function of the form $f(x) = b^x$, where b is a positive real number other than 1. In such a function, b is called the **base**.

The **domain** of an exponential function is all real numbers, and the **range** is all positive real numbers. There will always be a horizontal asymptote of $y = 0$ on one side. If b is greater than 1, then the graph will be increasing when moving to the right. If b is less than 1, then the graph will be decreasing when moving to the right. Exponential functions are one-to-one. The basic exponential function graph will go through the point $(0, 1)$.

The following example demonstartes this more clearly:

> Solve $5^{x+1} = 25$.
>
> The first step is to get the x out of the exponent by rewriting the equation $5^{x+1} = 5^2$ so that both sides have a base of 5. Since the bases are the same, the exponents must be equal to each other. This leaves $x + 1 = 2$ or $x = 1$. To check the answer, the x-value of 1 can be substituted back into the original equation.

Exponential growth and decay can be found in real-world situations. For example, if a piece of notebook paper is folded 25 times, the thickness of the paper can be found. To model this situation, a table can be used. The initial point is one-fold, which yields a thickness of 2 papers. For the second fold, the thickness is 4. Since the thickness doubles each time, the table below shows the thickness for the next few folds. Notice the thickness changes by the same factor each time. Since this change for a constant interval of folds is a factor of 2, the function is exponential. The equation for this is $y = 2^x$. For twenty-five folds, the thickness would be 33,554,432 papers.

x (folds)	y (paper thickness)
0	1
1	2
2	4
3	8
4	16
5	32

One exponential formula that is commonly used is the **interest formula**: $A = Pe^{rt}$. In this formula, interest is compounded continuously. A is the value of the investment after the time, t, in years. P is the initial amount of the investment, r is the interest rate, and e is the constant equal to approximately 2.718. Given an initial amount of \$200 and a time of 3 years, if interest is compounded continuously at a rate of 6%, the total investment value can be found by plugging each value into the formula. The invested value at the end is \$239.44. In more complex problems, the final investment may be given, and the rate may be the unknown. In this case, the formula becomes $239.44 = 200e^{r3}$. Solving for r requires isolating the exponential expression on one side by dividing by 200, yielding the equation $1.20 = e^{r3}$. Taking the natural log of both sides results in $\ln(1.2) = r3$. Using a calculator to evaluate the logarithmic expression, $r = 0.06 = 6\%$.

When working with logarithms and exponential expressions, it is important to remember the relationship between the two. In general, the logarithmic form is $y = log_b x$ for an exponential form $b^y = x$. Logarithms and exponential functions are inverses of each other.

Logarithmic Functions

A **logarithmic function** is an inverse for an exponential function. The inverse of the base b exponential function is written as $\log_b(x)$, and is called the **base b logarithm**. The domain of a logarithm is all positive real numbers. It has the properties that $\log_b(b^x) = x$. For positive real values of x, $b^{\log_b(x)} = x$.

When there is no chance of confusion, the parentheses are sometimes skipped for logarithmic functions: $\log_b(x)$ may be written as $\log_b x$. For the special number e, the base e logarithm is called the **natural logarithm** and is written as $\ln x$. Logarithms are one-to-one.

When working with logarithmic functions, it is important to remember the following properties. Each one can be derived from the definition of the logarithm as the inverse to an exponential function:

- $\log_b 1 = 0$
- $\log_b b = 1$
- $\log_b b^p = p$
- $\log_b MN = \log_b M + \log_b N$
- $\log_b \frac{M}{N} = \log_b M - \log_b N$
- $\log_b M^p = p \log_b M$

When solving equations involving exponentials and logarithms, the following fact should be used:

If f is a one-to-one function, $a = b$ is equivalent to $f(a) = f(b)$.

Using this, together with the fact that logarithms and exponentials are inverses, allows for manipulations of the equations to isolate the variable as is demonstrated in the following example:

Solve $4 = \ln(x - 4)$.

Using the definition of a logarithm, the equation can be changed to $e^4 = e^{\ln(x-4)}$. The functions on the right side cancel with a result of $e^4 = x - 4$. This then gives:

$$x = 4 + e^4$$

Rational Functions

A rational function is similar to an equation, but it includes two variables. In general, a rational function is in the form: $f(x) = \frac{p(x)}{q(x)}$, where $p(x)$ and $q(x)$ are polynomials. Rational functions are defined everywhere except where the denominator is equal to zero. When the denominator is equal to zero, this indicates either a hole in the graph or an asymptote. An asymptote can be either vertical, horizontal, or slant. A hole occurs when both the numerator and denominator are equal to 0 for a given value of x. A rational function can have at most one vertical asymptote and one horizontal or slant asymptote. An asymptote is a line such that the distance between the curve and the line tends toward 0, but never reaches it, as the line heads toward infinity. Examples of these types of functions are shown below. The

100

first graph shows a rational function with a vertical asymptote at $x = 0$. This can be found by setting the denominator equal to 0. In this case it is just $x = 0$.

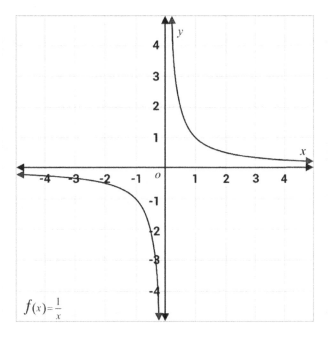

$$f(x) = \frac{1}{x}$$

The second graph shows a rational function with a vertical asymptote at $x = -0.5$. Again, this can be found by just setting the denominator equal to 0. So:

$$2x^2 + x = 0 \quad \rightarrow \quad 2x + 1 = 0 \quad \rightarrow \quad 2x = -1 \quad \rightarrow \quad x = -0.5$$

This graph also has a hole in the graph at $x = 0$. This is because both the numerator and denominator are equal to 0 when $x = 0$.

$$y = \frac{4x^2 + x}{2x^2 + x}$$

Hole at $x=0$

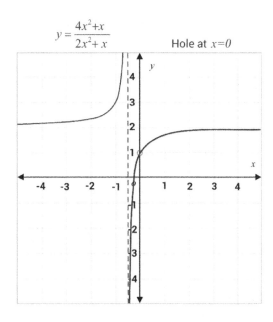

Piecewise Functions

A piecewise-defined function also has a different appearance on the graph. In the following function, there are three equations defined over different intervals. It is a function because there is only one y-value for each x-value, passing the Vertical Line Test. The domain is all real numbers less than or equal to 6. The range is all real numbers greater than zero. From left to right, the graph decreases to zero, then increases to almost 4, and then jumps to 6.

From input values greater than 2, the input decreases just below 8 to 4, and then stops.

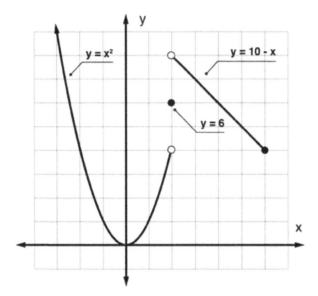

Trigonometric Functions

Trigonometric functions are built out of two basic functions, the **sine** and **cosine**, written as $\sin \theta$ and $\cos \theta$, respectively. Note that similar to logarithms, it is customary to drop the parentheses as long as the result is not confusing.

Sine and cosine are defined using the **unit circle**. If θ is the angle going counterclockwise around the origin from the x-axis, then the point on the unit circle in that direction will have the coordinates (cos θ, sin θ).

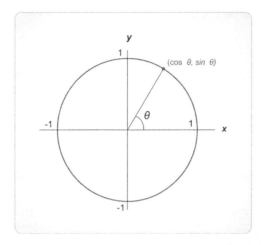

Since the angle returns to the start every 2π radians (or 360 degrees), the graph of these functions is **periodic**, with period 2π. This means that the graph repeats itself as one moves along the x-axis because $\sin \theta = \sin(\theta + 2\pi)$. Cosine works similarly.

From the unit circle definition, the sine function starts at 0 when $\theta = 0$. It grows to 1 as θ grows to $\pi/2$, and then back to 0 at $\theta = \pi$. Then it decreases to -1 as θ grows to $3\pi/2$, and goes back up to 0 at $\theta = 2\pi$.

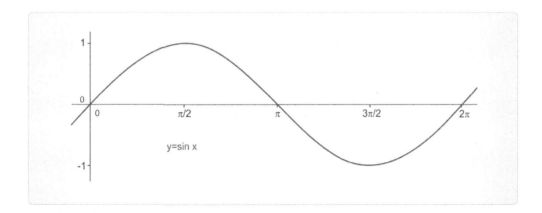

103

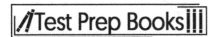
The graph of the cosine is similar. The cosine graph will start at 1, decreasing to 0 at $\frac{\pi}{2}$ and continuing to decrease to -1 at $\theta = \pi$. Then, it grows to 0 as θ grows to $\frac{3\pi}{2}$ and back up to 1 at $\theta = 2\pi$.

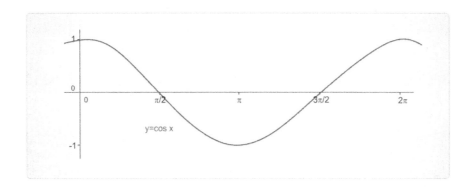

Another trigonometric function that is frequently used, is the **tangent** function. This is defined as the following equation: $\tan \theta = \frac{\sin \theta}{\cos \theta}$.

The tangent function is a period of π rather than 2π because the sine and cosine functions have the same absolute values after a change in the angle of π, but they flip their signs. Since the tangent is a ratio of the two functions, the changes in signs cancel.

The tangent function will be zero when sine is zero, and it will have a vertical asymptote whenever cosine is zero. The following graph shows the tangent function:

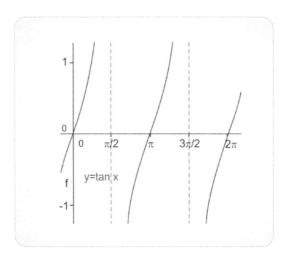

Three other trigonometric functions are sometimes useful. These are the **reciprocal** trigonometric functions, so named because they are just the reciprocals of sine, cosine, and tangent. They are the **cosecant**, defined as $\csc \theta = \frac{1}{\sin \theta}$, the **secant**, $\sec \theta = \frac{1}{\cos \theta}$, and the **cotangent**, $\cot \theta = \frac{1}{\tan \theta}$. Note that from the definition of tangent, $\cot \theta = \frac{\cos \theta}{\sin \theta}$.

In addition, there are three identities that relate the trigonometric functions to one another:

- $\cos\theta = \sin(\frac{\pi}{2} - \theta)$
- $\csc\theta = \sec\left(\frac{\pi}{2} - \theta\right)$
- $\cot\theta = \tan(\frac{\pi}{2} - \theta)$

Here is a list of commonly-needed values for trigonometric functions, given in radians, for the first quadrant:

Table for trigonometric functions

$\sin 0 = 0$	$\cos 0 = 1$	$\tan 0 = 0$
$\sin\frac{\pi}{6} = \frac{1}{2}$	$\cos\frac{\pi}{6} = \frac{\sqrt{3}}{2}$	$\tan\frac{\pi}{6} = \frac{\sqrt{3}}{3}$
$\sin\frac{\pi}{4} = \frac{\sqrt{2}}{2}$	$\cos\frac{\pi}{4} = \frac{\sqrt{2}}{2}$	$\tan\frac{\pi}{4} = 1$
$\sin\frac{\pi}{3} = \frac{\sqrt{3}}{2}$	$\cos\frac{\pi}{3} = \frac{1}{2}$	$\tan\frac{\pi}{3} = \sqrt{3}$
$\sin\frac{\pi}{2} = 1$	$\cos\frac{\pi}{2} = 0$	$\tan\frac{\pi}{2} = undefined$
$\csc 0 = undefined$	$\sec 0 = 1$	$\cot 0 = undefined$
$\csc\frac{\pi}{6} = 2$	$\sec\frac{\pi}{6} = \frac{2\sqrt{3}}{3}$	$\cot\frac{\pi}{6} = \sqrt{3}$
$\csc\frac{\pi}{4} = \sqrt{2}$	$\sec\frac{\pi}{4} = \sqrt{2}$	$\cot\frac{\pi}{4} = 1$
$\csc\frac{\pi}{3} = \frac{2\sqrt{3}}{3}$	$\sec\frac{\pi}{3} = 2$	$\cot\frac{\pi}{3} = \frac{\sqrt{3}}{3}$
$\csc\frac{\pi}{2} = 1$	$\sec\frac{\pi}{2} = undefined$	$\cot\frac{\pi}{2} = 0$

To find the trigonometric values in other quadrants, complementary angles can be used. The **complementary angle** is the smallest angle between the x-axis and the given angle.

Once the complementary angle is known, the following rule is used:

For an angle θ with complementary angle x, the absolute value of a trigonometric function evaluated at θ is the same as the absolute value when evaluated at x.

105

The correct sign for sine and cosine is determined by the x-and y-coordinates on the unit circle.

- Sine will be positive in quadrants I and II and negative in quadrants III and IV.
- Cosine will be positive in quadrants I and IV, and negative in II and III.
- Tangent will be positive in I and III, and negative in II and IV.

The signs of the reciprocal functions will be the same as the sign of the function of which they are the reciprocal. For example:

Find $\sin\frac{3\pi}{4}$.

The reference angle must be found first. This angle is in the II quadrant, and the angle between it and the x-axis is $\frac{\pi}{4}$. Now, $\sin\frac{\pi}{4} = \frac{\sqrt{2}}{2}$. Since this is in the II quadrant, sine takes on positive values (the y-coordinate is positive in the II quadrant). Therefore, $\sin\frac{3\pi}{4} = \frac{\sqrt{2}}{2}$.

In addition to the six trigonometric functions defined above, there are inverses for these functions. However, since the trigonometric functions are not one-to-one, one can only construct inverses for them on a restricted domain.

Usually, the domain chosen will be $[0, \pi)$ for cosine and $(-\frac{\pi}{2}, \frac{\pi}{2}]$ for sine. The inverse for tangent can use either of these domains. The inverse functions for the trigonometric functions are also called **arc functions**. In addition to being written with a -1 as the exponent to denote that the function is an inverse, they will sometimes be written with an "a" or "arc" in front of the function name, so $\cos^{-1}\theta = \mathrm{acos}\,\theta = \arccos\theta$.

When solving equations that involve trigonometric functions, there are often multiple solutions. For example, $2\sin\theta = \sqrt{2}$ can be simplified to $\sin\theta = \frac{\sqrt{2}}{2}$. This has solutions $\theta = \frac{\pi}{4}, \frac{3\pi}{4}$, but in addition, because of the periodicity, any integer multiple of 2π can also be added to these solutions to find another solution.

The full set of solutions is $\theta = \frac{\pi}{4} + 2\pi k, \frac{3\pi}{4} + 2\pi k$ for all integer values of k. It is very important to remember to find all possible solutions when dealing with equations that involve trigonometric functions.

The name *trigonometric* comes from the fact that these functions play an important role in the geometry of triangles, particularly right triangles. Consider the right triangle shown in this figure:

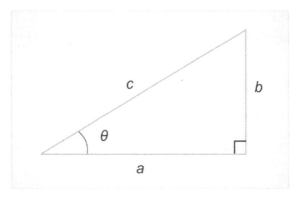

The following hold true:

- $c \sin \theta = b$
- $c \cos \theta = a$
- $\tan \theta = \dfrac{b}{a}$
- $b \csc \theta = c$
- $a \sec \theta = c$
- $\cot \theta = \dfrac{a}{b}$

It is important to remember that the angles of a triangle must add up to π radians (180 degrees).

Radical Functions

A radical function is any function involving a root. For instance, $y = \sqrt[n]{x}$ is a radical function with index n. If n is odd, the function represents an odd root, and its domain and range are both all real numbers. This is because the odd root of any real number is a real number. Radical functions, for example, $f(x) = \sqrt{x}$, have a restriction for the domain and range because there are no real negative inputs or outputs for this function. The domain can be stated as $x \geq 0$, and the range is $y \geq 0$.

Building a Function

Functions can be built out of the context of a situation. For example, the relationship between the money paid for a gym membership and the months that someone has been a member can be described through a function. If the one-time membership fee is $40 and the monthly fee is $30, then the function can be written:

$$f(x) = 30x + 40$$

The x-value represents the number of months the person has been part of the gym, while the output is the total money paid for the membership. The table below shows this relationship. It is a representation of the function because the initial cost is $40 and the cost increases each month by $30.

x (months)	y (money paid to gym)
0	40
1	70
2	100
3	130

Functions can also be built from existing functions. For example, a given function $f(x)$ can be transformed by adding a constant, multiplying by a constant, or changing the input value by a constant. The new function $g(x) = f(x) + k$ represents a vertical shift of the original function. In $f(x) = 3x - 2$, a vertical shift 4 units up would be:

$$g(x) = 3x - 2 + 4 = 3x + 2$$

Multiplying the function times a constant k represents a vertical stretch, based on whether the constant is greater than or less than 1. The function:

$$g(x) = kf(x) = 4(3x - 2) = 12x - 8$$

107

represents a stretch. Changing the input x by a constant, forms the function:

$$g(x) = f(x + k) = 3(x + 4) - 2$$

$$3x + 12 - 2 = 3x + 10$$

and this represents a horizontal shift to the left 4 units. If $(x - 4)$ was plugged into the function, it would represent a vertical shift.

A composition function can also be formed by plugging one function into another. In function notation, this is written:

$$(f \circ g)(x) = f(g(x))$$

For two functions $f(x) = x^2$ and $g(x) = x - 3$, the composition function becomes:

$$f(g(x)) = (x - 3)^2$$

$$x^2 - 6x + 9$$

The composition of functions can also be used to verify if two functions are inverses of each other. Given the two functions $f(x) = 2x + 5$ and $g(x) = \frac{x-5}{2}$, the composition function can be found $(f \circ g)(x)$. Solving this equation yields:

$$f(g(x)) = 2\left(\frac{x - 5}{2}\right) + 5$$

$$x - 5 + 5 = x$$

It also is true that $g(f(x)) = x$. Since the composition of these two functions gives a simplified answer of x, this verifies that $f(x)$ and $g(x)$ are inverse functions. The domain of $f(g(x))$ is the set of all x-values in the domain of $g(x)$ such that $g(x)$ is in the domain of $f(x)$. Basically, both $f(g(x))$ and $g(x)$ have to be defined.

To build an inverse of a function, $f(x)$ needs to be replaced with y, and the x and y values need to be switched. Then, the equation can be solved for y. For example, given the equation $y = e^{2x}$, the inverse can be found by rewriting the equation $x = e^{2y}$. The natural logarithm of both sides is taken down, and the exponent is brought down to form the equation:

$$\ln(x) = \ln(e)\, 2y$$

$\ln(e) = 1$, which yields the equation $\ln(x) = 2y$. Dividing both sides by 2 yields the inverse equation

$$\frac{\ln(x)}{2} = y = f^{-1}(x)$$

The domain of an inverse function is the range of the original function, and the range of an inverse function is the domain of the original function. Therefore, an ordered pair (x, y) on either a graph or a table corresponding to $f(x)$ means that the ordered pair (y, x) exists on the graph of $f^{-1}(x)$. Basically, if $f(x) = y$, then $f^{-1}(y) = x$. For a function to have an inverse, it must be one-to-one. That means it must pass the **Horizontal Line Test**, and if any horizontal line passes through the graph of the function twice, a function is not one-to-one. The domain of a function that is not one-to-one can be restricted to an interval in which the function is one-to-one, to be able to define an inverse function.

Functions can also be formed from combinations of existing functions.

Given $f(x)$ and $g(x)$, the following can be built:

$$f + g$$

$$f - g$$

$$fg$$

$$\frac{f}{g}$$

The domains of $f + g$, $f - g$, and fg are the intersection of the domains of f and g. The domain of $\frac{f}{g}$ is the same set, excluding those values that make $g(x) = 0$.

For example, if:

$$f(x) = 2x + 3$$

$$g(x) = x + 1$$

then

$$\frac{f}{g} = \frac{2x + 3}{x + 1}$$

Its domain is all real numbers except -1.

Comparing Functions

As mentioned, three common functions used to model different relationships between quantities are linear, quadratic, and exponential functions. **Linear functions** are the simplest of the three, and the independent variable x has an exponent of 1. Written in the most common form, $y = mx + b$, the coefficient of x indicates how fast the function grows at a constant rate, and the b-value denotes the starting point. A **quadratic** function has an exponent of 2 on the independent variable x. Standard form for this type of function is $y = ax^2 + bx + c$, and the graph is a parabola. These type functions grow at a changing rate. An **exponential** function has an independent variable in the exponent $y = ab^x$. The graph of these types of functions is described as **growth** or **decay**, based on whether the base, b, is greater than or less than 1. These functions are different from quadratic functions because the base stays constant. A common base is base e.

The following three functions model a linear, quadratic, and exponential function respectively: $y = 2x$, $y = x^2$, and $y = 2^x$. Their graphs are shown below. The first graph, modeling the linear function, shows that the growth is constant over each interval. With a horizontal change of 1, the vertical change is 2. It models constant positive growth. The second graph shows the quadratic function, which is a curve that is symmetric across the y-axis. The growth is not constant, but the change is mirrored over the axis. The last graph models the exponential function, where the horizontal change of 1 yields a vertical change that increases more and more with each iteration of horizontal change. The exponential graph gets very

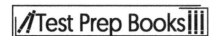
close to the x-axis, but never touches it, meaning there is an asymptote there. The y-value can never be zero because the base of 2 can never be raised to an input value that yields an output of zero.

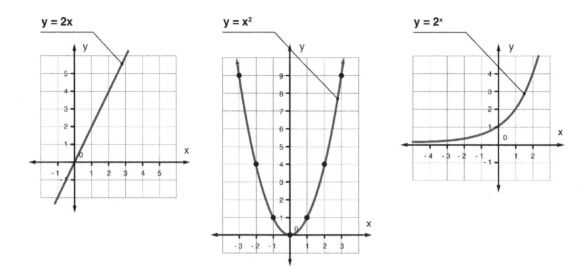

The three tables below show specific values for three types of functions. The third column in each table shows the change in the y-values for each interval. The first table shows a constant change of 2 for each equal interval, which matches the slope in the equation $y = 2x$. The second table shows an increasing change, but it also has a pattern. The increase is changing by 2 more each time, so the change is quadratic. The third table shows the change as factors of the base, 2. It shows a continuing pattern of factors of the base.

$y = 2x$		
x	y	Δy
1	2	
2	4	2
3	6	2
4	8	2
5	10	2

$y = x^2$		
x	y	Δy
1	1	
2	4	3
3	9	5
4	16	7
5	25	9

$y = 2^x$		
x	y	Δy
1	2	
2	4	2
3	8	4
4	16	8
5	32	16

Given a table of values, the type of function can be determined by observing the change in y over equal intervals. For example, the tables below model two functions. The changes in interval for the x-values is 1 for both tables. For the first table, the y-values increase by 5 for each interval. Since the change is constant, the situation can be described as a linear function. The equation would be:

$$y = 5x + 3$$

110

For the second table, the change for y is 20, 100, and 500, respectively. The increases are multiples of 5, meaning the situation can be modeled by an exponential function. The equation below models this situation:

$$y = 5^x + 3$$

$y = 5x + 3$	
x	y
1	8
2	13
3	18
4	23

$y = 5^x + 3$	
x	y
1	8
2	28
3	128
4	628

Evaluating Functions

To evaluate functions, plug in the given value everywhere the variable appears in the expression for the function. For example, find $g(-2)$ where:

$$g(x) = 2x^2 - \frac{4}{x}$$

To complete the problem, plug in -2 in the following way:

$$g(-2) = 2(-2)^2 - \frac{4}{-2}$$

$$2 \times 4 + 2$$

$$8 + 2 = 10$$

Geometry

Shapes and Solids

A **polygon** is a closed geometric figure in a plane (flat surface) consisting of at least 3 sides formed by line segments. These are often defined as two-dimensional shapes. Common two-dimensional shapes include circles, triangles, squares, rectangles, pentagons, and hexagons. Note that a circle is a two-dimensional shape without sides.

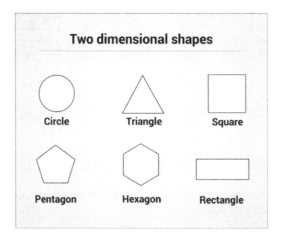

Polygons can be either convex or concave. A polygon that has interior angles all measuring less than 180° is convex. A concave polygon has one or more interior angles measuring greater than 180°. Examples are shown below.

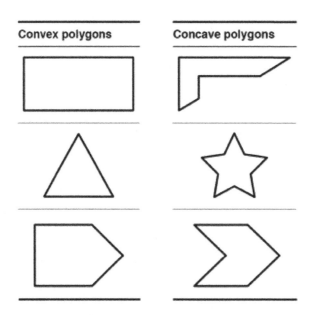

112

Polygons can be classified by the number of sides (also equal to the number of angles) they have. The following are the names of polygons with a given number of sides or angles:

# of Sides	Name of Polygon
3	Triangle
4	Quadrilateral
5	Pentagon
6	Hexagon
7	Septagon (or heptagon)
8	Octagon
9	Nonagon
10	Decagon

Equiangular polygons are polygons in which the measure of every interior angle is the same. The sides of equilateral polygons are always the same length. If a polygon is both equiangular and equilateral, the polygon is defined as a regular polygon.

Triangles can be further classified by their sides and angles. A triangle with its largest angle measuring 90° is a right triangle. A triangle with the largest angle less than 90° is an acute triangle. A triangle with the largest angle greater than 90° is an obtuse triangle. Below is an example of a right triangle.

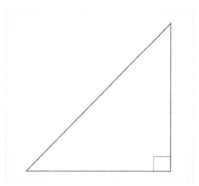

A triangle consisting of two equal sides and two equal angles is an isosceles triangle. A triangle with three equal sides and three equal angles is an equilateral triangle. A triangle with no equal sides or angles is a scalene triangle.

Isosceles triangle:

Equilateral triangle:

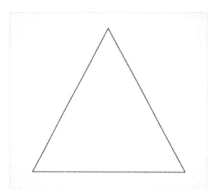

Scalene triangle:

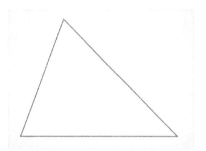

Quadrilaterals can be further classified according to their sides and angles. A quadrilateral with exactly one pair of parallel sides is called a trapezoid. A quadrilateral that shows both pairs of opposite sides parallel is a parallelogram. Parallelograms include rhombuses, rectangles, and squares. A rhombus has four equal sides. A rectangle has four equal angles (90° each). A square has four 90° angles and four equal sides. Therefore, a square is both a rhombus and a rectangle.

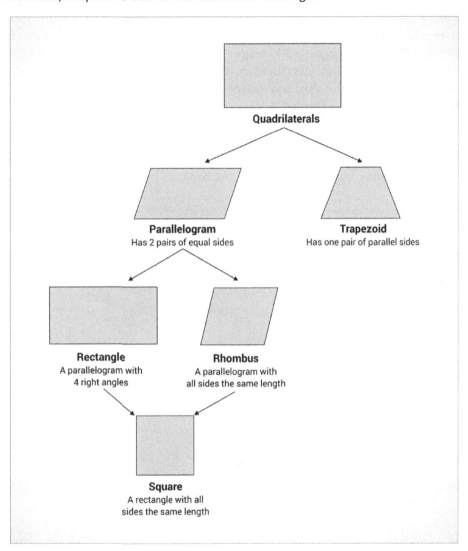

Angles and Diagonals

Diagonals are lines (excluding sides) that connect two vertices within a polygon. **Mutually bisecting diagonals** intersect at their midpoints. Parallelograms, rectangles, squares, and rhombuses have mutually bisecting diagonals. However, trapezoids don't have such lines. **Perpendicular diagonals** occur when they form four right triangles at their point of intersection. Squares and rhombuses have perpendicular diagonals, but trapezoids, rectangles, and parallelograms do not. Finally, **perpendicular bisecting diagonals** (also known as **perpendicular bisectors**) form four right triangles at their point of intersection, but this intersection is also the midpoint of the two lines. Both rhombuses and squares have perpendicular bisecting angles, but trapezoids, rectangles, and parallelograms do not. Knowing these definitions can help tremendously in problems that involve both angles and diagonals.

Polygons with More than Four Sides

A **pentagon** is a five-sided figure. A six-sided shape is a **hexagon**. A seven-sided figure is classified as a **heptagon**, and an eight-sided figure is called an **octagon**. An important characteristic is whether a polygon is regular or irregular. If it's **regular,** the side lengths and angle measurements are all equal. An **irregular** polygon has unequal side lengths and angle measurements. Mathematical problems involving polygons with more than four sides usually involve side length and angle measurements. The sum of all internal angles in a polygon equals $180(n-2)$ degrees, where n is the number of sides. Therefore, the total of all internal angles in a pentagon is 540 degrees because there are five sides so $180(5-2) = 540$ degrees. Unfortunately, area formulas don't exist for polygons with more than four sides. However, their shapes can be split up into triangles, and the formula for area of a triangle can be applied and totaled to obtain the area for the entire figure.

Solids

A solid is a three-dimensional figure that encloses a part of space. Common three-dimensional shapes include spheres, prisms, cubes, pyramids, cylinders, and cones.

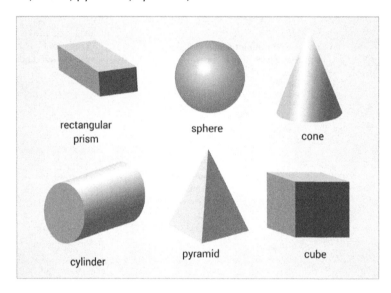

Solids consisting of all flat surfaces that are polygons are called polyhedrons. The two-dimensional surfaces that make up a polyhedron are called faces. Types of polyhedrons include prisms and pyramids. A prism consists of two parallel faces that are congruent (or the same shape and same size), and lateral faces going around (which are parallelograms). A prism is further classified by the shape of its base, as shown below:

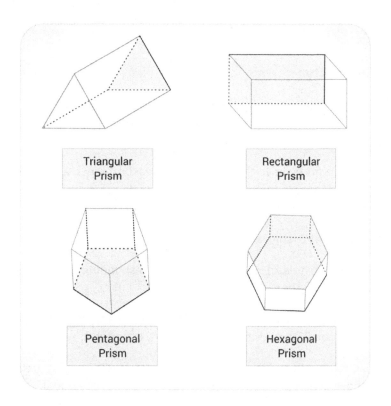

A pyramid consists of lateral faces (triangles) that meet at a common point called the vertex and one other face that is a polygon, called the base. A pyramid can be further classified by the shape of its base, as shown below.

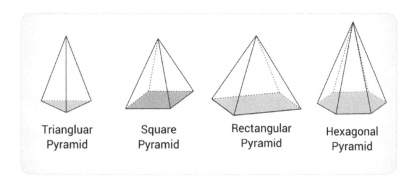

A tetrahedron is another name for a triangular pyramid. All the faces of a tetrahedron are triangles.

Solids that are not polyhedrons include spheres, cylinders, and cones. A sphere is the set of all points a given distance from a given center point. A sphere is commonly thought of as a three-dimensional circle.

A cylinder consists of two parallel, congruent (same size) circles and a lateral curved surface. A cone consists of a circle as its base and a lateral curved surface that narrows to a point called the vertex.

Similar polygons are the same shape but different sizes. More specifically, their corresponding angle measures are congruent (or equal) and the length of their sides is proportional. For example, all sides of one polygon may be double the length of the sides of another. Likewise, similar solids are the same shape but different sizes. Any corresponding faces or bases of similar solids are the same polygons that are proportional by a consistent value.

Congruence and Similarity

Sometimes, two figures are similar, meaning they have the same basic shape and the same interior angles, but they have different dimensions. If the ratio of two corresponding sides is known, then that ratio, or scale factor, holds true for all of the dimensions of the new figure.

Likewise, triangles are similar if they have the same angle measurements, and their sides are proportional to one another. Triangles are **congruent** if the angles of the triangles are equal in measurement and the sides of the triangles are equal in measurement.

There are five ways to show that triangles are congruent:

1. SSS (Side-Side-Side Postulate) – when all three corresponding sides are equal in length, then the two triangles are congruent.

2. SAS (Side-Angle-Side Postulate) – if a pair of corresponding sides and the angle in between those two sides are equal, then the two triangles are congruent.

3. ASA (Angle-Side-Angle Postulate) – if a pair of corresponding angles are equal and the side lengths within those angles are equal, then the two triangles are equal.

4. AAS (Angle-Angle-Side Postulate) – when a pair of corresponding angles for two triangles and a non-included side are equal, then the two triangles are congruent.

5. HL (Hypotenuse-Leg Theorem) – if two right triangles have the same hypotenuse length, and one of the other sides in each triangle are of the same length, then the two triangles are congruent.

If two triangles are discovered to be similar or congruent, this information can assist in determining unknown parts of triangles, such as missing angles and sides.

118

The example below involves the question of congruent triangles. The first step is to examine whether the triangles are congruent. If the triangles are congruent, then the measure of a missing angle can be found.

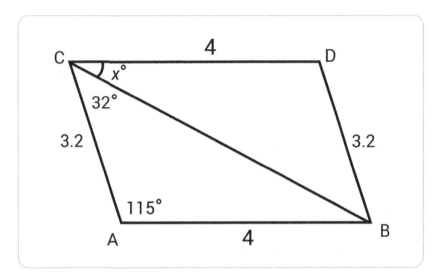

The above diagram provides values for angle measurements and side lengths in triangles *CAB* and *CDB*. Note that side *CA* is 3.2 and side *DB* is 3.2. Side *CD* is 4 and side *AB* is 4. Furthermore, line *CB* is congruent to itself by the reflexive property. Therefore, the two triangles are congruent by SSS (Side-Side-Side). Because the two triangles are congruent, all of the corresponding parts of the triangles are also congruent. Therefore, angle *x* is congruent to the inside of the angle for which a measurement is not provided in triangle *CAB*. Thus, 115º+32º=147º. A triangle's angles sum to 180º, therefore, 180º – 147º=33º. Angle *x* =33º, because the two triangles are reversed.

Transformations of a Plane
Given a figure drawn on a plane, many changes can be made to that figure, including rotation, translation, and reflection. **Rotations** turn the figure about a point, **translations** slide the figure, and **reflections** flip the figure over a specified line. When performing these transformations, the original figure is called the **pre-image**, and the figure after transformation is called the **image**.

More specifically, **translation** means that all points in the figure are moved in the same direction by the same distance. In other words, the figure is slid in some fixed direction. Of course, while the entire figure is slid by the same distance, this does not change any of the measurements of the figures involved. The result will have the same distances and angles as the original figure.

In terms of Cartesian coordinates, a translation means a shift of each of the original points (x, y) by a fixed amount in the x and y directions, to become $(x + a, y + b)$.

Another procedure that can be performed is called **reflection**. To do this, a line in the plane is specified, called the **line of reflection**. Then, take each point and flip it over the line so that it is the same distance from the line but on the opposite side of it. This does not change any of the distances or angles involved, but it does reverse the order in which everything appears.

To reflect something over the *x*-axis, the points (x, y) are sent to $(x, -y)$. To reflect something over the *y*-axis, the points (x, y) are sent to the points $(-x, y)$. Flipping over other lines is not something easy to

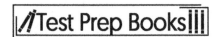
express in Cartesian coordinates. However, by drawing the figure and the line of reflection, the distance to the line and the original points can be used to find the reflected figure.

Example: Reflect this triangle with vertices $(-1, 0)$, $(2, 1)$, and $(2, 0)$ over the y-axis. The pre-image is shown below.

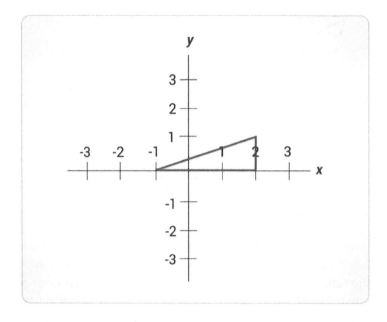

To do this, flip the x-values of the points involved to the negatives of themselves, while keeping the y-values the same. The image is shown here.

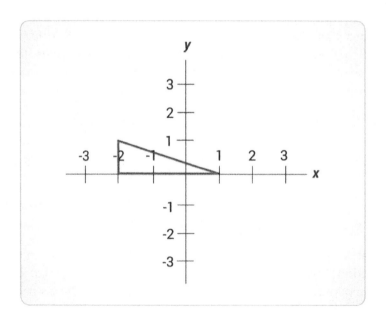

The new vertices will be $(1, 0)$, $(-2, 1)$, and $(-2, 0)$.

Another procedure that does not change the distances and angles in a figure is **rotation**. In this procedure, pick a center point, then rotate every vertex along a circle around that point by the same angle. This procedure is also not easy to express in Cartesian coordinates, and this is not a requirement on this test. However, as with reflections, it's helpful to draw the figures and see what the result of the rotation would look like. This transformation can be performed using a compass and protractor.

Each one of these transformations can be performed on the coordinate plane without changes to the original dimensions or angles.

If two figures in the plane involve the same distances and angles, they are called **congruent figures**. In other words, two figures are congruent when they go from one form to another through reflection, rotation, and translation, or a combination of these.

Remember that rotation and translation will give back a new figure that is identical to the original figure, but reflection will give back a mirror image of it.

To recognize that a figure has undergone a rotation, check to see that the figure has not been changed into a mirror image, but that its orientation has changed (that is, whether the parts of the figure now form different angles with the x- and y-axes).

To recognize that a figure has undergone a translation, check to see that the figure has not been changed into a mirror image, and that the orientation remains the same.

To recognize that a figure has undergone a reflection, check to see that the new figure is a mirror image of the old figure.

Keep in mind that sometimes a combination of translations, reflections, and rotations may be performed on a figure.

Dilation

A **dilation** is a transformation that preserves angles, but not distances. This can be thought of as stretching or shrinking a figure. If a dilation makes figures larger, it is called an **enlargement**. If a dilation makes figures smaller, it is called a **reduction**. The easiest example is to dilate around the origin. In this case, multiply the x- and y-coordinates by a **scale factor**, k, sending points (x, y) to (kx, ky).

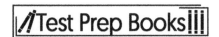
As an example, draw a dilation of the following triangle, whose vertices will be the points $(-1, 0)$, $(1, 0)$, and $(1, 1)$.

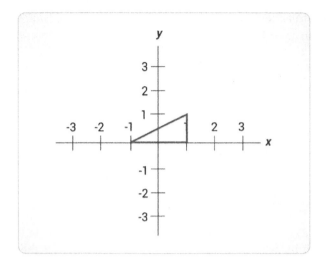

For this problem, dilate by a scale factor of 2, so the new vertices will be $(-2, 0)$, $(2, 0)$, and $(2, 2)$.

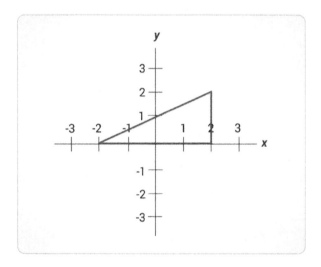

Note that after a dilation, the distances between the vertices of the figure will have changed, but the angles will remain the same. The two figures that are obtained by dilation, along with possibly translation, rotation, and reflection, are all *similar* to one another. Another way to think of this is that similar figures have the same number of vertices and edges, and their angles are all the same. Similar figures have the same basic shape but are different in size.

Surface Area and Volume

Surface area and volume are two- and three-dimensional measurements. Surface area measures the total surface space of an object, like the six sides of a cube. Questions about surface area will ask how much of something is needed to cover a three-dimensional object, like wrapping a present. **Volume** is the measurement of how much space an object occupies, like how much space is in the cube. Volume

questions will ask how much of something is needed to completely fill the object. The most common surface area and volume questions deal with spheres, cubes, and rectangular prisms.

The formula for a cube's surface area is $SA = 6 \times s^2$, where s is the length of a side. A cube has 6 equal sides, so the formula expresses the area of all the sides. Volume is simply measured by taking the cube of the length, so the formula is $V = s^3$.

The surface area formula for a rectangular prism or a general box is SA= $2(lw + lh + wh)$, where l is the length, h is the height, and w is the width. The volume formula is $V = l \times w \times h$, which is the cube's volume formula adjusted for the unequal lengths of a box's sides.

The formula for a sphere's surface area is $SA = 4\pi r^2$, where r is the sphere's radius. The surface area formula is the area for a circle multiplied by four. To measure volume, the formula is V= $\frac{4}{3}\pi r^3$.

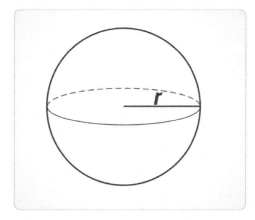

A **rectangular pyramid** is a figure with a rectangular base and four triangular sides that meet at a single vertex. If the rectangle has sides of lengths x and y, then the volume will be given by $V = \frac{1}{3}xyh$.

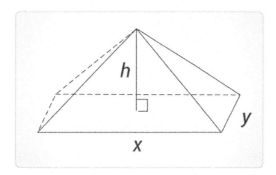

123

To find the surface area, the dimensions of each triangle must be known. However, these dimensions can differ depending on the problem in question. Therefore, there is no general formula for calculating total surface area.

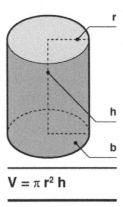

$$V = \pi r^2 h$$

The formula to find the volume of a cylinder is $\pi r^2 h$. This formula contains the formula for the area of a circle (πr^2) because the base of a cylinder is a circle. To calculate the volume of a cylinder, the slices of circles needed to build the entire height of the cylinder are added together. For example, if the radius is 5 feet and the height of the cylinder is 10 feet, the cylinder's volume is calculated by using the following equation: $\pi 5^2 \times 10$. Substituting 3.14 for π, the volume is 785.4 ft³.

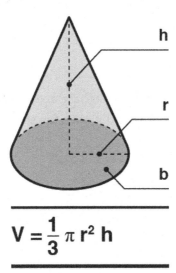

$$V = \frac{1}{3} \pi r^2 h$$

The formula used to calculate the volume of a cone is $\frac{1}{3}\pi r^2 h$. Essentially, the area of the base of the cone is multiplied by the cone's height. In a real-life example where the radius of a cone is 2 meters and the height of a cone is 5 meters, the volume of the cone is calculated by utilizing the formula:

$$\frac{1}{3}\pi 2^2 \times 5 = 21 \; m^3$$

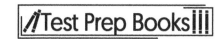

Solving for Missing Values in Shapes

Perimeter is the distance measurement around something. It can be thought of as the length of the boundary, like a fence. In contrast, area is the space occupied by a defined enclosure, like a field enclosed by a fence.

The perimeter of a square is measured by adding together all of the sides. Since a square has four equal sides, its perimeter can be calculated by multiplying the length of one side by 4. Thus, the formula is $P = 4 \times s$, where s equals one side. The area of a square is calculated by squaring the length of one side, which is expressed as the formula $A = s^2$.

Like a square, a rectangle's perimeter is measured by adding together all of the sides. But as the sides are unequal, the formula is different. A rectangle has equal values for its lengths (long sides) and equal values for its widths (short sides), so the perimeter formula for a rectangle is $P = l + l + w + w = 2l + 2w$, where l equals length and w equals width. The area is found by multiplying the length by the width, so the formula is $A = l \times w$.

A triangle's perimeter is measured by adding together the three sides, so the formula is $P = a + b + c$, where a, b, and c are the values of the three sides. The area is calculated by multiplying the length of the base times the height times ½, so the formula is:

$$A = \frac{1}{2} \times b \times h = \frac{bh}{2}$$

The base is the bottom of the triangle, and the height is the distance from the base to the peak. If a problem asks one to calculate the area of a triangle, it will provide the base and height.

A circle's perimeter—also known as its **circumference**—is measured by multiplying the **diameter** (the straight line measured from one side, through the center, to the direct opposite side of the circle) by π, so the formula is $\pi \times d$. This is sometimes expressed by the formula $C = 2 \times \pi \times r$, where r is the **radius** of the circle. These formulas are equivalent, as the radius equals half of the diameter. The area of a circle is calculated with the formula $A = \pi \times r^2$. The test will indicate either to leave the answer with π attached or to calculate to the nearest decimal place, which means multiplying by 3.14 for π.

The perimeter of a parallelogram is measured by adding the lengths and widths together. Thus, the formula is the same as for a rectangle:

$$P = l + l + w + w = 2l + 2w$$

However, the area formula differs from the rectangle. For a parallelogram, the area is calculated by multiplying the length by the height: $A = h \times l$

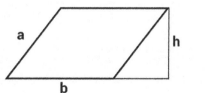

Area = bh

Perimeter = 2(a + b)

The perimeter of a trapezoid is calculated by adding the two unequal bases and two equal sides, so the formula is:

$$P = a + b_1 + c + b_2$$

Although unlikely to be a test question, the formula for the area of a trapezoid is $A = \frac{b_1 + b_2}{2} \times h$, where h equals height, and b_1 and b_2 equal the bases.

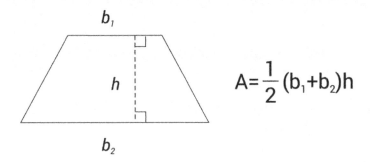

Using formulas such as perimeter and area for different shapes, it's possible to solve for missing side lengths.

Consider the following problem:

The total perimeter of a rectangular garden is 36 m. If the length of each side is 12 m, what is the width?

The formula for the perimeter of a rectangle is $P = 2L + 2W$, where P is the perimeter, L is the length, and W is the width. The first step is to substitute all of the data into the formula:

$$36 = 2(12) + 2W$$

Simplify by multiplying 2×12:

$$36 = 24 + 2W$$

Simplifying this further by subtracting 24 on each side gives:

$$36 - 24 = 24 - 24 + 2W$$

$$12 = 2W$$

Divide by 2:

$$6 = W$$

The width is 6 cm. Remember to test this answer by substituting this value into the original formula:

$$36 = 2(12) + 2(6)$$

More complicated situations can arise where missing side lengths can be calculated by using concepts of similarity and proportional relationships. Suppose that Lara is 5 feet tall and is standing 30 feet from the base of a light pole, and her shadow is 6 feet long. How high is the light on the pole? To figure this out, it helps to make a sketch of the situation:

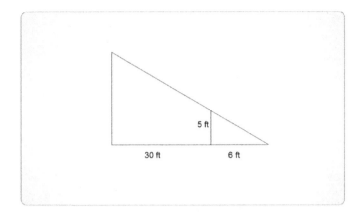

The light pole is the left side of the triangle. Lara is the 5-foot vertical line. Test takers should notice that there are two right triangles here, and that they have all the same angles as one another. Therefore, they form similar triangles. So, the ratio of proportionality between them must be found.

The bases of these triangles are known. The small triangle, formed by Lara and her shadow, has a base of 6 feet. The large triangle formed by the light pole along with the line from the base of the pole out to the end of Lara's shadow is $30 + 6 = 36$ feet long. So, the ratio of the big triangle to the little triangle is $\frac{36}{6} = 6$. The height of the little triangle is 5 feet. Therefore, the height of the big triangle will be $6 \times 5 = 30$ feet, meaning that the light is 30 feet up the pole.

Composite Shapes

The perimeter of an irregular polygon is found by adding the lengths of all of the sides. In cases where all of the sides are given, this will be very straightforward, as it will simply involve finding the sum of the provided lengths. Other times, a side length may be missing and must be determined before the perimeter can be calculated.

Consider the example below:

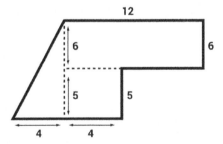

All of the side lengths are provided except for the angled side on the left. Test takers should notice that this is the hypotenuse of a right triangle. The other two sides of the triangle are provided (the base is 4 and the height is $6 + 5 = 11$). The Pythagorean Theorem can be used to find the length of the hypotenuse, remembering that $a^2 + b^2 = c^2$.

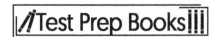
Substituting the side values provided yields:

$$(4)^2 + (11)^2 = c^2$$

Therefore:

$$c = \sqrt{16 + 121} = 11.7$$

Finally, the perimeter can be found by adding this new side length with the other provided lengths to get the total length around the figure:

$$4 + 4 + 5 + 8 + 6 + 12 + 11.7 = 50.7$$

Although units are not provided in this figure, remember that reporting units with a measurement is important.

The area of irregular polygons is found by decomposing, or breaking apart, the figure into smaller shapes. When the area of the smaller shapes is determined, the area of the smaller shapes will produce the area of the original figure when added together. Consider the earlier example:

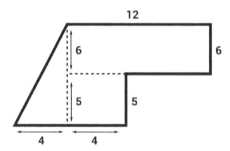

The irregular polygon is decomposed into two rectangles and a triangle. The area of the large rectangle ($A = l \times w \rightarrow A = 12 \times 6$) is 72 square units. The area of the small rectangle is 20 square units ($A = 4 \times 5$). The area of the triangle ($A = \frac{1}{2} \times b \times h \rightarrow A = \frac{1}{2} \times 4 \times 11$) is 22 square units. The sum of the areas of these figures produces the total area of the original polygon:

$$A = 72 + 20 + 22 \rightarrow A = 114 \text{ square units}$$

Here's another example:

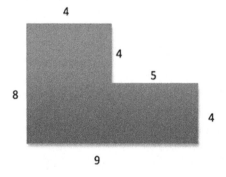

128

This irregular polygon is decomposed into two rectangles. The area of the large rectangle ($A = l \times w \rightarrow A = 8 \times 4$) is 32 square units. The area of the small rectangle is 20 square units ($A = 4 \times 5$). The sum of the areas of these figures produces the total area of the original polygon:

$$A = 32 + 20 \rightarrow A = 52 \text{ square units}$$

The Pythagorean Theorem and Right Triangles

Trigonometric Functions

From the unit circle, the trigonometric ratios were found for the special right triangle with a hypotenuse of 1.

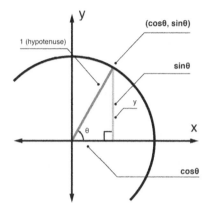

From this triangle, the following Pythagorean identities are formed:

$$\sin^2 \theta + \cos^2 \theta = 1$$

$$\tan^2 \theta + 1 = \sec^2 \theta$$

$$1 + \cot^2 \theta = \csc^2 \theta$$

The second two identities are formed by manipulating the first identity. Since identities are statements that are true for any value of the variable, then they may be used to manipulate equations. For example, a problem may ask for simplification of the expression:

$$\cos^2 x + \cos^2 x \tan^2 x$$

Using the fact that $\tan (x) = \frac{\sin x}{\cos x}$, $\frac{\sin^2 x}{\cos^2 x}$ can then be substituted in for $\tan^2 x$, making the expression:

$$\cos^2 x + \cos^2 x \frac{\sin^2 x}{\cos^2 x}$$

Then the two $\cos^2 x$ terms on top and bottom cancel each other out, simplifying the expression to $\cos^2 x + \sin^2 x$. By the first Pythagorean identity stated above, the expression can be turned into $\cos^2 x + \sin^2 x = 1$.

Another set of trigonometric identities are the double-angle formulas:

$$\sin 2\alpha = 2 \sin \alpha \, \cos \alpha$$

$$\cos 2\alpha = \begin{cases} \cos^2\alpha - \sin^2\alpha \\ 2\cos^2\alpha - 1 \\ 1 - 2\sin^2\alpha \end{cases}$$

Using these formulas, the following identity can be proved:

$$\sin 2x = \frac{2 \tan x}{1 + \tan^2 x}$$

By using one of the Pythagorean identities, the denominator can be rewritten as:

$$1 + \tan^2 x = \sec^2 x$$

By knowing the reciprocals of the trigonometric identities, the secant term can be rewritten to form the equation:

$$\sin 2x = \frac{2 \tan x}{1} \times \cos^2 x$$

Replacing tan (x), the equation becomes $\sin 2x = \frac{2 \sin x}{\cos x} \times \cos^2 x$, where the $\cos x$ can cancel out. The new equation is:

$$\sin 2x = 2 \sin x * \cos x$$

This final equation is one of the double-angle formulas.

Other trigonometric identities such as half-angle formulas, sum and difference formulas, and difference of angles formulas can be used to prove and rewrite trigonometric equations. Depending on the given equation or expression, the correct identities need to be chosen to write equivalent statements.

The graph of sine is equal to the graph of cosine, shifted $\frac{\pi}{2}$ units. Therefore, the function $y = \sin x$ is equal to:

$$y = \cos\left(\frac{\pi}{2} - x\right)$$

Within functions, adding a constant to the independent variable shifts the graph either left or right. By shifting the cosine graph, the curve lies on top of the sine function. By transforming the function, the two equations give the same output for any given input.

Complementary Angles

Angles that add up to 90 degrees are **complementary**. Within a right triangle, two complementary angles exist because the third angle is always 90 degrees. In this scenario, the **sine** of one of the complementary angles is equal to the **cosine** of the other angle. The opposite is also true. This relationship exists because sine and cosine will be calculated as the ratios of the same side lengths.

The Pythagorean Theorem

The **Pythagorean theorem** is an important concept in geometry. It states that for right triangles, the sum of the squares of the two shorter sides will be equal to the square of the longest side (also called the **hypotenuse**). The longest side will always be the side opposite to the 90° angle. If this side is called c, and the other two sides are a and b, then the Pythagorean theorem states that:

$$c^2 = a^2 + b^2$$

Since lengths are always positive, this also can be written as:

$$c = \sqrt{a^2 + b^2}$$

A diagram to show the parts of a triangle using the Pythagorean theorem is below.

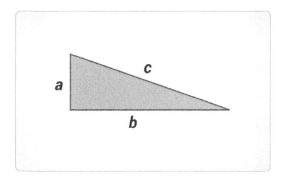

As an example of the theorem, suppose that Shirley has a rectangular field that is 5 feet wide and 12 feet long, and she wants to split it in half using a fence that goes from one corner to the opposite corner. How long will this fence need to be? To figure this out, note that this makes the field into two right triangles, whose hypotenuse will be the fence dividing it in half. Therefore, the fence length will be given by:

$$\sqrt{5^2 + 12^2} = \sqrt{169} = 13 \text{ feet long}$$

Translating Between a Geometric Description and an Equation for a Conic Section

Equation of a Circle

A **circle** can be defined as the set of all points that are the same distance (known as the **radius**, r) from a single point C (known as the center of the circle). The center has coordinates (h, k), and any point on the circle can be labelled with coordinates (x, y).

As shown below, a **right triangle** is formed with these two points:

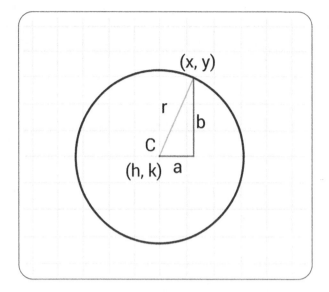

The **Pythagorean theorem** states that:

$$a^2 + b^2 = r^2$$

However, a can be replaced by $|x - h|$ and b can be replaced by $|y - k|$ by using the **distance formula** which is:

$$d = \sqrt{(x_2 - x_1)^2 + (y_2 - y_1)^2}$$

That substitution results in:

$$(x - h)^2 + (y - k)^2 = r^2$$

This is the formula for finding the equation of any circle with a center (h, k) and a radius r. Note that sometimes c is used instead of r.

Finding the Center and Radius
Circles aren't always given in the form of the circle equation where the center and radius can be seen so easily. Oftentimes, they're given in the more general format of:

$$ax^2 + by^2 + cx + dy + e = 0$$

This can be converted to the center-radius form using the algebra technique of completing the square in both variables. First, the constant term is moved over to the other side of the equals sign, and then the x- and y-variable terms are grouped together. Then the equation is divided through by a and, because this is the equation of a circle, $a = b$. At this point, the x-term coefficient is divided by 2, squared, and then added to both sides of the equation. This value is grouped with the x terms. The same steps then need to be completed with the y-term coefficient. The trinomial in both x and y can now be factored into a square of a binomial, which gives both:

$$(x - h)^2 \text{ and } (y - k)^2$$

Parabola Equations

A **parabola** is defined as a specific type of curve such that any point on it is the same distance from a fixed point (called the **foci**) and a fixed straight line (called the **directrix**). A parabola is the shape formed from the intersection of a cone with a plane that's parallel to its side. Every parabola has an **axis of symmetry**, and its **vertex** (h, k) is the point at which the axis of symmetry intersects the curve. If the parabola has an axis of symmetry parallel to the y-axis, the focus is the point $(h, k + f)$ and the directrix is the line $y = k - f$. For example, a parabola may have a vertex at the origin, focus $(0, f)$, and directrix $y = -f$. The equation of this parabola can be derived by using both the focus and the directrix. The distance from any coordinate on the curve to the focus is the same as the distance to the directrix, and the Pythagorean theorem can be used to find the length of d. The triangle has sides with length $|x|$ and $|y - f|$ and therefore:

$$d = \sqrt{x^2 + (y - f)^2}$$

By definition, the **vertex** is halfway between the focus and the directrix and $d = y + f$. Setting these two equations equal to one another, squaring each side, simplifying, and solving for y gives the equation of a parabola with the focus f and the vertex being the origin:

$$y = \frac{1}{4f}x^2$$

If the vertex (h, k) is not the origin, a similar process can be completed to derive the equation $(x - h)^2 = 4f(y - k)$ for a parabola with focus f.

Ellipse and Hyperbola Equations

An **ellipse** is the set of all points for which the sum of the distances from two fixed points (known as the *foci*) is constant. A **hyperbola** is the set of all points for which the difference between the distances from two fixed points (also known as the *foci*) is constant. The **distance formula** can be used to derive the formulas of both an ellipse and a hyperbola, given the coordinates of the foci. Consider an ellipse where its major axis is horizontal (i.e., it's longer along the x-axis) and its foci are the coordinates $(-c, 0)$ and $(c, 0)$. The distance from any point (x, y) to $(-c, 0)$ is

$$d_1 = \sqrt{(x + c)^2 + y^2}$$

The distance from the same point (x, y) to $(c, 0)$ is:

$$d_1 = \sqrt{(x - c)^2 + y^2}$$

Using the definition of an ellipse, it's true that the sum of the distances from the vertex a to each foci is equal to $d_1 + d_2$. Therefore:

$$d_1 + d_2 = (a + c) + (a - c) = 2a$$

and

$$\sqrt{(x + c)^2 + y^2} + \sqrt{(x - c)^2 + y^2} = 2a$$

133

After a series of algebraic steps, this equation can be simplified to $\frac{x^2}{a^2} + \frac{y^2}{b^2} = 1$, which is the equation of an ellipse with a horizontal major axis. In this case, $a > b$. When the ellipse has a vertical major axis, similar techniques result in $\frac{x^2}{b^2} + \frac{y^2}{a^2} = 1$, and $a > b$.

The equation of a hyperbola can be derived in a similar fashion. Consider a hyperbola with a horizontal major axis and its foci are also the coordinates $(-c, 0)$ and $(c, 0)$. Again, the distance from any point (x, y) to $(-c, 0)$ is:

$$d_1 = \sqrt{(x + c)^2 + y^2}$$

The distance from the same point (x, y) to $(c, 0)$ is:

$$d_1 = \sqrt{(x - c)^2 + y^2}$$

Using the definition of a hyperbola, it's true that the difference of the distances from the vertex a to each foci is equal to $d_1 - d_2$. Therefore:

$$d_1 - d_2 = (c + a) - (c - a) = 2a$$

This means that:

$$\sqrt{(x + c)^2 + y^2} - \sqrt{(x - c)^2 + y^2} = 2a$$

After a series of algebraic steps, this equation can be simplified to:

$$\frac{x^2}{a^2} - \frac{y^2}{b^2} = 1$$

This is the equation of a hyperbola with a horizontal major axis. In this case, $a > b$. Similar techniques result in the equation $\frac{x^2}{b} - \frac{y^2}{a^2} = 1$, where $a > b$, when the hyperbola has a vertical major axis.

Using Coordinate Geometry to Algebraically Prove Simple Geometric Theorems

Proving Theorems with Coordinates

Many important formulas and equations exist in geometry that use coordinates. The distance between two points (x_1, y_1) and (x_2, y_2) is:

$$d = \sqrt{(x_2 - x_1)^2 + (y_2 - y_1)^2}.$$

The slope of the line containing the same two points is:

$$m = \frac{y_2 - y_1}{x_2 - x_1}$$

Also, the midpoint of the line segment with endpoints (x_1, y_1) and (x_2, y_2) is:

$$M = \left(\frac{x_1 + x_2}{2}, \frac{y_1 + y_2}{2}\right)$$

The equations of a circle, parabola, ellipse, and hyperbola can also be used to prove theorems algebraically. Knowing when to use which formula or equation is extremely important, and knowing

134

which formula applies to which property of a given geometric shape is an integral part of the process. In some cases, there are a number of ways to prove a theorem; however, only one way is required.

Solving Problems with Parallel and Perpendicular Lines

Two lines can be parallel, perpendicular, or neither. If two lines are **parallel**, they have the same slope. This is proven using the idea of similar triangles. Consider the following diagram with two parallel lines, L1 and L2:

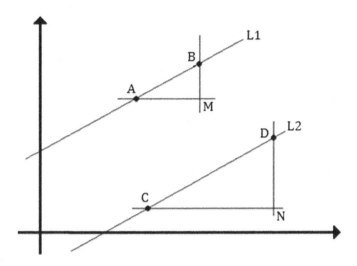

A and B are points on L1, and C and D are points on L2. Right triangles are formed with vertex M and N where lines BM and DN are parallel to the y-axis and AM and CN are parallel to the x-axis. Because all three sets of lines are parallel, the triangles are similar. Therefore:

$$\frac{BM}{DN} = \frac{MA}{NC}$$

This shows that the rise/run is equal for lines L1 and L2. Hence, their slopes are equal.

Secondly, if two lines are **perpendicular**, the product of their slopes equals -1. This means that their slopes are negative reciprocals of each other. Consider two perpendicular lines, l and n:

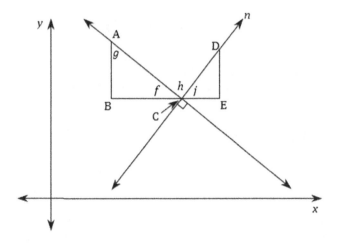

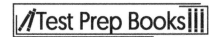

Right triangles ABC and CDE are formed so that lines BC and CE are parallel to the x-axis, and AB and DE are parallel to the y-axis. Because line BE is a straight line, angles:

$$f + h + i = 180 \text{ degrees}$$

However, angle h is a right angle, so:

$$f + j = 90 \text{ degrees}$$

By construction, $f + g = 90$, which means that $g = j$. Therefore, because angles $B = E$ and $g = j$, the triangles are similar and:

$$\frac{AB}{BC} = \frac{CE}{DE}$$

Because slope is equal to rise/run, the slope of line l is $-\frac{AB}{BC}$ and the slope of line n is $\frac{DE}{CE}$.

Multiplying the slopes together gives:

$$-\frac{AB}{BC} \cdot \frac{DE}{CE} = -\frac{CE}{DE} \cdot \frac{DE}{CE} = -1$$

This proves that the product of the slopes of two perpendicular lines equals -1. Both parallel and perpendicular lines can be integral in many geometric proofs, so knowing and understanding their properties is crucial for problem-solving.

Formulas for Ratios

If a line segment with endpoints (x_1, y_1) and (x_2, y_2) is partitioned into two equal parts, the formula for **midpoint** is used. Recall this formula is:

$$M = \left(\frac{x_1 + x_2}{2}, \frac{y_1 + y_2}{2} \right)$$

The ratio of line segments is 1:1. However, if the ratio needs to be anything other than 1:1, a different formula must be used. Consider a ratio that is $a:b$. This means the desired point that partitions the line segment is $\frac{a}{a+b}$ of the way from (x_1, y_1) to (x_2, y_2). The actual formula for the coordinate is:

$$\left(\frac{bx_1 + ax_2}{a+b}, \frac{by_1 + ay_2}{a+b} \right)$$

Computing Side Length, Perimeter, and Area

The side lengths of each shape can be found by plugging the endpoints into the distance formula between two ordered pairs (x_1, y_1) and (x_2, y_2).

As a reminder, this is the **distance formula**:

$$d = \sqrt{(x_2 - x_1)^2 + (y_2 - y_1)^2}$$

The distance formula is derived from the Pythagorean theorem. Once the side lengths are found, they can be added together to obtain the perimeter of the given polygon. Simplifications can be made for specific shapes such as squares and equilateral triangles. For example, one side length can be multiplied

136

by 4 to obtain the perimeter of a square. Also, one side length can be multiplied by 3 to obtain the perimeter of an equilateral triangle. A similar technique can be used to calculate areas. For polygons, both side length and height can be found by using the same distance formula. Areas of triangles and quadrilaterals are straightforward through the use of $A = \frac{1}{2}bh$ or $A = bh$, depending on the shape.

To find the area of other polygons, their shapes can be partitioned into rectangles and triangles. The areas of these simpler shapes can be calculated and then added together to find the total area of the polygon.

Statistics and Probability

Center and Spread of Distributions

Descriptive statistics are utilized to gain an understanding of properties of a data set. This entails examining the center, spread, and shape of the sample data.

Center

The **center** of the sample set can be represented by its mean, median or mode. The **mean** is the average of the data set. It is calculated by adding the data values together and dividing this sum by the sample size (the number of data points). The **median** is the value of the data point in the middle when the sample is arranged in numerical order. If the sample has an even number of data points, the mean of the two middle values is the median. The **mode** is the value which appears most often in a data set. It is possible to have multiple modes (if different values repeat equally as often) or no mode (if no value repeats).

Spread

Methods for determining the **spread** of the sample include calculating the range and standard deviation for the data. The *range* is calculated by subtracting the lowest value from the highest value in the set. The **standard deviation** of the sample can be calculated using the formula:

$$\sigma = \sqrt{\frac{\sum(x - \bar{x})^2}{n - 1}}$$

$\bar{x}$ = sample mean
n = sample size

Shape

The **shape** of the sample when displayed as a histogram or frequency distribution plot helps to determine if the sample is normally distributed (bell-shaped curve), symmetrical, or displays skewness (lack of symmetry), or kurtosis. **Kurtosis** is a measure of whether the data are heavy-tailed (high number of outliers) or light-tailed (low number of outliers).

Data Collection Methods

Statistical inference, based in probability theory, makes calculated assumptions about an entire population based on data from a sample set from that population.

Population Parameters

A population is the entire set of people or things of interest. For example, if researchers wanted to determine the number of hours of sleep per night for college females in the U.S, the population would consist of *every* college female in the country. A **sample** is a subset of the population that may be used for the study. A sample might consist of 100 students per school from 20 different colleges in the country. From the results of the survey, a sample statistic can be calculated. A **sample statistic** is a numerical characteristic of the sample data including mean and variance. A sample statistic can be used to estimate a corresponding **population parameter**, which is a numerical characteristic of the entire population.

Confidence Intervals

A population parameter estimated using a sample statistic may be very accurate or relatively inaccurate based on errors in sampling. A **confidence interval** indicates a range of values likely to include the true population parameter. A given confidence interval such as 95% means that the true population parameter will occur within the interval for 95% of samples.

Measurement Error

The accuracy of a population parameter based on a sample statistic may also be affected by measurement error. **Measurement error** can be divided into random error and systematic error. An example of **random error** for the previous scenario would be a student reporting 8 hours of sleep when she actually sleeps 7 hours per night. **Systematic errors** are those attributed to the measurement system. If the sleep survey gave response options of 2,4,6,8, or 10 hours. This would lead to systematic measurement error because certain values could not be accurately reported.

Evaluating Reports and Determining the Appropriateness of Data Collection Methods

The presentation of statistics can be manipulated to produce a desired outcome. For example, in the statement "four out of five dentists recommend our toothpaste", critical readers should wonder: *who are the five dentists?* While the wording is similar, this statement is very different from "four out of every five dentists recommend our toothpaste." The context of the numerical values allows one to decipher the meaning, intent, and significance of the survey or study.

When analyzing a report, the researchers who conducted the study and their intent must be considered. Was it performed by a neutral party or by a person or group with a vested interest? The sampling method and the data collection method should also be evaluated. Was it a true random sample of the population or was one subgroup over- or underrepresented? Lastly, the measurement system used to obtain the data should be assessed. Was the system accurate and precise or was it a flawed system?

Understanding and Modeling Relationships in Bivariate Data

In an experiment, variables are the key to analyzing data, especially when data is in a graph or table. Variables can represent anything, including objects, conditions, events, and amounts of time.

Covariance is a general term referring to how two variables move in relation to each other. Take for example an employee that gets paid by the hour. For them, hours worked and total pay have a positive covariance. As hours worked increases, so does pay.

Constant variables remain unchanged by the scientist across all trials. Because they are held constant for all groups in an experiment, they aren't being measured in the experiment, and they are usually ignored. Constants can either be controlled by the scientist directly like the nutrition, water, and

sunlight given to plants, or they can be selected by the scientist specifically for an experiment like using a certain animal species or choosing to investigate only people of a certain age group.

Independent variables are also controlled by the scientist, but they are the same only for each group or trial in the experiment. Each group might be composed of students that all have the same color of car or each trial may be run on different soda brands. The independent variable of an experiment is what is being indirectly tested because it causes change in the dependent variables.

Dependent variables experience change caused by the independent variable and are what is being measured or observed. For example, college acceptance rates could be a dependent variable of an experiment that sorted a large sample of high school students by an independent variable such as test scores. In this experiment, the scientist groups the high school students by the independent variable (test scores) to see how it affects the dependent variable (their college acceptance rates).

Note that most variables can be held constant in one experiment, but also serve as the independent variable or a dependent variable in another. For example, when testing how well a fertilizer aids plant growth, its amount of sunlight should be held constant for each group of plants, but if the experiment is being done to determine the proper amount of sunlight a plant should have, the amount of sunlight is an independent variable because it is necessarily changed for each group of plants.

Correlation

An **X-Y diagram**, also known as a scatter diagram, visually displays the relationship between two variables. The independent variable is placed on the **x-axis**, or horizontal axis, and the dependent variable is placed on the **y-axis**, or vertical axis.

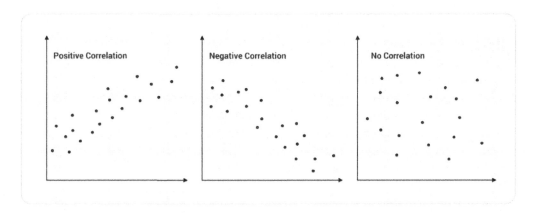

As shown in the figures above, an X-Y diagram may result in positive, negative, or no correlation between the two variables. So, in the first scatter plot as the Y factor increases the X factor increases as well. The opposite is true as well: as the X factor increases the Y factor also increases. Thus, there is a positive correlation because one factor appears to positively affect the other factor.

Correlation Coefficient

The **correlation coefficient** ® measures the association between two variables. Its value is between -1 and 1, where -1 represents a perfect negative linear relationship, 0 represents no relationship, and 1 represents a perfect positive linear relationship. A **negative linear relationship** means that as x-values

increase, y-values decrease. A **positive linear relationship** means that as x-values increase, y-values increase. The formula for computing the correlation coefficient is:

$$r = \frac{n(\sum xy) - (\sum x)(\sum y)}{\sqrt{n(\sum x^2) - (\sum x)^2}\sqrt{n(\sum y^2) - (\Sigma y)^2}}$$

n is the number of data points.

Both Microsoft Excel® and a graphing calculator can evaluate this easily once the data points are entered. A correlation greater than 0.8 or less than -0.8 is classified as "strong" while a correlation between -0.5 and 0.5 is classified as "weak."

Calculating Probabilities, Including Related Sample Spaces

Probability, represented by variable p, always has a value from 0 to 1. The total probability for all the possible outcomes (sample space) should equal 1.

Sample Spaces

Probabilities are based on observations of events. The probability of an event occurring is equal to the ratio of the number of favorable outcomes over the total number of possible outcomes. The total number of possible outcomes is found by constructing the sample space. The sum of probabilities of all possible distinct outcomes is equal to 1. A simple example of a sample space involves a deck of cards. They contain 52 distinct cards, and therefore the sample space contains each individual card. To find the probability of selecting a queen on one draw from the deck, the ratio would be equal to $\frac{4}{52} = \frac{1}{13}$, which equals 4 possible queens over the total number of possibilities in the sample space.

Verifying Independent Events

Two events aren't always independent. For example, having glasses and having brown hair aren't independent characteristics. There definitely can be overlap because people with brown hair can wear glasses. Also, two events that exist at the same time don't have to have a relationship. For example, even if everyone in a given sample is wearing glasses, the characteristics aren't related. In this case, the probability of a brunette wearing glasses is equal to the probability of a person being a brunette multiplied by the probability of a person wearing glasses. This mathematical test of $P(A \cap B) = P(A)P(B)$ verifies that two events are independent.

Simple and Compound Events

A **simple event** consists of only one outcome. The most popular simple event is flipping a coin, which results in either heads or tails. A **compound event** results in more than one outcome and consists of more than one simple event. An example of a compound event is flipping a coin while tossing a die. The result is either heads or tails on the coin and a number from one to six on the die. The probability of a simple event is calculated by dividing the number of possible outcomes by the total number of outcomes. Therefore, the probability of obtaining heads on a coin is $\frac{1}{2}$, and the probability of rolling a 6 on a die is $\frac{1}{6}$. The probability of compound events is calculated using the basic idea of the probability of simple events. If the two events are independent, the probability of one outcome is equal to the product

140

of the probabilities of each simple event. For example, the probability of obtaining heads on a coin and rolling a 6 is equal to:

$$\frac{1}{2} \times \frac{1}{6} = \frac{1}{12}$$

The probability of either A or B occurring is equal to the sum of the probabilities minus the probability that both A and B will occur. Therefore, the probability of obtaining either heads on a coin or rolling a 6 on a die is:

$$\frac{1}{2} + \frac{1}{6} - \frac{1}{12} = \frac{7}{12}$$

The two events aren't mutually exclusive because they can happen at the same time. If two events are mutually exclusive, and the probability of both events occurring at the same time is zero, the probability of event A or B occurring equals the sum of both probabilities. An example of calculating the probability of two mutually exclusive events is determining the probability of pulling a king or a queen from a deck of cards. The two events cannot occur at the same time.

Integrating Essential Skills

Using Ratios, Rates, Proportions, and Scale Drawings to Solve Single- and Multistep Problems

Ratios, rates, proportions, and scale drawings are used when comparing two quantities. Questions on this material will include expressing relationships in simplest terms and solving for missing quantities.

Ratios

A ratio is a comparison of two quantities that represent separate groups. For example, if a recipe calls for 2 eggs for every 3 cups of milk, it can be expressed as a ratio. Ratios can be written three ways: (1) with the word "to"; (2) using a colon; or (3) as a fraction. For the previous example, the ratio of eggs to cups of milk can be written as: 2 to 3, 2:3, or $\frac{2}{3}$. When writing ratios, the order is important. The ratio of eggs to cups of milk is not the same as the ratio of cups of milk to eggs, 3:2.

In simplest form, both quantities of a ratio should be written as integers. These should also be reduced just as a fraction would be. For example, 5:10 would reduce to 1:2. Given a ratio where one or both quantities are expressed as a decimal or fraction, both should be multiplied by the same number to produce integers. To write the ratio $\frac{1}{3}$ to 2 in simplest form, both quantities should be multiplied by 3. The resulting ratio is 1 to 6.

When a problem involving ratios gives a comparison between two groups, then: (1) a total should be provided and a part should be requested; or (2) a part should be provided and a total should be requested. Consider the following:

> The ratio of boys to girls in the 11th grade is 5:4. If there is a total of 270 11th grade students, how many are girls?

To solve this, the total number of "ratio pieces" first needs to be determined. The total number of 11th grade students is divided into 9 pieces. The ratio of boys to total students is 5:9; and the ratio of girls to

total students is 4:9. Knowing the total number of students, the number of girls can be determined by setting up a proportion:

$$\frac{4}{9} = \frac{x}{270}$$

Solving the proportion, it shows that there are 120 11th grade girls.

Rates

A rate is a ratio comparing two quantities expressed in different units. A unit rate is one in which the second is one unit. Rates often include the word *per*. Examples include miles per hour, beats per minute, and price per pound. The word *per* can be represented with a / symbol or abbreviated with the letter "p" and the units abbreviated. For example, miles per hour would be written mi/h. Given a rate that is not in simplest form (second quantity is not one unit), both quantities should be divided by the value of the second quantity. Suppose a patient had 99 heartbeats in 1½ minutes. To determine the heart rate, 1½ should divide both quantities. The result is 66 bpm.

Scale Drawings

Scale drawings are used in designs to model the actual measurements of a real-world object. For example, the blueprint of a house might indicate that it is drawn at a scale of 3 inches to 8 feet. Given one value and asked to determine the width of the house, a proportion should be set up to solve the problem. Given the scale of 3in:8ft and a blueprint width of 1 ft (12 in.), to find the actual width of the building, the proportion $\frac{3}{8} = \frac{12}{x}$ should be used. This results in an actual width of 32 ft.

Proportions

A proportion is a statement consisting of two equal ratios. Proportions will typically give three of four quantities and require solving for the missing value. The key to solving proportions is to set them up properly. Here's a sample problem:

If 7 gallons of gas costs $14.70, how many gallons can you get for $20?

The information should be written as equal ratios with a variable representing the missing quantity:

$$\left(\frac{gallons}{cost} = \frac{gallons}{cost}\right) : \frac{7}{14.70} = \frac{x}{20}$$

To solve, cross multiply (multiply the numerator of the first ratio by the denominator of the second and vice versa) is used, and the products are set equal to each other. Cross-multiplying results in:

$$(7)(20) = (14.7)(x)$$

Solving the equation for *x*, it can be determined that 9.5 gallons of gas can be purchased for $20.

For direct proportions, as one quantity increases, the other quantity also increases. For indirect proportions (also referred to as indirect variations, inverse proportions, or inverse variations), as one quantity increases, the other decreases. Direct proportions can be written:

$$\frac{y_1}{x_1} = \frac{y_2}{x_2}$$

142

Conversely, indirect proportions are written:

$$y_1x_1 = y_2x_2$$

Here's a sample problem:

> It takes 3 carpenters 10 days to build the frame of a house. How long should it take 5 carpenters to build the same frame?

In this scenario, as one quantity increases (number of carpenters), the other decreases (number of days building); therefore, this is an inverse proportion. To solve, the products of the two variables (in this scenario, the total work performed) are set equal to each other ($y_1x_1 = y_2x_2$). Using y to represent carpenters and x to represent days, the resulting equation is:

$$(3)(10) = (5)(x_2)$$

Solving for x_2, it is determined that it should take 5 carpenters 6 days to build the frame of the house.

Solving Single- and Multistep Problems Involving Percentages

The word percent means "per hundred." When dealing with percentages, it may be helpful to think of the number as a value in hundredths. For example, 15% can be expressed as "fifteen hundredths" and written as $\frac{15}{100}$ or .15.

Percent Problems

Material on percentages can include questions such as: What is 15% of 25? What percent of 45 is 3? Five is $\frac{1}{2}$% of what number? To solve these problems, the information should be rewritten as an equation where the following helpful steps are completed: (1) "what" is represented by a variable (x); (2) "is" is represented by an=sign; and (3) "of" is represented by multiplication. Any values expressed as a percent should be written as a decimal; and if the question is asking for a percent, the answer should be converted accordingly. Here are three sample problems based on the information above:

What is 15% of 25?	What percent of 45 is 3?	Five is $\frac{1}{2}$% of what number?
$x = 0.15 \times 25$	$x \times 45 = 3$	$5 = 0.005 \times x$
$x = 3.75$	$x = 0.0\overline{6}$	$x = 1{,}000$
	$x = 6.\overline{6}\%$	

Percent Increase/Decrease

Problems dealing with percentages may involve an original value, a change in that value, and a percentage change. A problem will provide two pieces of information and ask to find the third. To do so, this formula is used:

$$\frac{change}{original\ value} \times 100 = percent\ change$$

Here's a sample problem:

> Attendance at a baseball stadium has dropped 16% from last year. Last year's average attendance was 40,000. What is this year's average attendance?

143

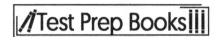

Using the formula and information, the change is unknown (x), the original value is 40,000, and the percent change is 16%. The formula can be written as:

$$\frac{x}{40,000} \times 100 = 16$$

When solving for x, it is determined the change was 6,400. The problem asked for this year's average attendance, so to calculate, the change (6,400) is subtracted from last year's attendance (40,000) to determine this year's average attendance is 33,600.

Percent More Than/Less Than

Percentage problems may give a value and what percent that given value is more than or less than an original unknown value. Here's a sample problem:

A store advertises that all its merchandise has been reduced by 25%. The new price of a pair of shoes is $60. What was the original price?

This problem can be solved by writing a proportion. Two ratios should be written comparing the cost and the percent of the original cost. The new cost is 75% of the original cost ($100\% - 25\%$); and the original cost is 100% of the original cost. The unknown original cost can be represented by x. The proportion would be set up as:

$$\frac{60}{75} = \frac{x}{100}$$

Solving the proportion, it is determined the original cost was $80.

Solving Single- and Multistep Problems Involving Measurement Quantities, Units, and Unit Conversion

Unit conversions apply to many real-world scenarios, including cooking, measurement, construction, and currency. Problems on this material can be solved similarly to those involving unit rates. Given the conversion rate, it can be written as a fraction (ratio) and multiplied by a quantity in one unit to convert it to the corresponding unit. For example, someone might want to know how many minutes are in 3½ hours. The conversion rate of 60 minutes to 1 hour can be written as:

$$\frac{60 \text{ min}}{1 \text{ h}}$$

Multiplying the quantity by the conversion rate results in:

$$3\frac{1}{2}\text{h} \times \frac{60 \text{ min}}{1 \text{ h}} = 210 \text{ min}$$

The "h" unit is canceled. To convert a quantity in minutes to hours, the fraction for the conversion rate would be flipped (to cancel the "min" unit). To convert 195 minutes to hours, the equation $195 \text{ min} \times \frac{1 \text{ h}}{60 \text{ min}}$ would be used. The result is $\frac{195 \text{ h}}{60}$, which reduces to $3\frac{1}{4}$ hours.

Converting units may require more than one multiplication. The key is to set up the conversion rates so that units cancel out each other and the desired unit is left. Suppose someone wants to convert 3.25 yards to inches, given that 1 yd = 3 ft and 12 in = 1 ft. To calculate, the equation use:

$$3.25 \text{ yd} \times \frac{3 \text{ ft}}{1 \text{ yd}} \times \frac{12 \text{ in}}{1 \text{ ft}}$$

The "yd" and "ft" units will cancel, resulting in 117 inches.

Area, Surface Area, and Volume

The area of a two-dimensional figure refers to the number of square units needed to cover the interior region of the figure. This concept is similar to wallpaper covering the flat surface of a wall. For example, if a rectangle has an area of 21 square centimeters (written 21 cm^2), it will take 21 squares, each with sides one centimeter in length, to cover the interior region of the rectangle. Note that area is measured in square units such as: square feet or ft^2; square yards or yd^2; square miles or mi^2.

The surface area of a three-dimensional figure refers to the number of square units needed to cover the entire surface of the figure. This concept is similar to using wrapping paper to completely cover the outside of a box. For example, if a triangular pyramid has a surface area of 17 square inches (written 17 in^2), it will take 17 squares, each with sides one inch in length, to cover the entire surface of the pyramid. Surface area is also measured in square units.

Many three-dimensional figures (solid figures) can be represented by nets consisting of rectangles and triangles. The surface area of such solids can be determined by adding the areas of each of its faces and bases. Finding the surface area using this method requires calculating the areas of rectangles and triangles. To find the area (A) of a rectangle, the length (l) is multiplied by the width:

$$(w) \rightarrow A = l \times w$$

The area of a rectangle with a length of 8 cm and a width of 4 cm is calculated:

$$A = (8 \text{ cm}) \times (4 \text{ cm}) \rightarrow A = 32 \text{ cm}^2.$$

To calculate the area (A) of a triangle, the product of $\frac{1}{2}$, the base (b), and the height (h) is found:

$$A = \frac{1}{2} \times b \times h$$

Note that the height of a triangle is measured from the base to the vertex opposite of it forming a right angle with the base. The area of a triangle with a base of 11cm and a height of 6 cm is calculated:

$$A = \frac{1}{2} \times (11 \text{ cm}) \times (6 \text{ cm}) \rightarrow A = 33 \text{ cm}^2$$

Consider the following triangular prism, which is represented by a net consisting of two triangles and three rectangles.

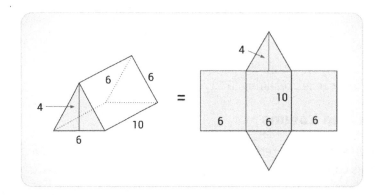

The surface area of the prism can be determined by adding the areas of each of its faces and bases. The surface area (SA) = area of triangle + area of triangle + area of rectangle + area of rectangle + area of rectangle.

$$SA = \left(\frac{1}{2} \times b \times h\right) + \left(\frac{1}{2} \times b \times h\right) + (l \times w) + (l \times w) + (l \times w)$$

$$SA = \left(\frac{1}{2} \times 6 \times 4\right) + \left(\frac{1}{2} \times 6 \times 4\right) + (6 \times 10) + (6 \times 10) + (6 \times 10)$$

$$SA = (12) + (12) + (60) + (60) + (60)$$

$$SA = 204 \text{ square units}$$

Effects of Changes to Dimensions on Area and Volume

Similar polygons are figures that are the same shape but different sizes. Likewise, similar solids are different sizes but are the same shape. In both cases, corresponding angles in the same positions for both figures are congruent (equal), and corresponding sides are proportional in length. For example, the triangles below are similar. The following pairs of corresponding angles are congruent: $\angle A$ and $\angle D$; $\angle B$ and $\angle E$; $\angle C$ and $\angle F$. The corresponding sides are proportional:

$$\frac{AB}{DE} = \frac{6}{3} = 2$$

$$\frac{BC}{EF} = \frac{9}{4.5} = 2$$

$$\frac{CA}{FD} = \frac{10}{5} = 2$$

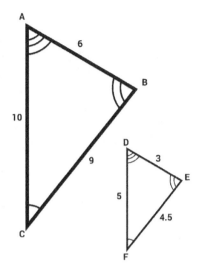

In other words, triangle *ABC* is the same shape but twice as large as triangle *DEF*.

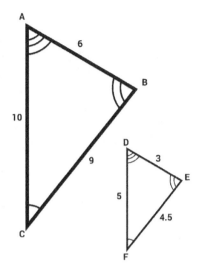

An example of similar triangular pyramids is shown below.

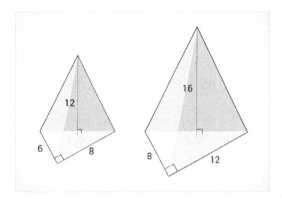

Given the nature of two- and three-dimensional measurements, changing dimensions by a given scale (multiplier) does not change the area of volume by the same scale. Consider a rectangle with a length of 5 centimeters and a width of 4 centimeters. The area of the rectangle is 20 cm². Doubling the dimensions of the rectangle (multiplying by a scale factor of 2) to 10 centimeters and 8 centimeters *does not* double the area to 40 cm². Area is a two-dimensional measurement (measured in square units). Therefore, the dimensions are multiplied by a scale that is squared (raised to the second power) to determine the scale of the corresponding areas. For the previous example, the length and width are multiplied by 2. Therefore, the area is multiplied by 2², or 4. The area of a 5 cm × 4 cm rectangle is 20 cm². The area of a 10 cm × 8 cm rectangle is 80 cm².

Volume is a three-dimensional measurement, which is measured in cubic units. Therefore, the scale between dimensions of similar solids is cubed (raised to the third power) to determine the scale between their volumes. Consider similar right rectangular prisms: one with a length of 8 inches, a width of 24 inches, and a height of 16 inches; the second with a length of 4 inches, a width of 12 inches, and a height of 8 inches. The first prism, multiplied by a scalar of $\frac{1}{2}$, produces the measurement of the second

147

prism. The volume of the first prism, multiplied by $\left(\frac{1}{2}\right)^3$, which equals $\frac{1}{8}$, produces the volume of the second prism. The volume of the first prism is 8 in × 24 in × 16 in which equals 3,072 in³. The volume of the second prism is 4 in × 12 in × 8 in which equals 384 in³ ($3,072 \text{ in}^3 \times \frac{1}{8} = 384 \text{ in}^3$).

The rules for squaring the scalar for area and cubing the scalar for volume only hold true for similar figures. In other words, if only one dimension is changed (changing the width of a rectangle but not the length) or dimensions are changed at different rates (the length of a prism is doubled and its height is tripled) the figures are not similar (same shape). Therefore, the rules above do not apply.

Average, Median, and Measures of Central Tendency

Suppose that X is a set of data points $(x_1, x_2, x_3, \dots x_n)$, and some description of the general properties of this data need to be found.

The first property that can be defined for this set of data is the **mean**. To find the mean, add up all the data points, then divide by the total number of data points. This can be expressed using **summation notation** as:

$$\bar{X} = \frac{x_1 + x_2 + x_3 + \cdots + x_n}{n} = \frac{1}{n} \sum_{i=1}^{n} x_i$$

For example, suppose that in a class of 10 students, the scores on a test were 50, 60, 65, 65, 75, 80, 85, 85, 90, 100. Therefore, the average test score will be:

$$\frac{1}{10}(50 + 60 + 65 + 65 + 75 + 80 + 85 + 85 + 90 + 100) = 75.5$$

The mean is a useful number if the distribution of data is normal (more on this later), which roughly means that the frequency of different outcomes has a single peak and is roughly equally distributed on both sides of that peak. However, it is less useful in some cases where the data might be split or where there are some **outliers**. Outliers are data points that are far from the rest of the data. For example, suppose there are 10 executives and 90 employees at a company. The executives make $1,000 per hour, and the employees make $10 per hour.

Therefore, the average pay rate will be:

$$\frac{\$1,000 \times 10 + \$10 \times 90}{100} = \$109 \text{ per hour}$$

In this case, this average is not very descriptive since it's not close to the actual pay of the executives or the employees.

Another useful measurement is the **median**. In a data set X consisting of data points $x_1, x_2, x_3, \dots x_n$, the median is the point in the middle. The middle refers to the point where half the data comes before it and half comes after, when the data is recorded in numerical order. If n is odd, then the median is:

$$x_{\frac{n+1}{2}}$$

148

If *n* is even, it is defined as:

$$\frac{1}{2}\left(x_{\frac{n}{2}} + x_{\frac{n}{2}+1}\right)$$

It is the mean of the two data points closest to the middle of the data points. In the previous example of test scores, the two middle points are 75 and 80. Since there is no single point, the average of these two scores needs to be found. The average is:

$$\frac{75 + 80}{2} = 77.5$$

The median is generally a good value to use if there are a few outliers in the data. It prevents those outliers from affecting the "middle" value as much as when using the mean.

Since an outlier is a data point that is far from most of the other data points in a data set, this means an outlier also is any point that is far from the median of the data set. The outliers can have a substantial effect on the mean of a data set, but they usually do not change the median or mode, or do not change them by a large quantity. For example, consider the data set (3, 5, 6, 6, 6, 8). This has a median of 6 and a mode of 6, with a mean of $\frac{34}{6} \approx 5.67$. Now, suppose a new data point of 1,000 is added so that the data set is now (3, 5, 6, 6, 6, 8, 1,000). The median and mode, which are both still 6, remain unchanged. However, the average is now $\frac{1,034}{7}$, which is approximately 147.7. In this case, the median and mode will be better descriptions for most of the data points.

The reason for outliers in a given data set is a complicated problem. It is sometimes the result of an error by the experimenter, but often they are perfectly valid data points that must be taken into consideration.

One additional measure to define for X is the **mode**. This is the data point that appears more frequently. If two or more data points all tie for the most frequent appearance, then each of them is considered a mode. In the case of the test scores, where the numbers were 50, 60, 65, 65, 75, 80, 85, 85, 90, 100, there are two modes: 65 and 85.

The **first quartile** of a set of data X refers to the largest value from the first $\frac{1}{4}$ of the data points. In practice, there are sometimes slightly different definitions that can be used, such as the median of the first half of the data points (excluding the median itself if there are an odd number of data points). The term also has a slightly different use: when it is said that a data point lies in the first quartile, it means it is less than or equal to the median of the first half of the data points. Conversely, if it lies *at* the first quartile, then it is equal to the first quartile.

When it is said that a data point lies in the **second quartile**, it means it is between the first quartile and the median.

The **third quartile** refers to data that lies between $\frac{1}{2}$ and $\frac{3}{4}$ of the way through the data set. Again, there are various methods for defining this precisely, but the simplest way is to include all of the data that lie between the median and the median of the top half of the data.

Data that lies in the **fourth quartile** refers to all of the data above the third quartile.

Percentiles may be defined in a similar manner to quartiles. Generally, this is defined in the following manner:

If a data point lies *in* the n-th percentile, this means it lies in the range of the first $n\%$ of the data.

If a data point lies *at* the n-th percentile, then it means that $n\%$ of the data lies below this data point.

Given a data set X consisting of data points $(x_1, x_2, x_3, \ldots x_n)$, the **variance of X** is defined to be:

$$\frac{\sum_{i=1}^{n}(x_i - \bar{X})^2}{n}$$

This means that the variance of X is the average of the squares of the differences between each data point and the mean of X. In the formula, $\bar{X}$ is the mean of the values in the data set, and x_i represents each individual value in the data set. The sigma notation indicates that the sum should be found with n being the number of values to add together. $i = 1$ means that the values should begin with the first value.

Given a data set X consisting of data points $(x_1, x_2, x_3, \ldots x_n)$, the **standard deviation of X** is defined to be:

$$s_x = \sqrt{\frac{\sum_{i=1}^{n}(x_i - \bar{X})^2}{n}}$$

In other words, the standard deviation is the square root of the variance.

Both the variance and the standard deviation are measures of how much the data tend to be spread out. When the standard deviation is low, the data points are mostly clustered around the mean. When the standard deviation is high, this generally indicates that the data are quite spread out, or else that there are a few substantial outliers.

As a simple example, compute the standard deviation for the data set (1, 3, 3, 5). First, compute the mean, which will be:

$$\frac{1 + 3 + 3 + 5}{4} = \frac{12}{4} = 3$$

Now, find the variance of X with the formula:

$$\sum_{i=1}^{4}(x_i - \bar{X})^2 = (1 - 3)^2 + (3 - 3)^2 + (3 - 3)^2 + (5 - 3)^2$$

$$-2^2 + 0^2 + 0^2 + 2^2 = 8$$

Therefore, the variance is $\frac{8}{4} = 2$. Taking the square root, the standard deviation will be $\sqrt{2}$.

Note that the standard deviation only depends upon the mean, not upon the median or mode(s). Generally, if there are multiple modes that are far apart from one another, the standard deviation will be high. A high standard deviation does not always mean there are multiple modes, however.

150

Representing Numbers in Various Ways

Concrete Models

Concrete objects are used to develop a tangible understanding of operations of rational numbers. Tools such as tiles, blocks, beads, and hundred charts are used to model problems. For example, a hundred chart (10×10) and beads can be used to model multiplication. If multiplying 5 by 4, beads are placed across 5 rows and down 4 columns producing a product of 20. Similarly, tiles can be used to model division by splitting the total into equal groups. If dividing 12 by 4, 12 tiles are placed one at a time into 4 groups. The result is 4 groups of 3. This is also an effective method for visualizing the concept of remainders.

Representations of objects can be used to expand on the concrete models of operations. Pictures, dots, and tallies can help model these concepts. Utilizing concrete models and representations creates a foundation upon which to build an abstract understanding of the operations.

Rational Numbers on a Number Line

A number line typically consists of integers (...3, 2, 1, 0, -1, -2, -3...), and is used to visually represent the value of a rational number. Each rational number has a distinct position on the line determined by comparing its value with the displayed values on the line. For example, if plotting -1.5 on the number line below, it is necessary to recognize that the value of -1.5 is .5 less than -1 and .5 greater than -2. Therefore, -1.5 is plotted halfway between -1 and -2.

Number lines can also be useful for visualizing sums and differences of rational numbers. Adding a value indicates moving to the right (values increase to the right), and subtracting a value indicates moving to the left (numbers decrease to the left). For example, $-3 - 2$ is displayed by starting at -3 and moving to the left 2 spaces, if the number line is in increments of 1. This will result in an answer of -5.

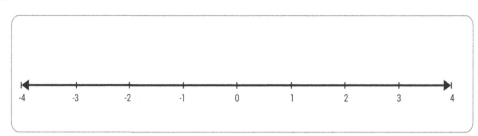

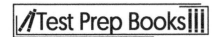
Rectangular Arrays and Area Models

Rectangular arrays include an arrangement of rows and columns that correspond to the factors and display product totals.

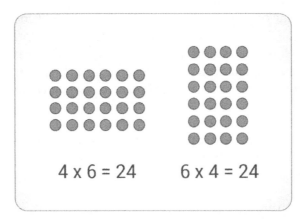

An area model is a rectangle that is divided into rows and columns that match up to the number of place values within each number. Take the example 29×65. These two numbers can be split into simpler numbers: $29 = 25 + 4$ and $65 = 60 + 5$. The products of those 4 numbers are found within the rectangle and then summed up to get the answer. The entire process is:

$$(60 \times 25) + (5 \times 25) + (60 \times 4) + (5 \times 4)$$

$$1,500 + 240 + 125 + 20 = 1,885$$

Here is the actual area model:

	25	**4**
60	60x25 1,500	60x4 240
5	5x25 125	5x4 20

```
        1 , 5 0 0
            2 4 0
            1 2 5
    +          2 0
        _____
        1 , 8 8 5
```

152

Practice Quiz

1.

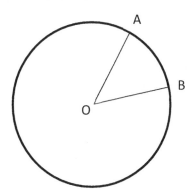

The length of arc $AB = 3\pi$ cm. The length of $\overline{OA} = 12$ cm. What is the degree measure of $\angle AOB$?
   a. 30 degrees
   b. 40 degrees
   c. 45 degrees
   d. 55 degrees

2. How will the following algebraic expression be simplified: $(5x^2 - 3x + 4) - (2x^2 - 7)$?
   a. x^5
   b. $3x^2 - 3x + 11$
   c. $3x^2 - 3x - 3$
   d. $x - 3$

3. What is the product of the following expression?
$$(3 + 2i)(5 - 4i).$$
   a. $23 - 2i$
   b. $15 - 8i$
   c. $15 - 8i^2$
   d. $15 - 10i$

4. An arc is intercepted by a central angle of 240°. What is the number of radians of that angle?
   a. $\dfrac{3\pi}{4}$

   b. $\dfrac{4\pi}{3}$

   c. $\dfrac{\pi}{4}$

   d. $\dfrac{\pi}{3}$

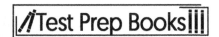

5. A shipping box has a length of 8 inches, a width of 14 inches, and a height of 4 inches. If all three dimensions are doubled, what is the relationship between the volume of the new box and the volume of the original box?

    a. The volume of the new box is double the volume of the original box.

    b. The volume of the new box is four times as large as the volume of the original box.

    c. The volume of the new box is six times as large as the volume of the original box.

    d. The volume of the new box is eight times as large as the volume of the original box.

See answers on next page.

Answer Explanations

1. C: The formula to find arc length is $s = \theta r$, where s is the arc length, θ is the radian measure of the central angle, and r is the radius of the circle. Substituting the given information produces

3π cm $= \theta 12$ cm. Solving for θ yields $\theta = \frac{\pi}{4}$. To convert from radian to degrees, multiply the radian measure by $\frac{180}{\pi}$:

$$\frac{\pi}{4} \times \frac{180}{\pi} = 45^\circ$$

2. B: $3x^2 - 3x + 11$. By distributing the implied one in front of the first set of parentheses and the -1 in front of the second set of parentheses, the parentheses can be eliminated:

$$1(5x^2 - 3x + 4) - 1(2x^2 - 7)$$

$$5x^2 - 3x + 4 - 2x^2 + 7$$

Next, like terms (same variables with same exponents) are combined by adding the coefficients and keeping the variables and their powers the same:

$$5x^2 - 3x + 4 - 2x^2 + 7$$

$$3x^2 - 3x + 11$$

3. A: The notation i stands for an imaginary number. The value of i is equal to $\sqrt{-1}$. When performing calculations with imaginary numbers, treat i as a variable, and simplify when possible. Multiplying the binomials by the FOIL method produces:

$$15 - 12i + 10i - 8i^2$$

Combining like terms yields $15 - 2i - 8i^2$. Since:

$$i = \sqrt{-1}, i^2 = (\sqrt{-1})^2 = -1$$

Therefore, substitute -1 for i^2:

$$15 - 2i - 8(-1)$$

Simplifying results in:

$$15 - 2i + 8 \rightarrow 23 - 2i$$

4. B: When you simplify $(240^\circ) \times \left(\frac{\pi}{180}\right)$, you get $\frac{4\pi}{3}$. Choice A is not the correct answer because it is the reciprocal of $\frac{4\pi}{3}$. Choices C and D are incorrect because they are not the correct reduction of the fraction.

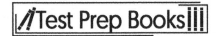

5. D: The formula for finding the volume of a rectangular prism is $V = l \times w \times h$, where l is the length, w is the width, and h is the height. The volume of the original box is calculated:

$$V = 8 \times 14 \times 4 = 448 \text{ in}^3$$

The volume of the new box is calculated:

$$V = 16 \times 28 \times 8 = 3{,}584 \text{ in}^3$$

The volume of the new box divided by the volume of the old box equals 8.

ACT Reading Test

What to Expect

The Reading test contains four passages that are 700-800 words in length. These passages represent the content categories of Literature, Humanities, Social Science, and Natural Science. Each passage has 10 multiple-choice questions associated with it. Test takers have 35 minutes to read the passages and answer the questions.

Tips for the Reading Test

- Play to your strengths. Start reading the passage that falls under the category or topic you are must comfortable with. This will boost your confidence and help you move through that portion of the section efficiently. Test takers often struggle with the fast pace of this section, so starting with something most familiar can help ensure you get a good jump on the Reading questions.

- Underline parts while you read. Key details, clues about the author's purpose, etc. may be revealed in the initial skim or read through. Marking these spots will save time finding them once the questions are addressed without needing to interrupt the flow of reading to stop and answer questions.

- Move along. Skim the passage first and then read the questions carefully. Eliminate the answer choices you know are wrong. If you can't figure it out in 30-45 seconds, mark the question and move on. After 9 minutes, move to the next passage in order to stay on pace. At the very end of the section, guess the answers to those questions you could not figure out or ran out of time to answer.

Key Ideas and Details

Central Ideas and Themes

Topic, Main Idea, Supporting Details, and Themes

The **topic** of a text is the overall subject, and the **main idea** more specifically builds on that subject. Consider a paragraph that begins with the following: "The United States government is made up of three branches: executive, judicial, and legislative." If this sentence is divided into its essential components, there is the topic (United States Government) and the main idea (the three branches of government).

A main idea must be supported with details, which usually appear in the form of quotations, paraphrasing, or analysis. Authors should connect details and analysis to the main point. Readers should always be cautious when accepting the validity of an argument and look for logical fallacies, such as slippery slope, straw man, and begging the question. It's okay for a reader to disagree with an author, because arguments may seem sound but are flawed upon further analysis.

It is important to remember that when most authors write, they want to make a point or send a message. The point, or message of a text, is known as the theme. Authors may state themes explicitly, like in *Aesop's Fables*. More often, especially in modern literature, readers must infer the theme based on textual details. Usually, after carefully reading and analyzing an entire text, the reader can identify

157

the theme. Typically, the longer the piece, the more numerous its themes, though often one theme dominates the rest, as evidenced by the author's purposeful revisiting of it throughout the passage.

Identifying Theme or Central Message

The **theme** is the central message of a fictional work, whether that work is structured as prose, drama, or poetry. It is the heart of what an author is trying to say to readers through the writing, and theme is largely conveyed through literary elements and techniques.

In literature, a theme can often be determined by considering the overarching narrative conflict within the work. Though there are several types of conflicts and several potential themes within them, the following are the most common:

- **Individual against the self**—relevant to themes of self-awareness, internal struggles, pride, coming of age, facing reality, fate, free will, vanity, loss of innocence, loneliness, isolation, fulfillment, failure, and disillusionment

- **Individual against nature**—relevant to themes of knowledge vs. ignorance, nature as beauty, quest for discovery, self-preservation, chaos and order, circle of life, death, and destruction of beauty

- **Individual against society**—relevant to themes of power, beauty, good, evil, war, class struggle, totalitarianism, role of men/women, wealth, corruption, change vs. tradition, capitalism, destruction, heroism, injustice, and racism

- **Individual against another individual**—relevant to themes of hope, loss of love or hope, sacrifice, power, revenge, betrayal, and honor

For example, in Hawthorne's *The Scarlet Letter*, one possible narrative conflict could be the individual against the self, with a relevant theme of internal struggles. This theme is alluded to through characterization—Dimmesdale's moral struggle with his love for Hester and Hester's internal struggles with the truth and her daughter, Pearl. It's also alluded to through plot—Dimmesdale's suicide and Hester helping the very townspeople who initially condemned her.

Sometimes, a text can convey a **message or universal lesson**—a truth or insight that the reader infers from the text, based on analysis of the literary and/or poetic elements. This message is often presented as a statement. For example, a potential message in Shakespeare's *Hamlet* could be "Revenge is what ultimately drives the human soul." This message can be immediately determined through plot and characterization in numerous ways, but it can also be determined through the setting of Norway, which is bordering on war.

How Authors Develop Theme

Authors employ a variety of techniques to present a theme. They may compare or contrast characters, events, places, ideas, or historical or invented settings to speak thematically. They may use analogies, metaphors, similes, allusions, or other literary devices to convey the theme. An author's use of diction, syntax, and tone can also help convey the theme. Authors will often develop themes through the development of characters, use of the setting, repetition of ideas, use of symbols, and through contrasting value systems. Authors of both fiction and nonfiction genres will use a variety of these techniques to develop one or more themes.

Regardless of the literary genre, there are commonalities in how authors, playwrights, and poets develop themes or central ideas.

Authors often do research, the results of which contributes to theme. In prose fiction and drama, this research may include real historical information about the setting the author has chosen or include elements that make fictional characters, settings, and plots seem realistic to the reader. In nonfiction, research is critical since the information contained within this literature must be accurate and, moreover, accurately represented.

In fiction, authors present a narrative conflict that will contribute to the overall theme. In fiction, this conflict may involve the storyline itself and some trouble within characters that needs resolution. In nonfiction, this conflict may be an explanation or commentary on factual people and events.

Authors will sometimes use character motivation to convey theme, such as in the example from *Hamlet* regarding revenge. In fiction, the characters an author creates will think, speak, and act in ways that effectively convey the theme to readers. In nonfiction, the characters are factual, as in a biography, but authors pay particular attention to presenting those motivations to make them clear to readers.

Authors also use literary devices as a means of conveying theme. For example, the use of moon symbolism in Mary Shelley's *Frankenstein* is significant as its phases can be compared to the phases that the Creature undergoes as he struggles with his identity.

The selected point of view can also contribute to a work's theme. The use of first-person point of view in a fiction or nonfiction work engages the reader's response differently than third person point of view. The central idea or theme from a first-person narrative may differ from a third-person limited text.

In literary nonfiction, authors usually identify the purpose of their writing, which differs from fiction, where the general purpose is to entertain. The purpose of nonfiction is usually to inform, persuade, or entertain the audience. The stated purpose of a nonfiction text will drive how the central message or theme, if applicable, is presented.

Authors identify an audience for their writing, which is critical in shaping the theme of the work. For example, the audience for J.K. Rowling's *Harry Potter* series would be different than the audience for a biography of George Washington. The audience an author chooses to address is closely tied to the purpose of the work. The choice of an audience also drives the choice of language and level of diction an author uses. Ultimately, the intended audience determines the level to which that subject matter is presented and the complexity of the theme.

Cultural Differences in Themes

Regardless of culture, place, or time, certain themes are universal to the human condition. Because all humans experience certain feelings and engage in similar experiences—birth, death, marriage, friendship, finding meaning, etc.—certain themes span cultures. However, different cultures have different norms and general beliefs concerning these themes. For example, the theme of maturing and crossing from childhood to adulthood is a global theme; however, the literature from one culture might imply that this happens in someone's twenties, while another culture's literature might imply that it happens in the early teenage years.

It's important for the reader to be aware of these differences. Readers must avoid being **ethnocentric**, which means believing the aspects of one's own culture to be superior to those of other cultures.

159

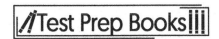

Summarizing Information Accurately

Summarizing is an effective way to draw a conclusion from a passage. A **summary** is a shortened version of the original text, written by the reader in their own words. Focusing on the main points of the original text and including only the relevant details can help readers reach a conclusion. It's important to retain the original meaning of the passage.

Like summarizing, **paraphrasing** can also help a reader fully understand different parts of a text. Paraphrasing calls for the reader to take a small part of the passage and list or describe its main points. However, paraphrasing is more than rewording the original passage; paraphrases should be written in the reader's own words, while still retaining the meaning of the original source. This will indicate an understanding of the original source, yet still help the reader expand on their interpretation.

Understanding Relationships

Inferences are useful in gaining a deeper understanding of how people, events, and ideas are connected in a passage. Readers can use the same strategies used with general inferences and analyzing texts— paying attention to details and using them to make reasonable guesses about the text—to read between the lines and get a more complete picture of how (and why) characters are thinking, feeling, and acting. Read the following passage from O. Henry's story "The Gift of the Magi":

> One dollar and eighty-seven cents. That was all. And sixty cents of it was in pennies. Pennies saved one and two at a time by bulldozing the grocer and the vegetable man and the butcher until one's cheeks burned with the silent imputation of parsimony that such close dealing implied. Three times Della counted it. One dollar and eighty-seven cents. And the next day would be Christmas.

> There was clearly nothing to do but flop down on the shabby little couch and howl. So Della did it.

These paragraphs introduce the reader to the character Della. Even though the author doesn't include a direct description of Della, the reader can already form a general impression of her personality and emotions. One detail that should stick out to the reader is repetition: "one dollar and eighty-seven cents." This amount is repeated twice in the first paragraph, along with other descriptions of money: "sixty cents of it was in pennies," "pennies saved one and two at a time." The story's preoccupation with money parallels how Della herself is constantly thinking about her finances—"three times Della counted" her meager savings.

Already the reader can guess that Della is having money problems. Next, think about her emotions. The first paragraph describes haggling over groceries "until one's cheeks burned"—another way to describe blushing. People tend to blush when they are embarrassed or ashamed, so readers can infer that Della is ashamed by her financial situation. This inference is also supported by the second paragraph, when she flops down and howls on her "shabby little couch." Clearly, she's in distress. Without saying, "Della has no money and is embarrassed to be poor," O. Henry is able to communicate the same impression to readers through his careful inclusion of details.

A character's **motive** is their reason for acting a certain way. Usually, characters are motivated by something that they want. In the passage, above, why is Della upset about not having enough money? There's an important detail at the end of the first paragraph: "the next day would be Christmas." Why is

160

money especially important around Christmas? Christmas is a holiday when people exchange gifts. If Della is struggling with money, she's probably also struggling to buy gifts. So a shrewd reader should be able to guess that Della's motivation is wanting to buy a gift for someone—but she's currently unable to afford it, leading to feelings of shame and frustration.

In order to understand characters in a text, readers should keep the following questions in mind:

- What words does the author use to describe the character? Are these words related to any specific emotions or personality traits (for example, characteristics like rude, friendly, unapproachable, or innocent)?

- What does the character say? Does their dialogue seem to be straightforward, or are they hiding some thoughts or emotions?

- What actions can be observed from this character? How do their actions reflect their feelings?

- What does the character want? What do they do to get it?

Drawing Logical Inferences and Conclusions

Making Inferences

Predictions
Some texts use suspense and foreshadowing to captivate readers. For example, an intriguing aspect of murder mysteries is that the reader is never sure of the culprit until the author reveals the individual's identity. Authors often build suspense and add depth and meaning to a work by leaving clues to provide hints or predict future events in the story; this is called foreshadowing. While some instances of foreshadowing are subtle, others are quite obvious.

Inferences
Another way to read actively is to identify examples of inference within text. Making an inference requires the reader to read between the lines and look for what is implied rather than what is explicitly stated. That is, using information that is known from the text, the reader is able to make a logical assumption about information that is *not* explicitly stated but is probably true.

Authors employ literary devices such as tone, characterization, and theme to engage the audience by showing details of the story instead of merely telling them. For example, if an author said *Bob is selfish*, there's little left to infer. If the author said, *Bob cheated on his test, ignored his mom's calls, and parked illegally*, the reader can infer Bob is selfish. Authors also make implications through character dialogue, thoughts, effects on others, actions, and looks. Like in life, readers must assemble all the clues to form a complete picture.

Read the following passage:

"Hey, do you wanna meet my new puppy?" Jonathan asked.

"Oh, I'm sorry but please don't—" Jacinta began to protest, but before she could finish, Jonathan had already opened the passenger side door of his car and a perfect white ball of fur came bouncing towards Jacinta.

161

"Isn't he the cutest?" beamed Jonathan.

"Yes—achoo!—he's pretty—aaaachooo!!—adora—aaa—aaaachoo!" Jacinta managed to say in between sneezes. "But if you don't mind, I—I—achoo!—need to go inside."

Which of the following can be inferred from Jacinta's reaction to the puppy?
a. she hates animals
b. she is allergic to dogs
c. she prefers cats to dogs
d. she is angry at Jonathan

An inference requires the reader to consider the information presented and then form their own idea about what is probably true. Based on the details in the passage, what is the best answer to the question? Important details to pay attention to include the tone of Jacinta's dialogue, which is overall polite and apologetic, as well as her reaction itself, which is a long string of sneezes. Answer choices (a) and (d) both express strong emotions ("hates" and "angry") that are not evident in Jacinta's speech or actions. Answer choice (c) mentions cats, but there is nothing in the passage to indicate Jacinta's feelings about cats. Answer choice (b), "she is allergic to dogs," is the most logical choice—based on the fact that she began sneezing as soon as a fluffy dog approached her, it makes sense to guess that Jacinta might be allergic to dogs. So even though Jacinta never directly states, "Sorry, I'm allergic to dogs!" using the clues in the passage, it is still reasonable to guess that this is true.

Making inferences is crucial for readers of literature because literary texts often avoid presenting complete and direct information to readers about characters' thoughts or feelings, or they present this information in an unclear way, leaving it up to the reader to interpret clues given in the text. In order to make inferences while reading, readers should ask themselves:

- What details are being presented in the text?
- Is there any important information that seems to be missing?
- Based on the information that the author *does* include, what else is probably true?
- Is this inference reasonable based on what is already known?

Conclusions

Active readers should also draw conclusions. When doing so, the reader should ask the following questions: What is this piece about? What does the author believe? Does this piece have merit? Do I believe the author? Would this piece support my argument? The reader should first determine the author's intent. Identify the author's viewpoint and connect relevant evidence to support it. Readers may then move to the most important step: deciding whether to agree and determining whether they are correct. Always read cautiously and critically. Interact with text, and record reactions in the margins. These active reading skills help determine not only what the author thinks, but what you think as the reader.

Determining conclusions requires being an active reader, as a reader must make a prediction and analyze facts to identify a conclusion. A reader should identify key words in a passage to determine the logical conclusion from the information presented. Consider the passage below:

Lindsay, covered in flour, moved around the kitchen frantically. Her mom yelled from another room, "Lindsay, we're going to be late!"

Readers can conclude that Lindsay's next steps are to finish baking, clean herself up, and head off somewhere with her baked goods. It's important to note that the conclusion cannot be verified factually. Many conclusions are not spelled out specifically in the text; thus, they have to be inferred and deduced by the reader.

Evaluating a Passage

Readers draw **conclusions** about what an author has presented. This helps them better understand what the writer has intended to communicate and whether or not they agree with what the author has offered. There are a few ways to determine a logical conclusion, but careful reading is the most important. It's helpful to read a passage a few times, noting details that seem important to the piece. Sometimes, readers arrive at a conclusion that is different than what the writer intended or they may come up with more than one conclusion.

Textual evidence helps readers draw a conclusion about a passage. **Textual evidence** refers to information—facts and examples—that support the main point; it will likely come from outside sources and can be in the form of quoted or paraphrased material. In order to draw a conclusion from evidence, it's important to examine the credibility and validity of that evidence as well as how (and if) it relates to the main idea.

If an author presents a differing opinion or a **counterargument**, in order to refute it, the reader should consider how and why the information is being presented. It is meant to strengthen the original argument and shouldn't be confused with the author's intended conclusion, but it should also be considered in the reader's final evaluation.

Sometimes, authors explicitly state the conclusion that they want readers to understand. Alternatively, a conclusion may not be directly stated. In that case, readers must rely on the implications to form a logical conclusion:

> On the way to the bus stop, Michael realized his homework wasn't in his backpack. He ran back to the house to get it and made it back to the bus just in time.

In this example, although it's never explicitly stated, it can be inferred that Michael is a student on his way to school in the morning. When forming a conclusion from implied information, it's important to read the text carefully to find several pieces of evidence to support the conclusion.

Sequential, Comparative, and Cause-Effect Relationships

Ideas within texts should be organized, connected, or related in some way. In sequential relationships, ideas or events have a temporal relationship; they occur in some sort of order. Every passage has a plot, whether it is from a short story, a manual, a newspaper article or editorial, or a history text. And each plot has a logical order, which is also known as a sequence. Some of the most straightforward sequences can be found in technology directions, science experiments, instructional materials, and recipes. These forms of writing list actions that must occur in a proper sequence in order to get sufficient results. Other forms of writing, however, use style and ideas in ways that completely change the sequence of events. Poetry, for instance, may introduce repetitions that make the events seem cyclical. Postmodern writers are famous for experimenting with different concepts of place and time, creating "cut scenes" that distort straightforward sequences and abruptly transport the audience to different contexts or times. Even everyday newspaper articles, editorials, and historical sources may experiment with different sequential forms for stylistic effect.

163

Most questions that call for test takers to apply their sequential knowledge use key words such as **sequence**, **sequence of events**, or **sequential order** to cue the test taker in to the task at hand. In social studies or history passages, the test questions might employ key words such as **chronology** or **chronological order** to cue the test taker. In some cases, sequence can be found through comprehension techniques. These literal passages number the sequences, or they use key words such as *firstly, secondly, finally, next,* or *then.* The sequences of these stories can be found by rereading the passage and charting these numbers or key words. In most cases, however, readers have to correctly order events through inferential and evaluative reading techniques; they have to place events in a logical order without explicit cues.

Ideas in a text can also have a **comparative** relationship wherein certain qualities are shown to overlap or be the same between two different things. In comparative relationships, similarities are drawn out. Words like *as, like, also, similarly, in the same way,* and *too* are often used.

Passages that have a **cause-and-effect** relationship demonstrate a specific type of connection between ideas or events wherein one (or multiple) caused another. Words such as *if, since, because, then,* or *consequently* indicate a relationship.

Understanding the Meaning and Purpose of Transition Words

The writer should act as a guide, showing the reader how all the sentences fit together. Consider this example:

> Seat belts save more lives than any other automobile safety feature. Many studies show that airbags save lives as well. Not all cars have airbags. Many older cars don't. Air bags aren't entirely reliable. Studies show that in 15% of accidents, airbags don't deploy as designed. Seat belt malfunctions are extremely rare.

There's nothing wrong with any of these sentences individually, but together they're disjointed and difficult to follow. The best way for the writer to communicate information is through the use of transition words. Here are examples of transition words and phrases that tie sentences together, enabling a more natural flow:

- To show causality: *as a result, therefore,* and *consequently*
- To compare and contrast: *however, but,* and *on the other hand*
- To introduce examples*: for instance, namely,* and *including*
- To show order of importance: *foremost, primarily, secondly,* and *lastly*

Note: This is not a complete list of transitions. There are many more that can be used; however, most fit into these or similar categories. The point is that the words should clearly show the relationship between sentences, supporting information, and the main idea.

Here is an update to the previous example using transition words. These changes make it easier to read and bring clarity to the writer's points:

> Seat belts save more lives than any other automobile safety feature. Many studies show that airbags save lives as well; however, not all cars have airbags. For instance, some older cars don't. Furthermore, air bags aren't entirely reliable. For example, studies show that in 15% of

accidents, airbags don't deploy as designed; but, on the other hand, seat belt malfunctions are extremely rare.

Also, be prepared to analyze whether the writer is using the best transition word or phrase for the situation. Take this sentence for example: "As a result, seat belt malfunctions are extremely rare." This sentence doesn't make sense in the context above because the writer is trying to show the contrast between seat belts and airbags, not the causality.

Craft and Structure

Word and Phrase Meanings

Most experts agree that learning new words is worth the time it takes. It helps readers understand what they are reading, and it expands their vocabulary. An extensive vocabulary improves one's ability to think. When words are added to someone's vocabulary, they are better able to make sense of the world.

One of the fastest ways to decode a word is through context. **Context**, or surrounding words, gives clues about what unknown words mean. Take the following example: *When the students in the classroom teased Johnny, he was so discombobulated that he couldn't finish a simple math problem.* Even though a reader might be unfamiliar with the word *discombobulated*, he or she can use context clues in the sentence to make sense of the word. In this case, it can be deduced that *discombobulated* means confused or distracted.

Although context clues provide a rudimentary understanding of a word, using a dictionary can provide the reader with a more comprehensive meaning. Printed dictionaries list words in alphabetical order, and all versions—including those online—include a word's multiple meanings. Typically, the first definition is the most widely used or known. The second, third, and subsequent entries move toward the more unusual or archaic. Dictionaries also indicate the part(s) of speech of each word, such as noun, verb, adjective, etc.

Dictionaries are not fixed in time. The English language today looks nothing like it did in Shakespeare's time, and Shakespeare's English is vastly different from Chaucer's. The English language is constantly evolving, as evidenced by the deletion of old words and the addition of new ones. *Ginormous* and *bling-bling*, for example, can both be found in *Merriam-Webster's* latest edition, yet they were not found in prior editions.

How Words Affect Tone

Tone refers to the writer's attitude toward the subject matter. For example, the tone conveys how the writer feels about the topic he or she is writing about. A lot of nonfiction writing has a neutral tone, which is an important tone for the writer to take. A neutral tone demonstrates that the writer is presenting a topic impartially and letting the information speak for itself. On the other hand, nonfiction writing can be just as effective and appropriate if the tone isn't neutral. For instance, consider this example:

Seat belts save more lives than any other automobile safety feature. Many studies show that airbags save lives as well; however, not all cars have airbags. For instance, some older cars don't. Furthermore, air bags aren't entirely reliable. For example, studies show that in 15% of accidents, airbags don't deploy as designed; but, on the other hand, seat belt malfunctions are extremely rare. The number of highway fatalities has plummeted since laws requiring seat belt usage were enacted.

In this passage, the writer mostly chooses to retain a neutral tone when presenting information. If the writer would instead include their own personal experience of losing a friend or family member in a car accident, the tone would change dramatically. The tone would no longer be neutral and would show that the writer has a personal stake in the content, allowing them to interpret the information in a different way. When analyzing tone, consider what the writer is trying to achieve in the text and how they *create* the tone using style.

An author's choice of words—also referred to as **diction**—helps to convey their meaning in a particular way. Through diction, an author can convey a particular tone—e.g., a humorous tone, a serious tone—in order to support the thesis in a meaningful way to the reader.

Connotation and Denotation

Connotation is when an author chooses words or phrases that invoke ideas or feelings other than their literal meaning. An example of the use of connotation is the word *cheap*, which suggests something is poor in value or negatively describes a person as reluctant to spend money. When something or someone is described this way, the reader is more inclined to have a particular image or feeling about it or him/her. Thus, connotation can be a very effective language tool in creating emotion and swaying opinion. However, connotations are sometimes hard to pin down because varying emotions can be associated with a word. Generally, though, connotative meanings tend to be fairly consistent within a specific cultural group.

Denotation refers to words or phrases that mean exactly what they say. It is helpful when a writer wants to present hard facts or vocabulary terms with which readers may be unfamiliar. Some examples of denotation are the words *inexpensive* and *frugal*. *Inexpensive* refers to the cost of something, not its value, and *frugal* indicates that a person is conscientiously watching their spending. These terms do not elicit the same emotions that *cheap* does.

Authors sometimes choose to use both, but what they choose and when they use it is what critical readers need to differentiate. One method isn't inherently better than the other; however, one may create a better effect, depending upon an author's intent. If, for example, an author's purpose is to inform, to instruct, and to familiarize readers with a difficult subject, their use of connotation may be helpful. However, it may also undermine credibility and confuse readers. An author who wants to create a credible, scholarly effect in their text would most likely use denotation, which emphasizes literal, factual meaning and examples.

Analyzing an Author's Rhetorical Choices

Authors utilize a wide range of techniques to tell a story or communicate information. Readers should be familiar with the most common of these techniques. Writing techniques are also known as **rhetorical devices**.

In nonfiction writing, authors employ argumentative techniques to present their opinions to readers in the most convincing way. Persuasive writing usually includes at least one type of **appeal**: an appeal to logic (**logos**), emotion (**pathos**), or credibility and trustworthiness (**ethos**). When writers appeal to logic, they are asking readers to agree with them based on research, evidence, and an established line of reasoning. An author's argument might also appeal to readers' emotions, perhaps by including personal stories and **anecdotes** (a short narrative of a specific event). A final type of appeal—appeal to authority—asks the reader to agree with the author's argument on the basis of their expertise or credentials. Three different approaches to arguing the same opinion are exemplified below:

Logic (Logos)

> Our school should abolish its current ban on campus cell phone use. The ban was adopted last year as an attempt to reduce class disruptions and help students focus more on their lessons. However, since the rule was enacted, there has been no change in the number of disciplinary problems in class. Therefore, the rule is ineffective and should be done away with.

The above is an example of an appeal to logic. The author uses evidence to disprove the logic of the school's rule (the rule was supposed to reduce discipline problems, but the number of problems has not been reduced; therefore, the rule is not working) and to call for its repeal.

Emotion (Pathos)

An author's argument might also appeal to readers' emotions, perhaps by including personal stories and anecdotes.

The next example presents an appeal to emotion. By sharing the personal anecdote of one student and speaking about emotional topics like family relationships, the author invokes the reader's empathy in asking them to reconsider the school rule.

> Our school should abolish its current ban on campus cell phone use. If students aren't able to use their phones during the school day, many of them feel isolated from their loved ones. For example, last semester, one student's grandmother had a heart attack in the morning. However, because he couldn't use his cell phone, the student didn't know about his grandmother's accident until the end of the day—when she had already passed away, and it was too late to say goodbye. By preventing students from contacting their friends and family, our school is placing undue stress and anxiety on students.

Credibility (Ethos)

Finally, an appeal to authority includes a statement from a relevant expert. In this case, the author uses a doctor in the field of education to support the argument. All three examples begin from the same opinion—the school's phone ban needs to change—but rely on different argumentative styles to persuade the reader.

> Our school should abolish its current ban on campus cell phone use. According to Dr. Bartholomew Everett, a leading educational expert, "Research studies show that cell phone usage has no real impact on student attentiveness. Rather, phones provide a valuable technological resource for learning. Schools need to learn how to integrate this new technology into their curriculum." Rather than banning phones altogether, our

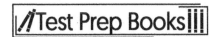

school should follow the advice of experts and allow students to use phones as part of their learning.

Figurative Language

Similes and **metaphors** are types of figurative language that are used as rhetorical devices. Both are comparisons between two things, but their formats differ slightly. A simile says that two things are similar and makes a comparison using "like" or "as"—*A* is like *B*, or *A* is as [some characteristic] as *B*— whereas a metaphor states that two things are exactly the same—*A* is *B*. In both cases, similes and metaphors invite the reader to think more deeply about the characteristics of the two subjects and

consider where they overlap. Sometimes the poet develops a complex metaphor throughout the entire poem; this is known as an extended metaphor. An example of metaphor can be found in the sentence: "His pillow was a fluffy cloud". An example of simile can be found in the first line of Robert Burns' famous poem:

My love is like a red, red rose

This is comparison using "like," and the two things being compared are love and a rose. Some characteristics of a rose are that it is fragrant, beautiful, blossoming, colorful, vibrant—by comparing his love to a red, red rose, Burns asks the reader to apply these qualities of a rose to his love. In this way, he implies that his love is also fresh, blossoming, and brilliant.

In addition to rhetorical devices that play on the *meanings* of words, there are also rhetorical devices that use the sounds of words. These devices are most often found in poetry, but may also be found in other types of literature and in nonfiction writing like texts for speeches.

Alliteration and **assonance** are both varieties of sound repetition. Other types of sound repetition include: **anaphora**—repetition that occurs at the beginning of the sentences; **epiphora**—repetition occurring at the end of phrases; antimetabole—repetition of words in a succession; and antiphrasis—a form of denial of an assertion in a text.

Alliteration refers to the repetition of the first sound of each word. Recall Robert Burns' opening line:

My love is like a red, red rose

This line includes two instances of alliteration: "love" and "like" (repeated *L* sound), as well as "red" and "rose" (repeated *R* sound). Next, assonance refers to the repetition of vowel sounds, and can occur anywhere within a word (not just the opening sound). Here is the opening of a poem by John Keats:

When I have fears that I may cease to be

Before my pen has glean'd my teeming brain

Assonance can be found in the words "fears," "cease," "be," "glean'd," and "teeming," all of which stress the long *E* sound. Both alliteration and assonance create a harmony that unifies the writer's language.

Another sound device is **onomatopoeia**—words whose spelling mimics the sound they describe. Words such as "crash," "bang," and "sizzle" are all examples of onomatopoeia. Use of onomatopoetic language adds auditory imagery to the text.

Readers are probably most familiar with the technique of using a **pun**. A pun is a play on words, taking advantage of two words that have the same or similar pronunciation. Puns can be found throughout Shakespeare's plays, for instance:

> Now is the winter of our discontent

> Made glorious summer by this son of York

These lines from *Richard III* contain a play on words. Richard III refers to his brother—the newly crowned King Edward IV—as the "son of York," referencing their family heritage from the house of York. However, while drawing a comparison between the political climate and the weather (times of political trouble were the "winter," but now the new king brings "glorious summer"), Richard's use of the word "son" also implies another word with the same pronunciation, "sun"—so Edward IV is also like the sun, bringing light, warmth, and hope to England. Puns are a clever way for writers to suggest two meanings at once.

Analyzing Text Structure

Organizational Structure within Literary Texts
Depending on what the author is attempting to accomplish, certain formats or text structures work better than others. For example, a sequence structure might work for narration but not for identifying similarities and differences between concepts. Similarly, a comparison-contrast structure is not useful for narration. It's the author's job to put the right information in the correct format.

Readers should be familiar with the five main literary structures:

1. **Sequence** structure (sometimes referred to as the order structure) is when the order of events proceeds in a predictable manner. In many cases, this means the text goes through the plot elements: exposition, rising action, climax, falling action, and resolution. Readers are introduced to characters, setting, and conflict in the exposition. In the rising action, there's an increase in tension and suspense. The climax is the height of tension and the point of no return. Tension decreases during the falling action. In the resolution, any conflicts presented in the exposition are solved, and the story concludes. An informative text that is structured sequentially will often go in order from one step to the next.

2. In the **problem-solution** structure, authors identify a potential problem and suggest a solution. This form of writing is usually divided into two paragraphs and can be found in informational texts. For example, cell phone, cable, and satellite providers use this structure in manuals to help customers troubleshoot or identify problems with services or products.

3. When authors want to discuss similarities and differences between separate concepts, they arrange thoughts in a **comparison-contrast** paragraph structure. **Venn diagrams** are an effective graphic organizer for comparison-contrast structures, because they feature two overlapping circles that can be used to organize and group similarities and differences. A comparison-contrast essay organizes one paragraph based on similarities and another based on differences. A comparison-contrast essay can also be arranged with the similarities and differences of individual traits addressed within individual paragraphs. Words such as *however*, *but*, and *nevertheless* help signal a contrast in ideas.

169

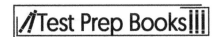

4. The **descriptive** writing structure is designed to appeal to one's senses. Much like an artist who constructs a painting, good descriptive writing builds an image in the reader's mind by appealing to the five senses: sight, hearing, taste, touch, and smell. However, overly descriptive writing can become tedious; whereas sparse descriptions can make settings and characters seem flat. Good authors strike a balance by applying descriptions only to passages, characters, and settings that are integral to the plot.

5. Passages that use the **cause and effect** structure are simply asking *why* by demonstrating some type of connection between ideas. Words such as *if, since, because, then, or consequently* indicate a cause-and-effect relationship. By switching the order of a complex sentence, the writer can rearrange the emphasis on different clauses. Saying, *If Sheryl is late, we'll miss the dance*, is different from saying, *We'll miss the dance if Sheryl is late*. One emphasizes Sheryl's tardiness while the other emphasizes missing the dance. Paragraphs can also be arranged in a cause and effect format. Since the format—before and after—is sequential, it is useful when authors wish to discuss the impact of choices. Researchers often apply this paragraph structure to the scientific method.

Organizational Structure within Informational Texts

Informational text is specifically designed to relate factual information, and although it is open to a reader's interpretation and application of the facts, the structure of the presentation is carefully designed to lead the reader to a particular conclusion or central idea. When reading informational text, it is important that readers are able to understand its organizational structure as the structure often directly relates to an author's intent to inform and/or persuade the reader.

The first step in identifying the text's structure is to determine the thesis or main idea. The thesis statement and organization of a work are closely intertwined. A **thesis statement** indicates the writer's purpose and may include the scope and direction of the text. It may be presented at the beginning of a text or at the end, and it may be explicit or implicit.

Once a reader has a grasp of the thesis or main idea of the text, he or she can better determine its organizational structure. Test takers are advised to read informational text passages more than once in order to comprehend the material fully. It is also helpful to examine any text features present in the text including the table of contents, index, glossary, headings, footnotes, and visuals. The analysis of these features and the information presented within them, can offer additional clues about the central idea and structure of a text. The following questions should be asked when considering structure:

- How does the author assemble the parts to make an effective whole argument?
- Is the passage linear in nature and if so, what is the timeline or thread of logic?
- What is the presented order of events, facts, or arguments? Are these effective in contributing to the author's thesis?
- How can the passage be divided into sections? How are they related to each other and to the main idea or thesis?
- What key terms are used to indicate the organization?

Next, test takers should skim the passage, noting the first line or two of each body paragraph—the **topic sentences**—and the conclusion. Key **transitional terms**, such as *on the other hand, also, because, however, therefore, most importantly*, and *first*, within the text can also signal organizational structure. Based on these clues, readers should then be able to identify what type of organizational structure is being used.

The following organizational structures are most common:

- **Problem/solution**—organized by an analysis/overview of a problem, followed by potential solution(s)

- **Cause/effect**—organized by the effects resulting from a cause or the cause(s) of a particular effect

- **Spatial order**—organized by points that suggest location or direction—e.g., top to bottom, right to left, outside to inside

- **Chronological/sequence order**—organized by points presented to indicate a passage of time or through purposeful steps/stages

- **Comparison/Contrast**—organized by points that indicate similarities and/or differences between two things or concepts

- **Order of importance**—organized by priority of points, often most significant to least significant or vice versa

Authorial Purpose and Perspective

No matter the genre or format, all authors are writing to persuade, inform, entertain, or express feelings. Often, these purposes are blended, with one dominating the rest. It's useful to learn to recognize the author's intent.

Persuasive writing is used to persuade or convince readers of something. It often contains two elements: the argument and the counterargument. The **argument** takes a stance on an issue, while the **counterargument** pokes holes in the opposition's stance. Authors rely on logic, emotion, and writer credibility to persuade readers to agree with them. If readers are opposed to the stance before reading, they are unlikely to adopt that stance. However, those who are undecided or committed to the same stance are more likely to agree with the author.

Informative writing tries to teach or inform. Workplace manuals, instructor lessons, statistical reports, and cookbooks are examples of informative texts. Informative writing is usually based on facts and does not use emotion and persuasion. Informative texts generally contain statistics, charts, and graphs. Although most informative texts lack a persuasive agenda, readers still must examine the text carefully to determine whether one exists within a given passage.

Stories or **narratives** are designed to entertain. When people go to the movies, they often want to escape for a few hours, not necessarily to think critically. **Entertaining** writing is designed to delight and engage the reader. However, sometimes this type of writing can be woven into more serious materials, such as persuasive or informative writing, to hook the reader before transitioning into a more scholarly discussion.

Emotional writing works to evoke the reader's feelings, such as anger, euphoria, or sadness. The connection between reader and author is an attempt to cause the reader to share the author's intended emotion or tone. Sometimes, in order to make a text more poignant, the author simply wants readers to feel the emotions that the author has felt. Other times, the author attempts to persuade or manipulate

171

the reader into adopting their stance. While it's okay to sympathize with the author, readers should be aware of the individual's underlying intent.

Characters' Point of View

Point of view is another important writing device to consider. In fiction writing, **point of view** refers to who tells the story or from whose perspective readers are observing the story. In nonfiction writing, the **point of view** refers to whether the author refers to himself or herself, their readers, or chooses not to mention either. Whether fiction or nonfiction, the author carefully considers the impact the perspective will have on the purpose and main point of the writing.

- **First-person** point of view: The story is told from the writer's perspective. In fiction, this would mean that the main character is also the narrator. First-person point of view is easily recognized by the use of personal pronouns such as *I, me, we, us, our, my*, and *myself*.

- **Third-person** point of view: In a more formal essay, this would be an appropriate perspective because the focus should be on the subject matter, not the writer or the reader. Third-person point of view is recognized by the use of the pronouns *he, she, they*, and *it*. In fiction writing, third-person point of view has a few variations.

  - **Third-person limited** point of view refers to a story told by a narrator who has access to the thoughts and feelings of just one character.

  - In **third-person omniscient** point of view, the narrator has access to the thoughts and feelings of all the characters.

  - In **third-person objective** point of view, the narrator is like a fly on the wall and can see and hear what the characters do and say but does not have access to their thoughts and feelings.

- **Second-person** point of view: This point of view isn't commonly used in fiction or nonfiction writing because it directly addresses the reader using the pronouns *you, your*, and *yourself*. Second-person perspective is more appropriate in direct communication, such as business letters or emails.

Point of View	Pronouns Used
First person	I, me, we, us, our, my, myself
Second person	You, your, yourself
Third person	He, she, it, they

Interpreting Authorial Decisions Rhetorically

There are a few ways for readers to engage actively with the text, such as making inferences and predictions. An **inference** refers to a point that is implied (as opposed to directly-stated) by the evidence presented:

> Bradley packed up all of the items from his desk in a box and said goodbye to his coworkers for the last time.

172

From this sentence, although it is not directly stated, readers can infer that Bradley is leaving his job. It's necessary to use inference in order to draw conclusions about the meaning of a passage. When making an inference about a passage, it's important to rely only on the information that is provided in the text itself. This helps readers ensure that their conclusions are valid.

Readers will also find themselves making predictions when reading a passage or paragraph. **Predictions** are guesses about what's going to happen next. This is a natural tendency, especially when reading a good story or watching a suspenseful movie. It's fun to try to figure out how it will end. Authors intentionally use suspenseful language and situations to keep readers interested:

A cat darted across the street just as the car came careening around the curve.

One unfortunate prediction might be that the car will hit the cat. Of course, predictions aren't always accurate, so it's important to read carefully to the end of the text to determine the accuracy of one's predictions.

Readers should pay attention to the **sequence**, or the order in which details are laid out in the text, as this can be important to understanding its meaning as a whole. Writers will often use transitional words to help the reader understand the order of events and to stay on track. Words like *next, then, after*, and *finally* show that the order of events is important to the author. In some cases, the author omits these transitional words, and the sequence is implied. Authors may even purposely present the information out of order to make an impact or have an effect on the reader. An example might be when a narrative writer uses **flashback** to reveal information.

Drawing conclusions is also important when actively reading a passage. **Hedge phrases** such as *will, might, probably*, and *appear to be* are used by writers who want to cover their bases and show there are exceptions to their statements. **Absolute phrasing**, such as *always* and *never*, should be carefully considered, as the use of these words and their intended meanings are often incorrect.

Differentiating Between Various Perspectives and Sources of Information

Primary sources contain firsthand documentation of a historical event or era. Primary sources are provided by people who have experienced an era or event. Primary sources capture a specific moment, context, or era in history. They are valued as eyewitness accounts and personal perspectives. Examples include diaries, memoirs, journals, letters, interviews, photographs, context-specific artwork, government documents, constitutions, newspapers, personal items, libraries, and archives. Another example of a primary source is the Declaration of Independence. This historical document captures the revolutionary sentiment of an era in American history.

Authors of secondary sources write about events, contexts, and eras in history with a relative amount of experiential, geographic, or temporal distance. Normally, secondary source authors aren't firsthand witnesses. In some cases, they may have experienced an event, but they are offering secondhand, retrospective accounts of their experience. All scholars and historians produce secondary sources—they gather primary source information and synthesize it for a new generation of students. Monographs, biographies, magazine articles, scholarly journals, theses, dissertations, textbooks, and encyclopedias are all secondary sources. In some rare instances, secondary sources become so enmeshed in their era of inquiry that they later become primary sources for future scholars and analysts.

Both primary and secondary sources of information are useful. They both offer invaluable insight that helps the writer learn more about the subject matter. However, researchers are cautioned to examine

the information closely and to consider the time period as well as the cultural, political, and social climate in which accounts were given. Learning to distinguish between reliable sources of information and questionable accounts is paramount to a quality research report.

Identifying the Appropriate Source for Locating Information

With a wealth of information at people's fingertips in this digital age, it's important to know not only the type of information one is looking for, but also in what medium one is most likely to find it. Information needs to be specific and reliable. For example, if someone is repairing a car, an encyclopedia would be mostly useless. While an encyclopedia might include information about cars, an owner's manual will contain the specific information needed for repairs. Information must also be credible, or trustworthy. A well-known newspaper may have reliable information, but a peer-reviewed journal article will have likely gone through a more rigorous check for validity. Determining **bias** can be helpful in determining credibility. If the information source (person, organization, or company) has something to gain from the reader forming a certain view on a topic, it's likely the information is skewed. For example, if trying to find the unemployment rate, the Bureau of Labor Statistics is a more credible source than a politician's speech.

Primary sources are best defined as records or items that serve as historical evidence. To be considered primary, the source documents or objects must have been created during the time period in which they reference. Examples include diaries, newspaper articles, speeches, government documents, photographs, and historical artifacts. In today's digital age, primary sources, which were once in print, are often embedded in secondary sources. **Secondary sources**—such as websites, history books, databases, or reviews—contain analysis or commentary on primary sources. Secondary sources borrow information from primary sources through the process of quoting, summarizing, or paraphrasing.

Today's students often complete research online through **electronic sources**. Electronic sources offer advantages over print and can be accessed on virtually any computer, while libraries or other research centers are limited to fixed locations and specific catalogs. Electronic sources are also efficient and yield massive amounts of data in seconds. The user can tailor a search based on key words, publication years, and article length. Lastly, many **databases** provide the user with instant citations, saving the user the trouble of manually assembling sources for a bibliography.

Although electronic sources yield powerful results, researchers must use caution. While there are many reputable and reliable sources on the internet, just as many are unreliable or biased sources. It's up to the researcher to examine and verify the reliability of sources. *Wikipedia*, for example, may or may not be accurate, depending on the contributor. Many databases, such as *EBSCO* or *SIRS*, offer peer-reviewed articles, meaning the publications have been reviewed for the quality and accuracy of their content.

Text Credibility

Credible sources are important when drawing conclusions because readers need to be able to trust what they are reading. Authors should always use credible sources to help gain the trust of their readers. A text is **credible** when it is believable and the author is objective and unbiased. If readers do not trust authors' words, they may simply dismiss the text completely. For example, if an author writes a persuasive essay, he or she is outwardly trying to sway readers' opinions to align with their own, providing readers with the liberty to do what they please with the text. Readers may agree or disagree with the author, which may, in turn, lead them to believe that the author is credible or not credible. Also, readers should keep in mind the source of the text. If readers review a journal about astronomy, would a more reliable source be a NASA employee or a plumber? Overall, text credibility is important

174

when drawing conclusions because readers want reliable sources that support the decisions they have made about the author's ideas.

Integration of Knowledge and Ideas

Understanding Authors' Claims

The goal of most persuasive and informative texts is to make a claim and support it with evidence. A **claim** is a statement made as though it is fact. Many claims are opinions; for example, "stealing is wrong." While this is generally true, it is arguable, meaning it is capable of being challenged. An initial reaction to "stealing is wrong" might be to agree; however, there may be circumstances in which it is warranted. If it is necessary for the survival of an individual or their loved ones (e.g., if they are starving and cannot afford to eat), then this assertion becomes morally ambiguous. While it may still be illegal, whether it is "wrong" is unclear.

When an assertion is made within a text, it is typically reinforced with supporting details as is exemplified in the following passage:

> The extinction of the dinosaurs has been a hot debate amongst scientists since the discovery of fossils in the eighteenth century. Numerous theories were developed in explanation, including extreme climate change, an epidemic of disease, or changes in the atmosphere. It wasn't until the late 1970s that a young geochemist, named Walter Alvarez, noticed significant changes in the soil layers of limestone he was studying in Italy. The layers contained fossilized remains of millions of small organisms within the layer that corresponded with the same period in which the dinosaurs lived. He noticed that the soil layer directly above this layer was suddenly devoid of any trace of these organisms. The soil layer directly above *this* layer was filled with an entirely new species of organisms. It seemed the first species had disappeared at the exact same time as the dinosaurs!

> With the help of his father, Walter Alvarez analyzed the soil layer between the extinct species and the new species and realized this layer was filled with an abnormal amount of *iridium* – a substance that is abundant in meteorites but almost never found on Earth. Unlike other elements in the fossil record, which take a long time to deposit, the iridium had been laid down very abruptly. The layer also contained high levels of soot, enough to account for all of the earth's forests burning to the ground at the same time. This led scientists to create the best-supported theory that the tiny organisms, as well as the dinosaurs and countless other species, had been destroyed by a giant asteroid that had slammed into Earth, raining tons of iridium down on the planet from a giant cosmic cloud.

Supporting Claims

Before beginning to answer questions, readers should summarize each. This will help in locating the supporting evidence. These summaries can be written down or completed mentally; full sentences are not necessary.

Paragraph 1: A layer of limestone shows that a species of organisms disappeared at the same time as the dinosaurs

Paragraph 2: The layer had high amounts of iridium and soot – scientists believe the dinosaurs were destroyed by an asteroid.

Simply by summarizing the text, it has been plainly outlined where there will be answers to relevant questions. Although there are often claims already embedded within an educational text, a claim will most likely be given, but the evidence to support it will need to be located. Take this example question:

> Q: What evidence within the text best supports the theory that the dinosaurs became extinct because of an asteroid?

The claim here is that the <u>dinosaurs went extinct because of an asteroid</u>. Because the text is already outlined in the summaries, it is easy to see that the evidence supporting this theory is in the second paragraph:

> With the help of his father, they analyzed the soil layer between the extinct species and the new species and realized <u>this layer was filled with an abnormal amount of *iridium*</u> – a substance that is <u>abundant is meteorites</u> but almost never found on Earth. Unlike other elements in the fossil record, which takes a long time to deposit, the iridium had been laid down very abruptly. <u>The layer also contained high levels of soot</u>, enough to account for all of the earth's forests burning to the ground at the same time. <u>This led scientists to create the best-supported theory</u> that the tiny organisms, as well as the dinosaurs and countless other species, had been <u>destroyed by a giant asteroid</u> that had slammed into Earth, <u>raining tons of iridium down on the planet</u> from a giant cosmic cloud.

Now that the evidence within the text that best supports the theory has been located, the answer choices can be evaluated:
a. Changes in climate and atmosphere caused an asteroid to crash into Earth.
b. Walter and Luis Alvarez studied limestone with fossilized organisms.
c. A soil layer lacking organisms that existed at the same time as the dinosaurs showed low levels of iridium.
d. A soil layer lacking organisms that existed at the same time as the dinosaurs showed high levels of iridium.

Answer choice (a) is clearly false as there is nothing within the text that claims that climate changes caused an asteroid to crash into Earth.. This kind of answer choice displays an incorrect use of detail. Although the passage may have contained the words "change," "climate," and "atmosphere," these terms were manipulated to form an erroneous answer.

Answer choice (b) is incorrect because while the scientists did study limestone with fossilized organisms, and in doing so they discovered evidence that led to the formation of the theory, this is not the actual evidence itself. This is an example of an out-of-scope answer choice: a true statement that may or may not have been in the passage, but that isn't the whole answer or isn't the point.

Answer choice (c) is incorrect because it is the opposite of the correct answer. Assuming the second paragraph was summarized correctly, it is already known that the soil layer contained *high* levels of iridium, not low levels. Even if the paragraph was not summarized that way, the final sentence states that "tons of iridium rained down on the planet." So, answer choice (c) is false.

Answer choice (d) is correct because it matches the evidence found in the second paragraph.

176

Differentiating Between Facts and Opinions

Fact and Opinion, Biases, and Stereotypes

It is important to distinguish between facts and opinions when reading a piece of writing. When an author presents **facts**, such as statistics or data, readers should be able to check those facts to verify that they are accurate. When authors share their own thoughts and feelings about a subject, they are expressing their **opinions**.

Authors often use words like *think, feel, believe,* or *in my opinion* when expressing an opinion, but these words won't always appear in an opinion piece, especially if it is formally written. An author's opinion may be backed up by facts, which gives it more credibility, but that opinion should not be taken as fact. A critical reader should be wary of an author's opinion, especially if it is only supported by other opinions.

Fact	Opinion
There are nine innings in a game of baseball.	Baseball games run too long.
James Garfield was assassinated on July 2, 1881.	James Garfield was a good president.
McDonald's® has stores in 118 countries.	McDonald's® has the best hamburgers.

Critical readers examine the facts used to support an author's argument. They check the facts against other sources to be sure those facts are correct. They also check the validity of the sources used to be sure those sources are credible, academic, and/or peer-reviewed. When an author uses another person's opinion to support their argument, even if it is an expert's opinion, it is still only an opinion and should not be taken as fact. A strong argument uses valid, measurable facts to support ideas. Even then, the reader may disagree with the argument.

An authoritative argument may use the facts to sway the reader. In the example of global warming, many experts differ in their opinions of which alternative fuels can be used to aid in offsetting it. Because of this, a writer may choose to only use the information and experts' opinions that supports their viewpoint. For example, if the argument is that wind energy is the best solution, the author will use facts that support this idea. That same author may leave out relevant facts on solar energy. The way the author uses facts can influence the reader, so it's important to consider the facts being used, how those facts are being presented, and what information might be left out.

Authors can also demonstrate **bias** if they ignore an opposing viewpoint or present their side in an unbalanced way. A strong argument considers the opposition and finds a way to refute it. Critical readers should look for an unfair or one-sided presentation of the argument and be skeptical, as a bias may be present. Even if this bias is unintentional, if it exists in the writing, the reader should be wary of the validity of the argument.

Readers should also look for the use of stereotypes that refer to specific groups. **Stereotypes** are often negative connotations about a person or place and should always be avoided. When a critical reader finds stereotypes in a piece of writing, he or she should immediately be critical of the argument and consider the validity of anything the author presents. Stereotypes reveal a flaw in the writer's thinking and may suggest a lack of knowledge or understanding about the subject.

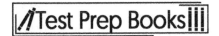

Using Evidence to Make Connections Between Different Texts

When analyzing two or more texts, there are several different aspects that need to be considered, particularly the styles (or the artful way in which the authors use diction to deliver a theme), points of view, and types of argument. In order to do so, one should compare and contrast the following elements between the texts:

- Style: narrative, persuasive, descriptive, informative, etc.
- Tone: sarcastic, angry, somber, humorous, etc.
- Sentence structure: simple (1 clause) compound (2 clauses), complex-compound (3 clauses)
- Punctuation choice: question marks, exclamation points, periods, dashes, etc.
- Point of view: first person, second person, third person
- Paragraph structure: long, short, both, differences between the two
- Organizational structure: compare/contrast, problem/solution, chronological, etc.

The following two passages concern the theme of death and are presented to demonstrate how to evaluate the above elements:

Passage I

Death occurs in several stages. The first stage is the pre-active stage, which occurs a few days to weeks before death, in which the desire to eat and drink decreases, and the person may feel restless, irritable, and anxious. The second stage is the active stage, where the skin begins to cool, breathing becomes difficult as the lungs become congested (known as the "death rattle"), and the person loses control of their bodily fluids.

Once death occurs, there are also two stages. The first is clinical death, when the heart stops pumping blood and breathing ceases. This stage lasts approximately 4-6 minutes, and during this time, it is possible for a victim to be resuscitated via CPR or a defibrillator. After 6 minutes however, the oxygen stores within the brain begin to deplete, and the victim enters biological death. This is the point of no return, as the cells of the brain and vital organs begin to die, a process that is irreversible.

Passage II

It was her sister Josephine who told her, in broken sentences; veiled hints that revealed in half concealing. Her husband's friend Richards was there, too, near her. It was he who had been in the newspaper office when intelligence of the railroad disaster was received, with Brently Mallard's name leading the list of "killed." He had only taken the time to assure himself of its truth by a second telegram, and had hastened to forestall any less careful, less tender friend in bearing the sad message.

She did not hear the story as many women have heard the same, with a paralyzed inability to accept its significance. She wept at once, with sudden, wild abandonment, in her sister's arms. When the storm of grief had spent itself she went away to her room alone. She would have no one follow her.

178

There stood, facing the open window, a comfortable, roomy armchair. Into this she sank, pressed down by a physical exhaustion that haunted her body and seemed to reach into her soul.

Excerpt from "The Story of an Hour" by Kate Chopin

Now, using the outline above, the similarities and differences between the two passages are considered:

1. **Style:** Passage I is an expository style, presenting purely factual evidence on death, completely devoid of emotion. Passage II is a narrative style, where the theme of death is presented to us by the reaction of the loved ones involved. This narrative style is full of emotional language and imagery.

2. **Tone:** Passage I has no emotionally-charged words of any kind, and seems to view death simply as a process that happens, neither welcoming nor fearing it. The tone in this passage, therefore, is neutral. Passage II does not have a neutral tone—it uses words like "disaster," "killed," "sad," "wept," "wild abandonment," and "physical exhaustion," implying an anxiety toward the theme of death.

3. **Sentence Structure:** Passage I contains many complex-compound sentences, which are used to accommodate lots of information. The structure of these sentences contributes to the overall informative nature of the selection. Passage II has several compound sentences and complex sentences on their own. It's also marked by the use of many commas in a single sentence, separating modifying words. Perhaps this variety is meant to match the sporadic emotion of the character's discovery of her husband's death.

4. **Punctuation Choice:** Passage I uses only commas and periods, which adds to the overall neutral tone of the selection. Passage II mostly uses commas and periods, and then one semicolon. Again, the excess of commas and semicolon in the first sentence may be said to mirror the character's anxiety.

5. **Point of View:** Passage I uses third-person point of view, as it avoids any first- or second-person pronouns. Passage II also uses third-person point of view, as the story is being told by a narrator about characters separate from the narrator.

6. **Paragraph Structure:** The first passage is told in an objective way, and each paragraph is focused on the topic brought up in the first sentence. The second passage has no specific topic per paragraph. It is organized in a sequential way, so the paragraphs flow into the next in a chronological order.

7. **Organizational Structure:** The structure of Passage I is told in a very objective, organized way. The first paragraph tells of the stages before death, and the second paragraph tells of the stages after death. The second passage is told in chronological order, as a sequence of events, like in a fictional story.

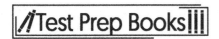

When analyzing the different structures, it may be helpful to make a table and use single words to compare and contrast the texts:

Elements	Passage I	Passage II
Style	Expository	Narrative
Tone	Neutral	Emotional
Sentence Structure	Long	Long/Sporadic
Punctuation Choice	.	. and ,
Point of View	Third	Third
Paragraph Structure	Focused	Sequential
Organizational Structure	Objective/Logical	Chronological

The main differences between the two selections are style, tone, and structure. Possibly the most noticeable difference is the style and tone, as one tone is more neutral, and the other tone is more emotional. This is due to the word choice used and how each passage treats the topic of death. These are only a handful of the endless possible interpretations the reader could make.

Analyzing How Authors Construct Arguments

Constructing Arguments Through Evidence

Using only one form of supporting evidence is not nearly as effective as using a variety to support a claim. Presenting only a list of statistics can be boring to the reader, but providing a true story that's both interesting and humanizing helps. In addition, one example isn't always enough to prove the writer's larger point, so combining it with other examples in the writing is extremely effective. Thus, when reading a passage, readers should not just look for a single form of supporting evidence.

For example, although most people can't argue with the statement, "Seat belts save lives", its impact on the reader is much greater when supported by additional content. The writer can support this idea by:

- Providing statistics on the rate of highway fatalities alongside statistics of estimated seat belt usage.

- Explaining the science behind car accidents and what happens to a passenger who doesn't use a seat belt.

- Offering anecdotal evidence or true stories from reliable sources on how seat belts prevent fatal injuries in car crashes.

Another key aspect of supporting evidence is a **reliable source**. Does the writer include the source of the information? If so, is the source well-known and trustworthy? Is there a potential for bias? For example, a seat belt study done by a seat belt manufacturer may have its own agenda to promote.

Logical Sequence

Even if the writer includes plenty of information to support their point, the writing is only effective when the information is in a logical order. **Logical sequencing** is really just common sense, but it's also an important writing technique. First, the writer should introduce the main idea, whether for a paragraph, a section, or the entire text. Then, they should present evidence to support the main idea by using transitional language. This shows the reader how the information relates to the main idea and to the sentences around it. The writer should then take time to interpret the information, making sure necessary connections are obvious to the reader. Finally, the writer can summarize the information in the closing section.

NOTE: Although most writing follows this pattern, it isn't a set rule. Sometimes writers change the order for effect. For example, the writer can begin with a surprising piece of supporting information to grab the reader's attention, and then transition to the main idea. Thus, if a passage doesn't follow the logical order, readers should not immediately assume it's wrong. However, most writing that has a nontraditional beginning usually settles into a logical sequence.

Evaluating Reasoning and Evidence

Making Generalizations Based on Evidence

One way to make generalizations is to look for main topics. When doing so, pay particular attention to any titles, headlines, or opening statements made by the author. Topic sentences or repetitive ideas can be clues in gleaning inferred ideas. For example, if a passage contains the phrase *While some consider DNA testing to be infallible, it is an inherently flawed technique,* the test taker can infer the rest of the passage will contain information that points to problems with DNA testing.

The test taker may be asked to make a generalization based on prior knowledge but may also be asked to make predictions based on new ideas. For example, the test taker may have no prior knowledge of DNA other than its genetic property to replicate. However, if the reader is given passages on the flaws of DNA testing with enough factual evidence, the test taker may arrive at the inferred conclusion or generalization that the author does not support the infallibility of DNA testing in all identification cases.

When making generalizations, it is important to remember that the critical thinking process involved must be fluid and open to change. While a reader may infer an idea from a main topic, general statement, or other clues, they must be open to receiving new information within a particular passage. New ideas presented by an author may require the test taker to alter a generalization. Similarly, when asked questions that require making an inference, it's important to read the entire test passage and all of the answer options. Often, a test taker will need to refine a generalization based on new ideas that may be presented within the text itself.

Textual evidence helps readers draw a conclusion about a passage. **Textual evidence** refers to information—facts and examples that support the main point; it will likely come from outside sources and can be in the form of quoted or paraphrased material. In order to draw a conclusion from evidence, it's important to examine the credibility and validity of that evidence as well as how (and if) it relates to the main idea.

If an author presents a differing opinion or a **counterargument** in order to refute it, the reader should consider how and why the information is being presented. It is meant to strengthen the original argument and shouldn't be confused with the author's intended conclusion, but it should also be considered in the reader's final evaluation.

181

The Steps of an Argument

Strong arguments tend to follow a fairly defined format. In the introduction, background information regarding the problem is shared, , the implications of the issue are stated, and the author's thesis or claims are given. Supporting evidence is then presented in the body paragraphs, along with the counterargument, which then gets refuted with specific evidence. Lastly, in the conclusion, the author summarizes the points and claims again.

Evidence Used to Support a Claim or Conclusion

Premises are the why, and **conclusions** are the what. Stated differently, premises are the evidence or facts supporting why the conclusion is logical and valid. ACT Reading questions do not require evaluation of the factual accuracy of the arguments; instead, the questions evaluate the test taker's ability to assess an argument's logical strength. For example, John eats all red food. Apples are red. Therefore, John eats apples. This argument is logically sound, despite having no factual basis in reality. Below is an example of a practice argument.

> Julie is an American track athlete. She's the star of the number one collegiate team in the country. Her times are consistently at the top of national rankings. Julie is extremely likely to represent the United States at the upcoming Olympics.

In this example, the conclusion, or the *what*, is that she will likely be on the American Olympic team. The author supports this conclusion with two premises. First, Julie is the star of an elite track team. Second, she runs some of the best times of the country. This is the *why* behind the conclusion. The following builds off this basic argument:

> Julie is an American track athlete. She's the star of the number one collegiate team in the country. Her times are consistently at the top of national rankings. Julie is extremely likely to represent the United States at the upcoming Olympics. Julie will continue to develop after the Olympic trials. She will be a frontrunner for the gold. Julie is likely to become a world-famous track star.

These additions to the argument make the conclusion different. Now, the conclusion is that Julie is likely to become a world-famous track star. The previous conclusion, Julie will likely be on the Olympic team, functions as a **sub-conclusion** in this argument. Like conclusions, premises must adequately support sub-conclusions. However, sub-conclusions function like premises, since sub-conclusions also support the overall conclusion.

Determining Whether Evidence is Relevant and Sufficient

A **hasty generalization** involves an argument relying on insufficient statistical data or inaccurately generalizing. One common generalization occurs when a group of individuals under observation have some quality or attribute that is asserted to be universal or true for a much larger number of people than actually documented. Here's an example of a hasty generalization:

> A man smokes a lot of cigarettes, but so did his grandfather. The grandfather smoked nearly two packs per day since his World War II service until he died at ninety years of age. Continuing to smoke cigarettes will clearly not impact the grandson's long-term health.

This argument is a hasty generalization because it assumes that one person's addiction and lack of consequences will naturally be reflected in a different individual. There is no reasonable justification for such extrapolation. It is common knowledge that any smoking is detrimental to everyone's health. The

182

fact that the man's grandfather smoked two packs per day and lived a long life has no logical connection with the grandson engaging in similar behavior. The hasty generalization doesn't take into account other reasons behind the grandfather's longevity. Nor does the author offer evidence that might support the idea that the man would share a similar lifetime if he smokes. It might be different if the author stated that the man's family shares some genetic trait rendering them immune to the effects of tar and chemicals on the lungs. If this were in the argument, we would assume it as truth and find the generalization to be valid rather than hasty. Of course, this is not the case in our example.

Determining Whether a Statement Is or Is Not Supported

The basic tenet of reading comprehension is the ability to read and understand a text. One way to understand a text is to look for information that supports the author's main idea, topic, or position statement. This information may be factual, or it may be based on the author's opinion. This section will focus on the test taker's ability to identify factual information, as opposed to opinionated bias. The ACT will ask test takers to read passages containing factual information, and then logically relate those passages by drawing conclusions based on evidence.

In order to identify factual information within one or more text passages, begin by looking for statements of fact. Factual statements can be either true or false. Identifying factual statements as opposed to opinion statements is important in demonstrating full command of evidence in reading. For example, the statement *The temperature outside was unbearably hot* may seem like a fact; however, it's not. While anyone can point to a temperature gauge as factual evidence, the statement itself reflects only an opinion. Some people may find the temperature unbearably hot. Others may find it comfortably warm. Thus, the sentence, *The temperature outside was unbearably hot,* reflects the opinion of the author who found it unbearable. If the text passage followed up the sentence with atmospheric conditions indicating heat indices above 140 degrees Fahrenheit, then the reader knows there is factual information that supports the author's assertion of *unbearably hot*.

In looking for information that can be proven or disproven, it's helpful to scan for dates, numbers, timelines, equations, statistics, and other similar data within any given text passage. These types of indicators will point to proven particulars. For example, the statement, *The temperature outside was unbearably hot on that summer day, July 10, 1913,* most likely indicates factual information, even if the reader is unaware that this is the hottest day on record in the United States. Be careful when reading biased words from an author. Biased words indicate opinion, as opposed to fact.

The following list contains a sampling of common biased words:

- Good/bad
- Great/greatest
- Better/best/worst
- Amazing
- Terrible/bad/awful
- Beautiful/handsome/ugly
- More/most
- Exciting/dull/boring
- Favorite
- Very
- Probably/should/seem/possibly

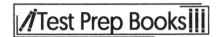

Remember, most of what is written is actually opinion or carefully worded information that seems like fact when it isn't. To say, *duplicating DNA results is not cost-effective* sounds like it could be a scientific fact, but it isn't. Factual information can be verified through independent sources.

The simplest type of test question may provide a text passage, then ask the test taker to distinguish the correct factual supporting statement that best answers the corresponding question on the test. However, be aware that most questions may ask the test taker to read more than one text passage and identify which answer best supports an author's topic. While the ability to identify factual information is critical, these types of questions require the test taker to identify chunks of details, and then relate them to one another.

Assessing Whether an Argument is Valid

Although different from conditions and If/Then Statements, **reasonableness** is another important foundational concept. Evaluating an argument for reasonableness and validity entails evaluating the evidence presented by the author to justify their conclusions. Everything contained in the argument should be considered, but remember to ignore outside biases, judgments, and knowledge. For the purposes of this test, the test taker is a one-person jury at a criminal trial using a standard of reasonableness under the circumstances presented by the argument.

These arguments are encountered on a daily basis through social media, entertainment, and cable news. An example is:

> Although many believe it to be a natural occurrence, some believe that the red tide that occurs in Florida each year may actually be a result of human sewage and agricultural runoff. However, it is arguable that both natural and human factors contribute to this annual phenomenon. On one hand, the red tide has been occurring every year since the time of explorers like Cabeza de Vaca in the 1500's. On the other hand, the red tide seems to be getting worse each year, and scientists from the Florida Fish & Wildlife Conservation say the bacteria found inside the tide feed off of nutrients found in fertilizer runoff.

The author's conclusion is that both natural phenomena and human activity contribute to the red tide that happens annually in Florida. The author backs this information up by historical data to prove the natural occurrence of the red tide, and then again with scientific data to back up the human contribution to the red tide. Both of these statements are examples of the premises in the argument. Evaluating the strength of the logical connection between the premises and conclusion is how reasonableness is determined. Another example is:

> The local railroad is a disaster. Tickets are exorbitantly priced, bathrooms leak, and the floor is sticky.

The author is clearly unhappy with the railroad service. They cite three examples of why they believe the railroad to be a disaster. An argument more familiar to everyday life is:

> Alexandra said the movie she just saw was amazing. We should go see it tonight.

Although not immediately apparent, this is an argument. The author is making the argument that they should go see the movie. This conclusion is based on the premise that Alexandra said the movie was amazing. There's an inferred note that Alexandra is knowledgeable on the subject, and she's credible

enough to prompt her friends to go see the movie. This seems like a reasonable argument. A less reasonable argument is:

> Alexandra is a film student, and she's written the perfect romantic comedy script. We should put our life savings toward its production as an investment in our future.

The author's conclusion is that they should invest their life savings into the production of a movie, and it is justified by referencing Alexandra's credibility and current work. However, the premises are entirely too weak to support the conclusion. Alexandra is only a film *student*, and the script is seemingly her first work. This is not enough evidence to justify investing one's life savings in the film's success.

Assumptions in an Argument

Think of assumptions as unwritten premises. Although they never explicitly appear in the argument, the author is relying on it to defend the argument, just like a premise. Assumptions are the most important part of an argument that will never appear in an argument.

An argument in the abstract is: The author concludes Z based on W and X premises. But the W and X premises actually depend on the unmentioned assumption of Y. Therefore, the author is really saying that X, W, and Y make Z correct, but Y is assumed.

People assume all of the time. Assumptions and inferences allow the human mind to process the constant flow of information. Many assumptions underlie even the most basic arguments. However, in the world of Legal Reasoning arguments, assumptions must be avoided. An argument must be fully presented to be valid; relying on an assumption is considered weak. The test requires that test takers identify these underlying assumptions. One example is:

> Peyton Manning is the most over-rated quarterback of all time. He lost more big games than anyone else. Plus, he allegedly assaulted his female trainer in college. Peyton clearly shouldn't make the Hall of Fame.

The author certainly relies on a lot of assumptions. A few assumptions are:

- Peyton Manning plays quarterback.

- He is considered to be a great quarterback by at least some people.

- He played in many big games.

- Allegations and past settlements without any admission of guilt from over a decade ago can be relied upon as evidence against Hall of Fame acceptance.

- The Hall of Fame voters factor in off-the-field incidents, even if true.

- The best players should make the Hall of Fame.

- Losing big games negates, at least in part, the achievement of making it to those big games

- Peyton Manning is retired, and people will vote on whether he makes the Hall of Fame at some point in the future.

The author is relying on all of these assumptions. Some are clearly more important to his argument than others. In fact, disproving a necessary assumption can destroy a premise and possibly an entire conclusion. For example, what if the Hall of Fame did not factor in any of the off-the-field incidents? Then the alleged assault no longer factors into the argument. Even worse, what if making the big games actually was more important than losing those games in the eyes of the Hall of Fame voters? Then the whole conclusion falls apart and is no longer justified if that premise is disproven.

Assumption questions test this exact point by asking the test taker to identify which assumption the argument relies upon. If the author is making numerous assumptions, then the most important assumption must be chosen.

If the author truly relies on an assumption, then the argument will completely fall apart if the assumption isn't true. **Negating** a necessary assumption will *always* make the argument fall apart. This is a universal rule of logic and should be the first thing done in testing answer choices.

Here are some ways that underlying assumptions will appear as questions:

- Which of the following is a hidden assumption that the author makes to advance his argument?
- Which assumption, if true, would support the argument's conclusion (make it more logical)?
- The strength of the argument depends on which of the following?
- Upon which of the following assumptions does the author rely?
- Which assumption does the argument presuppose?

An example is:

> Frank Underwood is a terrible president. The man is a typical spend, spend, spend liberal. His employment program would exponentially increase the annual deficit and pile on the national debt. Not to mention, Underwood is also on the verge of starting a war with Russia.

Upon which of the following assumptions does the author's argument most rely?
a. Frank Underwood is a terrible president.
b. The United States cannot afford Frank Underwood's policy plans without spending more than the country raises in revenue.
c. No spend, spend, spend liberal has ever succeeded as president.
d. Starting a war with Russia is beneficial to the United States.

Use the negation rule to find the correct answer in the choices below.

Choice *A* is not an assumption—it is the author's conclusion. This type of restatement will never be the correct answer, but test it anyway. After negating the choice, what remains is: *Frank Underwood is a fantastic president*. Does this make the argument fall apart? No, it just becomes the new conclusion. The argument is certainly worse since it does not seem reasonable for someone to praise a president for being a spend, spend, spend liberal or raising the national debt; however, the argument still makes *logical* sense. Eliminate this choice.

Choice *B* is certainly an assumption. It underlies the premises that the country cannot afford Underwood's economic plans. When reversed to: *The United States can afford Frank Underwood's policy plans without spending more than the country raises in revenue,* this destroys the argument. If the United States can afford his plans, then the annual deficit and national debt won't increase; therefore, Underwood being a terrible president would only be based on the final premise. The argument is much

186

weaker without the two sentences involving the financials. Keep it as a benchmark while working through the remaining choices.

Choice *C* is irrelevant. The author is not necessarily claiming that all loose-pocket liberals make for bad presidents. His argument specifically pertains to Underwood. Negate it— *Some spend, spend, spend liberals have succeeded as president.* This does not destroy the argument. Some other candidate could have succeeded as president. However, the author is pointing out that those policies would be disastrous considering the rising budget and debt. The author is not making an appeal to historical precedent. Although not a terrible choice, it is certainly weaker than Choice *B.* Eliminate this choice.

Choice *D* is definitely not an assumption made by the author. The author is assuming that a war with Russia is disastrous. Negate it anyway—*Starting a war with Russia is not beneficial for the United States.* This does not destroy the argument; it makes it stronger. Eliminate this choice.

Analyzing Two Arguments and Evaluating the Types of Evidence Used to Support Each Claim

Arguments use evidence and reasoning to support a position or prove a point. Claims are typically controversial and may be faced with some degree of contention. Thus, authors support claims with evidence. Two arguments might present different types of evidence that readers will need to evaluate for merit, worthiness, accuracy, relevance, and impact. Evidence can take on many forms such as numbers (statistics, measurements, numerical data, etc.), expert opinions or quotes, testimonies, anecdotal evidence or stories from individuals, and textual evidence, such as that obtained from documents like diaries, newspapers, and laws.

Practice Quiz

Questions 1-5 are based upon the following passage:

My gentleness and good behaviour had gained so far on the emperor and his court, and indeed upon the army and people in general, that I began to conceive hopes of getting my liberty in a short time. I took all possible methods to cultivate this favourable disposition. The natives came, by degrees, to be less apprehensive of any danger from me. I would sometimes lie down, and let five or six of them dance on my hand; and at last the boys and girls would venture to come and play at hide-and-seek in my hair. I had now made a good progress in understanding and speaking the language. The emperor had a mind one day to entertain me with several of the country shows, wherein they exceed all nations I have known, both for dexterity and magnificence. I was diverted with none so much as that of the rope-dancers, performed upon a slender white thread, extended about two feet, and twelve inches from the ground. Upon which I shall desire liberty, with the reader's patience, to enlarge a little.

This diversion is only practised by those persons who are candidates for great employments, and high favour at court. They are trained in this art from their youth, and are not always of noble birth, or liberal education. When a great office is vacant, either by death or disgrace (which often happens,) five or six of those candidates petition the emperor to entertain his majesty and the court with a dance on the rope; and whoever jumps the highest, without falling, succeeds in the office. Very often the chief ministers themselves are commanded to show their skill, and to convince the emperor that they have not lost their faculty. Flimnap, the treasurer, is allowed to cut a caper on the straight rope, at least an inch higher than any other lord in the whole empire. I have seen him do the summerset several times together, upon a trencher fixed on a rope which is no thicker than a common packthread in England. My friend Reldresal, principal secretary for private affairs, is, in my opinion, if I am not partial, the second after the treasurer; the rest of the great officers are much upon a par.

Excerpt from an adaptation of Jonathan Swift's Gulliver's Travels into Several Remote Nations of the World.

1. Which of the following statements best summarizes the central purpose of this text?
   a. Gulliver details his fondness for the archaic yet interesting practices of his captors.
   b. Gulliver conjectures about the intentions of the aristocratic sector of society.
   c. Gulliver becomes acquainted with the people and practices of his new surroundings.
   d. Gulliver's differences cause him to become penitent around new acquaintances.

2. What is the word *principal* referring to in the following text?
   My friend Reldresal, principal secretary for private affairs, is, in my opinion, if I am not partial, the second after the treasurer; the rest of the great officers are much upon a par.

   a. Primary or chief
   b. An acolyte
   c. An individual who provides nurturing
   d. One in a subordinate position

188

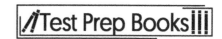

3. What can the reader infer from this passage?

> I would sometimes lie down, and let five or six of them dance on my hand; and at last the boys and girls would venture to come and play at hide-and-seek in my hair.

a. The children tortured Gulliver.
b. Gulliver traveled because he wanted to meet new people.
c. Gulliver is considerably larger than the children who are playing around him.
d. Gulliver has a genuine love and enthusiasm for people of all sizes.

4. What is the significance of the word *mind* in the following passage?

> The emperor had a mind one day to entertain me with several of the country shows, wherein they exceed all nations I have known, both for dexterity and magnificence.

a. The ability to think
b. A collective vote
c. A definitive decision
d. A mythological question

5. Which of the following assertions does NOT support the fact that games are a commonplace event in this culture?

a. My gentleness and good behavior . . . short time.
b. They are trained in this art from their youth . . . liberal education.
c. Very often the chief ministers themselves are commanded to show their skill . . . not lost their faculty.
d. Flimnap, the treasurer, is allowed to cut a caper on the straight rope . . . higher than any other lord in the whole empire.

See answers on next page.

Answer Explanations

1. C: Gulliver becomes acquainted with the people and practices of his new surroundings. Choice *C* is the correct answer because it most extensively summarizes the entire passage. While Choices *A* and *B* are reasonable possibilities, they reference portions of Gulliver's experiences, not the whole. Choice *D* is incorrect because Gulliver doesn't express repentance or sorrow in this particular passage.

2. A: Principal refers to *chief* or *primary* within the context of this text. Choice *A* is the answer that most closely aligns with this definition. Choices *B* and *D* make reference to a helper or followers while Choice *C* doesn't meet the description of Reldresal from the passage.

3. C: One can reasonably infer that Gulliver is considerably larger than the children who were playing around him because multiple children could fit into his hand. Choice *A* is incorrect because there is no indication of stress in Gulliver's tone. Choices *B* and *D* aren't the best answers because though Gulliver seems fond of his new acquaintances, he didn't travel there with the intentions of meeting new people or to express a definite love for them in this particular portion of the text.

4. C: The emperor made a *definitive decision* to expose Gulliver to their native customs. In this instance, the word *mind* was not related to a vote, question, or cognitive ability.

5. A: Choice *A* is correct. This assertion does *not* support the fact that games are a commonplace event in this culture because it mentions conduct, not games. Choices *B*, *C*, and *D* are incorrect because these do support the fact that games were a commonplace event.

ACT Science Test

Interpretation of Data

Manipulating and Analyzing Scientific Data Presented in Scientific Tables, Graphs, and Diagrams

Observations made during a scientific experiment are organized and presented as data. Data can be collected in a variety of ways, depending on the purpose of the experiment. In testing how light exposure affects plant growth, for example, the data collected would be changes in the height of the plant relative to the amount of light it received. The easiest way to organize collected data is to use a **data table**.

A data table always contains a title that relates the two variables in the experiment. Each column or row must contain the units of measurement in the heading only. See the below example (note: this is not actual data).

Plant Growth During Time Exposed to Light (130 Watts)	
Time (Hours)	Height (cm)
0	3.2
192	5.0
480	7.9
720	12.1

Data must be presented in a concise, coherent way. Most data are presented in graph form. The fundamental rule for creating a graph based on data is that the independent variable (i.e., amount of time exposed to light) is on the x-axis, and the dependent variable (i.e., height of plant) is on the y-axis.

There are many types of graphs that a person may choose to use depending on which best represents the data. Bar graphs, line graphs, scatterplots, and pie charts are among some of the most common graphics; these, and others, will be discussed in a subsequent section.

Recognizing Trends in Data

The most common relationship examined in an experiment is between two variables (independent and dependent), most often referred to as x and y. The independent variable (x) is displayed on the horizontal axis of a coordinate plane, and the dependent variable (y) is displayed on the vertical axis. The placement of the variables in this way provides a visual representation of what happens to y when x is manipulated. In analyzing trends, x is used to predict y, and since y is the result of x, then x comes before y in time. For example, in the experiment on plant growth, the hours the plant was exposed to light had to happen before growth could occur.

When analyzing the relationship between the variables, scientists will consider the following questions:

- Does y increase or decrease with x, or does it do both?

- If it increases or decreases, how fast does it change?

- Does y stay steady through certain values of x, or does it jump dramatically from one value to the other?

- Is there a strong relationship? If given a value of x, can one predict what will happen to y?

If, in general, y increases as x increases, or y decreases and x decreases, it is known as a **positive correlation**. The data from the plant experiment show a positive correlation—as time exposed to light (x) increases, plant growth (y) increases. If the variables trend in the opposite direction of each other—that is, if y increases as x decreases, or vice versa—it is called a **negative correlation**. If there doesn't seem to be any visible pattern to the relationship, it is referred to as **no** or **zero correlation**.

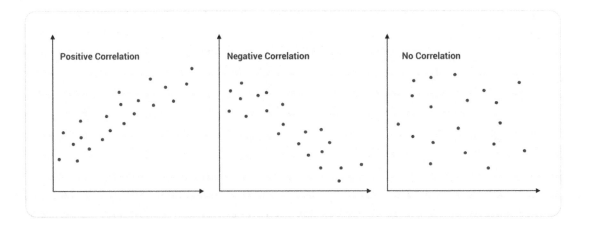

Experiments that show positive or negative correlation within their data indicate that the variables are related. This allows scientists to make predictions based on the data.

Estimating Data Points

Regression lines can be used to estimate data points not already given. For example, if an equation of a line is found that fit the temperature and beach visitor data set, its input is the average daily temperature and its output is the projected number of visitors. Thus, the number of beach visitors on a 100-degree day can be estimated. The output is a data point on the regression line, and the number of daily visitors is expected to be greater than on a 96-degree day because the regression line has a positive slope.

Interpreting the Regression Line

The formula for a regression line is $y = mx + b$, where m is the slope and b is the y-intercept. Both the slope and y-intercept are found in the **Method of Least Squares**, which is the process of finding the equation of the line through minimizing residuals. The slope represents the rate of change in y as x gets larger. Therefore, because y is the dependent variable, the slope actually provides the predicted values given the independent variable. The y-intercept is the predicted value for when the independent variable equals zero. In the temperature example, the y-intercept is the expected number of beach visitors for a very cold average daily temperature of zero degrees.

192

Correlation Coefficient

The **correlation coefficient** (r) measures the association between two variables. Its value is between -1 and 1, where -1 represents a perfect negative linear relationship, 0 represents no relationship, and 1 represents a perfect positive linear relationship. A **negative linear relationship** means that as x-values increase, y-values decrease. A **positive linear relationship** means that as x-values increase, y-values increase. The formula for computing the correlation coefficient is:

$$r = \frac{n(\sum xy) - (\sum x)(\sum y)}{\sqrt{n(\sum x^2) - (\sum x)^2}\sqrt{n(\sum y^2) - (\Sigma y)^2}}$$

n is the number of data points.

Both Microsoft Excel® and a graphing calculator can evaluate this easily once the data points are entered. A correlation greater than 0.8 or less than -0.8 is classified as "strong" while a correlation between -0.5 and 0.5 is classified as "weak."

Correlation Versus Causation

Correlation and causation have two different meanings. If two values are correlated, there is an association between them. However, correlation doesn't necessarily mean that one variable causes the other. **Causation** (or "cause and effect") occurs when one variable causes the other. Average daily temperature and number of beachgoers are correlated and have causation. If the temperature increases, the change in weather causes more people to go to the beach. However, alcoholism and smoking are correlated but don't have causation. The more someone drinks the more likely they are to smoke, but drinking alcohol doesn't cause someone to smoke.

Translating Tabular Data into Graphs

Tables provide an informative, organized way to look at the data that is collected from a scientific experiment. They contain every piece of data that is collected and organize it into categories. Graphs are useful tools for translating data presented in tables into a more visual presentation so that trends and results can be seen more readily. Depending on the type of data being collected, different types of graphs should be constructed.

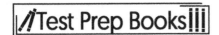
Pie charts show relative parts of a whole group. For example, if you wanted to observe the breakdown, or proportion, of different eye colors in a classroom, you could make a table to record the data, count the number of people with each eye color, enter the data in the table, and then create a pie chart.

Eye color	Number of students
Blue	5
Green	8
Brown	12
Total	*25*

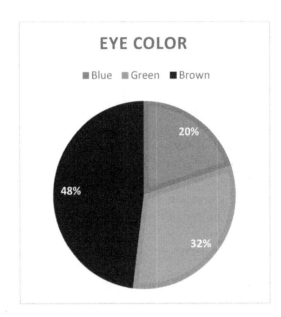

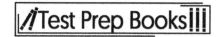

Bar graphs are useful for comparing different items in a related category, where only one variable is changing and being recorded. For example, the amount of interleukin-1β (IL-1β) that is secreted from cultured cells at a certain time point is recorded with different treatments.

	Cells alone	Cells+1 ng/ml dexamethasone	Cells+10 ng/ml dexamethasone
IL-1β (ng/ml)	35	15	5

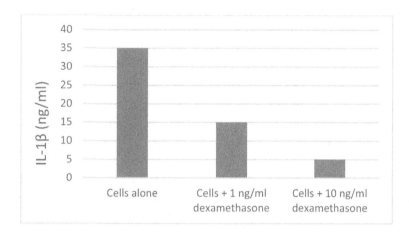

Line graphs are useful for showing changes over time or for a data set that has two changing variables. For example, Scientist A wants to see if a chemical reaction is exothermic, or releases heat, and takes the temperature of her solution every 15 minutes for two hours.

Time (min)	Temperature (°C)
0	22
15	22
30	25
45	30
60	37
75	37
90	35
105	33
120	31

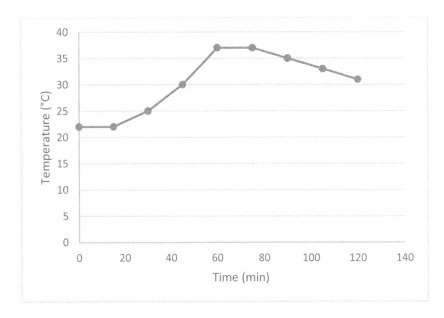

When turning tabular data into any type of graph, the variables must be translated over to the axes of the graph and then the scale of the graph is set. For example, for the line graph above dealing with temperature, the time was set as the *x* variable and the temperature was set as the *y* variable. For temperature, each major gridline was designated as a 5-degree increment. After that, data points from the table were plotted one at a time and then connected to help visualize the results.

Interpolating and Extrapolating

When collecting scientific data, it is often impossible to collect every single data point of interest. Therefore, scientists need to make reasonable, educated guesses to determine the values of the untested data points. For values that fall between the collected data, they use **interpolation**, and for values that fall outside of the collected data, they use **extrapolation**. When the data that is collected is plotted on a graph, the points can be connected using a mathematical and statistical method called **curve fitting**. Curve fitting uses the known data points to construct a curve that fits the trend of the

196

values. Using the continuous points of this curve, missing data points can be interpolated or extrapolated.

For example, Scientist A wants to determine how rapidly her test cells are doubling in number. She can count them every two hours while she is in the lab but will not be able to count them overnight. She can create a graph with points for every two hours that she counts them and can fit a curve to interpolate the number of cells between the two-hour readings and the longer overnight period. She can also extend the curve to extrapolate how many cells she would have after another day.

Time (hrs.)	Number of cells (10^3)
0	1
2	1.25
4	2
6	3
16	16
18	24
20	32
22	48
24	64

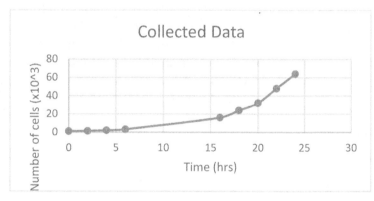

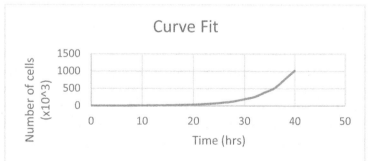

She can interpolate that there were approximately 10×10^3 cells after 13 hours. She can extrapolate that after 30 hours, there were 200×10^3 cells, since it appeared that the number of cells doubled every four hours.

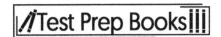

Reasoning Mathematically

Two types of mathematical reasoning that are often used to interpret scientific data are deductive and inductive reasoning. Deductive reasoning starts with a hypothesis, follows steps, and uses specific observations to draw a logical conclusion. The scientific method is an example of deductive reasoning because it starts with a hypothesis and then uses many observations and experimenting to draw a conclusion about the hypothesis. In deductive reasoning, a general premise is proposed, a second premise is made, and then an inference is made about the theory. For example, Sarah reads that when red blood cells are moon-shaped instead of flat and round, the person can have an iron deficiency in their blood. She analyzes a blood sample and finds that Patient A has lower iron levels than normal. She concludes that Patient A has moon-shaped red blood cells.

Inductive reasoning makes general conclusions based on specific observations. A specific set of data is collected and then a conclusion is drawn about the greater, general population. For example, Bill pulls three coins out of a bag. All three coins are quarters. He then induces that the entire bag contains only quarters.

Scientific Investigation

Experimental Tools, Procedures, and Design

Designing a Science Investigation

Human beings are, by nature, very curious. Since long before the scientific method was established, people have been making and predicting outcomes, manipulating the physical world to create extraordinary things—from the first man-made fire in 6000 B.C.E. to the satellite that orbited Pluto in 2016. Although the history of the scientific method is sporadic and attributed to many different people, it remains the most reliable way to obtain and utilize knowledge about the observable universe. Designing a science investigation is based on the scientific method, which consists of the following steps:

- Make an observation
- Create a question
- Form a hypothesis
- Conduct an experiment
- Collect and analyze data
- Form a conclusion

The first step is to identify a problem based on an observation—the who, what, when, where, why, and how. An **observation** is the analysis of information using basic human senses: sight, sound, touch, taste, and smell. Observations can be two different types—qualitative or quantitative. A **qualitative observation** describes what is being observed, such as the color of a house or the smell of a flower. **Quantitative observations** measure what is being observed, such as the number of windows on a house or the intensity of a flower's smell on a scale of 1–5.

Observations lead to the identification of a problem, also called an **inference**. For example, if a fire truck is barreling down a busy street, the inferences could be:

- There's a fire.
- Someone is hurt.

198

- Some kid pulled the fire alarm at a local school.

Inferences are logical predictions based on experience or education that lead to the formation of a hypothesis.

Forming and Testing a Hypothesis

A hypothesis is a testable explanation of an observed scenario and is presented in the form of a statement. It's an attempt to answer a question based on an observation, and it allows a scientist to predict an outcome. A hypothesis makes assumptions on the relationship between two different variables, and answers the question: "If I do this, what happens to that?"

In order to form a hypothesis, there must be an independent variable and a dependent variable that can be measured. The **independent variable** is the variable that is manipulated, and the **dependent variable** is the result of the change.

For example, suppose a student wants to know how light affects plant growth. Based upon what he or she already knows, the student proposes (hypothesizes) that the more light to which a plant is exposed, the faster it will grow.

- Observation: Plants exposed to lots of light seem to grow taller.
- Question: Will plants grow faster if there's more light available?
- Hypothesis: The more light the plant has, the faster it will grow.
- Independent variable: The amount of time exposed to light (able to be manipulated)
- Dependent variable: Plant growth (the result of the manipulation)

Once a hypothesis has been formed, it must be tested to determine whether it's true or false. (How to test a hypothesis is described in a subsequent section.) After it has been tested and validated as true over and over, then a hypothesis can develop into a theory, model, or law.

Experimental Design

To test a hypothesis, one must conduct a carefully designed experiment. There are four basic requirements that must be present for an experiment to be valid:

- A control
- Variables
- A constant
- Repeated and collected data

The control is a standard to which the resultant findings are compared. It's the baseline measurement that allows for scientists to determine whether the results are positive or negative. For the example of light affecting plant growth, the control may be a plant that receives no light at all.

The independent variable is manipulated (a good way to remember this is I manipulate the Independent variable), and the dependent variable is the result of changes to the independent variable. In the plant example, the independent variable is the amount of time exposed to light, and the dependent variable is the resulting growth (or lack thereof) of the plant. For this experiment, there may be three plants—one that receives a minimal amount of light, the control, and one that receives a lot of light.

Finally, there must be constants in an experiment. A constant is an element of the experiment that remains unchanged. Constants are extremely important in minimizing inconsistencies within the experiment that may lead to results outside the parameters of the hypothesis. For example, some constants in the above case are that all plants receive the same amount of water, all plants are potted in the same kind of soil, the species of the plant used in each condition is the same, and the plants are stored at the same temperature. If, for instance, the plants received different amounts of water as well as light, it would be impossible to tell whether the plants responded to changes in water or light.

Once the experiment begins, a disciplined scientist must always record the observations in meticulous detail, usually in a journal. A good journal includes dates, times, and exact values of both variables and constants. Upon reading this journal, a different scientist should be able to clearly understand the experiment and recreate it exactly. The journal includes all collected data, or any observed changes. In this case, the data is rates of plant growth, as well as any other phenomena that occurred as a result of the experiment. A well-designed experiment also includes repetition in order to get the most accurate possible readings and to account for any errors, so several trials may be conducted.

Even in the presence of diligent constants, there are an infinite number of reasons that an experiment can (and will) go wrong, known as sources of error. All experimental results are inherently accepted as imperfect, if ever so slightly, because experiments are conducted by human beings, and no instrument can measure anything perfectly. The goal of scientists is to minimize those errors to the best of their ability.

Identifying Controls and Variables

In an experiment, variables are the key to analyzing data, especially when data is in a graph or table. Variables can represent anything, including objects, conditions, events, and amounts of time.

Covariance is a general term referring to how two variables move in relation to each other. Take for example an employee that gets paid by the hour. For them, hours worked and total pay have a positive covariance. As hours worked increases, so does pay.

Constant variables remain unchanged by the scientist across all trials. Because they are held constant for all groups in an experiment, they aren't being measured in the experiment, and they are usually ignored. Constants can either be controlled by the scientist directly like the nutrition, water, and sunlight given to plants, or they can be selected by the scientist specifically for an experiment like using a certain animal species or choosing to investigate only people of a certain age group.

Independent variables are also controlled by the scientist, but they are the same only for each group or trial in the experiment. Each group might be composed of students that all have the same color of car or each trial may be run on different soda brands. The independent variable of an experiment is what is being indirectly tested because it causes change in the dependent variables.

Dependent variables experience change caused by the independent variable and are what is being measured or observed. For example, college acceptance rates could be a dependent variable of an experiment that sorted a large sample of high school students by an independent variable such as test scores. In this experiment, the scientist groups the high school students by the independent variable (test scores) to see how it affects the dependent variable (their college acceptance rates).

Note that most variables can be held constant in one experiment, but also serve as the independent variable or a dependent variable in another. For example, when testing how well a fertilizer aids plant

200

growth, its amount of sunlight should be held constant for each group of plants, but if the experiment is being done to determine the proper amount of sunlight a plant should have, the amount of sunlight is an independent variable because it is necessarily changed for each group of plants.

Comparing, Extending, and Modifying Experiments

Predicting the Results of Additional Trials

Science is amazing in that it actually allows people to predict the future and see into the past with a certain degree of accuracy. Using numerical correlations created from quantitative data, one can see in a general way what will happen to *y* when something happens to *x*.

The best way to get a useful overview of quantitative data to facilitate predictions is to use a scatter plot, which plots each data point individually. As shown above, there may be slight fluctuations from the correlation line, so one may not be able to predict what happens with *every* change, but he or she will be able to have a general idea of what is going to happen to *y* with a change in *x*. To demonstrate, the graph with a line of best fit created from the plant growth experiment is below.

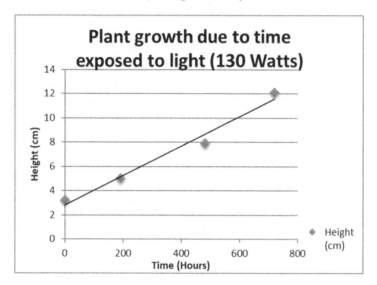

Using the trend line within the data, one can estimate what will happen to plant growth at a given length of time exposed to light. For example, it can be estimated that with 700 hours of time, the plant is expected to grow to a height of about 11 cm. The plant may not grow to exactly 11 cm, but it will likely grow to about that height based on previous data. This process allows scientists to draw conclusions based on data.

Identifying and Improving Hypotheses for Science Investigations

When presented with fundamental, scientific concepts, it is important to read for understanding. The most basic skill in achieving this literacy is to understand the concept of hypothesis and moreover, to be able to identify it in a particular passage. A **hypothesis** is a proposed idea that needs further investigation in order to be proven true or false. While it can be considered an educated guess, a hypothesis goes more in depth in its attempt to explain something that is not currently accepted within scientific theory. It requires further experimentation and data gathering to test its validity and is subject to change, based on scientifically conducted test results. Being able to read a science passage and understand its main purpose, including any hypotheses, helps the test taker understand data-driven

evidence. It helps the test taker to be able to correctly answer questions about the science excerpt they are asked to read.

When reading to identify a hypothesis, a test taker should ask, "What is the passage trying to establish? What is the passage's main idea? What evidence does the passage contain that either supports or refutes this idea?" Asking oneself these questions will help identify a hypothesis. Additionally, hypotheses are logical statements that are testable and use very precise language.

Review the following hypothesis example:

> Consuming excess sugar in the form of beverages has a greater impact on childhood obesity and subsequent weight gain than excessive sugar from food.

While this is likely a true statement, it is still only a conceptual idea in a text passage regarding sugar consumption in childhood obesity, unless the passage also contains tested data that either proves or disproves the statement. A test taker could expect the rest of the passage to cite data proving that children who drink empty calories gain more weight, and are more likely to be obese, than children who eat sugary snacks.

A hypothesis goes further in that, given its ability to be proven or disproven, it may result in further hypotheses that require extended research. For example, the hypothesis regarding sugar consumption in drinks, after undergoing rigorous testing, may lead scientists to state another hypothesis such as the following:

> Consuming excess sugar in the form of beverages as opposed to food items is a habit found in mostly sedentary children.

This new, working hypothesis further focuses not just on the source of an excess of calories, but tries an "educated guess" that empty caloric intake has a direct, subsequent impact on physical behavior.

The data-driven chart below is similar to an illustration a test taker might see in relation to the hypothesis on sugar consumption in children:

Behaviors of Healthy and Unhealthy Kids

[Line chart titled "Behaviors of Healthy and Unhealthy Kids" with y-axis from 0 to 100 and x-axis categories: Exercise daily, Video games daily, Fruits daily, Vegetables daily, Chips daily, Sugar daily. Two lines shown: Healthful and Unhealthful.]

While this guide will address other data-driven passages a test taker could expect to see within a given science excerpt, note that the hypothesis regarding childhood sugar intake and rate of exercise has undergone scientific examination and yielded results that support its truth.

When reading a science passage to determine its hypothesis, a test taker should look for a concept that attempts to explain a phenomenon, is testable, logical, precisely worded, and yields data-driven results. The test taker should scan the presented passage for any word or data-driven clues that will help identify the hypothesis, and then be able to correctly answer test questions regarding the hypothesis based on their critical thinking skills.

Identifying Possible Errors in a Science Investigation and Changing the Design to Correct Them

For a hypothesis to be proven true or false, all experiments are subject to multiple trials in order to verify accuracy and precision. A measurement is **accurate** if the observed value is close to the "true value." For example, if someone measured the pH of water at 6.9, this measurement would be considered accurate (the pH of water is 7). On the other hand, a measurement is **precise** if the measurements are consistent—that is, if they are reproducible. If someone had a series of values for a pH of water that were 6.9, 7.0, 7.2, and 7.3, their measurements would not be precise. However, if all measured values were 6.9, or the average of these values was 6.9 with a small range, then their measurements would be precise. Measurements can fall into the following categories:

- Both accurate and precise
- Accurate but not precise
- Precise but not accurate

203

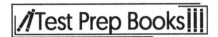

- Neither accurate nor precise

The accuracy and precision of observed values most frequently correspond to the amount of error present in the experiment. Aside from general carelessness, there are two primary types of error: random and systematic. **Random errors** are unpredictable variations in the experiment that occur by chance. They can be difficult to detect, but they can often be nullified using a statistical analysis and minimized by taking repeated measurements and taking an average. **Systematic errors** occur when there are imperfections in the design of the experiment itself—usually errors that affect the accuracy of the measurements. These errors can be minimized by using the most accurate equipment available and by taking proper care of instruments and measuring techniques. Common examples of errors are listed below.

Random	Systematic
Environmental factors (random changes in vibration, temperature, humidity, etc.)	Poorly maintained instruments
	Old or out-of-date instruments
Differences in instrument use among scientists	Faulty calibration of instruments
Errors in judgment—can be affected by state of mind	Reading the instruments at an angle (parallax error) or other faulty reading errors
Incorrectly recorded observations	Not accounting for lag time

The most basic method to account for the possibility of errors is to take an average (also called a **mean**) of all observed values. To do so, one must divide the number of measurements taken from the sum of all measurements.

$$\frac{Sum\ of\ Measurements}{Total\ \#\ of\ Measurements}$$

For the above example of the pH values, the average is calculated by finding the sum of the pH values ascertained and dividing by the number of values recorded.

$$\frac{6.9 + 7.0 + 7.2 + 7.3}{4} = 7.1$$

The more observations recorded, the greater the precision. It's important to first assess the accuracy of measurements before proceeding to collect multiple trials of data. If a particular trial results in measurements that are vastly different from the average, it may indicate that a random or systematic error occurred during the trial. When this happens, a scientist might decide to "throw out" the trial and run the experiment again.

Identifying the Strengths and Weaknesses of Different Types of Science Investigations

In order to address the strengths and weaknesses of different types of scientific investigations, ACT test takers must first strengthen their capacity for scientific literacy and numeracy. It is important to familiarize oneself with methods for decoding highly specialized scientific terms, formulas, and symbols. Additionally, test takers can take the following suggestions to help identify unique weaknesses and strengths in different types of scientific investigations:

- Using critical analysis, test takers begin asking questions about the accuracy of the methods used to collect, analyze, and display data. They should carefully look at text and graphics that show scientific findings.

- Test takers should determine whether or not the words, data, and symbols provided by the author actually offer information that is relevant for testing a hypothesis or making an inference.

- When two or more passages on the same topic are offered, test takers should cross-analyze the findings to determine what data is accurate or relevant and which findings are most objective.

- Although scientific research strives for objectivity, test takers should highlight any subjective biases that may be embedded in a text. In particular, they should be aware of certain historical or ethical biases that might appear.

- Test takers should double check for any computational inaccuracies.

- Test takers should make suggestions for better ways to present the findings in both texts and visual images.

Evaluation of Models, Inferences, and Experimental Results

Judging the Validity of Scientific Information

Valid science information must have sufficient, credible, accurate evidence that fully support the claims and conclusions. Critical readers examine the facts and evidence used to support an author's claim. They check the facts against other sources to be sure those facts are correct. They also check the validity of the sources used to be sure those sources are credible, academic, and/or peer-reviewed. Consider that when an informative science passage uses another person's opinion to support their argument, even if it is an expert's opinion, it is still only an opinion and should not be taken as fact. A trustworthy study or science report uses valid, measurable facts to support ideas. Even then, the reader may disagree with the argument as it may be rooted in their personal beliefs.

An authoritative argument may use the facts to sway the reader. For example, in a paper on global warming, many experts differ in their opinions of what alternative fuels can be used to aid in offsetting it. Because of this, a writer may choose to only use the information and expert opinion that supports their viewpoint.

Students must be able to distinguish between reliable and unreliable sources in order to develop a well-written research report. When choosing print sources, typically published works that have been edited and clearly identify the author or authors are considered credible sources. Peer-reviewed journals and research conducted by scholars are likewise considered to be credible sources of information.

When deciding on what Internet sources to use, it is also a sound practice for researchers to look closely at each website's universal resource locator, the *URL*. Generally speaking, websites with .edu, .gov, or .org as the Top Level Domain are considered reliable, but the researcher must still question any possible political or social bias. Personal blogs, tweets, personal websites, online forums, and any site that clearly demonstrates bias, strong opinions, or persuasive language are considered unreliable sources.

Science is often a process of checks and balances, and ACT students are expected to carry out this process of checks and balances as they analyze and compare information that differs between various science sources. Science demands a high degree of communication, which, in turn, demands a high degree of scientific literacy and numeracy. ACT students must be prepared to analyze the different data

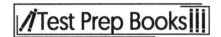

and written conclusions of various texts. Contrary to popular belief, science is not an authoritarian field—scientific worldviews and inquiries can be wrong. It is more fruitful to think of science as a living library that is shaped by the complex activities carried out by different groups in different places. This living library is filled with ideas that are shaped by various sources and methods of research. The explanations, inferences, and discussions carried out by scientists are filled with facts that may be flawed or biased. Science, like any other field, cannot completely escape bias. Even though science is meant to be objective, its findings can still lend themselves to biases.

Thus, it is important for ACT students to get in the practice of not only making sense of information that differs between various science sources, but also to begin synthesizing this information into a unique worldview. The peer review process is also necessary to ensure checks and balances within the scientific field. The key to making this happen while taking the ACT is to maintain an acute awareness of when and where information or data differs. Pay close attention to the ways in which each scientist uses specific words or data to back their overall conclusions.

Below are some key reasons why data and interpretations can differ:

- Historical bias
- Cultural bias
- Interpretation or personal bias
- Lack of implementation and data collection fidelity
- Different data collection approaches
- Different data collection and data analysis tools
- Weak hypotheses
- Compounding variables
- Failure to recognize certain variables
- User error
- Changes in the environment between two studies
- Computation or statistical errors
- Interpretive blind spots
- Lack of understanding of context or environment

Formulating Conclusions and Predictions Based on Scientific Information

Deciding Whether Conclusions are Supported by Data

Drawing conclusions is the process of analyzing patterns in data and determining whether the relationship is **causal**, meaning that one variable is the cause of the change in the other. There are many correlations that aren't casual, such as a city where alcohol sales increase as crime increases. Although there's a positive correlation between the two, crime may not be the factor that causes an increase in alcohol sales. There could be other factors, such as an increase in unemployment, which increases both alcohol sales and crime rates. Although crime and alcohol sales are positively correlated, they aren't causally correlated.

For this reason, it's important for scientists to carefully design their experiments with all the appropriate constants to ensure that the relationships are causal. If a relationship is determined to be causal by isolating the variables from all other factors, only then can conclusions be drawn based on data. In the plant growth experiment, the conclusion is that light affects plant growth because the data shows they are causally correlated since the two variables were entirely isolated.

Making Conclusions Based on Data

The Science section of the ACT will contain one data-driven science passage that requires the test taker to examine evidence within a particular type of graphic. The test taker will then be required to interpret the data and answer questions demonstrating their ability to draw logical conclusions.

In general, there are two types of data: qualitative and quantitative. Science passages may contain both, but simply put, **quantitative** data is reflected numerically and qualitative is not. **Qualitative** data is based on its qualities. In other words, qualitative data tends to present information more in subjective generalities (for example, relating to size or appearance). Quantitative data is based on numerical findings such as percentages. Quantitative data will be described in numerical terms. While both types of data are valid, the test taker will more likely be faced with having to interpret quantitative data through one or more graphic(s), and then be required to answer questions regarding the numerical data. A test taker should take the time to learn the skills it takes to interpret quantitative data so that they can make sound conclusions.

An example of a line graph is as follows:

Cell Phone Use in Kiteville, 2000-2006

A **line graph** presents quantitative data on both horizontal (side to side) and vertical (up and down) axes. It requires the test taker to examine information across varying data points. When reading a line graph, a test taker should pay attention to any headings, as these indicate a title for the data it contains. In the above example, the test taker can anticipate the line graph contains numerical data regarding the use of cellphones during a certain time period. From there, a test taker should carefully read any outlying words or phrases that will help determine the meaning of data within the horizontal and vertical axes. In this example, the vertical axis displays the total number of people in increments of 5,000. Horizontally, the graph displays yearly markers, and the reader can assume the data presented accounts for a full calendar year. In addition, the line graph also uses different shapes to mark its data points. Some data points represent the number of men. Some data points represent the number of women, and a third type of data point represents the number of both sexes combined.

A test taker may be asked to read and interpret the graph's data, then answer questions about it. For example, the test may ask, *In which year did men seem to decrease cellphone use?* then require the test

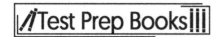
taker to select the correct answer. Similarly, the test taker may encounter a question such as *Which year yielded the highest number of cellphone users overall?* The test taker should be able to identify the correct answer as 2006.

A **bar graph** presents quantitative data through the use of lines or rectangles. The height and length of these lines or rectangles corresponds to the magnitude of the numerical data for that particular category or attribute. The data presented may represent information over time, showing shaded data over time or over other defined parameters. A bar graph will also utilize horizontal and vertical axes.

An example of a bar graph is as follows:

Population Growth in Major U.S. Cities

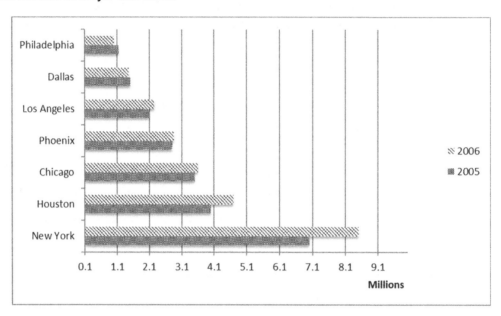

Reading the data in a bar graph is similar to the skills needed to read a line graph. The test taker should read and comprehend all heading information, as well as information provided along the horizontal and vertical axes. Note that the graph pertains to the population of some major U.S. cities. The "values" of these cities can be found along the left side of the graph, along the vertical axis. The population values can be found along the horizontal axes. Notice how the graph uses shaded bars to depict the change in population over time, as the heading indicates. Therefore, when the test taker is asked a question such as, *Which major U.S. city experienced the greatest amount of population growth during the depicted two year cycle,* the reader should be able to determine a correct answer of New York. It is important to pay particular attention to color, length, data points, and both axes, as well as any outlying header information in order to be able to answer graph-like test questions.

A **circle graph** (also sometimes referred to as a **pie chart**) presents quantitative data in the form of a circle. The same principles apply: the test taker should look for numerical data within the confines of the circle itself but also note any outlying information that may be included in a header, footer, or to the side of the circle. A circle graph will not depict horizontal or vertical axis information but will instead rely on the reader's ability to visually take note of segmented circle pieces and apply information accordingly.

An example of a circle graph is as follows:

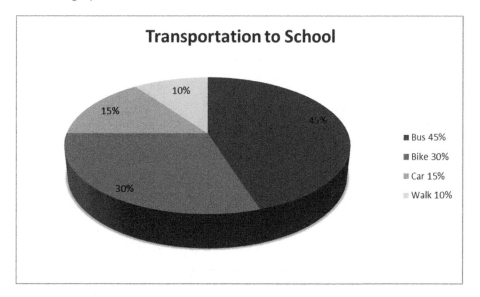

Notice the heading "Transportation to School." This should indicate to the test taker that the topic of the circle graph is how people traditionally get to school. To the right of the graph, the reader should comprehend that the data percentages contained within it directly correspond to the method of transportation. In this graph, the data is represented through the use shades and pattern. Each transportation method has its own shade. For example, if the test taker was then asked, *Which method of school transportation is most widely utilized,* the reader should be able to identify school bus as the correct answer.

Be wary of test questions that ask test takers to draw conclusions based on information that is not present. For example, it is not possible to determine, given the parameters of this circle graph, whether the population presented is of a particular gender or ethnic group. This graph does not represent data from a particular city or school district. It does not distinguish between student grade levels and, although the reader could infer that the typical student must be of driving age if cars are included, this is not necessarily the case. Elementary school students may rely on parents or others to drive them by personal methods. Therefore, do not read too much into data that is not presented. Only rely on the quantitative data that is presented in order to answer questions.

A **scatter plot** or **scatter diagram** is a graph that depicts quantitative data across plotted points. It will involve at least two sets of data.

It will also involve horizontal and vertical axes.

An example of a scatter plot is as follows:

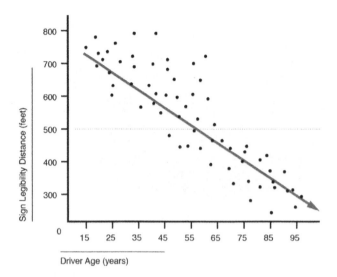

The skills needed to address a scatter plot are essentially the same as in other graph examples. Note any topic headings, as well as horizontal or vertical axis information. In the sample above, the reader can determine the data addresses a driver's ability to correctly and legibly read road signs as related to their age. Again, note the information that is absent. The test taker is not given the data to assess a time period, location, or driver gender. It simply requires the reader to note an approximate age to the ability to correctly identify road signs from a distance measured in feet. Notice that the overall graph also displays a trend. In this case, the data indicates a negative one and possibly supports the hypothesis that as a driver ages, their ability to correctly read a road sign at over 500 feet tends to decline over time. If the test taker were to be asked, *At what approximation in feet does a sixteen-year-old driver correctly see and read a street sign,* the answer would be the option closest to 700 feet.

Reading and examining scientific data in excerpts involves all of a reader's contextual reading, data interpretation, drawing logical conclusions based only on the information presented, and their application of critical thinking skills across a set of interpretive questions. Thorough comprehension and attention to detail is necessary to achieve test success.

Determining Which Explanation for a Scientific Phenomenon is Supported by New Findings

Finding Evidence that Supports a Finding

Science is one of the most objective, straightforward fields of study. Thus, it is no surprise that scientists and science articles are focused on **evidence**. When reading science passages, test takers are sometimes asked to find supporting evidence that reinforces a particular finding. A **finding** in science is a result of the investigation; it is what scientists find out. The majority of science passages tend to avoid opinions; instead, they focus on facts. Although no results are infallible just because the texts are scientific, most results are quantified. Quantified results mean they are expressed in numbers or measurements. Thus, when in doubt, go straight to the data, or numbers, that are offered. Sometimes data is embedded in the text; other times it appears in charts, tables, or graphs. These tools use numbers to demonstrate the

patterns discussed in scientific texts, and they help readers to visualize concrete patterns. In order to find evidence to support a finding in scientific passage, all test takers should try collecting and analyzing the relevant data offered. Regardless of whether the data is coming from the text or a graph, it is helpful when making conclusions.

The following steps are helpful for identifying evidence that supports a finding in a science passage:

- Apply critical analysis and critical thinking by asking the right questions.
- Determine the weight of the information by figuring out its relevance.
- Identify trends in the numbers.
- Make inferences.
- Determine the most appropriate methods for either quantifying or communicating inferences.

Types of Passages and Tips

The ACT science exam tests analytical skills associated with interpreting scientific principles of the natural world. The content may be from biology, the earth sciences, chemistry, or physics. The test presents scientific concepts in the form of passages of three different formats. A total of 40 multiple-choice questions related to the passage are to be completed in 35 minutes.

Test-takers are often surprised to discover that detailed knowledge of science content isn't required to achieve success on the ACT science test. In fact, the test is designed to determine how well an individual is able to analyze, compare, and generalize information. For example, the test doesn't seek to determine if one possesses an extensive knowledge of elephant biology. Instead, the exam might ask one to compare two scientists' differing opinions about elephant communication. In this case, the test taker is *not* required to possess any knowledge about elephants or the manner in which they communicate. All of the information needed to answer the questions will be presented in the passage. The test taker must read the passage, compare the differing hypotheses, analyze the graphical information, and generate conclusions.

Three Types of Passages

Data Representation
Scientific data will be presented in tables, graphs, diagrams, or models. These passages account for 30% to 40% of the ACT Science Test. These passages typically contain 5 or 6 questions designed to test one's ability to interpret scientific data represented in a graphical format instead of written text. These questions do *not* necessarily examine scientific content knowledge (e.g., the equation for photosynthesis); rather, they test students' ability to interpret raw data represented in a table or graph. Therefore, it's possible to do well on this portion of the exam without a detailed understanding of the scientific topic at hand. Questions may ask for factual information, identification of data trends, or graph calculations. For example:

- Based on the attached graph, how did Study 1 differ from Study 2?
- What is the nature of the relationship between Experiment 1 and Experiment 2?
- What is x at the given y-value?

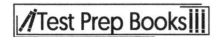

Research summaries

These passages account for 45% to 55% of the ACT Science Test. Passages present the design, implementation, and conclusion of various scientific experiments. These passages typically contain 5 or 6 questions designed to test one's ability to identify the following:

- What question is the experiment trying to answer?
- What is the researcher's predicted answer to the question?
- How did the researchers test the hypotheses?
- Based on data obtained from the experiments, was the prediction correct?
- What would happen if . . .?
- 2 X 2 Matrix questions: "Yes, because . . ." or "No, because . . ."

Conflicting viewpoints

This section will present a disagreement between two scientists about a specific scientific hypothesis or concept. These passages account for 15% to 20% of the ACT Science Test. The opinions of each researcher are presented in two separate passages. There are two formats for these questions. The test taker must demonstrate an understanding of the content or compare and contrast the main differences between the two opinions. For example:

- Based on the data presented by Scientist 1, which of the following is correct?
- What is the main difference between the conclusions of Expert A and Expert B?

Elements of Science Passages

Short answer questions

Short answer questions are usually one to five words long and require the reader to recall basic facts presented in the passage.

An example answer choice: "Research group #1 finished last."

Long answer questions

Long answer questions are composed of one to three sentences that require the reader to make comparisons, summaries, generalizations, or conclusions about the passage.

An example answer choice: "Scientist 2 disagreed with Scientist 1 on the effects of Bisphenol A pollution and its presumed correlation to birth defects in mice and humans. Scientist 2 proposes that current environmental Bisphenol A levels are not sufficient to cause adverse effects on human health."

Fact questions

Fact questions are the most basic type of question on the test. They ask the reader to recall a specific term, definition, number, or meaning.

An example question/answer: "Which of the following organisms was present in fresh water samples from Pond #1?"
   a. Water flea
   b. Dragonfly nymph
   c. Snail
   d. Tadpole

Graphics

There are several different types of graphics used in the ACT Science Test to represent the passage data. There will be at least one of each of the following types included in the test: tables, illustrative diagrams, bar graphs, scatter plots, line graphs, and region graphs. Most ACT Science passages will include two or more of these graphics.

The **illustrative diagram** provides a graphic representation or picture of some process. Questions may address specific details of the process depicted in the graphic. For example, "At which stage of the sliding filament theory of muscle contraction does the physical length of the fibers shorten (and contract)?"

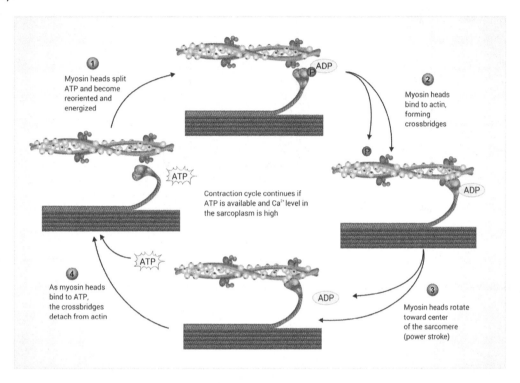

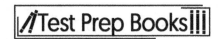

Bar graphs depict the passage data as parallel lines of varying heights. ACT bar graphs will be printed in black and white. Data may be oriented vertically or horizontally. Questions may ask, "During the fall season, in what habitat do bears spend the most time?"

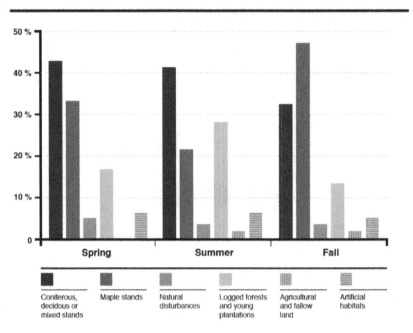

Bar graphs can also be horizontal, like the graph below.

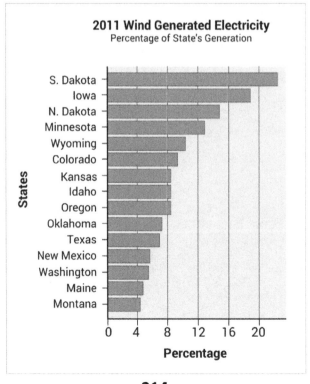

214

Scatter plots provide a visual representation of the passage data along the x- and y-axes. This representation indicates the nature of the relationship between the two variables. It is important to note that correlation doesn't equal causation. The relationship may be linear, curvilinear, positive, negative, inverse, or there may be no relationship. Questions may ask "What is the relationship between x and y?"

Line graphs are scatter plots that compare and contrast the relationships between two or more data sets. The horizontal axis represents the passage data sets that are compared over time. The vertical axis is the scale for measurement of that data. The scale points are equidistant from one another. There will always be a title for the line graph. Questions related to line graphs might ask," Which of the following conclusions is supported by the provided graph of tropical storms?"

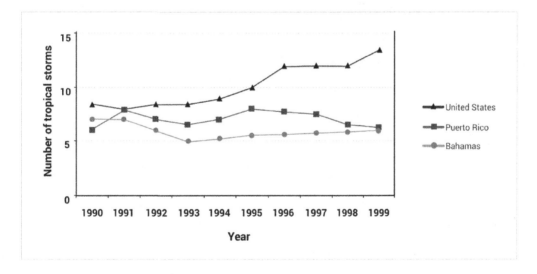

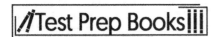
A **region graph** is a visual representation of the passage data set used to display the properties of a given substance under different conditions or at different points in time. Questions relating to this graph may ask, "According to the figure, what is the temperature range associated with liquid nitrogen?"

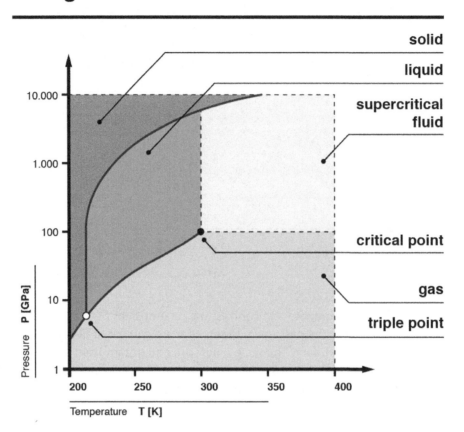

Nitrogen Phases

216

Tables

ACT Science Test tables present passage data sets in tabular form. The **independent variable** is positioned on the left side, while the **dependent variable** is on the right side of the table. The content of ACT Science tables is always discussed in the corresponding passage. Knowledge of all table content isn't required.

Sample Table for Analysis

Data type	Seismic sources							
	Individual faults						Area/volume sources	
	Location	Activity	Length	Dip	Depth	Style	Area	Depth
Geological/Remote Sensing								
Detailed mapping	X	X	X	X		X		
Geomorphic data	X	X	X			X	X	
Quatenary surface rupture	X	X	X			X		
Fault trenching data	X	X		X		X		
Paleoliquefaction data	X	X					X	
Borehole data	X	X		X		X		
Aerial photography	X	X	X					
Low sun-angle photography	X	X	X					
Satellite imagery	X		X				X	
Regional structure	X			X		X	X	
Balanced Cross Section	X			X	X		X	
Geophysical/Geodetic								
Regional potential field data	X		X				X	X
Local potential field data	X		X	X	X	X		
High resolution reflection data	X	X		X		X		
Standard reflexing data	X			X		X		
Deep crustal reflection data	X			X	X		X	X
Tectonic geodetic/strain data	X	X		X	X	X	X	X
Regional stress data						X	X	
Seismological								
Reflected crustal phase data							X	X
Pre-instrumental earthquake data	X	X			X	X	X	
Teleseismic earthquake data							X	
Regional network seismicity data	X	X	X	X	X		X	X
Local network seismicity data	X	X	X	X	X			X
Focal mechanism data				X		X		

Answer Choice Elimination Techniques

The ability to eliminate incorrect answer choices quickly and effectively is one of the most important skills to develop before sitting for the exam. The following tips and strategies are designed to help in this effort.

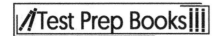

First, test takers should look for answer choices that make absolute "all-or-nothing" statements, as they are usually incorrect answers. Key word clues to incorrect answer choices include: always, never, everyone, no one, all, must, and none. An example of a possible incorrect answer choice is provided below:

"The use of antibiotics should be discontinued indefinitely as they are always over-prescribed."

An example of a possible correct answer choice:

"The use of antibiotics should be closely monitored by physician review boards in order to prevent the rise of drug-resistant bacteria."

Test takers should look for unreasonable, awkward, or irrational answer choices and they should pay special attention to irrelevant information that isn't mentioned in the passage. If the answer choice relates to an idea or position that isn't clearly presented in the passage, it's likely incorrect.

Answer choices that seem too broad or generic and also those that are very narrow or specific are also important to note. For example, if a question relates to a summarization of the passage, test takers should look for answers that encompass a broad representation of the presented ideas, facts, concepts, etc. On the other hand, if a question asks about a specific word, number, data point, etc. the correct answer will likely be more narrow or specific.

Highly Technical Questions

The goal of the ACT Science Test is to measure scientific reasoning skills, not scientific content knowledge. Therefore, candidates shouldn't "cram" for this section using complex scientific concepts from textbooks or online courses. Instead, they should focus on understanding the format of the exam and the manner in which ideas are presented and questions are asked.

Example question about two scientists' conflicting viewpoints:

<u>Scientist 1</u>: Reproductive success in red-tailed hawks has been drastically reduced as a consequence of widespread release of endocrine-disrupting chemicals such as dichloro-diphenyl-trichloroethane (DDT).

<u>Scientist 2</u>: The reproductive fitness of red-tailed hawks is only mildly reduced by the weak effects of DDT, but it is highly sensitive to another class of chemicals called polychlorinated biphenyls (PCBs).

Considering the two viewpoints of the passage, which of the following statements is true?
a. Red-tailed hawks are an endangered species due the effects of over-hunting and the release of toxic chemicals such as DDT and PCBs.
b. PCBs must not be the cause of red-tailed hawk reproductive problems because polychlorinated biphenyls do not affect female reproductive organs.
c. Scientist 2 proposes that PCBs are likely the cause of red-tailed hawk reproductive problems since DDT is only mildly toxic.
d. DDT is a persistent organic pesticide and should be avoided.

Answer A: INCORRECT. This answer is irrational. Neither scientist mentioned anything about hunting or red-tailed hawks being endangered.

Answer B: INCORRECT. This answer is also irrational. Neither scientist proposes that PCBs do not affect female reproductive organs.

Answer C: CORRECT. This answer makes the most sense. It's true that Scientist 2 believes that PCBs cause reproductive problems in red-tailed hawks because DDT is only mildly toxic.

Answer D: INCORRECT. This answer is very narrow and specific. The phrase "persistent organic pesticide" isn't mentioned at all in the passage.

Again, the reader didn't need to know anything about dichloro-diphenyl-trichloroethane, polychlorinated biphenyls, red-tailed hawks, reproductive biology, or endocrine-disrupting chemicals to answer the question correctly. Instead, the test taker must consider both viewpoints and make comparisons or generalizations between the two.

Time Management

Using time efficiently is a critical factor for success on the ACT Science Test. Test takers may find the following strategies to be helpful when preparing for the exam:

- There are 40 questions and only 35 minutes, which leaves about 50 seconds for each question. This may seem daunting; however, it's important to consider that multiple questions apply to a single passage, graph, etc. Therefore, it may be possible to answer some in less than 50 seconds, leaving extra time for more demanding questions.
- It's important to read the entire passage before answering the questions and to consider all facts, conflicting viewpoints, hypotheses, conclusions, opinions, etc.
- Be sure to review only the information presented in the passages, as the questions will relate solely to this content.
- Don't get stuck on difficult questions. The exam is designed with a mix of easy and hard questions. Make sure to get all the easy ones answered, and then go back to focus on more difficult questions.
- Try to quickly eliminate answer choices that are obviously incorrect.

General Tips for Success

Before taking the exam, successful test takers practice answering questions from all of the different formats. Being able to quickly identify what one is being asked to do saves valuable time.

Test takers should read each passage completely and make notes or underline important information, such as:

- What is the hypothesis of an experiment?
- What is the result of the experiment?
- What is the experimental question?
- What information led to the researcher's viewpoint?
- What is the main difference between the two experiments?
- What is the main difference of opinion between two researchers?

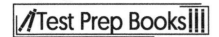

Test takers should be mindful of the time. There are 40 questions that must be completed in 35 minutes. It is recommended that test takers quickly look at the questions before reading the associated passage. This will provide a general idea of which parts of the passage to read carefully. Test takers should answer all of the questions.

Practice Quiz

Questions 1-5 pertain to the following information:

Scientists disagree about the cause of Bovine Spongiform Encephalopathy (BSE), also known as "mad cow disease." Two scientists discuss different explanations about the cause of the disease.

<u>Scientist 1</u>

Mad cow disease is a condition that results in the deterioration of brain and spinal cord tissue. This deterioration manifests as sponge-like defects or holes that result in irreversible damage to the brain. The cause of this damage is widely accepted to be the result of an infectious type of protein, called a prion. Normal proteins are located in the cell wall of the central nervous system and function to preserve the myelin sheath around the nerves. Prions are capable of turning normal proteins into other prions by a process that is still unclear, thereby causing the proteins to be "refolded" in abnormal and harmful configurations. Unlike viruses and bacteria, the harmful prions possibly don't contain DNA or RNA, based on the observation of infected tissues in the laboratory that remain infected after immersion in formaldehyde or exposure to ultraviolet light. The transformation from normal to abnormal protein structure and function in a given individual is thought to occur as the result of proteins that are genetically weak or abnormally prone to mutation, or through transmission from another host through food, drugs or organ transplants from infected animals. The abnormal prions also don't trigger an immune response. After prions accumulate in large enough numbers, they form damaging conglomerations that result in the sponge-like holes in tissues, which eventually cause the loss of proper brain function and death.

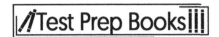
Figure 1 depicts formation of abnormal prions that results from the abnormal (right) folding of amino acids.

Figure 1:

Configurations of Normal and Abnormal Proteins

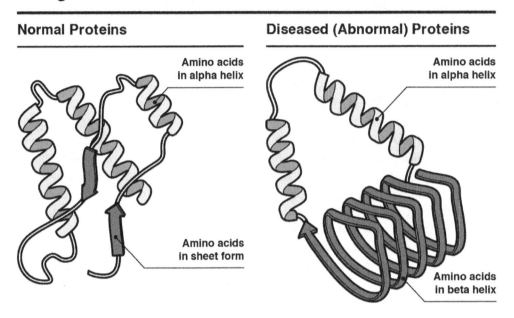

Normal Proteins

Amino acids in alpha helix

Amino acids in sheet form

Diseased (Abnormal) Proteins

Amino acids in alpha helix

Amino acids in beta helix

Scientist 2

The degeneration of brain tissue in animals afflicted with mad cow disease is widely considered to be the result of prions. This theory fails to consider other possible causes, such as viruses. Recent studies have shown that infected tissues often contain small particles that match the size and density of viruses. In order to demonstrate that these viral particles are the cause of mad cow disease, researchers used chemicals to inactivate the viruses. When the damaged, inactivated viruses were introduced into healthy tissue, no mad cow disease symptoms were observed. This result indicates that viruses are likely the cause of mad cow disease. In addition, when the infected particles from an infected animal are used to infect a different species, the resulting particles are identical to the original particles. If the infecting agent was a protein, the particles would not be identical because proteins are species-specific. Instead, the infective agent is viewed as some form of a virus that has its own DNA or RNA configuration and can reproduce identical infective particles.

1. Which statement below best characterizes a point of agreement between the two scientists' opinions?
   a. Mad cow disease is caused by a virus.
   b. Mad cow disease causes the deterioration of brain tissue.
   c. Mad cow disease is caused by prions.
   d. It is unclear what causes mad cow disease.

2. Which of the following arguments from Scientist 1 would best support the conclusion that viruses do NOT cause mad cow disease?

    a. Infected tissues remain infected after immersion in formaldehyde or exposure to ultraviolet light.

    b. Prions are capable of turning normal proteins into other prions.

    c. Abnormal prions don't trigger an immune response.

    d. When prions accumulate in large enough numbers, they eventually cause death.

3. Which argument best supports the claim of Scientist 2 that prions do NOT cause mad cow disease?

    a. The prion theory fails to consider other possible causes, such as viruses.

    b. Recent studies have shown that infected tissues often contain small particles that match the size and density of viruses.

    c. When damaged, inactivated viruses were introduced into healthy tissue, no mad cow disease symptoms were observed.

    d. If the infecting agent was a protein, the particles would be identical because proteins are not species-specific.

4. According to Figure 1 above, which configuration in a diseased protein is abnormal?

    a. Amino acids in sheet form

    b. Amino acids in alpha helix

    c. Amino acids in beta helix

    d. There is not enough information in Figure 1 to answer the question.

5. Which of the following statements is supported by one or both of these passages?

    a. The brain damage from mad cow disease can be reversed.

    b. Scientists can trace the process by which prions create abnormal proteins.

    c. Only a few scientists believe that prions cause mad cow disease.

    d. Prions cause damaging conglomerations.

See answers on next page.

Answer Explanations

1. B: The only point on which both scientists agree is that mad cow disease causes brain deterioration. Choices *A* and *C* are incorrect because the main difference in the scientists' opinions is related to whether prions or viruses cause mad cow disease. Choice *D* is incorrect because both scientists' arguments indicate that they think they know what causes mad cow disease. Neither passage indicates a lack of clarity in the author's opinion.

2. A: All viruses contain either DNA or RNA. According to Scientist 1, infected tissues remain infected after exposure to formaldehyde or ultraviolet light, both of which destroy the DNA in viruses. Therefore, this is the best argument from Scientist 1 to prove that viruses do not cause mad cow disease. Choice *B* does not address viruses at all, although prions do seem to replicate in a similar fashion to some viruses. Choice *C* is the second-best response because viruses often do trigger an immune response and the lack of one here might indicate that mad cow disease is not caused by viruses; however, Scientist 1 does not tie this fact to viruses in the argument provided. Choice *D* is incorrect because, like Choice *B*, it does not address viruses at all, although high enough concentrations of viruses can also produce death.

3. C: Scientist 2 specifically argues that the lack of mad cow disease symptoms in healthy tissue after being injected with damaged, inactivated viruses indicates that mad cow disease is likely caused by viruses, which would invalidate the theory that mad cow disease is caused by prions. Choice *A* is incorrect because this statement does not contain any evidence for or against prions as the cause of mad cow disease. Also, Scientist 1 does address viruses to some extent. Choice *B* is incorrect because the presence of small particles that could be viruses is not evidence that prions do not cause mad cow disease. Choice *D* is incorrect because it is the exact opposite of the argument that Scientist 2 makes.

4. C: The configuration of the amino acids in beta helix is what causes the protein to be diseased or abnormal. When comparing the normal and abnormal proteins in Figure 1, the configuration of the amino acid in either sheet form or beta helix is the only difference shown between a normal and abnormal protein. Choice *A* is incorrect because amino acids in sheet form is the configuration of a healthy protein. Choice *B* is incorrect because amino acids in alpha helix is the same in both a normal and abnormal protein. Choice *D* is incorrect because the different configuration of amino acids (sheet form versus beta helix) is clearly shown as the difference between a normal and abnormal protein.

5. D: The only statement that is supported by either passage is that prions cause damaging conglomerations. Choice *A* is incorrect because Passage 1 clearly states that the damage from mad cow disease is irreversible. Choice *B* is incorrect because Passage 1 indicates that the process by which prions form abnormal proteins is still unclear. Choice *C* is incorrect because both passages state that it is a widely held belief that prions cause mad cow disease.

ACT Writing Test

For some people, a writing test can seem very intimidating, perhaps even as scary as public speaking. However, with a little planning and practice, there's no reason to be afraid. Let's look at some strategies to help test takers do their best.

What to Expect

The test contains a topic followed by three possible viewpoints. Read everything carefully and brainstorm an opinion on the topic. Then, write an essay that clearly evaluates all three viewpoints and states and supports the opinion using relevant facts and personal experiences along with creativity and critical thinking.

The assignment must be completed within a 30-minute time frame. Thirty minutes may not seem like a lot of time, but it is sufficient for organizing thoughts and putting the best words forward. Keep in mind that there is no right or wrong answer to the writing test. The important thing is to approach the response in an organized, clear, and direct way. In other words, be sure the writing makes sense.

So, how is that done?

Before the Big Day

Practice. Practice. Practice. While the concept of practice may seem unappealing, it is important to be aware of its value. Just as skills in any sport will likely improve with practice, creating sample writings will exercise "writing muscles" and will likely elevate skills and proficiency. Any kind of writing practice is advantageous, but essay writing is particularly relevant.

It also helps to be aware of how long it takes to comprehend and complete an essay assignment such as the ACT Test to determine if it is necessary to work faster.

Another tip is to ask others for their opinion. Feedback is a very important tool for becoming aware of strengths and weaknesses. Ultimately, the best opportunity for success is to work on being both a reader and a writer.

Keys to Good Writing

Use proper grammar, spelling, punctuation, and other formal writing techniques. This isn't an email or a text to send to friends with *lol* and *l8r*, where the only punctuation marks are in emojis, and the only capital letters are for shouting. There's nothing wrong with typing that way in a text, but this is a different kind of writing. It's closer to a speech, so start thinking more formally about how to express thoughts.

Explain thoughts in an organized way. Writers shouldn't assume that readers share the same knowledge or thoughts. It is necessary to explain the opinion that an idea is "bad" or "good," even if it seems obvious. Make sure the reasons are relevant and consistent—writing won't be credible if an argument contradicts a previous statement.

On Test Day

Brainstorm

Don't just start writing! Writing lacks direction if thoughts and ideas aren't organized first. So, before writing a single sentence of the opening paragraph, take a few minutes to **brainstorm**. Write down anything and everything related to the topic. Don't filter out anything, no matter how silly it might seem; it's impossible to know what ideas might grow into a full argument. It might be a good idea to use the scratch paper provided to jot down ideas and organize them, grouping similar ideas together. At this point, keep in mind that the people scoring the test will be looking for variety, creativity, and imagination—in the examples, in the ways the points are made, and especially in the perspectives.

While forming thoughts on the topic, imagine someone who disagrees. What arguments would that person make? How would he or she see the topic? Write down those ideas. Keep in mind that there are often many ways to justify the same position. So, imagine people who may agree but for completely different reasons, and write down what they might say as well. Including diverse viewpoints will show a well-rounded understanding of the topic.

Lastly, when brainstorming, don't forget that, although covering multiple viewpoints is key to good writing, truly *great* writing comes from bringing personal experience to the content. If the topic can be related to something personal (and still make a relevant, organized point), the writing will be more memorable—and probably earn a higher score.

Inventory

Keep brainstorming until the ideas stop flowing (but keep an eye on the clock—don't go over five minutes, or it may be difficult to get the actual writing done). Then, take a deep breath, and look at the ideas. Look for those that have a lot of information and strategies to support them, even if they're not the most exciting ones. At this point, it may be necessary to start cutting ideas that don't have enough material to back them up.

An **angle**, or pattern, should start to emerge—a common theme to pull the most promising ideas together. Keep this overarching direction in mind while deciding what to keep and what to drop. Once again, good writing comes from having well-developed and supported ideas, but *great* writing finds a way to connect all those ideas into a single big idea.

Organize

After deciding what written material to use, start putting it all in order. Look for ideas that flow logically. Seek out similarities or differences that draw certain thoughts together into a natural sequence. If one area looks weak or needs more support, either come up with some convincing evidence to strengthen it or take it out. Don't include anything that can't be backed up or that doesn't fit in the flow of the main idea.

Manage the Clock

Don't let the clock be the enemy. By now, it should be possible to see how many points there are and how much time is left. Do some simple math to figure out how much time there is to develop each idea.

Don't forget to leave some time to review and proofread the writing (proofreading will be covered later).

Write

After all the preparation work is done, writers should have a clear idea of what they want to say. Keep in mind that there are certain things the scorers are looking for to show that the writing is well-thought-out. Also, be sure to write legibly, as the score could be lowered if the handwriting is poor.

Introduction

The opening paragraph is the **introduction**. It should include the following basic components:

- **A short restatement of the topic.** Don't just copy the writing prompt; rephrase it to suit the ideas. Make it look like the topic was created to make the points.

- **A personal opinion, or a statement of the overall big theme.** This will help set up the reader to understand how the smaller ideas fit into the big picture.

- **Smaller ideas.** They will serve as road maps for the audience. Telling readers how to navigate the ideas is like letting them see a "movie trailer" for the writing. They'll know what the writing is about, and they'll be interested to see how the ideas are developed.

Body

This is the meat of the writing and what all the brainstorming time has been spent preparing for. But by now, the ideas aren't bouncing around; they're neatly lined up, in order, ready to be released on the page. So, start writing!

Don't rush. With all these ideas, it's easy to start rushing to get them all down at once. This can lead to long, complicated, hard-to-follow sentences with lots of ideas crammed in. That's not good writing. Remember, hard work went into organizing the thoughts, and all the ideas are there. So, slow down. Make each point, one at a time, in the clearest, most direct way possible. Look for ways to connect ideas. Transition sentences that lead from one concept to another are a great way to provide flow and can prevent the writing from sounding like a collection of unrelated statements.

Conclusion

All the points have been made, developed, and connected to one another. Now it's time to write a **conclusion**. Conclusions sometimes seem silly and repetitive, but they really do serve an important purpose. State the opinion again and the main reasons behind it. Revisit the big idea here, and possibly restate the small ideas in a very basic way. Don't go through the details again—that's already been done. Also, don't present any *new* information or ideas in the conclusion. Simply summarize what's been said and wrap it up into a neat package for the reader.

Proofread

Everyone makes mistakes in the heat of writing on an exam: a misspelled word, a sentence that doesn't make sense, or a paragraph that seems disjointed and confusing. Be sure to leave a few minutes (at the end) to go back and reread the writing. Read slowly, trying to hear the words. It may feel silly, but moving the lips will help internalize the flow and make it easier to catch writing problems. Most mistakes are quick fixes, and any writer will be glad to have gone back and corrected them.

Also, be sure to delete any notes left while working through the assignment or any text from the brainstorming session. The formatting (indented paragraphs, for example) should be consistent. Leave readers with a document that looks appealing and "clean"—without mistakes—before they read a single word.

Final Thoughts

When time runs out, it will probably feel like there was room for improvement. That's normal. In fact, scorers understand the difficulties of creating organized, coherent writing in a timed situation under pressure. No one expects the writing to be perfect. With that in mind, here are some ideas for test takers to consider while working through the writing test:

- **Don't panic**. This is doable. Stop if it feels like brain overload is setting in and drawing a blank is imminent. Take a deep breath and remember the process. Don't force it. It's even okay to stop for a 30-second "mental vacation" to clear the mind.

- **Make the clock work**. Brainstorming and dividing the task into smaller chunks allows for viewing the remaining time in the least stressful way. If writing an entire essay in 30 minutes is overwhelming, just focus on finishing the next paragraph.

- **Don't try to impress anyone**. Don't use fancy words just because they're familiar—writers shouldn't use any word that they're not 100 percent sure about. Also, don't add more writing just to make the essay longer. What's important is clear, organized writing. If the ideas have been brainstormed, developed, and written in a logical order, it will be possible to put a lot of meaning into very few words.

In the end, by following these procedures, writing an easy-to-follow and well-thought-out response on the test should be no trouble. Remember: This can be done!

Good luck, and good writing!

Writing Prompt

Writing

Directions

Write an organized, coherent essay about the passage below. In your essay, make sure you:

- Clearly state your own opinion on the issue and analyze the relationships between your perspective and at least one other perspective
- Develop and support your ideas with evidence
- Organize your ideas logically
- Communicate your ideas in standard English

Prompt

People who share their lives on social media sites are edging into dangerous territory. Social media sites such as TikTok, Instagram, and Snapchat are black holes for those easily addicted to validation and acceptance. Society should be wary of allowing their kids to have open access to social media sites.

Perspectives

1. Although there are many negative side effects to social media, such as predatory accounts, cyberbullying, and identity theft, there are many positive sides to social media as well. Carrying around information 24/7 has its perks and can't be all bad—in fact, we are a society thriving on technology and connection.

2. People should take care to stay away from social media and get their validation and acceptance from entities that truly matter, like from themselves or a larger purpose. Being outside and getting exercise is a good alternative to staring at a screen all day. Those who get out and expand their worlds will definitely experience happier lives.

3. People should not be afraid of social media when it's able to bring so much opportunity to society. Staying in touch with family and friends, supporting political campaigns, and creating business opportunities are just some of the ways social media is beneficial to the community.

ACT Practice Test #1

English

Questions 1–9 are based on the following passage:

While all dogs (1) <u>descend through gray wolves</u>, it's easy to notice that dog breeds come in a variety of shapes and sizes. With such a (2) <u>drastic range of traits, appearances and body types</u> dogs are one of the most variable and adaptable species on the planet. (3) <u>But why so many differences.</u> The answer is that humans have actually played a major role in altering the biology of dogs. (4) <u>This was done through a process called selective breeding.</u>

(5) <u>Selective breeding which is also called artificial selection is the processes</u> in which animals with desired traits are bred in order to produce offspring that share the same traits. In natural selection, (6) <u>animals must adapt to their environments increase their chance of survival</u>. Over time, certain traits develop in animals that enable them to thrive in these environments. Those animals with more of these traits, or better versions of these traits, gain an (7) <u>advantage over others of their species.</u> Therefore, the animal's chances to mate are increased and these useful (8) <u>genes are passed into their offspring.</u> With dog breeding, humans select traits that are desired and encourage more of these desired traits in other dogs by breeding dogs that already have them.

The reason for different breeds of dogs is that there were specific needs that humans wanted to fill with their animals. For example, scent hounds are known for their extraordinary ability to track game through scent. These breeds are also known for their endurance in seeking deer and other prey. Therefore, early hunters took dogs that displayed these abilities and bred them to encourage these traits. Later, these generations took on characteristics that aided these desired traits. (9) <u>For example, Bloodhounds</u> have broad snouts and droopy ears that fall to the ground when they smell. These physical qualities not only define the look of the Bloodhound, but also contribute to their amazing tracking ability. The broad snout is able to define and hold onto scents longer than many other breeds. The long, floppy ears serve to collect and hold the scents the earth holds so that the smells are clearer and able to be distinguished.

1. Which of the following would be the best choice for this sentence (reproduced below)?

While all dogs (1) <u>descend through gray wolves</u>, it's easy to notice that dog breeds come in a variety of shapes and sizes.

a. NO CHANGE
b. descend by gray wolves
c. descend from gray wolves
d. descended through gray wolves

2. Which of the following would be the best choice for this sentence (reproduced below)?

With such a (2) <u>drastic range of traits, appearances and body types,</u> dogs are one of the most variable and adaptable species on the planet.

a. NO CHANGE
b. drastic range of traits, appearances, and body types,
c. drastic range of traits and appearances and body types,
d. drastic range of traits, appearances, as well as body types,

3. Which of the following would be the best choice for this sentence (reproduced below)?

(3) <u>But why so many differences.</u>

a. NO CHANGE
b. But are there so many differences?
c. But why so many differences are there.
d. But why so many differences?

4. Which of the following would be the best choice for this sentence (reproduced below)?

(4) <u>This was done through a process called selective breeding.</u>

a. NO CHANGE
b. This was done, through a process called selective breeding.
c. This was done, through a process, called selective breeding.
d. This was done through selective breeding, a process.

5. Which of the following would be the best choice for this sentence (reproduced below)?

(5) <u>Selective breeding which is also called artificial selection is the processes</u> in which animals with desired traits are bred in order to produce offspring that share the same traits.

a. NO CHANGE
b. Selective breeding, which is also called artificial selection is the processes
c. Selective breeding which is also called, artificial selection, is the processes
d. Selective breeding, which is also called artificial selection, is the processes

6. Which of the following would be the best choice for this sentence (reproduced below)?

In natural selection, (6) animals must adapt to their environments increase their chance of survival.

a. NO CHANGE
b. animals must adapt to their environments to increase their chance of survival.
c. animals must adapt to their environments, increase their chance of survival.
d. animals must adapt to their environments, increasing their chance of survival.

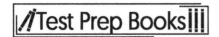

7. Which of the following would be the best choice for this sentence (reproduced below)?

Those animals with more of these traits, or better versions of these traits, gain an (7) <u>advantage over others of their species.</u>

a. NO CHANGE
b. advantage over others, of their species.
c. advantages over others of their species.
d. advantage over others.

8. Which of the following would be the best choice for this sentence (reproduced below)?

Therefore, the animal's chances to mate are increased and these useful (8) <u>genes are passed into their offspring.</u>

a. NO CHANGE
b. genes are passed onto their offspring.
c. genes are passed on to their offspring.
d. genes are passed within their offspring.

9. Which of the following would be the best choice for this sentence (reproduced below)?

(9) <u>For example, Bloodhounds</u> have broad snouts and droopy ears that fall to the ground when they smell.

a. NO CHANGE
b. For example, Bloodhounds,
c. For example Bloodhounds
d. For example, bloodhounds

Questions 10–18 are based on the following passage:

I'm not alone when I say that it's hard to pay attention sometimes. I can't count how many times I've sat in a classroom, lecture, speech, or workshop and (10) <u>been bored to tears or rather sleep</u>. (11) <u>Usually I turn to doodling in order to keep awake</u>. This never really helps; I'm not much of an artist. Therefore, after giving up on drawing a masterpiece, I would just concentrate on keeping my eyes open and trying to be attentive. This didn't always work because I wasn't engaged in what was going on.

(12) <u>Sometimes in particularly dull seminars,</u> I'd imagine comical things going on in the room or with the people trapped in the room with me. Why? (13) <u>Because I wasn't invested in what was going on I wasn't motivated to listen.</u> I'm not going to write about how I conquered the difficult task of actually paying attention in a difficult or unappealing class—it can be done, sure. I have sat through the very epitome of boredom (in my view at least) several times and come away learning something. (14) <u>Everyone probably has had to at one time do this</u>. What I want to talk about is that profound moment when curiosity is sparked (15) <u>in another person drawing them to pay attention to what is before them</u> and expand their knowledge.

What really makes people pay attention? (16) <u>Easy it's interest</u>. This doesn't necessarily mean (17) <u>embellishing subject matter drawing people's attention.</u> This won't always work. However, an individual can present material in a way that is clear to understand and actually engages the audience. Asking questions to the audience or class will make them a part of the topic at hand. Discussions that make people think about the content and (18) <u>how it applies to there lives world and future is key.</u> If math is being discussed, an instructor can explain the purpose behind the equations or perhaps use real-world applications to show how relevant the topic is. When discussing history, a lecturer can prompt students to imagine themselves in the place of key figures and ask how they might respond. The bottom line is to explore the ideas rather than just lecture. Give people the chance to explore material from multiple angles, and they'll be hungry to keep paying attention for more information.

10. Which of the following would be the best choice for this sentence (reproduced below)?

I can't count how many times I've sat in a classroom, lecture, speech, or workshop and (10) <u>been bored to tears or rather sleep.</u>

a. NO CHANGE
b. been bored to, tears, or rather sleep.
c. been bored, to tears or rather sleep.
d. been bored to tears or, rather, sleep.

11. Which of the following would be the best choice for this sentence (reproduced below)?

(11) <u>Usually I turn to doodling in order to keep awake.</u>

a. NO CHANGE
b. Usually, I turn to doodling in order to keep awake.
c. Usually I turn to doodling, in order, to keep awake.
d. Usually I turned to doodling in order to keep awake.

12. Which of the following would be the best choice for this sentence (reproduced below)?

(12) <u>Sometimes in particularly dull seminars,</u> I'd imagine comical things going on in the room or with the people trapped in the room with me.

a. NO CHANGE
b. Sometimes, in particularly, dull seminars,
c. Sometimes in particularly dull seminars
d. Sometimes, in particularly, dull seminars,

13. Which of the following would be the best choice for this sentence (reproduced below)?

(13) <u>Because I wasn't invested in what was going on I wasn't motivated to listen.</u>

a. NO CHANGE
b. Because I wasn't invested, in what was going on, I wasn't motivated to listen.
c. Because I wasn't invested in what was going on. I wasn't motivated to listen.
d. I wasn't motivated to listen because I wasn't invested in what was going on.

233

14. Which of the following would be the best choice for this sentence (reproduced below)?

(14) <u>Everyone probably has had to at one time do this.</u>

a. NO CHANGE
b. Everyone probably has had to, at one time. Do this.
c. Everyone's probably had to do this at some time.
d. At one time everyone probably has had to do this.

15. Which of the following would be the best choice for this sentence (reproduced below)?

What I want to talk about is that profound moment when curiosity is sparked (15) <u>in another person drawing them to pay attention to what is before them</u> and expand their knowledge.

a. NO CHANGE
b. in another person, drawing them to pay attention
c. in another person; drawing them to pay attention to what is before them.
d. in another person, drawing them to pay attention to what is before them.

16. Which of the following would be the best choice for this sentence (reproduced below)?

(16) <u>Easy it's interest.</u>

a. NO CHANGE
b. Easy it is interest.
c. Easy. It's interest.
d. Easy—it's interest.

17. Which of the following would be the best choice for this sentence (reproduced below)?

This doesn't necessarily mean (17) <u>embellishing subject matter drawing people's attention.</u>

a. NO CHANGE
b. embellishing subject matter which draws people's attention.
c. embellishing subject matter to draw people's attention.
d. embellishing subject matter for the purpose of drawing people's attention.

18. Which of the following would be the best choice for this sentence (reproduced below)?

Discussions that make people think about the content and (18) <u>how it applies to there lives world and future is key.</u>

a. NO CHANGE
b. how it applies to their lives, world, and future is key.
c. how it applied to there lives world and future is key.
d. how it applies to their lives, world and future is key.

Questions 19–27 are based on the following passage:

Since the first discovery of dinosaur bones, (19) <u>scientists has made strides in technological development and methodologies used to investigate</u> these extinct animals. We know more about dinosaurs than ever before and are still learning fascinating new things about how they looked and lived. However, one has to ask, (20) <u>how if earlier perceptions of dinosaurs</u> continue to influence people's understanding of these creatures? Can these perceptions inhibit progress towards further understanding of dinosaurs?

(21) <u>The biggest problem with studying dinosaurs is simply that there are no living dinosaurs to observe.</u> All discoveries associated with these animals are based on physical remains. To gauge behavioral characteristics, scientists cross-examine these (22) <u>finds with living animals that seem similar in order to gain understanding.</u> While this method is effective, these are still deductions. Some ideas about dinosaurs can't be tested and confirmed simply because humans can't replicate a living dinosaur. For example, a Spinosaurus has a large sail, or a finlike structure that grows from its back. Paleontologists know this sail exists and have ideas for the function of (23) <u>the sail however they are uncertain of which idea is the true function.</u> Some scientists believe (24) <u>the sail serves to regulate the Spinosaurus' body temperature and yet others believe its used to attract mates.</u> Still, other scientists think the sail is used to intimidate other predatory dinosaurs for self-defense. These are all viable explanations, but they are also influenced by what scientists know about modern animals. (25) <u>Yet, it's quite possible</u> that the sail could hold a completely unique function.

While it's (26) <u>plausible, even likely that dinosaurs share many</u> traits with modern animals, there is the danger of overattributing these qualities to a unique, extinct species. For much of the early nineteenth century, when people first started studying dinosaur bones, the assumption was that they were simply giant lizards. (27) <u>For the longest time this image was the prevailing view on dinosaurs,</u> until evidence indicated that they were more likely warm blooded. Scientists have also discovered that many dinosaurs had feathers and actually share many traits with modern birds.

19. Which of the following would be the best choice for this sentence (reproduced below)?

Since the first discovery of dinosaur bones, (19) <u>scientists has made strides in technological development and methodologies used to investigate</u> these extinct animals.

a. NO CHANGE
b. scientists has made strides in technological development, and methodologies, used to investigate
c. scientists have made strides in technological development and methodologies used to investigate
d. scientists, have made strides in technological development and methodologies used, to investigate

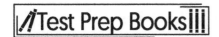

20. Which of the following would be the best choice for this sentence (reproduced below)?

However, one has to ask, (20) how if earlier perceptions of dinosaurs continue to influence people's understanding of these creatures?

a. NO CHANGE
b. how perceptions of dinosaurs
c. how, if, earlier perceptions of dinosaurs
d. whether earlier perceptions of dinosaurs

21. Which of the following would be the best choice for this sentence (reproduced below)?

(21) The biggest problem with studying dinosaurs is simply that there are no living dinosaurs to observe.

a. NO CHANGE
b. The biggest problem with studying dinosaurs is simple, that there are no living dinosaurs to observe.
c. The biggest problem with studying dinosaurs is simple. There are no living dinosaurs to observe.
d. The biggest problem with studying dinosaurs, is simply that there are no living dinosaurs to observe.

22. Which of the following would be the best choice for this sentence (reproduced below)?

To gauge behavioral characteristics, scientists cross-examine these (22) finds with living animals that seem similar in order to gain understanding.

a. NO CHANGE
b. finds with living animals to explore potential similarities.
c. finds with living animals to gain understanding of similarities.
d. finds with living animals that seem similar, in order, to gain understanding.

23. Which of the following would be the best choice for this sentence (reproduced below)?

Paleontologists know this sail exists and have ideas for the function of (23) the sail however they are uncertain of which idea is the true function.

a. NO CHANGE
b. the sail however, they are uncertain of which idea is the true function.
c. the sail however they are, uncertain, of which idea is the true function.
d. the sail; however, they are uncertain of which idea is the true function.

24. Which of the following would be the best choice for this sentence (reproduced below)?

Some scientists believe (24) <u>the sail serves to regulate the Spinosaurus' body temperature and yet others believe its used to attract mates.</u>

a. NO CHANGE
b. the sail serves to regulate the Spinosaurus' body temperature, yet others believe it's used to attract mates.
c. the sail serves to regulate the Spinosaurus' body temperature and yet others believe it's used to attract mates.
d. the sail serves to regulate the Spinosaurus' body temperature however others believe it's used to attract mates.

25. Which of the following would be the best choice for this sentence (reproduced below)?

(25) <u>Yet, it's quite possible</u> that the sail could hold a completely unique function.

a. NO CHANGE
b. Yet, it's quite possible,
c. It's quite possible,
d. Its quite possible

26. Which of the following would be the best choice for this sentence (reproduced below)?

While it's (26) <u>plausible, even likely that dinosaurs share many</u> traits with modern animals, there is the danger of over attributing these qualities to a unique, extinct species.

a. NO CHANGE
b. plausible, even likely that, dinosaurs share many
c. plausible, even likely, that dinosaurs share many
d. plausible even likely that dinosaurs share many

27. Which of the following would be the best choice for this sentence (reproduced below)?

(27) <u>For the longest time this image was the prevailing view on dinosaurs</u>, until evidence indicated that they were more likely warm blooded.

a. NO CHANGE
b. For the longest time this was the prevailing view on dinosaurs
c. For the longest time, this image, was the prevailing view on dinosaurs
d. For the longest time this was the prevailing image of dinosaurs

Questions 28–36 are based on the following passage:

Everyone has heard the (28) <u>idea of the end justifying the means; that would be Weston's philosophy.</u> Weston is willing to cross any line, commit any act no matter how heinous, to achieve success in his goal. (29) <u>Ransom is reviled by this fact, seeing total evil in Weston's plan.</u> To do an evil act in order (30) <u>to gain a result that's supposedly good would ultimately warp the final act.</u> (31) <u>This opposing viewpoints immediately distinguishes Ransom as the hero.</u> In the conflict with Un-man, Ransom remains true to his moral principles, someone who refuses to be

237

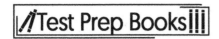

compromised by power. Instead, Ransom makes it clear that by allowing such processes as murder and lying dictate how one attains a positive outcome, (32) the righteous goal becomes corrupted. The good end would not be truly good, but a twisted end that conceals corrupt deeds.

(33) This idea of allowing necessary evils to happen, is very tempting, it is what Weston fell prey to. (34) The temptation of the evil spirit Un-man ultimately takes over Weston and he is possessed. However, Ransom does not give into temptation. He remains faithful to the truth of what is right and incorrect. This leads him to directly face Un-man for the fate of Perelandra and its inhabitants.

Just as Weston was corrupted by the Un-man, (35) Un-man after this seeks to tempt the Queen of Perelandra to darkness. Ransom must literally (36) show her the right path, to accomplish this, he does this based on the same principle as the "means to an end" argument—that good follows good, and evil follows evil. Later in the plot, Weston/Un-man seeks to use deceptive reasoning to turn the queen to sin, pushing the queen to essentially ignore Melildil's rule to satisfy her own curiosity. In this sense, Un-man takes on the role of a false prophet, a tempter. Ransom must shed light on the truth, but this is difficult; his adversary is very clever and uses brilliant language. Ransom's lack of refinement heightens the weight of Un-man's corrupted logic, and so the Queen herself is intrigued by his logic.

Based on an excerpt from *Perelandra* by C.S. Lewis

28. Which of the following would be the best choice for this sentence (reproduced below)?

Everyone has heard the (28) idea of the end justifying the means; that would be Weston's philosophy.

a. NO CHANGE
b. idea of the end justifying the means; this is Weston's philosophy.
c. idea of the end justifying the means, this is the philosophy of Weston
d. idea of the end justifying the means. That would be Weston's philosophy.

29. Which of the following would be the best choice for this sentence (reproduced below)?

(29) Ransom is reviled by this fact, seeing total evil in Weston's plan.

a. NO CHANGE
b. Ransom is reviled by this fact; seeing total evil in Weston's plan.
c. Ransom, is reviled by this fact, seeing total evil in Weston's plan.
d. Ransom reviled by this, sees total evil in Weston's plan.

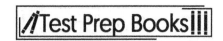

30. Which of the following would be the best choice for this sentence (reproduced below)?

To do an evil act in order (30) <u>to gain a result that's supposedly good would ultimately warp the final act.</u>

a. NO CHANGE
b. for an outcome that's for a greater good would ultimately warp the final act.
c. to gain a final act would warp its goodness.
d. to achieve a positive outcome would ultimately warp the goodness of the final act.

31. Which of the following would be the best choice for this sentence (reproduced below)?

(31) <u>This opposing viewpoints immediately distinguishes Ransom as the hero.</u>

a. NO CHANGE
b. This opposing viewpoints immediately distinguishes Ransom, as the hero.
c. This opposing viewpoint immediately distinguishes Ransom as the hero.
d. Those opposing viewpoints immediately distinguishes Ransom as the hero.

32. Which of the following would be the best choice for this sentence (reproduced below)?

Instead, Ransom makes it clear that by allowing such processes as murder and lying dictate how one attains a positive outcome, (32) <u>the righteous goal becomes corrupted.</u>

a. NO CHANGE
b. the goal becomes corrupted and no longer righteous.
c. the righteous goal becomes, corrupted.
d. the goal becomes corrupted, when once it was righteous.

33. Which of the following would be the best choice for this sentence (reproduced below)?

(33) <u>This idea of allowing necessary evils to happen, is very tempting, it is what Weston fell prey to.</u>

a. NO CHANGE
b. This idea of allowing necessary evils to happen, is very tempting. This is what Weston fell prey to.
c. This idea, allowing necessary evils to happen, is very tempting, it is what Weston fell prey to.
d. This tempting idea of allowing necessary evils to happen is what Weston fell prey to.

34. Which of the following would be the best choice for this sentence (reproduced below)?

(34) <u>The temptation of the evil spirit Un-man ultimately takes over Weston and he is possessed.</u>

a. NO CHANGE
b. The temptation of the evil spirit Un-man ultimately takes over and possesses Weston.
c. Weston is possessed as a result of the temptation of the evil spirit Un-man ultimately, who takes over.
d. The temptation of the evil spirit Un-man takes over Weston and he is possessed ultimately.

35. Which of the following would be the best choice for this sentence (reproduced below)?

Just as Weston was corrupted by the Un-man, (35) <u>Un-man after this seeks to tempt the Queen of Perelandra</u> to darkness.

a. NO CHANGE
b. Un-man, after this, would tempt the Queen of Perelandra
c. Un-man, after this, seeks to tempt the Queen of Perelandra
d. Un-man then seeks to tempt the Queen of Perelandra

36. Which of the following would be the best choice for this sentence (reproduced below)?

Ransom must literally (36) <u>show her the right path, to accomplish this, he does this based on the same principle as the "means to an end" argument</u>—that good follows good, and evil follows evil.

a. NO CHANGE
b. show her the right path. To accomplish this, he uses the same principle as the "means to an end" argument
c. show her the right path; to accomplish this he uses the same principle as the "means to an end" argument
d. show her the right path, to accomplish this, the same principle as the "means to an end" argument is applied

Questions 37–45 are based on the following passage:

(37) <u>What's clear about the news is today is that the broader the media </u>the more ways there are to tell a story. Even if different news groups cover the same story, individual newsrooms can interpret or depict the story differently than other counterparts. Stories can also change depending on the type of (38) <u>media in question incorporating different styles and unique</u> ways to approach the news. (39) <u>It is because of these respective media types that ethical and news-related subject matter can sometimes seem different or altered.</u> But how does this affect the narrative of the new story?

I began by investigating a written newspaper article from the Baltimore Sun. Instantly striking are the bolded headlines. (40) <u>These are clearly meant for direct the viewer </u>to the most exciting and important stories the paper has to offer. What was particularly noteworthy about this edition was that the first page dealt with two major ethical issues. (41) <u>On a national level there was a story</u> on the evolving Petraeus scandal involving his supposed affair. The other article was focused locally in Baltimore, a piece questioning the city's Ethics Board and their current director. Just as a television newscaster communicates the story through camera and dialogue, the printed article applies intentional and targeted written narrative style. More so than any of the mediums, a news article seems to be focused specifically on a given story without need to jump to another. Finer details are usually expanded on (42) <u>in written articles, usually people who</u> read newspapers or go online for web articles want more than a quick blurb. The diction of the story is also more precise and can be either straightforward or suggestive (43) <u>depending in earnest on the goal of the writer.</u> However, there's still plenty of room for opinions to be inserted into the text.

240

Usually, all news (44) <u>outlets have some sort of bias, it's just a question of how much</u> bias clouds the reporting. As long as this bias doesn't withhold information from the reader, it can be considered credible. (45) <u>However an over use of bias</u>, opinion, and suggestive language can rob readers of the chance to interpret the news events for themselves.

37. Which of the following would be the best choice for this sentence (reproduced below)?

(37) <u>What's clear about the news today is that the broader the media</u> the more ways there are to tell a story.

a. NO CHANGE
b. What's clear, about the news today, is that the broader the media
c. What's clear about today's news is that the broader the media
d. The news today is broader than earlier media

38. Which of the following would be the best choice for this sentence (reproduced below)?

Stories can also change depending on the type of (38) <u>media in question incorporating different styles and unique</u> ways to approach the news.

a. NO CHANGE
b. media in question; each incorporates unique styles and unique
c. media in question. To incorporate different styles and unique
d. media in question, incorporating different styles and unique

39. Which of the following would be the best choice for this sentence (reproduced below)?

(39) <u>It is because of these respective media types that ethical and news-related subject matter can sometimes seem different or altered.</u>

a. NO CHANGE
b. It is because of these respective media types, that ethical and news-related subject matter, can sometimes seem different or altered.
c. It is because of these respective media types, that ethical and news-related subject matter can sometimes seem different or altered.
d. It is because of these respective media types that ethical and news-related subject matter can sometimes seem different. Or altered.

40. Which of the following would be the best choice for this sentence (reproduced below)?

(40) <u>These are clearly meant for direct the viewer</u> to the most exciting and important stories the paper has to offer.

a. NO CHANGE
b. These are clearly meant for the purpose of giving direction to the viewer
c. These are clearly meant to direct the viewer
d. These are clearly meant for the viewer to be directed

241

41. Which of the following would be the best choice for this sentence (reproduced below)?

(41) <u>On a national level there was a story</u> on the evolving Petraeus scandal involving his supposed affair.

a. NO CHANGE
b. On a national level a story was there
c. On a national level; there was a story
d. On a national level, there was a story

42. Which of the following would be the best choice for this sentence (reproduced below)?

Finer details are usually expanded on (42) <u>in written articles, usually people who</u> read newspapers or go online for web articles want more than a quick blurb.

a. NO CHANGE
b. in written articles. People who usually
c. in written articles, usually, people who
d. in written articles usually people who

43. Which of the following would be the best choice for this sentence (reproduced below)?

The diction of the story is also more precise and can be either straightforward or suggestive (43) <u>depending in earnest on the goal of the writer.</u>

a. NO CHANGE
b. depending; in earnest on the goal of the writer.
c. depending, in earnest, on the goal of the writer.
d. the goal of the writer, in earnest, depends on the goal of the writer.

44. Which of the following would be the best choice for this sentence (reproduced below)?

Usually, all news (44) <u>outlets have some sort of bias, it's just a question of how much</u> bias clouds the reporting.

a. NO CHANGE
b. outlets have some sort of bias. Just a question of how much
c. outlets have some sort of bias it can just be a question of how much
d. outlets have some sort of bias, its just a question of how much

45. Which of the following would be the best choice for this sentence (reproduced below)?

(45) <u>However an over use of bias,</u> opinion, and suggestive language can rob readers of the chance to interpret the news events for themselves.

a. NO CHANGE
b. However, an over use of bias,
c. However, with too much bias,
d. However, an overuse of bias,

242

Questions 46–54 are based on the following passage:

(46) One of the icon's of romantic and science fiction literature remains Mary Shelley's classic, *Frankenstein, or The Modern Prometheus*. Schools throughout the world still teach the book in literature and philosophy courses. Scientific communities also engage in discussion on the novel. But why? Besides the novel's engaging (47) writing style the story's central theme remains highly relevant in a world of constant discovery and moral dilemmas. Central to the core narrative is the (48) struggle between enlightenment and the cost of overusing power.

The subtitle, *The Modern Prometheus*, encapsulates the inner theme of the story more than the main title of *Frankenstein*. As with many romantic writers, Shelley invokes the classical myths and (49) symbolism of Ancient Greece and Rome to high light core ideas. Looking deeper into the myth of Prometheus sheds light not only on the character of Frankenstein (50) but also poses a psychological dilemma to the audience. Prometheus is the titan who gave fire to mankind. (51) However, more than just fire he gave people knowledge and power. The power of fire advanced civilization. Yet, for giving fire to man, Prometheus is (52) punished by the gods bound to a rock and tormented for his act. This is clearly a parallel to Frankenstein—he is the modern Prometheus.

Frankenstein's quest for knowledge becomes an obsession. It leads him to literally create new life, breaking the bounds of conceivable science to illustrate that man can create life out of nothing. (53) Yet he ultimately faltered as a creator, abandoning his progeny in horror of what he created. Frankenstein then suffers his creature's wrath, (54) the result of his pride, obsession for power and lack of responsibility.

Shelley isn't condemning scientific achievement. Rather, her writing reflects that science and discovery are good things, but, like all power, it must be used wisely. The text alludes to the message that one must have reverence for nature and be mindful of the potential consequences. Frankenstein did not take responsibility or even consider how his actions would affect others. His scientific brilliance ultimately led to suffering.

Based on an excerpt from Frankenstein by Mary Shelley

46. Which of the following would be the best choice for this sentence (reproduced below)?

(46) One of the icon's of romantic and science fiction literature remains Mary Shelley's classic, *Frankenstein, or The Modern Prometheus*.

a. NO CHANGE
b. One of the icons of romantic and science fiction literature
c. One of the icon's of romantic, and science fiction literature,
d. The icon of romantic and science fiction literature

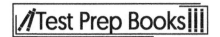

47. Which of the following would be the best choice for this sentence (reproduced below)?

Besides the novel's engaging (47) writing style the story's central theme remains highly relevant in a world of constant discovery and moral dilemmas.

a. NO CHANGE
b. writing style the central theme of the story
c. writing style, the story's central theme
d. the story's central theme's writing style

48. Which of the following would be the best choice for this sentence (reproduced below)?

Central to the core narrative is the (48) struggle between enlightenment and the cost of overusing power.

a. NO CHANGE
b. struggle between enlighten and the cost of overusing power.
c. struggle between enlightenment's cost of overusing power.
d. struggle between enlightening and the cost of overusing power.

49. Which of the following would be the best choice for this sentence (reproduced below)?

As with many romantic writers, Shelley invokes the classical myths and (49) symbolism of Ancient Greece and Rome to high light core ideas.

a. NO CHANGE
b. symbolism of Ancient Greece and Rome to highlight core ideas.
c. symbolism of ancient Greece and Rome to highlight core ideas.
d. symbolism of Ancient Greece and Rome highlighting core ideas.

50. Which of the following would be the best choice for this sentence (reproduced below)?

Looking deeper into the myth of Prometheus sheds light not only on the character of Frankenstein (50) but also poses a psychological dilemma to the audience.

a. NO CHANGE
b. but also poses a psychological dilemma with the audience.
c. but also poses a psychological dilemma for the audience.
d. but also poses a psychological dilemma there before the audience.

51. Which of the following would be the best choice for this sentence (reproduced below)?

(51) However, more than just fire he gave people knowledge and power.

a. NO CHANGE
b. However, more than just fire he gave people, knowledge, and power.
c. However, more than just fire, he gave people knowledge and power.
d. Besides actual fire, Prometheus gave people knowledge and power.

244

52. Which of the following would be the best choice for this sentence (reproduced below)?

Yet, for giving fire to man, Prometheus is (52) <u>punished by the gods bound to a rock and tormented for his act.</u>

a. NO CHANGE
b. punished by the gods, bound to a rock and tormented for his act.
c. bound to a rock and tormented as punishment by the gods.
d. punished for his act by being bound to a rock and tormented as punishment from the gods.

53. Which of the following would be the best choice for this sentence (reproduced below)?

(53) <u>Yet he ultimately faltered as a creator,</u> abandoning his progeny in horror of what he created.

a. NO CHANGE
b. Yet, he ultimately falters as a creator by
c. Yet, he ultimately faltered as a creator,
d. Yet he ultimately falters as a creator by

54. Which of the following would be the best choice for this sentence (reproduced below)?

Frankenstein then suffers his creature's wrath, (54) <u>the result of his pride, obsession for power and lack of responsibility.</u>

a. NO CHANGE
b. the result of his pride, obsession for power and lacking of responsibility.
c. the result of his pride, obsession for power, and lack of responsibility.
d. the result of his pride and also his obsession for power and lack of responsibility.

Questions 55–63 are based on the following passage:

The power of legends continues to enthrall our imagination, provoking us both to wonder and explore. (55) <u>Who doesnt love a good legend?</u> Some say legends never (56) <u>die and this is certainly the case</u> for the most legendary creature of all, Bigfoot. To this day, people still claim sightings of the illusive cryptid. Many think of Bigfoot as America's monster, yet many nations have legends of a similar creature. In my own research I have found that Australia has the Yowie, China has the Yerin, and Russia has the Almas. (57) <u>Their all over the world, the</u> bigfoots and the legends tied to them. Does this mean they could exist?

There are many things to consider when addressing (58) <u>this question but the chief factor</u> is whether there is credible evidence. (59) <u>For science to formally recognize that such a species exists, there needs to be physical proof.</u> While people have found supposed footprints and even (60) <u>captured photos and film of the creature, this validity of such evidence is up for debate.</u> There is room for uncertainty. Most visual evidence is out of focus, thus (61) <u>there is often skepticism whether such images are real.</u> Some researchers have even claimed to have hair and blood samples, but still there is doubt in the scientific community. The reason is simple: there needs to be a body or living specimen found and actively studied in order to prove the Bigfoots' existence.

Yet, one cannot ignore the fact that (62) <u>hundreds of witnesses continuing to describe a creature</u> with uniform features all over the world. These bigfoot sightings aren't a modern occurrence either. Ancient civilizations have reported (63) <u>seeing Bigfoot as well including Native Americans</u>. It is from Native Americans that we gained the popular term Sasquatch, which is the primary name for the North American bigfoot. How does their testimony factor in? If indigenous people saw these animals, could they not have existed at some point? After all, when Europeans first arrived in Africa, they disbelieved the native accounts of the gorilla. But sure enough, Europeans eventually found gorillas and collected a body.

55. Which of the following would be the best choice for this sentence (reproduced below)?

(55) <u>Who doesnt love a good legend?</u>

a. NO CHANGE
b. Who does not love a good legend?
c. A good legend, who doesn't love one?
d. Who doesn't love a good legend?

56. Which of the following would be the best choice for this sentence (reproduced below)?

Some say legends never (56) <u>die and this is certainly the case</u> for the most legendary creature of all, Bigfoot.

a. NO CHANGE
b. die, and this is certainly the case
c. die; this is certainly the case
d. die. This is certainly the case

57. Which of the following would be the best choice for this sentence (reproduced below)?

(57) <u>Their all over the world, the</u> bigfoots and the legends tied to them.

a. NO CHANGE
b. There all over the world, the
c. They're all over the world, the
d. All over the world they are, the

58. Which of the following would be the best choice for this sentence (reproduced below)?

There are many things to consider when addressing (58) <u>this question but the chief factor</u> is whether there is credible evidence.

a. NO CHANGE
b. this question, but the chief factor
c. this question however the chief factor
d. this question; but the chief factor

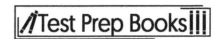

59. Which of the following would be the best choice for this sentence (reproduced below)?

(59) <u>For science to formally recognize that such a species exists, there needs to be physical proof.</u>

a. NO CHANGE
b. Physical proof are needed in order for science to formally recognize that such a species exists.
c. For science to formally recognize that such a species exists there needs to be physical proof.
d. For science, to formally recognize that such a species exists, there needs to be physical proof.

60. Which of the following would be the best choice for this sentence (reproduced below)?

While people have found supposed footprints and even (60) <u>captured photos and film of the creature, this validity of such evidence is up for debate.</u>

a. NO CHANGE
b. captured photos and film of the creature. This validity of such evidence is up for debate.
c. captured photos and film of the creature, the validities of such evidence is up for debate.
d. captured photos and film of the creature, the validity of such evidence is up for debate.

61. Which of the following would be the best choice for this sentence (reproduced below)?

Most visual evidence is out of focus, thus (61) <u>there is often skepticism whether such images are real.</u>

a. NO CHANGE
b. often skepticism whether such images are real.
c. there is often skepticism, whether such images are real.
d. there is often skepticism weather such images are real.

62. Which of the following would be the best choice for this sentence (reproduced below)?

Yet, one cannot ignore the fact that (62) <u>hundreds of witnesses continuing to describe a creature</u> with uniform features all over the world.

a. NO CHANGE
b. hundreds of witnesses continuing to describing a creature
c. hundreds of witnesses continue to describe a creature
d. hundreds of the witnesses continue to described a creature

63. Which of the following would be the best choice for this sentence (reproduced below)?

Ancient civilizations have reported (63) <u>seeing Bigfoot as well including Native Americans.</u>

a. NO CHANGE
b. seeing Bigfoot, Native Americans as well.
c. seeing Bigfoot also the Native Americans.
d. seeing Bigfoot, including Native Americans.

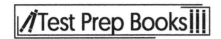

Questions 64–70 are based on the following passage:

I have to admit that when my father bought a recreational vehicle (RV), I thought he was making a huge mistake. I didn't really know anything about RVs, but I knew that my dad was as big a "city slicker" as there was. (64) <u>In fact, I even thought he might have gone a little bit crazy.</u> On trips to the beach, he preferred to swim at the pool, and whenever he went hiking, he avoided touching any plants for fear that they might be poison ivy. Why would this man, with an almost irrational fear of the outdoors, want a 40-foot camping behemoth?

(65) <u>The RV</u> was a great purchase for our family and brought us all closer together. Every morning (66) <u>we would wake up, eat breakfast, and broke camp.</u> We laughed at our own comical attempts to back The Beast into spaces that seemed impossibly small. (67) <u>We rejoiced as "hackers."</u> When things inevitably went wrong and we couldn't solve the problems on our own, we discovered the incredible helpfulness and friendliness of the RV community. (68) <u>We even made some new friends in the process.</u>

(69) <u>Above all, it allowed us to share adventures. While traveling across America,</u> which we could not have experienced in cars and hotels. Enjoying a campfire on a chilly summer evening with the mountains of Glacier National Park in the background or waking up early in the morning to see the sun rising over the distant spires of Arches National Park are memories that will always stay with me and our entire family. (70) <u>Those are also memories that my siblings and me</u> have now shared with our own children.

64. Which of the following would be the best choice for this sentence (reproduced below)?

(64) <u>In fact, I even thought he might have gone a little bit crazy.</u>

a. NO CHANGE
b. Move the sentence so that it comes before the preceding sentence.
c. Move the sentence to the end of the first paragraph.
d. Omit the sentence.

65. In context, which is the best version of the underlined portion of this sentence (reproduced below)?

(65) <u>The RV</u> was a great purchase for our family and brought us all closer together.

a. NO CHANGE
b. Not surprisingly, the RV
c. Furthermore, the RV
d. As it turns out, the RV

66. Which is the best version of the underlined portion of this sentence (reproduced below)?

Every morning (66) <u>we would wake up, eat breakfast, and broke camp.</u>

a. NO CHANGE
b. we would wake up, eat breakfast, and break camp.
c. would we wake up, eat breakfast, and break camp?
d. we are waking up, eating breakfast, and breaking camp.

248

67. Which is the best version of the underlined portion of this sentence (reproduced below)?

(67) We rejoiced as "hackers."

a. NO CHANGE
b. To a nagging problem of technology, we rejoiced as "hackers."
c. We rejoiced when we figured out how to "hack" a solution to a nagging technological problem.
d. To "hack" our way to a solution, we had to rejoice.

68. Which is the best version of the underlined portion of this sentence (reproduced below)?

(68) We even made some new friends in the process.

a. NO CHANGE
b. In the process was the friends we were making.
c. We are even making some new friends in the process.
d. We will make new friends in the process.

69. Which is the best version of the underlined portion of this sentence (reproduced below)?

(69) Above all, it allowed us to share adventures. While traveling across America, which we could not have experienced in cars and hotels.

a. NO CHANGE
b. Above all, it allowed us to share adventures while traveling across America
c. Above all, it allowed us to share adventures; while traveling across America
d. Above all, it allowed us to share adventures—while traveling across America

70. Which is the best version of the underlined portion of this sentence (reproduced below)?

(70) Those are also memories that my siblings and me have now shared with our own children.

a. NO CHANGE
b. Those are also memories that me and my siblings
c. Those are also memories that my siblings and I
d. Those are also memories that I and my siblings

Questions 71–75 are based on the following passage:

We live in a savage world; that's just a simple fact. It is a time of violence, when the need for self-defense is imperative. (71) Martial arts, like Jiu-Jitsu, still play a vital role in ones survival. (72) Jiu-Jitsu, however doesn't justify kicking people around, even when being harassed or attacked. Today, laws prohibit the (73) use of unnecessary force in self-defense; these serve to eliminate beating someone to a pulp once they have been neutralized. Such laws are needed. Apart from being unnecessary to continually strike a person when (74) their down, its immoral. Such over-aggressive retaliation turns the innocent into the aggressor. Jiu-Jitsu provides a way for defending oneself while maintaining the philosophy of restraint and self-discipline. (75) Integrated into its core philosophy, Jiu-Jitsu tempers the potential to do great physical harm with respect for that power and for life.

249

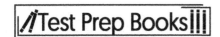

71. Which of the following would be the best choice for this sentence (reproduced below)?

(71) <u>Martial arts, like Jiu-Jitsu, still play a vital role in ones survival.</u>

a. NO CHANGE
b. Martial arts, like Jiu-Jitsu, still play a vital role in one's survival.
c. Martial arts, like Jiu-Jitsu still play a vital role in ones survival.
d. Martial arts, like Jiu-Jitsu, still plays a vital role in one's survival.

72. Which of the following would be the best choice for this sentence (reproduced below)?

(72) <u>Jiu-Jitsu, however doesn't justify kicking people around,</u> even when being harassed or attacked.

a. NO CHANGE
b. Jiu-Jitsu, however, isn't justified by kicking people around,
c. However, Jiu-Jitsu doesn't justify kicking people around,
d. Jiu-Jitsu however doesn't justify kicking people around,

73. Which of the following would be the best choice for this sentence (reproduced below)?

Today, laws prohibit the (73) <u>use of unnecessary force in self-defense; these serve to eliminate</u> beating someone to a pulp once they have been neutralized.

a. NO CHANGE
b. use of unnecessary force in self-defense serving to eliminate
c. use of unnecessary force, in self-defense, these serve to eliminate
d. use of unnecessary force. In self-defense, these serve to eliminate

74. Which of the following would be the best choice for this sentence (reproduced below)?

Apart from being unnecessary to continually strike a person when (74) <u>their down, its immoral.</u>

a. NO CHANGE
b. their down, it's immoral.
c. they're down, its immoral.
d. they're down, it's immoral.

75. Which of the following would be the best choice for this sentence (reproduced below)?

(75) <u>Integrated into its core philosophy,</u> Jiu-Jitsu tempers the potential to do great physical harm with respect for that power, and for life.

a. NO CHANGE
b. Integrated into its core philosophy
c. Integrated into it's core philosophy
d. Integrated into its' core philosophy,

250

Math

1. $3.4 + 2.35 + 4 =$
   - a. 5.35
   - b. 9.2
   - c. 9.75
   - d. 10.25
   - e. 11.15

2. $5.88 \times 3.2 =$
   - a. 18.816
   - b. 16.44
   - c. 20.352
   - d. 17
   - e. 19.25

3. $\frac{3}{25} =$
   - a. 0.15
   - b. 0.1
   - c. 0.9
   - d. 0.75
   - e. 0.12

4. Which of the following is largest?
   - a. 0.45
   - b. 0.096
   - c. 0.3
   - d. 0.313
   - e. 0.25

5. Which of the following is NOT a way to write 40 percent of N?
   - a. $(0.4)N$
   - b. $\frac{2}{5}N$
   - c. $40N$
   - d. $\frac{4N}{10}$
   - e. $\frac{8N}{20}$

6. Which is closest to 17.8×9.9?
   - a. 140
   - b. 180
   - c. 200
   - d. 350
   - e. 400

251

7. A student gets an 85% on a test with 20 questions. How many answers did the student solve correctly?

    a. 15

    b. 16

    c. 17

    d. 18

    e. 19

8. Four people split a bill. The first person pays for $\frac{1}{5}$, the second person pays for $\frac{1}{4}$, and the third person pays for $\frac{1}{3}$. What fraction of the bill does the fourth person pay?

    a. $\frac{13}{60}$

    b. $\frac{47}{60}$

    c. $\frac{1}{4}$

    d. $\frac{4}{15}$

    e. $\frac{1}{2}$

9. 6 is 30% of what number?

    a. 18

    b. 20

    c. 24

    d. 26

    e. 22

10. $3\frac{2}{3} - 1\frac{4}{5} =$

    a. $1\frac{13}{20}$

    b. $\frac{14}{15}$

    c. $2\frac{2}{3}$

    d. $\frac{4}{5}$

    e. $1\frac{13}{15}$

11. What is $\frac{420}{98}$ rounded to the nearest integer?

    a. 4

    b. 3

    c. 5

    d. 6

    e. 2

12. $4\frac{1}{3} + 3\frac{3}{4} =$

    a. $6\frac{5}{12}$

    b. $8\frac{1}{12}$

    c. $8\frac{2}{3}$

    d. $7\frac{7}{12}$

    e. $9\frac{1}{12}$

13. Five of six numbers have a sum of 25. The average of all six numbers is 6. What is the sixth number?
    a. 8
    b. 10
    c. 11
    d. 12
    e. 13

14. $52.3 \times 10^{-3} =$
    a. 0.00523
    b. 0.0523
    c. 0.523
    d. 523
    e. 5,230

15. If $\frac{5}{2} \div \frac{1}{3} = n$, then n is between:
    a. 5 and 7
    b. 1 and 3
    c. 9 and 11
    d. 3 and 5
    e. 7 and 9

16. A closet is filled with red, blue, and green shirts. If $\frac{1}{3}$ of the shirts are green and $\frac{2}{5}$ are red, what fraction of the shirts are blue?

    a. $\frac{4}{15}$

    b. $\frac{1}{5}$

    c. $\frac{7}{15}$

    d. $\frac{1}{2}$

    e. $\frac{1}{3}$

17. Shawna buys $2\frac{1}{2}$ gallons of paint. If she uses $\frac{1}{3}$ of it on the first day, how much does she have left?

    a. $1\frac{5}{6}$ gallons

    b. $1\frac{1}{2}$ gallons

    c. $1\frac{2}{3}$ gallons

    d. 2 gallons

    e. $2\frac{2}{3}$ gallons

18. If $6t + 4 = 16$, what is t?

    a. 1
    b. 2
    c. 3
    d. 4
    e. 5

19. There are $4x + 1$ treats in each party favor bag. If a total of $60x + 15$ treats is distributed, how many bags are given out?

    a. 15
    b. 16
    c. 20
    d. 22
    e. 24

20. In an office, there are 50 workers. A total of 60% of the workers are women, and the chances of a woman wearing a skirt is 50%. If no men wear skirts, how many workers are wearing skirts?

    a. 12
    b. 15
    c. 16
    d. 20
    e. 21

21. If $2x + 6 = 20$, what is x?

    a. 3
    b. 4
    c. 7
    d. 9
    e. 11

22. The variable y is directly proportional to x. If $y = 3$ when $x = 5$, then what is y when $x = 20$?

    a. 10
    b. 12
    c. 14
    d. 16
    e. 18

23. Apples cost $2 each, while oranges cost $3 each. Maria purchased 10 fruits in total and spent $22. How many apples did she buy?

   a. 5
   b. 6
   c. 7
   d. 4
   e. 8

24. What are the polynomial roots of $x^2 + x - 2$?

   a. 1 and -2
   b. -1 and 2
   c. 2 and -2
   d. 9 and 13
   e. 3 and 9

25. What is the y-intercept of $y = x^{5/3} + (x - 3)(x + 1)$?

   a. 3.5
   b. 7.6
   c. -3
   d. -15.1
   e. 3

26. Suppose $\frac{x+2}{x} = 2$. What is x?

   a. -1
   b. 0
   c. 2
   d. 4
   e. -2

27. A rectangle has a length that is 5 feet longer than three times its width. If the perimeter is 90 feet, what is the length in feet?

   a. 10
   b. 20
   c. 25
   d. 35
   e. 40

28. Five students take a test. The scores of the first four students are 80, 85, 75, and 60. If the median score is 80, which of the following could NOT be the score of the fifth student?

   a. 60
   b. 80
   c. 85
   d. 100
   e. 90

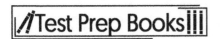

29. Change $3\frac{3}{5}$ to a decimal.

    a. 3.6

    b. 4.67

    c. 5.3

    d. 0.28

    e. 6.3

30. If a car can travel 300 miles in 4 hours, how far can it go in an hour and a half?

    a. 100 miles

    b. 112.5 miles

    c. 135.5 miles

    d. 150 miles

    e. 155 miles

31. Which measure for the center of a small sample set is most affected by outliers?

    a. Mean

    b. Median

    c. Mode

    d. Range

    e. None of these

32. Given the value of a given stock at monthly intervals, which graph should be used to best represent the trend of the stock?

    a. Box plot

    b. Line plot

    c. Scatter plot

    d. Circle graph

    e. Line graph

33. What is the probability of randomly picking the winner and runner-up from a race of four horses and distinguishing which is the winner?

    a. $\frac{1}{4}$

    b. $\frac{1}{2}$

    c. $\frac{1}{16}$

    d. $\frac{1}{12}$

    e. $\frac{1}{3}$

34. Which of the following could be used in the classroom to show $\frac{3}{7} < \frac{5}{6}$ is a true statement?

    a. A bar graph

    b. A number line

    c. An area model

    d. Base 10 blocks

    e. A line graph

35. Add $103,678 + 487$
    a. 103,191
    b. 103,550
    c. 104,265
    d. 104,165
    e. 105,143

36. Add $1.001 + 5.629$
    a. 4.472
    b. 4.628
    c. 5.630
    d. 6.245
    e. 6.630

37. Add $143.77 + 5.2$
    a. 138.57
    b. 148.97
    c. 138.97
    d. 148.57
    e. 149.087

38. What is the next number in the following series: $1, 3, 6, 10, 15, 21, \ldots$?
    a. 26
    b. 27
    c. 28
    d. 29
    e. 30

39. Add and express in reduced form $\frac{14}{33} + \frac{10}{11}$.
    a. $\frac{2}{11}$
    b. $\frac{6}{11}$
    c. $\frac{4}{3}$
    d. $\frac{44}{33}$
    e. $\frac{3}{4}$

40. 32 is 25% of what number?
    a. 64
    b. 128
    c. 12.65
    d. 8
    e. 155

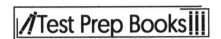

41. Subtract $112,076 - 1,243$.
   a. 109,398
   b. 113,319
   c. 113,833
   d. 110,833
   e. 111,485

42. Carey bought 184 pounds of fertilizer to use on her lawn. Each segment of her lawn required $11\frac{1}{2}$ pounds of fertilizer to do a sufficient job. If a student were asked to determine how many segments could be fertilized with the amount purchased, what operation would be necessary to solve this problem?
   a. Multiplication
   b. Division
   c. Addition
   d. Subtraction
   e. Exponents

43. Subtract $701.1 - 52.33$.
   a. 753.43
   b. 648.77
   c. 652.77
   d. 638.43
   e. 786.34

44. Which of the following expressions best exemplifies the additive and subtractive identity?
   a. $5 + 2 - 0 = 5 + 2 + 0$
   b. $6 + x = 6 - 6$
   c. $9 - 9 = 0$
   d. $8 + 2 = 10$
   e. $7 + 8 = 15$

45. Which of the following is an equivalent measurement for 1.3 cm?
   a. 0.13 m
   b. 13 m
   c. 0.13 mm
   d. 0.013 mm
   e. 0.013 m

46. Divide $1,015 \div 1.4$.
   a. 7,250
   b. 0.725
   c. 7.25
   d. 725
   e. 575

47. At the store, Jan spends $90 on apples and oranges. Apples cost $1 each and oranges cost $2 each. If Jan buys the same number of apples as oranges, how many oranges did she buy?

    a. 20

    b. 25

    c. 30

    d. 35

    e. 40

48. Multiply 12.4×0.2.

    a. 12.6

    b. 2.48

    c. 12.48

    d. 2.6

    e. 4.28

49. Multiply $1,987 \times 0.05$.

    a. 9.935

    b. 99.35

    c. 993.5

    d. 999.35

    e. 93.95

50. A clock reads 5:00 am. What is the measure of the angle formed by the two hands of that clock?

    a. 300 degrees

    b. 150 degrees

    c. 75 degrees

    d. 210 degrees

    e. 285 degrees

51. Divide, express with a remainder $1,202 \div 44$.

    a. $27\frac{2}{7}$

    b. $2\frac{7}{22}$

    c. $7\frac{2}{7}$

    d. $27\frac{7}{22}$

    e. $22\frac{7}{22}$

52. What is the volume of a box with rectangular sides 5 feet long, 6 feet wide, and 3 feet high?

    a. 60 cubic feet

    b. 75 cubic feet

    c. 80 cubic feet

    d. 14 cubic feet

    e. 90 cubic feet

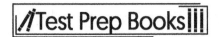

53. Divide 702 ÷ 2.6.
   a. 27
   b. 207
   c. 2.7
   d. 270
   e. 2700

54. A train traveling 50 miles per hour takes a trip lasting 3 hours. If a map has a scale of 1 inch per 10 miles, how many inches apart are the train's starting point and ending point on the map?
   a. 14
   b. 12
   c. 13
   d. 15
   e. 16

55. A traveler takes an hour to drive to a museum, spends 3 hours and 30 minutes there, and takes half an hour to drive home. What percentage of their time was spent driving?
   a. 15%
   b. 30%
   c. 40%
   d. 60%
   e. 70%

56. A truck is carrying three cylindrical barrels. Their bases have a diameter of 2 feet, and they have a height of 3 feet. What is the total volume of the three barrels in cubic feet?
   a. 3π
   b. 9π
   c. 12π
   d. 15π
   e. 18π

57. Greg buys a $10 lunch with 5% sales tax. He leaves a $2 tip after his bill. How much money does he spend?
   a. $12.50
   b. $12
   c. $13
   d. $13.25
   e. $13.50

58. Add 5,089 + 10,323
   a. 15,402
   b. 15,412
   c. 5,234
   d. 15,234
   e. 16,001

59. A teacher is showing students how to evaluate $5 \times 6 + 4 \div 2 - 1$. Which operation should be completed first?
  a. Multiplication
  b. Addition
  c. Division
  d. Subtraction
  e. Exponent

60. What is the definition of a factor of the number 36?
  a. A number that can be divided by 36 and have no remainder
  b. A number that can be added to 36 with no remainder
  c. A prime number that is multiplied times 36
  d. A number that 36 can be divided by and have no remainder
  e. A number that 36 can be multiplied by and have no remainder

Reading

Fiction

Questions 1–10 are based upon the following passage:

"Did you ever come across a protégé of his—one Hyde?" He asked.

"Hyde?" repeated Lanyon. "No. Never heard of him. Since my time."

That was the amount of information that the lawyer carried back with him to the great, dark bed on which he tossed to and fro until the small hours of the morning began to grow large. It was a night of little ease to his toiling mind, toiling in mere darkness and besieged by questions.

Six o'clock struck on the bells of the church that was so conveniently near to Mr. Utterson's dwelling, and still he was digging at the problem. Hitherto it had touched him on the intellectual side alone; but now his imagination also was engaged, or rather enslaved; and as he lay and tossed in the gross darkness of the night in the curtained room, Mr. Enfield's tale went by before his mind in a scroll of lighted pictures. He would be aware of the great field of lamps in a nocturnal city; then of the figure of a man walking swiftly; then of a child running from the doctor's; and then these met, and that human Juggernaut trod the child down and passed on regardless of her screams. Or else he would see a room in a rich house, where his friend lay asleep, dreaming and smiling at his dreams; and then the door of that room would be opened, the curtains of the bed plucked apart, the sleeper recalled, and, lo! There would stand by his side a figure to whom power was given, and even at that dead hour he must rise and do its bidding. The figure in these two phases haunted the lawyer all night; and if at any time he dozed over, it was but to see it glide more stealthily through sleeping houses, or move the more swiftly, and still the more smoothly, even to dizziness, through wider labyrinths of lamplighted city, and at every street corner crush a child and leave her screaming. And still the figure had no face by which he might know it; even in his dreams it had no face, or one that baffled him and melted before his eyes; and thus it was that there sprung up and grew apace in the lawyer's mind a singularly strong,

almost an inordinate, curiosity to behold the features of the real Mr. Hyde. If he could but once set eyes on him, he thought the mystery would lighten and perhaps roll altogether away, as was the habit of mysterious things when well examined. He might see a reason for his friend's strange preference or bondage, and even for the startling clauses of the will. And at least it would be a face worth seeing: the face of a man who was without bowels of mercy: a face which had but to show itself to raise up, in the mind of the unimpressionable Enfield, a spirit of enduring hatred.

From that time forward, Mr. Utterson began to haunt the door in the by-street of shops. In the morning before office hours, at noon when business was plenty and time scarce, at night under the face of the full city moon, by all lights and at all hours of solitude or concourse, the lawyer was to be found on his chosen post.

"If he be Mr. Hyde," he had thought, "I should be Mr. Seek."

Excerpt from The Strange Case of Dr. Jekyll and Mr. Hyde *by Robert Louis Stevenson*

1. What is the purpose of the use of repetition in the following passage?

It was a night of little ease to his toiling mind, toiling in mere darkness and besieged by questions.

a. It serves as a demonstration of the mental state of Mr. Lanyon.
b. It is reminiscent of the church bells that are mentioned in the story.
c. It mimics Mr. Utterson's ambivalence.
d. It emphasizes Mr. Utterson's anguish in failing to identify Hyde's whereabouts.

2. What is the setting of the story in this passage?
a. In the city
b. On the countryside
c. In a jail
d. In a mental health facility

3. What can one infer about the meaning of the word *Juggernaut* from the author's use of it in the passage?
a. It is an apparition that appears at daybreak.
b. It scares children.
c. It is associated with space travel.
d. Mr. Utterson finds it soothing.

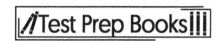

4. What is the definition of the word *haunt* in the following passage?

From that time forward, Mr. Utterson began to haunt the door in the by-street of shops. In the morning before office hours, at noon when business was plenty and time scarce, at night under the face of the full city moon, by all lights and at all hours of solitude or concourse, the lawyer was to be found on his chosen post.

a. To levitate
b. To constantly visit
c. To terrorize
d. To daunt

5. The phrase *labyrinths of lamplighted city* contains an example of what?
a. Hyperbole
b. Simile
c. Juxtaposition
d. Alliteration

6. What can one reasonably conclude from the final comment of this passage?

"If he be Mr. Hyde," he had thought, "I should be Mr. Seek."

a. The speaker is considering a name change.
b. The speaker is experiencing an identity crisis.
c. The speaker has mistakenly been looking for the wrong person.
d. The speaker intends to continue to look for Hyde.

7. The author's attitude toward the main subject of this passage can be described as:
a. Intrigue
b. Elation
c. Animosity
d. Rigidity

8. According to the passage, what is Mr. Utterson struggling with as he tosses and turns in bed?
a. A murderer who is stalking Mr. Utterson since he moved to the city.
b. The mystery surrounding a dark figure and the terrible crimes he commits.
c. The cases he is involved in as a detective.
d. A chronic illness that is causing Mr. Utterson to hallucinate.

9. According to the passage, why did Mr. Utterson start to haunt the doors by the street shops?
a. He was looking for a long, lost love who he kept dreaming about.
b. He was recently homeless, and the street shops offered him food to eat when he was hungry.
c. He was looking for the dark, mysterious figure who he had been obsessing over in his sleep.
d. He was looking for a thief that would regularly steal out of stores.

263

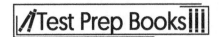
10. What point of view is the passage written in?

    a. First person

    b. Second person

    c. Third person limited

    d. Third person omniscient

Social Science

Questions 11–20 are based on the following passages:

Passage I

Lethal force, or deadly force, is defined as the physical means to cause death or serious harm to another individual. The law holds that lethal force is only accepted when you or another person are in immediate and unavoidable danger of death or severe bodily harm. For example, a person could be beating someone in such a way that the victim is suffering severe trauma that could result in death or serious harm. This would be an instance where lethal force would be acceptable and possibly the only way to save the victim from irrevocable damage.

Another example of when to use lethal force would be when someone enters your home with a deadly weapon. The intruder's presence and possession of the weapon indicate mal-intent and the ability to inflict death or severe injury to you and your loved ones. Again, lethal force can be used in this situation. Lethal force can also be applied to prevent the harm of another individual. If a woman is being brutally assaulted and is unable to fend off an attacker, lethal force can be used to defend her as a last-ditch effort. If she is in immediate jeopardy of rape, harm, and/or death, lethal force could be the only response that could effectively deter the assailant.

The key to understanding the concept of lethal force is the term *last resort*. Deadly force cannot be taken back; it should be used only to prevent severe harm or death. The law does distinguish whether the means of one's self-defense is fully warranted, or if the individual goes out of control in the process. If you continually attack the assailant after they are rendered incapacitated, this would be causing unnecessary harm, and the law can bring charges against you. Likewise, if you kill an attacker unnecessarily after defending yourself, you can be charged with murder. This would move lethal force beyond necessary defense, making it no longer a last resort but rather a use of excessive force.

Passage II

Assault is the unlawful attempt of one person to apply apprehension on another individual by an imminent threat or by initiating offensive contact. Assaults can vary, encompassing physical strikes, threatening body language, and even provocative language. In the case of the latter, even if a hand has not been laid, it is still considered an assault because of its threatening nature.

Let's look at an example: A homeowner is angered because his neighbor blows fallen leaves into his freshly mowed lawn. Irate, the homeowner gestures a fist to his neighbor and threatens to bash his head in for littering on his lawn. The homeowner's physical

motions and verbal threats herald a physical threat against the other neighbor. These factors classify the homeowner's reaction as an assault. If the angry neighbor hits the threatening homeowner in retaliation, that would constitute an assault as well because he physically hit the homeowner.

Assault also centers on the involvement of weapons in a conflict. If someone fires a gun at another person, this could be interpreted as an assault unless the shooter acted in self-defense. If an individual drew a gun or a knife on someone with the intent to harm them, that would be considered assault. However, it's also considered an assault if someone simply aimed a weapon, loaded or not, at another person in a threatening manner.

11. What is the purpose of the second passage?
    a. To inform the reader about what assault is and how it is committed
    b. To inform the reader about how assault is a minor example of lethal force
    c. To disprove the previous passage concerning lethal force
    d. The author is recounting an incident in which they were assaulted

12. Which of the following situations, according to the passages, would not constitute an illegal use of lethal force?
    a. A disgruntled cashier yells obscenities at a customer.
    b. A thief is seen running away with stolen cash.
    c. A man is attacked in an alley by another man with a knife.
    d. A woman punches another woman in a bar.

13. Given the information in the passages, which of the following must be true about assault?
    a. Assault charges are more severe than unnecessary use of force charges.
    b. There are various forms of assault.
    c. Smaller, weaker people cannot commit assaults.
    d. Assault is justified only as a last resort.

14. Which of the following, if true, would most seriously undermine the explanation proposed by the author of Passage I in the third paragraph?
    a. An instance of lethal force in self-defense is not absolutely absolved from blame. The law considers the necessary use of force at the time it is committed.
    b. An individual who uses lethal force under necessary defense is in direct compliance of the law under most circumstances.
    c. Lethal force in self-defense should be forgiven in all cases for the peace of mind of the primary victim.
    d. The use of lethal force is not evaluated on the intent of the user but rather the severity of the primary attack that warranted self-defense.

15. Based on the passages, what can be inferred about the relationship between assault and lethal force?
   a. An act of lethal force always leads to a type of assault.
   b. An assault will result in someone using lethal force.
   c. An assault with deadly intent can lead to an individual using lethal force to preserve their well-being.
   d. If someone uses self-defense in a conflict, it is called deadly force; if actions or threats are intended, it is called assault.

16. Which of the following best describes the way the passages are structured?
   a. Both passages open by defining a legal concept and then continue to describe situations that further explain the concept.
   b. Both passages begin with situations, introduce accepted definitions, and then cite legal ramifications.
   c. Passage I presents a long definition while the Passage II begins by showing an example of assault.
   d. Both cite specific legal doctrines, then proceed to explain the rulings.

17. What can be inferred about the role of intent in lethal force and assault?
   a. Intent is irrelevant. The law does not take intent into account.
   b. Intent is vital for determining the lawfulness of using lethal force.
   c. Intent is very important for determining both lethal force and assault; intent is examined in both parties and helps determine the severity of the issue.
   d. The intent of the assailant is the main focus for determining legal ramifications; it is used to determine if the defender was justified in using force to respond.

18. The author uses the example in the second paragraph of Passage II in order to do what?
   a. To demonstrate two different types of assault by showing how each specifically relates to the other
   b. To demonstrate a single example of two different types of assault, then adding in the third type of assault in the example's conclusion
   c. To prove that the definition of lethal force is altered when the victim in question is a homeowner and his property is threatened
   d. To suggest that verbal assault can be an exaggerated crime by the law and does not necessarily lead to physical violence

19. As it is used in the second passage, the word *apprehension* most nearly means:
   a. Pain
   b. Exhaustion
   c. Fear
   d. Honor

20. One of the main purposes of the last paragraph in the first passage is to state:
   a. How assault is different when used in the home versus when it is used out in public.
   b. A specific example of lethal force so that the audience will know what it looks like.
   c. Why police officers defend those who use lethal force but do not defend those who use assault.
   d. The concept of lethal force as a last resort and the point at which it can cross a line from defense to manslaughter.

Humanities

Questions 21–30 are based upon the following passage:

My Good Friends,—When I first imparted to the committee of the projected Institute my particular wish that on one of the evenings of my readings here the main body of my audience should be composed of working men and their families, I was animated by two desires; first, by the wish to have the great pleasure of meeting you face to face at this Christmas time, and accompany you myself through one of my little Christmas books; and second, by the wish to have an opportunity of stating publicly in your presence, and in the presence of the committee, my earnest hope that the Institute will, from the beginning, recognise one great principle—strong in reason and justice—which I believe to be essential to the very life of such an Institution. It is, that the working man shall, from the first unto the last, have a share in the management of an Institution which is designed for his benefit, and which calls itself by his name.

I have no fear here of being misunderstood—of being supposed to mean too much in this. If there ever was a time when any one class could of itself do much for its own good, and for the welfare of society—which I greatly doubt—that time is unquestionably past. It is in the fusion of different classes, without confusion; in the bringing together of employers and employed; in the creating of a better common understanding among those whose interests are identical, who depend upon each other, who are vitally essential to each other, and who never can be in unnatural antagonism without deplorable results, that one of the chief principles of a Mechanics' Institution should consist. In this world, a great deal of the bitterness among us arises from an imperfect understanding of one another. Erect in Birmingham a great Educational Institution, properly educational; educational of the feelings as well as of the reason; to which all orders of Birmingham men contribute; in which all orders of Birmingham men meet; wherein all orders of Birmingham men are faithfully represented—and you will erect a Temple of Concord here which will be a model edifice to the whole of England.

Contemplating as I do the existence of the Artisans' Committee, which not long ago considered the establishment of the Institute so sensibly, and supported it so heartily, I earnestly entreat the gentlemen—earnest I know in the good work, and who are now among us—by all means to avoid the great shortcoming of similar institutions; and in asking the working man for his confidence, to set him the great example and give him theirs in return. You will judge for yourselves if I promise too much for the working man, when I say that he will stand by such an enterprise with the utmost of his patience, his perseverance, sense, and support; that I am sure he will need no charitable aid or condescending patronage; but will readily and cheerfully pay for the advantages which it confers; that he will prepare himself in individual cases where he feels that the adverse circumstances around him have rendered it necessary; in a word, that he will feel his responsibility like an honest man, and will most honestly and manfully discharge it. I now proceed to the pleasant task to which I assure you I have looked forward for a long time.

From Charles Dickens' speech in Birmingham in England on December 30, 1853 on behalf of the Birmingham and Midland Institute.

267

21. Which word is most closely synonymous with the word *patronage* as it appears in the following statement?

   ...that I am sure he will need no charitable aid or condescending patronage

   a. Auspices
   b. Aberration
   c. Acerbic
   d. Adulation

22. Which term is most closely aligned with the definition of the term *working man* as it is defined in the following passage?

   You will judge for yourselves if I promise too much for the working man, when I say that he will stand by such an enterprise with the utmost of his patience, his perseverance, sense, and support...

   a. Athlete
   b. Viscount
   c. Entrepreneur
   d. Bourgeois

23. Which of the following statements most closely correlates with the definition of the term *working man* as it is defined in Question 22?
   a. A working man is not someone who works for institutions or corporations, but someone who is well-versed in the workings of the soul.
   b. A working man is someone who is probably not involved in social activities because the physical demand for work is too high.
   c. A working man is someone who works for wages among the middle class.
   d. The working man has historically taken to the field, to the factory, and now to the screen.

24. Based upon the contextual evidence provided in the passage above, what is the meaning of the term *enterprise* in the third paragraph?
   a. Company
   b. Courage
   c. Game
   d. Cause

25. The speaker addresses his audience as *My Good Friends.* What kind of credibility does this salutation give to the speaker?
   a. The speaker is an employer addressing his employees, so the salutation is a way for the boss to bridge the gap between himself and his employees.
   b. The speaker's salutation is one from an entertainer to his audience and uses the friendly language to connect to his audience before a serious speech.
   c. The salutation is used ironically to give a somber tone to the serious speech that follows.
   d. The speech is one from a politician to the public, so the salutation is used to grab the audience's attention.

26. According to the passage, what is the speaker's second desire for his time in front of the audience?
    a. To read a Christmas story
    b. For the working man to have a say in his institution, which is designed for his benefit
    c. To have an opportunity to stand in their presence
    d. For the life of the institution to be essential to the audience as a whole

27. The speaker's tone in the passage can be described as:
    a. Happy and gullible
    b. Lazy and entitled
    c. Confident and informed
    d. Angry and frustrated

28. One of the main purposes of the last paragraph is:
    a. To persuade the audience to support the Institute no matter what since it provided so much support to the working class.
    b. To market the speaker's new book while at the same time supporting the activities of the Institute.
    c. To inform the audience that the Institute is corrupt and will not help them out when the time comes to give them compensation.
    d. To provide credibility to the working man and share confidence in their ability to take on responsibilities if they are compensated appropriately.

29. According to the passage, what does the speaker wish to erect in Birmingham?
    a. An Educational Institution
    b. The Temple of Concord
    c. A Writing Workshop
    d. A VA Hospital

30. As it is used in the second paragraph, the word *antagonism* most nearly means:
    a. Conformity
    b. Opposition
    c. Affluence
    d. Scarcity

Natural Science

Questions 31–40 are based upon the following passage:

Three years ago, I think there were not many bird-lovers in the United States who believed it possible to prevent the total extinction of both egrets from our fauna. All the known rookeries accessible to plume-hunters had been totally destroyed. Two years ago, the secret discovery of several small, hidden colonies prompted William Dutcher, President of the National Association of Audubon Societies, and Mr. T. Gilbert Pearson, Secretary, to attempt the protection of those colonies. With a fund contributed for the purpose, wardens were hired and duly commissioned. As previously stated, one of those wardens was shot dead in cold blood by a plume hunter. The task of guarding swamp rookeries from the attacks of money-hungry desperadoes to whom the accursed plumes were worth their weight in gold, is a very chancy proceeding. There is now one warden in Florida who says that "before they get my rookery they will first have to get me."

Thus far the protective work of the Audubon Association has been successful. Now there are twenty colonies, which contain all told, about 5,000 egrets and about 120,000 herons and ibises which are guarded by the Audubon wardens. One of the most important is on Bird Island, a mile out in Orange Lake, central Florida, and it is ably defended by Oscar E. Baynard. To-day, the plume hunters who do not dare to raid the guarded rookeries are trying to study out the lines of flight of the birds, to and from their feeding-grounds, and shoot them in transit. Their motto is—"Anything to beat the law, and get the plumes." It is there that the state of Florida should take part in the war.

The success of this campaign is attested by the fact that last year a number of egrets were seen in eastern Massachusetts—for the first time in many years. And so to-day the question is, can the wardens continue to hold the plume-hunters at bay?

Excerpt from *Our Vanishing Wildlife* by William T. Hornaday

31. The author's use of first-person pronouns in the following text does NOT have which of the following effects?

Three years ago, I think there were not many bird-lovers in the United States who believed it possible to prevent the total extinction of both egrets from our fauna.

a. The phrase *I think* acts as a sort of hedging, where the author's tone is less direct and/or absolute.
b. It allows the reader to more easily connect with the author.
c. It encourages the reader to empathize with the egrets.
d. It distances the reader from the text by overemphasizing the story.

32. What purpose does the quote serve at the end of the first paragraph?
a. The quote shows proof of a hunter threatening one of the wardens.
b. The quote lightens the mood by illustrating the colloquial language of the region.
c. The quote provides an example of a warden protecting one of the colonies.
d. The quote provides much needed comic relief in the form of a joke.

270

33. What is the meaning of the word *rookeries* in the following text?

> To-day, the plume hunters who do not dare to raid the guarded rookeries are trying to study out the lines of flight of the birds, to and from their feeding-grounds, and shoot them in transit.

    a. Houses in a slum area
    b. A place where hunters gather to trade tools
    c. A place where wardens go to trade stories
    d. A colony of breeding birds

34. What is on Bird Island?
    a. Hunters selling plumes
    b. An important bird colony
    c. Bird Island Battle between the hunters and the wardens
    d. An important egret with unique plumes

35. What is the main purpose of the passage?
    a. To persuade the audience to act in preservation of the bird colonies
    b. To show the effect hunting egrets has had on the environment
    c. To argue that the preservation of bird colonies has had a negative impact on the environment
    d. To demonstrate the success of the protective work of the Audubon Association

36. According to the passage, why are hunters trying to study the lines of flight of the birds?
    a. To study ornithology, one must know the lines of flight that birds take.
    b. To help wardens preserve the lives of the birds
    c. To have a better opportunity to hunt the birds
    d. To build their homes under the lines of flight because they believe it brings good luck

37. A year before the passage was written, where were a number of egrets seen?
    a. California
    b. Florida
    c. Eastern Massachusetts
    d. Western Texas

38. As it is used in the first paragraph, the word *commissioned* most nearly means:
    a. Appointed
    b. Compelled
    c. Beguiled
    d. Fortified

39. What happened two years before the passage was written?
    a. The plume hunters didn't dare to raid the rookeries, as they are heavily guarded.
    b. Twenty colonies have emerged as thousands of egrets are protected and make their homes in safe havens.
    c. The plume hunters tried to shoot the birds in their line of flight.
    d. Several hidden colonies were found which prompted Dutcher and Pearson to protect them.

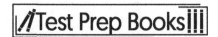

40. As it is used in the second paragraph, the phrase *in transit* most nearly means:
    a. On a journey or trip
    b. To give authority to
    c. On the way to the destination
    d. To make angry

Science

Passage 1

Questions 1–5 pertain to Passage 1:

Scientists use the scientific method to investigate a theory or solve a problem. It includes four steps: observation, hypothesis, experiment, and conclusion. Observation occurs when the scientist uses one of their senses to identify what they want to study. A hypothesis is a conclusive sentence about what the scientist wants to research. It generally includes an explanation for the observations, can be tested experimentally, and predicts the outcome. The experiment includes the parameters for the testing that will occur. The conclusion will state whether or not the hypothesis was supported.

Scientist A would like to know how sunlight affects the growth of a plant. She says that more sunlight will cause the plant to grow faster. She sets up her experimental groups and tests her hypothesis over 11 days.

Figure 1 below shows the experimental data Scientist A collected over 11 days.

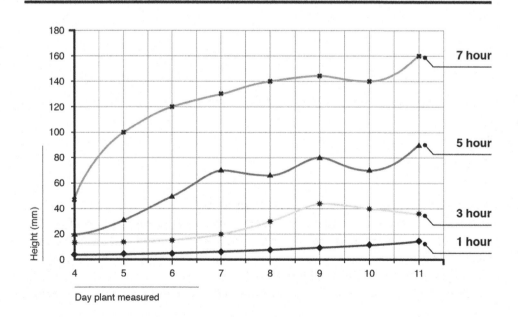

Length and height of plants in the sunlight

272

Figure 2 below represents the process of photosynthesis that occurs in plants.

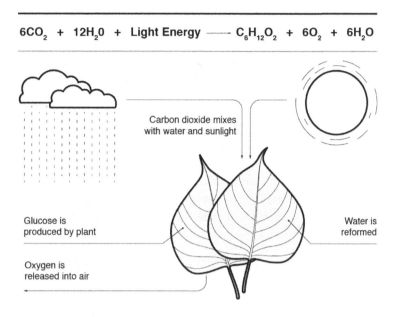

$$6CO_2 + 12H_2O + Light\ Energy \longrightarrow C_6H_{12}O_2 + 6O_2 + 6H_2O$$

Carbon dioxide mixes
with water and sunlight

Glucose is
produced by plant

Water is
reformed

Oxygen is
released into air

1. What is her hypothesis?
   a. More sunlight will cause the plant to grow faster.
   b. She will test her theory over 11 days.
   c. How sunlight affects plant growth.
   d. Plants do not grow well with one hour of sunlight per day.

2. How many experimental groups does she have?
   a. 1
   b. 3
   c. 4
   d. 11

3. What type of chart is represented in the first figure?
   a. Bar graph
   b. Line graph
   c. Pie chart
   d. Pictogram

4. What part of the photosynthesis reaction is provided directly by sunlight?
   a. Light energy
   b. H_2O
   c. CO_2
   d. Glucose

5. What should her conclusion be based on her experimental data?
   a. 5 hours of sunlight is optimal for plant growth.
   b. Plants should only be measured for 11 days.
   c. Less sunlight is better for plant growth.
   d. Providing plants with more sunlight makes them grow bigger.

273

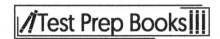
Passage 2

Questions 6–10 pertain to Passage 2:

The periodic table contains all known 118 chemical elements. The first 98 elements are found naturally while the remaining were synthesized by scientists. The elements are ordered according to the number of protons they contain, also known as their atomic number. For example, hydrogen has an atomic number of one and is found in the top left corner of the periodic table, whereas radon has an atomic number of 86 and is found closer on the right side of the periodic table, several rows down. The rows are called periods and the columns are called groups. The elements are arranged by similar chemical properties.

Each chemical element represents an individual atom. When atoms are linked together, they form molecules. The smallest molecule contains just two atoms, but molecules can also be very large and contain hundreds of atoms. In order to find the mass of a molecule, the atomic mass of each individual atom in the molecule must be added together.

Figure 1 below depicts the trends and commonalities between the elements that can be seen in the periodic table.

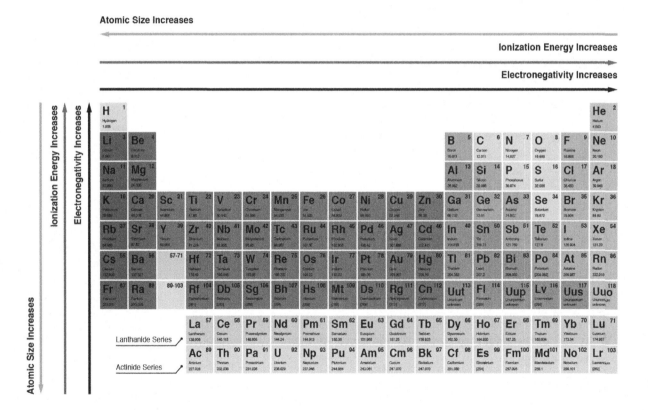

Figure 2 below shows what the information in each element's box represents.

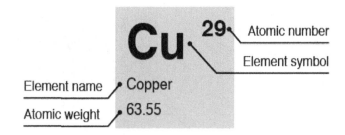

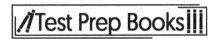
Figure 3 below shows the periodic table with color coding according to the groups and periods.

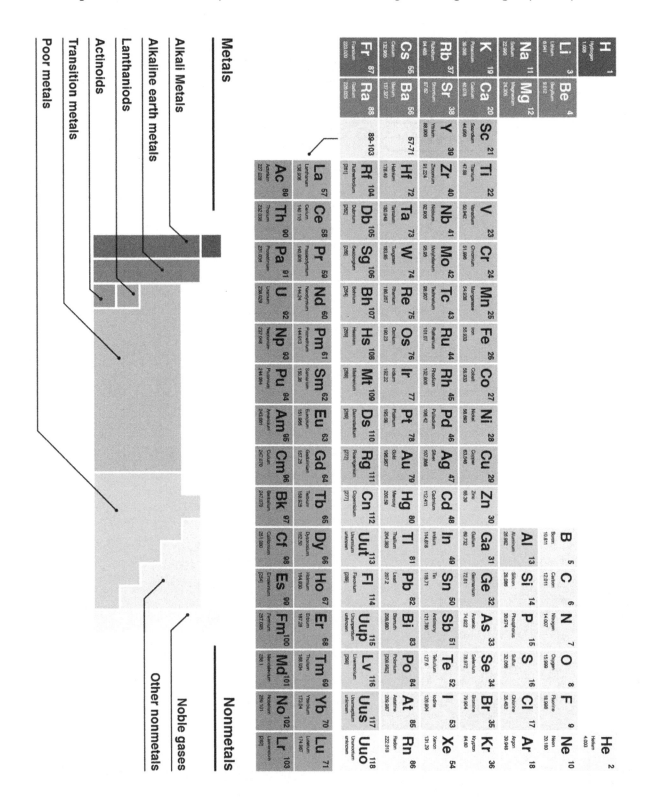

276

6. What is the atomic mass of NaCl?
    a. 23
    b. 58.5
    c. 35.5
    d. 71

7. Which of the following elements is most electronegative?
    a. Ununoctium (Uuo)
    b. Francium (Fr)
    c. Hydrogen (H)
    d. Helium (He)

8. Which of the following elements has the lowest ionization energy?
    a. Potassium (K)
    b. Gallium (Ga)
    c. Sodium (Na)
    d. Aluminum (Al)

9. Which element has the fewest number of protons?
    a. Radon (Rn)
    b. Boron (B)
    c. Nitrogen (N)
    d. Hydrogen (H)

10. Scientist A needs a noble gas for her experiment. Which of these elements should she consider using?
    a. Nitrogen (N)
    b. Radon (Rn)
    c. Copper (Cu)
    d. Boron (B)

Passage 3

Questions 11–15 pertain to Passage 3:

Physical characteristics are controlled by genes. Each gene has two alleles, or variations. Generally, one allele is more dominant than the other allele and when one of each allele is present on the gene, the physical trait of the dominant allele will be expressed. The allele that is not expressed is called the recessive allele. Recessive alleles are expressed only when both alleles present on the gene are the recessive allele.

Punnett squares are diagrams that can predict the outcome of crossing different traits. In these diagrams, dominant alleles are represented by uppercase letters and recessive alleles are represented by lowercase letters.

Scientist A wants to grow white flowered plants and is doing a series of crossbreeding experiments. She had each plant genetically tested so she knows which alleles comprise each plant. The dominant flowers are red (A) and the recessive allele (a) produces white flowers.

Figure 1 below represents the different flowers that underwent crossbreeding during Round #1A

Round #1A

Crossbreeding #1A		Crossbreeding #2A		Crossbreeding #2A	
A	**a**	**a**	**a**	**a**	**a**
A AA	Aa	**A** Aa	Aa	**A** Aa	Aa
A AA	Aa	**A** Aa	Aa	**a** aa	aa

Figure 2 below represents the number of flowers that were red and white after the first round of crossbreeding experiments.

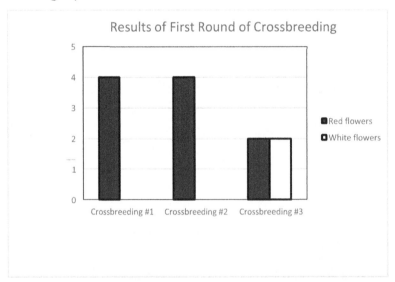

During her second round of crossbreeding, she adds in a plant of unknown genetic makeup with red flowers. She crosses it with a white-flowering plant. The results of her experiment are represented in the next figure.

Figure 3 represents the genetic results from the second round of crossbreeding.

Round #2		
	a	a
?	Aa	Aa
?	aa	aa

Scientist A takes offspring plants from Round #1A and crossbreeds them with each other and calls this Round #1B.

Figure 4 below represents the results of crossbreeding from Round #1B.

Crossbreeding #1B			Crossbreeding #2B			Crossbreeding #2B		
	A	a		A	a		a	a
A	AA	Aa	A	AA	Aa	a	aa	aa
A	AA	Aa	a	Aa	aa	a	aa	aa

11. Crossbreeding which two plants will give her the highest likelihood of obtaining some white plants right away in Round #1A?
    a. AA×Aa
    b. Aa×aa
    c. AA×aa
    d. AA×AA

12. What percentage of plants are white after the first crossbreeding reactions?
    a. 12
    b. 50
    c. 16.7
    d. 25

13. What is the genetic makeup of the unknown plant from the second round of crossbreeding?
    a. aa
    b. Aa
    c. AA
    d. Cannot be determined

279

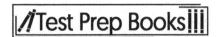
14. From which group of crossbreeding in Round #1B can she obtain 100% white flowers by the second generation?
    a. They are all equal.
    b. 1B
    c. 2B
    d. 3B

15. Which of her five senses did she use for the observation step of the scientific method here?
    a. Sight
    b. Smell
    c. Touch
    d. Hearing

Passage 4

Questions 16–20 pertain to Passage 4:

Rainforests cover approximately 6% of the Earth's surface. Tropical rainforests are found in five major areas of the world: Central America, South America, Central Africa, Asia stretching from India to islands in the Pacific Ocean, and Australia. All of these areas are warm and wet areas within ten degrees of the equator. They do not have a substantial dry season during the year.

Rainforests are large areas of jungle that get an abundance of rain. They comprise four layers, each with unique characteristics. The emergent layer is the highest layer and is made up of the tops of the tall trees. There is very good sunlight in this layer. The canopy layer is the next layer, just under the emergent layer. Here, there is some sun but not as much as the emergent layer. The next layer is the understory layer. This layer does not receive very much sunlight. The plants in this layer need to grow very large leaves to reach the sun. The bottom-most layer is the forest floor. Sunlight generally does not reach this layer, so plants do not grow here.

Figure 1 below represents the different layers of the rainforest.

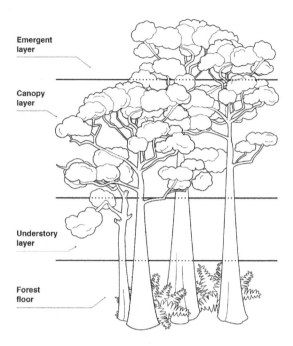

Figure 2 below is a map of the rainforests on Earth and a map of Central America.

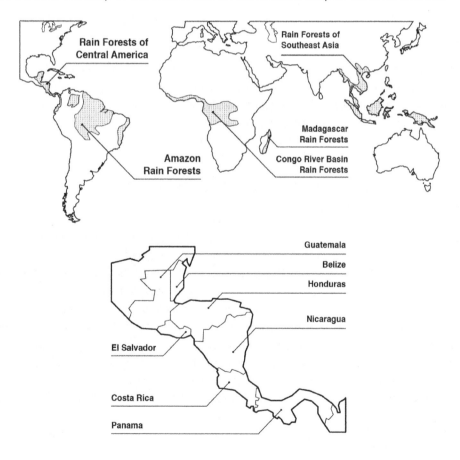

281

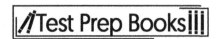

16. What essential part of photosynthesis, which is necessary for plant growth, is lacking on the forest floor and does not allow for plants to grow?
    a. Carbon
    b. Water
    c. Oxygen
    d. Sunlight

17. Which is a country in Central America that contains a rainforest?
    a. India
    b. Panama
    c. Madagascar
    d. Brazil

18. In which layer of the rainforest would birds fly around the most?
    a. Forest floor
    b. Understory layer
    c. Emergent layer
    d. Canopy layer

19. Giant taro plants have the largest leaves in the world that are approximately ten feet in length. In which layer of the rainforest do they reside?
    a. Emergent layer
    b. Canopy layer
    c. Forest floor
    d. Understory layer

20. Which of these plants, based on their listed requirements, would thrive in a rainforest climate?
    a. Giant water lily: warm temperatures, wet environment, has ability to grow large leaves
    b. Cactus: dry environment, long, hot season for growth
    c. Pine tree: dry and sandy soil, lots of sunlight
    d. Black-eyed susan: very hot temperatures, slightly moist soil

Passage 5

Questions 21–25 pertain to Passage 5:

An eclipse occurs when the light from one object in the solar system is completely or partially blocked by another object in the solar system. In 2017, the Earth was a part of two different types of eclipses. One was a solar eclipse, which occurs when the moon passes between the Sun and the Earth and blocks the Sun's light, making it dark during the daytime for several minutes. A total solar eclipse occurs when the moon completely covers the Sun. A partial solar eclipse occurs when the moon only covers part of the Sun. Solar eclipses should not be looked at directly because the Sun's rays can damage a person's eyes even though they appear to be dim while the eclipse is happening. Special viewing devices can be used to look at a solar eclipse indirectly, such as a pinhole camera facing away from the eclipse that allows light from the eclipse to pass through a hole in a piece of cardboard and its image to be reflected on a piece of white paper.

The other type of eclipse that the Earth was a part of was a lunar eclipse. This type of eclipse occurs when the moon passes behind the Earth, into its shadow. The moon is illuminated by the light of the sun, so when it is in the Earth's shadow, the moon becomes dim for a few hours during the night. This type of eclipse is safe to look at without any protection for your eyes.

Figure 1 below represents a solar eclipse.

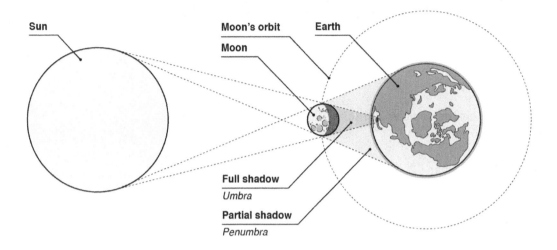

Figure 2 below represents a lunar eclipse.

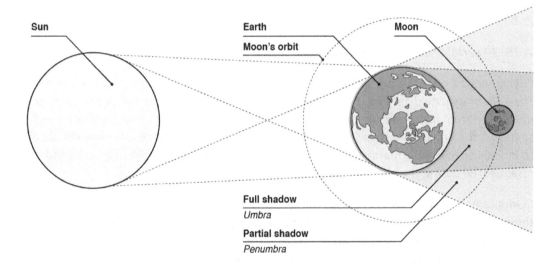

21. Which apparatus would be best to use to look at a solar eclipse?
    a. A telescope facing the eclipse
    b. A pinhole camera facing away from the eclipse
    c. Sunglasses facing the eclipse
    d. Binoculars facing the eclipse

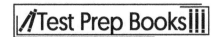

22. What type of eclipse occurs when the moon comes between the Earth and Sun and covers the Sun's light completely?
    a. Total solar eclipse
    b. Partial lunar eclipse
    c. Total lunar eclipse
    d. Partial solar eclipse

23. What object in the solar system becomes dim during a lunar eclipse?
    a. Sun
    b. Earth
    c. Moon
    d. Earth and moon

24. Which type of eclipse could you observe directly using a telescope?
    a. Neither solar nor lunar
    b. Lunar only
    c. Both solar and lunar
    d. Solar only

25. Which type of eclipse is viewed during the daytime?
    a. Both solar and lunar
    b. Solar only
    c. Partial lunar
    d. Total lunar

Passage 6

Questions 26–30 pertain to Passage 6:

Phylogenetic trees are diagrams that map out the proposed evolutionary history of a species. They are branching diagrams that make it easy to see how scientists believe certain species developed from other species. The most recent proposed common ancestor between two species is the one before their lineages branch in the diagram. These diagrams do not attempt to include specific information about physical traits that were thought to be retained or disappeared during the evolutionary process.

Cladograms classify organisms based on their proposed common ancestry but are focused on their common physical traits. Branching points on these diagrams represent when a group of organisms is thought to have developed a new trait. Analogous features are those that have the same function but were not derived from a common ancestor. Homologous features have anatomical similarities, even if the function is no longer the same, due to a proposed common ancestor.

284

Figure 1 below is a phylogenetic tree of the Carnivora order.

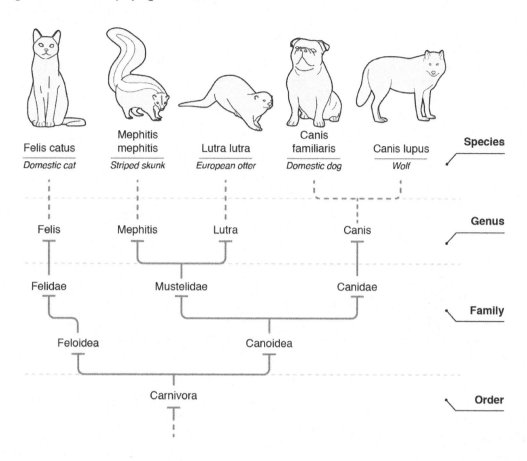

Figure 2 below is a cladogram.

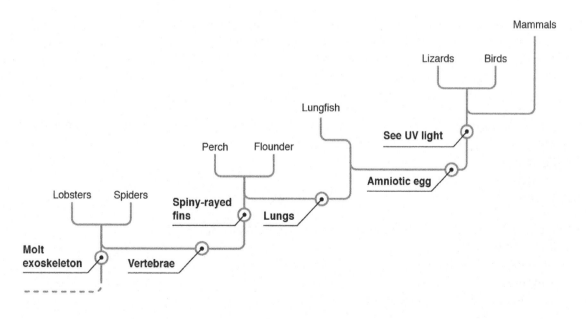

Figure 3 below shows a homologous feature between four different species with a proposed common ancestor.

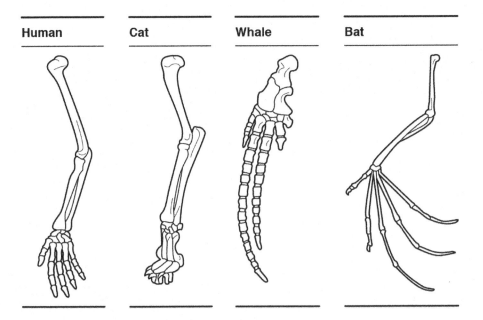

26. Which tool would you use to find out when a common ancestor of two species supposedly developed lungs?
    a. Phylogenetic tree
    b. Cladogram
    c. Punnett square
    d. Photographs

27. According to the earlier details, how are human arms and whale fins related?
    a. They are homologous structures from a common ancestor.
    b. They both have the same number of bones.
    c. They are analogous features.
    d. They are both covered in the same type of skin.

28. According to Figure 1, what common ancestry group do the striped skunk and European otter share?
    a. Mephitis
    b. Felidae
    c. Canidae
    d. Mustelidae

29. What trait do lizards and birds have in common according to Figure 2?
    a. Both see UV light
    b. Both have spiny-rayed fins
    c. Both molt an exoskeleton
    d. They do not have any traits in common.

30. According to Figure 1, at what level of organization are domestic cats and wolves related?
   a. Family
   b. Genus
   c. Order
   d. Species

Passage 7

Questions 31–35 pertain to Passage 7:

Scientists often use an assay called an enzyme-linked immunosorbent assay, or ELISA, to quantify specific substances within a larger sample. An ELISA works based on the specificity of an antibody to an antigen. One type of ELISA is called a sandwich ELISA. In this type of ELISA, a plate is coated with a capture antibody that adheres the antigen in the sample when it is added. Then the primary antibody is added and sticks to any antigen bound to the capture antibody. Next, a secondary antibody is added. Once it attaches to the primary antibody, it releases a colored tag that can be detected by a piece of laboratory equipment. If more color is released, it is indicative of more antigen having been present in the sample.

Figure 1 below describes how a sandwich ELISA works.

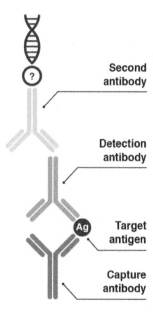

The cytokine protein IL-1β is a marker of inflammation in the body. Scientist A took samples from different locations within the body to find out where there was elevated inflammation in a patient.

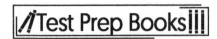
Figure 2 below is a picture of the ELISA plate from Scientist A's experiment.

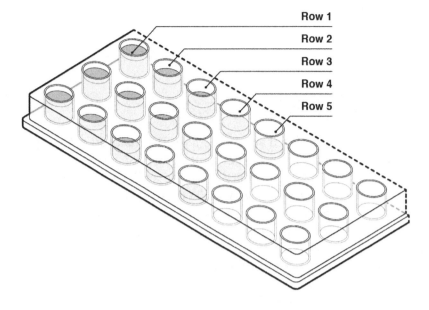

Figure 3 below is a graph of the results of Scientist A's experiment.

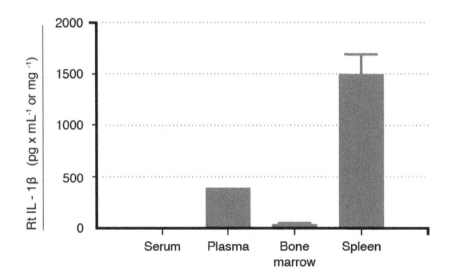

31. Which step of the ELISA allows for the color to be released for detection of the antigen?
    a. Addition of the antigen
    b. Addition of the primary antibody
    c. The presence of the capture antibody
    d. Addition of the secondary antibody

32. According to Figure 2, which row had the largest amount of antigen in the sample?
    a. Row 2
    b. Row 1
    c. Row 5
    d. Row 3

33. According to the ELISA results in Figure 3, which area of the body had the most inflammation?
    a. Serum
    b. Plasma
    c. Spleen
    d. Bone marrow

34. Which two antibodies sandwich the antigen in a sandwich ELISA?
    a. Capture antibody and secondary antibody
    b. Capture antibody and primary antibody
    c. Primary antibody and secondary antibody
    d. Two units of the secondary antibody

35. What is the purpose of an ELISA?
    a. Quantify specific substances within a larger sample
    b. Quantify all substances within a larger sample
    c. To create a colorful pattern with the samples
    d. To develop different antibodies

Passage 8

Questions 36–40 pertain to Passage 8:

Natural selection is the idea that certain traits make an individual have longer survival and higher reproduction rates than other individuals. It is based on the **phenotype**, or physical appearance, of the individual and not the **genotype**, or genetic makeup. There are three ways in which a phenotype can change due to natural selection. Directional selection occurs when one extreme of a phenotype is favored. Disruptive selection occurs when both extremes of a phenotype are favored. Stabilizing selection occurs when an intermediate phenotype is favored over either extreme phenotype.

Scenario 1: Mice live in an environment that has a mix of light and dark colored rocks. To avoid predators, the mice with intermediate color fur survive longer and produce more offspring.

Scenario 2: The Galapagos Islands experienced a drought and large, tough seeds became abundant. Finches developed large beaks to break up these seeds.

Scenario 3: In Cameroon, seeds are either large or small. Finches in Cameroon have either large beaks or small beaks. They are not found with medium-sized beaks.

36. What type of selection is described in Scenario 1?
    a. Stabilizing selection
    b. Directional selection
    c. Disruptive selection
    d. Color selection

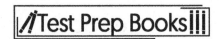

37. What type of selection is described in Scenario 2?
   a. Beak-type
   b. Disruptive
   c. Stabilizing
   d. Directional

38. Why would it be hard for small-beaked finches in the Galapagos Island to survive after the drought?
   a. Too much sand got caught in the small beaks
   b. Beaks would not be able to break up large seeds
   c. Large-beaked finches would attack them
   d. Two extreme phenotypes can never be selected by natural selection

39. What type of selection is described in Scenario 3?
   a. Stabilizing
   b. Directional
   c. Disruptive
   d. Beak-type

40. Which statement is true about natural selection?
   a. Individuals are selected based on their genotype.
   b. An extreme phenotype is always selected.
   c. It only occurs after a drought.
   d. Individuals are selected based on phenotypes that are advantageous for survival and reproduction.

Writing

Directions

Write an organized, coherent essay about the passage below. In your essay, make sure you:

- Clearly state your own opinion on the issue and analyze the relationships between your perspective and at least one other perspective
- Develop and support your ideas with evidence
- Organize your ideas logically
- Communicate your ideas in standard English

Prompt

A common societal expectation is that high school students will pursue a college degree after they graduate. Some may argue that is hard to get a high-paying job or be successful without a college degree, but others disagree, saying that pursuing a vocational trade will make more money in the long run because training for such jobs is much more affordable than the traditional four-year degree. Even others may advocate for a gap year so that young adults can get work experience and determine what career path they would like to pursue.

290

Perspectives

1. Many jobs require a college degree, so individuals who do not attend will have more limited career options. College graduates may even pursue a career outside of their degree programs because many hiring managers simply look for candidates with a bachelor's degree, regardless of its specific field. Furthermore, those who have aspirations to become doctors, lawyers, professors, etc., will need to attend graduate school, so of course undergraduate school is a necessity.

2. Some students are not enthralled by academics or motivated by grades, and therefore might have difficulty in a traditional college program. Instead of wasting money on tuition and other college fees, these individuals can pursue trade school or a vocation that does not require a degree. Trade schools offer shorter programs and sometimes allow students to begin making money right away, and other careers such as professional cleaning or nannying may not require any specific schooling.

3. Often, high school graduates do not know exactly what they want to do with their futures. Instead of going right to school, they may want to take a gap year to work, travel, or participate in a more formal gap year program designed to help young people find clarity and direction. Some may discover a passion for a certain area of work that they were unfamiliar with before.

Answer Explanations #1

English

1. C: Choice *C* correctly uses *from* to describe the fact that dogs are related to wolves. The word *through* is incorrectly used here, so Choice *A* is incorrect. Choice *B* makes no sense. Choice *D* unnecessarily changes the verb tense in addition to incorrectly using *through*.

2. B: Choice *B* is correct because the Oxford comma is applied, clearly separating the specific terms. Choice *A* lacks this clarity. Choice *C* is correct but too wordy since commas can be easily applied. Choice *D* doesn't flow with the sentence's structure.

3. D: Choice *D* correctly uses the question mark, fixing the sentence's main issue. Thus, Choice *A* is incorrect because questions do not end with periods. Choice *B,* although correctly written, changes the meaning of the original sentence. Choice *C* is incorrect because it completely changes the direction of the sentence, disrupts the flow of the paragraph, and lacks the crucial question mark.

4. A: Choice *A* is correct since there are no errors in the sentence. Choices *B* and *C* both have extraneous commas, disrupting the flow of the sentence. Choice *D* unnecessarily rearranges the sentence.

5. D: Choice *D* is correct because the commas serve to distinguish that *artificial selection* is just another term for *selective breeding* before the sentence continues. The structure is preserved, and the sentence can flow with more clarity. Choice *A* is incorrect because the sentence needs commas to avoid being a run-on. Choice *B* is close but still lacks the required comma after *selection*, so this is incorrect. Choice *C* is incorrect because the comma to set off the aside should be placed after *breeding* instead of *called*.

6. B: Choice *B* is correct because the sentence is talking about a continuing process. Therefore, the best modification is to add the word *to* in front of *increase*. Choice *A* is incorrect because this modifier is missing. Choice *C* is incorrect because, with the additional comma, the present tense of *increase* is inappropriate. Choice *D* makes more sense, but the tense is still not the best to use.

7. A: The sentence has no errors, so Choice *A* is correct. Choice *B* is incorrect because it adds an unnecessary comma. Choice *C* is incorrect because *advantage* should not be plural in this sentence without the removal of the singular *an*. Choice *D* is very tempting. While this would make the sentence more concise, this would ultimately alter the context of the sentence, which would be incorrect.

8. C: Choice *C* correctly uses *on to*, describing the way genes are passed generationally. The use of *into* is inappropriate for this context, which makes Choice *A* incorrect. Choice *B* is close, but *onto* refers to something being placed on a surface. Choice *D* doesn't make logical sense.

9. D: Choice *D* is correct, since only proper names should be capitalized. Because the name of a dog breed is not a proper name, Choice *A* is incorrect. In terms of punctuation, only one comma after *example* is needed, so Choices *B* and *C* are incorrect.

10. D: Choice *D* is the correct answer because "rather" acts as an interrupting word here and thus should be separated by commas. Choices *B* and *C* use commas unwisely, breaking the flow of the sentence.

11. B: Since the sentence can stand on its own without *Usually*, separating it from the rest of the sentence with a comma is correct. Choice *A* needs the comma after *Usually*, while Choice *C* uses commas incorrectly. Choice *D* is tempting, but changing *turn* to past tense goes against the rest of the paragraph.

12. A: In Choice *A*, the dependent clause *Sometimes in particularly dull seminars* is seamlessly attached with a single comma after *seminars*. Choice *B* contains too many commas. Choice *C* does not correctly combine the dependent clause with the independent clause. Choice *D* introduces too many unnecessary commas.

13. D: Choice *D* rearranges the sentence to be more direct and straightforward, so it is correct. Choice *A* needs a comma after *on*. Choice *B* introduces unnecessary commas. Choice *C* creates an incomplete sentence, since *Because I wasn't invested in what was going on* is a dependent clause.

14. C: Choice *C* is fluid and direct, making it the best revision. Choice *A* is incorrect because the construction is awkward and lacks parallel structure. Choice *B* is incorrect because of the unnecessary comma and period. Choice *D* is close, but its sequence is still awkward and overly complicated.

15. B: Choice *B* correctly adds a comma after *person* and cuts out the extraneous writing, making the sentence more streamlined. Choice *A* is poorly constructed, lacking proper grammar to connect the sections of the sentence correctly. Choice *C* inserts an unnecessary semicolon and doesn't enable this section to flow well with the rest of the sentence. Choice *D* is better but still unnecessarily long.

16. D: This sentence, though short, is a complete sentence. The only thing the sentence needs is an em-dash after "Easy." In this sentence the em-dash works to add emphasis to the word "Easy" and also acts in place of a colon, but in a less formal way. Therefore, Choice *D* is correct. Choices *A* and *B* lack the crucial comma, while Choice *C* unnecessarily breaks the sentence apart.

17. C: Choice *C* successfully fixes the construction of the sentence, changing *drawing* into *to draw*. Keeping the original sentence disrupts the flow, so Choice *A* is incorrect. Choice *B*'s use of *which* offsets the whole sentence. Choice *D* is incorrect because it unnecessarily expands the sentence content and makes it more confusing.

18. B: Choice *B* fixes the homophone issue. Because the author is talking about people, *their* must be used instead of *there*. This revision also appropriately uses the Oxford comma, separating and distinguishing *lives, world, and future*. Choice *A* uses the wrong homophone and is missing commas. Choice *C* neglects to fix these problems and unnecessarily changes the tense of *applies*. Choice *D* fixes the homophone but fails to properly separate *world* and *future*.

19. C: Choice *C* is correct because it fixes the core issue with this sentence: the singular *has* should not describe the plural *scientists*. Thus, Choice *A* is incorrect. Choices *B* and *D* add unnecessary commas.

20. D: Choice *D* correctly conveys the writer's intention of asking if, or *whether*, early perceptions of dinosaurs are still influencing people. Choice *A* makes no sense as worded. Choice *B* is better, but *how* doesn't coincide with the context. Choice *C* adds unnecessary commas.

21. A: Choice *A* is correct, as the sentence does not require modification. Choices *B* and *C* implement extra punctuation unnecessarily, disrupting the flow of the sentence. Choice *D* incorrectly adds a comma in an awkward location.

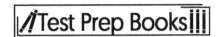

22. B: Choice *B* is the strongest revision, as adding *to explore* is very effective in both shortening the sentence and maintaining, even enhancing, the point of the writer. To explore is to seek understanding in order to gain knowledge and insight, which coincides with the focus of the overall sentence. Choice *A* is not technically incorrect, but it is overcomplicated. Choice *C* is a decent revision, but the sentence could still be more condensed and sharpened. Choice *D* fails to make the sentence more concise and inserts unnecessary commas.

23. D: Choice *D* correctly applies a semicolon to introduce a new line of thought while remaining in a single sentence. The comma after *however* is also appropriately placed. Choice *A* is a run-on sentence. Choice *B* is also incorrect because the single comma is not enough to fix the sentence. Choice *C* adds commas around *uncertain* which are unnecessary.

24. B: Choice *B* not only fixes the homophone issue from *its*, which is possessive, to *it's*, which is a contraction of *it is*, but also streamlines the sentence by adding a comma and eliminating *and*. Choice *A* is incorrect because of these errors. Choices *C* and *D* only fix the homophone issue.

25. A: Choice *A* is correct, as the sentence is fine the way it is. Choices *B* and *C* add unnecessary commas, while Choice *D* uses the possessive *its* instead of the contraction *it's*.

26. C: Choice *C* is correct because the phrase *even likely* is flanked by commas, creating a kind of aside, which allows the reader to see this separate thought while acknowledging it as part of the overall sentence and subject at hand. Choice *A* is incorrect because it seems to ramble after *even* due to a missing comma after *likely*. Choice *B* is better but inserting a comma after *that* warps the flow of the writing. Choice *D* is incorrect because there must be a comma after *plausible*.

27. D: Choice *D* strengthens the overall sentence structure while condensing the words. This makes the subject of the sentence, and the emphasis of the writer, much clearer to the reader. Thus, while Choice *A* is technically correct, the language is choppy and over-complicated. Choice *B* is better but lacks the reference to a specific image of dinosaurs. Choice *C* introduces unnecessary commas.

28. B: Choice *B* correctly joins the two independent clauses. Choice *A* is decent, but "that would be" is too verbose for the sentence. Choice *C* incorrectly changes the semicolon to a comma. Choice *D* splits the clauses effectively but is not concise enough.

29. A: Choice *A* is correct, as the original sentence has no error. Choices *B* and *C* employ unnecessary semicolons and commas. Choice *D* would be an ideal revision, but it lacks the comma after *Ransom* that would enable the sentence structure to flow.

30. D: By reorganizing the sentence, the context becomes clearer with Choice *D*. Choice *A* has an awkward sentence structure. Choice *B* offers a revision that doesn't correspond well with the original sentence's intent. Choice *C* cuts out too much of the original content, losing the full meaning.

31. C: Choice *C* fixes the disagreement between the singular *this* and the plural *viewpoints*. Choice *A*, therefore, is incorrect. Choice *B* introduces an unnecessary comma. In Choice *D, those* agrees with *viewpoints*, but neither agrees with *distinguishes*.

32. A: Choice *A* is direct and clear, without any punctuation errors. Choice *B* is well-written but too wordy. Choice *C* adds an unnecessary comma. Choice *D* is also well-written but much less concise than Choice *A*.

33. D: Choice *D* rearranges the sentence to improve clarity and impact, with *tempting* directly describing *idea*. On its own, Choice *A* is a run-on. Choice *B* is better because it separates the clauses, but it keeps an unnecessary comma. Choice *C* is also an improvement but still a run-on.

34. B: Choice *B* is the best answer simply because the sentence makes it clear that Un-man takes over and possesses Weston. In Choice *A*, these events sounded like two different things, instead of an action and result. Choices *C* and *D* make this relationship clearer, but the revisions don't flow very well grammatically.

35. D: Changing the phrase *after this* to *then* makes the sentence less complicated and captures the writer's intent, making Choice *D* correct. Choice *A* is awkwardly constructed. Choices *B* and *C* misuse their commas and do not adequately improve the clarity.

36. B: By starting a new sentence, the run-on issue is eliminated, and a new line of reasoning can be seamlessly introduced, making Choice *B* correct. Choice *A* is thus incorrect. While Choice *C* fixes the run-on via a semicolon, a comma is still needed after *this*. Choice *D* contains a comma splice. The independent clauses must be separated by more than just a comma, even with the rearrangement of the second half of the sentence.

37. C: Choice *C* condenses the original sentence while being more active in communicating the emphasis on changing times/media that the author is going for, so it is correct. Choice *A* is clunky because it lacks a comma after *today* to successfully transition into the second half of the sentence. Choice *B* inserts unnecessary commas. Choice *D* is a good revision of the underlined section, but not only does it not fully capture the original meaning, it also does not flow into the rest of the sentence.

38. B: Choice *B* clearly illustrates the author's point, with a well-placed semicolon that breaks the sentence into clearer, more readable sections. Choice *A* lacks punctuation. Choice *C* is incorrect because the period inserted after *question* forms an incomplete sentence. Choice *D* is a very good revision but does not make the author's point clearer than the original.

39. A: Choice *A* is correct: while the sentence seems long, it actually doesn't require any commas. The conjunction "that" successfully combines the two parts of the sentence without the need for additional punctuation. Choices *B* and *C* insert commas unnecessarily, incorrectly breaking up the flow of the sentence. Choice *D* alters the meaning of the original text by creating a new sentence, which is only a fragment.

40. C: Choice *C* correctly replaces *for* with *to*, the correct preposition for the selected area. Choice *A* is not the answer because of this incorrect preposition. Choice *B* is unnecessarily long and disrupts the original sentence structure. Choice *D* is also too wordy and lacks parallel structure.

41. D: Choice *D* is the answer because it inserts the correct punctuation to fix the sentence, linking the dependent and independent clauses. Choice *A* is therefore incorrect. Choice *B* is also incorrect since this revision only adds content to the sentence while lacking grammatical precision. Choice *C* overdoes the punctuation; only a comma is needed, not a semicolon.

42. B: Choice *B* correctly separates the section into two sentences and changes the word order to make the second part clearer. Choice *A* is incorrect because it is a run-on. Choice *C* adds an extraneous comma, while Choice *D* makes the run-on worse and does not coincide with the overall structure of the sentence.

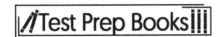

43. C: Choice *C* is the best answer because of how the commas are used to flank *in earnest*. This distinguishes the side thought (*in earnest*) from the rest of the sentence. Choice *A* needs punctuation. Choice *B* inserts a semicolon in a spot that doesn't make sense, resulting in a fragmented sentence and lost meaning. Choice *D* is unnecessarily repetitive and creates a run-on.

44. A: Choice *A* is correct because the sentence contains no errors. The comma after *bias* successfully links the two halves of the sentence, and the use of *it's* is correct as a contraction of *it is*. Choice *B* creates a sentence fragment, while Choice *C* creates a run-on. Choice *D* incorrectly changes *it's* to *its*.

45. D: Choice *D* correctly inserts a comma after *However* and fixes *over use* to *overuse*—in this usage, it is one word. Choice *A* is therefore incorrect, as is Choice *B*. Choice *C* is a good revision but does not fit well with the rest of the sentence.

46. B: Choice *B* is correct because it removes the apostrophe from *icon's*, since the noun *icon* is not possessing anything. This conveys the author's intent of setting *Frankenstein* apart from other icons of the romantic and science fiction genres. Choices *A* and *C* are therefore incorrect. Choice *D* is a good revision but alters the meaning of the sentence—*Frankenstein* is one of the icons, not the sole icon.

47 C: Choice *C* correctly adds a comma after *style*, successfully joining the dependent and the independent clauses as a single sentence. Choice *A* is incorrect because the dependent and independent clauses remain unsuccessfully combined without the comma. Choices *B* and *D* do nothing to fix this.

48. A: Choice *A* is correct, as the sentence doesn't require changes. Choice *B* incorrectly changes the noun *enlightenment* into the verb *enlighten*. Choices *C* and *D* alter the original meaning of the sentence.

49. B: Choice *B* is correct, fixing the incorrect split of *highlight*. This is a polyseme, a word combined from two unrelated words to make a new word. On their own, *high* and *light* make no sense for the sentence, making Choice *A* incorrect. Choice *C* incorrectly decapitalizes *Ancient*—since it modifies *Greece* and works with the noun to describe a civilization, *Ancient Greece* functions as a proper noun, which should be capitalized. Choice *D* uses *highlighting*, a gerund, but the present tense of *highlight* is what works with the rest of the sentence; to make this change, a comma would be needed after *Rome*.

50. A: Choice *A* is correct, as *not only* and *but also* are correlative pairs. In this sentence, *but* successfully transitions the first part into the second half, making punctuation unnecessary. Additionally, the use of *to* indicates that an idea or challenge is being presented to the reader. Choice *B*'s *with*, *C*'s *for*, and *D*'s *there before* are not as active, meaning these revisions weaken the sentence.

51. D: Choice *D* is correct, adding finer details to help the reader understand exactly what Prometheus did and his impact: fire came with knowledge and power. Choice *A* lacks a comma after *fire*. Choice *B* inserts unnecessary commas since *people* is not part of the list *knowledge and power*. Choice *C* is a strong revision but could be confusing, hinting that the fire was knowledge and power itself, as opposed to being symbolized by the fire.

52. C: Choice *C* reverses the order of the section, making the sentence more direct. Choice *A* lacks a comma after *gods*, and although Choice *B* adds this, the structure is too different from the first half of the sentence to flow correctly. Choice *D* is overly complicated and repetitious in its structure even though it doesn't need any punctuation.

53. B: Choice *B* fixes the two problems of the sentence, changing *faltered* to present tense in agreement with the rest of the passage, and correctly linking the two dependent clauses. Choice *A* is therefore

296

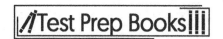

incorrect. Choice *C* does not correct the past tense of *faltered*. Choice *D* correctly adds the conjunction *by*, but it lacks a comma after the conjunction *Yet*.

54. C: Choice *C* successfully applies a comma after *power*, distinguishing the causes of Frankenstein's suffering and maintaining parallel structure. Choice *A* is thus incorrect. Choice *B* lacks the necessary punctuation and unnecessarily changes *lack* to a gerund. Choice *D* adds unnecessary wording, making the sentence more cumbersome.

55. D: Choice *D* correctly inserts an apostrophe into the contraction *doesn't*. Choice *A* is incorrect because of this omission. Choices *B* and *C* are better than the original but do not fit well with the informal tone of the passage.

56. B: Choice *B* is correct, successfully combining the two independent clauses of this compound sentence by adding a comma before "and" to create the effective pause and transition between clauses. Choice *A* does not join the independent clauses correctly. Choices *C* and *D* offer alternate ways of joining these clauses, but since "and" is already part of the sentence, adding the comma is the most logical choice. This also keeps the informal tone set by the rest of the passage.

57. C: Choice *C* correctly fixes the homophone issue of *their* and *they're*. *Their* implies ownership, which is not needed here. The author intends *they're*, a contraction of *they are*. Thus, Choice *A* is incorrect, as is Choice *B*, using the homophone *there*. Choice *D* eliminates the homophone issue altogether, but the sentence becomes more clunky because of that.

58. B: Choice *B* correctly joins the two independent clauses with a comma before *but*. Choice *A* is incorrect because, without the comma, it is a run-on sentence. Choice *C* also lacks punctuation and uses *however*, which should be reserved for starting a new sentence or perhaps after a semicolon. Choice *D* is incorrect because the semicolon throws off the sentence structure and is incorrectly used; the correct revision would have also removed *but*.

59. A: Choice *A* is correct because the sentence does not require modification. Choice *B* is incorrect because it uses the faulty subject/verb agreement, "Physical proof are." Choice *C* is incorrect because a comma would need to follow *exists*. Choice *D* is incorrect because the comma after *science* is unnecessary.

60. D: Choice *D* correctly changes *this* to *the* and retains *validity*, making it the right choice. Choices *A* and *B* keep *this*, which is not as specific as "the." Choice *C* incorrectly pluralizes *validity*.

61. A: Choice *A* is correct because the sentence is fine without revisions. Choice *B* is incorrect, since removing *there is* is unnecessary and confusing. Choice *C* is incorrect since it inserts an unnecessary comma. Choice *D* introduces a homophone issue: *weather* refers to climatic states and atmospheric events, while *whether* expresses doubt, which is the author's intent.

62. C: Choice *C* correctly changes *continuing* to the present tense. Choice *A* is incorrect because of this out-of-place gerund use. Choice *B* not only does not fix this issue but also incorrectly changes *describe* into a gerund. While Choice *D* correctly uses *continue*, *describe* is incorrectly put in the past tense.

63. D: Choice *D* is correct, since it eliminates the unnecessary *as well* and adds a comma to separate the given example, making the sentence more direct. Choice *A* seems repetitive with *as well*, since it has *including*, and at the least needs punctuation. Choice *B* is poorly constructed, taking out the clearer *including*. Choice *C* also makes little sense.

64. B: For this question, place the underlined sentence in each prospective choice's position. Leaving the sentence in place is incorrect because the father "going crazy" doesn't logically follow the fact that he was a "city slicker." Choice *C* is incorrect because the sentence in question is not a concluding sentence and does not transition smoothly into the second paragraph. Choice *D* is incorrect because the sentence doesn't necessarily need to be omitted since it logically follows the very first sentence in the passage.

65. D: Choice *D* is correct because "As it turns out" indicates a contrast from the previous sentiment, that the RV was a great purchase. Choice *A* is incorrect because the sentence needs an effective transition from the paragraph before. Choice *B* is incorrect because the text indicates it *is* surprising that the RV was a great purchase because the author was skeptical beforehand. Choice *C* is incorrect because the transition "furthermore" does not indicate a contrast.

66. B: This sentence calls for parallel structure. Choice *B* is correct because the verbs "wake," "eat," and "break" are consistent in tense and parts of speech. Choice *A* is incorrect because the words "wake" and "eat" are present tense while the word "broke" is in past tense. Choice *C* is incorrect because this turns the sentence into a question, which doesn't make sense within the context. Choice *D* is incorrect because it breaks tense with the rest of the passage. "Waking," "eating," and "breaking" are all present participles, and the context around the sentence is in past tense.

67. C: Choice *C* is correct because it is clear and fits within the context of the passage. Choice *A* is incorrect because "We rejoiced as 'hackers'" does not explain what was meant by "hackers" or why it was a cause for rejoicing. Choice *B* is incorrect because it does not mention a solution being found and is therefore not specific enough. Choice *D* is incorrect because the meaning is eschewed by the helping verb "had to rejoice," and the sentence suggests that rejoicing was necessary to "hack" a solution.

68. A: The original sentence is correct because the verb tense and the meaning both align with the rest of the passage. Choice *B* is incorrect because the order of the words makes the sentence more confusing than it otherwise would be. Choice *C* is incorrect because "We are even making" is in present tense. Choice *D* is incorrect because "We will make" is future tense. The surrounding text of the sentence is in past tense.

69. B: Choice *B* is correct because there is no punctuation needed if a dependent clause ("while traveling across America") is located behind the independent clause ("it allowed us to share adventures"). Choice *A* is incorrect because there are two dependent clauses connected and no independent clause, and a complete sentence requires at least one independent clause. Choice *C* is incorrect because of the same reason as Choice *A*. Semicolons have the same function as periods: there must be an independent clause on either side of the semicolon. Choice *D* is incorrect because the dash simply interrupts the complete sentence.

70. C: The rule for "me" and "I" is that one should use "I" when it is the subject pronoun of a sentence, and "me" when it is the object pronoun of the sentence. Break the sentence up to see if "I" or "me" should be used. To say "Those are memories that I have now shared" is correct, rather than "Those are memories that me have now shared." Choice *D* is incorrect because "my siblings" should come before "I."

71. B: Choice *B* is correct because it adds an apostrophe to *ones*, which indicates *one's* possession of *survival*. Choice *A* doesn't do this, so it is incorrect. This is the same for Choice *C*, but that option also takes out the crucial comma after *Jiu-Jitsu*. Choice *D* is incorrect because it changes *play* to *plays*. This

298

disagrees with the plural *Martial arts*, exemplified by having an example of its many forms, *Jiu-Jitsu*. Therefore, *play* is required.

72. C: Choice *C* is the best answer because it most clearly defines the point that the author is trying to make. The original sentence would need a comma after *however* in order to continue the sentence fluidly—but this option isn't available. Choice *B* is close, but this option changes the meaning of the sentence. Therefore, the best alternative is to begin the sentence with *However* and have a comma follow right after it in order to introduce a new idea. The original context is still maintained, but the flow of the language is more streamlined. Thus, Choice *A* is incorrect. Choice *D* would need a comma before and after *however*, so it is also incorrect.

73. A: Choice *A* is the best answer for several reasons. To begin, the section is grammatically correct in using a semicolon to connect the two independent clauses. This allows the two ideas to be connected without separating them. In this context, the semicolon makes more sense for the overall sentence structure and passage as a whole. Choice *B* is incorrect because it forms a run-on. Choice *C* applies a comma in incorrect positions. Choice *D* separates the sentence in a place that does not make sense for the context.

74. D: Choice *D* is the correct answer because it fixes two key issues. First, *their* is incorrectly used. *Their* is a possessive indefinite pronoun and also an antecedent—neither of these fit the context of the sentence, so Choices *A* and *B* are incorrect. What should be used instead is *they're*, which is the contraction of *they are*, emphasizing action or the result of action in this case. Choice *D* also corrects another contraction-related issue with *its*. Again, *its* indicates possession, while *it's* is the contraction of *it is*. The latter is what's needed for the sentence to make sense and be grammatically correct. Thus, Choice *C* is also incorrect.

75. A: Choice *A* is correct because the section contains no errors and clearly communicates the writer's point. Choice *B* is incorrect because it lacks a comma after *philosophy*, needed to link the first clause with the second. Choice *C* also has this issue but additionally alters *its* to *it's*; since *it is* does not make sense in this sentence, this is incorrect. Choice *D* is incorrect because *its* is already plural possessive and does not need an apostrophe on the end.

Math

1. C: The decimal points are lined up, with zeroes put in as needed. Then, the numbers are added just like integers:

$$
\begin{array}{r}
3.40 \\
2.35 \\
+4.00 \\
\hline
9.75
\end{array}
$$

2. A: This problem can be multiplied as 588×32, except at the end, the decimal point needs to be moved three places to the left. Performing the multiplication will give 18,816, and moving the decimal place over three places results in 18.816.

3. E: The fraction is converted so that the denominator is 100 by multiplying the numerator and denominator by 4, to get $\frac{3}{25} = \frac{12}{100}$. Dividing a number by 100 just moves the decimal point two places to the left, with a result of 0.12.

4. A: Figure out which is largest by looking at the first non-zero digits. Choice *B*'s first non-zero digit is in the hundredths place. The other four all have non-zero digits in the tenths place, so it must be *A, C, D,* or *E*. Of these, *A* has the largest first non-zero digit.

5. C: $40N$ would be 4,000% of N. All of the other coefficients are equivalent to $\frac{40}{100}$ or 40%.

6. B: Instead of multiplying these out, the product can be estimated by using $18 \times 10 = 180$. The error here should be lower than 15, since it is rounded to the nearest integer, and the numbers add to something less than 30.

7. C: 85% of a number means multiplying that number by 0.85. So:

$$0.85 \times 20 = \frac{85}{100} \times \frac{20}{1}$$

which can be simplified to:

$$\frac{17}{20} \times \frac{20}{1} = 17$$

8. A: To find the fraction of the bill that the first three people pay, the fractions need to be added, which means finding the common denominator. The common denominator will be 60.

$$\frac{1}{5} + \frac{1}{4} + \frac{1}{3} = \frac{12}{60} + \frac{15}{60} + \frac{20}{60} = \frac{47}{60}$$

The remainder of the bill is:

$$1 - \frac{47}{60} = \frac{60}{60} - \frac{47}{60} = \frac{13}{60}$$

9. B: 30% is $\frac{3}{10}$. The equation to represent this question is $6 = \frac{3}{10}x$. To find the value of x, multiply both sides by $\frac{10}{3}$. This results in $20 = x$, so 20 is 30% of 6.

$$\frac{10}{3} \times 6 = 10 \times 2 = 20$$

10. E: These numbers to improper fractions: $\frac{11}{3} - \frac{9}{5}$. Then, convert the fractions to have a common denominator of 15, subtract, and convert the answer back to a mixed number.

$$\frac{11}{3} - \frac{9}{5} = \frac{55}{15} - \frac{27}{15} = \frac{28}{15} = 1\frac{13}{15}$$

11. A: Dividing by 98 can be approximated by dividing by 100, which would mean shifting the decimal point of the numerator to the left by 2. The result is 4.2 and rounds to 4.

12. B: $4\frac{1}{3} + 3\frac{3}{4} = 4 + 3 + \frac{1}{3} + \frac{3}{4} = 7 + \frac{1}{3} + \frac{3}{4}$

Adding the fractions gives:

$$\frac{1}{3} + \frac{3}{4} = \frac{4}{12} + \frac{9}{12} = \frac{13}{12} = 1 + \frac{1}{12}$$

Thus:

$$7 + \frac{1}{3} + \frac{3}{4} = 7 + 1 + \frac{1}{12} = 8\frac{1}{12}$$

13. C: The average is calculated by adding all six numbers, then dividing by 6. The first five numbers have a sum of 25. If the total divided by 6 is equal to 6, then the total itself must be 36. The sixth number must be $36 - 25 = 11$.

14. B: Multiplying by 10^{-3} means moving the decimal point three places to the left, putting in zeros as necessary.

15. E: $\frac{5}{2} \div \frac{1}{3} = \frac{5}{2} \times \frac{3}{1} = \frac{15}{2} = 7.5$.

16. A: The total fraction taken up by green and red shirts will be:

$$\frac{1}{3} + \frac{2}{5} = \frac{5}{15} + \frac{6}{15} = \frac{11}{15}$$

The remaining fraction is:

$$1 - \frac{11}{15} = \frac{15}{15} - \frac{11}{15} = \frac{4}{15}$$

17. C: If she has used $\frac{1}{3}$ of the paint, she has $\frac{2}{3}$ remaining. The mixed fraction can be converted because $2\frac{1}{2}$ gallons is the same as $\frac{5}{2}$ gallons. The calculation is:

$$\frac{2}{3} \times \frac{5}{2} = \frac{5}{3} = 1\frac{2}{3} \text{ gal}$$

18. B: First, subtract 4 from each side. This yields $6t = 12$. Now, divide both sides by 6 to obtain $t = 2$.

19. A: Each bag contributes $4x + 1$ treats. The total treats will be in the form $4nx + n$ where n is the total number of bags. The total is in the form $60x + 15$, from which it is known $n = 15$.

20. B: If 60% of 50 workers are women, then there are 30 women working in the office. If half of them are wearing skirts, then that means 15 women wear skirts. Since none of the men wear skirts, this means there are 15 people wearing skirts.

21. C: Begin by subtracting 6 from both sides to get $2x = 14$. Dividing both sides by 2 results in $x = 7$.

22. B: To be directly proportional means that $y = kx$. If x is changed from 5 to 20, the value of x is multiplied by 4. Applying the same rule to the y-value, also multiply the value of y by 4. Therefore:

$$y = 12$$

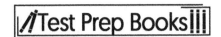

23. E: Let a be the number of apples and o the number of oranges. Then, the total cost is:

$$2a + 3o = 22$$

It also known that $a + o = 10$. Using the knowledge of systems of equations, cancel the o-variables by multiplying the second equation by -3.

This makes the equation:

$$-3a - 3o = -30$$

Adding this to the first equation, the b-values cancel to get $-a = -8$, which simplifies to $a = 8$.

24. A: Finding the roots means finding the values of x when y is zero. The quadratic formula could be used, but in this case, it is possible to factor by hand, since the numbers -1 and 2 add to 1 and multiply to -2. So, factor:

$$x^2 + x - 2 = (x - 1)(x + 2) = 0$$

Then, set each factor equal to zero. Solving for each value gives the values $x = 1$ and $x = -2$.

25. C: To find the y-intercept, substitute zero for x, which gives us:

$$y = 0^{5/3} + (0 - 3)(0 + 1) = 0 + (-3)(1) = -3$$

26. C: Multiply both sides by x to get $x + 2 = 2x$, which simplifies to $-x = -2$, or $x = 2$.

27. D: Denote the width as w and the length as l. Then, $l = 3w + 5$. The perimeter is:

$$2w + 2l = 90$$

Substituting the first expression for l into the second equation yields:

$$2(3w + 5) + 2w = 90$$

$$6w + 10 + 2w = 90$$

$$8w = 80$$

$$w = 10$$

Putting this into the first equation, it yields:

$$l = 3(10) + 5 = 35$$

28. A: Lining up the given scores provides the following list: 60, 75, 80, 85, and one unknown. Because the median needs to be 80, it means 80 must be the middle data point out of these five. Therefore, the unknown data point must be the fourth or fifth data point, meaning it must be greater than or equal to 80. The only answer that fails to meet this condition is 60.

29. A: 3.6

Divide 3 by 5 to get 0.6 and add that to the whole number 3, to get 3.6. An alternative is to incorporate the whole number 3 earlier on by creating an improper fraction: $\frac{18}{5}$. Then dividing 18 by 5 to get 3.6.

30. B: 300 miles in 4 hours is $\frac{300}{4} = 75$ miles per hour. In 1.5 hours, the car will go 1.5×75 miles, or 112.5 miles.

31. A: Mean. An outlier is a data value that is either far above or far below the majority of values in a sample set. The mean is the average of all the values in the set. In a small sample set, a very high or very low number could drastically change the average of the data points. Outliers will have no more of an effect on the median (the middle value when arranged from lowest to highest) than any other value above or below the median. If the same outlier does not repeat, outliers will have no effect on the mode (value that repeats most often).

32. E: Line graph. The scenario involves data consisting of two variables, month and stock value. Box plots display data consisting of values for one variable. Therefore, a box plot is not an appropriate choice. Both line plots and circle graphs are used to display frequencies within categorical data. Neither can be used for the given scenario. Scatter plots compare the values of two variables to see if there are any patterns present. Line graphs display two numerical variables on a coordinate grid and show trends among the variables.

33. D: $\frac{1}{12}$. The probability of picking the winner of the race is $\frac{1}{4}$ or:

$$\left(\frac{number\ of\ favorable\ outcomes}{number\ of\ total\ outcomes} \right)$$

Assuming the winner was picked on the first selection, three horses remain from which to choose the runner-up (these are dependent events). Therefore, the probability of picking the runner-up is $\frac{1}{3}$. To determine the probability of multiple events, the probability of each event is multiplied:

$$\frac{1}{4} \times \frac{1}{3} = \frac{1}{12}$$

34. B: This inequality can be seen with the use of a number line. $\frac{3}{7}$ is close to $\frac{1}{2}$.

$\frac{5}{6}$ is close to 1, but less than 1, and $\frac{8}{7}$ is greater than 1. Therefore, $\frac{3}{7}$ is less than $\frac{5}{6}$.

35. D: 104,165

Set up the problem and add each column, starting on the far right (ones). Add, carrying anything over 9 into the next column to the left. Solve from right to left.

36. E: 6.630

Set up the problem, with the larger number on top and numbers lined up at the decimal. Add, carrying anything over 9 into the next column to the left. Solve from right to left.

37. B: 148.97

Set up the problem, with the larger number on top and numbers lined up at the decimal. Insert 0 in any blank spots to the right of the decimal as placeholders. Add, carrying anything over 9 into the next column to the left.

38. C: Each number in the sequence is adding one more than the difference between the previous two.

For example, $10 - 6 = 4, 4 + 1 = 5$.

Therefore, the next number after 10 is $10 + 5 = 15$.

Going forward, $21 - 15 = 6, 6 + 1 = 7$. The next number is:

$$21 + 7 = 28$$

Therefore, the difference between numbers is the set of whole numbers starting at 2: 2, 3, 4, 5, 6, 7....

39. C: $\frac{4}{3}$

Set up the problem and find a common denominator for both fractions:

$$\frac{14}{33} + \frac{10}{11}$$

Multiply each fraction across by 1 to convert to a common denominator:

$$\frac{14}{33} \times \frac{1}{1} + \frac{10}{11} \times \frac{3}{3}$$

Once over the same denominator, add across the top. The total is over the common denominator:

$$\frac{14 + 30}{33} = \frac{44}{33}$$

Reduce by dividing both numerator and denominator by 11:

$$\frac{44 \div 11}{33 \div 11} = \frac{4}{3}$$

40. B: 128

This question involves the percent formula:

$$\frac{32}{x} = \frac{25}{100}$$

We multiply the diagonal numbers, 32 and 100, to get 3,200. Dividing by the remaining number, 25, gives us 128.

The percent formula does not have to be used for a question like this. Since 25% is ¼ of 100, you know that 32 needs to be multiplied by 4, which yields 128.

304

41. D: 110,833

Set up the problem, with the larger number on top. Begin subtracting with the far-right column (ones). Borrow 10 from the column to the left, when necessary.

42. B: This is a division problem because the original amount needs to be split up into equal amounts. The mixed number $11\frac{1}{2}$ should be converted to an improper fraction first:

$$11\frac{1}{2} = \frac{(11 \times 2) + 1}{2} = \frac{23}{2}$$

Carey needs to determine how many times $\frac{23}{2}$ goes into 184. This is a division problem:

$$184 \div \frac{23}{2} = ?$$

The fraction can be flipped, and the problem turns into the multiplication:

$$184 \times \frac{2}{23} = \frac{368}{23}$$

This improper fraction can be simplified into 16 because $368 \div 23 = 16$. The answer is 16 lawn segments.

43. B: 648.77

Set up the problem, with the larger number on top and numbers lined up at the decimal. Insert 0 in any blank spots to the right of the decimal as placeholders. Begin subtracting with the far-right column. Borrow 10 from the column to the left, when necessary.

44. A: The additive and subtractive identity is 0. When added or subtracted to any number, 0 does not change the original number.

45. E: 100 cm is equal to 1 m. 1.3 divided by 100 is 0.013. Therefore, 1.3 cm is equal to 0.013 m. Because 1 cm is equal to 10 mm, 1.3 cm is equal to 13 mm.

46. D: 725

Set up the division problem.

$$1. \quad 4\overline{)\begin{array}{cccc} 1 & 0 & 1 & 5 \end{array}}$$

Move the decimal over one place to the right in both numbers.

$$1 \quad 4\overline{)\begin{array}{ccccc} 1 & 0 & 1 & 5 & 0 \end{array}}$$

305

14 does not go into 1 or 10 but does go into 101 so start there.

```
                          7   2   5
    1   4|  1   0   1   5   0
           -  9   8
                      3   5
                   -  2   8
                          7   0
                       -  7   0
                              0
```

The result is 725.

47. C: The best way to solve this problem is by using a system of equations. We know that Jan bought $90 worth of apples ($a$) and oranges ($o$) at $1 and $2 respectively. That means our first equation is:

$$1(a) + 2(o) = 90$$

We also know that she bought an equal number of apples and oranges, which gives us our second equation $a = o$. We can then replace a with o in the first equation to give:

$$1(o) + 2(o) = 90 \text{ or } 3(o) = 90$$

Which yields:

$$o = 30$$

Thus, Jan bought 30 oranges (and 30 apples).

48. B: 2.48

Set up the problem, with the larger number on top. Multiply as if there are no decimal places. Add the answer rows together. Count the number of decimal places that were in the original numbers:

$$1 + 1 = 2$$

Place the decimal 2 places to the right for the final solution.

49. B: 99.35

Set up the problem, with the larger number on top. Multiply as if there are no decimal places. Add the answer rows together. Count the number of decimal places that were in the original numbers (2).

Place the decimal in that many spots from the right for the final solution.

50. B: Each hour on the clock represents 30 degrees. For example, 3:00 represents a right angle. Therefore, 5:00 represents 150 degrees.

51. D: $27\frac{7}{22}$

Set up the division problem.

```
    4   4|  1   2   0   2
```

306

44 does not go into 1 or 12 but will go into 120 so start there.

```
                    2   7
    4   4| 1   2   0   2
          -   8   8
              3   2   2
          -   3   0   8
                  1   4
```

The answer is $27\frac{14}{44}$.

Reduce the fraction for the final answer.

$$27\frac{7}{22}$$

52. E: The formula for The volume of a box with rectangular sides is the length times the width times the height, so:

$$5 \times 6 \times 3 = 90 \text{ cubic feet}$$

53. D: 270

Set up the division problem.

```
    2.   6| 7   0   2
```

Move the decimal over one place to the right in both numbers.

```
    2   6| 7   0   2   0
```

26 does not go into 7 but does go into 70 so start there.

```
                2   7   0
    2   6| 7    0   2   0
          -  5  2
             1  8   2
          -  1  8   2
                    0
```

The result is 270.

54. D: First, the train's journey in the real world is:

$$3\,\text{h} \times 50\,\frac{\text{mi}}{\text{h}} = 150 \text{ mi}$$

On the map, 1 inch corresponds to 10 miles, so that is equivalent to:

$$150 \text{ mi} \times \frac{1\,\text{in}}{10\,\text{mi}} = 15 \text{ in}$$

Therefore, the start and end points are 15 inches apart on the map.

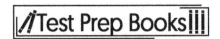

55. B: The total trip time is:

$$1 + 3.5 + 0.5 = 5 \text{ hours}$$

The total time driving is $1 + 0.5 = 1.5$ hours. So, the fraction of time spent driving is $\frac{1.5}{5}$, or $\frac{3}{10}$. To get the percentage, convert this to a fraction out of 100. The numerator and denominator are multiplied by 10, with a result of $\frac{30}{100}$. The percentage is the numerator in a fraction out of 100, so 30%.

56. B: The formula for the volume of a cylinder is $\pi r^2 h$, where r is the radius and h is the height. The diameter is twice the radius, so these barrels have a radius of 1 foot. That means each barrel has a volume of:

$$\pi \times 1^2 \times 3 = 3\pi \text{ cubic feet}$$

Since there are three of them, the total is:

$$3 \times 3\pi = 9\pi \text{ cubic feet}$$

57. A: The tip is not taxed, so he pays 5% tax only on the $10. 5% of $10 is $0.05 \times 10 = \$0.50$. Add up $10 + \$2 + \$0.50$ to get $12.50.

58. B: 15,412

Set up the problem and add each column, starting on the far right (ones). Add, carrying anything over 9 into the next column to the left. Solve from right to left.

59. A: Using the order of operations, multiplication and division are computed first from left to right. Multiplication is on the left; therefore, multiplication should be performed first.

60. D: A factor of 36 is any number that can be divided into 36 and have no remainder. $36 = 36 \times 1, 18 \times 2, 9 \times 4,$ and 6×6. Therefore, it has 7 unique factors: 36, 18, 9, 6, 4, 2, and 1.

Reading

1. D: It emphasizes Mr. Utterson's anguish in failing to identify Hyde's whereabouts. Context clues indicate that Choice *D* is correct because the passage provides great detail of Mr. Utterson's feelings about locating Hyde. Choice *A* does not fit because there is no mention of Mr. Lanyon's mental state. Choice *B* is incorrect; although the text does make mention of bells, Choice *B* is not the *best* answer overall. Choice *C* is incorrect because the passage clearly states that Mr. Utterson was determined, not unsure.

2. A: The word *city* appears in the passage several times, thus establishing the location for the reader.

3. B: The passage states that the Juggernaut causes the children to scream. Choices *A* and *D* don't apply because the text doesn't mention either of these instances specifically. Choice *C* is incorrect because there is nothing in the text that mentions space travel.

4. B: The mention of *morning*, *noon*, and *night* make it clear that the word *haunt* refers to frequent appearances at various times. Choice *A* doesn't work because the text makes no mention of levitating. Choices *C* and *D* are not correct because the text makes mention of Mr. Utterson's anguish and disheartenment because of his failure to find Hyde but does not make mention of Mr. Utterson's feelings negatively affecting anyone else.

308

5. D: This is an example of alliteration. Choice *D* is the correct answer because of the repetition of the *L*-words. Hyperbole is an exaggeration, so Choice *A* doesn't work. No comparison is being made, so no simile or juxtaposition is being used, thus eliminating Choices *B* and *C*.

6. D: The speaker invokes the game of hide and seek to indicate they will continue their search for Hyde. Choices *A* and *B* are not possible answers because the text doesn't refer to any name changes or an identity crisis, despite Mr. Utterson's extreme obsession with finding Hyde. The text also makes no mention of a mistaken identity when referring to Hyde, so Choice *C* is also incorrect.

7. A: The author's attitude toward the main subject can be described as *intrigue*. Although this is fiction and we are seeing the passage through the eyes of a character, the author still is in control of word choice and tone. *Intrigue* means to arouse curiosity, so we are confronted with words and phrases such as "besieged by questions," "digging," "imagination," and "haunt." Choice *B*, elation, means joy. Choice *C*, animosity, means strong dislike. Choice *D*, rigidity, means stiff or unyielding.

8. B: Mr. Utterson is struggling with the mystery surrounding a dark figure and the terrible crimes he commits. As Mr. Utterson tosses and turns in bed in the long paragraph, we see him wanting to discern the figure's face as he imagines him committing the crimes, but Mr. Utterson has no idea who the figure is.

9. C: Choice *C* is the best answer because of the chronological aspect of the passage. By the transition "From that time forward," we know that Mr. Utterson haunted storefronts *after* his night visions of the mysterious figure, and we also see that Mr. Utterson's dialogue at the very end is a promise to find "Mr. Hyde," whoever he may be.

10. C: The passage is in third person limited, which means we see the thoughts of one character only by the use of the pronouns "he" or "she." First person is characterized by the use of "I." Second person is characterized by the use of "you." Third person omniscient is when we see the thoughts of all the characters in the story, and the author uses the pronouns "he" or "she."

11. A: The purpose is to inform the reader about what assault is and how it is committed. Choice *B* is incorrect because the passage does not state that assault is a lesser form of lethal force, only that an assault can use lethal force, or alternatively, lethal force can be utilized to counter a dangerous assault. Choice *C* is incorrect because the passage is informative and does not have a set agenda. Finally, Choice *D* is incorrect because although the author uses an example in order to explain assault, it is not indicated that this is the author's personal account.

12. C: If the man being attacked in an alley by another man with a knife used self-defense by lethal force, it would not be considered illegal. The presence of a deadly weapon indicates mal-intent and because the individual is isolated in an alley, lethal force in self-defense may be the only way to preserve his life. Choices *A* and *B* can be ruled out because in these situations, no one is in danger of immediate death or bodily harm by someone else. Choice *D* is an assault and does exhibit intent to harm, but this situation isn't severe enough to merit lethal force; there is no intent to kill.

13. B: As discussed in the second passage, there are several forms of assault, like assault with a deadly weapon, verbal assault, or threatening posture or language. Choice *A* is incorrect because the author does mention what the charges are on assaults; therefore, we cannot assume that they are more or less than unnecessary use of force charges. Choice *C* is incorrect because anyone is capable of assault; the

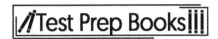

author does not state that one group of people cannot commit assault. Choice *D* is incorrect because assault is never justified. Self-defense resulting in lethal force can be justified.

14. D: The use of lethal force is not evaluated on the intent of the user, but rather on the severity of the primary attack that warranted self-defense. This statement most undermines the last part of the passage because it directly contradicts how the law evaluates the use of lethal force. Choices *A* and *B* are stated in the paragraph, so they do not undermine the explanation from the author. Choice *C* does not necessarily undermine the passage, but it does not support the passage either. It is more of an opinion that does not offer strength or weakness to the explanation.

15. C: An assault with deadly intent can lead to an individual using lethal force to preserve their well-being. Choice *C* is correct because it clearly establishes what both assault and lethal force are and gives the specific way in which the two concepts meet. Choice *A* is incorrect because lethal force doesn't necessarily result in assault. This is also why Choice *B* is incorrect. Not all assaults would necessarily be life-threatening to the point where lethal force is needed for self-defense. Choice *D* is compelling but ultimately too vague; the statement touches on aspects of the two ideas but fails to present the concrete way in which the two are connected to each other.

16. A: Both passages open by defining a legal concept and then continue to describe situations in order to further explain the concept. Choice *D* is incorrect because while the passages utilize examples to help explain the concepts discussed, the author doesn't indicate that they are specific court cases. It's also clear that the passages don't open with examples, but instead, they begin by defining the terms addressed in each passage. This eliminates Choice *B,* and ultimately reveals Choice *A* to be the correct answer. Choice *A* accurately outlines the way both passages are structured. Because the passages follow a nearly identical structure, the Choice *C* can easily be ruled out.

17. C: Intent is very important for determining both lethal force and assault; intent is examined in both parties and helps determine the severity of the issue. Choices *A* and *B* are incorrect because it is clear in both passages that intent is a prevailing theme in both lethal force and assault. Choice *D* is compelling, but if a person uses lethal force to defend himself or herself, the intent of the defender is also examined in order to help determine if there was excessive force used. Choice *C* is correct because it states that intent is important for determining both lethal force and assault, and that intent is used to gauge the severity of the issues. Remember, just as lethal force can escalate to excessive use of force, there are different kinds of assault. Intent dictates several different forms of assault.

18. B: The example is used to demonstrate a single example of two different types of assault, then adding in a third type of assault to the example's conclusion. The example mainly provides an instance of "threatening body language" and "provocative language" with the homeowner gesturing threats to his neighbor. It ends the example by adding a third type of assault: physical strikes. This example is used to show the variant nature of assaults. Choice *A* is incorrect because it doesn't mention the "physical strike" assault at the end and is not specific enough. Choice *C* is incorrect because the example does not say anything about the definition of lethal force or how it might be altered. Choice *D* is incorrect, as the example mentions nothing about cause and effect.

19. C: The word *apprehension* most nearly means fear. The passage indicates that "assault is the unlawful attempt of one person to apply fear/anxiety on another individual by an imminent threat." The creation of fear in another individual seems to be a property of assault.

310

20. D: Choice *D* is the best answer, "The concept of lethal force as a last resort and the point at which it can cross a line from defense to manslaughter." The last paragraph of the first passage states what the term "last resort" means and how it's distinguished in the eyes of the law.

21. A: The word *patronage* most nearly means *auspices*, which means *protection* or *support*. Choice *B*, *aberration*, means *deformity* and does not make sense within the context of the sentence. Choice *C*, *acerbic*, means *bitter* and also does not make sense in the sentence. Choice *D*, *adulation*, is a positive word meaning *praise*, and thus does not fit with the word *condescending* in the sentence.

22. D: *Working man* is most closely aligned with Choice *D*, *bourgeois*. In the context of the speech, the word *bourgeois* means *working* or *middle class*. Choice *A*, *athlete*, does suggest someone who works hard, but it does not make sense in context. Choice *B*, *viscount*, is a European title used to describe a specific degree of nobility. Choice *C*, *entrepreneur*, is a person who operates their own business.

23. C: In the context of the speech, the term *working man* most closely correlates with Choice *C*, "A working man is someone who works for wages among the middle class." Choice *A* is not mentioned in the passage and is off-topic. Choice *B* may be true in some cases, but it does not reflect the sentiment described for the term *working man* in the passage. Choice *D* may also be arguably true. However, it is not given as a definition but as *acts* of the working man, and the topics of *field, factory,* and *screen* are not mentioned in the passage.

24. D: *Enterprise* most closely means *cause*. Choices *A, B,* and *C* are all related to the term *enterprise*. However, Dickens speaks of a *cause* here, not a company, courage, or a game. "He will stand by such an enterprise" is a call to stand by a cause to enable the working man to have a certain autonomy over his own economic standing. The very first paragraph ends with the statement that the working man "shall . . . have a share in the management of an institution which is designed for his benefit."

25. B: The speaker's salutation is one from an entertainer to his audience and uses the friendly language to connect to his audience before a serious speech. Recall in the first paragraph that the speaker is there to "accompany [the audience] . . . through one of my little Christmas books," making him an author there to entertain the crowd with his own writing. The speech preceding the reading is the passage itself, and, as the tone indicates, a serious speech addressing the "working man." Although the passage speaks of employers and employees, the speaker himself is not an employer of the audience, so Choice *A* is incorrect. Choice *C* is also incorrect, as the salutation is not used ironically, but sincerely, as the speech addresses the well-being of the crowd. Choice *D* is incorrect because the speech is not given by a politician, but by a writer.

26. B: Choice *A* is incorrect because that is the speaker's *first* desire, not his second. Choices *C* and *D* are tricky because the language of both of these is mentioned after the word *second*. However, the speaker doesn't get to the second wish until the next sentence. Choices *C* and *D* are merely prepositions preparing for the statement of the main clause, Choice *B*, for the working man to have a say in his institution, which is designed for his benefit.

27. C: The speaker's tone can best be described as *confident and informed*. The speaker addresses the audience as "My good friends," and says, "I have no fear of being misunderstood," which implies confidence. Additionally, the speaker's knowledge of the proposal and topic can be seen in the text as well, especially in the second paragraph.

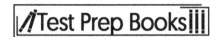

28. D: To provide credibility to the working man and share confidence in their ability to take on responsibilities if they are compensated appropriately. The speaker provides credibility by saying "he will stand by such an enterprise with the utmost of his patience," and displays their responsibilities by saying "he will feel his responsibility like an honest man."

29. A: The speaker says to "Erect in Birmingham a great Education Institution, properly educational." Choice *B* is close, but the speaker uses the name "Temple of Concord" in the passage as a metaphor, so this is incorrect. The other two choices aren't mentioned in the passage.

30. B: The word *antagonism* most nearly means opposition. Choice *A, conformity*, is the opposite of antagonism. Choice *C, affluence*, means abundance. Choice *D, scarcity*, means being deficient in something.

31. D: The use of "I" could serve to have a "hedging" effect, allow the reader to connect with the author in a more personal way, and cause the reader to empathize more with the egrets. However, it doesn't distance the reader from the text, making Choice *D* the answer to this question.

32. C: The quote provides an example of a warden protecting one of the colonies. Choice *A* is incorrect because the speaker of the quote is a warden, not a hunter. Choice *B* is incorrect because the quote does not lighten the mood but shows the danger of the situation between the wardens and the hunters. Choice *D* is incorrect because there is no humor found in the quote.

33. D: A *rookery* is a colony of breeding birds. Although *rookery* could mean Choice *A,* houses in a slum area, it does not make sense in this context. Choices *B* and *C* are both incorrect, as this is not a place for hunters to trade tools or for wardens to trade stories.

34. B: An important bird colony. The previous sentence is describing "twenty colonies" of birds, so what follows should be a bird colony. Choice *A* may be true, but we have no evidence of this in the text. Choice *C* does touch on the tension between the hunters and wardens, but there is no official "Bird Island Battle" mentioned in the text. Choice *D* does not exist in the text.

35. D: To demonstrate the success of the protective work of the Audubon Association. The text mentions several different times how and why the association has been successful and gives examples to back this fact. Choice *A* is incorrect because although the article, in some instances, calls certain people to act, it is not the purpose of the entire passage. There is no way to tell if Choices *B* and *C* are correct, as they are not mentioned in the text.

36. C: To have a better opportunity to hunt the birds. Choice *A* might be true in a general sense, but it is not relevant to the context of the text. Choice *B* is incorrect because the hunters are not studying lines of flight to help wardens, but to hunt birds. Choice *D* is incorrect because nothing in the text mentions that hunters are trying to build homes underneath lines of flight of birds for good luck.

37. C: The passage states in the third paragraph that a year before, "a number of egrets were seen in eastern Massachusetts." Florida is mentioned in the passage as a place where bird colonies reside. The other two locations are not mentioned in the passage.

38. A: The word *commissioned* most nearly means *appointed*. Choice *B, compelled*, means forced. Choice *C, beguiled*, means entertained. Choice *D, fortified*, means defended.

39. D: Several hidden colonies were found which prompted Dutcher and Pearson to protect them. This information is presented in the first paragraph starting with the sentence "Two years ago." The other answer choices are current to the passage.

40. C: *In transit* means on the way to the destination. Choice *A* is the definition of *travelling*. Choice *B* is the definition of *delegate.* Choice *D* is the definition of *provoke*.

Science

1. A: The hypothesis is the sentence that describes what the scientist wants to research with a conclusive expected finding. Choice *A* describes how she believes sunlight will affect plant growth. Choice *B* includes details about the experiment. Choice *C* is not a conclusive theory. Choice *D* describes the data that she found after conducting the experiment.

2. C: Looking at Figure 1, four experimental groups are shown on the graph for which data were collected: plants that received 1 hour of sunlight, 3 hours of sunlight, 5 hours of sunlight, and 7 hours of sunlight. Choices *A* and *B* could be describing two of the experimental groups and how much sunlight they received. Choice *D* describes how many days' data was collected.

3. B: After the data was collected, it was compiled into a line graph. The data points were collected, and then a line was drawn between the points. Data is represented by horizontal or vertical bars in bar graphs, Choice *A*. Pie charts are circular charts, with the data being represented by different wedges of the circle, Choice *C*. Pictograms use pictures to describe their subject, Choice *D.*

4. A: Looking at Figure 2, the sun provides light energy that drives forward the process of photosynthesis, which is how plants make their own source of energy and nutrients. Choices *B* and *C* are found in the environment around the plants. They combine with light energy to make the photosynthesis reaction work. Choice *D* is a product of photosynthesis.

5. D: Looking at the Figure 1, the experimental group that received 7 hours of sunlight every day grew taller than any of the other groups that received less sunlight per day. Therefore, it is reasonable to conclude that more sunlight makes plants grow bigger. Choice *A* is not a reasonable conclusion because it did not have the tallest plants. The scientist decided to measure the plants only for 11 days, but that does not describe a conclusion for the experiment, Choice *B*. Choice *C* is the opposite of the correct conclusion and does not have evidence to support it.

6. B: The atomic mass of a molecule can be found by adding the atomic mass of each component together. Looking at Figure 2, the atomic mass of each element is found below its symbol. The atomic mass of Na is 23, Choice *A,* and the atomic mass of Cl is 35.5, Choice *C*. The sum of those two components is 58.5, Choice *B*. Choice *D* is equal to two Cl atoms joined together.

7. D: Figure 1 shows the trends of the periodic table. Looking at the black arrows representing electronegativity, it is shown that electronegativity increases going towards the top row of the table and also increases going towards the right columns of the table. Therefore, the most electronegative element would be found in the top right corner of the table, which is where the element Helium is found. Choices *A* and *B* are found at the bottom of the table. Choice *D* is found on the left side of the table.

be raised by others. In a modern trial, the judge and (64) <u>jury would see these as kidnapping and</u> ultimately condemn the philosopher. (65) <u>As parents and emotional beings, this seems like</u> <u>cruelty</u>. However, the reason Plato makes this suggestion is to benefit both society and the individual. The reason for this confiscation and placement is for the child to grow to the best of their potential. If the child is brilliant and placed with a (66) <u>similar family than the child will</u> <u>have access to</u> more opportunities. Prosperous or intellectual parents could help develop the child's talents. The child would be placed in an (67) <u>environment that encourage growth.</u> This brilliant child—developed through this different upbringing—would then grow to be a positive presence in the community, a force that would benefit everyone. Thus, in this scenario, Plato *is* thinking of the individual, but resorting to extreme means to *help* them fully develop talents for the good of all the republic.

While our modern views may oppose this idea, we have to acknowledge that this isn't an evil idea. Rather, this is a suggestion to help society through the sacrifice of a few individual liberties. However, one must question how much sacrifice is needed to attain true freedom.

59. Which of the following would be the best choice for this sentence (reproduced below)?

Our modern society (59) <u>would actually look down on some</u> of Plato's ideas in *The Republic*.

a. NO CHANGE
b. would actually look down upon some
c. would actually be looking down on some
d. would actually look down on something

60. Which of the following would be the best choice for this sentence (reproduced below)?

(60) <u>Certainly his ideas could help create a more orderly and fair system, but at what cost?</u>

a. NO CHANGE
b. Certainly, his ideas could help create a more orderly and fair system, at what cost?
c. Certainly, his ideas could help create a more orderly and fair system, but at what cost?
d. Certainly his ideas could help create a more orderly and fair system, at what cost?

61. Which of the following would be the best choice for this sentence (reproduced below)?

Plato's ideal society is one that places human (61) <u>desire aside to focuses on</u> what will benefit the entire community.

a. NO CHANGE
b. desire aside to focus on
c. desire aside focusing on
d. desire aside, focuses on

8. A: Looking at Figure 1, the ionization energy increases as it goes right and up on the periodic table. Of the choices given, potassium (K) is found in the first column, fourth row. Each of the other choices is found above or to the right of potassium, so they would tend to have higher ionization energy. Since we're looking for the element with the lowest ionization energy, Choice *A*, potassium, is correct.

9. D: The atomic number of an element represents the number of protons. Looking at Figure 2, the atomic number is located at the top of the box, above the element's symbol. Hydrogen (H) has an atomic number of 1 and has the least number of protons of any other element in the periodic table. Radon (Rn), Choice *A*, has 86 protons. Boron (B), Choice *B*, has 5 protons. Nitrogen (N), Choice *C*, has 7 protons.

10. B: Looking at Figure 3, the elements are color coded in periods and groups according to their similar properties. Noble gases are located in the right most column of the table. Radon (Rn) is the only one of the element choices marked as a noble gas and would be the right choice for Scientist A. Nitrogen (N) and Boron (B), Choices *A* and *D*, are nonmetals. Copper (Cu), Choice *C*, is a transition metal.

11. B: Looking at Figures 1 and 2, crossbreeding experiment #3 in round #1 produces plants that are completely recessive and would have white flowers. Choices *A* and *C*, crossbreeding experiments #1 and 2, respectively, only produce flowers with a dominant allele present, making red flowers. Choice *D* does not have any recessive alleles, so white flowers are not a possibility.

12. C: Looking at Figure 2, which represents the number of plants that were produced from each crossbreeding experiment, it can be seen that only 2 plants produced white flowers out of 12 plants total, 4 from each experiment. To find the percentage, divide 2 by 12 and multiply by 100. The result is 16.7%. Choice *A* is the total number of plants that were produced. Choice *B* represents the percentage of white flowers in experiment #3 alone.

13. B: In a Punnett Square, each box represents one allele from each of the parent's genes. To find the genetic makeup of the second parent, take out the allele that was contributed from the first parent. Here, the first parent contributed a recessive allele, a, to each offspring. In the top row, that leaves a dominant allele, A, and in the bottom row, that leaves a recessive allele, a. Therefore, the genetic makeup of the second parent is Aa.

14. D: Crossbreeding the plants with only recessive alleles will result in 100% white flowering plants. All four offspring have white flowering plants. Choice *B* gives 100% red flowering plants. Choice *C* gives 25%, 1 out of 4 plants, with white flowers.

15. A: The observation step of the scientific method involves using your senses to identify the results of the experiment. In this case, the experiment depended on identifying the color of the flowers. This was done using sight. If the experiment had involved different scents produced by the flowers, Choice *B* would have worked. If it has involved different textures of the flowers, Choice *C* would have worked. Flowers generally do not make any noise, so Choice *D* would not have been useful.

16. D: The process of photosynthesis requires carbon dioxide and water to combine with sunlight to produce glucose, which is used as an energy source by plants. The forest floor does not get a lot of sunlight since it is shaded by the growth of so many trees and plants in the rainforest. Carbon, Choice *A*, is available through the air. Plants expel carbon dioxide. Water, Choice *B*, is abundant in the humid climate of the rainforest. Oxygen, Choice *C*, is always available in the Earth's atmosphere.

314

17. B: Central America is one of the five major areas of the world that has a rainforest. Looking at Figure 2, it can be seen that the southern countries of Central America contain rainforests. Comparing this map to the map of Central America, it is clear that Panama is a country that has rainforests. Choices *A*, *C*, and *D* are not found in Central America.

18. C: Birds fly above the trees of the rainforest the most. There, they have unobstructed skies, unlike the dense growth of the trees and plants in the other layers of the rainforest.

19. D: The understory layer is the third layer from the top of the rainforest. It does not receive much sunlight, so the plants need to grow large leaves to absorb as much sunlight as possible. Giant taro leaves would grow well in this layer since they have large leaves. The emergent layer, Choice *A*, gets plenty of sunlight since it is the topmost layer. The canopy layer, Choice *B*, receives enough sunlight for plants to grow without needing to increase their leaf size. The forest floor, Choice *C*, does not receive sunlight, and plants generally do not grow here.

20. A: Rainforests have warm and wet climates. They do not have long dry seasons and tend to have temperate temperatures. The giant water lily is ideal for the rainforest because it can grow large leaves and needs a wet environment to grow in. They grow in the shallow basins of rainforest rivers. Choices *B* and *C* need dry environments. Choice *D* needs a very hot environment, which is not characteristic of rainforests.

21. B: Solar eclipses should not be looked at directly. The rays of the Sun do not seem as bright as normal but can still cause damage to the eyes. A pinhole camera facing away from the eclipse allows the viewer to see a reflection of the eclipse instead of the actual eclipse. Choices *A*, *C*, and *D* all require looking directly at the solar eclipse.

22. A: When the moon comes between the Earth and Sun, a solar eclipse occurs. If the sun is far enough away and is completely blocked by the moon, it is a total solar eclipse. If it is only partially blocked by the moon, it is a partial solar eclipse, Choice *D*. A lunar eclipse occurs when the moon is on the opposite side of the Earth as the Sun and the Sun creates a shadow of the Earth on the moon, so that the moon becomes completely dark, Choice *C*, or partially dark, Choice *B*.

23. C: During a lunar eclipse, the Sun and moon are on opposite sides of the Earth. They line up so that the Sun's light that normally illuminates the moon is blocked by the Earth. This causes the moon to become dim. Sunlight can still be seen, Choice *A*, and the Earth does not become dark, Choices *B* and *D*.

24. B: The moon does not produce harmful light rays that can damage the eyes, so lunar eclipses can be viewed directly. A telescope would allow the lunar eclipse to be magnified and seen more clearly. During a solar eclipse, the Sun's rays appear to be dim and easy to see directly but they are still harmful to the eyes.

25. B: Solar eclipses are viewed during the daytime because they involve viewing the Sun while it is out during normal daytime hours. Lunar eclipses, Choices *C* and *D*, are viewed at nighttime when the moon is in the sky during its normal hours. The moon is normally illuminated by the Sun that is on the other side of the Earth. When the Sun is on the other side of the earth, it is nighttime for people looking at the moon.

26. B: A cladogram is a diagram that organizes proposed ancestral relations based on the development of physical features. A branching point would be seen on the cladogram where the development of lungs was noted. A phylogenetic tree, Choice *A*, does not note phenotypic features on it. Punnett

315

squares, Choice *C*, are used to determine the possible genetic makeup of offspring and are not related to evolution. Photographs, Choice *D*, may reveal species that look alike but would not reveal if they truly had a common ancestor.

27. A: According to Figure 3, human arms and whale fins are homologous structures that were derived from a common ancestor. They have anatomical similarities, although their function is not the same. They have different numbers of bones, so Choice *B* is incorrect. Since they are proposed to be developed from a common ancestor, they are not analogous features, Choice *C*. Whales have blubber covering their bodies and not layered skin like humans, so Choice *D* is incorrect.

28. D: According to the phylogenetic tree in Figure 1, the common ancestor of the striped skunk and European otter is the one that is noted before they branch into separate lineages, which is Mustelidae. Mephitis, Choice *A*, is the genus for only the striped skunk. Felidae, Choice *B*, and Canidae, Choice *C*, are completely different branches of the Carnivora order than the one that leads to the striped skunk and European otter.

29. A: According to Figure 2, the common trait that is listed on the branch of the cladogram that leads to lizards and birds is seeing UV light. They also have the common traits listed on the main branch of the cladogram before their lineages are branched off, which are vertebrae, lungs, and amniotic eggs. Perch and flounder branch from the main common ancestor and develop spiny-rayed fins, Choice *B*. Lobsters and spiders branch from the main common ancestor and develop the ability to molt an exoskeleton, Choice *C*.

30. C: Domestic cats and wolves are proposed to be related at the point where they share a common line before any branching occurs to separate their lineages. Figure 1 shows this as Carnivora, which is noted as the Order on the left side of the figure.

31. D: The color reagent is attached to the secondary antibody. It is released only when the secondary antibody attaches to the activated primary antibody. The antigen, primary antibody, and capture antibody, Choices *A*, *B*, and *C*, do not have any color reagent attached to them, so only the secondary antibody can cause the color reaction.

32. B: The color reagent is attached to the secondary antibody. If more antigen is present, more primary and secondary antibody will be attached to it and more color reagent will be released. Row 1 has the darkest green color of all the samples tested in the plate in Figure 2.

33. C: Looking at the graph in Figure 3, the highest amount of IL-1β is found in the spleen. IL-1β is a marker of inflammation and indicates that the spleen had the most inflammation of the areas tested. Serum, Choice *A*, had no IL-1β in the sample. Plasma, Choice *B*, had the second highest amount of IL-1β in the sample, and bone marrow, Choice *D*, had the second lowest amount of IL-1β.

34. B: Looking at the diagram in Figure 1, the antigen is located between the capture antibody and the primary antibody. The capture antibody keeps the antigen attached to the surface of the plate. The primary antibody recognizes the specific antigen. The secondary antibody generally recognizes the primary antibody is not specific to the antigen.

35. A: ELISAs are used to analyze specific substances within a larger sample. The antibodies used in an ELISA are designed specifically for a particular antigen. Sandwich ELISAs are generally used to quantify one antigen and not all substances in a larger sample, making Choice *B* incorrect. When used to quantify

316

an antigen, the antibodies need to already be developed and able to detect the antigen, making Choice *D* incorrect.

36. A: Stabilizing selection occurs when an intermediate phenotype is favored over two extreme phenotypes. In Scenario 1, the mice develop an intermediate colored fur so that they can blend in with the rocks in their environment. Developing one or both extremes, Choices *B* and *C,* would make them more visible to predators. Color selection, Choice *D,* is not a type of natural selection.

37. D: Directional selection occurs when one extreme of a phenotype is favored. In Scenario 2, large beaks are favored over medium- or small-sized beaks. The large beaks help the finches break up the tough seeds that became abundant after the drought. Finches with medium and small beaks had trouble breaking up the large seeds and did not survive as well as those with large beaks.

38. B: Small-beaked finches had trouble breaking up the large seeds after the drought, and therefore could not gain enough nutrition for survival. Natural selection is based on the idea that the individuals who adapt to their environment in the best way are the ones that have enhanced survival and reproduction. Finches with large beaks were most able to adapt to the large seeds and continue with their regular feeding schedule. There was no evidence of Choices *A* or *C* in the passage. Two extremes can be selected by natural selection in disruptive selection but that was not the case here, Choice *D.*

39. C: Disruptive selection occurs when both extremes of a phenotype are selected. In Cameroon, the finches had both large and small beaks, but did not survive well with medium beaks. If medium beaks were selected, it would have been stabilizing selection, Choice *A.* If only one of the extremes had been favored, it would have been directional selection, Choice *B.*

40. D: Natural selection is the idea that individuals are selected to survive and reproduce based on their ability to adapt to the environment. Their phenotypes are advantageous for survival and reproduction over those of other individuals. It is solely based on the phenotype of the individual, not the genotype, Choice *A.* Extreme phenotypes, Choice *B,* may be selected but are not always the most advantageous. It occurs all time, not just in extreme weather conditions, such as a drought, Choice *C.*

ACT Practice Test #2

English

Questions 1–9 are based on the following passage:

The name "Thor" has always been associated with great power. (1) <u>Arguably, Norse Mythologies most</u> popular and powerful god is Thor of the Aesir. My first experience of Thor was not like most of today's generation. I grew up reading Norse mythology where (2) <u>Thor wasn't a comic book superhero but even mightier.</u> There are stories of Thor destroying mountains, (3) <u>defeating scores of giants and lifting up the world's largest creature the Midgard Serpent.</u> But always, Thor was a protector.

Like in modern comics and movies, Thor was the god of thunder and wielded (4) <u>the hammer Mjolnir however there are several differences</u> between the ancient legend and modern hero. (5) <u>For example, Loki, the god of mischief, isn't Thor's brother.</u> Loki is actually Thor's servant, but this doesn't stop the trickster from causing chaos, chaos that Thor has to then quell. In all of his incarnations, Thor is a god that reestablishes order by tempering the chaos around him. (6) <u>This is also symbolized in his prized weapon Mjolnir a magic hammer.</u> A hammer is both a weapon and a (7) <u>tool, but why would a god favor a seemingly everyday object?</u>

A hammer is used to shape metal and create change. The hammer tempers raw iron, (8) <u>ore that is in an chaotic state of impurities and shapelessness,</u> to create an item of worth. Thus, a hammer is in many ways a tool that brings a kind of order to the world—like Thor. Hammers were also tools of everyday people, which further endeared Thor to the common man. Therefore, it's no surprise that Thor remains an iconic hero to this day.

I began thinking to myself, why is Thor so prominent in our culture today even though many people don't follow the old religion? (9) <u>Well the truth is that every culture throughout time, including ours,</u> needs heroes. People need figures in their lives that give them hope and make them aspire to be great. We need the peace of mind that chaos will eventually be brought to order and that good can conquer evil. Thor was a figure of hope and remains so to this day.

1. Which of the following would be the best choice for this sentence (reproduced below)?

   (1) <u>Arguably, Norse Mythologies most</u> popular and powerful god is Thor of the Aesir.

   a. NO CHANGE
   b. Arguably Norse Mythologies most
   c. Arguably, Norse mythology's most
   d. Arguably, Norse Mythology's most

2. Which of the following would be the best choice for this sentence (reproduced below)?

I grew up reading Norse mythology where (2) <u>Thor wasn't a comic book superhero but even mightier.</u>

a. NO CHANGE
b. Thor wasn't a comic book superhero. He was even mightier.
c. Thor wasn't a comic book superhero, but even mightier.
d. Thor wasn't a comic book superhero, he was even mightier.

3. Which of the following would be the best choice for this sentence (reproduced below)?

There are stories of Thor destroying mountains, (3) <u>defeating scores of giants and lifting up the world's largest creature the Midgard Serpent.</u>

a. NO CHANGE
b. defeating scores of giants, and lifting up the world's largest creature, the Midgard Serpent.
c. defeating scores of giants, and lifting up the world's largest creature the Midgard Serpent.
d. defeating scores, of giants, and lifting up the world's largest creature the Midgard Serpent.

4. Which of the following would be the best choice for this sentence (reproduced below)?

Like in modern comics and movies, Thor was the god of thunder and wielded (4) <u>the hammer Mjolnir however there are several differences</u> between the ancient legend and modern hero.

a. NO CHANGE
b. the hammer Mjolnir, however there are several differences
c. the hammer Mjolnir. However there are several differences
d. the hammer Mjolnir. However, there are several differences

5. Which of the following would be the best choice for this sentence (reproduced below)?

(5) <u>For example, Loki, the god of mischief, isn't Thor's brother.</u>

a. NO CHANGE
b. For example, Loki the god of mischief isn't Thor's brother.
c. For example, Loki the god of mischief, isn't Thor's brother.
d. For example Loki, the god of mischief, isn't Thor's brother.

6. Which of the following would be the best choice for this sentence (reproduced below)?

(6) <u>This is also symbolized in his prized weapon Mjolnir a magic hammer.</u>

a. NO CHANGE
b. This is also symbolized in his prized weapon, Mjolnir a magic hammer.
c. This is also symbolized in his prized weapon, Mjolnir, a magic hammer.
d. This is also symbolized in his prized weapon Mjolnir, a magic hammer.

319

7. Which of the following would be the best choice for this sentence (reproduced below)?

A hammer is both a weapon and a (7) tool, but why would a god favor a seemingly everyday object?

a. NO CHANGE
b. tool; why would a god favor a seemingly everyday object?
c. tool, but, why would a god favor a seemingly everyday object?
d. tool, however, why would a god favor a seemingly everyday object?

8. Which of the following would be the best choice for this sentence (reproduced below)?

The hammer tempers raw iron, (8) ore that is in an chaotic state of impurities and shapelessness, to create an item of worth.

a. NO CHANGE
b. ore that is in a chaotic state of impurities and shapelessness
c. ore that has the impurities and shapelessness of a chaotic state
d. ore that is in an chaotic state, of impurities and shapelessness,

9. Which of the following would be the best choice for this sentence (reproduced below)?

(9) Well the truth is that every culture throughout time, including ours, needs heroes.

a. NO CHANGE
b. Well, the truth is, every culture throughout time, including ours,
c. Well, every culture throughout time, including ours, in truth
d. Well, the truth is that every culture throughout time, including ours,

Questions 10–18 are based on the following passage:

In our essay and class discussion, (10) we came to talking about mirrors. It was an excellent class in which we focused on an article written by Salman Rushdie that compared the homeland to a mirror. (11) Essentially this mirror was an metaphor for us and our homeland. (12) When we look at our reflection we see the culture, our homeland staring back at us. An interesting analogy, but the conversation really began when we read that Rushdie himself stated that the cracked mirror is more valuable than a whole one. But why?

(13) After reflecting on the passage I found the answer to be simple. The analogy reflects the inherent nature of human individuality. The cracks in the mirror represent different aspects of our own being. Perhaps it is our personal views, our hobbies, or our differences with other people, but (14) whatever it is that makes us unique defines us, even while we are part of a big culture. (15) What this tells us is that we can have a homeland, but ultimately we ourselves are each different in it.

Just because one's (16) mirror is cracked, the individuals isn't disowned from the actual, physical homeland and culture within. It means that the homeland is uniquely perceived by the (17) individual beholding it and that there are in fact many aspects to culture itself. Like the various

320

cracks, a culture has religion, language, and many other factors that form to make it whole. What this idea does is invite the viewer to accept their own view of their culture as a whole.

Like in Chandra's *Love and Longing in Bombay*, a single homeland has many stories to tell. Whether one is a cop or a retired war veteran, the individual will perceive the different aspects of the world with unduplicated eyes. (18) <u>Rushdie, seems to be urging his readers</u> to love their culture but to not be pressured by the common crowd. Again, the cracks represent differences which could easily be interpreted as views about the culture, so what this is saying is to accept the culture but accept oneself as well.

From the essay "Portals to Homeland: Mirrors"

10. Which of the following would be the best choice for this sentence (reproduced below)?

In our essay and class discussion, (10) <u>we came to talking about</u> mirrors.

a. NO CHANGE
b. we were talking about
c. we talked about
d. we came to talk about

11. Which of the following would be the best choice for this sentence (reproduced below)?

(11) <u>Essentially this mirror is an metaphor for us and our homeland.</u>

a. NO CHANGE
b. Essentially, this mirror is a metaphor for us and our homeland.
c. Essentially, this mirror is an metaphor for us and our homeland.
d. Essentially this mirror is an metaphor, for us and our homeland.

12. Which of the following would be the best choice for this sentence (reproduced below)?

(12) <u>When we look at our reflection we see the culture, our homeland staring back at us.</u>

a. NO CHANGE
b. When we look at our reflection we see our culture our homeland staring back at us.
c. When we look at our reflection we saw our culture, our homeland, staring back at us.
d. Looking at our reflection we see our culture as our homeland is staring back at us.

13. Which of the following would be the best choice for this sentence (reproduced below)?

(13) <u>After reflecting on the passage I found the answer to be simple.</u>

a. NO CHANGE
b. After reflecting on the passage; I found the answer to be simple.
c. After reflecting on the passage I finding the answer to be simple.
d. After reflecting on the passage, I found the answer to be simple.

321

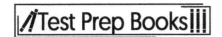

14. Which of the following would be the best choice for this sentence (reproduced below)?

Perhaps it is our personal views, our hobbies, or our differences with other people, but (14) <u>whatever it is that makes us unique defines us, even while we are part of a big culture.</u>

a. NO CHANGE
b. whatever it is, that makes us unique, defines us, even while we are part of a big culture.
c. whatever it is that makes us unique also defines us, even while we are part of a bigger culture.
d. whatever it is that makes us unique defines us, even though we are part of a big culture.

15. Which of the following would be the best choice for this sentence (reproduced below)?

(15) <u>What this tells us is that we can have a homeland, but ultimately we ourselves are each different in it.</u>

a. NO CHANGE
b. What this tells us is that we can have a homeland, but ultimately, we ourselves are each different in it.
c. What this tells us is that we can have a homeland, however, ultimately, we ourselves are each different in it.
d. What this tells us is that we can have a homeland, ultimately we ourselves are each different in it.

16. Which of the following would be the best choice for this sentence (reproduced below)?

Just because one's (16) <u>mirror is cracked, the individuals isn't disowned</u> from the actual, physical homeland and culture within.

a. NO CHANGE
b. mirror is cracked, the individuals will not be disowned
c. mirror is cracked, the individuals aren't disowned
d. mirror is cracked, the individual isn't disowned

17. Which of the following would be the best choice for this sentence (reproduced below)?

It means that the homeland is uniquely perceived by the (17) <u>individual beholding it and that there are, in fact, many aspects</u> of culture itself.

a. NO CHANGE
b. individual beholding it; and that there are in fact many aspects
c. individual beholding it and that there is, in fact, many aspects
d. individual beholding it and there's in fact, many aspects

18. Which of the following would be the best choice for this sentence (reproduced below)?

(18) <u>Rushdie, seems to be urging his readers</u> to love their culture but to not be pressured by the common crowd.

a. NO CHANGE
b. Rushdie seemed to be urging his readers
c. Rushdie, seeming to urge his readers,
d. Rushdie seems to be urging his readers

Questions 19–27 are based on the following passage:

The Odyssey reading performed by Odds Bodkin (19) <u>was an especially rewarding experience</u>. Myths continue to help us (20) <u>understood ancient cultures</u> while still helping us connect to real-world lessons through narrative. (21) <u>While myths were not read exactly the way Bodkin performed *The Odyssey*,</u> his performance truly combined ancient and modern artistic styles.

(22) <u>Originally, myths were not written down instead, stories like The Odyssey</u> were transferred to written form thousands of years after they were originally told. *Told* is a (23) <u>key term here: myths were passing on to generations orally</u>. They were sung, or at least accompanied by music. Of course, we no longer gather in halls to hear (24) <u>myths; we read it, or</u> perhaps listen to audio versions. The Odds Bodkin reading was unique in that it offered a traditional glimpse into what it might have been like to receive a myth in its original form of delivery.

What I thought was especially interesting, was that Bodkin used his guitar to build an atmosphere or tempo around the story. In points of action, like when the wooden horse was being moved into Troy, or when Odysseus leads his men in search of the missing crew (lotus episode), he played a signature tune. (25) <u>This creates a kind of soundtrack for the story,</u> providing a unique feeling for the scene. While (26) <u>there is no visual stimuli like in motion picture</u>, one is moved by the guitar's playing. Accompanied by his dramatic reading, the music reflects the action of the plot and even emotions/insights of the characters. Interestingly, Bodkin also used physical gestures to tell the story as well. He occasionally acted out scenes with his hands and sometimes with sound effects.

The best scene was when Bodkin played the Cyclops, Polyphemus, grabbing and gorging himself on Odysseus' men. (27) <u>In addition from bringing a kind of animation</u> to the presentation, it linked the story to the physical world too. He wasn't just reading, he was acting. It gave this a three-dimensional aspect of the telling of *The Odyssey* that I thought was especially great.

19. Which of the following would be the best choice for this sentence (reproduced below)?

The Odyssey reading performed by Odds Bodkin (19) <u>was an especially rewarding experience.</u>

a. NO CHANGE
b. was, an especially, rewarding experience.
c. was a especially rewarding experience.
d. was an especially rewarded experience.

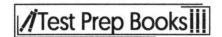

20. Which of the following would be the best choice for this sentence (reproduced below)?

Myths continue to help us (20) <u>understood ancient cultures</u> while still helping us connect to real-world lessons through narrative.

a. NO CHANGE
b. understand ancient cultures
c. understood ancient cultures,
d. understanding ancient cultures

21. Which of the following would be the best choice for this sentence (reproduced below)?

(21) <u>While myths were not read exactly the way Bodkin performed The Odyssey,</u> his performance truly combined ancient and modern artistic styles.

a. NO CHANGE
b. While myths were not exactly the way Bodkin read/performed *The Odyssey*,
c. While myths were not read, exactly, the way Bodkin performed *The Odyssey*,
d. While myths were not read exactly the way Bodkin performed *The Odyssey*.

22. Which of the following would be the best choice for this sentence (reproduced below)?

(22) <u>Originally, myths were not written down instead, stories like The Odyssey</u> were transferred to written form thousands of years after they were originally told.

a. NO CHANGE
b. Myths, originally, were not written down instead, stories like *The Odyssey*
c. Originally myths were not written down; instead stories like *The Odyssey*
d. Originally, myths were not written down. Instead, stories like *The Odyssey*

23. Which of the following would be the best choice for this sentence (reproduced below)?

Told is a (23) <u>key term here: myths were passing on to generations orally.</u>

a. NO CHANGE
b. key term here: myths were passed on to generations orally.
c. key term here: myths passed on to generations orally.
d. key term here: myths pass on to generations orally.

24. Which of the following would be the best choice for this sentence (reproduced below)?

Of course, we no longer gather in halls to hear (24) <u>myths, we read it, or</u> perhaps listen to audio versions.

a. NO CHANGE
b. myths; we read it or
c. myths; they are read, or
d. myths; we read them, or

324

25. Which of the following would be the best choice for this sentence (reproduced below)?

(25) <u>This creates a kind of soundtrack for the story,</u> providing a unique feeling for the scene.

a. NO CHANGE
b. This creates a kind of soundtrack for the story;
c. This creates, a kind of soundtrack, for the story,
d. This creates a kinds of soundtrack for the story,

26. Which of the following would be the best choice for this sentence (reproduced below)?

While (26) <u>there is no visual stimuli like in motion picture,</u> one is moved by the guitar's playing.

a. NO CHANGE
b. there is no visual stimuli, like in motion picture,
c. there are no visual stimuli, like in motion pictures,
d. there are no visual stimuli like in motion picture,

27. Which of the following would be the best choice for this sentence (reproduced below)?

(27) <u>In addition from bringing a kind of animation</u> to the presentation, it linked the story to the physical world too.

a. NO CHANGE
b. In addition to bringing a kind of animation
c. In addition too bringing, a kind of animation,
d. In addition for bringing a kind of animation

Questions 28–36 are based on the following passage:

Quantum mechanics, which describes how the universe works on its smallest scale, is inherently weird. Even the founders of the field (28) <u>including Max Planck, Werner Heisenberg, and Wolfgang Pauli unsettled by the new theory's implications.</u> (29) <u>Instead of a deterministic world where everything can be predicted by equations,</u> events at the quantum scale are purely probabilistic. (30) <u>Every outcome exist simultaneously,</u> while the actual act of observation forces nature to choose one path.

In our everyday lives, (31) <u>this concept of determinism, is actually expressed</u> in the thought experiment of Schrödinger's cat. Devised by Erwin Schrödinger, one of the founders of quantum mechanics, (32) <u>it's purpose is to show how truly strange</u> the framework is. Picture a box containing a cat, a radioactive element, and a vial of poison. (33) <u>If the radioactive element decays, it will release the poison and kill the cat.</u> The box is closed, so there is no way for anyone outside to know what is happening inside. Since the cat's status—alive and dead—are mutually exclusive, only one state can exist. (34) <u>What quantum mechanics says however</u> is that the cat is simultaneously alive and dead, existing in both states until the box's lid is removed and one outcome is chosen.

(35) <u>Further confounding our sense of reality, Louis de Broglie proposed that, on the smallest scales, particles and waves are indistinguishable.</u> This builds on Albert Einstein's famous theory

325

that matter and energy are interchangeable. Although there isn't apparent evidence for this in our daily lives, various experiments have shown the validity of quantum mechanics. One of the most famous experiments is the double-slit experiment, which initially proved the wave nature of light. When shone through parallel slits onto a screen, (36) light creates a interference pattern of alternating bands of light and dark. But when electrons were fired at the slits, the act of observation changed the outcome. If observers monitored which slit the electrons travelled through, only one band was seen on the screen. This is expected, since we know electrons act as particles. However, when they monitored the screen only, an interference pattern is created— implying that the electrons behaved as waves!

28. Which of the following would be the best choice for this sentence (reproduced below)?

(28) Even the founders of the field including Max Planck, Werner Heisenberg, and Wolfgang Pauli unsettled by the new theory's implications.

a. NO CHANGE
b. including Max Planck, Werner Heisenberg, and Wolfgang Pauli; unsettled by the new theory's implications.
c. including Max Planck, Werner Heisenberg, and Wolfgang Pauli were unsettled by the new theories' implications.
d. including Max Planck, Werner Heisenberg, and Wolfgang Pauli were unsettled by the new theory's implications.

29. Which of the following would be the best choice for this sentence (reproduced below)?

(29) Instead of a deterministic world where everything can be predicted by equations, events at the quantum scale are purely probabilistic.

a. NO CHANGE
b. Instead, of a deterministic world where everything can be predicted by equations,
c. Instead of a deterministic world where everything can be predicting by equations,
d. Instead of a deterministic world, where everything can be predicted by equations,

30. Which of the following would be the best choice for this sentence (reproduced below)?

(30) Every outcome exist simultaneously, while the actual act of observation forces nature to choose one path.

a. NO CHANGE
b. Each of these outcome exist simultaneously,
c. Every outcome, existing simultaneously,
d. Every outcome exists simultaneously,

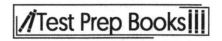

31. Which of the following would be the best choice for this sentence (reproduced below)?

In our everyday lives, (31) this concept of determinism, is actually expressed in the thought experiment of Schrödinger's cat.

a. NO CHANGE
b. this concept of determinism is actually expressed
c. this, concept of determinism, is actually expressed
d. this concept of determinism, is expressed actually

32. Which of the following would be the best choice for this sentence (reproduced below)?

Devised by Erwin Schrödinger, one of the founders of quantum mechanics, (32) it's purpose is to show how truly strange the framework is.

a. NO CHANGE
B. its purposes is to show how truly strange
c. its purpose is to show how truly strange
d. it's purpose, showing how truly strange

33. Which of the following would be the best choice for this sentence (reproduced below)?

(33) If the radioactive element decays, it will release the poison and kill the cat.

a. NO CHANGE
b. If, the radioactive element decays, it will release the poison and kill the cat.
c. If the radioactive element decays. It will release the poison and kill the cat.
d. If the radioactive element decays, releasing the poison and kill the cat.

34. Which of the following would be the best choice for this sentence (reproduced below)?

(34) What quantum mechanics says however is that the cat is simultaneously alive and dead, existing in both states until the box's lid is removed and one outcome is chosen.

a. NO CHANGE
b. What quantum mechanics says however, is
c. What quantum mechanics says. However, is
d. What quantum mechanics says, however, is

35. Which of the following would be the best choice for this sentence (reproduced below)?

(35) <u>Further confounding our sense of reality, Louis de Broglie proposed that, on the smallest scales, particles and waves are indistinguishable.</u>

a. NO CHANGE
b. Further confounding our sense of reality Louis de Broglie proposed that on the smallest scales, particles and waves are indistinguishable.
c. Further confounding our sense of reality, Louis de Broglie proposed that on the smallest scales, particles and waves are indistinguishable.
d. Further, confounding our sense of reality, Louis de Broglie proposed that, on the smallest scales, particles and waves are indistinguishable.

36. Which of the following would be the best choice for this sentence (reproduced below)?

When shone through parallel slits onto a screen, (36) <u>light creates a interference</u> pattern of alternating bands of light and dark.

a. NO CHANGE
b. light created an interference
c. lights create a interference
d. light, creating an interference,

Questions 37–45 are based on the following passage:

(37) <u>As the adage goes knowledge is power.</u> Those who are smart and understand the world as it is are the most fit to lead. Intelligence (38) <u>doesn't necessarily require</u> a deep understanding of complex scientific principles. Rather, having the basic knowledge of how the world works, particularly how people go about gaining what they need to survive and thrive, (39) <u>are more important.</u>

Any leadership position, whether on the job or informally, tends to be fraught with politics. (40) <u>Smart leaders will engage in critical thinking allowing them to discern ulterior motives and identify propaganda.</u> Besides catching negative intentions, (41) <u>these practice will serve to highlight</u> the positives in group interactions. Gaining insights into different viewpoints will make leaders more (42) <u>receptive to constructive criticism and ideas from unexpected sources.</u> As with many aspects of being a good and well-rounded person, the seeds for this trait are sown in pre-school. Besides facts and figures, students need to be taught critical thinking skills to survive in a world flooded with subliminal messages and scams. (43) <u>Sadly our current society is plagued by many inconvenient truths that are attacked as lies.</u> Wise leaders should recognize when someone is trying to save the world or merely push a political agenda.

Just as important as the knowledge of how the world works (44) <u>is understood of how humanity operates.</u> Leaders should be able to tactfully make friends and influence people using the doctrines of psychology. People who say whatever comes into their heads without thinking demonstrate a lack of basic diplomatic understanding, not to mention a deficiency of self-control and lack of respect. Breaches of courtesy, whether intentional or otherwise, strain relations and can ruin potential alliances.

328

While the best leaders are tolerant of other (45) cultural practices and diverse perspectives, those who exhibit disregard and unwarranted contempt for others shouldn't be expected to find favor. Knowledge extends past textbook learning to practical awareness, encompassing skills for a successful life as a decent human being all around. These skills include risk management and creative solutions. Someone who fails to hone these abilities—or neglects to apply their knowledge—will likely be overthrown by those they are supposed to lead.

37. Which of the following would be the best choice for this sentence (reproduced below)?

(37) As the adage goes knowledge is power.

a. NO CHANGE
b. Knowledge is power as the adage goes.
c. As the adage goes, "knowledge is power."
d. As, the adage goes, knowledge is power.

38. Which of the following would be the best choice for this sentence (reproduced below)?

Intelligence (38) doesn't necessarily require a deep understanding of complex scientific principles.

a. NO CHANGE
b. doesn't, necessarily, require
c. doesn't require necessarily
d. aren't necessarily require

39. Which of the following would be the best choice for this sentence (reproduced below)?

Rather, having the basic knowledge of how the world works, particularly how people go about gaining what they need to survive and thrive, (39) are more important.

a. NO CHANGE
b. is more important.
c. are the most important.
d. is most important.

40. Which of the following would be the best choice for this sentence (reproduced below)?

(40) Smart leaders will engage in critical thinking allowing them to discern ulterior motives and identify propaganda.

a. NO CHANGE
b. Smart leaders will engage in critical thinking allowing them to discern ulterior motives, and identify propaganda.
c. Smart leaders will engage in critical thinking, allowing them to discern ulterior motives and identify propaganda.
d. Smart leaders will engage in critical thinking allows them to discern ulterior motives and identify propaganda.

41. Which of the following would be the best choice for this sentence (reproduced below)?

Besides catching negative intentions, (41) these practice will serve to highlight the positives in group interactions.

a. NO CHANGE
b. this practices will serve to highlight
c. these practice serve to highlight
d. this practice will serve to highlight

42. Which of the following would be the best choice for this sentence (reproduced below)?

Gaining insights into different viewpoints will make leaders more (42) receptive to constructive criticism and ideas from unexpected sources.

a. NO CHANGE
b. receptive for constructive criticism and ideas from unexpected sources.
c. receptive from unexpected sources to construct criticism and ideas.
d. receptive, to constructive criticism and ideas, from unexpected sources.

43. Which of the following would be the best choice for this sentence (reproduced below)?

(43) Sadly our current society is plagued by many inconvenient truths that are attacked as lies.

a. NO CHANGE
b. Sadly, our current society is plagued by many inconvenient truths that are attacked as lies.
c. Sadly our current society is plagued by many inconvenient truths, that are attacked as lies.
d. Sadly our current society is plaguing by many inconvenient truths that are attacking as lies.

44. Which of the following would be the best choice for this sentence (reproduced below)?

Just as important as the knowledge of how the world works (44) is understood of how humanity operates.

a. NO CHANGE
b. is to understand of how humanity operates.
c. is understanding of how humanity operates.
d. is an understanding of how humanity operates.

45. Which of the following would be the best choice for this sentence (reproduced below)?

While the best leaders are tolerant of other (45) cultural practices and diverse perspectives, those who exhibit disregard and unwarranted contempt for others shouldn't be expected to find favor.

a. NO CHANGE
b. cultural practices and diverse perspectives. Those who exhibit disregard
c. cultural practices, and diverse perspectives, those who exhibit disregard
d. cultural practices and diverse perspectives, those whom exhibit disregard

330

Questions 46–54 are based on the following passage:

While the various tales do take on the individual perspectives, (46) <u>Chaucer's internal character retain a unique presence throughout the text.</u> *The Canterbury Tales* provides the ultimate example of a story (47) <u>about stories also being a story containing multiple stories.</u> (48) <u>Chaucer does these by compiling embedded narratives</u> from multiple sources while delivering them through a single, primary voice. From the (49) <u>beginning, it's clear that Chaucer</u> is the source of the text. Yet, Chaucer is more than just a storyteller; he's an honest storyteller. Chaucer provides bold character descriptions of (50) <u>these individual, including their faults</u>. This can be seen when Chaucer sheds light on the nature of the Prioress. He describes that, (51) <u>while her supposed to be a pious nun</u>, she is actually a walking façade. The prioress is noted for counterfeiting courtly behavior so that people think highly of her.

With Chaucer providing such detailed observations, the readers have a more complete picture of what is going on and who the other characters really are. Another example of this is (52) <u>the sarcastic and brutal honest description</u> of the miller: "The millere, that for drunken was al pale." This description of the (53) <u>miller's drunkenness shed's light on</u> why he seems so crazy. It's because he's a drunk. Thus, Chaucer's own narrative gives readers a reliable perspective amongst a host of questionable storytellers. He also provides information on the characters that can help the reader grasp their tales more fully.

One of the signature methods of Chaucer's storytelling is that he doesn't just tell a story, his characters do as well. As a writer, Chaucer actually immerses himself into the collective character discussions. In many ways, Chaucer is a vehicle for the characters to tell their individual stories. Chaucer actually takes on the styles and voice of the characters. A good, eloquent tale like the *Knight's Tale* is written that way because that's how the knight would have told it. (54) <u>Likewise, it's also why several tales are poorly written</u>, have cross delivery, or lack a driven plotline. The *Miller's Tale* is rather crazy and cross because he is drunk while telling it. Chaucer seeks to tell the story in the way his drunken character would have.

46. Which of the following would be the best choice for this sentence (reproduced below)?

While the various tales do take on the individual perspectives, (46) <u>Chaucer's internal character retain a unique presence throughout the text.</u>

a. NO CHANGE
b. Chaucer's internal character retains a unique presence throughout the text.
c. Chaucer's internal character retaining a unique presence throughout the text.
d. Chaucer's internal character retained a unique presence throughout the text.

47. Which of the following would be the best choice for this sentence (reproduced below)?

The Canterbury Tales provides the ultimate example of a story (47) <u>about stories also being a story containing multiple stories.</u>

a. NO CHANGE
b. about stories; not to mention stories within a single story.
c. about stories, also being a story containing multiple stories.
d. about stories, as well as being a story containing multiple stories.

48. Which of the following would be the best choice for this sentence (reproduced below)?

(48) <u>Chaucer does these by compiling embedded narratives</u> from multiple sources while delivering them through a single, primary voice.

a. NO CHANGE
b. Chaucer does this, compiling embedded narratives
c. Chaucer does this by compiling embedded narratives
d. Chaucer does these through compiling embedded narratives

49. Which of the following would be the best choice for this sentence (reproduced below)?

From the (49) <u>beginning, it's clear that Chaucer</u> is the source of the text.

a. NO CHANGE
b. beginning. It's clear that Chaucer
c. beginning, Chaucer clearly
d. beginning, it's clear, that Chaucer

50. Which of the following would be the best choice for this sentence (reproduced below)?

Chaucer provides bold character descriptions of (50) <u>these individual, including their faults.</u>

a. NO CHANGE
b. these individuals, including their faults
c. these individual including their faults
d. these individuals; including their faults

51. Which of the following would be the best choice for this sentence (reproduced below)?

He describes that, (51) <u>while her supposed to be a pious nun,</u> she is actually a walking façade.

a. NO CHANGE
b. her supposed nun's piety,
c. while her is supposed to be a pious nun,
d. while she's supposed to be a pious nun,

332

52. Which of the following would be the best choice for this sentence (reproduced below)?

Another example of this is (52) <u>the sarcastic and brutal honest description of</u> the miller: "The millere, that for drunken was al pale."

a. NO CHANGE
b. the sarcastic, and brutal, honest description of
c. the sarcastic and brutally honest description of
d. the sarcastic, brutal honest description of

53. Which of the following would be the best choice for this sentence (reproduced below)?

This description of the (53) <u>miller's drunkenness shed's light on</u> why he seems so crazy.

a. NO CHANGE
b. miller's drunkenness sheds light on
c. miller's drunk, which sheds light on
d. miller's drunkenness, shed's light on

54. Which of the following would be the best choice for this sentence (reproduced below)?

<u>Likewise, it's also why several tales are poorly written,</u> have crass delivery, or lack a driven plotline.

a. NO CHANGE
b. Likewise it's also why several tales are poorly written,
c. Likewise it's also why several tales are, poorly written,
d. Likewise, it's also why several tales are, poorly written,

Questions 55–58 are based on the following passage:

(55) <u>Practitioner of Ju-jitsu, and other martial arts, strive away</u> from the act of total violence. We tend not to be violent individuals in the first place because of our training. From the first day on the mat, physical restraint is emphasized. The moves we learn are inherently harmful, (56) <u>so them should used sparingly</u> and not to advance our own satisfaction. The lessons taught in Ju-juitsu urge people to be mindful of their capabilities while also being decisive when defense is required. Having grace, even in the face of danger, is a central theme within martial arts studies.

Everything we do, whether striking a blow or undertaking a certain task, carries responsibility. One must be motivated by pure intention because action cannot be taken back. Life is precious, and its preservation must be top priority. Even when defending against someone who seeks to end your own life, a true Ju-jitsu practitioner should strive to defend themselves while not ending the opponent's life. To abuse this power would only stain the soul and demine the art. (57) <u>Having restraint is testament to how one values life and the possibilities within.</u> Life is about growth, like the study of Ju-jitsu. Ju-jitsu is all about a process of learning and relearning, dedication, struggle, and then understanding. The study (58) <u>of Ju-jitsu, like any trial throughout one's life,</u> is a test of faith and willpower. The end result benefits others as well as oneself.

From the essay "Morality and the Warrior's Path"

333

55. Which of the following would be the best choice for this sentence (reproduced below)?

(55) <u>Practitioner of Ju-jitsu, and other martial arts, strive away</u> from the act of total violence.

a. NO CHANGE
b. Practitioners of Ju-jitsu, and other martial arts, strive away
c. Practitioners of Ju-jitsu, and other martial arts strive away
d. Practitioner of Ju-jitsu, and other martial arts, strives away

56. Which of the following would be the best choice for this sentence (reproduced below)?

The moves we learn are inherently harmful, (56) <u>so them should used sparingly</u> and not to advance our own satisfaction.

a. NO CHANGE
b. so them should be used sparingly
c. so they should used sparingly
d. so they should be used sparingly

57. Which of the following would be the best choice for this sentence (reproduced below)?

(57) <u>Having restraint is testament to how one values life and the possibilities within.</u>

a. NO CHANGE
b. Having restraint is an testament to how one values life and the possibilities within.
c. Having restraint is a testament to how one values life and the possibilities within.
d. Having restraint is testament to how one values life and the possibilities, within.

58. Which of the following would be the best choice for this sentence (reproduced below)?

The study (58) <u>of Ju-jitsu, like any trial throughout one's life</u> is a test of faith and willpower.

a. NO CHANGE
b. of Ju-jitsu like any trial throughout one's life
c. of Ju-jitsu, like, any trial throughout one's life
d. of Ju-jitsu, like any trial throughout one's life,

Questions 59–67 are based on the following passage:

Our modern society (59) <u>would actually look down on some</u> of Plato's ideas in *The Republic.* But why? (60) <u>Certainly his ideas could help create a more orderly and fair system, but at what cost?</u> The simple truth is that in many of his examples, we see that Plato has taken the individual completely out of the equation. Plato's ideal society is one that places human (61) <u>desire aside to focuses on</u> what will benefit the entire community. To enforce these ideas, Plato seeks to use government to regulate and mandate these rules. This may seem to (62) <u>equalize the population, its possible that this is</u> actually the greatest breech of freedom.

Today, people would think Plato's (63) <u>suggestion to confiscate citizens children</u> and place them in different homes is utterly barbaric. We cannot imagine the pain of losing one's own child to

334

62. Which of the following would be the best choice for this sentence (reproduced below)?

This may seem to (62) equalize the population, its possible that this is actually the greatest breech of freedom.

a. NO CHANGE
b. equalize the population it's possible that this is
c. equalize the population, but it's possible that this is
d. equalize the population, however possible that this is

63. Which of the following would be the best choice for this sentence (reproduced below)?

Today, people would think Plato's (63) suggestion to confiscate citizens children and place them in different homes is utterly barbaric.

a. NO CHANGE
b. suggestion for confiscating citizens children
c. suggestion for confiscating citizen's children
d. suggestion to confiscate citizens' children

64. Which of the following would be the best choice for this sentence (reproduced below)?

In a modern trial, the judge and (64) jury would see these as kidnapping and ultimately condemn the philosopher.

a. NO CHANGE
b. jury would see this as kidnapping and
c. jury would see these kidnappings
d. jury would see those as kidnapping and

65. Which of the following would be the best choice for this sentence (reproduced below)?

(65) As parents and emotional beings, this seems like cruelty.

a. NO CHANGE
b. As parents and emotional beings this seems like cruelty.
c. As parents and emotional beings; this seems like cruelty.
d. As parents and emotional beings those seems like cruelty.

66. Which of the following would be the best choice for this sentence (reproduced below)?

If the child is brilliant and placed with a (66) similar family than he will have access to more opportunities.

a. NO CHANGE
b. similar family, than the child will have access to
c. similar family then the child will access to
d. similar family, the child will have access to

336

67. Which of the following would be the best choice for this sentence (reproduced below)?
The child would be placed in an (67) environment that encourage growth.

    a. NO CHANGE
    b. environment encouraging growth.
    c. environment that encourages growth.
    d. environment which encourage growth.

Questions 68–75 are based on the following passage:

Early in my career, (68) a master's teacher shared this thought with me "Education is the last bastion of civility." While I did not completely understand the scope of those words at the time, I have since come to realize the depth, breadth, truth, and significance of what he said. (69) Education provides society with a vehicle for (70) raising it's children to be civil, decent, human beings with something valuable to contribute to the world. It is really what makes us human and what (71) distinguishes us as civilised creatures.

Being "civilized" humans means being "whole" humans. Education must address the mind, body, and soul of students. (72) It would be detrimental to society, only meeting the needs of the mind, if our schools were myopic in their focus. As humans, we are multi-dimensional, multi-faceted beings who need more than head knowledge to survive. (73) The human heart and psyche have to be fed in order for the mind to develop properly, and the body must be maintained and exercised to help fuel the working of the brain. Education is a basic human right, and it allows us to sustain a democratic society in which participation is fundamental to its success. It should inspire students to seek better solutions to world problems and to dream of a more equitable society. Education should never discriminate on any basis, and it should create individuals who are self-sufficient, patriotic, and tolerant of (74) others' ideas.

(75) All children can learn. Although not all children learn in the same manner. All children learn best, however, when their basic physical needs are met, and they feel safe, secure, and loved. Students are much more responsive to a teacher who values them and shows them respect as individual people. Teachers must model at all times the way they expect students to treat them and their peers. If teachers set high expectations for their students, the students will rise to that high level. Teachers must make the well-being of students their primary focus and must not be afraid to let students learn from their own mistakes.

From the essay "Education is Essential to Civilization"

68. Which is the best version of the underlined portion of this sentence (reproduced below)?

Early in my career, (68) a master's teacher shared this thought with me "Education is the last bastion of civility."

    a. NO CHANGE
    b. a master's teacher shared this thought with me: "Education is the last bastion of civility."
    c. a master's teacher shared this thought with me: "Education is the last bastion of civility".
    d. a master's teacher shared this thought with me. "Education is the last bastion of civility."

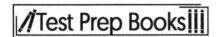

69. Which is the best version of the underlined portion of this sentence (reproduced below)?

(69) <u>Education provides</u> society with a vehicle for raising it's children to be civil, decent, human beings with something valuable to contribute to the world.

    a. NO CHANGE
    b. Education provide
    c. Education will provide
    d. Education providing

70. Which is the best version of the underlined portion of this sentence (reproduced below)?

Education provides society with a vehicle for (70) <u>raising it's children to be</u> civil, decent, human beings with something valuable to contribute to the world.

    a. NO CHANGE
    b. raises its children to be
    c. raising its' children to be
    d. raising its children to be

71. Which of these, if any, is misspelled?

It is really what makes us human and what (71) <u>distinguishes</u> us as <u>civilised creatures</u>.

    a. NO CHANGE
    b. distinguishes
    c. civilised
    d. creatures

72. Which is the best version of the underlined portion of this sentence (reproduced below)?

(72) <u>It would be detrimental to society, only meeting the needs of the mind, if our schools were myopic in their focus.</u>

    a. NO CHANGE
    b. It would be detrimental to society if our schools were myopic in their focus, only meeting the needs of the mind.
    c. Only meeting the needs of our mind, our schools were myopic in their focus, detrimental to society.
    d. Myopic is the focus of our schools, being detrimental to society for only meeting the needs of the mind.

73. Which of these sentences, if any, should begin a new paragraph?

(73) <u>The human heart and psyche have to be fed in order for the mind to develop properly, and the body must be maintained and exercised to help fuel the working of the brain. Education is a basic human right, and it allows us to sustain a democratic society in which participation is fundamental to its success. It should inspire students to seek better solutions to world problems and to dream of a more equitable society.</u>

a. NO CHANGE
b. The human heart and psyche have to be fed in order for the mind to develop properly, and the body must be maintained and exercised to help fuel the working of the brain.
c. Education is a basic human right, and it allows us to sustain a democratic society in which participation is fundamental to its success.
d. It should inspire students to seek better solutions to world problems and to dream of a more equitable society.

74. Which is the best version of the underlined portion of this sentence (reproduced below)?

Education should never discriminate on any basis, and it should create individuals who are self-sufficient, patriotic, and tolerant of <u>others' ideas</u>.

a. NO CHANGE
b. other's ideas
c. others ideas
d. others's ideas

75. Which is the best version of the underlined portion of this sentence (reproduced below)?

(75) <u>All children can learn. Although not all children learn in the same manner.</u>

a. NO CHANGE
b. All children can learn although not all children learn in the same manner.
c. All children can learn although, not all children learn in the same manner.
d. All children can learn, although not all children learn in the same manner.

Math

1. Which of the following numbers has the greatest value?
   a. 1.43785
   b. 1.07548
   c. 1.43592
   d. 0.89409
   e. 0.94739

2. The value of 6×12 is the same as:

    a. $2 \times 4 \times 4 \times 2$

    b. $7 \times 4 \times 3$

    c. $6 \times 6 \times 3$

    d. $3 \times 3 \times 4 \times 2$

    e. $5 \times 9 \times 8$

3. This chart indicates how many sales of CDs, vinyl records, and MP3 downloads occurred over the last year. Approximately what percentage of the total sales was from CDs?

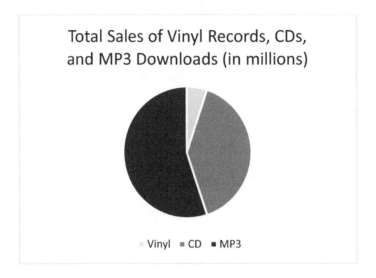

Total Sales of Vinyl Records, CDs, and MP3 Downloads (in millions)

Vinyl   CD   MP3

    a. 55%

    b. 25%

    c. 40%

    d. 5%

    e. 15%

4. Alan currently weighs 200 pounds, but he wants to lose weight to get down to 175 pounds. What is this difference in kilograms? (1 pound is approximately equal to 0.45 kilograms.)

    a. 9 kg

    b. 18.55 kg

    c. 78.75 kg

    d. 90 kg

    e. 11.25 kg

5. Johnny earns $2,334.50 from his job each month. He pays $1,437 for monthly expenses. Johnny is planning a vacation in 3 months that he estimates will cost $1,750 total. How much will Johnny have left over from three months of saving once he pays for his vacation?

    a. $948.50

    b. $584.50

    c. $852.50

    d. $942.50

    e. $742.50

6. Solve the following:

$$\left(\sqrt{36} \times \sqrt{16}\right) - 3^2$$

a. 30
b. 21
c. 15
d. 13
e. 25

7. In Jim's school, there are 3 girls for every 2 boys. There are 650 students in total. Using this information, how many students are girls?

a. 260
b. 130
c. 65
d. 390
e. 410

8. Kimberley earns $10 an hour babysitting, and after 10 p.m., she earns $12 an hour, with the amount paid being rounded to the nearest hour accordingly. On her last job, she worked from 5:30 p.m. to 11 p.m. In total, how much did Kimberley earn on her last job?

a. $45
b. $57
c. $62
d. $42
e. $53

9. Arrange the following numbers from least to greatest value:

$$0.85, \frac{4}{5}, \frac{2}{3}, \frac{91}{100}$$

a. $0.85, \frac{4}{5}, \frac{2}{3}, \frac{91}{100}$

b. $\frac{4}{5}, 0.85, \frac{91}{100}, \frac{2}{3}$

c. $\frac{2}{3}, \frac{4}{5}, 0.85, \frac{91}{100}$

d. $0.85, \frac{91}{100}, \frac{4}{5}, \frac{2}{3}$

e. $\frac{4}{5}, \frac{91}{100}, \frac{2}{3}, 0.85$

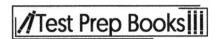

10. Keith's bakery had 252 customers go through its doors last week. This week, that number increased to 378. Express this increase as a percentage.

    a. 26%

    b. 50%

    c. 35%

    d. 12%

    e. 18%

11. Simplify the following expression:

$$4\frac{2}{3} - 3\frac{4}{9}$$

    a. $1\frac{1}{3}$

    b. $1\frac{3}{8}$

    c. 1

    d. $1\frac{2}{3}$

    e. $1\frac{2}{9}$

12. Jessica buys 10 cans of paint. Red paint costs $1 per can and blue paint costs $2 per can. In total, she spends $16. How many red cans did she buy?

    a. 2

    b. 3

    c. 4

    d. 5

    e. 6

13. Six people apply to work for Janice's company, but she only needs four workers. How many different groups of four employees can Janice choose?

    a. 6

    b. 10

    c. 15

    d. 36

    e. 42

14. Which of the following is equivalent to the value of the digit 3 in the number 792.134?

    a. 3×10

    b. 3×100

    c. $\frac{3}{10}$

    d. $\frac{3}{100}$

    e. $100 \div 3$

15. In the following expression, which operation should be completed first? $5 \times 6 + (5 + 4) \div 2 - 1$.
    a. Multiplication
    b. Addition
    c. Division
    d. Parentheses
    e. Exponents

16. How will the number 847.89632 be written if rounded to the nearest hundredth?
    a. 847.90
    b. 900
    c. 847.89
    d. 847.896
    e. 850

17. The perimeter of a 6-sided polygon is 56 cm. The length of three of the sides are 9 cm each. The length of two other sides are 8 cm each. What is the length of the missing side?
    a. 11 cm
    b. 12 cm
    c. 13 cm
    d. 10 cm
    e. 9 cm

18. Which of the following is a mixed number?
    a. $16\frac{1}{2}$
    b. 16
    c. $\frac{16}{3}$
    d. $\frac{1}{4}$
    e. $\frac{90}{80}$

19. Change 9.3 to a fraction.
    a. $9\frac{3}{7}$
    b. $\frac{903}{1,000}$
    c. $\frac{9.03}{100}$
    d. $3\frac{9}{10}$
    e. $9\frac{3}{10}$

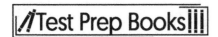

20. What is the value of b in this equation?

$$5b - 4 = 2b + 17$$

    a. 13
    b. 24
    c. 7
    d. 21
    e. 15

21. What is 39% of 164?
    a. 63.96
    b. 23.78
    c. 6,396
    d. 2.38
    e. .0987

22. Katie works at a clothing company and sold 192 shirts over the weekend. One-third of the shirts that were sold were patterned and the rest were solid. Which mathematical expression would calculate the number of solid shirts Katie sold over the weekend?

    a. $192 \times \frac{1}{3}$

    b. $192 \div \frac{1}{3}$

    c. $192 \times (1 - \frac{1}{3})$

    d. $192 \div 3$

    e. $192 \times (1 + \frac{1}{3})$

23. Which four-sided shape is always a rectangle?
    a. Rhombus
    b. Square
    c. Parallelogram
    d. Quadrilateral
    e. Trapezoid

24. A rectangle was formed out of pipe cleaner. Its length was $\frac{1}{2}$ ft, and its width was $\frac{11}{2}$ inches. What is its area in square inches?

    a. $\frac{11}{4}$ inch^2

    b. $\frac{11}{2}$ inch^2

    c. 22 inches^2

    d. $27\frac{1}{3}$ inches^2

    e. 33 inches^2

25. How will $\frac{4}{5}$ be written as a percent?

    a. 40%

    b. 125%

    c. 90%

    d. 80%

    e. 25%

26. If Danny takes 48 minutes to walk 3 miles, how long should it take him to walk 5 miles maintaining the same speed?

    a. 32 min

    b. 64 min

    c. 80 min

    d. 96 min

    e. 105 min

27. A solution needs 5 ml of saline for every 8 ml of medicine given. How much saline is needed for 45 ml of medicine?

    a. $\frac{225}{8}$ ml

    b. 72 ml

    c. 28 ml

    d. $\frac{45}{8}$ ml

    e. 84 ml

28. What unit of volume is used to describe the following 3-dimensional shape?

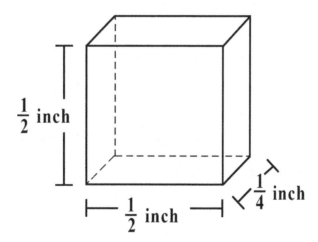

    a. Square inches

    b. Inches

    c. Cubic inches

    d. Squares

    e. Cubic feet

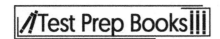

29. Which common denominator would be used in order to evaluate $\frac{2}{3} + \frac{4}{5}$?

    a. 15

    b. 3

    c. 5

    d. 10

    e. 12

30. The diameter of a circle measures 5.75 centimeters. What tool could be used to draw such a circle?

    a. Ruler

    b. Meter stick

    c. Compass

    d. Yard stick

    e. Protractor

31. A piggy bank contains 12 dollars' worth of nickels. A nickel weighs 5 grams, and the empty piggy bank weighs 1,050 grams. What is the total weight of the full piggy bank?

    a. 1,110 grams

    b. 1,200 grams

    c. 2,150 grams

    d. 2,250 grams

    e. 2,500 grams

32. Last year, the New York City area received approximately $27\frac{3}{4}$ inches of snow. The Denver area received approximately 3 times as much snow as New York City. How much snow fell in Denver?

    a. $71\frac{3}{4}$ inches

    b. $27\frac{1}{4}$ inches

    c. $89\frac{1}{4}$ inches

    d. $83\frac{1}{4}$ inches

    e. $64\frac{3}{4}$ inches

33. Which of the following would be an instance in which ordinal numbers are used?

    a. Katie scored a 9 out of 10 on her quiz.

    b. Matthew finished second in the spelling bee.

    c. Jacob missed one day of school last month.

    d. Kim was 5 minutes late to school this morning.

    e. Katrina lost 10 lbs. over the summer.

34. How will the following number be written in standard form: $(1 \times 10^4) + (3 \times 10^3) + (7 \times 10^1) + (8 \times 10^0)$
   a. 137
   b. 13,780
   c. 1,378
   d. 13,078
   e. 3,780

35. What is the area of the regular hexagon shown below?

   a. 72
   b. 124.68
   c. 374.04
   d. 748.08
   e. 676.79

36. The area of a given rectangle is 24 square centimeters. If the measure of each side is multiplied by 3, what is the area of the new figure?
   a. 48 cm^2
   b. 72 cm^2
   c. 111 cm^2
   d. 13,824 cm^2
   e. 216 cm^2

37. Which of the following is the definition of a prime number?
   a. A number that factors only into itself and 1
   b. A number greater than one that factors only into itself and 1
   c. A number less than 10
   d. A number divisible by 10
   e. Any number that's greater than 1

38. Add and express in reduced form $\frac{5}{12} + \frac{4}{9}$.
   a. $\frac{9}{17}$
   b. $\frac{1}{3}$
   c. $\frac{31}{36}$
   d. $\frac{3}{5}$
   e. $\frac{9}{21}$

39. Which of the following is the correct order of operations that could be used on a difficult math problem that contained grouping symbols?
    a. Parentheses, Exponents, Multiplication, Division, Addition, Subtraction
    b. Exponents, Parentheses, Multiplication, Division, Addition, Subtraction
    c. Parentheses, Exponents, Addition, Multiplication, Division, Subtraction
    d. Parentheses, Exponents, Division, Addition, Subtraction, Multiplication
    e. Multiplication, Parentheses, Exponents, Division, Subtraction, Addition

40. Convert $\frac{5}{8}$ to a decimal.
    a. 0.62
    b. 1.05
    c. 0.63
    d. 1.60
    e. 1.25

41. Subtract $9,576 - 891$.
    a. 10,467
    b. 9,685
    c. 8,325
    d. 8,685
    e. 7,564

42. If a teacher was showing a class how to round 245.2678 to the nearest thousandth, which place value would be used to decide whether to round up or round down?
    a. Ten-thousandth
    b. Thousandth
    c. Hundredth
    d. Thousand
    e. Hundred

43. Subtract $50.888 - 13.091$.
    a. 63.799
    b. 63.979
    c. 37.979
    d. 37.797
    e. 36.697

44. Students should line up decimal places within the given numbers before performing which of the following?
    a. Multiplication
    b. Division
    c. Subtraction
    d. Exponents
    e. Parentheses

45. Subtract and express in reduced form $\frac{23}{24} - \frac{1}{6}$.

    a. $\frac{22}{18}$

    b. $\frac{11}{9}$

    c. $\frac{19}{24}$

    d. $\frac{4}{5}$

    e. $\frac{1}{2}$

46. Subtract and express in reduced form $\frac{43}{45} - \frac{11}{15}$.

    a. $\frac{10}{45}$

    b. $\frac{16}{15}$

    c. $\frac{32}{30}$

    d. $\frac{5}{9}$

    e. $\frac{2}{9}$

47. Change 0.56 to a fraction.

    a. $\frac{5.6}{100}$

    b. $\frac{14}{25}$

    c. $\frac{56}{1,000}$

    d. $\frac{56}{10}$

    e. $\frac{100}{56}$

48. Multiply $13,114 \times 191$.

    a. 2,504,774

    b. 250,477

    c. 150,474

    d. 2,514,774

    e. 1,759,492

49. Marty wishes to save $150 over a 4-day period. How much must Marty save each day on average?

    a. $37.50

    b. $35

    c. $45.50

    d. $41

    e. $43.50

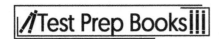

50. A teacher cuts a pie into 6 equal pieces and takes one away. What topic would she be introducing to the class by using such a visual?
    a. Decimals
    b. Addition
    c. Subtraction
    d. Fractions
    e. Exponents

51. Multiply and reduce $\frac{15}{23} \times \frac{54}{127}$.

    a. $\frac{810}{2,921}$

    b. $\frac{81}{292}$

    c. $\frac{69}{150}$

    d. $\frac{810}{2929}$

    e. $\frac{2921}{810}$

52. Which of the following represent one hundred eighty-two billion, thirty-six thousand, four hundred twenty-one and three hundred fifty-six thousandths?
    a. 182,036,421.356
    b. 182,036,421.0356
    c. 182,000,036,421.0356
    d. 182,000,036,421.356
    e. 182,360,000,421.356

53. Divide, express with a remainder 188 ÷ 16.

    a. $1\frac{3}{4}$

    b. $111\frac{3}{4}$

    c. $10\frac{3}{4}$

    d. $11\frac{3}{4}$

    e. $3\frac{4}{11}$

54. What other operation could be utilized to teach the process of dividing 9453 by 24 besides division?
    a. Multiplication
    b. Addition
    c. Exponents
    d. Subtraction
    e. Parentheses

55. Bernard can make $80 per day. If he needs to make $300 and only works full days, how many days will this take?

    a. 6

    b. 3

    c. 5

    d. 2

    e. 4

56. A couple buys a house for $150,000. They sell it for $165,000. By what percentage did the house's value increase?

    a. 18%

    b. 13%

    c. 15%

    d. 12%

    e. 10%

57. What operation is repeated to evaluate an expression involving an exponent?

    a. Addition

    b. Multiplication

    c. Division

    d. Subtraction

    e. Parentheses

58. Which of the following formulas would correctly calculate the perimeter of a legal-sized piece of paper that is 14 inches long and $8\frac{1}{2}$ inches wide?

    a. $P = 14 + 8\frac{1}{2}$

    b. $P = 14 + 8\frac{1}{2} + 14 + 8\frac{1}{2}$

    c. $P = 14 \times 8\frac{1}{2}$

    d. $P = 14 \times \frac{17}{2}$

    e. $P = 14 - \frac{17}{2}$

59. Which of the following are units that would be taught in a lecture covering the metric system?

    a. Inches, feet, miles, pounds

    b. Millimeters, centimeters, meters, pounds

    c. Kilograms, grams, kilometers, meters

    d. Teaspoons, tablespoons, ounces

    e. Stone, quart, gallon, foot, yard

60. Which important mathematical property is shown in the expression: $(7 \times 3) \times 2 = 7 \times (3 \times 2)$?

    a. Distributive property

    b. Commutative property

    c. Additive inverse

    d. Associative property

    e. Multiplicative Identity property

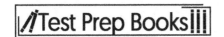

Reading

Fiction

Questions 1–10 are based on the following passage:

As long ago as 1860 it was the proper thing to be born at home. At present, so I am told, the high gods of medicine have decreed that the first cries of the young shall be uttered upon the anesthetic air of a hospital, preferably a fashionable one. So young Mr. and Mrs. Roger Button were fifty years ahead of style when they decided, one day in the summer of 1860, that their first baby should be born in a hospital. Whether this anachronism had any bearing upon the astonishing history I am about to set down will never be known.

I shall tell you what occurred, and let you judge for yourself.

The Roger Buttons held an enviable position, both social and financial, in ante-bellum Baltimore. They were related to the This Family and the That Family, which, as every Southerner knew, entitled them to membership in that enormous peerage which largely populated the Confederacy. This was their first experience with the charming old custom of having babies— Mr. Button was naturally nervous. He hoped it would be a boy so that he could be sent to Yale College in Connecticut, at which institution Mr. Button himself had been known for four years by the somewhat obvious nickname of "Cuff."

On the September morning <u>consecrated</u> to the enormous event he arose nervously at six o'clock, dressed himself, adjusted an impeccable stock, and hurried forth through the streets of Baltimore to the hospital, to determine whether the darkness of the night had borne in new life upon its bosom.

When he was approximately a hundred yards from the Maryland Private Hospital for Ladies and Gentlemen he saw Doctor Keene, the family physician, descending the front steps, rubbing his hands together with a washing movement—as all doctors are required to do by the unwritten ethics of their profession.

Mr. Roger Button, the president of Roger Button & Co., Wholesale Hardware, began to run toward Doctor Keene with much less dignity than was expected from a Southern gentleman of that picturesque period. "Doctor Keene!" he called. "Oh, Doctor Keene!"

The doctor heard him, faced around, and stood waiting, a curious expression settling on his harsh, medicinal face as Mr. Button drew near.

"What happened?" demanded Mr. Button, as he came up in a gasping rush. "What was it? How is she? A boy? Who is it? What—"

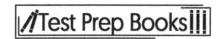

"Talk sense!" said Doctor Keene sharply. He appeared somewhat irritated.

"Is the child born?" begged Mr. Button.

Doctor Keene frowned. "Why, yes, I suppose so—after a fashion." Again he threw a curious glance at Mr. Button.

From The Curious Case of Benjamin Button by F.S. Fitzgerald, 1922.

1. According to the passage, what major event is about to happen in this story?
   a. Mr. Button is about to go to a funeral.
   b. Mr. Button's wife is about to have a baby.
   c. Mr. Button is getting ready to go to the doctor's office.
   d. Mr. Button is about to go shopping for new clothes.

2. What kind of tone does the above passage have?
   a. Nervous and Excited
   b. Sad and Angry
   c. Shameful and Confused
   d. Grateful and Joyous

3. As it is used in the fourth paragraph, the word *consecrated* most nearly means:
   a. Numbed
   b. Chained
   c. Dedicated
   d. Moved

4. What does the author mean to do by adding the following statement?

   "rubbing his hands together with a washing movement—as all doctors are required to do by the unwritten ethics of their profession."

   a. Suggesting that Mr. Button is tired of the doctor.
   b. Trying to explain the detail of the doctor's profession.
   c. Hinting to readers that the doctor is an unethical man.
   d. Giving readers a visual picture of what the doctor is doing.

5. Which of the following best describes the development of this passage?
   a. It starts in the middle of a narrative in order to transition smoothly to a conclusion.
   b. It is a chronological narrative from beginning to end.
   c. The sequence of events is backwards—we go from future events to past events.
   d. To introduce the setting of the story and its characters.

6. Which of the following is an example of an imperative sentence?
   a. "Oh, Doctor Keene!"
   b. "Talk sense!"
   c. "Is the child born?"
   d. "Why, yes, I suppose so—"

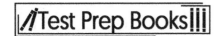

7. As it is used in the first paragraph, the word *anachronism* most nearly means:
    a. Comparison
    b. Misplacement
    c. Aberration
    d. Amelioration

8. This passage can best be described as what type of text?
    a. Expository
    b. Descriptive
    c. Narrative
    d. Persuasive

9. The main purpose of the first paragraph is:
    a. To explain the setting of the narrative and give information about the story.
    b. To present the thesis so that the audience can determine which points are valid later in the text.
    c. To introduce a counterargument so that the author can refute it in the next paragraph.
    d. To provide a description of the speaker's city and the building in which he works.

10. The end of the passage implies to the audience that:
    a. There is bad weather coming.
    b. The doctor thinks Mr. Button is annoying.
    c. The baby and the mother did not make it through labor.
    d. Something is unusual about the birth of the baby.

Social Science

Questions 11–20 are based on the following passage:

I heartily accept the motto, "That government is best which governs least"; and I should like to see it acted up to more rapidly and systematically. Carried out, it finally amounts to this, which also I believe—"That government is best which governs not at all"; and when men are prepared for it, that will be the kind of government which they will have. Government is at best but an expedient; but most governments are usually, and all governments are sometimes, inexpedient. The objections which have been brought against a standing army, and they are many and weighty, and deserve to prevail, may also at last be brought against a standing government. The standing army is only an arm of the standing government. The government itself, which is only the mode which the people have chosen to execute their will, is equally liable to be abused and perverted before the people can act through it. Witness the present Mexican war, the work of comparatively a few individuals using the standing government as their tool; for, in the outset, the people would not have consented to this measure.

This American government—what is it but a tradition, though a recent one, endeavoring to transmit itself unimpaired to posterity, but each instant losing some of its integrity? It has not the vitality and force of a single living man; for a single man can bend it to his will. It is a sort of wooden gun to the people themselves. But it is not the less necessary for this; for the people must have some complicated machinery or other, and hear its din, to satisfy that idea of government which they have. Governments show thus how successfully men can be imposed on, even impose on themselves, for their own advantage. It is excellent, we must all allow. Yet this government never of itself furthered any enterprise, but by the alacrity with which it got out

354

of its way. It does not keep the country free. It does not settle the West. It does not educate. The character inherent in the American people has done all that has been accomplished; and it would have done somewhat more, if the government had not sometimes got in its way. For government is an expedient by which men would fain succeed in letting one another alone; and, as has been said, when it is most expedient, the governed are most let alone by it. Trade and commerce, if they were not made of India-rubber, would never manage to bounce over the obstacles which legislators are continually putting in their way; and, if one were to judge these men wholly by the effects of their actions and not partly by their intentions, they would deserve to be classed and punished with those mischievous persons who put obstructions on the railroads.

But, to speak practically and as a citizen, unlike those who call themselves no-government men, I ask for, not at once no government, but at once a better government. Let every man make known what kind of government would command his respect, and that will be one step toward obtaining it.

Excerpt from Civil Disobedience *by Henry David Thoreau*

11. Which phrase best encapsulates Thoreau's use of the term *expedient* in the first paragraph?
    a. A dead end
    b. A state of order
    c. A means to an end
    d. Rushed construction

12. Which best describes Thoreau's view on the Mexican War?
    a. Government is inherently corrupt because it must wage war.
    b. Government can easily be manipulated by a few individuals for their own agenda.
    c. Government is a tool for the people, but it can also act against their interest.
    d. The Mexican War was a necessary action, but not all the people believed this.

13. What is Thoreau's purpose for writing?
    a. His goal is to illustrate how government can function if ideals are maintained.
    b. He wants to prove that true democracy is the best government, but it can be corrupted easily.
    c. Thoreau reflects on the stages of government abuses.
    d. He is seeking to prove that government is easily corruptible and inherently restrictive of individual freedoms that can simultaneously affect the whole state.

14. Which example best supports Thoreau's argument?
    a. A vote carries in the Senate to create a new road tax.
    b. The president vetoes the new FARM bill.
    c. Prohibition is passed to outlaw alcohol.
    d. Trade is opened between the United States and Iceland.

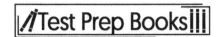

15. Which best summarizes this section from the following passage?

"This American government—what is it but a tradition, though a recent one, endeavoring to transmit itself unimpaired to posterity, but each instant losing some of its integrity? It has not the vitality and force of a single living man; for a single man can bend it to his will. It is a sort of wooden gun to the people themselves."

a. The government may be instituted to ensure the protections of freedoms, but this is weakened by the fact that it is easily manipulated by individuals.
b. Unlike an individual, government is uncaring.
c. Unlike an individual, government has no will, making it more prone to be used as a weapon against the people.
d. American government is modeled after other traditions but actually has greater potential to be used to control people.

16. According to Thoreau, what's the main reason why government eventually fails to achieve progress?
a. There are too many rules.
b. Legislation eventually becomes a hindrance to the lives and work of everyday people.
c. Trade and wealth eventually become the driving factor of those in government.
d. Government doesn't separate religion and state.

17. What type of passage is this?
a. Narrative
b. Descriptive
c. Persuasive
d. Expository

18. As it is used in the first paragraph, the word *liable* most nearly means:
a. Paramount
b. Inconceivable
c. Susceptible
d. Detrimental

19. According to the passage, which government is Thoreau talking about?
a. Mexican
b. American
c. Chinese
d. British

20. As it is used in the second paragraph, the word *posterity* most nearly means:
a. Persons of royal lineage.
b. All future generations of people.
c. A person involved in directing education.
d. A person who offers views on important life questions

356

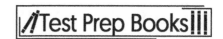

Humanities

Questions 21–30 are based on the following passage:

Four hundred years ago, in 1612, the north-west of England was the scene of England's biggest peacetime witch trial: the trial of the Lancashire witches. Twenty people, mostly from the Pendle area of Lancashire, were imprisoned in the castle as witches. Ten were hanged, one died in gaol, one was sentenced to stand in the pillory, and eight were acquitted. The 2012 anniversary sees a small flood of commemorative events, including works of fiction by Blake Morrison, Carol Ann Duffy, and Jeanette Winterson. How did this witch trial come about, and what accounts for its enduring fame?

We know so much about the Lancashire Witches because the trial was recorded in unique detail by the clerk of the court, Thomas Potts, who published his account soon afterwards as *The Wonderful Discovery of Witches in the County of Lancaster*. I have recently published a modern-English edition of this book, together with an essay piecing together what we know of the events of 1612. It has been a fascinating exercise, revealing how Potts carefully edited the evidence, and also how the case against the "witches" was constructed and manipulated to bring about a spectacular show trial. It all began in mid-March when a pedlar from Halifax named John Law had a frightening encounter with a poor young woman, Alizon Device, in a field near Colne. He refused her request for pins and there was a brief argument during which he was seized by a fit that left him with "his head … drawn awry, his eyes and face deformed, his speech not well to be understood; his thighs and legs stark lame." We can now recognize this as a stroke, perhaps triggered by the stressful encounter. Alizon Device was sent for and surprised all by confessing to the bewitching of John Law and then begged for forgiveness.

When Alizon Device was unable to cure the pedlar, the local magistrate, Roger Nowell was called in. Characterized by Thomas Potts as "God's justice" he was alert to instances of witchcraft, which were regarded by the Lancashire's puritan-inclined authorities as part of the cultural rubble of "popery"—Roman Catholicism—long overdue to be swept away at the end of the country's very slow protestant reformation. "With weeping tears" Alizon explained that she had been led astray by her grandmother, "old Demdike," well-known in the district for her knowledge of old Catholic prayers, charms, cures, magic, and curses. Nowell quickly interviewed Alizon's grandmother and mother, as well as Demdike's supposed rival, "old Chattox" and her daughter Anne. Their panicky attempts to explain themselves and shift the blame to others eventually only ended up incriminating them, and the four were sent to Lancaster gaol in early April to await trial at the summer assizes. The initial picture revealed was of a couple of poor, marginal local families in the forest of Pendle with a longstanding reputation for magical powers, which they had occasionally used at the request of their wealthier neighbours. There had been disputes but none of these were part of ordinary village life. Not until 1612 did any of this come to the attention of the authorities.

The net was widened still further at the end of April when Alizon's younger brother James and younger sister Jennet, only nine years old, came up between them with a story about a "great meeting of witches" at their grandmother's house, known as Malkin Tower. This meeting was presumably to discuss the plight of those arrested and the threat of further arrests, but according to the evidence extracted from the children by the magistrates, a plot was hatched to blow up Lancaster castle with gunpowder, kill the gaoler, and rescue the imprisoned witches. It was, in short, a conspiracy against royal authority to rival the gunpowder plot of 1605—

357

something to be expected in a county known for its particularly strong underground Roman Catholic presence.

Those present at the meeting were mostly family members and neighbours, but they also included Alice Nutter, described by Potts as "a rich woman [who] had a great estate, and children of good hope: in the common opinion of the world, of good temper, free from envy or malice." Her part in the affair remains mysterious, but she seems to have had Catholic family connections, and may have been one herself, providing an added motive for her to be prosecuted.

"The Lancashire Witches 1612–2012" by Robert Poole.

21. What's the point of this passage, and why did the author write it?
    a. The author is documenting a historic witchcraft trial while uncovering/investigating the role of suspicion and anti-Catholicism in the events.
    b. The author seeks long-overdue reparations for the ancestors of those accused and executed for witchcraft in Lancashire.
    c. The author is educating the reader about actual occult practices of the 1600s.
    d. The author argues that the Lancashire witch trials were more brutal than the infamous Salem trials.

22. Which term best captures the meaning of the author's use of *enduring* in the first paragraph?
    a. Un-original
    b. Popular
    c. Wicked
    d. Circumstantial

23. What textual information is present within the passage that most lends itself to the author's credibility?
    a. His prose is consistent with the time.
    b. This is a reflective passage; the author doesn't need to establish credibility.
    c. The author cites specific quotes.
    d. The author has published a modern account of the case and has written on the subject before.

24. What might the following excerpt suggest about the trial or, at the very least, Thomas Potts' account of the trial(s)?

"It has been a fascinating exercise, revealing how Potts carefully edited the evidence, and also how the case against the 'witches' was constructed and manipulated to bring about a spectacular show trial."

a. The events were so grand that the public was allowed access to such a spectacular set of cases.
b. Sections may have been exaggerated or stretched to create notoriety on an extraordinary case.
c. Evidence was faked, making the trial a total farce.
d. The trial was corrupt from the beginning.

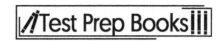

25. Which statement best describes the political atmosphere of the 1600s that influenced the Alizon Device witch trial/case?
    a. Fear of witches was prevalent during this period.
    b. Magistrates were seeking ways to cement their power during this period of unrest.
    c. In a highly superstitious culture, the Protestant church and government were highly motivated to root out any potential sources that could undermine the current regime.
    d. Lancashire was originally a prominent area for pagan celebration, making the modern Protestants very weary of whispers of witchcraft and open to witch trials to resolve any potential threats to Christianity.

26. Which best describes the strongest "evidence" used in the case against Alizon and the witches?
    a. Knowledge of the occult and witchcraft
    b. "Spectral evidence"
    c. Popular rumors of witchcraft and Catholic association
    d. Self-incriminating speech

27. What type of passage is this?
    a. Persuasive
    b. Expository
    c. Narrative
    d. Descriptive

28. According to the passage, how many people were arrested as witches in the Lancashire trials?
    a. 10
    b. 20
    c. 30
    d. 40

29. As it is used in the first paragraph, the word *commemorative* most nearly means:
    a. Associated with being acquitted
    b. An act of disloyalty
    c. A circumstance to be disliked
    d. In honor of something

30. According to the passage, what is Malkin tower?
    a. The building where the trial of the Lancashire witches took place.
    b. The grandmother's house of the peddler who sought revenge on Alizon.
    c. Alizon's grandmother's house where a meeting of witches was held.
    d. The residence of a jury member who witnessed the cursing of the peddler.

Natural Science

Questions 31–40 are based upon the following passage:

Insects as a whole are preeminently creatures of the land and the air. This is shown not only by the possession of wings by a vast majority of the class, but by the mode of breathing to which reference has already been made, a system of branching air-tubes carrying atmospheric air with its combustion-supporting oxygen to all the insect's

tissues. The air gains access to these tubes through a number of paired air-holes or spiracles, arranged segmentally in series.

It is of great interest to find that, nevertheless, a number of insects spend much of their time under water. This is true of not a few in the perfect winged state, as for example aquatic beetles and water-bugs ('boatmen' and 'scorpions') which have some way of protecting their spiracles when submerged, and, possessing usually the power of flight, can pass on occasion from pond or stream to upper air. But it is advisable in connection with our present subject to dwell especially on some insects that remain continually under water till they are ready to undergo their final molt and attain the winged state, which they pass entirely in the air. The preparatory instars of such insects are aquatic; the adult instar is aerial. All may-flies, dragon-flies, and caddis-flies, many beetles and two-winged flies, and a few moths thus divide their life-story between the water and the air. For the present we confine attention to the Stone-flies, the May-flies, and the Dragon-flies, three well-known orders of insects respectively called by systematists the Plecoptera, the Ephemeroptera, and the Odonata.

In the case of many insects that have aquatic larvae, the latter are provided with some arrangement for enabling them to reach atmospheric air through the surface-film of the water. But the larva of a stone-fly, a dragon-fly, or a may-fly is adapted more completely than these for aquatic life; it can, by means of gills of some kind, breathe the air dissolved in water.

Excerpt from *The Life-Story of Insects* by Geo H. Carpenter

31. Which statement best details the central idea in this passage?
    a. It introduces certain insects that transition from water to air.
    b. It delves into entomology, especially where gills are concerned.
    c. It defines what constitutes insects' breathing.
    d. It invites readers to have a hand in the preservation of insects.

32. Which definition most closely relates to the usage of the word *molt* in the passage?
    a. An adventure of sorts, especially underwater
    b. Mating act between two insects
    c. The act of shedding part or all of the outer shell
    d. Death of an organism that ends in a revival of life

33. What is the purpose of the first paragraph in relation to the second paragraph?
    a. The first paragraph serves as a cause, and the second paragraph serves as an effect.
    b. The first paragraph serves as a contrast to the second.
    c. The first paragraph is a description for the argument in the second paragraph.
    d. The first and second paragraphs are merely presented in a sequence.

34. What does the following sentence most nearly mean?

The preparatory instars of such insects are aquatic; the adult instar is aerial.

a. The volume of water is necessary to prep the insect for transition rather than the volume of the air.
b. The abdomen of the insect is designed like a star in the water as well as the air.
c. The early stages in between periods of molting are acted out in the water, while the last stage is in the air.
d. These insects breathe first in the water through gills yet continue to use the same organs to breathe in the air.

35. Which of the statements reflect information that one could reasonably infer based on the author's tone?

a. The author's tone is persuasive and attempts to call the audience to action.
b. The author's tone is passionate due to excitement over the subject and personal narrative.
c. The author's tone is informative and exhibits interest in the subject of the study.
d. The author's tone is somber, depicting some anger at the state of insect larvae.

36. Which statement best describes stoneflies, mayflies, and dragonflies?

a. They are creatures of the land and the air.
b. They have a way of protecting their spiracles when submerged.
c. Their larvae can breathe the air dissolved in water through gills of some kind.
d. The preparatory instars of these insects are aerial.

37. According to the passage, what is true of "boatmen" and "scorpions"?

a. They have no way of protecting their spiracles when submerged.
b. They have some way of protecting their spiracles when submerged.
c. They usually do not possess the power of flight.
d. They remain continually under water till they are ready to undergo their final molt.

38. The last paragraph indicates that the author believes

a. That the stonefly, dragonfly, and mayfly larvae are better prepared to live beneath the water because they have gills that allow them to do so.
b. That the stonefly is different from the mayfly because the stonefly can breathe underwater and the mayfly can only breathe above water.
c. That the dragonfly is a unique species in that its larvae lives mostly underwater for most of its young life.
d. That the stonefly larvae can breathe only by reaching the surface film of the water.

39. According to the passage, why are insects as a whole preeminently creatures of the land and the air?

a. Because insects are born on land but eventually end up adapting to life underwater for the rest of their adult lives.
b. Because most insects have legs made for walking on land and tube-like structures on their bellies for skimming the water.
c. Because a vast majority of insects have wings and also have the ability to breathe underwater.
d. Because most insects have a propulsion method specifically designed for underwater use, but they can only breathe on land.

361

40. As it is used in the first paragraph, the word *preeminently* most nearly means:
    a. Unknowingly
    b. Above all
    c. Most truthfully
    d. Not importantly

Science

Passage 1

Questions 1–5 pertain to Passage 1:

Predators are animals that eat other animals. Prey are animals that are eaten by a predator. Predators and prey have a distinct relationship. Predators rely on the prey population for food and nutrition. They evolve physically to catch their prey. For example, they develop a keen sense of sight, smell, or hearing. They may also be able to run very fast or camouflage to their environment in order to sneak up on their prey. Likewise, the prey population may develop these features to escape and hide from their predators. As predators catch more prey, the prey population dwindles. With fewer prey to catch, the predator population also dwindles. This happens in a cyclical manner over time.

Figure 1 below shows the cyclical population growth in a predator-prey relationship.

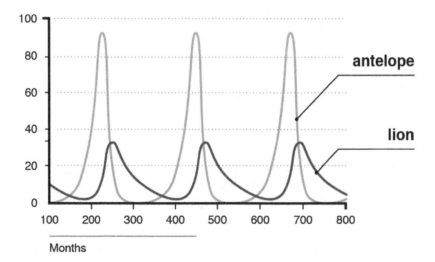

Figure 2 below shows a predator-prey cycle in a circular picture diagram

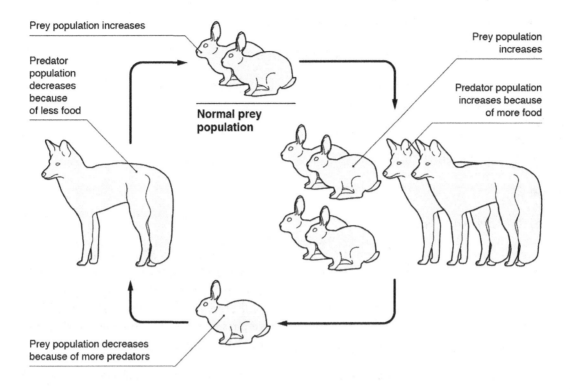

Prey population increases

Predator population decreases because of less food

Normal prey population

Prey population increases

Predator population increases because of more food

Prey population decreases because of more predators

1. Looking at Figure 1, approximately how long is one cycle of the prey population, which includes the population being low, reaching a peak, and then becoming low again?
    a. 300 months
    b. 200 months
    c. 800 months
    d. 400 months

2. In Figure 2, which animal is the predator?
    a. Both the fox and rabbit
    b. Fox only
    c. Rabbit only
    d. Neither the fox nor the rabbit

3. What causes the predator population to decrease?
    a. When there's an increase in the prey population
    b. When winter arrives
    c. When the prey start attacking the predators
    d. When there are fewer prey to find

363

4. What causes the prey population to increase?
    a. When the predator population decreases, so more prey survive and reproduce.
    b. When there's an increase in the predator population
    c. When there's more sunlight
    d. The prey population always remains the same size.

5. Which is NOT a feature that a prey population can develop to hide from their predator?
    a. Keen sense of smell
    b. Camouflage ability
    c. A loud voice
    d. Keen sense of hearing

Passage 2

Questions 6–10 pertain to Passage 2:

Greenhouses are glass structures that people grow plants in. They allow plants to survive and grow even in the cold winter months by providing light and trapping warm air inside. Light is allowed in through the clear glass walls and roof. Warm air comes in as sunlight through the glass roof. The sunlight is converted into heat, or infrared energy, by the surfaces inside the greenhouse. This heat energy then takes longer to pass back through the glass surfaces and causes the interior of the greenhouse to feel warmer than the outside climate.

Plants may grow better inside a greenhouse versus outside for several reasons. There is more control of the temperature and humidity of the environment inside the greenhouse. The carbon dioxide produced by plants is trapped inside the greenhouse and can increase the rate of photosynthesis of the plants. There are also fewer pests and diseases inside the greenhouse.

Figure 1 below shows how a greenhouse works.

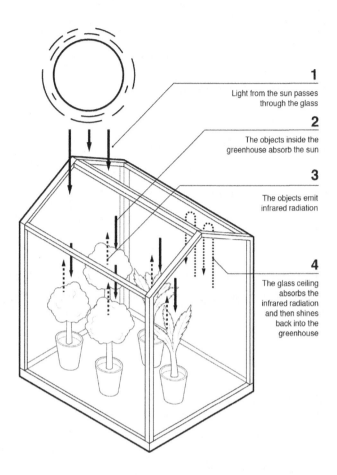

1
Light from the sun passes through the glass

2
The objects inside the greenhouse absorb the sun

3
The objects emit infrared radiation

4
The glass ceiling absorbs the infrared radiation and then shines back into the greenhouse

Scientist A wants to compare how a tomato plant grows inside a greenhouse versus outside a greenhouse.

Figure 2 below shows a graph of her results over 3 months.

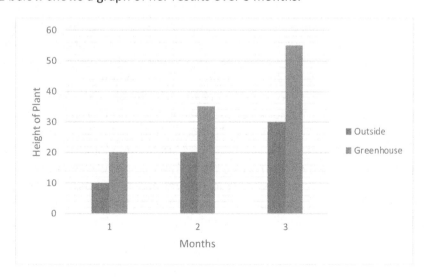

365

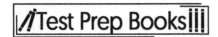

6. Looking at Figure 1, what gets trapped inside the greenhouse that helps plants grow?
    a. Short-wavelength IR
    b. Long-wavelength IR
    c. Cold air
    d. Water

7. Which plant grew taller from Scientist A's experiment?
    a. Outside
    b. Both grew to the same height.
    c. They both remained the same height for 3 months.
    d. Greenhouse

8. What gets converted to heat inside a greenhouse?
    a. Water
    b. Sunlight
    c. Plants
    d. Oxygen

9. What type of wavelength moves through the greenhouse glass easily according to Figure 1?
    a. Short-wavelength IR
    b. Oxygen
    c. Carbon dioxide
    d. Long-wavelength IR

10. What is one reason that plants may grow better inside a greenhouse?
    a. Colder air
    b. Less photosynthesis occurs in the greenhouse
    c. Fewer pests
    d. Less sunlight comes into the greenhouse

Passage 3

Questions 11–15 pertain to Passage 3:

> In chemistry, a titration is a method that is used to determine the concentration of an unknown solution. Generally, a known volume of a solution of known concentration is mixed with the unknown solution. Once the reaction of the two solutions has been completed, the concentration of the unknown solution can be calculated. When acids and bases are titrated, the progress of the reaction is monitored by changes in the pH of the known solution. The equivalence point is when just enough of the unknown solution has been added to neutralize the known solution. A color reaction may also occur so that with the drop of solution that causes complete neutralization, the solution turns bright pink, for example. For acids that only have one proton, usually a hydrogen atom, the halfway point between the beginning of the curve and the equivalence point is where the amount of acid and base are equal in the solution. At this point, the pH is equal to the pK_a, or the acid dissociation constant.

Figure 1 below shows a general titration curve of a strong acid with a strong base.

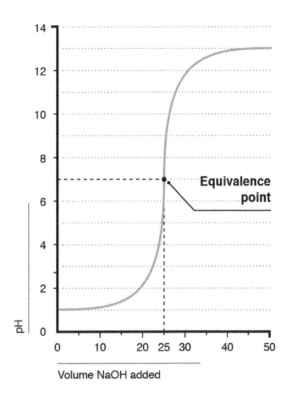

Figure 2 below shows the chemical reaction of a strong acid with a strong base.

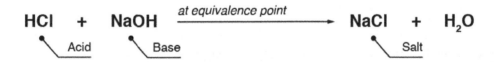

Figure 3 shows the titration curve for acetic acid.

Titration Curve of Acetic Acid

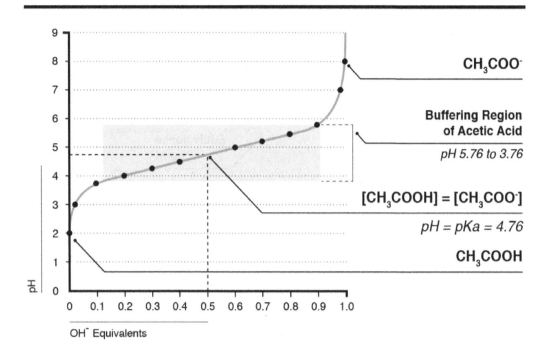

OH⁻ Equivalents

11. How much NaOH is added to the HCl solution to reach the equivalence point in Figure 1?
    a. 10
    b. 40
    c. 50
    d. 25

12. What is the acid dissociation constant of the titration curve in the Figure 3?
    a. 4.21
    b. 3.50
    c. 4.76
    d. 6.52

13. What is the pH of the acetic acid before the titration has started in Figure 3?
    a. 2
    b. 4.76
    c. 7
    d. 6

14. What is one of the products of the chemical equation in Figure 2?
    a. HCl
    b. NaCl
    c. NaOH
    d. Cl⁻

15. How would you describe the solution at the equivalence point in Figure 1?
    a. Neutral
    b. Acidic
    c. Basic
    d. Unknown

Passage 4

Questions 16–20 pertain to Passage 4:

The heart is a muscle that is responsible for pumping blood through the body. It is divided into four chambers: the right atrium, right ventricle, left atrium, and left ventricle. Blood enters the atria and is then pumped into the ventricles below them. There is a valve between the atria and ventricles that prevents the blood from flowing back into the atria. The valve between the right atrium and ventricle has three folds whereas the valve between the left atrium and ventricle has two folds. Arteries carry oxygen-rich blood away from the heart to the body. Veins carry oxygen-poor blood from the body back to the heart. From there, the blood gets pumped to the lungs to get re-oxygenated and then back to the heart before circulating to the body. The heart beats every second of the day. For an adult, the normal heartrate is between 60 and 100 beats per minute. For a child, a normal heartrate is between 90 and 120 beats per minute.

Figure 1 below shows how blood gets pumped through the body.

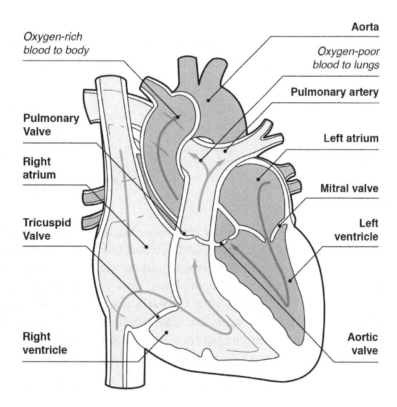

369

16. Where is the oxygen-poor blood pumped to before returning to the heart to get circulated to the rest of the body?
    a. Lungs
    b. Brain
    c. Stomach
    d. Kidney

17. Which heart valve has two folds?
    a. Pulmonary artery
    b. Tricuspid valve
    c. Mitral valve
    d. Aorta

18. If the aorta contains oxygen-rich blood, what type of vessel is it?
    a. Vein
    b. Pulmonary
    c. Airway
    d. Artery

19. Which heartrate (beats per minute) would be considered normal for a child during resting conditions?
    a. 85
    b. 125
    c. 100
    d. 60

20. The aorta is the artery that breaks into smaller vessels to transport blood to the rest of the body. Looking at the figure, which is the final chamber that the blood flows through before entering the aorta?
    a. Right ventricle
    b. Left ventricle
    c. Right atrium
    d. Left atrium

Passage 5

Questions 21–25 pertain to Passage 5:

There are three types of rocks: sedimentary, metamorphic, and igneous. Sedimentary rock is formed from sediment, such as sand, shells, and pebbles. The sediment gathers together and hardens over time. It is generally soft and breaks apart easily. This is the only type of rock that contains fossils, which are the remains of animals and plants that lived a long time ago. Metamorphic rock forms under the surface of the earth due to changes in heat and pressure. These rocks usually have ribbon-like layers and may contain shiny crystals. Igneous rock forms when molten rock, or magma, cools and hardens. An example of molten rock is lava, which escapes from an erupting volcano. This type of rock looks shiny and glasslike.

Figure 1 below is a chart of different types of rocks.

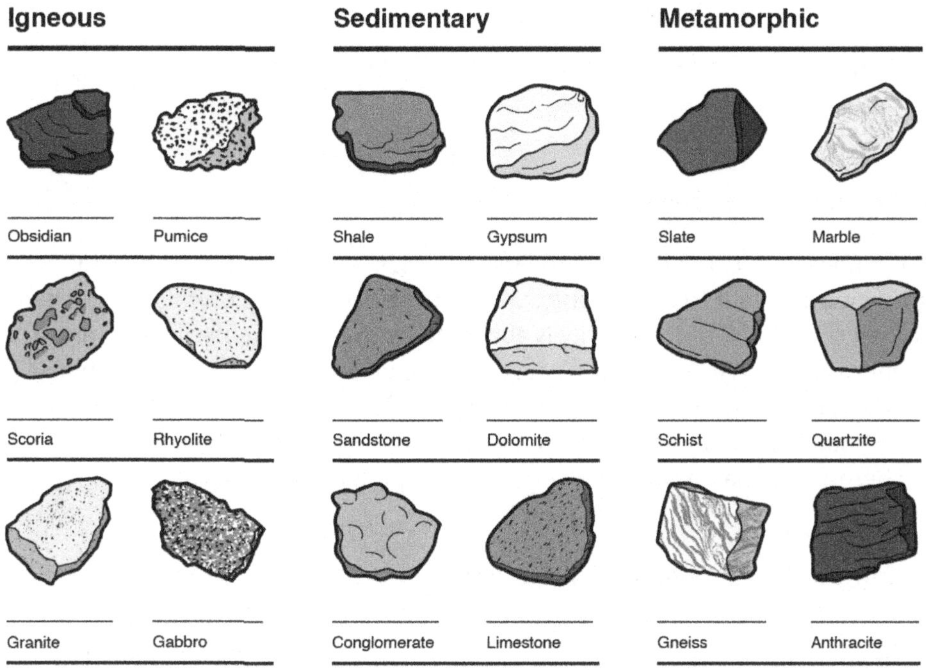

21. A volcano erupts and lava comes out and hardens once it is cooled. What type of rock is formed?
    A. Sedimentary
    B. Metamorphic
    C. Igneous
    D. Lava does not cool

22. Scientist A found a piece of granite rock, as seen in Figure 1. What type of rock is it?
    a. Igneous
    b. Metamorphic
    c. Sedimentary
    d. Fossil

23. Which type of rock could a fossil be found in?
    a. Igneous
    b. Bone
    c. Metamorphic
    d. Sedimentary

24. Which is an example of a metamorphic rock in the figure?
    a. Sandstone
    b. Slate
    c. Granite
    d. Limestone

371

25. What type of rock would most likely be formed at and found on the beach?
   a. Sedimentary
   b. Shells
   c. Igneous
   d. Metamorphic

Passage 6

Questions 26–30 pertain to Passage 6:

The greenhouse effect is a natural process that warms the Earth's surface, similar to what occurs in a greenhouse meant to grow plants. Solar energy reaches the Earth's atmosphere and warms the air and land. Some of the energy is absorbed by the greenhouse gases found in the Earth's atmosphere and by the land, and the rest is reflected back into space. Greenhouse gases include water vapor, carbon dioxide, methane, nitrous oxide, and chlorofluorocarbons. In recent decades, human activity has increased the amount of greenhouse gases present in the Earth's atmosphere, which has created a warmer atmosphere than normal and increased the Earth's temperature.

Figure 1 below shows the process of the greenhouse effect.

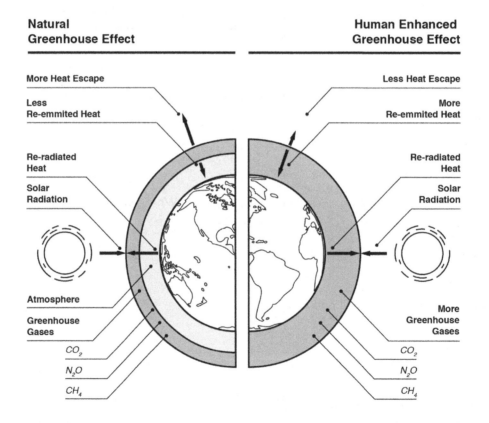

372

Figure 2 below describes the greenhouse gases that are produced from human activity.

Major Greenhouse Gases from People's Activities

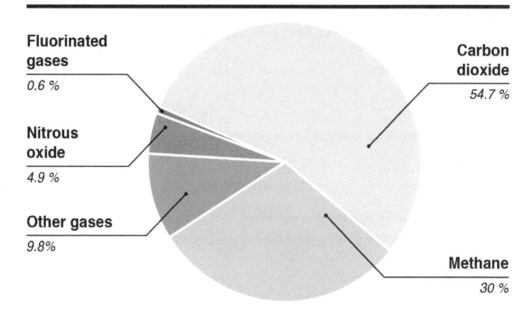

Fluorinated gases
0.6 %

Nitrous oxide
4.9 %

Other gases
9.8%

Carbon dioxide
54.7 %

Methane
30 %

Figure 3 below describes the human activities that produce carbon dioxide.

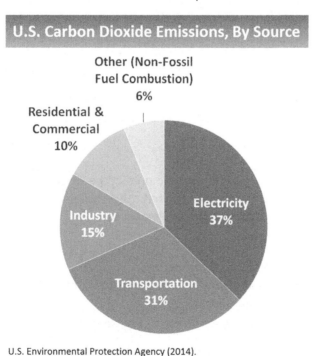

U.S. Carbon Dioxide Emissions, By Source

Other (Non-Fossil Fuel Combustion)
6%

Residential & Commercial
10%

Industry
15%

Electricity
37%

Transportation
31%

U.S. Environmental Protection Agency (2014).
U.S. Greenhouse Gas Inventory Report: 1990-2014.

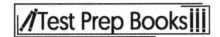

26. Which is not an example of a greenhouse gas?
   a. Methane
   b. Carbon dioxide
   c. Nitrous oxide
   d. Helium gas

27. Looking at Figure 3, what could a person do to decrease how much carbon dioxide they produce?
   a. Leave lights on all the time
   b. Walk instead of drive a car
   c. Always drive in their own car everywhere
   d. Leave the television on all the time

28. Looking at Figure 2, which is the second highest greenhouse gas produced by human activity?
   a. Methane
   b. Fluorinated gases
   c. Nitrous oxide
   d. Carbon dioxide

29. Looking at Figure 1, what gets increasingly trapped in the Earth's atmosphere with increased human activity?
   a. Space
   b. The Sun
   c. Heat
   d. Water vapor

30. What type of charts are found in Figures 2 and 3?
   a. Scatter plots
   b. Line graphs
   c. Bar graphs
   d. Pie charts

Passage 7

Questions 31–35 pertain to Passage 7:

A meteorologist uses many different tools to predict the weather. They study the atmosphere and changes that are occurring to predict what the weather will be like in the future. Listed below are some of the tools that a meteorologist uses:

- Thermometer: measures air temperature
- Barometer: measures air pressure
- Rain gauge: measures rainfall over a specific time
- Anemometer: measures air speed
- Wind vane: shows which direction the wind is blowing

374

Figure 1 below shows data that is collected by a meteorologist.

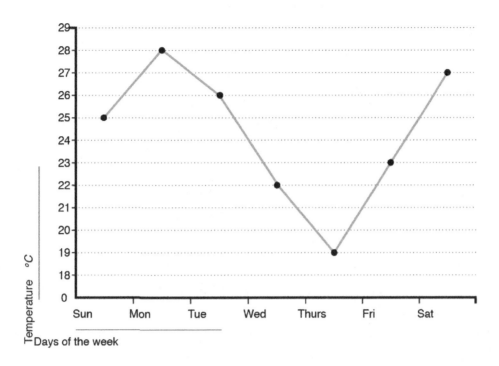

Figure 2 below shows data collected from a rain gauge.

Rainfall

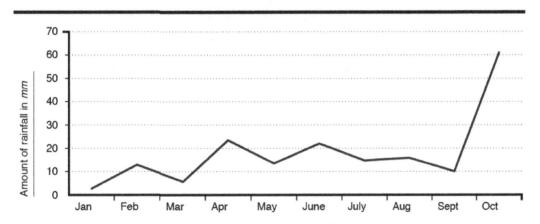

31. What tool would a meteorologist use to find out how fast the wind is blowing?
    a. Anemometer
    b. Barometer
    c. Thermometer
    d. Wind vane

375

32. What tool was used to collect the data shown in Figure 1?
    a. Rain gauge
    b. Thermometer
    c. Barometer
    d. Anemometer

33. The wind vane is pointing north. What does this tell us?
    a. Wind is blowing in an eastern direction.
    b. A storm is coming.
    c. The wind is blowing in a northern direction.
    d. The wind is blowing in a southern direction.

34. Looking at Figure 2, which month had the lowest rainfall?
    a. January
    b. April
    c. September
    d. October

35. Looking at Figure 2, what was the approximate amount of rain that fell in June?
    a. 0 mm
    b. 10 mm
    c. 50 mm
    d. 20 mm

Passage 8

Questions 36–40 pertain to Passage 8:

Cells are the smallest functional unit of living organisms. Organisms can be single-celled or multicellular. Each cell contains organelles that are responsible for distinct functions and are essential for the organism's life. Plants and animals have different necessities for generating energy and nutrients. Their cells are similar but also have unique features.

Figure 1 below is a depiction of the organelles in an animal cell.

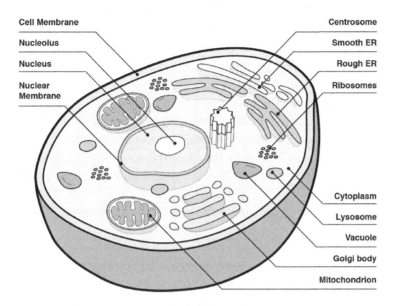

Figure 2 below depicts the organelles of a plant cell.

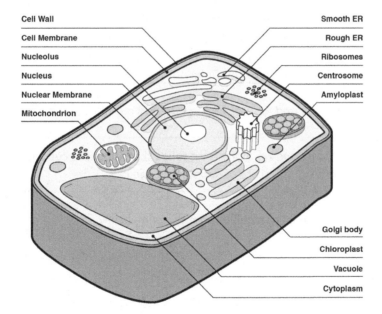

Figure 3 below describes the function of many important organelles.

Cell Organelle	Function
Cell wall	*(Plants only)* Maintains the shape of the cell and is a protective barrier for the internal contents of the cell.
Chloroplasts	*(Plants only)* Site of photosynthesis, which converts sunlight energy to glucose storage energy.
Nucleus	*(Plants and Animals)* Contains the cell's DNA.
Ribosomes	*(Plants and Animals)* Puts together long chains of amino acids to build proteins. Smallest organelle in the cell.
Mitochondria	*(Plants and Animals)* The powerhouse of the cell. Converts the stored glucose energy to ATP energy, which drives forward almost all of the cell's reactions.
Cell membrane	*(Plants and Animals)* Regulates what molecules can move in and out of the cell. Made of a phospholipid bilayer.
Cytoplasm	*(Plants and Animals)* The liquid that fills the inside of the cell.
Vacuole	*(Plants and Animals)* A membranous sac that encloses anything in the cell that needs to be kept separate, such as food and water.
Golgi Body	*(Plants and Animals)* Receives products produced by the endoplasmic reticulum (ER) and adds final changes to them.
Lysosomes	*(Plants and Animals)* A membranous sac that is full of digestive juices. Breaks down larger molecules into smaller parts so that they can be used to build new parts of the cell.
Rough endoplasmic reticulum (ER)	*(Plants and Animals)* A large folded membrane that is covered with ribosomes. Helps fold and modify the proteins built by the ribosomes before sending them to the Golgi body.
Smooth endoplasmic reticulum (ER)	*(Plants and Animals)* A large folded membrane that puts together lipids.
Microtubules and microfilaments	*(Plants and Animals)* Long tubes that allow the cell to move and provide an internal structure of support for the cell.

36. Which is an organelle found in a plant cell but not an animal cell?
    a. Mitochondria
    b. Chloroplast
    c. Golgi body
    d. Nucleus

37. Where is the nucleolus located in both plant and animal cells?
    a. Near the chloroplast
    b. Inside the mitochondria
    c. Inside the nucleus
    d. Attached to the cell membrane

38. Which organelle is responsible for generating energy for the cell and is referred to as the powerhouse of the cell?
    a. Mitochondria
    b. Nucleus
    c. Ribosomes
    d. Cell wall

39. What does the cell membrane do?
    a. Builds proteins
    b. Breaks down large molecules
    c. Contains the cell's DNA
    d. Controls which molecules are allowed in and out of the cell

40. What are chloroplasts responsible for in plant cells?
    a. Maintaining the cell's shape
    b. Containing the cell's DNA
    c. Converting energy from sunlight to glucose
    d. Building proteins

Writing

Directions

Write an organized, coherent essay about the passage below. In your essay, make sure you:

- Clearly state your own opinion on the issue and analyze the relationships between your perspective and at least one other perspective
- Develop and support your ideas with evidence
- Organize your ideas logically
- Communicate your ideas in standard English

Prompt

An ongoing debate within college athletics has been whether or not collegiate athletes should receive compensation for their performance. While many athletes receive scholarship money or room and board stipends, some people claim that such compensation is not enough.

Perspectives

1. College sports have the potential to attract large crowds of spectators. Division I sports in particular are often televised, maintain loyal fan bases, and attract millions of attendees across the country. Even smaller schools draw in paying spectators, whether it be locals, alumni, or family and friends. However, none of this revenue goes to the athletes, even though they are who the fans are paying to see.

2. Athletes are compensated adequately by the scholarship money they receive. In fact, athletes often have additional scholarship opportunities not afforded to other students (e.g., they can receive both academic and athletic scholarship money). Additionally, college administrations want their athletes to perform well academically, and allowing them the opportunity to get paid

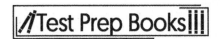

for their athletic performance could cause students to focus disproportionately on athletics, thereby neglecting academics.

3. College athletes are often too busy to hold a job throughout the year because practice, conditioning, and competition require such a significant time commitment. Even when their sport is not in session, athletes have to work hard to maintain strength, endurance, and form. This could even extend into the summer, preventing them from working or getting an internship. Therefore, they should be able to earn money on their performance when afforded the opportunity.

Answer Explanations #2

English

1. C: Choice *C* is correct, changing *Mythologies* to *mythology's*. Since one myth system is being referred to—and one particular component of it—the possessive is needed. Additionally, *Mythology's* does not need to be capitalized, since only the culture represents a proper noun. Choice *A* therefore is incorrect, with Choice *B* failing to fix the plural and Choice *D* having extraneous capitalization.

2. A: Choice *A* is correct because the sentence has no issues. While Choice *B* separates the sentence correctly, it makes more sense in this context of a direct comparison to keep the sentence intact. Choice *C* is incorrect because the sentence inserts an unnecessary comma after *superhero*. Choice *D* is unnecessarily long and lacks the word *but* that helps the author differentiate ideas.

3. B: Choice *B* is correct because it adds the two commas needed to clarify key subjects individually and establish a better flow to the sentence. Since *destroying mountains*, *defeating scores of giants*, and *lifting up the world's largest creature* are separate feats, commas are needed to separate them. Also, because *the world's largest creature* can stand alone in the sentence, a comma needs to proceed its name; *the Midgard Serpent* is not necessary to the sentence but rather provides extra information as an aside. Choice *A* is unclear and thus incorrect. Choice *C* is still missing a comma, while Choice *D* put an extraneous one in an incorrect place.

4. D: Choice *D* is correct since the sentence is lengthy as originally presented and should be split into two. Additionally, *however*, being a conjunction, needs a comma afterwards. Choice *A* is therefore incorrect due to missing punctuation. Choice *B* is an improvement but could separate the sentence's ideas better and more clearly. Choice *C* lacks the necessary comma after *However*.

5. A: Choice *A* is correct because this sentence has no issues with punctuation, content, or sentence construction. While there are three commas used, they serve to appropriately introduce an idea, an individual person, and transition into another line of thinking. Choices *B* and *C* miss commas needed to offset Loki's title as *the god of mischief*, while Choice *D* misses the comma needed to introduce the example.

6. C: Choice *C* is correct because the sentence needs two commas to emphasize the proper name of Mjolnir. Since Mjolnir is being talked about, directly addressed, and then explained, it must be flanked by commas to signify its role in the sentence. Choice *A* lacks necessary punctuation and is confusing. Choices *B* and *D* miss commas on either side of *Mjolnir*.

7. A: Choice *A* is correct, as this is an example of a compound sentence written correctly. Because of the conjunction *but* and the proceeding comma, the two independent clauses are able to form a single sentence coherently. While Choice *B* makes the question more direct, it doesn't go well with the remainder of the sentence. Choice *C* applies a comma after *but*, which is incorrect and confusing. Choice *D* inserts *however*, which is out of place and makes the sentence awkward.

8. B: Choice *B* correctly changes *an* to *a*, since *an* is only required when *a* precedes a word that begins with a vowel. Choice *A* therefore uses the incorrect form of *a*. Choice *C* fixes the issue but unnecessarily reverses the structure of the sentence, making it less direct and more confusing. Choice *D* does not fix the error and adds extraneous commas.

9. D: Choice *D* is correct, simply applying a comma after *Well* to introduce an idea. Choice *A* is therefore incorrect. Choice *B* introduces too many commas, resulting in a fractured sentence structure. Choice *C* applies a comma after *Well*, which is correct, but interrupts the flow of the sentence by switching the structure of the sentence. This makes the sentence lack fluidity and serves to confuse the reader.

10. C: Choice *C* is simple and straightforward, describing the event clearly for the reader to follow; talked is past tense, which is consistent with the rest of the passage. Choice *A* is incorrect, since we came to talking about confuses the tense of the sentence and the verb talk. Choices *B* and *D* are wordy and not as straightforward as Choice *C.*

11. B: Choice *B* is the correct answer because it adds a comma after *Essentially* and changes *an* to *a*. This is called the indefinite article, when an unspecified thing or quantity is referred to. However, *an* doesn't agree with *metaphor*, since *an* should only be used when the next word starts with a vowel. Choice *A* uses the article *an* and lacks the crucial comma after *Essentially*. Choice *C* is incorrect because it only provides the comma after *Essentially*, neglecting the indefinite article disagreement. Choice *D* is incorrect because neither issue is fixed and an unnecessary comma is introduced.

12. A: Choice *A* is correct because there are no errors present in the sentence. Choice *B* is a run on, because the clauses are not broken up by commas. Choice *C* has a verbal disagreement: *look* and *saw* are different tenses. Choice *D* changes the structure of the sentence but fails to add a transition to make this correct.

13. D: Choice *D* is correct because it uses a comma after the word *passage*, successfully connecting the dependent clause with its independent clause to form a complete thought/sentence. Choice *A* is therefore incorrect. Choice *B* uses a semicolon unwisely. The two clauses need to be connected to each other in order to make sense, otherwise they are just two fragments improperly combined. Choice *C* does not have the required comma and changes *found* to *finding*, an inappropriate tense for the verb in this sentence.

14. C: Choice *C* is correct because it fixes two major flaws in the original portion of the sentence. First, it inserts the adverb *also* to show the connection between *whatever it is that makes us unique* and *defines us*. Without this adverb, the sentence lacks clarity, and the connection is lost. Second, *big* is incorrect in this context. The sentence needs the superlative *bigger* in order to communicate the scope and scale of the author's assessment of how people relate to others on a grand scale. Choice *A* is therefore incorrect, Choice *B* inserts unnecessary commas, and Choice *D* subtly alters the original meaning.

15. B: Choice *B* is correct because a comma is correctly inserted after *ultimately*. This serves to express a side thought that helps transition into the rest of the sentence without having to break it apart. Choice *A* is incorrect because it lacks the comma after *ultimately*. Choice *C* uses too many commas and is overly complicated. Choice *D* lacks the necessary conjunction after the comma (*but*) before *ultimately*, making it a run-on sentence. It also lacks the important comma after *ultimately*.

16. D: Choice *D* corrects the subject-verb disagreement. *One's* is the possessive form of *one*, a single individual, not the plural *individuals. Isn't* is the singular contraction of *is not*, which conflicts with *individuals*. To correct this, either *isn't* must change to *aren't* or *individuals* should become the singular *individual*. The latter is correct because of the context of the sentence. Choice *A* is incorrect because of the subject-verb disagreement. Choice *B* uses the future tense, while Choice *C's aren't* conflicts with *one's*, which is possessive singular.

17. A: Choice *A* contains no grammatical errors and communicates the writer's message clearly. Choice *B* inserts an unnecessary semicolon. Choice *C* uses *is*, which disagrees with the plural *aspects*. *Are* must be used because it is plural. This is the same for Choice *D*, which uses *there's* (*there is*).

18. D: Choice *D* is the correct answer because it removes the comma after *Rushdie*. Adding a comma after the proper name in this case is incorrect because *Rushdie* is not being addressed directly. Rather, the writer is talking about Rushdie. Therefore, Choices *A* disrupts the construction of the sentence. Choice *B* is incorrect because *seemed*, in this context, should be present tense. The author is talking about a theme and idea that *Rushdie* had but that is still relevant and being actively studied. Choice *C* fails to remove the comma after Rushdie and applies the gerund *seeming* incorrectly.

19. A: Choice *A* is the correct answer. The sentence requires no punctuation and clearly communicates the author's idea. Choice *B* is incorrect because it misuses multiple commas. Choice *C* is incorrect because it uses *a* instead of *an*, which is necessary because the next word (*essentially*) begins with a vowel. Choice *D* changes *rewarding* to *rewarded*, which clashes with the earlier use of *was*, indicating past tense, making it incorrect.

20. B: Choice *B* is correct because it uses the present tense of *understand* instead of the past tense *understood*. *Continues* emphasizes something ongoing. Therefore, the present tense of *understand* is needed. Choice *A* therefore has tense disagreement. Choice *C* uses an extraneous comma. While Choice *D's* use of the gerund is a better option, *in* would need to be added before *understanding* for correctness.

21. A: Choice *A* is correct; the dependent and independent clauses are successfully combined to form a sentence. Choice *A* is also the most concise and straightforward option, presenting the information appropriately so as not to be confusing. Choice *B* can be eliminated because it changes the meaning of the sentence. Choice *C* unnecessarily flanks *exactly* with commas. Choice *D* is incorrect because a period after the underlined phrase would result in an incomplete sentence.

22. D: Choice *D* is correct because of how it successfully connects the two sentences. By starting a new sentence with *instead*, the two ideas are clearly and correctly presented. Choice *A* is a run-on. Choice *B* is incorrect because the commas used are misplaced and confusing. Choice *C* is incorrect because there needs to be a comma after *originally*.

23. B: Choice *B* correctly uses the word *passed* instead of *passing*. The word *were* is being used as a past tense modifier; therefore, it disagrees with the *passing* participle. Combining the helping verb *were* with the past tense *passed* creates the correct past tense compound verb, *were passed*, which is needed to be grammatically consistent with the rest of the sentence. Choices *A, C,* and *D* thus have incongruent tenses.

24. D: Choice *D* is correct because it corrects the subject-verb disagreement between the plural *myths* and the singular *it*. This is done by changing *it* to *them*, reflecting that more than one type of *myths* are being talked about. Because of the subject-verb disagreement, Choice *A* is incorrect. Choice *B* does not correct this at all. Choice *C* addresses this disagreement, but at the cost of maintaining parallel structure within the sentence.

25. A: Choice *A* is correct because this sentence contains no grammatical errors, unlike the others. Choice *B* uses the semicolon when only a comma is required. Choice *C* uses commas to unnecessarily

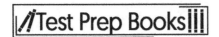

isolate *a kind of soundtrack* from its connected phrase. Choice *D* is incorrect because the plural *kinds* disagrees with the singular pronoun *This*.

26. C: Choice *C* is the correct answer because the plural *are* and *motion pictures* agree with the subject *stimuli* (the plural form of *stimulus*). All verbs and nouns in the sentence should be in agreement with each other in tense and number. Choices *A, B,* and *D* all violate this number agreement.

27. B: Choice *B* correctly replaces the preposition *from* with the correct proposition *to*. *To* is used to emphasize an action or idea being presented rather than received. This is why Choice *A* is incorrect. Choice *C* is incorrect because it uses the adverb *too*, which emphasizes a higher level of something or the addition of something in a sentence; this isn't relevant here. Choice *D* uses the preposition *for* instead of *to*.

28. D: Choice *D* is correct because it adds the helping verb *were* to modify *unsettled*. This allows the sentence to reflect that the founders were unsettled by the implications. Without *were* to connect the founders to *unsettled*, the sentence doesn't make sense. Choice *A* lacks the crucial helping verb, making it incorrect. Choice *B* is incorrect because of its unnecessary semicolon. Choice *C* changes *theory's*, which is singular possessive, to *theories'* (plural possessive), which isn't consistent with the sentence's context.

29. A: Choice *A* is correct because it contains no errors and requires no additional punctuation to form a coherent sentence. The single comma, used successfully, unites the two clauses and enables a solid grammatical structure. Choice *B* incorrectly places a comma after *Instead*, Choice *C* incorrectly changes *predicted* to *predicting*, and Choice *D* incorrectly separates *where everything can be predicted by equations* from the rest of the sentence.

30. D: Choice *D* is correct because it fixes the subject-verb disagreement with *Every outcome* and *exist*. *Exists* is third person present but also appropriate to reflect multiple outcomes, as indicated by *every outcome*. Choices *A* and *B* use *exist*, not *exists*, which makes them both incorrect. Choice *C* is fine on its own but does not fit with the rest of the sentence.

31. B: Choice *B* is correct because the comma after *determinism* isn't needed. Adding a comma in the selected area actually breaks up the independent clause of the sentence, thus compromising the overall structure of the sentence. Choices *A, C,* and *D* are therefore incorrect.

32. C: Choice *C* is the correct answer because it removes the contraction of *it is, it's*. Choice *A*, which is incorrect, originally used *it's*—note the apostrophe before *s*. *It's* simply means *it is*, while *its* (no apostrophe) shows possession. In this sentence, *its* is referring to the idea devised by Schrödinger, giving ownership of the purpose to the idea. Choice *B* is incorrect because *purpose* should remain singular. Choice *D* is incorrect because it uses *it's*.

33. A: Choice *A* is correct because the sentence is well-formed and grammatically correct. Choice *B* is incorrect because it adds an unnecessary comma after *if*. Choice *C* breaks the sentence apart, creating a sentence fragment. Choice *D* is incorrect because it changes *release* to a gerund and fails to make a coherent sentence, leaving only two dependent clauses.

34. D: Choice *D* is the correct answer. This is a tricky question, but Choice *D* is correct because, in the context of this sentence, it's important to have *however* flanked by commas. This is because the use of *however* is basically an aside to the reader, addressing an idea and then redirecting the reader to an alternative outcome or line of reasoning. Choice *A* is therefore confusing, with *however* floating in the

384

sentence aimlessly. Choice *B* only uses one comma, which is incorrect. Choice *C* creates two incomplete sentences.

35. A: Choice *A* is correct. The sentence uses a lot of commas, but these are used effectively to highlight key points while continuing to focus on a central idea. Choice *B* is incorrect because the commas after *reality* and *that* are required. Choice *C* is incorrect because there should be a comma after *that* because *on the smallest scales* elaborates on the idea itself but not necessarily what Broglie said. Choice *D* puts a comma after *further*, which is unnecessary in this context.

36. B: Choice *B* correctly uses *an* instead of *a* to modify *interference*. The indefinite article *an* must be used before words that start with a vowel sound. The verb *created* is also in agreement with the tense of the story. Choice *C* incorrectly changes *creates* to *create* and pluralizes *light*, which is inconsistent with the rest of the sentence. Choice *D* modifies *creates* inappropriately and adds an incorrect comma after *light*.

37. C: Choice *C* is correct because it applies the single comma needed to combine the independent clause with the dependent clause, forming a functional sentence. It also includes quotes. Choice *A* is an awkward, disjointed sentence because it lacks a comma after *goes*. The other answers result in oddly constructed sentences (Choice *B*), and a misused comma after *As* (Choice *D*).

38. A: Choice *A* is the correct answer because the proper contraction for does not (doesn't) is used. There is also no need for commas or punctuation here as well, making Choices *B* and *C* incorrect. Choice *D* needlessly changes *doesn't* to *aren't*.

39. B: Choice *B* is correct because it fixes the subject-verb disagreement between the subject *the basic knowledge* and the verb *are*. Because *knowledge* is singular, the verb *are*, which is plural, is incorrect. Instead, the singular *is* must be used in place of *are*. This makes Choices *A* and *C* incorrect. Choice *D* is incorrect because it changes the meaning of the sentence.

40. C: Choice *C* is the correct answer because it employs a comma to effectively combine the independent clause with the dependent clause to form a complete sentence. Choice *A* lacks the comma after *thinking* needed to unite the two parts of the sentence. The independent clause is *Smart leaders will engage in critical thinking*, while the independent clause is *allowing them to discern ulterior motives and identify propaganda*. Choice *B* incorrectly adds a comma after *motives*. Choice *D* is incorrect because it still lacks connective punctuation and incorrectly alters the gerund *allowing* to *allows*; this would be fine if a comma and *which* were added before *allows* to effectively combine the clauses.

41. D: Choice *D* is the best answer because it changes *these* to *this*, making it properly modify the singular *practice*. Choice *A* is incorrect because of this lack of numerical agreement. Choice *B* is incorrect for the same reason—*this* is singular while *practices* is plural. Choice *C* is also incorrect because it doesn't fix *these* and takes out *will*, which is important for the tense of the overall sentence.

42. A: Choice *A* is correct because the sentence is fine as it is. Commas are not necessary here. Choices *B* and *C* replace *to* with *for* and *from*, respectively, which don't work in the context of the sentence: if leaders are *receptive*, they are receiving something, so *to* is appropriate. Choice *D* introduces unnecessary commas.

43. B: Choice *B* is the correct answer because it appropriately applies a comma after the opening word *Sadly*. This is because the author is introducing an idea or feeling, then transitioning into an elaborative explanation. *Sadly* is an aside, so there must be a comma afterwards to transition between thoughts and

385

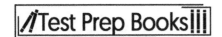

avoid a long-winded sentence. Choice *A* lacks the comma, so it is incorrect. Choice *C* incorrectly separates *that are attacked as lies* from the rest of the sentence, breaking its flow. Choice *D* still lacks the comma and incorrectly changes the two past tense verbs, *plagued* and *attacked*, into gerunds.

44. D: Choice *D* is the correct answer because the tense of *understanding* best applies to the context of the sentence. *Understanding* is also preceded by the modifier *an*. The combined *an understanding* forms a compound noun that is the direct object and focus of the sentence. Choices *A* and *B* use *understand* as a verb, which doesn't complement the sentence. Choice *C* lacks the modifying *an*.

45. A: Choice *A* is the best option. There are no errors in the original sentence, as both parts of the sentence (dependent and independent clauses) are combined through the central comma. Choice *B* creates two new sentences, the first of which is not complete with *While* still present. Choice *C* introduces an unnecessary comma after *practices*. Choice *D* uses *whom* instead of *who*, which is the correct form for this sentence.

46. B: Choice *B* is the correct answer because it corrects the subject-verb disagreement between *character* and *retain* by using *retains* instead. *Retain* is plural, which clashes with the singular *character*, making Choice *A* incorrect. *Retains* is the correct form because it is third person singular, meaning that Choice *C* is also incorrect. Choice *D* is possible as a revision but does not agree with the tense of *do take on* earlier in the sentence.

47. D: Choice *D* is the correct answer because it uses a comma to link the two halves of the sentence and adds the phrase *as well as* to help transition into the dependent clause. *As well as* is also used to communicate that *The Canterbury Tales* shares other qualities besides being *a story about stories*. Choice *A* is incorrect because it is a run on. In particular, *stories also being a story* is very unclear, necessitating the swap of *also* for *as well as*. Choice *B* has an awkward construction and uses the semicolon unwisely; this is certainly not the best option. Choice *C* uses the correct comma but lacks the phrase *as well as*.

48. C: Choice *C* is the correct answer because *these* is the incorrect pronoun for this particular section of the sentence; instead, the singular pronoun *this* should be used. Therefore, Choice *A* is incorrect. While Choice *B* correctly uses *this*, it also inserts a comma afterwards, which disrupts the flow of the sentence. Choice *D* is incorrect because it uses *these* and incorrectly uses *through* instead of *by*.

49. A: Choice *A* is correct. The original sentence has no issues and the author's thoughts are communicated clearly. Choice *B* incorrectly separates the sentence into two sentences, which creates a sentence fragment. Choice *C* rearranges the section in a way that clashes with the rest of the sentence. Choice *D* is incorrect because of the comma inserted after *clear,* breaking up the sentence unnecessarily.

50. B: Choice *B* is the correct answer because it corrects the subject-verb disagreement within the underlined portion. *These* is plural, so it must modify a plural noun. Thus, the plural *individuals* is required. Another clue for this is the fact that *descriptions* is also plural. Choice *A* is therefore incorrect. Choice *C* removes the necessary comma, while Choice *D* inserts an unnecessary semicolon.

51. D: Choice *D* is correct for two reasons. The incorrect pronoun *her* is replaced with the appropriate pronoun *she*. More specifically, Choice *D* uses *she's*, the contraction of *she is*. This emphasizes that the subject, *she,* is acting in a certain way or doing something. Clearly, the author is describing the nun's actions or characteristics. Choice *A* is incorrect because *her* is an inappropriate pronoun in this context,

and there is no form of *is* to express what the nun is doing. Choices *B* and *C* still use *her*, so they are incorrect, with the former also altering the sentence completely.

52. C: Choice *C* is the answer, correctly changing the adjective *brutal* to the adverb *brutally* so it can properly modify the adjective *honest*. Without this change, the sentence makes no sense because it presents a stream of adjectives that don't cleanly fit together. Thus, Choice *A* is incorrect. Choice *B* introduces too many commas and remains incoherent, while Choice *D* fails to modify *brutal*.

53. B: Choice *B* is the correct choice because it fixes the confusion of *shed's*. In this context, *shed* is not used as a noun but as a verb, and a verb cannot be possessive. What the sentence should have is *sheds*, the third-person simple singular present form of the verb to complete the phrase: *sheds light on*. This means Choice *A* is incorrect. Choice *C* alters the section in a way that clashes with the whole sentence. Choice *D* fails to correct *shed's* and introduces an unnecessary comma.

54. A: Choice *A* is the correct answer because there are no issues with this section of the sentence. The whole sentence is clear and uses proper punctuation. Choice *B* lacks an introductory comma after *likewise*, which is incorrect. Choices *C* and *D* add unnecessary commas.

55. B: Choice *B* is correct because it makes *Practitioners* plural, enabling it to agree with the verb *strive*. Making *Practitioners* plural also matches the context of the sentence. Therefore, Choice *A* is incorrect. Choice *C* is incorrect because it takes away a necessary comma. Choice *D* makes *Practitioner* and *strives* both singular, but without a modifier like *A* or *The* in front of *practitioner*, the sentence is not correct.

56. D: Choice *D* is the best answer because it corrects the two key errors in the section. *Them* is not the proper pronoun to use in this sentence. *They*, the third-person plural personal pronoun, should be used instead. Choices *A* and *B* are thus incorrect. Choice *D* also adds *be* to modify the main verb *used*, forming the appropriate compound verb. Choice *C* is missing this essential component.

57. C: Choice *C* is correct because the sentence requires the presence of *a* to introduce and modify the noun *testament*. *Testament* is a noun meaning evidence of quality or belief; it's not a verb, which is how Choice *A* uses it. This makes Choice *A* incorrect. Choice *B* uses *an* instead of *a*, which is not necessary because *testament* begins with a consonant. Choice *D* adds an unneeded comma after *possibilities*.

58. D: Choice *D* is the answer because it applies the two commas needed around *like any trial throughout one's life* in order to introduce a side thought in the sentence clearly, without breaking up the flow. The direct object is *test*. Therefore, the commas implemented before and after the phrase are required. Choice *A* doesn't contain the comma after *life*. Choice *B* lacks both the needed commas. Choice *C* applies the second comma incorrectly after *like*, which disrupts the construction of the sentence.

59. A: Choice *A* is correct because it contains no errors that mar the grammar or flow of the sentence. Choice *B* is incorrect because *upon* is incorrectly used to replace *on*. *Upon* refers specifically to a surface, which is not appropriate for this sentence. The preposition *on* is needed here. Choice *C* alters the sentence unnecessarily, confusing the tense and focus of the sentence by using *looking* instead of *look*. Choice *D* changes *some* to *something*, which makes no sense for the rest of the sentence.

60. C: Choice *C* is the correct answer because it adds a comma after *Certainly*. This is important because the author is addressing the audience before moving on to explore *his ideas*. Choice *A* is incorrect because the lack of a comma makes this sentence a run-on. Choices *B* and *D* are incorrect because,

while the former applies the comma after *Certainly*, they both take away the *but* that modifies *at what costs*.

61. B: Choice *B* corrects the verb tense of *focuses*. The phrase *to focuses* is not an appropriate infinitive; the best replacement is *to focus*. The sentence is not providing the reason why *Plato's ideal society is one that places human desire*, so Choice *A* is incorrect. Using *focus* allows the prepositional phrase *to focus on* to fluidly transition into the second half of the sentence. Choice *C* is not a bad option, but it lacks the comma needed to transition into *focusing on*. Choice *D* incorrectly eliminates *to*.

62. C: Choice *C* is the correct answer because it replaces the possessive *its* with the contraction *it's* and adds a transition to an alternate viewpoint. *But* should be added as a conjunction after the comma, linking the dependent clause and independent clause. Choices *A* and *B* are therefore incorrect. Choice *D* adds a transition but incorrectly removes *its*, rendering the sentence incoherent.

63. D: Choice *D* is the correct answer because it adds an apostrophe to *citizens*, making it *citizens'*. This gives ownership to *citizens*, which clearly indicates the idea of many citizens having their children confiscated. Choices *A, B*, and *C* are all incorrect because they don't give ownership to citizens: the latter adds the apostrophe in a place that indicates only one citizen is impacted.

64. B: Choice *B* is correct because it changes the plural *these* to the singular *this* in order to agree with the singular noun *kidnapping*. Choice *A* is incorrect because of this number disagreement. Choice *C* would be a good alternative, but it lacks the adverb *as* to clarify the use of *kidnappings* and eliminates *and*, which serves as the connection to the rest of the sentence. Choice *D* is incorrect because *those* is plural while *kidnapping* remains singular.

65. A: Choice *A* is correct because the sentence lacks grammatical errors and successfully joins the dependent clause with the independent clause by inserting a single comma after *beings*. Choice *B* is incorrect because it needs a comma to connect the dependent clause and independent clause. Choice *C* uses a semicolon instead of a simple comma. Choice *D* is incorrect because the plural *those* replaces *this*. *This* is singular to describe a single event, which agrees with *seems*.

66. D: Choice *D* is the correct choice because it fixes two issues with the underlined section that cause confusion for the whole sentence. First, *than* is incorrectly used in the original section. *Than* is a conjunction used to make a comparison, while *then* (acting as an adverb) serves to express a result of something, like a sequence of events. Therefore, Choices *A* and *B* are incorrect. However, therein lies the trickiness of the question because none of the answer choices use *then* without altering the meaning of the sentence (Choice *C*). Choice *D* compensates for this by replacing *than/then* with a simple comma to link the two clauses and transition from the central idea to the potential outcome of the idea (the child having more opportunities).

67. C: Choice *C* corrects the only flaw in this sentence by fixing the tense of *encourage*. *Encourages* is the third person present form of the original verb and as such fits much better because the sentence is written in the third person. Choice *A* is incorrect because the tense of *encourage* doesn't sync with the rest of the sentence. Choice *B* is incorrect; the gerund form of *encourage* is unnecessary. Choice *D* uses the conjunction *which* instead *that*, which is incorrect, in addition to not fixing the tense of *encourage*.

68. B: Choice *B* is correct. Here, a colon is used to introduce an explanation. Colons either introduce explanations or lists. Additionally, the quote ends with the punctuation inside the quotes, unlike Choice *C*.

69. A: The verb tense in this passage is predominantly in the present tense, so Choice *A* is the correct answer. Choice *B* is incorrect because the subject and verb do not agree. It should be *Education provides,* not *Education provide*. Choice *C* is incorrect because the passage is in present tense, and *Education will provide* is future tense. Choice *D* doesn't make sense when placed in the sentence.

70. D: The possessive form of the word *it* is *its*. The contraction *it's* denotes *it is*. Thus, Choice *A* is incorrect. The word *raises* in Choice *B* makes the sentence grammatically incorrect. Choice *C* adds an apostrophe at the end of *its*. While adding an apostrophe to most words would indicate possession, adding *'s* to the word *it* indicates a contraction.

71. C: The word *civilised* should be spelled *civilized.* The words *distinguishes* and *creatures* are both spelled correctly.

72. B: Choice *B* is correct because it provides clarity by describing what *myopic* means right after the word itself. Choice *A* is incorrect because the explanation of *myopic* comes before the word; thus, the meaning is skewed. It's possible that Choice *C* makes sense within context. However, it's not the best way to say this because the commas create too many unnecessary phrases. Choice *D* is confusingly worded. Using *myopic focus* is not detrimental to society; however, the way *D* is worded makes it seem that way.

73. C: Again, we see where the second paragraph can be divided into two parts due to separate topics. The paragraph's first main focus is education addressing the mind, body, and soul. This first section, then, could end with the concluding sentence, "The human heart and psyche . . ." The next sentence to start a new paragraph would be "Education is a basic human right." The rest of this paragraph talks about what education is and some of its characteristics.

74. A: Choice *A* is correct because the phrase *others' ideas* is both plural and indicates possession. Choice *B* is incorrect because *other's* indicates only one *other* that's in possession of *ideas*, which is incorrect. Choice *C* is incorrect because no possession is indicated. Choice *D* is incorrect because the word *other* does not end in *s*. Others's is not a correct form of the plural possessive word.

75. D: This sentence must have a comma before *although* because the word *although* is connecting two independent clauses. Thus, Choices *B* and *C* are incorrect. Choice *A* is incorrect because the second sentence in the underlined section is a fragment.

Math

1. A: Compare each number after the decimal point to figure out which overall number is greatest. In Choices *A* (1.43785) and *C* (1.43592), both have the same tenths place (4) and hundredths place (3). However, the thousandths place is greater in Choice *A* (7), so *A* has the greatest value overall.

2. D: By grouping the four numbers in the answer into factors of the two numbers of the question (6 and 12), it can be determined that:

$$(3 \times 2) \times (4 \times 3) = 6 \times 12$$

Alternatively, you could find the prime factorization of each answer choices and compare it to the original value. 6×12 has a value of 72 and a prime factorization of $2^3 \times 3^2$. The answer choices respectively have values of 64, 84, 108, 72, and 360, so Choice *D* is correct.

3. C: The sum total percentage of a pie chart must equal 100%. Since the CD sales take up less than half of the chart (50%) and more than a quarter (25%), it can be determined to be 40% overall. This can also be measured with a protractor. The angle of a circle is 360°. Since 25% of 360° would be 90° and 50% would be 180°, the angle percentage of CD sales falls in between; therefore, it would be Choice *C*.

4. B: Using the conversion rate, multiply the projected weight loss of 25 lb. by $0.45 \frac{\text{kg}}{\text{lb}}$ to get the amount in kilograms (11.25 kg).

5. D: First, subtract $1,437 from $2,334.50 to find Johnny's monthly savings; this equals $897.50. Then, multiply this amount by 3 to find out how much he will have in three months before he pays for his vacation; this equals $2,692.50. Finally, subtract the cost of the vacation ($1,750) from this amount to find how much Johnny will have left: $942.50.

6. C: Follow the order of operations in order to solve this problem. Solve the parentheses first, following the order of operations inside the parentheses as well. First, simplify the square roots:

$$(6 \times 4) - 3^2$$

Then, multiply inside the parentheses:

$$24 - 3^2$$

Next, simplify the exponents:

$$24 - 9$$

Finally, subtract to get 15, Choice *C*.

7. D: Three girls for every two boys can be expressed as a ratio: 3 : 2. This can be visualized as splitting the school into 5 groups: 3 girl groups and 2 boy groups. The number of students that are in each group can be found by dividing the total number of students by 5:

$$\frac{650 \text{ students}}{5 \text{ groups}} = \frac{130 \text{ students}}{\text{group}}$$

To find the total number of girls, multiply the number of students per group (130) by the number of girl groups in the school (3). This equals 390, Choice *D*.

8. C: Kimberley worked 4.5 hours at the rate of $10 / h and 1 hour at the rate of $12 / h. The problem states that her pay is rounded to the nearest hour, so the 4.5 hours would round up to 5 hours at the rate of $10 / h.

$$(5 \text{ h}) \times \left(\frac{\$10}{\text{h}}\right) + (1 \text{ h}) \times \left(\frac{\$12}{\text{h}}\right) = \$50 + \$12 = \$62$$

9. C: The first step is to depict each number using decimals:

$$\frac{91}{100} = 0.91$$

390

Dividing the numerator by denominator of $\frac{4}{5}$ to convert it to a decimal yields 0.80, while $\frac{2}{3}$ becomes 0.66 recurring. Rearrange each expression in ascending order, as found in Choice *C*.

10. B: First, calculate the difference between the larger value and the smaller value:

$$378 - 252 = 126$$

To calculate this difference as a percentage of the original value, and thus calculate the percentage *increase*, divide 126 by 252, then multiply by 100 to reach the percentage 50%, Choice *B*.

11. E: Simplify each mixed number of the problem into a fraction by multiplying the denominator by the whole number and adding the numerator:

$$\frac{14}{3} - \frac{31}{9}$$

Since the first denominator is a multiple of the second, simplify it further by multiplying both the numerator and denominator of the first expression by 3 so that the denominators of the fractions are equal:

$$\frac{42}{9} - \frac{31}{9} = \frac{11}{9}$$

Simplifying this further, divide the numerator 11 by the denominator 9; this leaves 1 with a remainder of 2. To write this as a mixed number, place the remainder over the denominator, resulting in $1\frac{2}{9}$.

12. C: We are trying to find x, the number of red cans. The equation can be set up like this:

$$x + 2(10 - x) = 16$$

The left x is actually multiplied by \$1, the price per red can. Since we know Jessica bought 10 total cans, $10 - x$ is the number blue cans that she bought. We multiply the number of blue cans by \$2, the price per blue can.

That should all equal \$16, the total amount of money that Jessica spent. Working that out gives us:

$$x + 20 - 2x = 16$$

$$20 - x = 16$$

$$x = 4$$

13. C: Janice will be choosing 4 employees out of a set of 6 applicants, so this will be given by the choice function. The following equation shows the choice function worked out:

$$\binom{6}{4} = \frac{6!}{4!\,(6-4)!} = \frac{6!}{4!\,(2)!}$$

$$\frac{6 \times 5 \times 4 \times 3 \times 2 \times 1}{4 \times 3 \times 2 \times 1 \times 2 \times 1} = \frac{6 \times 5}{2} = 15$$

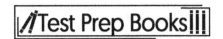

14. D: $\frac{3}{100}$

Each digit to the left of the decimal point represents a higher multiple of 10 and each digit to the right of the decimal point represents a quotient of a higher multiple of 10 for the divisor.

The first digit to the right of the decimal point is equal to the value divided by 10. The second digit to the right of the decimal point is equal to the value divided by (10×10), or the value divided by 100.

15. D: Using the order of operations, items inside of parentheses are sorted out first. Therefore, the teacher should resolve the parentheses first. In this expression, multiplication and division are computed next from left to right, followed by addition and subtraction.

16. A: 847.90

The hundredths place value is located two digits to the right of the decimal point (the digit 9 in the original number). The digit to the right of the place value is examined to decide whether to round up or keep the digit. In this case, the digit 6 is 5 or greater, so the hundredths place is rounded up. When rounding up, if the digit to be increased is a 9, the digit to its left is increased by one and the digit in the desired place value is made a zero. Therefore, the number is rounded to 847.90.

17. C: The perimeter is found by calculating the sum of all sides of the polygon:

$$9 + 9 + 9 + 8 + 8 + s = 56$$

s is the missing side length. Therefore, $43 + s = 56$. The missing side length is 13 cm.

18. A: $16\frac{1}{2}$

A mixed number contains both a whole number and either a fraction or a decimal. Therefore, the mixed number is $16\frac{1}{2}$.

19. E: $9\frac{3}{10}$

To convert a decimal to a fraction, remember that any number to the left of the decimal point will be a whole number. Then, since 0.3 goes to the tenths place, it can be placed over 10.

20. C: To solve for the value of b, isolate the variable b on one side of the equation.

Start by moving the lower value of -4 to the other side by adding 4 to both sides:

$$5b - 4 = 2b + 17$$

$$5b - 4 + 4 = 2b + 17 + 4$$

$$5b = 2b + 21$$

Then subtract $2b$ from both sides:

$$5b - 2b = 2b + 21 - 2b$$

$$3b = 21$$

392

Then divide both sides by 3 to get the value of b:

$$\frac{3b}{3} = \frac{21}{3}$$

$$b = 7$$

21. A: 63.96

This question involves the percent formula. Since we're beginning with a percent, also known as a number over 100, we'll put 39 on the right side of the equation:

$$\frac{x}{164} = \frac{39}{100}$$

Now, multiply 164 and 39 to get 6,396, which then needs to be divided by 100.

$$6,396 \div 100 = 63.96$$

22. C: $\frac{1}{3}$ of the shirts sold were patterned. Therefore, $1 - \frac{1}{3} = \frac{2}{3}$ of the shirts sold were solid. Anytime "of" a quantity appears in a word problem, multiplication needs to be used. Therefore,

$$192 \times \frac{2}{3} = 192 \times \frac{2}{3} = \frac{384}{3} = 128 \text{ solid shirts were sold}$$

The entire expression is $192 \times \left(1 - \frac{1}{3}\right)$.

23. B: A rectangle is a specific type of parallelogram. It has 4 right angles. A square is a rhombus that has 4 right angles. Therefore, a square is always a rectangle because it has two sets of parallel lines and 4 right angles.

24. E: Recall the formula for area of a rectangle, area = length × width. The answer must be in square inches, so all values must be converted to inches. Half of a foot is equal to 6 inches. Therefore, the area of the rectangle is equal to:

$$6 \text{ in} \times \frac{11}{2} \text{ in} = \frac{66}{2} \text{ in}^2 = 33 \text{ in}^2$$

25. D: 80%

To convert a fraction to a percent, the fraction is first converted to a decimal. To do so, the numerator is divided by the denominator: $4 \div 5 = 0.8$. To convert a decimal to a percent, the number is multiplied by 100:

$$0.8 \times 10 = 80\%$$

26. C: 80 min

To solve the problem, a proportion is written consisting of ratios comparing distance and time. One way to set up the proportion is:

$$\frac{3}{48} = \frac{5}{x} \left(\frac{distance}{time} = \frac{distance}{time} \right)$$

393

x represents the unknown value of time. To solve a proportion, the ratios are cross-multiplied:

$$(3)(x) = (5)(48) \rightarrow 3x = 240$$

The equation is solved by isolating the variable, or dividing by 3 on both sides, to produce $x = 80$.

27. A: Every 8 ml of medicine requires 5 ml. The 45 ml first needs to be split into portions of 8 ml. This results in $\frac{45}{8}$ portions. Each portion requires 5 ml. Therefore,

$$\frac{45}{8} \times 5 = 45 \times \frac{5}{8} = \frac{225}{8} \text{ ml is necessary}$$

28. C: Volume of this 3-dimensional figure is calculated using $length \times width \times height$. Each measure of length is in inches. Therefore, the answer would be labeled in cubic inches.

29. A: A common denominator must be found. The least common denominator is 15 because it has both 5 and 3 as factors. The fractions must be rewritten using 15 as the denominator.

30. C: A compass is a tool that can be used to draw a circle. The compass would be drawn by using the length of the radius, which is half of the diameter.

31. D: A dollar contains 20 nickels. Therefore, if there are 12 dollars' worth of nickels, there are:

$$12 \times 20 = 240 \text{ nickels}$$

Each nickel weighs 5 grams. Therefore, the weight of the nickels is:

$$240 \times 5 = 1,200 \text{ grams}$$

Adding in the weight of the empty piggy bank, the filled bank weighs 2,250 grams.

32. D: To find Denver's total snowfall, 3 must be multiplied by $27\frac{3}{4}$. In order to easily do this, the mixed number should be converted into an improper fraction.

$$27\frac{3}{4} = \frac{27 \times 4 + 3}{4} = \frac{111}{4}$$

Therefore, Denver had approximately $\frac{3 \times 111}{4} = \frac{333}{4}$ inches of snow. The improper fraction can be converted back into a mixed number through division.

$$\frac{333}{4} = 83\frac{1}{4} \text{ inches}$$

33. B: Ordinal numbers represent a ranking. Placing second in a competition is a ranking among the other participants of the spelling bee.

34. D: 13,078

The power of 10 by which a digit is multiplied corresponds with the number of zeros following the digit when expressing its value in standard form. Therefore:

$$(1 \times 10^4) + (3 \times 10^3) + (7 \times 10^1) + (8 \times 10^0)$$

$$10,000 + 3,000 + 70 + 8 = 13,078$$

35. C: 374.04

The formula for finding the area of a regular polygon is $A = \frac{1}{2} \times a \times P$ where a is the length of the apothem (from the center to any side at a right angle), and P is the perimeter of the figure. The apothem a is given as 10.39, and the perimeter can be found by multiplying the length of one side by the number of sides (since the polygon is regular): $P = 12 \times 6 \rightarrow P = 72$. To find the area, substitute the values for a and P into the formula:

$$A = \frac{1}{2} \times a \times P$$

$$A = \frac{1}{2} \times (10.39) \times (72) \rightarrow A = 374.04$$

36. E: 216 cm^2

Because area is a two-dimensional measurement, the dimensions are multiplied by a scale factor that is squared to determine the scale factor of the corresponding areas. The dimensions of the rectangle are multiplied by a scale factor of 3. Therefore, the area is multiplied by a scale factor of 3^2 (which is equal to 9):

$$24 \text{ cm}^2 \times 9 = 216 \text{ cm}^2$$

37. B: A number is prime because its only factors are itself and 1. Positive numbers (greater than one) can be prime numbers.

38. C: $\frac{31}{36}$

Set up the problem and find a common denominator for both fractions.

$$\frac{5}{12} + \frac{4}{9}$$

Multiply each fraction across by 1 to convert to a common denominator.

$$\frac{5}{12} \times \frac{3}{3} + \frac{4}{9} \times \frac{4}{4}$$

Once over the same denominator, add across the top. The total is over the common denominator.

$$\frac{15 + 16}{36} = \frac{31}{36}$$

395

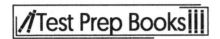

39. A: Order of operations follows PEMDAS—Parentheses, Exponents, Multiplication and Division from left to right, and Addition and Subtraction from left to right.

40. C: 0.63

Divide 5 by 8, which results in 0.63.

41. D: 8,685

Set up the problem, with the larger number on top. Begin subtracting with the far-right column (ones). Borrow 10 from the column to the left, when necessary.

42. A: The place value to the right of the thousandth place, which would be the ten-thousandth place, is what gets used. The value in the thousandth place is 7. The number in the place value to its right is 5 or greater, so the 7 gets bumped up to 8. Everything to its right turns to a zero, and the final zero is dropped because it is part of the decimal. 245.2678 rounded to the nearest thousandth is 245.268.

43. D: 37.797

Set up the problem, larger number on top and numbers lined up at the decimal. Begin subtracting with the far-right column. Borrow 10 from the column to the left, when necessary.

44. C: Numbers should be lined up by decimal places before subtraction is performed. This is because subtraction is performed within each place value. The other operations, such as multiplication, division, and exponents (which is a form of multiplication), involve ignoring the decimal places at first and then including them at the end.

45. C: $\frac{19}{24}$

Set up the problem and find a common denominator for both fractions.

$$\frac{23}{24} - \frac{1}{6}$$

Multiply each fraction across by 1 to convert to a common denominator.

$$\frac{23}{24} \times \frac{1}{1} - \frac{1}{6} \times \frac{4}{4}$$

Once over the same denominator, subtract across the top.

$$\frac{23 - 4}{24} = \frac{19}{24}$$

46. E: $\frac{2}{9}$

Set up the problem and find a common denominator for both fractions.

$$\frac{43}{45} - \frac{11}{15}$$

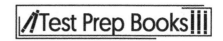

Multiply each fraction across by 1 to convert to a common denominator.

$$\frac{43}{45} \times \frac{1}{1} - \frac{11}{15} \times \frac{3}{3}$$

Once over the same denominator, subtract across the top.

$$\frac{43 - 33}{45} = \frac{10}{45}$$

Reduce:

$$\frac{10 \div 5}{45 \div 5} = \frac{2}{9}$$

47. B: $\frac{14}{25}$

Since 0.56 goes to the hundredths place, it can be placed over 100:

$$\frac{56}{100}$$

Essentially, the way we got there is by multiplying the numerator and denominator by 100:

$$\frac{0.56}{1} \times \frac{100}{100} = \frac{56}{100}$$

Then, the fraction can be simplified down to $\frac{14}{25}$:

$$\frac{56}{100} \div \frac{4}{4} = \frac{14}{25}$$

48. A: 2,504,774

Line up the numbers (the number with the most digits on top) to multiply. Begin with the right column on top and the right column on bottom.

Move one column left on top and multiply by the far-right column on the bottom. Remember to add the carry over after you multiply. Continue that pattern for each of the numbers on the top row.

Starting on the far-right column on top repeat this pattern for the next number left on the bottom. Write the answers below the first line of answers; remember to begin with a zero placeholder. Continue for each number in the top row.

Starting on the far-right column on top, repeat this pattern for the next number left on the bottom. Write the answers below the first line of answers. Remember to begin with zero placeholders.

Once completed, ensure the answer rows are lined up correctly, then add.

49. A: In order to determine the savings needed per day, $\frac{150}{4} = 37.5$, so she needs to save an average of $37.50 per day.

50. D: The teacher would be introducing fractions. If a pie was cut into 6 pieces, each piece would represent $\frac{1}{6}$ of the pie. If one piece was taken away, $\frac{5}{6}$ of the pie would be left over.

51. A: $\frac{810}{2921}$

Line up the fractions.

$$\frac{15}{23} \times \frac{54}{127}$$

Multiply across the top and across the bottom:

$$\frac{15 \times 54}{23 \times 127} = \frac{810}{2921}$$

52. D: There are no millions, so the millions period consists of all zeros. 182 is in the billions period, 36 is in the thousands period, 421 is in the hundreds period, and 356 is the decimal.

53. D: $11\frac{3}{4}$

Set up the division problem.

$$1 \quad 6 \overline{\smash{\big)}\ 1 \quad 8 \quad 8}$$

16 does not go into 1 but does go into 18 so start there.

$$
\begin{array}{r}
1 \quad 1 \\
1 \quad 6 \overline{\smash{\big)}\ 1 \quad 8 \quad 8} \\
-\ 1 \quad 6 \\
\hline
2 \quad 8 \\
-\ 1 \quad 6 \\
\hline
1 \quad 2 \\
\end{array}
$$

The result is $11\frac{12}{16}$

Reduce the fraction for the final answer.

$$11\frac{3}{4}$$

54. D: Division can be computed as a repetition of subtraction problems by subtracting multiples of 24.

55. E: The number of days can be found by taking the total amount Bernard needs to make and dividing it by the amount he earns per day:

$$\frac{300}{80} = \frac{30}{8} = \frac{15}{4} = 3.75$$

398

But Bernard is only working full days, so he will need to work 4 days, since 3 days is not a sufficient amount of time.

56. E: The value went up by:

$$\$165,000 - \$150,000 = \$15,000$$

Out of \$150,000, this is $\frac{15,000}{150,000} = \frac{1}{10}$. Convert this to having a denominator of 100, the result is $\frac{10}{100}$ or 10%.

57. B: A number raised to an exponent is a compressed form of multiplication.

For example,

$$10^3 = 10 \times 10 \times 10$$

58. B: The perimeter of a rectangle is the sum of all four sides.

Therefore, the answer is:

$$P = 14 + 8\frac{1}{2} + 14 + 8\frac{1}{2}$$

$$14 + 14 + 8 + \frac{1}{2} + 8 + \frac{1}{2} = 45 \text{ square inches}$$

59. C: Kilograms, grams, kilometers, and meters. Inches, pounds, and baking measurements, such as tablespoons, are not part of the metric system. Kilograms, grams, kilometers, and meters are part of the metric system.

60. D: It shows the associative property of multiplication. The order of multiplication does not matter, and the grouping symbols do not change the final result once the expression is evaluated.

Reading

1. B: Mr. Button's wife is about to have a baby. The passage begins by giving the reader information about traditional birthing situations. Then, we are told that Mr. and Mrs. Button decide to go against tradition to have their baby in a hospital. The next few passages are dedicated to letting the reader know how Mr. Button dresses and goes to the hospital to welcome his new baby. There is a doctor in this excerpt, as Choice *C* indicates, and Mr. Button does put on clothes, as Choice *D* indicates. However, Mr. Button is not going to the doctor's office nor is he about to go shopping for new clothes.

2. A: The tone of the above passage is nervous and excited. We are told in the fourth paragraph that Mr. Button "arose nervously." We also see him running without caution to the doctor to find out about his wife and baby—this indicates his excitement. We also see him stuttering in a nervous yet excited fashion as he asks the doctor if it's a boy or girl. Though the doctor may seem a bit abrupt at the end, indicating a bit of anger or shame, neither of these choices is the overwhelming tone of the entire passage. Despite the circumstances, joy and gratitude are not the main tone in the passage.

3. C: Dedicated. Mr. Button is dedicated to the task before him. Choice *A*, numbed, Choice *B*, chained, and Choice *D*, moved, all could grammatically fit in the sentence. However, they are not synonyms with *consecrated* like Choice *C* is.

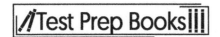

4. D: Giving readers a visual picture of what the doctor is doing. The author describes a visual image—the doctor rubbing his hands together—first and foremost. The author may be trying to make a comment about the profession; however, the author does not "explain the detail of the doctor's profession" as Choice *B* suggests.

5. D: To introduce the setting of the story and its characters. We know we are being introduced to the setting because we are given the year in the very first paragraph along with the season: "one day in the summer of 1860." This is a classic structure of an introduction of the setting. We are also getting a long explanation of Mr. Button, what his work is, who is related to him, and what his life is like in the third paragraph.

6. B: "Talk sense!" is an example of an imperative sentence. An imperative sentence gives a command. The doctor is commanding Mr. Button to talk sense. Choice *A* is an example of an exclamatory sentence, which expresses excitement. Choice *C* is an example of an interrogative sentence—these types of sentences ask questions. Choice *D* is an example of a declarative sentence. This means that the character is simply making a statement.

7. B: The word *anachronism* most nearly means misplacement. Choice *A*, comparison, is an analogy or similarity to something. Choice *C*, *aberration*, means abnormality. Choice *D*, *amelioration*, means improvement.

8. C: This passage can best be described as a narrative, which is a type of passage that tells a story. Choice *A*, expository, is a text organized logically to investigate a problem. Choice *B*, descriptive, is a text that mostly goes about describing something or someone in detail. Choice *D*, persuasive, is a text that is organized as an argument and meant to persuade the audience to do something.

9. A: To explain the setting of the narrative and give information about the story. The setting of a narrative is the time and place. We see from the first paragraph that the year is 1860. We also can discern that it is summer, and Mr. and Mrs. Button are about to have a baby. This tells us both the setting and information about the story.

10. D: Something is unusual about the birth of the baby. The word "curious" is thrown in at the end twice, which tells us the doctor is suspicious about something having to do with the birth of the baby, since that is the most recent event to happen. Mr. Button is acting like a father who is expecting a baby, and the doctor seems confused about something.

11. C: This is a tricky question, but it can be solved through careful context analysis and vocabulary knowledge. One can infer that the use of "expedient," while not necessarily very positive, isn't inherently bad in this context either. Note how in the next line, he says, "but most governments are usually, and all governments are sometimes, inexpedient." This use of "inexpedient" indicates that a government becomes a hindrance rather than a solution; it slows progress rather than helps facilitate progress. Thus, Choice *A* and Choice *D* can be ruled out because they are hindrances or problems and would work better with inexpedient rather than expedient. Choice *B* makes no logical sense. Therefore, Choice *C* is the best description of *expedient*.

12. B: Choice *B* is the most accurate representation of Thoreau's views. Essentially, Thoreau brings to light the fact that the few people in power can twist government and policy for their own needs. Choices *A* and *C* are also correct to a degree, but the answer asks for the best description, which is

400

Choice *B*. While Choice *D* is the only answer that mentions the Mexican War directly, Thoreau clearly thinks the war is unnecessary because the people generally didn't consent to the war.

13. D: Choices *A* and *B* are completely incorrect. Thoreau is not defending government in any way. His views are set against government. As mentioned in the text, he appreciates little government but favors having no government structure at all. The text is reflective by nature but not reflective on the stages of government abuses as Choice *C* suggests. Choice *D* is the more appropriate answer because of the presence of evidence in the text. Thoreau cites current events and uses them to illustrate the point he's trying to make.

14. C: One of Thoreau's biggest criticisms of government is its capacity to impose on the people's freedoms and liberties, enacting rules that the people don't want and removing power from the individual. None of the scenarios directly impose specific regulations or restrictions on the people, except Prohibition. Prohibition removed the choice to consume alcohol in favor of abstinence, which was favored by the religious conservatives of the time. Thus, Thoreau would point out that this is a clear violation of free choice and an example of government meddling.

15. A: Choice *B* is totally irrelevant. Choice *C* is also incorrect; Thoreau never personifies government. Also, this doesn't coincide with his wooden gun analogy. Choice *D* is compelling because of its language but doesn't define the statement. Choice *A* is the most accurate summary of the main point of Thoreau's statement.

16. B: Thoreau specifically cites that legislators "are continually putting in their way." This reflects his suspicion and concern of government intervention. Recall that Thoreau continually mentions that government, while meant as a way to establish freedom, is easily used to suppress freedom, piling on regulations and rules that inhibit progress. Choice *B* is the answer that most directly states how Thoreau sees government getting in the way of freedom.

17. D: This passage is an expository essay, which means that an idea is investigated and then expanded upon. Thoreau is investigating the idea of government here and how the U.S. government works in relation to the people.

18. C: The word *liable* most nearly means susceptible. The text says, "The government itself, which is only the mode which the people have chosen to execute their will, is equally liable to be abused and perverted before the people can act through it." Thoreau is saying here that the government is vulnerable enough to be abused. Choice *A*, *paramount*, means having importance. Choice *B*, *inconceivable*, means unbelievable. Choice *D*, *detrimental*, means damaging.

19. B: Thoreau is talking about the American government. We see this information in the beginning of the second paragraph. The passage mentions the Mexican War, but the passage itself does not relay the vulnerabilities of the Mexican government. The other two countries are not mentioned in the passage.

20. B: Posterity means all future generations of people. The sentence would say, "The American government—what is it but a tradition, though a recent one, endeavoring to transmit itself unimpaired to all future generations of people . . ." Choice *A* would be the definition of *royalty*. Choice *C* would be the definition of an *educator*. Choice *D* would be the definition of a *philosopher*.

21. A: Choice *D* can be eliminated because the Salem witch trials aren't mentioned. While sympathetic to the plight of the accused, the author doesn't demand or urge the reader to demand reparations to the descendants; therefore, Choice *B* can also be ruled out. It's clear that the author's main goal is to

401

educate the reader and shed light on the facts and hidden details behind the case. However, his focus isn't on the occult, but the specific Lancashire case itself. He goes into detail about suspects' histories and ties to Catholicism, revealing how the fears of the English people at the time sealed the fate of the accused witches. Choice *A* is correct.

22. B: It's important to note that these terms may not be an exact analog for *enduring*. However, through knowledge of the definition of *enduring*, as well as the context in which it's used, an appropriate synonym can be found. Plugging "circumstantial" into the passage in place of "enduring" doesn't make sense. Nor does "un-original" work, since this particular case of witchcraft stands out in history. "Wicked" is very descriptive, but this is an attribute applied to people, not events; therefore, this is an inappropriate choice as well. *Enduring* literally means long lasting, referring to the continued interest in this particular case of witchcraft. Therefore, it's a popular topic of 1600s witch trials, making "popular," Choice *B,* the best choice.

23. D: Choices *A* and *B* are irrelevant and incorrect. The use of quotes lends credibility to the author. However, the presence of quotes alone doesn't necessarily mean that the author has a qualified perspective. What establishes the writer as a reliable voice is that the author's previous writing on the subject has been published before. This qualification greatly establishes the author's credentials as a historical writer, making Choice *D* the correct answer.

24. B: Choice *B* is the best answer because it ultimately encompasses the potentiality of Choices *C* and *D*. Choice *A* is incorrect because it takes the statement literally. For Choice *C,* it's possible that evidence was tampered with or even falsified, but this statement doesn't refer to this. While the author alludes that there may have been evidence tampering and potentially corruption (Choice *D*), what the writer is directly saying is that the documentation of the court indicates an elaborate trial.

25. C: Several of these answers could have contributed to the fear and political motivations around the Lancashire witch trials. What this answer's looking for is very specific: political motivations and issues that played a major role in the case. Choice *C* clearly outlines the public fears of the time. It also describes how the government can use this fear to weed out and eliminate traces of Catholicism (and witchcraft too). Catholicism and witchcraft were seen as dangerous and undermining to English Protestantism and governance. Choice *D* can be eliminated; while this information may have some truth and is certainly consistent with the general fear of witchcraft, the details about Lancashire's ancient history aren't mentioned in the text. Choice *A* is true but not necessarily political in nature. Choice *B* is very promising, though not outright mentioned.

26. D: The best evidence comes from Alizon herself. The text mentions that she confessed to bewitching John Law, thinking that she did him harm. From here she names her grandmother, who she believes corrupted her. Choice *B* can be ruled out; spectral evidence isn't mentioned. The case draws on knowledge of superstition of witchcraft, but this in itself can't be considered evidence, so Choice *A* is incorrect. Choice *C* isn't evidence in a modern sense; rumors have no weight in court and therefore are not evidence. While this is used as evidence to some degree, this still isn't the *best* evidence against Alizon and the witches.

27. B: This type of passage would be considered expository, which is an informative passage. Choice *A,* persuasive, means to take a side of an argument, and this essay is merely divulging information. Choice *C,* narrative, means to tell a story. Although a story is being told indirectly, the essay doesn't follow a traditional narrative. Choice *D,* descriptive, means a detailed description of a person or place.

28. B: According to the passage, 20 people were arrested as witches in the Lancashire trials. The essay tells us that "ten were hanged, one died in goal (jail), one was sentenced to death in the pillory, and eight were acquitted."

29. D: The word *commemorative* means in honor of something. The context clue here includes the "works of fiction" by the authors Blake Morrison, Ann Duffy, and Jeanette Winterson, no doubt to celebrate the preserved history of the famous trial.

30. C: Malkin tower is the house of Alizon's grandmother. It is also a place where a meeting of witches was said to be held in the passage. The passage says, "The net was widened still further at the end of April when Alizon's younger brother James and younger sister Jennet, only nine years old, came up between them with a story about a "great meeting of witches" at their grandmother's house, known as Malkin Tower."

31. A: It introduces certain insects that transition from water to air. Choice *B* is incorrect because although the passage talks about gills, it is not the central idea of the passage. Choices *C* and *D* are incorrect because the passage does not "define" or "invite," but only serves as an introduction to stoneflies, dragonflies, and mayflies and their transition from water to air.

32. C: To molt is to shed part or all of the outer shell, as noted in Choice *C*. Choices *A, B,* and *D* are incorrect. The word in the passage is mentioned here: "But it is advisable in connection with our present subject to dwell especially on some insects that remain continually under water till they are ready to undergo their final molt and attain the winged state, which they pass entirely in the air."

33. B: The first paragraph serves as a contrast to the second. Notice how the first paragraph goes into detail describing how insects are able to breathe air. The second paragraph acts as a contrast to the first by stating "[i]t is of great interest to find that, nevertheless, a number of insects spend much of their time under water." Watch for transition words such as "nevertheless" to help find what type of passage you're dealing with.

34: C: *Instars* are the phases between two periods of molting, and the text explains when these transitions occur. The preparatory stages are acted out in the water while the last stage is in the air. Choices *A, B,* and *D* are all incorrect.

35. C: The author's tone is informative and exhibits interest in the subject of the study. Overall, the author presents us with information on the subject. One moment where personal interest is depicted is when the author states, "It is of great interest to find that, nevertheless, a number of insects spend much of their time under water."

36. C: Their larva can breathe the air dissolved in water through gills of some kind. This is stated in the last paragraph. Choice *A* is incorrect because the text mentions this in a general way at the beginning of the passage concerning "insects as a whole." Choice *B* is incorrect because this is stated of beetles and water-bugs, and not the insects in question. Choice *D* is incorrect because this is the opposite of what the text says of instars.

37. B: According to the passage, boatmen and scorpions have some way of protecting their spiracles when submerged. We see this in the second paragraph, which says "(boatmen and scorpions) which have some way of protecting their spiracles when submerged."

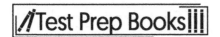

38. A: The best answer Choice is *A*: the author believes that the stonefly, dragonfly, and mayfly larvae are better prepared to live beneath the water because they have gills that allow them to do so. We see this when the author says "But the larva of a stone-fly, a dragon-fly, or a may-fly is adapted more completely than these for aquatic life; it can, by means of gills of some kind, breathe the air dissolved in water."

39. C: Because a vast majority of insects have wings and also have the ability to breathe underwater. The entire first paragraph talks of how insects have wings, and how insects also have "a system of branching air-tubes" that carries oxygen to the insect's tissues.

40. B: The word *preeminently* most nearly means *above all* or *in particular*. The author is saying that above all, insects are creatures of both land and water.

Science

1. A: One cycle takes 300 months. It starts with the population being low, rising and reaching a peak, and then falling again. It takes 200 months to reach the peak, Choice *B*. Three cycles could be completed in 800 months, Choice *C*, and the second cycle would have started by 400 months, Choice *D*.

2. B: Looking at Figure 2, the fox is the predator. When the diagram notes that the predator population decreases on the left side, there is only one fox left. As it increases, as noted on the right side, there are two foxes drawn. Foxes are also much larger than rabbits and would be able to catch them much easier than the other way around.

3. D: When the prey population decreases, the predators have less food, i.e., prey, to feed on. This causes the predator population to dwindle. An increase in the prey population, Choice *A*, would actually increase the predator population because they would have more food, which would lengthen survival and increase reproduction. Seasons do not affect the predator population in this situation, Choice *B*. Generally, prey do not have the ability to attack their predators, Choice *C*, due to physical constraints, such as differences in size.

4. A: When the predator population decreases, the rate of survival of the prey population increases, and they can then also reproduce more. An increase in the predator population, Choice *B*, would cause the prey population to decrease. Weather and amount of sunlight, Choice *C*, does not affect the growth of the prey population. The prey population is cyclical and does not remain the same size, Choice *D*.

5. C: Prey populations can develop different features to try and hide from and escape the predator population. The features help them blend into their environment, such as Choice *B*, or help them identify predators early and quickly, Choices *A* and *D*. Choice *C* would just allow the predators to hear the prey easily.

6. B: Sunlight comes into the greenhouse as short-wavelength IR. As it is absorbed by surfaces in the greenhouse, it is converted to long-wavelength IR. The long-wavelength IR gets trapped inside the greenhouse and bounces off the surfaces and glass and remains inside the greenhouse. Since short-wavelength IR can enter the greenhouse, it also has the ability to leave the greenhouse, making Choice *A* incorrect. The greenhouse feels warmer, not cooler, than outside, so Choice *C* is incorrect. Water is not involved in the reaction noted in Figure 1, so Choice *D* is also incorrect.

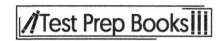

7. D: Looking at the graph in Figure 2, the greenhouse plant grew taller than the outside plant. The bars representing the greenhouse plant are taller at 3 time points that Scientist A measured. Greenhouses trap sunlight, warm air, and gases, such as CO_2 inside the greenhouse, so plants have an increased rate of photosynthesis, allowing them to grow faster. The plants are also protected from pests inside the greenhouse.

8. B: Sunlight enters the greenhouse as short-wavelength IR and gets converted to long-wavelength IR. This process also gives off heat and makes the greenhouse feel warmer than the outside climate. Water and oxygen, Choices *A* and *D*, are not involved in this reaction. The plants remain the same and do not get converted into anything else, Choice *C*.

9. A: Short-wavelength IR enters the greenhouse in the form of sunlight. It can pass easily through the glass and can therefore pass easily back out to the outside environment. The long-wavelength IR, Choice *D*, gets trapped inside the greenhouse.

10. C: The plants inside a greenhouse are protected from many pests that can be found in the outside environment. The air is warmer in the greenhouse, so Choice *A* is incorrect. More photosynthesis occurs because of the increased sunlight energy that stays in the greenhouse, making Choices *B* and *D* incorrect.

11. D: The equivalence point occurs when just enough of the unknown solution is added to completely neutralize the known solution. In Figure 1, at the halfway point of the curve, the equivalence point is when 25 volumes of NaOH have been added to the solution. The pH is 7 at this point also, which is a neutralization of the HCl, strong acid.

12. C: The acid dissociation constant is the pK_a of the solution. It is found at the halfway point between the beginning of the curve and the equivalence point, where the solution would have a pH of 7 and be completely neutralized. In Figure 3, it is marked as 4.76.

13. A: Looking at Figure 3, the vertical axis on the left side has information about the pH of the solution. The horizontal axis at the bottom has information about how much basic solution containing OH^- is being added to the acetic acid. When the OH^- is at 0, and none has been added yet, the pH of the acetic acid is marked as 2.

14. B: Looking at the chemical equation in Figure 2, the reactants are on the left side and the products are on the right side. HCl and NaOH, Choices *A* and *C*, are the reactants of the equation. NaCl is the salt that is formed as one of the products of the reaction. The chloride ion, Choice *D*, is not formed in this reaction.

15. A: The equivalence point occurs in all titration reactions when the solution is neutralized. If an acid and base are being titrated, the solution is no longer acidic or basic, Choices *B* and *C*. It reaches a pH of 7 and is considered neutral.

16. A: Oxygen-poor blood is pumped to the lungs before returning to the heart. Oxygen is transferred from the airways of the lungs into the blood. The blood becomes rich with oxygen and then returns to the heart so that it can bring oxygen and nutrients to other organs of the body, such as the brain, stomach, and kidney, Choices *B*, *C*, and *D*.

17. C: The mitral valve has two folds. The tricuspid valve, Choice *B*, has three folds. The valve between the left atrium and ventricle has two valves, as was noted in the descriptive passage. Correlating this

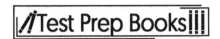

information to Figure 1, the name of the valve between these two chambers is the mitral valve. Choices A and D are vessels that carry blood through them and are not names of valves.

18. D: Arteries carry oxygen-rich blood away from the heart to the rest of the body. The aorta is the largest artery in the body. Veins, Choice A, carry oxygen-poor blood to the heart and lungs. Airway, Choice C, is found in the respiratory system and carries air in and out of the body.

19. C: A normal heartrate for a child is between 90 and 120 beats per minute. Choice C, 100 beats per minute, falls within this range. Choices A and D are within the normal range for an adult but not for a child. Children's hearts pump blood faster than adults' hearts through the body. Choice B, 125, is higher than the normal range for children.

20. B: Looking at Figure 1 and following the red arrow in the aorta backwards, the left ventricle is where the blood is coming from directly before it enters the aorta. Blood flows from the atria to the ventricles, so it enters the left atrium before the left ventricle and then the aorta, Choice D. Oxygen-poor blood is on the right side of the heart and flows from the right atrium to the right ventricle before flowing to the lungs to get re-oxygenated, Choices A and C.

21. C: Lava is a type of molten rock. When molten rock cools down and hardens, it forms igneous rock. Sedimentary and metamorphic rocks, Choices A and B, are not formed from molten rock. Choice D is incorrect because lava does cool down eventually and becomes hard.

22: A: Looking at Figure 1, the granite is found in column A. The description of the rocks in these columns says that these rocks were formed from molten rock. When molten rock cools, it forms igneous rock. Column C describes how metamorphic rocks are formed, Choice B. Column B describes how sedimentary rocks are formed, Choice C. Fossils, Choice D, are not rocks but are formed into sedimentary rock.

23: D: Sedimentary rocks are formed from soft materials, such as sand, shells, and pebbles. This allows for fossils to form because the remains of animals or plants can be pressed into the softer rock material and leave their imprint. Fossils cannot form in igneous, Choice A, or metamorphic, Choice C, rocks. Bones are something that can actually make a fossil imprint, Choice B.

24. B: Rocks that are formed by changes in heat and pressure are called metamorphic rocks, which is how the rocks in Column C are described. Slate is found in Column C of Figure 1. Sandstone and limestone, Choices A and D, are both found in Column B, which describes sedimentary rock. Granite, Choice B, is found in Column A, which describes sedimentary rock.

25. A: Sedimentary rock is formed from sand, shells, and pebbles, all of which are found in abundance at the beach. Shells, Choice B, are something that contribute to the formation of sedimentary rock. Igneous rock, Choice C, is formed from molten rock, which would likely be much too hot to be found on most beaches. The surface environment of a beach likely does not undergo changes in heat and pressure enough to form metamorphic rock, Choice D.

26. D: Helium gas is not one of the major direct or indirect greenhouse gases. Looking at Figure 2, Choices A, B, and C are part of the pie chart as greenhouse gases found in the atmosphere.

27. B: The two major wedges of the pie chart in Figure 3 are Transportation and Electricity. Using a car, Choice C, produces a lot of carbon dioxide. Walking instead of driving a car would not produce any

406

carbon dioxide. Choices *A* and *D* use electricity and leaving either the lights or the television on would need a constant source of electricity, producing lots of carbon dioxide.

28. A: Looking at Figure 2, carbon dioxide, Choice *D*, takes up the largest wedge of the pie chart at 54.7%. The next largest wedge is methane at 30%. Nitrous oxide, Choice *C*, takes up only 4.9% and fluorinated gases, Choice *B*, takes up 0.6%.

29. C: Looking at Figure 1, in the right picture where there are more greenhouse gases, the re-emitted heat arrow is larger as more heat gets trapped in the Earth's atmosphere. Space and the Sun, Choices *A* and *B*, remain outside the Earth's atmosphere. Water vapor, Choice *D*, is not a part of the diagrams for the greenhouse effect.

30. D: Figures 2 and 3 are pie charts. Circular charts that are broken up into wedges, or pie pieces, are called pie charts. Scatter plots, Choice *A*, have specific point markers to mark each data point. In line graphs, Choice *B*, data are represented by connecting lines. In bar graphs, Choice *C*, data are represented by vertical or horizontal bars.

31. A: An anemometer measures air speed. Wind is the movement of air, so an anemometer would be able to measure wind speed. A barometer, Choice *B*, measures air pressure. A thermometer, Choice *C*, measures temperature. A wind vane, Choice *D*, shows which direction the wind is blowing.

32. B: Figure 1 is a graph showing the temperature on different days. Temperature is measured using a thermometer. A rain gauge, Choice *A*, would allow a meteorologist to record amounts of rainfall. A barometer, Choice *C*, measures air pressure. An anemometer, Choice *D*, measures air speed.

33. C: A wind vane shows which direction the wind is blowing. If it is pointing north, the wind is blowing in a northern direction. It would not be blowing in an eastern direction, Choice *A*, or a southern direction, Choice *D*, since that is the opposite direction of north. A wind vane simply tells wind direction and does not determine whether a storm is coming, Choice *B*.

34. A: Looking at the line graph in Figure 2, the lowest point is marked for January, with approximately 2 mm of rainfall. April, Choice *B*, has approximately 23 mm rainfall, September, Choice *C*, has 10 mm of rainfall, and October, Choice *D*, has the highest rainfall at 60 mm.

35. D: Reading the graph in Figure 2, at June, the rainfall is approximately 20 mm. The trend line marks all of the data collected for each month. For June, the trend line is just about at the 20 mm mark from the vertical axis on the left side of the graph.

36. B: Plants use chloroplasts to turn light energy into glucose. Animal cells do not have this ability. Comparing Figures 1 and 2, chloroplasts can be found in the plant cell but not the animal cell.

37. C: The nucleolus is always located inside the nucleus. It contains important hereditary information about the cell that is critical for the reproductive process. Chloroplasts, Choice *A*, are only located in plant cells. It is not found in the mitochondria, Choice *B*, or attached to the cell membrane, Choice *D*.

38. A: Looking at the table in Figure 3, each organelle is described, and mitochondria is described as the powerhouse of the cell. The nucleus, Choice *B*, contains the cell's DNA. The ribosomes, Choice *C*, build proteins. The cell wall, Choice *D*, maintains the shape of plant cells and protects its contents.

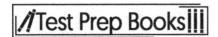

39. D: Figure 3 describes the functions of the organelles. The cell membrane surrounds the cell and regulates which molecules can move in and out of the cell. Ribosomes build proteins, Choice *A*. Lysosomes, Choice *B*, break down large molecules. The nucleus, Choice *C*, contains the cell's DNA.

40. C: Figure 3 describes the functions of the organelles. Chloroplasts are responsible for photosynthesis in plant cells, which is the process of converting sunlight energy to glucose energy. The cell wall helps maintain the cell's shape, Choice *A*. The nucleus contains the cell's DNA, Choice *B*. Ribosomes build proteins, Choice *D*.

ACT Practice Test #3

English

Questions 1–15 are based on the following passage:

The knowledge of an aircraft engineer is acquired through years of education, and special (1) licenses are required. Ideally, an individual will begin their preparation for the profession in high school (2) by taking chemistry physics trigonometry and calculus. Such curricula will aid in (3) one's pursuit of a bachelor's degree in aircraft engineering, which requires several physical and life sciences, mathematics, and design courses.

(4) Some of universities provide internship or apprentice opportunities for the students enrolled in aircraft engineer programs. A bachelor's in aircraft engineering is commonly accompanied by a master's degree in advanced engineering or business administration. Such advanced degrees enable an individual to position himself or herself for executive, faculty, and/or research opportunities. (5) These advanced offices oftentimes require a Professional Engineering (PE) license which can be obtained through additional college courses, professional experience, and acceptable scores on the Fundamentals of Engineering (FE) and Professional Engineering (PE) standardized assessments.

(6) Once the job begins, this lines of work requires critical thinking, business skills, problem solving, and creativity. This level of (7) expertise (8) allows aircraft engineers to (9) apply mathematical equation and scientific processes to aeronautical and aerospace issues or inventions. (10) For example, aircraft engineers may test, design, and construct flying vessels such as airplanes, space shuttles, and missile weapons. As a result, aircraft engineers are compensated with generous salaries. In fact, in May 2014, the lowest 10 percent of all American aircraft engineers earned less than $60,110 while the highest paid ten-percent of all American aircraft engineers earned $155,240. (11) In May 2015, the United States Bureau of Labor Statistics (BLS) reported that the median annual salary of aircraft engineers was $107,830. (12) Conversely, (13) employment opportunities for aircraft engineers are projected to decrease by 2 percent by 2024. This decrease may be the result of a decline in the manufacturing industry. (14) Nevertheless aircraft engineers who know how to utilize modeling and simulation programs, fluid dynamic software, and robotic engineering tools (15) is projected to remain the most employable.

1. Which of the following would be the best choice for this sentence (reproduced below)?

The knowledge of an aircraft engineer is acquired through years of education, and special (1) licenses are required.

a. NO CHANGE
b. licenses will be required
c. licenses may be required
d. licenses should be required

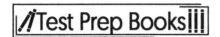

2. Which of the following would be the best choice for this sentence (reproduced below)?

Ideally, an individual will begin their preparation for the profession in high school (2) by taking chemistry physics trigonometry and calculus.

a. NO CHANGE
b. by taking chemistry; physics; trigonometry; and calculus.
c. by taking chemistry, physics, trigonometry, and calculus.
d. by taking chemistry, physics, trigonometry, calculus.

3. Which of the following would be the best choice for this sentence (reproduced below)?

Such curricula will aid in (3) one's pursuit of a bachelor's degree in aircraft engineering, which requires several physical and life sciences, mathematics, and design courses.

a. NO CHANGE
b. ones pursuit of a bachelors degree
c. one's pursuit of a bachelors degree
d. ones pursuit of a bachelor's degree

4. Which of the following would be the best choice for this sentence (reproduced below)?

(4) Some of universities provide internship or apprentice opportunities for the students enrolled in aircraft engineer programs.

a. NO CHANGE
b. Some of universities provided internship or apprentice opportunities
c. Some of universities provide internship or apprenticeship opportunities
d. Some universities provide internship or apprenticeship opportunities

5. Which of the following would be the best choice for this sentence (reproduced below)?

(5) These advanced offices oftentimes require a Professional Engineering (PE) license which can be obtained through additional college courses, professional experience, and acceptable scores on the Fundamentals of Engineering (FE) and Professional Engineering (PE) standardized assessments.

a. NO CHANGE
b. These advanced positions oftentimes require acceptable scores on the Fundamentals of Engineering (FE) and Professional Engineering (PE) standardized assessments in order to achieve a Professional Engineering (PE) license. Additional college courses and professional experience help.
c. These advanced offices oftentimes require acceptable scores on the Fundamentals of Engineering (FE) and Professional Engineering (PE) standardized assessments to gain the Professional Engineering (PE) license which can be obtained through additional college courses, professional experience.
d. These advanced positions oftentimes require a Professional Engineering (PE) license which is obtained by acceptable scores on the Fundamentals of Engineering (FE) and Professional Engineering (PE) standardized assessments. Further education and professional experience can help prepare for the assessments.

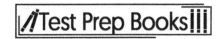

6. Which of the following would be the best choice for this sentence (reproduced below)?

(6) <u>Once the job begins, this lines of work</u> requires critical thinking, business skills, problem solving, and creativity.

a. NO CHANGE
b. Once the job begins, this line of work
c. Once the job begins, these line of work
d. Once the job begin, this line of work

7. Which of the following would be the best choice for this sentence (reproduced below)?

This level of (7) <u>expertise</u> allows aircraft engineers to apply mathematical equation and scientific processes to aeronautical and aerospace issues or inventions.

a. NO CHANGE
b. expertis
c. expirtise
d. excpertise

8. Which of the following would be the best choice for this sentence (reproduced below)?

This level of expertise (8) <u>allows</u> aircraft engineers to apply mathematical equation and scientific processes to aeronautical and aerospace issues or inventions.

a. NO CHANGE
b. Inhibits
c. Requires
d. Should

9. Which of the following would be the best choice for this sentence (reproduced below)?

This level of expertise allows aircraft engineers to (9) <u>apply mathematical equation and scientific processes</u> to aeronautical and aerospace issues or inventions.

a. NO CHANGE
b. apply mathematical equations and scientific process
c. apply mathematical equation and scientific process
d. apply mathematical equations and scientific processes

10. Which of the following would be the best choice for this sentence (reproduced below)?

(10) <u>For example,</u> aircraft engineers may test, design, and construct flying vessels such as airplanes, space shuttles, and missile weapons.

a. NO CHANGE
b. Therefore,
c. However,
d. Furthermore,

11. Which of the following would be the best choice for this sentence (reproduced below)?

(11) <u>In May 2015, the United States Bureau of Labor Statistics (BLS) reported that the median annual salary of aircraft engineers was $107,830.</u>

a. NO CHANGE
b. May of 2015, the United States Bureau of Labor Statistics (BLS) reported that the median annual salary of aircraft engineers was $107,830.
c. In May of 2015 the United States Bureau of Labor Statistics (BLS) reported that the median annual salary of aircraft engineers was $107,830.
d. In May, 2015, the United States Bureau of Labor Statistics (BLS) reported that the median annual salary of aircraft engineers was $107,830.

12. Which of the following would be the best choice for this sentence (reproduced below)?

(12) <u>Conversely,</u> employment opportunities for aircraft engineers are projected to decrease by 2 percent by 2024.

a. NO CHANGE
b. Similarly,
c. In other words,
d. Accordingly,

13. Which of the following would be the best choice for this sentence (reproduced below)?

Conversely, (13) <u>employment opportunities for aircraft engineers are projected to decrease by 2 percent by 2024.</u>

a. NO CHANGE
b. employment opportunities for aircraft engineers will be projected to decrease by 2 percent by 2024.
c. employment opportunities for aircraft engineers is projected to decrease by 2 percent by 2024.
d. employment opportunities for aircraft engineers was projected to decrease by 2 percent by 2024.

14. Which of the following would be the best choice for this sentence (reproduced below)?

(14) <u>Nevertheless aircraft engineers who know how to utilize</u> modeling and simulation programs, fluid dynamic software, and robotic engineering tools is projected to remain the most employable.

a. NO CHANGE
b. Nevertheless; aircraft engineers who know how to utilize
c. Nevertheless, aircraft engineers who know how to utilize
d. Nevertheless—aircraft engineers who know how to utilize

15. Which of the following would be the best choice for this sentence (reproduced below)?

Nevertheless aircraft engineers who know how to utilize modeling and simulation programs, fluid dynamic software, and robotic engineering tools (15) is projected to remain the most employable.

a. NO CHANGE
b. am projected to remain
c. was projected to remain
d. are projected to remain

Questions 16–30 are based on the following passage:

On September 11th, 2001, a group of terrorists hijacked four American airplanes. The terrorists crashed the planes into the World Trade Center in New York City, the Pentagon in Washington D.C., and a field in Pennsylvania. Nearly 3,000 people died during the attacks, which propelled the United States into a (16) "War on Terror".

About the Terrorists

(17) Terrorists commonly uses fear and violence to achieve political goals. The nineteen terrorists who orchestrated and implemented the attacks of September 11th were militants associated with al-Qaeda, an Islamic extremist group founded by Osama bin Laden, Abdullah Azzam, and others in the late 1980s. (18) Bin Laden orchestrated the attacks as a response to what he felt was American injustice against Islam and hatred towards Muslims. In his words, "Terrorism against America deserves to be praised."

Islam is the religion of Muslims, (19) who live mainly in south and southwest Asia and Sub-Saharan Africa. The majority of Muslims practice Islam peacefully. However, fractures in Islam have led to the growth of Islamic extremists who strictly oppose Western influences. They seek to institute stringent Islamic law and destroy those who violate Islamic code.

In November 2002, bin Laden provided the explicit motives for the 9/11 terror attacks. According to this list, (20) Americas support of Israel, military presence in Saudi Arabia, and other anti-Muslim actions were the causes.

The Timeline of the Attacks

The morning of September 11 began like any other for most Americans. Then, at 8:45 a.m., a Boeing 767 plane (21) crashed into the north tower of the World Trade Center in New York City. Hundreds were instantly killed. Others were trapped on higher floors. The crash was initially thought to be a freak accident. When a second plane flew directly into the south tower eighteen minutes later, it was determined that America was under attack.

At 9:45 a.m., (22) slamming into the Pentagon was a third plane, America's military headquarters in Washington D.C. The jet fuel of this plane caused a major fire and partial building collapse that resulted in nearly 200 deaths. By 10:00 a.m., the south tower of the World Trade Center collapsed. Thirty minutes later, the north tower followed suit.

While this was happening, a fourth plane that departed from New Jersey, United Flight 93, was hijacked. The passengers learned of the attacks that occurred in New York and Washington D.C. and realized that they faced the same fate as the other planes that crashed. The passengers were determined to overpower the terrorists in an effort to prevent the deaths of additional innocent American citizens. Although the passengers were successful in (23) diverging the plane, it crashed in a western Pennsylvania field and killed everyone on board. The plane's final target remains uncertain, (24) but believed by many people was the fact that United Flight 93 was heading for the White House.

Heroes and Rescuers

(25) Close to 3,000 people died in the World Trade Center attacks. This figure includes 343 New York City firefighters and paramedics, 23 New York City police officers, and 37 Port Authority officers. Nevertheless, thousands of men and women in service worked (26) valiantly to evacuate the buildings, save trapped workers, extinguish infernos, uncover victims trapped in fallen rubble, and tend to nearly 10,000 injured individuals.

About 300 rescue dogs played a major role in the after-attack salvages. Working twelve-hour shifts, the dogs scoured the rubble and alerted paramedics when they found signs of life. While doing so, the dogs served as a source of comfort and therapy for the rescue teams.

Initial Impacts on America

The attacks of September 11, 2001 resulted in the immediate suspension of all air travel. No flights could take off from or land on American soil. (27) American airports and airspace closed to all national and international flights. Therefore, over five hundred flights had to turn back or be redirected to other countries. Canada alone received 226 flights and thousands of stranded passengers. (28) Needless to say, as cancelled flights are rescheduled, air travel became backed up and chaotic for quite some time.

At the time of the attacks, George W. Bush was the president of the United States. President Bush announced that "We will make no distinction between the terrorists who committed these acts and those who harbor them." The rate of hate crimes against American Muslims spiked, despite President Bush's call for the country to treat them with respect.

Additionally, relief funds were quickly arranged. The funds were used to support families of the victims, orphaned children, and those with major injuries. In this way, the tragic event brought the citizens together through acts of service towards those directly impacted by the attack.

Long-Term Effects of the Attacks

Over the past fifteen years, the attacks of September 11th have transformed the United States' government, travel safety protocols, and international relations. Anti-terrorism legislation became a priority for many countries as law enforcement and intelligence agencies teamed up to find and defeat alleged terrorists.

Present George W. Bush announced a War on Terror. He (29) <u>desired</u> to bring bin Laden and al-Qaeda to justice and prevent future terrorist networks from gaining strength. The War in Afghanistan began in October of 2001 when the United States and British forces bombed al-Qaeda camps. (30) <u>The Taliban, a group of fundamental Muslims who protected Osama bin Laden, was overthrown on December 9, 2001. However, the war continued in order to defeat insurgency campaigns in neighboring countries.</u> Ten years later, the United State Navy SEALS killed Osama bin Laden in Pakistan. During 2014, the United States declared the end of its involvement in the War on Terror in Afghanistan.

Museums and memorials have since been erected to honor and remember the thousands of people who died during the September 11th attacks, including the brave rescue workers who gave their lives in the effort to help others.

16. Which of the following would be the best choice for this sentence (reproduced below)?

Nearly 3,000 people died during the attacks, which propelled the United States into a (16) <u>"War on Terror"</u>.

a. NO CHANGE
b. "war on terror".
c. "war on terror."
d. "War on Terror."

17. Which of the following would be the best choice for this sentence (reproduced below)?

(17) <u>Terrorists commonly uses fear and violence to achieve political goals.</u>

a. NO CHANGE
b. Terrorist's commonly use fear and violence to achieve political goals.
c. Terrorists commonly use fear and violence to achieve political goals.
d. Terrorists commonly use fear and violence to achieves political goals.

18. Which of the following would be the best choice for this sentence (reproduced below)?

(18) <u>Bin Laden orchestrated the attacks as a response to what he felt was American injustice against Islam and hatred towards Muslims.</u>

a. NO CHANGE
b. Bin Laden orchestrated the attacks as a response to what he felt was American injustice against Islam, and hatred towards Muslims.
c. Bin Laden orchestrated the attacks, as a response to what he felt was American injustice against Islam and hatred towards Muslims.
d. Bin Laden orchestrated the attacks as responding to what he felt was American injustice against Islam and hatred towards Muslims.

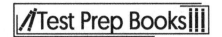

19. Which of the following would be the best choice for this sentence (reproduced below)?

Islam is the religion of Muslims, (19) who live mainly in south and southwest Asia and Sub-Saharan Africa.

a. NO CHANGE
b. who live mainly in the South and Southwest Asia
c. who live mainly in the south and Southwest Asia
d. who live mainly in the south and southwest asia

20. Which of the following would be the best choice for this sentence (reproduced below)?

According to this list, (20) Americas support of Israel, military presence in Saudi Arabia, and other anti-Muslim actions were the causes.

a. NO CHANGE
b. America's support of israel,
c. Americas support of Israel
d. America's support of Israel,

21. Which of the following would be the best choice for this sentence (reproduced below)?

Then, at 8:45 a.m., a Boeing 767 plane (21) crashed into the north tower of the World Trade Center in New York City.

a. NO CHANGE
b. crashes into the north tower of the World Trade Center
c. crashing into the north tower of the World Trade Center
d. crash into the north tower of the World Trade Center

22. Which of the following would be the best choice for this sentence (reproduced below)?

At 9:45 a.m., (22) slamming into the Pentagon was a third plane, America's military headquarters in Washington D.C.

a. NO CHANGE
b. into the Pentagon slammed a third plane,
c. a third plane slammed into the Pentagon,
d. the Pentagon was slamming by a third plane,

23. Which of the following would be the best choice for this sentence (reproduced below)?

Although the passengers were successful in (23) diverging the plane, it crashed in a western Pennsylvania field and killed everyone on board.

a. NO CHANGE
b. Diverting
c. Converging
d. Distracting

416

24. Which of the following would be the best choice for this sentence (reproduced below)?

The plane's final target remains uncertain, (24) but believed by many people was the fact that United Flight 93 was heading for the White House.

a. NO CHANGE
b. but many believe that United Flight 93 was heading for the White House.
c. also heading for the white house United Flight 93 was believed to be.
d. then many believe that United Flight 93 was heading for the White House.

25. Which of the following would be the best choice for this sentence (reproduced below)?

(25) Close to 3,000 people died in the World Trade Center attacks.

a. NO CHANGE
b. 3,000 people in the World Trade Center attacks died.
c. Dying in the World Trade Center attacks were around 3,000 people.
d. In the World Trade Center attacks were around 3,000 people dying.

26. Which of the following would be the best choice for this sentence (reproduced below)?

Nevertheless, thousands of men and women in service worked (26) valiantly to evacuate the buildings, save trapped workers, extinguish infernos, uncover victims trapped in fallen rubble, and tend to nearly 10,000 injured individuals.

a. NO CHANGE
b. valiently
c. valently
d. vanlyantly

27. Which of the following would be the best choice for this sentence (reproduced below)?

(27) American airports and airspace closed to all national and international flights.

a. NO CHANGE
b. American airports and airspace close to all national and international flights.
c. American airports and airspaces closed to all national and international flights.
d. American airspace and airports were closed to all national and international flights.

417

28. Which of the following would be the best choice for this sentence (reproduced below)?

(28) Needless to say, <u>as cancelled flights are rescheduled, air travel became backed up and chaotic for quite some time.</u>

a. NO CHANGE
b. As cancelled flights are rescheduled, air travel became backed up and chaotic for quite some time.
c. Needless to say, as cancelled flights were rescheduled, air travel became backed up and chaotic for quite some time.
d. Needless to say, as cancelled flights are rescheduled, air travel became backed up and chaotic over a period of time.

29. Which of the following would be the best choice for this sentence (reproduced below)?

He (29) <u>desired</u> to bring bin Laden and al-Qaeda to justice and prevent future terrorist networks from gaining strength.

a. NO CHANGE
b. Perceived
c. Intended
d. Assimilated

30. Which of the following would be the best choice for this sentence (reproduced below)?

(30) <u>The Taliban, a group of fundamental Muslims who protected Osama bin Laden, was overthrown on December 9, 2001. However, the war continued in order to defeat insurgency campaigns in neighboring countries.</u>

a. NO CHANGE
b. The Taliban was overthrown on December 9, 2001. They were a group of fundamental Muslims who protected Osama bin Laden. However, the war continued in order to defeat insurgency campaigns in neighboring countries.
c. The Taliban, a group of fundamental Muslims who protected Osama bin Laden, on December 9, 2001 was overthrown. However, the war continued in order to defeat insurgency campaigns in neighboring countries.
d. Osama bin Laden's fundamental Muslims who protected him were called the Taliban and overthrown on December 9, 2001. Yet the war continued in order to defeat the insurgency campaigns in neighboring countries.

Questions 31–46 are based on the following passage:

(31) <u>Seeing a lasting social change for African American people Fred Hampton desired to see</u> through nonviolent means and community recognition. (32) <u>As a result, he became an African American activist</u> during the American Civil Rights Movement and led the Chicago chapter of the Black Panther Party.

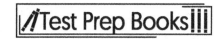

Hampton's Education

(33) <u>Born and raised in Maywood of Chicago, Illinois in 1948 was Hampton.</u> (34) <u>He was gifted academically and a natural athlete,</u> he became a stellar baseball player in high school. (35) <u>After graduating from Proviso East High School in 1966, he later went on to study law at Triton Junior College.</u>

While studying at Triton, Hampton joined and became a leader of the National Association for the Advancement of Colored People (NAACP). (36) <u>The NAACP gained more than 500 members resulting from his membership.</u> Hampton worked relentlessly to establish recreational facilities in the Maywood neighborhood and improve the educational resources provided to the impoverished black community.

The Black Panthers

The Black Panther Party (BPP) was another activist group that formed around the same time as the NAACP. Hampton was quickly attracted to the Black Panther's approach to the fight for equal rights for African Americans. (37) <u>Hampton eventually joined the chapter, and relocated</u> to downtown Chicago to be closer to its headquarters.

His charismatic personality, organizational abilities, sheer determination, and rhetorical skills enabled him to (38) <u>quickly risen</u> through the chapter's ranks. (39) <u>Hampton soon became the leader of the Chicago chapter of the BPP where he organized rallies, taught political education classes, and established a free medical clinic.</u> He also took part in the community police supervision project and played an instrumental role in the BPP breakfast program for impoverished African American children.

(40) <u>Leading the BPP Hampton's greatest achievement</u> may be his fight against street gang violence in Chicago. In 1969, (41) <u>Hampton was held by a press conference</u> where he made the gangs agree to a nonaggression pact known as the Rainbow Coalition. As a result of the pact, a multiracial alliance between blacks, Puerto Ricans, and poor youth was developed.

Assassination

As the Black Panther Party's popularity and influence grew, the Federal Bureau of Investigation (FBI) placed the group under constant surveillance. In an attempt to (42) <u>neutralize</u> the party, the FBI launched several harassment campaigns against the BPP, raided its headquarters in Chicago three times, and arrested over one hundred of the group's members. (43) <u>During such a raid that occurred Hampton was shot</u> on the morning of December 4th 1969.

In 1976, seven years after the event, it was revealed that William O'Neal, Hampton's trusted bodyguard, was an undercover FBI agent. (44) <u>O'Neal provided the FBI with detailed</u> floor plans of the BPP's headquarters, identifying the exact location of Hampton's bed. (45) <u>It was because of these floor plans that the police were able to target and kill Hampton.</u>

419

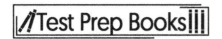

The assassination of Hampton fueled outrage amongst the African American community. It was not until years after the assassination that the police admitted wrongdoing. The Chicago City Council now (46) commemorates December 4th as Fred Hampton Day.

31. Which of the following would be the best choice for this sentence (reproduced below)?

(31) Seeing a lasting social change for African American people Fred Hampton desired to see through nonviolent means and community recognition.

a. NO CHANGE
b. Desiring to see a lasting social change for African American people, Fred Hampton
c. Fred Hampton desired to see lasting social change for African American people
d. Fred Hampton desiring to see last social change for African American people

32. Which of the following would be the best choice for this sentence (reproduced below)?

(32) As a result, he became an African American activist during the American Civil Rights Movement and led the Chicago chapter of the Black Panther Party.

a. NO CHANGE
b. As a result he became an African American activist
c. As a result: he became an African American activist
d. As a result of, he became an African American activist

33. Which of the following would be the best choice for this sentence (reproduced below)?

(33) Born and raised in Maywood of Chicago, Illinois in 1948 was Hampton.

a. NO CHANGE
b. Hampton was born and raised in Maywood of Chicago, Illinois in 1948.
c. Hampton is born and raised in Maywood of Chicago, Illinois in 1948.
d. Hampton was born and raised in Maywood of Chicago Illinois in 1948.

34. Which of the following would be the best choice for this sentence (reproduced below)?

(34) He was gifted academically and a natural athlete, he became a stellar baseball player in high school.

a. NO CHANGE
b. A natural athlete and gifted though he was,
c. A natural athlete, and gifted,
d. Gifted academically and a natural athlete,

35. Which of the following would be the best choice for this sentence (reproduced below)?

(35) After graduating from Proviso East High School in 1966, he later went on to study law at Triton Junior College.

420

a. NO CHANGE

b. He later went on to study law at Triton Junior College graduating from Proviso East High School in 1966.

c. Graduating from Proviso East High School and Triton Junior College went to study.

d. Later at Triton Junior College, studying law, from Proviso East High School in 1966.

36. Which of the following would be the best choice for this sentence (reproduced below)?

(36) The NAACP gained more than 500 members resulting from his membership.

a. NO CHANGE

b. A gain of 500 members happened to the NAACP due to his membership.

c. As a result of his leadership, the NAACP gained more than 500 members.

d. 500 members were gained due to his NAACP membership.

37. Which of the following would be the best choice for this sentence (reproduced below)?

(37) Hampton eventually joined the chapter, and relocated to downtown Chicago to be closer to its headquarters.

a. NO CHANGE

b. Hampton eventually joined the chapter; and relocated to downtown Chicago to be closer to its headquarters.

c. Hampton eventually joined the chapter relocated to downtown Chicago to be closer to its headquarters.

d. Hampton eventually joined the chapter and relocated to downtown Chicago to be closer to its headquarters.

38. Which of the following would be the best choice for this sentence (reproduced below)?

His charismatic personality, organizational abilities, sheer determination, and rhetorical skills enabled him to (38) quickly risen through the chapter's ranks.

a. NO CHANGE

b. quickly rise

c. quickly rose

d. quickly rosed

39. Which of the following would be the best choice for this sentence (reproduced below)?

(39) Hampton soon became the leader of the Chicago chapter of the BPP where he organized rallies, taught political education classes, and established a free medical clinic.

a. NO CHANGE

b. As the leader of the BPP, Hampton: organized rallies, taught political education classes, and established a free medical clinic.

c. As the leader of the BPP, Hampton; organized rallies, taught political education classes, and established a free medical clinic.

d. As the leader of the BPP, Hampton—organized rallies, taught political education classes, and established a medical free clinic.

40. Which of the following would be the best choice for this sentence (reproduced below)?

(40) <u>Leading the BPP Hampton's greatest achievement</u> may be his fight against street gang violence in Chicago.

a. NO CHANGE
b. Greatest achievement of Hampton leading the BPP
c. Hampton's greatest achievement as the leader of the BPP
d. Leader of the BPP Hampton and greatest achievement

41. Which of the following would be the best choice for this sentence (reproduced below)?

In 1969, (41) <u>Hampton was held by a press conference</u> where he made the gangs agree to a nonaggression pact known as the Rainbow Coalition.

a. NO CHANGE
b. a press conference held Hampton
c. held by a press conference was Hampton
d. Hampton held a press conference

42. Which of the following would be the best choice for this sentence (reproduced below)?

In an attempt to (42) <u>neutralize</u> the party, the FBI launched several harassment campaigns against the BPP, raided its headquarters in Chicago three times, and arrested over one hundred of the group's members.

a. NO CHANGE
b. Accommodate
c. Assuage
d. Praise

43. Which of the following would be the best choice for this sentence (reproduced below)?

(43) <u>During such a raid that occurred Hampton was shot</u> on the morning of December 4th 1969.

a. NO CHANGE
b. A raid, occurring because Hampton was shot
c. Hampton was shot during such a raid that occurred
d. Such a raid that occurred, Hampton was shot at

44. Which of the following would be the best choice for this sentence (reproduced below)?

(44) <u>O'Neal provided the FBI with detailed</u> floor plans of the BPP's headquarters, identifying the exact location of Hampton's bed.

a. NO CHANGE
b. O'Neal is providing
c. O'Neal provides
d. O'Neal provided

45. Which of the following would be the best choice for this sentence (reproduced below)?

(45) It was because of these floor plans that the police were able to target and kill Hampton.

a. NO CHANGE
b. These floor plans made it possible for the police to target and kill Hampton.
c. For the police to target and kill Hampton, these floor plans made it possible.
d. These floor plans make it possible for the police to target and kill Hampton.

46. Which of the following would be the best choice for this sentence (reproduced below)?

The Chicago City Council now (46) commemorates December 4th as Fred Hampton Day.

a. NO CHANGE
b. disparages
c. exculpates
d. brandishes

Questions 47–60 are based on the following passage:

A flood occurs when an area of land that is normally dry becomes submerged with water. Floods have affected Earth since the (47) beginning of time, and are caused by many different factors. Flooding can occur slowly or within seconds and can submerge small regions or extend over vast areas of land. Their impact on society and the environment can be harmful or helpful.

What Causes Flooding?

Floods may be caused by natural phenomenon, induced by the activities of humans and other animals, or the failure of an infrastructure. (48) Areas located near bodies of water are prone to flooding as are low-lying regions.

Global warming is the result of air pollution (49) that prevents the suns radiation from being emitted back into space. Instead, the radiation is trapped in Earth and results in global warming. The warming of the Earth has resulted in climate changes. As a result, floods have been occurring with increasing regularity. Some claim that the increased temperatures on Earth may cause the icebergs to melt. They fear that the melting of icebergs will cause the (50) oceans levels to rise and flood coastal regions.

Most commonly, flooding is caused by excessive rain. The ground is not able to absorb all the water produced by a sudden heavy rainfall or rainfall that occurs over a prolonged period of time. Such rainfall (51) may cause to overflow the water in rivers and other bodies of water. The excess water can cause dams to break. Such events can cause flooding of the surrounding riverbanks or coastal regions.

Flash flooding can occur without warning and without rainfall. Flash floods may be caused by a river being blocked by (52) a glacier; avalanche; landslide; logjam; a beaver's obstruction; construction; or dam. Water builds behind such a blockage. Eventually, the mass and force of the built-up water become so extreme that it causes the obstruction to break. Thus, enormous amounts of water rush out towards the surrounding areas.

423

Areal or urban flooding occurs because the land has become hardened. The hardening of land may result from urbanization or drought. Either way, the hardened land prevents water from seeping into the ground. Instead, the water resides on top of the land.

(53) <u>Finally, flooding may result after severe hurricanes, tsunamis, then tropical cyclones.</u> Local defenses and infrastructures are no matches for the tidal surges and waves caused by these natural phenomena. Such events are bound to result in the flooding of nearby coastal regions or estuaries.

A Flood's After-Effects

Flooding can result in severe devastation of nearby areas. Flash floods and tsunamis can result in sweeping waters that travel at destructive speeds. Fast-moving water has the power to demolish all obstacles in its path such as homes, trees, bridges, and buildings. Animals, plants, and humans may all lose their lives during a flood.

Floods can also cause pollution and infection. Sewage may seep from drains or septic tanks and contaminate drinking water or surrounding lands. Similarly, toxins, fuels, debris from annihilated buildings, and other hazardous materials can leave water unusable for consumption. (54) <u>As the water begins to drain, mold may begin to grow.</u> As a result, residents of flooded areas may be left without power, drinkable water, or be exposed to toxins and other diseases.

(55) <u>Although often associated with devastation, not all flooding results</u> in adverse circumstances. (56) <u>For thousands of years, people have inhabited floodplains of rivers.</u> (57) <u>Examples include the Mississippi Valley of the United States, the Nile River in Egypt, and the Tigris River of the Middle East</u>. The flooding of such rivers (58) <u>caused</u> nutrient-rich silts to be deposited on the floodplains. Thus, after the floods recede, an extremely fertile soil is left behind. This soil is conducive to the agriculture of bountiful crops and has sustained the diets of humans for millennium.

Proactive Measures Against Flooding

Technologies now allow scientists to predict where and when flooding is likely to occur. Such technologies can also be used (59) <u>to project</u> the severity of an anticipated flood. In this way, local inhabitants can be warned and take preventative measures such as boarding up their homes, gathering necessary provisions, and moving themselves and their possessions to higher grounds.

The (60) <u>picturesque</u> views of coastal regions and rivers have long enticed people to build near such locations. Due to the costs associated with the repairs needed after the flooding of such residencies, many governments now require inhabitants of flood-prone areas to purchase flood insurance and build flood-resistant structures. Pictures of all items within a building or home should be taken so that proper reimbursement for losses can be made in the event that a flood does occur.

Staying Safe During a Flood

If a forecasted flood does occur, (60) <u>so people</u> should retreat to higher ground such as a mountain or roof. Flooded waters may be contaminated, contain hidden debris, or travel at high speeds. Therefore, people should not attempt to walk or drive through a flooded area. To prevent electrocution, electrical outlets and downed power lines need to be avoided.

The Flood Dries Up

Regardless of the type or cause of a flood, floods can result in detrimental alterations to nearby lands and serious injuries to nearby inhabitants. By understanding flood cycles, civilizations can learn to take advantage of flood seasons. By taking the proper precautionary measures, people can stay safe when floods occur. Thus, proper knowledge can lead to safety and prosperity during such an adverse natural phenomenon.

47. Which of the following would be the best choice for this sentence (reproduced below)?

Floods have affected Earth since the (47) <u>beginning of time, and are caused</u> by many different factors.

a. NO CHANGE
b. beginning of time and are causing
c. beginning of time so to cause
d. beginning of time and are caused

48. Which of the following would be the best choice for this sentence (reproduced below)?

(48) <u>Areas located near bodies of water are prone to flooding as are low-lying regions.</u>

a. NO CHANGE
b. Low-lying regions are prone to flooding, areas located near bodies of water are prone to flooding.
c. Areas located near bodies of water are prone to flooding, as are low-lying regions.
d. Near bodies of water are areas that are prone to flooding and areas near low-lying regions are prone to flooding.

49. Which of the following would be the best choice for this sentence (reproduced below)?

Global warming is the result of air pollution (49) <u>that prevents the suns radiation</u> from being emitted back into space.

a. NO CHANGE
b. that which prevents the sun's radiation
c. the sun's radiation being prevented
d. that prevents the sun's radiation

50. Which of the following would be the best choice for this sentence (reproduced below)?

They fear that the melting of icebergs will cause the (50) oceans levels to rise and flood coastal regions.

a. NO CHANGE
b. ocean levels
c. ocean's levels
d. levels of the oceans

51. Which of the following would be the best choice for this sentence (reproduced below)?

Such rainfall (51) may cause to overflow the water in rivers and other bodies of water.

a. NO CHANGE
b. may been causing the rivers and other bodies of water to overflow.
c. may cause the rivers and other bodies of water to overflow.
d. may cause other bodies of water and water in rivers to overflow.

52. Which of the following would be the best choice for this sentence (reproduced below)?

Flash floods may be caused by a river being blocked by (52) a glacier; avalanche; landslide; logjam; a beaver's obstruction; construction; or dam.

a. NO CHANGE
b. a glacier avalanche landslide logjam a beaver's obstruction construction or dam.
c. a glacier, avalanche, landslide, logjam, a beavers obstruction, construction, or dam.
d. a glacier, avalanche, landslide, logjam, a beaver's obstruction, construction, or dam.

53. Which of the following would be the best choice for this sentence (reproduced below)?

(53) Finally, flooding may result after severe hurricanes, tsunamis, then tropical cyclones.

a. NO CHANGE
b. Finally, flooding may result after severe hurricanes, tsunamis, or tropical cyclones.
c. Finally, flooding may result after severe hurricanes, tsunamis, so tropical cyclones.
d. Finally, flooding may result after severe hurricanes, tsunamis, but tropical cyclones.

54. Which of the following would be the best choice for this sentence (reproduced below)?

(54) As the water begins to drain, mold may begin to grow.

a. NO CHANGE
b. As the waters begins to drain, mold may begin to grow.
c. Mold may begin grow as the water begins to drain.
d. The water will begin to drain and mold will begin to grow.

426

55. Which of the following would be the best choice for this sentence (reproduced below)?

(55) Although often associated with devastation, not all flooding results in adverse circumstances.

a. NO CHANGE
b. Although often associated with devastation not all flooding results
c. Although often associated with devastation. Not all flooding results
d. While often associated with devastation, not all flooding results

56. Which of the following would be the best choice for this sentence (reproduced below)?

(56) For thousands of years, people have inhabited floodplains of rivers.

a. NO CHANGE
b. For thousands of years, people have inhabited river floodplains.
c. For thousands of years people have inhabited river floodplains.
d. For thousand's of years, people have inhabited floodplains of rivers.

57. Which of the following would be the best choice for this sentence (reproduced below)?

(57) Examples include the Mississippi Valley of the United States, the Nile River in Egypt, and the Tigris River of the Middle East.

a. NO CHANGE
b. Examples of floodplains include the Mississippi Valley of the United States, the Nile River in Egypt, and the Tigris River of the Middle East.
c. Examples include the Mississippi Valley of the United States . . . the Nile River in Egypt . . . and the Tigris River of the Middle East.
d. Examples of floodplains include the Mississippi Valley of the United States the Nile River in Egypt and the Tigris River of the Middle East.

58. Which of the following would be the best choice for this sentence (reproduced below)?

The flooding of such rivers (58) caused nutrient-rich silts to be deposited on the floodplains.

a. NO CHANGE
b. Cause
c. Causing
d. Causes

59. Which of the following would be the best choice for this sentence (reproduced below)?

Such technologies can also be used (59) to project the severity of an anticipated flood.

a. NO CHANGE
b. Projecting
c. Project
d. Projected

427

60. Which of the following would be the best choice for this sentence (reproduced below)?

If a forecasted flood does occur, (60) so people should retreat to higher ground such as a mountain or roof.

a. NO CHANGE
b. then people
c. and people
d. for people

Questions 61–75 are based on the following passage:

In (61) "The Odyssey," Odysseus develops out of his experiences and the people he meets along his journey home. Many of his encounters involve female characters, some of whom offer Odysseus aid in his journey. (62) However, several of these characters deceive and even pose great danger to the hero. (63) This makes his journey home harder, it forces Odysseus himself to change and adapt in order to deal with the challenges. (64) For the time Odysseus reaches home, he has become notably distrustful of women and even those who have true intentions. It is this sense of caution that ultimately serves Odysseus in successfully defeating the suitors of Penelope upon his return home.

Odysseus would not have been able to defeat the suitors without stealth and deception. He had (65) to conceal himself in order to achieve revenge. This is something we see earlier in Odysseus' encounter with Polyphemus the Cyclops. While not female, Polyphemus displayed feminine qualities characterized by his "womb-like cave." (66) Entering into the dwelling Odysseus directly demanded hospitality Polyphemus instead butchered his men in spite of custom. In order to survive the encounter, Odysseus (67) relinquishes his true identity by telling Polyphemus his name is "Nobody." After the carnage of his men, he does not entrust the Cyclops with his true name. Rather, Odysseus uses disguise and cunning to trick Polyphemus into reopening the cave. When he emerges, he is then reborn again as "Odysseus."

This pattern is echoed again when Odysseus reaches Ithaca: "I look for endless ground to be spattered by the blood and brains of the suitors, these men who are eating all your substance away. But come now, let me make you so that no mortal can recognize you." Here, Athena reveals her plan to disguise Odysseus as he makes his move against the suitors. Why would Odysseus embrace the idea? With Polyphemus, Odysseus entered the cave trusting he would be received as a welcomed guest, but he wasn't. (68) Clearly, Odysseus isn't making the same mistake twice in trusting people to automatically abide by custom. Using a disguise allows Odysseus to apply strategy in a similar manner he had with Polyphemus. (69) This passage specifically described the suitors as eating away at Odysseus' substance, seeming to further the parallel with Polyphemus who devoured Odysseus' men. (70) Also like with Polyphemus, Odysseus only reveals his true identity when he knows his plan has succeeded. The disguise concept presents a strategic role, but it also sheds further light on the impact of Odysseus' travels. To conceal (71) ones identity is to withhold trust.

428

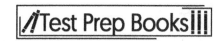

The Circe episode matches Odysseus against someone he already knows to be untrustworthy. It is known that Circe welcomes all men who (72) enter upon her island with food and drink, but this is a deception meant to ensnare them. This xenia, or hospitality, that Odysseus would have been accustomed to, turns out to be farce. She violates the trust of her guests by turning them into swine, thus making her a deceitful host and a woman Odysseus cannot trust. In order to (73) assure his and the crew's safety, Odysseus must look past her empty courtesy and deceive her in a way that will remedy the situation. With the knowledge of Circe's dark intentions (and Hermes' instructions), Odysseus attempts to out-maneuver Circe by making her think he will kill her. By doing this, he is taking on deceitful qualities so as to ensure he can bend her to proper behavior, which works. Still untrusting of Circe's submission, Odysseus makes her swear a formal oath: "I would not be willing to go to bed with you unless you can bring yourself, O goddess, to swear me a great oath that there is no other evil hurt you devise against me" (10:342-344). Even though Odysseus tames Circe, he is still distrustful. The oath becomes a final assurance that she is sincere. Until he knows for certain that no more treachery can befall him (the oath), he does not partake in showing any form of trust.

In the Land of the Dead, Odysseus encounters Agamemnon, who describes his own murder at the hand of his wife, Klytaimestra. Not only is this an example of a wife's betrayal, but a betrayal that appears close to Odysseus' own situation. Like Agamemnon, Odysseus (74) is returning home to his wife. However, Agamemnon didn't realize his wife had foul intentions, he trusted her to receive him with open arms:

> See, I had been thinking that I would be welcome to my children and thralls of my household when I came home, but she with thoughts surpassing grisly splashed the shame on herself and on the rest of her sex, on women still to come, even on the one whose acts are virtuous.

Clearly this is a cautionary story for Odysseus. After telling Odysseus of Klytaimestra's betrayal, Agamemnon warns Odysseus that all women are inherently distrustful. By this time, Odysseus has already been deceived and nearly killed by female/female-like characters. Agamemnon's logic seems to back up what he already experienced. (75) As the text progresses, Odysseus encounters the Sirens and Calypso, who seem to corroborate the idea that women are bad news. However, what is most impressionable on Odysseus is Agamemnon's distrust of even virtuous women, "even on the one whose acts are virtuous." Who is to say that they cannot turn against him like Klytaimestra did against Agamemnon. This seems to cement in Odysseus a fear of betrayal.

61. Which of the following would be the best choice for this sentence (reproduced below)?

In (61) "The Odyssey," Odysseus develops out of his experiences and the people he meets along his journey home.

a. NO CHANGE
b. 'The Odyssey'
c. *The Odyssey*
d. The Odyssey

62. Which of the following would be the best choice for this sentence (reproduced below)?

(62) <u>However, several of these</u> characters deceive and even pose great danger to the hero.

   a. NO CHANGE
   b. However these
   c. However several of these
   d. Several of these

63. Which of the following would be the best choice for this sentence (reproduced below)?

(63) <u>This makes his journey home harder, it forces Odysseus himself to change and adapt</u> in order to deal with the challenges.

   a. NO CHANGE
   b. This makes his journey home harder it forces Odysseus himself to change and adapt
   c. This makes his journey home harder which forces Odysseus to change and adapt
   d. This makes his journey home harder, forcing Odysseus to change and adapt

64. Which of the following would be the best choice for this sentence (reproduced below)?

(64) <u>For the time Odysseus reaches home,</u> he has become notably distrustful of women and even those who have true intentions.

   a. NO CHANGE
   b. When the time Odysseus reaches home,
   c. By the time Odysseus reaches home,
   d. At the time Odysseus reaches home,

65. Which of the following would be the best choice for this sentence (reproduced below)?

He had (65) <u>to conceal</u> himself in order to achieve revenge.

   a. NO CHANGE
   b. To be concealed
   c. Conceals
   d. Concealing

66. Which of the following would be the best choice for this sentence (reproduced below)?

(66) <u>Entering into the dwelling Odysseus directly demanded hospitality Polyphemus instead butchered his men in spite of custom.</u>

   a. NO CHANGE
   b. Entering into the dwelling, Odysseus directly demanded hospitality. Polyphemus instead butchered his men in spite of custom.
   c. Entering into the dwelling, Odysseus directly demanded hospitality, Polyphemus instead butchered his men in spite of custom.
   d. Entering into the dwelling; Odysseus directly demanded hospitality; Polyphemus instead butchered his men in spite of custom.

67. Which of the following would be the best choice for this sentence (reproduced below)?

In order to survive the encounter, Odysseus (67) relinquishes his true identity by telling Polyphemus his name is "Nobody."

a. NO CHANGE
b. Conceals
c. Withholds
d. Surrenders

68. Which of the following would be the best choice for this sentence (reproduced below)?

(68) Clearly, Odysseus isn't making the same mistake twice in trusting people to automatically abide by custom.

a. NO CHANGE
b. Clearly Odysseus isn't making the same mistake twice in trusting people to automatically abide by custom.
c. Clearly, Odysseus isn't making the same mistake twice; trusting people to automatically abide by custom.
d. Odysseus isn't making the same mistake twice in trusting people, clearly, to automatically abide by custom.

69. Which of the following would be the best choice for this sentence (reproduced below)?

(69) This passage specifically described the suitors as eating away at Odysseus' substance, seeming to further the parallel with Polyphemus who devoured Odysseus' men.

a. NO CHANGE
b. This passages specifically describes
c. This passage specifically describes
d. These passage specifically describes

70. Which of the following would be the best choice for this sentence (reproduced below)?

(70) Also like with Polyphemus, Odysseus only reveals his true identity when he knows his plan has succeeded.

a. NO CHANGE
b. As he did with Polyphemus
c. As he did before
d. With the exact method as he had with Polyphemus

71. Which of the following would be the best choice for this sentence (reproduced below)?

To conceal (71) ones identity is to withhold trust.

a. NO CHANGE
b. One's
c. Someone's
d. Oneself

431

72. Which of the following would be the best choice for this sentence (reproduced below)?

It is known that Circe welcomes all men who (72) <u>enter upon</u> her island with food and drink, but this is a deception meant to ensnare them.

a. NO CHANGE
b. Land upon
c. Arrive on
d. Crash on

73. Which of the following would be the best choice for this sentence (reproduced below)?

In order to (73) <u>assure</u> his and the crew's safety, Odysseus must look past her empty courtesy and deceive her in a way that will remedy the situation.

a. NO CHANGE
b. Ensure
c. Prevent
d. Vindicate

74. Which of the following would be the best choice for this sentence (reproduced below)?

Like Agamemnon, Odysseus (74) <u>is returning</u> home to his wife.

a. NO CHANGE
b. returns
c. returned
d. was returned

75. Which of the following would be the best choice for this sentence (reproduced below)?

(75) <u>As the text progresses, Odysseus</u> encounters the Sirens and Calypso, who seem to corroborate the idea that women are bad news.

a. NO CHANGE
b. As the text progresses Odysseus
c. The text progresses with Odysseus
d. As Odysseus progresses in the text

Math

1. At the beginning of the day, Xavier has 20 apples. At lunch, he meets his sister Emma and gives her half of his apples. After lunch, he stops by his neighbor Jim's house and gives him 6 of his apples. He then uses $\frac{3}{4}$ of his remaining apples to make an apple pie for dessert at dinner. At the end of the day, how many apples does Xavier have left?

a. 4
b. 6
c. 2
d. 1
e. 3

2. What is the product of two irrational numbers?
   a. Irrational
   b. Rational
   c. Irrational or rational
   d. Complex and imaginary
   e. Imaginary

3. The graph shows the position of a car over a 10-second time interval. Which of the following is the correct interpretation of the graph for the interval 1 to 3 seconds?

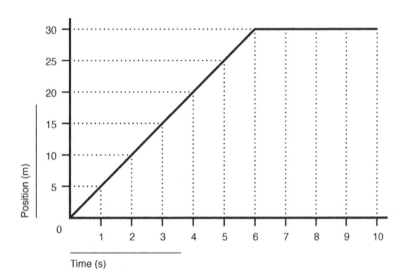

a. The car remains in the same position.
b. The car is traveling at a speed of 5 m/s.
c. The car is traveling up a hill.
d. The car is traveling at 5 mph.
e. The car accelerates at a rate of 5 m/s.

4. Being as specific as possible, how is the number -4 classified?
   a. Real, rational, integer, whole, natural
   b. Real, rational, integer, natural
   c. Real, rational, integer
   d. Real, irrational, complex
   e. Real, irrational, whole

5. After a 20% discount, Frank purchased a new refrigerator for $850. How much did he save from the original price?
   a. $170
   b. $212.50
   c. $105.75
   d. $200
   e. $187.50

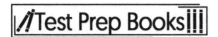

6. Store brand coffee beans cost $1.23 per pound. A local coffee bean roaster charges $1.98 per $1\frac{1}{2}$ pounds. How much more would 5 pounds from the local roaster cost than 5 pounds of the store brand?
    a. $0.55
    b. $1.55
    c. $1.45
    d. $0.45
    e. $0.35

7. What is the solution to the following problem in decimal form?
$$\frac{3}{5} \times \frac{7}{10} \div \frac{1}{2}$$
    a. 0.042
    b. 84%
    c. 0.84
    d. 0.42
    e. 42%

8. Dwayne has received the following scores on his math tests: 78, 92, 83, and 97. What score must Dwayne get on his next math test to have an overall average of 90?
    a. 89
    b. 98
    c. 95
    d. 94
    e. 100

9. What are all the factors of 12?
    a. 12, 24, 36
    b. 1, 2, 4, 6, 12
    c. 12, 24, 36, 48
    d. 1, 2, 3, 4, 6, 12
    e. 0, 1, 12

10. Which of the following augmented matrices represents the system of equations below?

$$2x - 3y + z = -5$$
$$4x - y - 2z = -7$$
$$-x + 2z = -1$$

a. $\begin{bmatrix} 2 & -3 & 1 & 5 \\ 4 & -1 & 0 & -7 \\ -1 & 0 & 2 & 1 \end{bmatrix}$

b. $\begin{bmatrix} 2 & 4 & -1 \\ -3 & -1 & 0 \\ 1 & -2 & 2 \\ -5 & -7 & -1 \end{bmatrix}$

c. $\begin{bmatrix} 2 & 4 & -1 & -5 \\ -3 & -1 & 0 & -7 \\ 2 & -2 & 2 & -1 \end{bmatrix}$

d. $\begin{bmatrix} 2 & -3 & 1 \\ 4 & -1 & -2 \\ -1 & 0 & 2 \end{bmatrix}$

e. $\begin{bmatrix} 2 & -3 & 1 & -5 \\ 4 & -1 & -2 & -7 \\ -1 & 0 & 2 & -1 \end{bmatrix}$

11. What are the zeros of the function: $f(x) = x^3 + 4x^2 + 4x$?
   a. -2
   b. 0, -2
   c. 2
   d. 0, 2
   e. 0

12. If $g(x) = x^3 - 3x^2 - 2x + 6$ and $f(x) = 2$, then what is $g(f(x))$?
   a. -26
   b. 6
   c. $2x^3 - 6x^2 - 4x + 12$
   d. -2
   e. $2x^2 - 6$

13. What is the solution to the following system of equations?

$$x^2 - 2x + y = 8$$
$$x - y = -2$$

   a. $(-2, 3)$
   b. There is no solution.
   c. $(-2, 0) \ (1, 3)$
   d. $(-2, 0) \ (3, 5)$
   e. $(2, 0) \ (-1, 3)$

14. Which of the following is the result after simplifying the expression: $(7n + 3n^3 + 3) + (8n + 5n^3 + 2n^4)$?
    a. $9n^4 + 15n - 2$
    b. $2n^4 + 5n^3 + 15n - 2$
    c. $9n^4 + 8n^3 + 15n$
    d. $2n^4 + 8n^3 + 15n + 3$
    e. $2n^4 + 5n^3 + 15n - 3$

15. What is the product of the following expression?
$$(4x - 8)(5x^2 + x + 6)$$
    a. $20x^3 - 36x^2 + 16x - 48$
    b. $6x^3 - 41x^2 + 12x + 15$
    c. $20x^4 + 11x^2 - 37x - 12$
    d. $2x^3 - 11x^2 - 32x + 20$
    e. $20x^3 - 40x^2 + 24x - 48$

16. How could the following equation be factored to find the zeros?
$$y = x^3 - 3x^2 - 4x$$
    a. $0 = x^2(x - 4), x = 0, 4$
    b. $0 = 3x(x + 1)(x + 4), x = 0, -1, -4$
    c. $0 = x(x + 1)(x + 6), x = 0, -1, -6$
    d. $0 = 3x(x + 1)(x - 4), x = 0, 1, -4$
    e. $0 = x(x + 1)(x - 4), x = 0, -1, 4$

17. The hospital has a nurse-to-patient ratio of 1:25. If there is a maximum of 325 patients admitted at a time, how many nurses are there?
    a. 13 nurses
    b. 25 nurses
    c. 325 nurses
    d. 12 nurses
    e. 5 nurses

18. Which of the following is the solution for the given equation?
$$\frac{x^2 + x - 30}{x - 5} = 11$$
    a. $x = -6$
    b. All real numbers.
    c. $x = 16$
    d. $x = 5$
    e. There is no solution.

19. Mom's car drove 72 miles in 90 minutes. How fast did she drive in feet per second?
(1 mile = 5,280 ft)
    a. 0.8 feet per second
    b. 48.9 feet per second
    c. 0.009 feet per second
    d. 70.4 feet per second
    e. 21.3 feet per second

20. Solve $V = lwh$ for h.

    a. $lwV = h$

    b. $h = \dfrac{V}{lw}$

    c. $h = \dfrac{Vl}{w}$

    d. $h = \dfrac{Vw}{l}$

    e. $h = \dfrac{Vl}{w}$

21. What is the domain for the function $y = \sqrt{x}$?

    a. All real numbers

    b. $x \geq 0$

    c. $x > 0$

    d. $y \geq 0$

    e. $x < 0$

22. If Sarah reads at an average rate of 21 pages in four nights, how long will it take her to read 140 pages?

    a. 6 nights

    b. 26 nights

    c. 8 nights

    d. 27 nights

    e. 21 nights

23. The phone bill is calculated each month using the equation $c = 50g + 75$. The cost of the phone bill per month is represented by c, and g represents the gigabytes of data used that month. Identify and interpret the slope of this equation.

    a. 75 dollars per day

    b. 75 gigabytes per day

    c. 50 dollars per day

    d. 50 dollars per gigabyte

    e. The slope cannot be determined

24. What is the function that forms an equivalent graph to $y = \cos(x)$?

    a. $y = \tan(x)$

    b. $y = \csc(x)$

    c. $y = \sin\left(x + \dfrac{\pi}{2}\right)$

    d. $y = \sin\left(x - \dfrac{\pi}{2}\right)$

    e. $y = \tan\left(x + \dfrac{\pi}{2}\right)$

25. If $\sqrt{1 + x} = 4$, what is x?

    a. 10

    b. 15

    c. 20

    d. 25

    e. 36

26. What is the inverse of the function $f(x) = 3x - 5$?

    a. $f^{-1}(x) = \frac{x}{3} + 5$

    b. $f^{-1}(x) = \frac{5x}{3}$

    c. $f^{-1}(x) = 3x + 5$

    d. $f^{-1}(x) = \frac{x+5}{3}$

    e. $f^{-1}(x) = \frac{x}{3} - 5$

27. What are the zeros of $f(x) = x^2 + 4$?

    a. $x = -4$

    b. $x = \pm 2i$

    c. $x = \pm 2$

    d. $x = \pm 4i$

    e. $x = 2, 4$

28. Twenty is 40% of what number?

    a. 60

    b. 8

    c. 200

    d. 70

    e. 50

29. What is the simplified form of the expression $1.2 \times 10^{12} \div 3.0 \times 10^8$?

    a. 0.4×10^4

    b. 4.0×10^4

    c. 4.0×10^3

    d. 3.6×10^{20}

    e. 4.0×10^2

30. You measure the width of your door to be 36 inches. The true width of the door is 35.75 inches. What is the relative error in your measurement?

    a. 0.7%

    b. 0.007%

    c. 0.99%

    d. 0.1%

    e. 7.0%

31. What is the y-intercept for $y = x^2 + 3x - 4$?

    a. $y = 1$

    b. $y = -4$

    c. $y = 3$

    d. $y = 4$

    e. $y = -3$

32. Is the following function even, odd, neither, or both?
$$y = \frac{1}{2}x^4 + 2x^2 - 6$$

    a. Even
    b. Odd
    c. Neither
    d. Both
    e. Even for all negative x-values and odd for all positive x-values

33. Which equation is not a function?
    a. $y = |x|$
    b. $y = \sqrt{x}$
    c. $x = 3$
    d. $y = 4$
    e. $y = 3x$

34. How could the following function be rewritten to identify the zeros?
$$y = 3x^3 + 3x^2 - 18x$$
    a. $y = 3x(x + 3)(x - 2)$
    b. $y = x(x - 2)(x + 3)$
    c. $y = 3x(x - 3)(x + 2)$
    d. $y = (x + 3)(x - 2)$
    e. $y = 3x(x + 3)(x + 2)$

35. A six-sided die is rolled. What is the probability that the roll is 1 or 2?
    a. $\frac{1}{6}$

    b. $\frac{1}{4}$

    c. $\frac{1}{3}$

    d. $\frac{1}{2}$

    e. $\frac{1}{36}$

36. A line passes through the origin and through the point (-3, 4). What is the slope of the line?
    a. $-\frac{4}{3}$

    b. $-\frac{3}{4}$

    c. $\frac{4}{3}$

    d. $\frac{3}{4}$

    e. $\frac{1}{3}$

37. What type of function is modeled by the values in the following table?

x	$f(x)$
1	2
2	4
3	8
4	16
5	32

    a. Linear
    b. Exponential
    c. Quadratic
    d. Cubic
    e. Logarithmic

38. An investment of $2,000 is made into an account with an annual interest rate of 5%, compounded continuously. What is the total value of the investment after eight years?
    a. $2,954.91
    b. $3,000
    c. $2,983.65
    d. $2,800
    e. $1,977.61

39. A ball is drawn at random from a ball pit containing 8 red balls, 7 yellow balls, 6 green balls, and 5 purple balls. What's the probability that the ball drawn is yellow?
    a. $\frac{1}{26}$

    b. $\frac{19}{26}$

    c. $\frac{14}{26}$

    d. 1

    e. $\frac{7}{26}$

40. Two cards are drawn from a shuffled deck of 52 cards. What's the probability that both cards are kings if the first card isn't replaced after it's drawn?
    a. $\frac{1}{169}$

    b. $\frac{1}{221}$

    c. $\frac{1}{13}$

    d. $\frac{4}{13}$

    e. $\frac{1}{104}$

41. What's the probability of rolling a 6 exactly once in two rolls of a die?

    a. $\frac{1}{3}$

    b. $\frac{1}{36}$

    c. $\frac{1}{6}$

    d. $\frac{1}{12}$

    e. $\frac{11}{36}$

42. Given the set $A = \{1, 2, 3, 4, 5, 6, 7, 8, 9, 10\}$ and $B = \{1, 2, 3, 4, 5\}$, what is $A - (A \cap B)$?

    a. $\{6, 7, 8, 9, 10\}$
    b. $\{1, 2, 3, 4, 5\}$
    c. $\{1, 2, 3, 4, 5, 6, 7, 8, 9, 10\}$
    d. $\emptyset$
    e. $\{-1, -2, -3, -4, -5\}$

43. An equilateral triangle has a perimeter of 18 feet. If a square whose sides have the same length as one side of the triangle is built, what will be the area of the square?

    a. 6 square feet
    b. 36 square feet
    c. 256 square feet
    d. 1,000 square feet
    e. 324 square feet

44. In a group of 20 men, the median weight is 180 pounds and the range is 30 pounds. If each man gains 10 pounds, which of the following would be true?

    a. The median weight will increase, and the range will remain the same.
    b. The median weight and range will both remain the same.
    c. The median weight will stay the same, and the range will increase.
    d. The median weight and range will both increase.
    e. The median weight will increase, and the range will decrease.

45. For the following similar triangles, what are the values of x and y (rounded to one decimal place)?

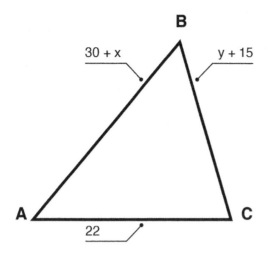
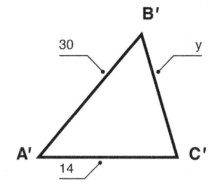

a. $x = 16.5, y = 25.1$
b. $x = 19.5, y = 24.1$
c. $x = 17.1, y = 26.3$
d. $x = 26.3, y = 17.1$
e. $x = 24.1, y = 19.5$

46. On Monday, Robert mopped the floor in 4 hours. On Tuesday, he did it in 3 hours. If on Monday, his average rate of mopping was p sq. ft. per hour, what was his average rate on Tuesday?

a. $\frac{4}{3}p$ sq. ft. per hour
b. $\frac{3}{4}p$ sq. ft. per hour
c. $\frac{5}{4}p$ sq. ft. per hour
d. $p + 1$ sq. ft. per hour
e. $\frac{1}{3}p$ sq. ft. per hour

47. Which of the following inequalities is equivalent to $3 - \frac{1}{2}x \geq 2$?

a. $x \geq 2$
b. $x \leq 2$
c. $x \geq 1$
d. $x \leq 1$
e. $x \leq -2$

48. For which of the following are $x = 4$ and $x = -4$ solutions?

a. $x^2 + 16 = 0$
b. $x^2 + 4x - 4 = 0$
c. $x^2 - 2x - 2 = 0$
d. $x^2 - x - 16 = 0$
e. $x^2 - 16 = 0$

49. What are the center and radius of a circle with equation $4x^2 + 4y^2 - 16x - 24y + 51 = 0$?

    a. Center (3, 2) and radius $\frac{1}{2}$

    b. Center (2, 3) and radius $\frac{1}{2}$

    c. Center (3, 2) and radius $\frac{1}{4}$

    d. Center (2, 3) and radius $\frac{1}{4}$

    e. Center (2, 2) and radius $\frac{1}{4}$

50. If the ordered pair $(-3, -4)$ is reflected over the x-axis, what's the new ordered pair?

    a. $(-3, -4)$

    b. $(3, -4)$

    c. $(3, 4)$

    d. $(-3, 4)$

    e. $(-4, -3)$

51. If the volume of a sphere is 288π cubic meters, what are the radius and surface area of the same sphere?

    a. Radius: 6 meters, Surface Area: 144π square meters

    b. Radius: 36 meters, Surface Area: 144π square meters

    c. Radius: 6 meters, Surface Area: 12π square meters

    d. Radius: 36 meters, Surface Area: 12π square meters

    e. Radius: 12 meters, Surface Area: 144π square meters

52. The triangle shown below is a right triangle. What's the value of x?

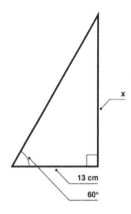

13 cm

60°

    a. $x = 1.73$

    b. $x = 0.57$

    c. $x = 13$

    d. $x = 14.73$

    e. $x = 22.52$

53. Ten students take a test. Five students get a 50. Four students get a 70. If the average score is 55, what was the last student's score?

    a. 20

    b. 40

    c. 50

    d. 60

    e. 62

54. A sample data set contains the following values: 1, 3, 5, 7. What's the standard deviation of the set?

    a. 2.58

    b. 4

    c. 6.23

    d. 1.1

    e. 0.25

55. A company invests \$50,000 in a building where they can produce saws. If the cost of producing one saw is \$40, then which function expresses the amount of money the company pays? The variable y is the money paid and x is the number of saws produced.

    a. $y = 50{,}000x + 40$

    b. $y + 40 = x - 50{,}000$

    c. $y = 40x - 50{,}000$

    d. $y = 40x + 50{,}000$

    e. $y = 4x + 50{,}000$

56. A pair of dice is thrown, and the sum of the two scores is calculated. What's the expected value of the roll?

    a. 5

    b. 6

    c. 7

    d. 8

    e. 9

57. A line passes through the point $(1, 2)$ and crosses the y-axis at $y = 1$. Which of the following is an equation for this line?

    a. $y = 2x$

    b. $y = x + 1$

    c. $x + y = 1$

    d. $y = \frac{x}{2} - 2$

    e. $y = x - 1$

58. $x^4 - 16$ can be simplified to which of the following?

    a. $(x^2 - 4)(x^2 + 4)$

    b. $(x^2 + 4)(x^2 + 4)$

    c. $(x^2 - 4)(x^2 - 4)$

    d. $(x^2 - 2)(x^2 + 4)$

    e. $(x^2 - 2)(x^2 + 2)$

59. $(4x^2y^4)^{\frac{3}{2}}$ can be simplified to which of the following?

    a. $8x^3y^6$

    b. $4x^{\frac{5}{2}}y$

    c. $4xy$

    d. $32x^{\frac{7}{2}}y^{\frac{11}{2}}$

    e. x^3y^6

60. A ball is thrown from the top of a high hill, so that the height of the ball as a function of time is $h(t) = -16t^2 + 4t + 6$, in feet. What is the maximum height of the ball in feet?

    a. 6
    b. 6.25
    c. 6.5
    d. 6.75
    e. 6.8

Reading

Fiction

Questions 1–10 are based on the following passage:

"Mademoiselle Eugénie is pretty—I think I remember that to be her name."

"Very pretty, or rather, very beautiful," replied Albert, "but of that style of beauty which I don't appreciate; I am an ungrateful fellow."

"Really," said Monte Cristo, lowering his voice, "you don't appear to me to be very enthusiastic on the subject of this marriage."

"Mademoiselle Danglars is too rich for me," replied Morcerf, "and that frightens me."

"Bah," exclaimed Monte Cristo, "that's a fine reason to give. Are you not rich yourself?"

"My father's income is about 50,000 francs per annum; and he will give me, perhaps, ten or twelve thousand when I marry."

"That, perhaps, might not be considered a large sum, in Paris especially," said the count; "but everything doesn't depend on wealth, and it's a fine thing to have a good name, and to occupy a high station in society. Your name is celebrated, your position magnificent; and then the Comte de Morcerf is a soldier, and it's pleasing to see the integrity of a Bayard united to the poverty of a Duguesclin; disinterestedness is the brightest ray in which a noble sword can shine. As for me, I consider the union with Mademoiselle Danglars a most suitable one; she will enrich you, and you will ennoble her."

Albert shook his head, and looked thoughtful. "There is still something else," said he.

445

"I confess," observed Monte Cristo, "that I have some difficulty in comprehending your objection to a young lady who is both rich and beautiful."

"Oh," said Morcerf, "this repugnance, if repugnance it may be called, isn't all on my side."

"Whence can it arise, then? for you told me your father desired the marriage."

"It's my mother who dissents; she has a clear and penetrating judgment, and doesn't smile on the proposed union. I cannot account for it, but she seems to entertain some prejudice against the Danglars."

"Ah," said the count, in a somewhat forced tone, "that may be easily explained; the Comtesse de Morcerf, who is aristocracy and refinement itself, doesn't relish the idea of being allied by your marriage with one of ignoble birth; that is natural enough."

Excerpt from *The Count of Monte Cristo* by Alexandre Dumas

1. The meaning of the word *repugnance* is closest to:
    a. Strong resemblance
    b. Strong dislike
    c. Extreme shyness
    d. Extreme dissimilarity

2. What can be inferred about Albert's family?
    a. Their finances are uncertain.
    b. Albert is the only son in his family.
    c. Their name is more respected than the Danglars'.
    d. Albert's mother and father both agree on their decisions.

3. What is Albert's attitude towards his impending marriage?
    a. Pragmatic
    b. Romantic
    c. Indifferent
    d. Apprehensive

4. What is the best description of the Count's relationship with Albert?
    a. He's like a strict parent, criticizing Albert's choices.
    b. He's like a wise uncle, giving practical advice to Albert.
    c. He's like a close friend, supporting all of Albert's opinions.
    d. He's like a suspicious investigator, asking many probing questions.

5. Which sentence is true of Albert's mother?
    a. She belongs to a noble family.
    b. She often makes poor choices.
    c. She is primarily occupied with money.
    d. She is unconcerned about her son's future.

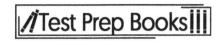

6. Based on this passage, what is probably NOT true about French society in the 1800s?
   a. Children often received money from their parents.
   b. Marriages were sometimes arranged between families.
   c. The richest people in society were also the most respected.
   d. People were often expected to marry within their same social class.

7. Why is the Count puzzled by Albert's attitude toward his marriage?
   a. He seems reluctant to marry Eugénie, despite her wealth and beauty.
   b. He is marrying against his father's wishes, despite usually following his advice.
   c. He appears excited to marry someone he doesn't love, despite being a hopeless romantic.
   d. He expresses reverence towards Eugénie, despite being from a higher social class than her.

8. The passage is made up mostly of what kind of text?
   a. Narration
   b. Dialogue
   c. Description
   d. Explanation

9. What does the word *ennoble* mean in the middle of the passage?
   a. To create beauty in another person
   b. To endow someone with wealth
   c. To make someone chaste again
   d. To give someone a noble rank or title

10. Why is the count said to have a "forced tone" in the last paragraph?
    a. Because he is in love with Mademoiselle Eugénie and is trying to keep it a secret.
    b. Because he finally agrees with Albert's point of view but still doesn't understand it.
    c. Because he finally understands Albert's point of view but still doesn't agree with it.
    d. Because he is only pretending that Albert is his friend to get information out of him.

Social Science

Questions 11–20 are based upon the following passage:

MANKIND being originally equals in the order of creation, the equality could only be destroyed by some subsequent circumstance; the distinctions of rich, and poor, may in a great measure be accounted for, and that without having recourse to the harsh, ill-sounding names of oppression and avarice. Oppression is often the CONSEQUENCE , but seldom or never the MEANS of riches; and though avarice will preserve a man from being necessitously poor, it generally makes him too timorous to be wealthy.

But there is another and greater distinction, for which no truly natural or religious reason can be assigned, and that is, the distinction of men into KINGS and SUBJECTS. Male and female are the distinctions of nature, good and bad the distinctions of heaven; but how a race of men came into the world so exalted above the rest, and distinguished like some new species, is worth enquiring into, and whether they are the means of happiness or of misery to mankind.

In the early ages of the world, according to the scripture chronology, there were no kings; the consequence of which was, there were no wars; it is the pride of kings which

447

throw mankind into confusion. Holland without a king hath enjoyed more peace for this last century than any of the monarchical governments in Europe. Antiquity favors the same remark; for the quiet and rural lives of the first patriarchs hath a happy something in them, which vanishes away when we come to the history of Jewish royalty.

Government by kings was first introduced into the world by the Heathens, from whom the children of Israel copied the custom. It was the most prosperous invention the Devil ever set on foot for the promotion of idolatry. The Heathens paid divine honors to their deceased kings, and the Christian world hath improved on the plan, by doing the same to their living ones. How impious is the title of sacred majesty applied to a worm, who in the midst of his splendor is crumbling into dust!

As the exalting one man so greatly above the rest cannot be justified on the equal rights of nature, so neither can it be defended on the authority of scripture; for the will of the Almighty, as declared by Gideon and the prophet Samuel, expressly disapproves of government by kings. All anti-monarchical parts of scripture have been very smoothly glossed over in monarchical governments, but they undoubtedly merit the attention of countries which have their governments yet to form. RENDER UNTO CAESAR THE THINGS WHICH ARE CAESAR'S is the scripture doctrine of courts, yet it is no support of monarchical government, for the Jews at that time were without a king, and in a state of vassalage to the Romans.

Now three thousand years passed away from the Mosaic account of the creation, till the Jews under a national delusion requested a king. Till then their form of government (except in extraordinary cases, where the Almighty interposed) was a kind of republic administered by a judge and the elders of the tribes. Kings they had none, and it was held sinful to acknowledge any being under that title but the Lord of Hosts. And when a man seriously reflects on the idolatrous homage which is paid to the persons of kings, he need not wonder that the Almighty, ever jealous of his honor, should disapprove of a form of government which so impiously invades the prerogative of heaven.

Excerpt from "Common Sense" by Thomas Paine

11. According to the passage, what role does avarice, or greed, play in poverty?
    a. Avarice makes a man poor.
    b. Avarice is the consequence of wealth.
    c. Avarice prevents a man from being poor, but makes him too fearful to be wealthy.
    d. Avarice is what drives a person to be wealthy.

12. Of these distinctions, which does the author believe to be beyond natural or religious reason?
    a. Good and bad
    b. Male and female
    c. Human and animal
    d. King and subjects

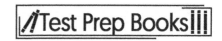

13. According to the passage, what are the Heathens responsible for?
    a. Government by kings
    b. Quiet and rural lives of patriarchs
    c. Paying divine honors to their living kings
    d. Equal rights of nature

14. Which of the following best states Paine's rationale for the denouncement of the monarchy?
    a. It is against the laws of nature.
    b. It is against the equal rights of nature and is denounced in scripture.
    c. Despite scripture, a monarchal government is unlawful.
    d. Neither the law nor scripture denounce monarchy.

15. Based on the passage, what is the best definition of the word *idolatrous*?
    a. Worshipping kings
    b. Being deceitful
    c. Sinfulness
    d. Engaging in illegal activities

16. What is the essential meaning of lines 41–44?

    And when a man seriously reflects on the idolatrous homage which is paid to the persons of kings, he need not wonder that the Almighty, ever jealous of his honor, should disapprove of a form of government which so impiously invades the prerogative of heaven.

    a. God disapproves of the irreverence of a monarchical government.
    b. With careful reflection, men should realize that heaven is not promised.
    c. God will punish those that follow a monarchical government.
    d. Belief in a monarchical government cannot coexist with belief in God.

17. Based on the passage, what is the best definition of the word *timorous* in the first paragraph?
    a. Being full of fear
    b. A characteristic of shyness
    c. Being able to see through someone
    d. Being full of anger and hatred

18. The author's attitude toward the subject can best be described as:
    a. Indifferent and fatigued
    b. Impassioned and critical
    c. Awed and enchanted
    d. Enraged and sulky

19. The main purpose of the fourth paragraph is:
    a. To persuade the audience that heathens were more advanced than Christians.
    b. To explain how monarchs came into existence and how Christians adopted the same system.
    c. To describe the divination of English monarchs and how it is their birthright to be revered.
    d. To counteract the preceding paragraph by giving proof of the damage monarchs can cause.

20. In the last paragraph, what does the author mean by the "Mosaic account of creation"?
    a. The author means that creation is based on individuals composed of cells of two genetically different types.
    b. The author implies that the work of God is like a mosaic painting due to the various formations of creation.
    c. The author means that the kings of the past developed a system in which to maintain accounts of creation.
    d. The author implies that the recorded history of creation is a collection, collage, or pattern taken from various accounts of cultures.

Humanities

Questions 21–30 are based on the following two passages:

Passage 1

Shakespeare and His Plays

People who argue that William Shakespeare is not responsible for the plays attributed to his name are known as anti-Stratfordians (from the name of Shakespeare's birthplace, Stratford-upon-Avon). The most common anti-Stratfordian claim is that William Shakespeare simply was not educated enough or from a high enough social class to have written plays overflowing with references to such a wide range of subjects like history, the classics, religion, and international culture. William Shakespeare was the son of a glove-maker, he only had a basic grade school education, and he never set foot outside of England—so how could he have produced plays of such sophistication and imagination? How could he have written in such detail about historical figures and events, or about different cultures and locations around Europe? According to anti-Stratfordians, the depth of knowledge contained in Shakespeare's plays suggests a well-traveled writer from a wealthy background with a university education, not a countryside writer like Shakespeare. But in fact, there is not much substance to such speculation, and most anti-Stratfordian arguments can be refuted with a little background about Shakespeare's time and upbringing.

First of all, those who doubt Shakespeare's authorship often point to his common birth and brief education as stumbling blocks to his writerly genius. Although it is true that Shakespeare did not come from a noble class, his father was a very *successful* glove-maker and his mother was from a very wealthy land-owning family—so while Shakespeare may have had a country upbringing, he was certainly from a well-off family and would have been educated accordingly. Also, even though he did not attend university, grade school education in Shakespeare's time was actually quite rigorous and exposed students to classic drama through writers like Seneca and Ovid. It is not unreasonable to believe that Shakespeare received a very solid foundation in poetry and literature from his early schooling.

Next, anti-Stratfordians tend to question how Shakespeare could write so extensively about countries and cultures he had never visited before (for instance, several of his most famous works like *Romeo and Juliet* and *The Merchant of Venice* were set in Italy, on the opposite side of Europe!). But again, this criticism does not hold up under scrutiny. For one thing, Shakespeare was living in London, a bustling metropolis of international trade, the most populous city in England, and a political and cultural hub of Europe. In the daily crowds of people, Shakespeare

450

would certainly have been able to meet travelers from other countries and hear firsthand accounts of life in their home country. And, in addition to the influx of information from world travelers, this was also the age of the printing press, a jump in technology that made it possible to print and circulate books much more easily than in the past. This also allowed for a freer flow of information across different countries, allowing people to read about life and ideas from throughout Europe. One needn't travel the continent in order to learn and write about its culture.

Passage 2

The following passage is from The Shakespeare Problem Restated *by G.G. Greenwood*

Now there is very good authority for saying, and I think the truth is so, that at least two of the plays published among the works of Shakespeare are not his at all; that at least three others contain very little, if any, of his writing; and that of the remainder, many contain long passages that are non-Shakespearean. But when we have submitted them all the crucible of criticism we have a magnificent residuum of the purest gold. Here is the true Shakespeare; here is the great magician who, by a wave of his wand, could transmute brass into gold, or make dry bones live and move and have immortal being. Who was this great magician—this mighty dramatist who was "not of an age, but for all time"? Who was the writer of *Venus* and *Lucrece* and the *Sonnets* and *Lear* and *Hamlet*? Was it William Shakespeare of Stratford, the Player? So it is generally believed, and that hypothesis I had accepted in unquestioning faith till my love of the works naturally led me to an examination of the life of the supposed author of them. Then I found that as I read my faith melted away "into thin air." It was not, certainly, that I had (nor have I now) any wish to disbelieve. I was, and I am, altogether willing to accept the Player as the immortal poet if only my reason would allow me to do so. Why not? . . . But the question of authorship is, nevertheless, a most fascinating one. If it be true, as the Rev. Leonard Bacon wrote that "The great world does not care sixpence who wrote *Hamlet*," the great world must, at the same time, be a very small world, and many of us must be content to be outside it. Having given, then, the best attention I was able to give to the question, and more time, I fear, than I ought to have devoted to it, I was brought to the conclusion, as many others have been, that the man who is, truly enough, designated by Messrs. Garnett and Gosse as a "Stratford rustic" is not the true Shakespeare. . .

That Shakespeare the "Stratford rustic and London actor" should have acquired this learning, this culture, and this polish; that *he* should have travelled into foreign lands, studied the life and topography of foreign cities, and the manners and customs of all sorts and conditions of men; that *he* should have written some half-dozen dramas . . . besides qualifying himself as a professional actor; that *he* should have done all this and a good deal more between 1587 and 1592 is a supposition so wild that it can only be entertained by those who are prepared to accept it as a miracle. "And miracles do not happen!"

21. Which sentence contains the author's thesis in the first passage?
    a. People who argue that William Shakespeare is not responsible for the plays attributed to his name are known as anti-Stratfordians.
    b. But in fact, there is not much substance to such speculation, and most anti-Stratfordian arguments can be refuted with a little background about Shakespeare's time and upbringing.
    c. It is not unreasonable to believe that Shakespeare received a very solid foundation in poetry and literature from his early schooling.
    d. Next, anti-Stratfordians tend to question how Shakespeare could write so extensively about countries and cultures he had never visited before.

22. In the first paragraph in Passage 1, "How could he have written in such detail about historical figures and events, or about different cultures and locations around Europe?" is an example of which of the following?
    a. Hyperbole
    b. Onomatopoeia
    c. Rhetorical question
    d. Appeal to authority

23. In Passage 1, how does the author respond to the claim that Shakespeare was not well-educated because he did not attend university?
    a. By insisting upon Shakespeare's natural genius.
    b. By explaining grade school curriculum in Shakespeare's time.
    c. By comparing Shakespeare with other uneducated writers of his time.
    d. By pointing out that Shakespeare's wealthy parents probably paid for private tutors.

24. In Passage 1, the word *bustling* in the third paragraph most nearly means which of the following?
    a. Busy
    b. Foreign
    c. Expensive
    d. Undeveloped

25. In passage 2, the following sentence is an example of what?

    Here is the true Shakespeare; here is the great magician who, by a wave of his wand, could transmute brass into gold, or make dry bones live and move and have immortal being.

    a. Personification
    b. Metaphor
    c. Simile
    d. Allusion

26. In passage 2, the author's attitude toward Stratfordians can be described as which of the following?
    a. Accepting and forgiving
    b. Uncaring and neutral
    c. Uplifting and admiring
    d. Disbelieving and critical

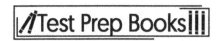

27. What is the relationship between these two sentences from Passage 2?

Sentence 1: So it is generally believed, and that hypothesis I had accepted in unquestioning faith till my love of the works naturally led me to an examination of the life of the supposed author of them.

Sentence 2: Then I found that as I read my faith melted away "into thin air."

a. Sentence 2 explains the main idea in Sentence 1.
b. Sentence 2 continues the definition begun in Sentence 1.
c. Sentence 2 analyzes the comment in Sentence 1.
d. Sentence 2 is a contrast to the idea in Sentence 1.

28. The writing style of Passage 1 could be best described as what?
a. Expository
b. Persuasive
c. Narrative
d. Descriptive

29. In passage 2, the word *topography* in the second paragraph most nearly means which of the following?
a. Climate features of an area.
b. Agriculture specific to place.
c. Shape and features of the Earth.
d. Aspects of humans within society.

30. The authors of the passages differ in their opinion of Shakespeare in that the author of Passage 2
a. Believes that Shakespeare the actor did not write the plays.
b. Believes that Shakespeare the playwright did not in act in the plays.
c. Believes that Shakespeare was both the actor and the playwright.
d. Believes that Shakespeare was neither the actor nor the playwright.

Natural Science

Questions 31–40 are based on the following passage:

In the quest to understand existence, modern philosophers must question if humans can fully comprehend the world. Classical western approaches to philosophy tend to hold that one can understand something, be it an event or object, by standing outside of the phenomena and observing it. It is then by unbiased observation that one can grasp the details of the world. This seems to hold true for many things. Scientists conduct experiments and record their findings, and thus many natural phenomena become comprehendible. However, several of these observations were possible because humans used tools in order to make these discoveries.

This may seem like an extraneous matter. After all, people invented things like microscopes and telescopes in order to enhance their capacity to view cells or the movement of stars. While humans are still capable of seeing things, the question remains if human beings have the capacity to fully observe and see the world in order to understand it. It would not be an impossible stretch to argue that what humans see through a microscope is not the exact thing itself, but a human interpretation of it.

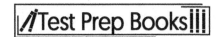

This would seem to be the case in the "Business of the Holes" experiment conducted by Richard Feynman. To study the way electrons behave, Feynman set up a barrier with two holes and a plate. The plate was there to indicate how many times the electrons would pass through the hole(s). Rather than casually observe the electrons acting under normal circumstances, Feynman discovered that electrons behave in two totally different ways depending on whether or not they are observed. The electrons that were observed had passed through either one of the holes or were caught on the plate as particles. However, electrons that weren't observed acted as waves instead of particles and passed through both holes. This indicated that electrons have a dual nature. Electrons seen by the human eye act like particles, while unseen electrons act like waves of energy.

This dual nature of the electrons presents a conundrum. While humans now have a better understanding of electrons, the fact remains that people cannot entirely perceive how electrons behave without the use of instruments. We can only observe one of the mentioned behaviors, which only provides a partial understanding of the entire function of electrons. Therefore, we're forced to ask ourselves whether the world we observe is objective or if it is subjectively perceived by humans. Or, an alternative question: can man understand the world only through machines that will allow them to observe natural phenomena?

Both questions humble man's capacity to grasp the world. However, those ideas don't consider that many phenomena have been proven by human beings without the use of machines, such as the discovery of gravity. Like all philosophical questions, whether man's reason and observation alone can understand the universe can be approached from many angles.

31. The word *extraneous* in paragraph 2 can be best interpreted as referring to which one of the following?
    a. Indispensable
    b. Bewildering
    c. Superfluous
    d. Exuberant

32. What is the author's motivation for writing the passage?
    a. To bring to light an alternative view on human perception by examining the role of technology in human understanding.
    b. To educate the reader on the latest astroparticle physics discovery and offer terms that may be unfamiliar to the reader.
    c. To argue that humans are totally blind to the realities of the world by presenting an experiment that proves that electrons are not what they seem on the surface.
    d. To reflect on opposing views of human understanding.

33. Which of the following most closely resembles the way in which paragraph four is structured?
    a. It offers one solution, questions the solution, and then ends with an alternative solution.
    b. It presents an inquiry, explains the details of that inquiry, and then offers a solution.
    c. It presents a problem, explains the details of that problem, and then ends with more inquiry.
    d. It gives a definition, offers an explanation, and then ends with an inquiry.

34. For the classical approach of understanding to hold true, which of the following must be required?
    a. A telescope
    b. A recording device
    c. Multiple witnesses present
    d. The person observing must be unbiased

35. Which best describes how the electrons in the experiment behaved like waves?
    a. The electrons moved up and down like actual waves.
    b. The electrons passed through both holes and then onto the plate.
    c. The electrons converted to photons upon touching the plate.
    d. Electrons were seen passing through one hole or the other.

36. The author mentions "gravity" in the last paragraph in order to do what?
    a. To show that different natural phenomena test man's ability to grasp the world.
    b. To prove that since man has not measured it with the use of tools or machines, humans cannot know the true nature of gravity.
    c. To demonstrate an example of natural phenomena humans discovered and understood without the use of tools or machines.
    d. To show an alternative solution to the nature of electrons that humans have not thought of yet.

37. Which situation best parallels the revelation of the dual nature of electrons discovered in Feynman's experiment?
    a. A man is born color-blind and grows up observing everything in lighter or darker shades. With the invention of special goggles he puts on, he discovers that there are other colors in addition to different shades.
    b. The coelacanth was thought to be extinct, but a live specimen was just recently discovered. There are now two living species of coelacanth known to man, and both are believed to be endangered.
    c. In the Middle Ages, blacksmiths added carbon to iron, thus inventing steel. The consequences of this important discovery would have its biggest effects during the industrial revolution.
    d. In order to better examine and treat broken bones, the x-ray machine was invented and put to use in hospitals and medical centers.

38. Which statement about technology would the author likely disagree with?
    a. Technology can help expand the field of human vision.
    b. Technology renders human observation irrelevant.
    c. Developing tools used in observation and research indicates growing understanding of our world itself.
    d. Studying certain phenomena necessitates the use of tools and machines.

39. As it is used in paragraph 4, the word *conundrum* most nearly means:
    a. Platitude
    b. Enigma
    c. Solution
    d. Hypothesis

455

40. What is the author's purpose in paragraph 3?

a. To prove to the audience the thesis of the passage by providing evidence suggesting that electrons behave differently when observed by the human eye.

b. To propose that the experiment conducted was not ethically done and to provide evidence that a new experiment should be conducted in order to reach the truth.

c. To introduce the topic to the audience in a manner that puts it into a practical as well as historical understanding.

d. To pose a question relating to the topic about whether humans fully observe phenomena in an objective or subjective sense.

Science

Passage 1

Questions 1–5 pertain to the following information:

Worldwide, fungal infections of the lung account for significant mortality in individuals with compromised immune function. Three of the most common infecting agents are *Aspergillus*, *Histoplasma*, and *Candida*. Successful treatment of infections caused by these agents depends on an early and accurate diagnosis. Three tests used to identify specific markers for these mold species include ELISA (enzyme-linked immunosorbent assay), GM Assay (Galactomannan Assay), and PCR (polymerase chain reaction).

Two important characteristics of these tests include sensitivity and specificity. Sensitivity relates to the probability that the test will identify the presence of the infecting agent, resulting in a true positive result. Higher sensitivity equals fewer false-positive results. Specificity relates to the probability that if the test doesn't detect the infecting agent, the test is truly negative for that agent. Higher specificity equals fewer false-negatives.

Figure 1 shows the timeline for the process of infection from exposure to the pathogen to recovery or death.

Figure 1:
Natural History of the Process of Infection

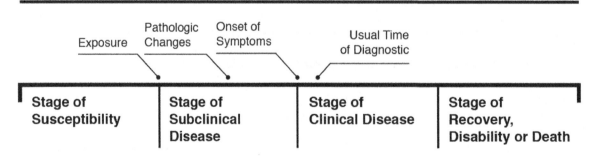

456

Figure 2 (below) shows the sensitivity and specificity for ELISA, GM assay and PCR related to the diagnosis of infection by *Aspergillus*, *Histoplasma* and *Candida*.

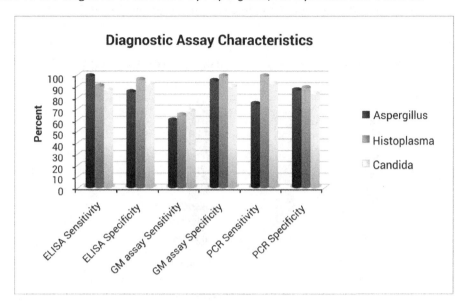

The table below identifies the process of infection in days from exposure for each of the species.

Process of Infection – Days Since Pathogen Exposure			
	Aspergillus	Histoplasma	Candida
Sub-clinical Disease	Day 90	Day 28	Day 7
Detection Possible	Day 118	Day 90	Day 45
Symptoms Appear	Day 145	Day100	Day 120

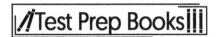

Figure 3 (below) identifies the point at which each test can detect the organism. Time is measured in days from the time an individual is exposed to the pathogen.

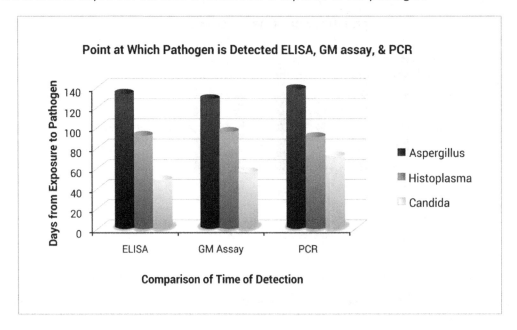

1. Which of the following statements is supported by Figure 2?
    a. For *Candida*, the GM assay will provide the most reliable results.
    b. ELISA testing for *Aspergillus* is the most specific of the three tests.
    c. PCR is the most sensitive method for testing *Histoplasma*.
    d. True positive rates were greater than 75% for all three testing methods.

2. In reference to the table and Figure 3, which pathogen can be detected earlier in the disease process, and by which method?
    a. *Candida* by PCR testing
    b. *Aspergillus* by ELISA testing
    c. *Candida* by GM assay
    d. *Histoplasma* by PCR testing

3. In reference to Figure 2, which statement is correct?
    a. There is a 20% probability that ELISA testing will NOT correctly identify the presence of *Histoplasma*.
    b. When GM assay testing for *Candida* is conducted, there is a 31% probability that it will NOT be identified if the organism is present.
    c. The probability that GM assay testing for *Aspergillus* will correctly identify the presence of the organism is 99%.
    d. The false-negative probabilities for each of the three testing methods identified in Figure 2 indicate that the organism will be detected when present less than 70% of the time.

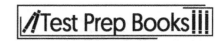

4. Physicians caring for individuals with suspected *Histoplasma* infections order diagnostic testing prior to instituting treatment. PCR testing results will not be available for 10 days. GM assay results can be obtained more quickly. The physicians opt to wait for the PCR testing. Choose the best possible rationale for that decision.

   a. The treatment will be the same regardless of the test results.

   b. The individual was not exhibiting any disease symptoms.

   c. The probability of PCR testing identifying the presence of the organism is greater than the GM assay.

   d. The subclinical disease phase for *Histoplasma* is more than 100 days.

5. Referencing the data in Figures 2 and 3, if ELISA testing costs twice as much as PCR testing, why might it still be the best choice to test for *Candida*?

   a. ELISA testing detects the presence of *Candida* sooner than PCR testing.

   b. ELISA testing has fewer false-positives than PCR testing.

   c. There is only a 69% probability that PCR testing will correctly identify the presence of *Candida*.

   d. PCR testing is less sensitive than ELISA testing for *Candida*.

Passage 2

Questions 6–12 pertain to the following information:

> Scientists disagree about the cause of Bovine Spongiform Encephalopathy (BSE), also known as "mad cow disease." Two scientists discuss different explanations about the cause of the disease.

Scientist 1

Mad cow disease is a condition that results in the deterioration of brain and spinal cord tissue. This deterioration manifests as sponge-like defects or holes that result in irreversible damage to the brain. The cause of this damage is widely accepted to be the result of an infectious type of protein, called a prion. Normal proteins are located in the cell wall of the central nervous system and function to preserve the myelin sheath around the nerves. Prions are capable of turning normal proteins into other prions by a process that is still unclear, thereby causing the proteins to be "refolded" in abnormal and harmful configurations. Unlike viruses and bacteria, the harmful prions possibly don't contain DNA or RNA, based on the observation of infected tissues in the laboratory that remain infected after immersion in formaldehyde or exposure to ultraviolet light. The transformation from normal to abnormal protein structure and function in a given individual is thought to occur as the result of proteins that are genetically weak or abnormally prone to mutation, or through transmission from another host through food, drugs or organ transplants from infected animals. The abnormal prions also don't trigger an immune response. After prions accumulate in large enough numbers, they form damaging conglomerations that result in the sponge-like holes in tissues, which eventually cause the loss of proper brain function and death.

459

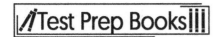
Figure 1 depicts formation of abnormal prions that results from the abnormal (right) folding of amino acids.

Figure 1:

Configurations of Normal and Abnormal Proteins

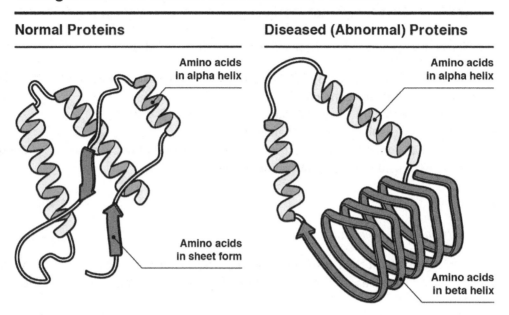

Scientist 2

The degeneration of brain tissue in animals afflicted with mad cow disease is widely considered to be the result of prions. This theory fails to consider other possible causes, such as viruses. Recent studies have shown that infected tissues often contain small particles that match the size and density of viruses. In order to demonstrate that these viral particles are the cause of mad cow disease, researchers used chemicals to inactivate the viruses. When the damaged, inactivated viruses were introduced into healthy tissue, no mad cow disease symptoms were observed. This result indicates that viruses are likely the cause of mad cow disease. In addition, when the infected particles from an infected animal are used to infect a different species, the resulting particles are identical to the original particles. If the infecting agent was a protein, the particles would not be identical because proteins are species-specific. Instead, the infective agent is viewed as some form of a virus that has its own DNA or RNA configuration and can reproduce identical infective particles.

6. Which statement below best characterizes the main difference in the scientists' opinions?
   a. The existence of species-specific proteins
   b. Transmission rates of mad cow disease
   c. The conversion process of normal proteins into prions
   d. The underlying cause of mad cow disease

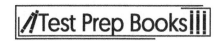

7. Which of the following statements is INCORRECT?
   a. Scientist 2 proposes that viruses aren't the cause of mad cow disease because chemicals inactivated the viruses.
   b. Scientist 1 suggests that infectious proteins called prions are the cause of mad cow disease.
   c. Scientist 1 indicates that the damaging conglomerations formed by prions eventually result in death.
   d. Scientist 2 reports that infected tissues often contain particles that match the size profile of viruses.

8. Which of the following is true according to Scientist 1?
   a. Normal proteins accumulate in large numbers to produce damaging conglomerations.
   b. Prions can change normal proteins into prions.
   c. Species-specific DNA sequences of infected tissues indicate that proteins cause mad cow disease.
   d. Prions are present only in the peripheral nervous system of mammals.

9. Which of the following statements would be consistent with the views of BOTH scientists?
   a. Resulting tissue damage is reversible.
   b. The infecting agent is composed of sheets of amino acids in an alpha helix configuration.
   c. Species-specific DNA can be isolated from infected tissue.
   d. Cross-species transmission of the illness is possible.

10. How does the *conglomeration* described in the passage affect function?
    a. Synapses are delayed
    b. Sponge-like tissue formations occur
    c. Space-occupying lesions compress the nerves
    d. The blood supply to surrounding tissues is decreased

11. What evidence best supports the views of Scientist 2?
    a. Species-specific DNA is present in the infected particles.
    b. Prions are present in the cell membrane.
    c. Prions can trigger an immune response.
    d. The infected particles were inactivated and didn't cause disease.

12. Which of the following statements is supported by this passage?
    a. Scientist 1 favors the claim that viruses are the cause of mad cow disease.
    b. Prions are a type of infectious virus.
    c. The process that results in the formation of the abnormal prion is unclear.
    d. Mad cow disease is caused by normal proteins.

Passage 3

Questions 13–17 pertain to the following information:

> Scientists have long been interested in the effect of sleep deprivation on overeating and obesity in humans. Recently, scientists discovered that increased levels of the endocannabinoid 2-Arachidonoylglycerol (2-AG) in the human body is related to overeating. The endocannabinoids play an important role in memory, mood, the reward system, and metabolic processes including glucose metabolism and generation of energy. The endocannabinoid receptors CB1-R and CB2-R are protein receptors located

461

on the cell membrane in the brain, the spinal cord and, to a lesser extent, in the peripheral neurons and the organs of the immune system. The two principal endogenous endocannabinoids are AEA (Anandamide) and 2-Arachidonoylglycerol (2-AG). The endocannabinoids can affect the body's response to chronic stress, mediate the pain response, decrease GI motility, and lessen the inflammatory response in some cancers.

Figure 1 (below) identifies the chemical structure of the endogenous cannabinoids including 2-AG.

Figure 1:
Chemical Structure of Common Endogenous Cannabinoids

The Five-Best known Endocannabinoids Showing the Common 19 - C Backbone Structure and specific R-group Constituents

Anandamide	2 - Arachidonoyl- glycerol	Noladin Ether

N-arachidonoyl-dopamine	Virodhamine	EC backbone structure

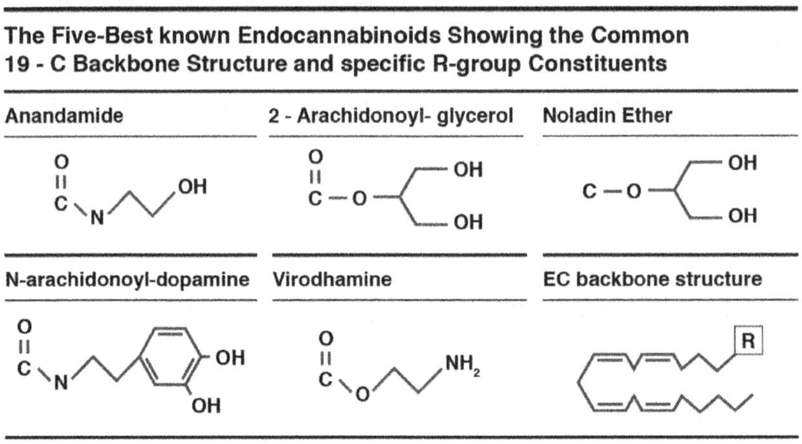

Recent research has also examined the relationship between sleep deprivation and the levels of 2-AG present in blood, as these conditions relate to obesity. The circadian fluctuations of 2-AG are well-known. Levels normally increase in late afternoon and evening. This physiological increase is thought to contribute to late-day snacking behaviors even after adequate calories have been consumed. The relationship between sleep deprivation and 2-AG appears to relate to the effect of 2-AG on the stress response, represented by sleep deprivation in this study. In order to examine this relationship, university scientists conducted an experiment to identify the influence of injections of 2-AG and sleep deprivation on overeating in a population of non-obese male and female participants that ranged in age from 20–40 years old. To accomplish this, human research subjects (participants) were allowed to eat their favorite junk foods in addition to consuming sufficient calories each day. All of the participants were injected daily with a solution of either sterile normal saline or 2-AG. Daily weight gain was recorded for the three treatment groups that included: participants A–E who received sterile normal saline injections, participants F–J who received 2-AG injections, and participants K–O who received 2-AG injections and were limited to 4.5 hours of sleep each night for 7 nights. The results of the three trials are shown below.

Figure 2 identifies the daily weight gain (in grams) of participants receiving sterile normal saline injections.

Daily Weight Gain for Patients Receiving Sterile Normal Saline Injections

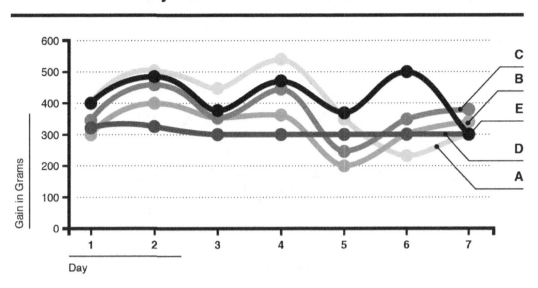

Figure 3 identifies the daily weight gain for participants receiving 2-AG injections.

Figure 3:
Daily Weight Gain for Participants Receiving Daily 2-AG Injections

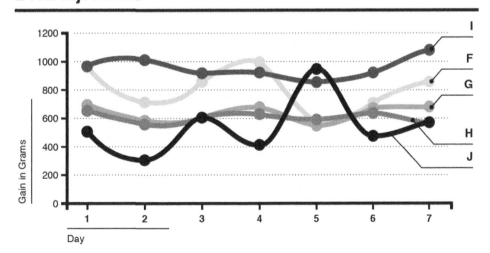

Figure 4 identifies the daily weight gain for participants receiving daily injections of 2-AG who were also limited to 4.5 hours sleep per night for 7 consecutive nights.

Figure 4:

Daily Weight Gain for Participants Receiving Daily 2-AG Injections Who Were Limited to 4.5 Hours of Sleep Per Night for 7 Consecutive Nights

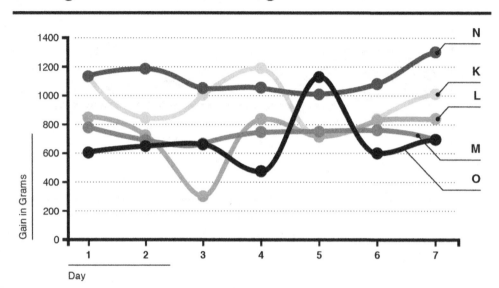

Figure 5 (below) identifies the participants' average daily weight gain by trial.

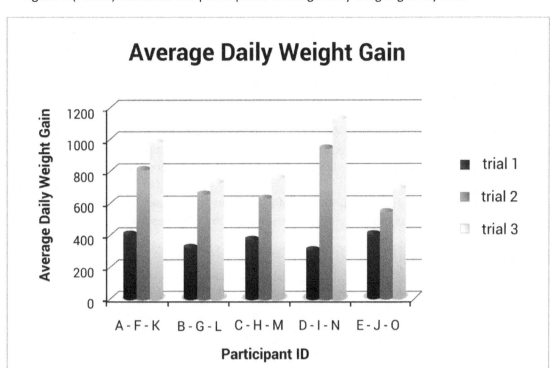

13. What was the main hypothesis for this study?
   a. 2-AG injections combined with sleep deprivation will result in weight gain.
   b. 2-AG injections will increase food intake beyond satiety.
   c. Sleep deprivation will result in weight gain.
   d. The placebo effect of the sterile normal saline will influence eating behavior.

14. Do the study results support the hypothesis? Choose the best answer.
   a. No, participants in trials 1 and 3 all gained weight.
   b. Yes, participants in trial 1 gained more weight daily than participants in trial 3.
   c. No, the average weight gain of participants in trial 2 and trial 3 was the same.
   d. Yes, all trial 3 participants gained more weight than trial 1 participants.

15. Describe the study results for participants D and H.
   a. Participant H gained more than one pound each day.
   b. Weight gain for each participant was inconsistent with the study hypothesis.
   c. There was significant fluctuation in the daily weight gain for both participants.
   d. Participant D's average daily weight was two times participant H's average daily weight gain.

16. According to the researchers, which of the following best describes the influence of sleep deprivation on eating behaviors?

a. The total number of sleep hours is unrelated to the degree of body stress.

b. Sleep deprivation stimulates the release of endogenous cannabinoids that may increase food intake.

c. Deprivation of any variety triggers the hunger response.

d. Sleep deprivation increases eating behaviors in the early morning hours.

17. According to the passage, how does 2-AG influence eating behaviors?

a. Circadian fluctuations result in increased levels of 2-AG in the afternoon and evening.

b. Endogenous cannabinoids like 2-AG increase gastric motility, which stimulates the hunger response.

c. The sedation that results from the presence of 2-AG limits food intake.

d. Endogenous cannabinoids block the opioid system, which decreases food-seeking behaviors.

Passage 4

Questions 18–22 pertain to the following passage:

A national wholesale nursery commissioned research to conduct a cost/benefit analysis of replacing existing fluorescent grow lighting systems with newer LED lighting systems. LEDs (light-emitting diodes) are composed of various semi-conductor materials that allow the flow of current in one direction. This means that LEDs emit light in a predictable range, unlike conventional lighting systems that give off heat and light in all directions. The wavelength of light of a single LED is determined by the properties of the specific semi-conductor. For instance, the indium gallium nitride system is used for blue, green, and cyan LEDs. As a result, growing systems can be individualized for the specific wavelength requirements for different plant species. In addition, LEDs don't emit significant amounts of heat compared to broadband systems, so plant hydration can be controlled more efficiently.

Figure 1 identifies the visible spectrum with the wavelength expressed in nanometers.

Figure 1:
The Visible Spectrum (Wavelength in Nanometers)

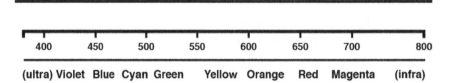

466

Figure 2 (below) identifies the absorption rates of different wavelengths of light.

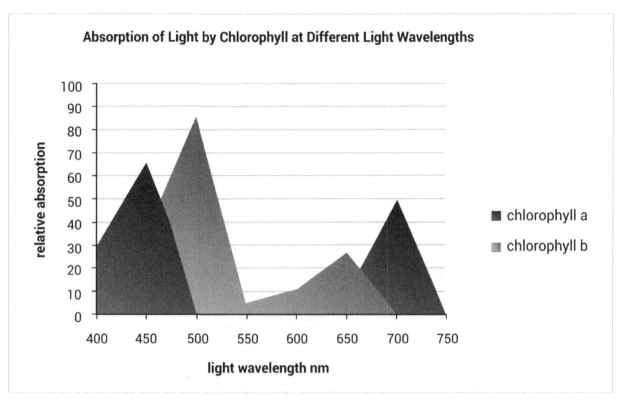

Researchers conducted three trials and hypothesized that LEDs would result in greater growth rates than conventional lighting or white light. They also hypothesized that using a combination of red, blue, green, and yellow wavelengths in the LED lighting system would result in a greater growth rate than using red or blue wavelengths alone. Although green and yellow wavelengths are largely reflected by the plant (Figure 2), the absorption rate is sufficient to make a modest contribution to plant growth. Fifteen Impatiens walleriana seed samples were planted in the same growing medium. Temperature, hydration, and light intensity were held constant. Plant height in millimeters was recorded as follows.

467

Figure 3 identifies the plant growth rate in millimeters with light wavelengths of 440 nanometers.

Figure 3:
Plant Growth Rate (mm) with Light wavelengths of 440 nm

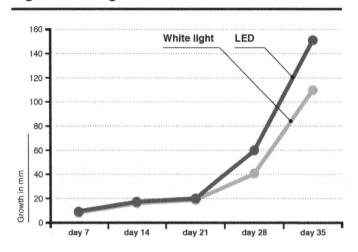

Figure 4 (below) identifies the plant growth rate in mm with light wavelengths of 650 nanometers.

Figure 4:
Plant Growth Rate (mm) with Light wavelengths of 650 nm

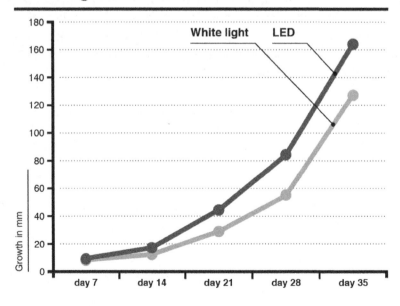

Figure 5 (below) identifies the plant growth rate in millimeters with combined light wavelengths of 440, 550, and 650 nanometers.

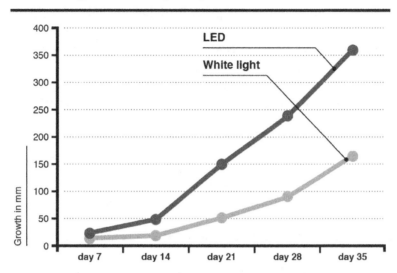

Figure 5:
Plant Growth Rate (mm) with Combined Light wavelengths of 440, 550, and 650 nm

Figure 6 (below) identifies average daily plant growth rate in millimeters.

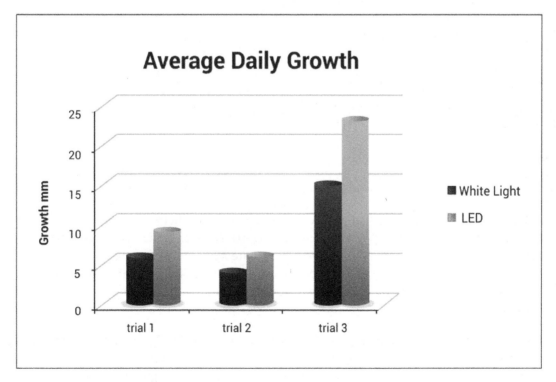

469

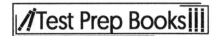

18. If the minimum plant height required for packaging a plant for sale is 150 millimeters, based on plant growth, how much sooner will the LED plants be packaged compared to the white light plants?

    a. 14 days

    b. 21 days

    c. 35 days

    d. 42 days

19. Plants reflect green and yellow light wavelengths. Do the results of the three trials support the view that plants also absorb and use green and yellow light wavelengths for growth?

    a. Yes, green and yellow light wavelengths were responsible for plant growth in trial 3.

    b. No, white light alone was responsible for measurable plant growth.

    c. Yes, the growth rates in trial 3 were greater than the rates in trials 1 and 2.

    d. No, only the red and blue wavelengths were effective in stimulating plant growth.

20. When did the greatest rate of growth occur for both groups in trial 1 and trial 2?

    a. From 7 days to 14 days

    b. From 28 days to 35 days

    c. From 21 days to 28 days

    d. From 14 days to 21 days

21. If an LED lighting system costs twice as much as a white light system, based only on the average daily growth rate as noted above, would it be a wise investment?

    a. No, because multiple different semi-conductors would be necessary.

    b. Yes, growth rates are better with LEDs.

    c. No, the LED average daily growth rate was not two times greater than the white light rate.

    d. Yes, LEDs use less electricity and water.

22. If the researchers conducted an additional trial, trial 4, to measure the effect of green and yellow wavelengths on plant growth, what would be the probable result?

    a. The growth rate would exceed trial 1.

    b. The growth rate would equal trial 3.

    c. The growth rate would be the same as trial 2.

    d. The growth rate would be less than trial 1 or trial 2.

Passage 5

Questions 23–28 pertain to the following passage:

> Mangoes are a tropical fruit that grow on trees native to Southern Asia called the *Mangifera*. Mangoes are now grown in most frost-free tropical and subtropical locations around the world. India and China harvest the greatest numbers of mangoes. A major problem the mango industry faces each year is the destruction of fruit after harvest. This destruction is the result of spoilage or rotting that occurs during long shipping and storage times.
>
> To prevent the spoilage of mangoes, fruits are stored and shipped in climate-controlled containers. Ideally, mangoes should be stored at around 5 °C, which is about the same temperature as a home refrigerator. Although storage at 5 °C is highly effective at

470

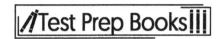

preventing spoilage, the monetary costs associated with maintaining this temperature during long shipping times are prohibitive.

Fruit companies spend large amounts of money to learn about the underlying cause of spoilage and possible methods to prevent loss of their product. Anthracnose, an infection that causes mango decay, is caused by *Colletotrichum,* a type of fungus that has been identified as a major contributor to mango spoilage. This fungus, which may remain dormant on green fruit, grows on the surface of the mango and can penetrate the skin and cause spoilage. The infection first appears during the flowering period as small black dots that progress to dark brown or black areas as ripening occurs. Humidity and excessive rainfall increase the severity of this infection. Previous studies established that colony sizes smaller than 35 millimeters after 4 weeks of travel resulted in acceptable amounts of spoilage.

Currently, several additional pre-treatment measures aimed at prevention are employed to slow decay of the fruit from the harvest to the marketplace. Industry researchers examined the individual and collective benefits of two of these processes, including post-harvest hot water treatment and air cooling at varied transport temperatures in order to identify optimum post-harvest procedures.

Table 1 identifies the observed mango decay in millimeters at 5 °C, 7.5 °C, and 10 °C with two pre-treatment processes over time measured in days since harvest of the fruit.

Table 1: Days Since Harvest

	2	4	6	8	10	12	14	16	18	20	22	24	26	28
5° C														
Water	1	4	7	9	11	12	14	19	22	23	25	27	28	30
Air	0	2	3	6	8	9	11	12	13	15	16	17	18	19
7.5°C														
Water	2	3	4	5	6	8	9	11	12	13	14	15	16	27
Air	0	2	5	6	7	9	10	15	22	23	24	27	32	39
10°C														
Water	2	3	5	7	8	11	12	14	22	35	42	44	47	62
Air	1	2	4	6	7	9	10	15	19	23	27	29	35	44

Figure 1 (below) identifies the observed mango decay of fruit stored at 5 °C measured in millimeters, with two pretreatment processes, over time measured in days since harvest of the fruit.

Figure 1:
5 °C Mango Decay Rates

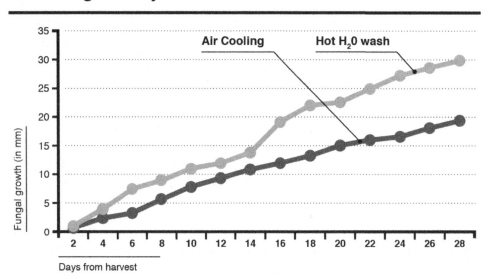

Figures 2 (below) identifies the observed mango decay of fruit stored at 7.5 °C, measured in millimeters, with two pretreatment processes, over time measured in days since harvest of the fruit.

Figure 2:
7.5 °C Mango Decay Rates

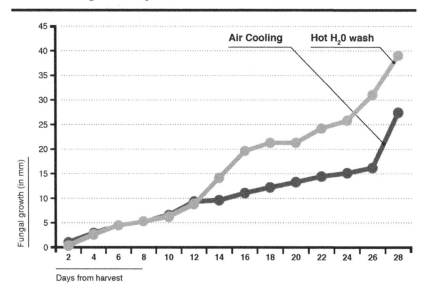

Figures 3 (below) identifies the observed mango decay of fruit stored at 10 °C measured in millimeters, with two pretreatment processes, over time measured in days since harvest of the fruit.

Figure 3:
10 °C Mango Decay Rates

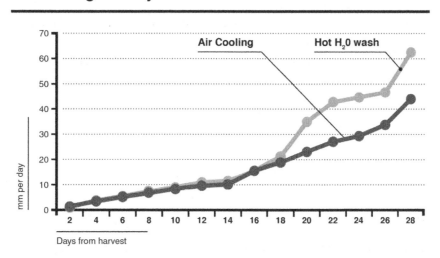

Figure 4 (below) identifies fruit decay measured in millimeters at 5 °C, 7.5 °C, and 10 °C with the combined pre-treatments over 28 days.

Figure 4:
Mango Decay Rates at 5 °C, 7.5 °C, and 10 °C with the Combined Pre-Treatments (Air Cooling & Water Bath)

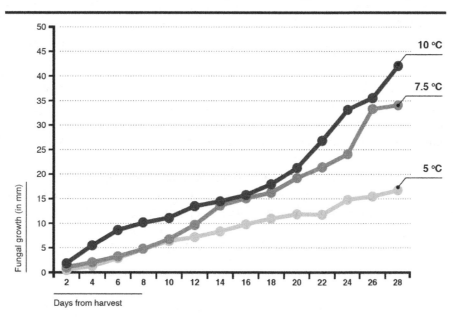

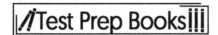

23. According to the passage above, which of the following statements is false?
    a. The optimal temperature for storing mangos is 5 °C.
    b. *Anacardiaceae Mangifera* is responsible for mango spoilage.
    c. Storing fruit at 5 °C is costly.
    d. Long distance shipping is a critical factor in mango spoilage.

24. If the mangoes were shipped from India to the U.S., and the trip was expected to take 20 days, which model would be best according to the data in Table 1?
    a. The 10 °C model, because fungal levels were acceptable for both pre-treatments.
    b. The 5 °C, model because it's more cost-effective.
    c. The 7.5 °C model, because this temperature is less expensive to maintain, and the fungal levels were acceptable.
    d. No single model is better than the other two models.

25. According to Figures 1–3 above, the largest one-day increase in fruit decay occurred under which conditions?
    a. Air cooling at 10 °C
    b. Hot water wash at 10 °C
    c. Air cooling at 7.5 °C
    d. Hot water wash at 7.5 °C

26. Which pre-treatment method reached unacceptable fungal levels first?
    a. Hot water wash at 7.5 °C
    b. Air cooling at 5 °C
    c. Hot water wash at 10 °C
    d. Air cooling at 10 °C

27. The researchers were attempting to identify the best shipping conditions for mangoes for a 28-day trip from harvest to market. Referencing Figures 1–4, which conditions would be the most cost-effective?
    a. Air cooling pre-treatment at 5 °C
    b. Air cooling and hot water wash pre-treatment at 5 °C
    c. Air cooling pre-treatment at 7.5 °C
    d. Air cooling pre-treatment at 10 °C

28. Shipping mangoes at 5 °C is costly. According to the researchers' findings, is shipping mangoes at 5 °C more cost effective than 7.5 °C for trips lasting more than 28 days when combined air cooling and hot water wash treatments are applied?
    a. Yes, shipping at 7.5 °C combined with both pre-treatments resulted in an unacceptable fungal infection rate.
    b. Yes, fungal infection rates were below 35 mm for both pre-treatments 5 °C.
    c. No, air cooling pre-treatment was acceptable at 10 °C, and it's less expensive to ship fruit at 10 °C.
    d. No, hot water wash rates were lower than air cooling at 5 °C.

Passage 6

Questions 29–34 pertain to the following passage:

Scientists recently discovered that circadian rhythms help regulate sugar consumption by brown adipose tissue. The results of this study suggest that circadian rhythms and fat cells work together to warm the body in preparation for early morning activities involving cold weather. A circadian rhythm refers to life processes controlled by an internal "biological clock" that maintains a 24-hour rhythm. Sleep is controlled by one's circadian rhythm. To initiate sleep, the circadian rhythm stimulates the pineal gland to release the hormone melatonin, which causes sleepiness. Importantly, the circadian rhythm discerns when to begin the process of sleep based on the time of day. During the daytime, sunlight stimulates special cells within the eye, photosensitive retinal ganglion cells, which, in turn, allow the "biological clock" to keep track of how many hours of sunlight there are in a given day.

Brown adipose tissue (BAT) is a type of fat that plays an important role in thermogenesis, a process that generates heat. In humans and other mammals, there are two basic types of thermogenesis: shivering thermogenesis and non-shivering thermogenesis. Shivering thermogenesis involves physical movements, such as shaky hands or clattering teeth. Heat is produced as a result of energy being burned during physical activity. Non-shivering thermogenesis doesn't require physical activity; instead, it utilizes brown adipose tissue to generate heat. Brown fat cells appear dark because they contain large numbers of mitochondria, the organelles that burn sugar to produce energy and heat.

Researchers know that brown adipose tissue (BAT) is essential for maintaining body temperature. A new discovery in humans has shown that circadian rhythms cause BAT to consume more sugar in the early-morning hours. This spike in sugar consumption causes more heat to be produced in BAT. Scientists propose that our human ancestors could have benefited from extra body heat during cold hunts in the morning.

Perhaps more significantly, these new findings may suggest a role for BAT in the prevention of Type 2 Diabetes. Two important questions remain; to what degree does BAT affect blood glucose levels, and is it possible to increase BAT in a given individual? The demonstrated increase in sugar consumption and heat production of BAT is thought to be related to insulin-sensitivity. To examine the first question, researchers conducted three trials to examine the relationship between brown fat and blood glucose levels at different points in the day. PET scanning was used to estimate total body brown fat in 18 non-diabetic participants. Total body brown fat expressed as a proportion of total body fat (either 5%, 10%, or 20%) was the basis for group selection. The researchers hypothesized that the blood glucose levels would be inversely related to the percentage of BAT. Resulting data is included below.

Figure 1 (below) identifies the circadian cycle of blood glucose.

Figure 1:
Normal Circadian Plasma Glucose Levels

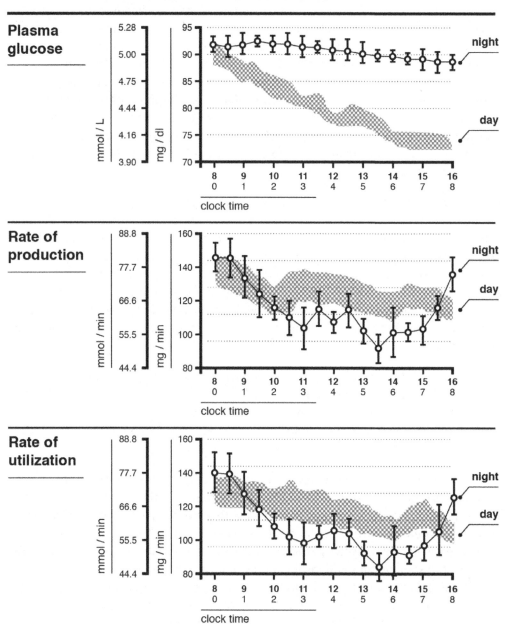

476

Figure 2 (below) identifies the resulting blood glucose measurements for participants with 5% total brown body fat.

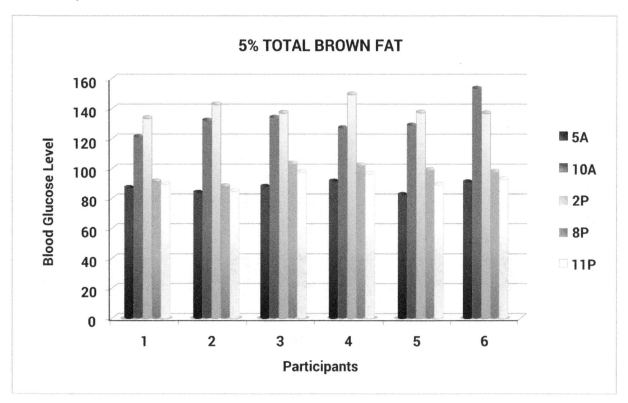

Figure 3 (below) identifies the resulting blood glucose measurements for participants with 10% total brown body fat.

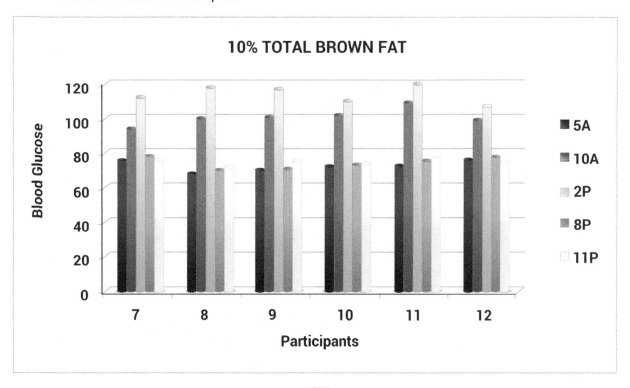

477

Figure 4 (below) identifies the resulting blood glucose measurements for participants with 20% total brown body fat.

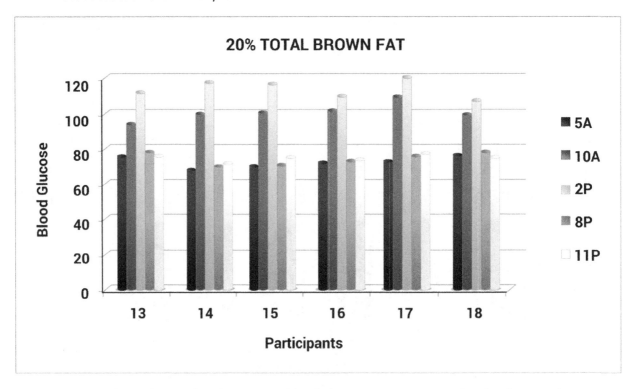

Figure 5 (below) identifies the average blood glucose measurements for the three trials.

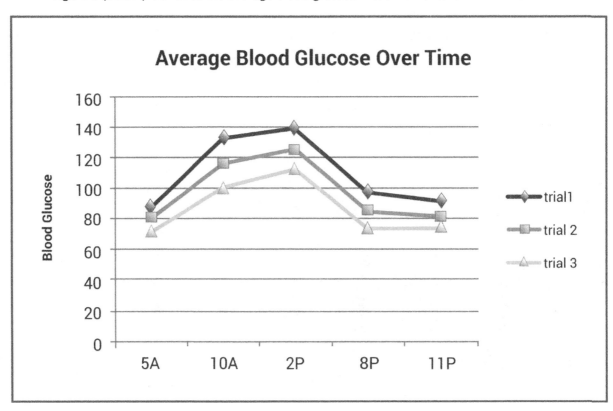

29. Which of the following describes the relationship of the research results in Figure 5?
    a. Positive correlation among the three trials
    b. Curvilinear relationship
    c. Weak negative relationship
    d. No demonstrated relationship

30. Which of the following statements concerning mitochondria is INCORRECT?
    a. Mitochondrial function is diminished in the presence of elevated blood glucose levels.
    b. Mitochondria are responsible for the color of brown fat.
    c. Mitochondria are capable of reproduction in response to energy needs.
    d. Mitochondria are responsible for binding oxygen in mature red blood cells.

31. According to Figure 5, participants' blood sugars were highest at what time of day?
    a. 5 a.m., because heat is generated early in the morning
    b. 8 p.m., because the participants ate less for dinner than lunch
    c. 11 p.m., because brown adipose tissue is not active at night
    d. 2 p.m., because the effects of the early-morning activity of the brown adipose tissue had diminished

32. Circadian rhythms control sleep by doing which of the following?
    a. Stimulating the pineal gland to release ganglia
    b. Stimulating the release of melatonin
    c. Suppressing shivering during cold mornings
    d. Instructing brown adipose tissue to release sugar

33. Which Participant in trial 1 had the highest average blood sugar for the group?
    a. 1
    b. 3
    c. 4
    d. 6

34. Is the data in Figure 5 consistent with the daytime plasma glucose trend in Figure 1?
    a. Yes, Figure 5 blood glucose readings declined from a morning to afternoon.
    b. No, blood glucose readings peaked at 2 p.m..
    c. Yes, morning glucose readings were higher in group 1.
    d. No, nighttime levels fluctuated between 100 and 110.

Passage 7

Questions 35–40 pertain to the following passage:

A biome is a major terrestrial or aquatic environment that supports diverse life forms. Freshwater biomes—including lakes, streams and rivers, and wetlands—account for 0.01% of the Earth's fresh water. Collectively, they are home to 6% of all recognized species. Standing water bodies may vary in size from small ponds to the Great Lakes. Plant life in lakes is specific to the zone of the lake that provides the optimal habitat for a specific species, based on the depth of the water as it relates to light. The photic layer is the shallower layer where light is available for photosynthesis. The aphotic layer is deeper, and the levels of sunlight are too low for photosynthesis. The benthic layer is

the bottom-most layer, and its inhabitants are nourished by materials from the photic layer. Light-sensitive cyanobacteria and microscopic algae are two forms of phytoplankton that exist in lakes. As a result of nitrogen and phosphorus from agriculture and sewage run-off, algae residing near the surface can multiply abnormally so that available light is diminished to other species. Oxygen supplies may also be reduced when large numbers of algae die.

Recently, concerns have been raised about the effects of agriculture and commercial development on the quality of national freshwater bodies. In order to estimate the effect of human impact on freshwater, researchers examined plant life from the aphotic layer of three freshwater lakes of approximately the same size located in three different environments. Lake A was located in a remote forested area of western Montana. Lake B was located in central Kansas. Lake C was located in a medium-size city on the west coast of Florida. The researchers hypothesized that the microscopic algae and cyanobacteria populations from Lake A would approach appropriate levels for the size of the lake. They also hypothesized that the remaining two samples would reveal abnormal levels of the phytoplankton. In addition, the researchers measured the concentration of algae at different depths at four different times in another lake identified as having abnormal algae growth. These measurements attempted to identify the point at which light absorption in the photic layer was no longer sufficient for the growth of organisms in the aphotic layer. Resulting data is identified below.

Figure 1 (below) illustrates the zones of the freshwater lake.

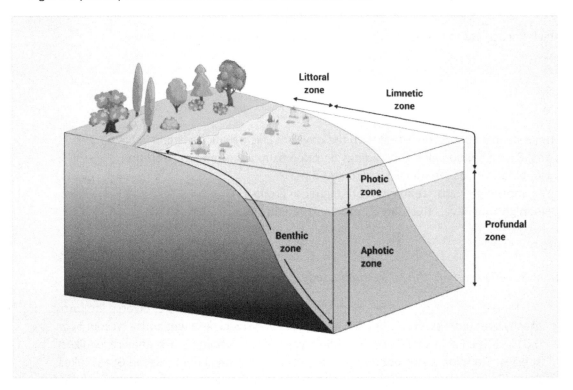

Figure 2 (below) identifies algae and cyanobacteria levels in parts per million for Lake A over six measurements.

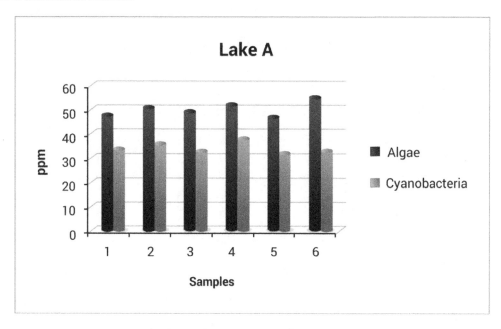

normal: Algae 50 p.p.m. Cyanobacteria 35 p.p.m.

Figure 3 (below) identifies algae and cyanobacteria levels in parts per million for Lake B over six measurements.

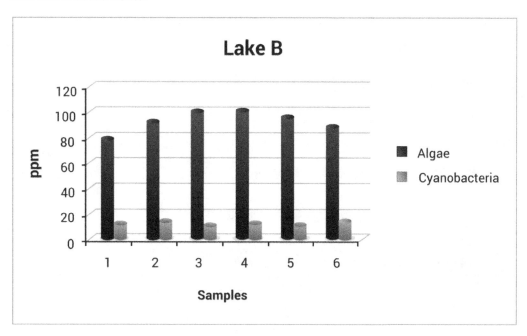

normal: Algae 50 p.p.m. Cyanobacteria 35 p.p.m.

481

Figure 4 (below) identifies algae and cyanobacteria levels in parts per million for Lake C over six measurements.

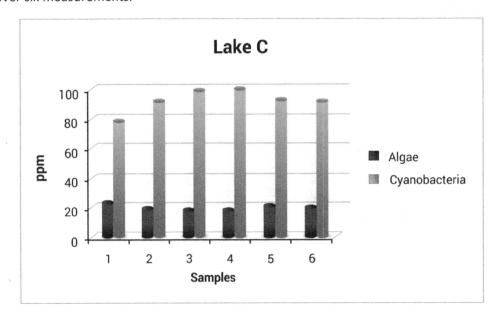

normal: Algae 50 p.p.m. Cyanobacteria 35 p.p.m.

Figure 5 (below) identifies cyanobacteria levels at different depths over time.

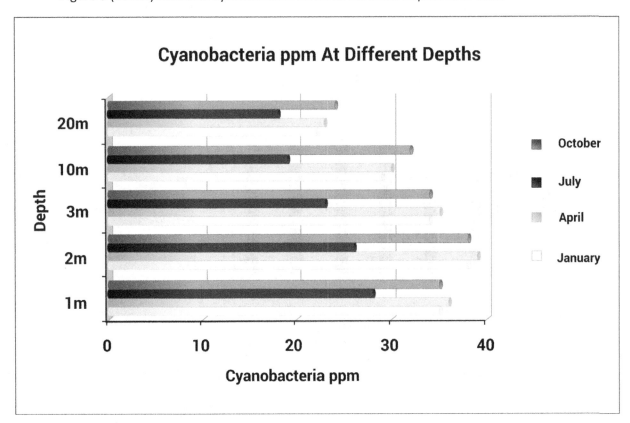

35. Based on Figure 2, was the researchers' hypothesis confirmed?
   a. No, the phytoplankton levels were not elevated in the first trial.
   b. Yes, the phytoplankton levels were raised above normal in each sample.
   c. No, the Lake A numbers were normal.
   d. Yes, algae levels were above normal in Lake C.

36. In Lake B, cyanobacteria were decreased and algae were increased. Which of the following is a possible explanation for this finding?
   a. The overgrowth of algae decreased the light energy available for cyanobacteria growth.
   b. Lake B experienced severe flooding, causing the water levels in the lake to rise above normal.
   c. Agricultural chemical residue depleted the food source for cyanobacteria.
   d. Cyanobacteria cannot survive in the cold winter weather in Lake B.

37. What common factor might explain the results for Lake B and Lake C?
   a. Population concentration
   b. Average humidity of the locations
   c. Average heat index
   d. Excess nitrogen and phosphorus in the ground water

38. As algae levels increase above normal, what happens to organisms in the aphotic level?
   a. Growth is limited but sustained.
   b. Species eventually die due to decreased oxygenation.
   c. Cyanobacteria increase to unsafe levels.
   d. Aerobic bacteria multiply.

39. Referencing Figures 3 and 4, which environment would favor organisms in the benthic layer of the corresponding lake?
   a. Figure 4, because the cyanobacteria are protective.
   b. Figure 3, because increased numbers of algae provide more light.
   c. Figure 4, because cyanobacteria are able to survive.
   d. Figure 3, because the levels of both species are normal.

40. Which of the following statements is supported by the data in Figure 5?
   a. Algae growth is greater in July than April.
   b. Cyanobacteria can't exist at 20 meters in this lake.
   c. There's insufficient light in the aphotic layer at 3 meters to support algae growth.
   d. Cyanobacteria growth rates are independent of algae growth at 1 meter.

Writing

Directions

Write an organized, coherent essay about the passage below. In your essay, make sure you:

- Clearly state your own opinion on the issue and analyze the relationships between your perspective and at least one other perspective
- Develop and support your ideas with evidence
- Organize your ideas logically
- Communicate your ideas in standard English

483

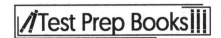

Prompt

Technology has been invading cars for the last several years, but there are some new high-tech trends that are pretty amazing. It is now standard in many car models to have a rear-view camera, hands-free phone and text, and a touch screen digital display. Music can be streamed from a paired cell phone, and some displays can even be programmed with a personal photo. Sensors beep to indicate there is something in the driver's path when reversing and changing lanes. Rain-sensing windshield wipers and lights are automatic, leaving the driver with little to do but watch the road and enjoy the ride. The next wave of technology will include cars that automatically parallel park, and self-driving cars are on the horizon. These technological advances make it a good time to be a driver.

Perspectives

1. Some technological features could become distracting or cause the driver to rely too heavily on the car's automation instead of paying close attention to road conditions. Either way, these features can inadvertently cause a safety hazard. For example, solely utilizing the rear-view camera instead of turning around to check the surroundings could give a driver false confidence that there are no obstacles in the way, even though the camera may not pick up on something outside of its lens. Another example is a digital display showing music choices and incoming text messages that could draw the driver's attention away from the road.

2. New technological features make driving more enjoyable and much easier. Hands-free phone features prevent drivers from looking at their phone screens for prolonged periods of time and provide an easy way to communicate in the case of an emergency. Rearview cameras and other sensors allow drivers to become more aware of their surroundings and help adjust for human error. Features like these actually make driving much safer.

3. Technological advances in the automotive industry bring in more profit for that sector, but they may end up having an overall detrimental impact economically. Many people earn a living by driving others from one place to another, and if highly automated or completely self-driving cars become widespread enough, then they will replace the individuals performing those jobs.

Answer Explanations #3

English

1. C: The next paragraph states that "These advanced offices oftentimes require a Professional Engineering (PE) license which can be obtained through additional college courses, professional experience, and acceptable scores on the Fundamentals of Engineering (FE) and Professional Engineering (PE) standardized assessments." Since the word *oftentimes* is used instead of *always*, Choice *C* is the best response.

2. C: The best answer is Choice *C*. Items in a list should be separated by a comma. Choice *A* is incorrect because there are no commas within the list to separate the items. Choice *B* is incorrect; a semicolon is used in a series only when a comma is present within the list itself. Choice *D* is incorrect because the conjunction *and* is missing before the word *calculus*.

3. A: The sentence is correct as-is. The words *one* and *bachelor* have apostrophe *-s* at the end because they show possession for the words that come after. The other answer choices do not indicate possession is being shown.

4. D: To begin, *of* is not required here. *Apprenticeship* is also more appropriate in this context than *apprentice opportunities*; *apprentice* describes an individual in an apprenticeship, not an apprenticeship itself. Both of these changes are needed, making Choice *D* the correct answer.

5. D: Choice *D* is correct because it breaks the section into coherent sentences and emphasizes the main point the author is trying to communicate: the PE license is required for some higher positions, it's obtained by scoring well on the two standardized assessments, and college and experience can be used to prepare for the assessments in order to gain the certification. The original sentence is a run-on and contains confusing information, so Choice *A* is incorrect. Choice *B* fixes the run-on aspect, but the sentence is indirect and awkward in construction. Choice *C* is incorrect for the same reason as Choice *B*, and it is a run on.

6. B: *Once the job begins, this line of work* is the best way to phrase this sentence. Choice *A* is incorrect because *lines* does not match up with *this*; it would instead match up with the word *these*. Choice *C* is incorrect; *these line* should say *this line*. Choice *D* is incorrect; *job begin* is faulty subject/verb agreement.

7. A: The word is spelled correctly as it is: *expertise*.

8. C: *Allows* is inappropriate because it does not stress what those in the position of aircraft engineers actually need to be able to do. *Requires* is the only alternative that fits because it actually describes necessary skills of the job.

9. D: The words *equations* and *processes* in this sentence should be plural. Choices *A, B,* and *C* have one or both words as singular, which is incorrect.

10. A: The correct response is Choice *A* because this statement's intent is to give examples as to how aircraft engineers apply mathematical equations and scientific processes towards aeronautical and aerospace issues and/or inventions. The answer is not *Therefore*, Choice *B*, or *Furthermore*, Choice *D*,

because no causality is being made between ideas. Two items are neither being compared nor contrasted, so *However*, Choice *C*, is also not the correct answer.

11. A: No change is required. The comma is properly placed after the introductory phrase *In May of 2015.* Choice *B* is missing the word *In*. Choice *C* does not separate the introductory phrase from the rest of the sentence. Choice *D* places an extra comma prior to 2015.

12. A: The word *conversely* best demonstrates the opposite sentiments in this passage. Choice *B* is incorrect because it denotes agreement with the previous statement. Choice *C* is incorrect because the sentiment is not restated but opposed. Choice *D* is incorrect because the previous statement is not a cause for the sentence in question.

13. A: The correct answer is Choice *A, are projected*. The present tense *are* matches with the rest of the sentence. The verb *are* also matches with the plural *employment opportunities*. Choice *B* uses *will be projected*, which is incorrect because the statistic is being used as evidence, which demands a present or past tense verb. In this case it is present tense to maintain consistency. Choice *C* is incorrect because the singular verb *is* does not match with the plural subject *employment opportunities*. Choice *D* is incorrect because the past tense verb *were* does not maintain consistency with the present tense in the rest of the passage.

14. C: Choice *C* is the best answer because introductory words like "Nevertheless" are always succeeded by a comma.

15. D: The main subject and verb in this sentence are far apart from each other. The subject is *engineers* and the subject is *are projected*. Although there is a clause which interrupts the subject and the verb, they still must agree with each other.

16. D: The correct phrase should be "War on Terror." The phrase is capitalized because it was part of the campaign phrase that was launched by the U.S. government after September 11. Punctuation should always be used inside double quotes as well, making Choice *D* the best answer.

17. C: Terrorists commonly use fear and violence to achieve political goals. Choice *A* is incorrect because the subject *Terrorists* is plural while the verb *uses* is singular, so the subject and verb do not agree with each other. Choice *B* is incorrect because the word *Terrorist's* with the apostrophe *-s* shows possession, but the terrorists aren't in possession of anything in this sentence. Choice *D* is incorrect because the word *achieves* should be *achieve*.

18. A: No change is needed. Choices *B* and *C* utilize incorrect comma placements. Choice *D* utilizes an incorrect verb tense (*responding*).

19. B: The best answer Choice is *B, who live mainly in the South and Southwest Asia*. The directional terms *South Asia* and *Southwest Asia* are integral parts of a proper name and should therefore be capitalized.

20. D: This is the best answer choice because *America's* with the apostrophe *-s* shows possession of the word *support*, and *Israel* should be capitalized because it is a country and therefore a proper noun. Choice *A* does not show possession in the word *Americas*. Choice *B* does not capitalize the word *Israel*. Choice *C* does not show possession and does not include the necessary comma at the end of the phrase.

21. A: This sentence is correct as-is. The verb tense should be in the past—the other three answer choices either have a present or continuous verb tense, so these are incorrect.

22. C: Choice *C* is the most straightforward version of this independent clause, because it follows the "subject+verb+prepositional phrase" order which usually provides the most clarity.

23. B: Although *diverging* means to separate from the main route and go in a different direction, it is used awkwardly and unconventionally in this sentence. Therefore, Choice *A* is not the answer. Choice *B* is the correct answer because it implies that the passengers distracted the terrorists, which caused a change in the plane's direction. *Converging*, Choice *C*, is incorrect because it implies that the plane met another in a central location. Although the passengers may have distracted the terrorists, they did not distract the plane. Therefore, Choice *D* is incorrect.

24. B: Choice *B* is the best answer because it is straightforward and clear. Choice *A* is incorrect because the phrase *the fact that* is redundant. Choice *C* is inverted and doesn't make much sense because the subject comes after the verb. Choice *D* is incorrect because it does not have the appropriate transition, *but*, which is intended to show a contrast to the *uncertainty* phrase that comes before it.

25. A: Choice *A* is the best choice for this sentence because it is the most straightforward and easiest to understand. Choice *B* is incorrect because it leaves out the hedging language. Choice *C* keeps the hedging language, but the sentence begins with a verb which is not the best decision for clarity. Choice *D* is incorrect because it begins with a preposition which is not the best choice for a straightforward presentation of the facts.

26. A: The word *valiantly* is spelled correctly in the original sentence.

27. D: Airspace and airports must be closed by people; they don't just close themselves, so it is proper to include an action to indicate that they were sealed off. Choice *B* is incorrect because the verb *close* is in the incorrect tense. Choice *C* is also incorrect because *airspace* does not need to become *airspaces* and the issue still remains: while there is action, it is not in the proper form to indicate human action. Choice *D* is correct because it correctly uses the helping verb *were*, which indicates human action.

28. C: This sentence contains improper verb agreement in the fragment *as cancelled flights are rescheduled. Are* is a present-tense verb while *rescheduled* is a past-tense verb. Because the attacks occurred in the past, both verbs need to be written in the past tense, as done in Choice *C*.

29. C: Intended means planned or meant to. Intended is a far better choice than desired, because it would communicate goals and strategy more than simply saying that Bush desired to do something. *Desired* communicates wishing or direct motive. Choices *B* and *D* have irrelevant meanings and wouldn't serve the sentence at all.

30. A: The original structure of the two sentences is correct. Choice *B* lacks the direct nature that the original sentence has. By breaking up the sentences, the connection between the Taliban's defeat and the ongoing war is separated by an unnecessary second sentence. Choice *C* corrects this problem, but the fluidity of the sentence is marred because of the awkward construction of the first sentence. Choice *D* begins well but lacks the use of *was* before *overthrown*.

31. C: Choice *C* is the best answer choice here because we have "subject+verb+prepositional phrases" which is usually the most direct sentence combination. Choice *A* is incorrect because the verbs *seeing* and *see* are repetitive. Choice *B* is incorrect because the subject and verb are separated, which is not the

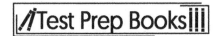
best way to divulge information in this particular sentence. Choice *D* is incorrect because the sentence uses a continuous verb form instead of past tense.

32. A: The comma after *result* is necessary for the sentence structure, making it an imperative component. The original sentence is correct, making Choice *A* correct. Choice *B* is incorrect because it lacks the crucial comma that introduces a new idea. Choice *C* is incorrect because a colon is unnecessary, and Choice *D* is incorrect because the addition of the word *of* is unnecessary when applied to the rest of the sentence.

33. B: Hampton was born and raised in Maywood of Chicago, Illinois in 1948. Choice *A* is incorrect because the subject and verb are at the end, and this is not the most straightforward syntax. Choice *C* is incorrect because the rest of the passage is in past tense. Choice *D* is incorrect because there should be a comma between the names of a city and a state.

34. D: Choice *D* is the best answer because it fixes the comma splice in the original sentence by creating a modifying clause at the beginning of the sentence. Choice *A* is incorrect because it contains a comma splice. Choice *B* is too wordy. Choice *C* has an unnecessary comma.

35. A: The sentence is correct as-is. Choice *B* is incorrect because we are missing the chronological signpost *after*. Choice *C* is incorrect because there is no subject represented in this sentence. Choice *D* is incorrect because it also doesn't have a subject.

36. C: Choice *C* is the best sentence because it is a compound sentence with the appropriate syntax. Choice *A* is incorrect because *resulting* is not as clear as the phrase *as a result*. Choice *B* is incorrect because the syntax is clunky—to say something happened to the NAACP rather than the NAACP making the gain is awkward. Choice *D* is incorrect because this is passive voice; active voice would be better to use here as in Choice *C*.

37. D: Choice *D* is the best answer. Choice *A* is incorrect; if the second clause was independent we would need a comma in the middle, but the two clauses have the same single subject, so a comma is unnecessary. Choice *B* is incorrect; semicolons go in between two independent clauses without conjunctions. Choice *C* is incorrect; there needs to be a conjunction before the word *relocated*.

38. B: *enabled him to quickly rise* is the best answer. Although the passage is in past tense, the verb *enabled* is followed by the "to+infinitive." The infinitive is the base form of the verb; that's why *rise* is the best answer choice, because the verb follows *to* and represents the infinitive after the verb *enabled*.

39. A: No change is needed. The list of events should be separated by a comma. Choice *B* is incorrect. Although a colon can be used to introduce a list of items, it is not a conventional choice for separating items within a series. Semicolons are used to separate at least three items in a series that have an internal comma. Therefore, Choice *C* is incorrect. Choice *D* is incorrect because a dash is not a conventional choice for punctuating items in a series.

40. C: *Hampton's greatest achievement as the leader of the BPP* is the best way to phrase this sentence because it is the most straightforward and clear. Choice *A* is incorrect because the sentence starts out with a gerund when it could start out with Hampton, reducing confusion as to who is leading the BPP. Choice *B* is incorrect for the same reason; the sentence starts off with the subject inside the preposition, which is not the best syntax. Choice *D* is incorrect because it doesn't signify that the achievement was Hampton's.

41. D: Choice *D* is the most straightforward answer, "Hampton held a press conference." Choice *A* is incorrect because usually one isn't held "by" a press conference. Choice *B* is incorrect because likewise, a press conference doesn't "hold" someone, but someone would "hold" a press conference. Choice *C* is incorrect because again, someone isn't held "by" a press conference, and the syntax is inverted here.

42. A: The term *neutralize* means to counteract, or render ineffective, which is exactly what the FBI is wanting to do. Accommodate means to be helpful or lend aid, which is the opposite of *neutralize*. Therefore, Choice *B* is incorrect. *Assuage* means to ease, while *praise* means to express warm feeling, so they are in no way close to the needed context. Therefore, *neutralize* is the best option, making Choice *A* the correct answer.

43. C: Choice *C* is the most straightforward answer choice. Choice *A* is incorrect because the sentence is inverted and not very clear. Choice *B* is incorrect because the change in syntax changes the meaning in the sentence. Choice *D* isn't the best way to organize the sentence because it creates wordiness.

44. D: Choice *D* is the best answer choice because it matches with the past tense of the passage. The other answer choices are either in present tense or a present continuous tense.

45. B: Choice *B* is the most straightforward sentence, beginning with the subject and verb, then leading off with two prepositions. Choice *A* is incorrect because the sentence is passive and thus more wordy than the active voice in Choice *B*. Choice *C* is incorrect because the sentence starts out with two prepositions which isn't the best syntax for clarity here. Choice *D* is incorrect because the verb is in present tense instead of past tense.

46. A: Choice *A* is the best answer because *commemorates* means to show respect for something through recognition. Choice *B*, *disparages*, means to discourage, so this is incorrect. Choice *C*, *exculpates*, means to show that someone is not guilty of wrongdoing, and this does not make sense within the context of the sentence. Choice *D*, *brandish*, means to swing or flaunt, and is not the best choice here.

47. D: Choice *D* is the best answer. Choice *A* is incorrect; the comma is not necessary here because both clauses use the same subject, *Floods*. Choice *B* is incorrect because *causing by* is not an appropriate verb phrase. Choice *C* is incorrect because *so to cause by* is also not an appropriate verb phrase.

48. C: The sentence is best written with a comma before the clause *as are low-lying regions*. Choice *A* is incorrect because the comma before the clause is missing. Choice *B* is incorrect; there is a comma splice and this sentence is repetitive. Choice *D* is incorrect because the syntax is not straightforward, and it also is repetitive.

49. D: Choice *D* is the best arrangement of the sentence. Choice *A* is incorrect; *sun* should be possessive of *radiation* and thus have an apostrophe *-s* at the end of the word. Choice *B* is incorrect; the addition of the word *which* adds unnecessary wordiness to the sentence. Choices *C* is incorrect; the word *being* is used twice which creates repetition.

50. B: In this sentence, the word *ocean* does not require an *s* after it to make it plural because *ocean levels* is plural. Therefore, Choices *A* and *C* are incorrect. Because the sentence is referring to multiple— if not all ocean levels—*ocean* does not require an apostrophe ('s) because that would indicate that only one ocean is the focus, which is not the case. Choice *D* does not fit well into the sentence and, once again, we see that *ocean* has an *s* after it. This leaves Choice *B*, which correctly completes the sentence and maintains the intended meaning.

51. C: Choice *C* is the best answer. Choice *A* is incorrect because *the water* is doing the overflowing, so it should come before the phrase *to overflow*. Choice *B* is incorrect because *may been causing* isn't an appropriate verb phrase. Choice *D* is incorrect because the word *water* is used repetitively.

52. D: Choice *A* is incorrect; semicolons separate items in a list only when an item in the list contains a comma itself. Choice *B* is incorrect; items in a list should always be separated by commas. Choice *C* is incorrect because the word *beavers* is missing a possessive -'s at the end.

53. B: The best conjunction to use in this sentence is the word *or*. The other conjunctions used, *then, so,* and *but*, do not fit in the context of the sentence here.

54. A: Choice *A* is the best answer. Choice *B* is incorrect because it has incorrect subject/verb agreement, *waters begins*. Choice *C* is incorrect because it is missing the word *to* in front of the word *grow*. Choice *D* is incorrect; technically this sentence is grammatically correct, but by using the conjunction *and,* it implies that water begins to drain and mold grows at the same time, which is not what the passage intended.

55. A: Choice *C* can be eliminated because creating a new sentence with *not* is grammatically incorrect, and it throws off the rest of the sentence. Choice *B* is incorrect because a comma is needed after *devastation* in the sentence. Choice *D* is also incorrect because *while* is a poor substitute for *although*. *Although* in this context is meant to show contradiction with the idea that floods are associated with devastation. Therefore, none of these choices would be suitable revisions because the original was correct.

56. B: Choice *B* is the best answer because it is the most straightforward syntax. Choice *A* is incorrect because *floodplains of rivers* is unnecessarily long. Choice *C* is incorrect because a comma is missing after the prepositional phrase. Choice *D* is incorrect because the word *thousands* is plural and therefore should not have an apostrophe.

57. B: Choice *B* is the best answer here. Choice *A* is incorrect because the text should specify what type of examples are about to be named. Choice *C* is incorrect because items in a list should be separated by commas, not by ellipses. Choice *D* is incorrect because, again, items in a list should be separated by commas.

58. D: Choice *D* is correct because it is in the indefinite present tense and is consistent with the passage. Choice *A* is incorrect because *caused* is inconsistent with the rest of the verb tense in the passage. Choice *B* is incorrect because this does not agree with the subject *the flooding*. *Causing*, Choice *C,* is in the present continuous tense which does not fit with the subject, *Flooding . . . causing*.

59. A: To *project* means to anticipate or forecast. This goes very well with the sentence because it describes how new technology is trying to estimate flood activity in order to prevent damage and save lives. *Project* in this case needs to be assisted by *to* in order to function in the sentence. Therefore, Choice *A* is correct. Choices *B* and *D* are the incorrect tenses. Choice *C* is incorrect because it lacks *to*.

60. B: The correct conjunction is *then*. The word *then* implies *after that* or *afterward*.

61. C: Choice *C* is the correct answer. Shorter poems should be in quotation marks, but tiles of long, epic poems like *The Odyssey* should be written with italics.

490

62. A: Choice *A* is the best answer. *However* is an appropriate word to begin this sentence since it illustrates the idea of contrast: some of the females Odysseus encountered were helpful, *however* some were clearly not. Therefore, we can eliminate Choice *D*. Choice *B* is also incorrect because it eliminates the word *several*, which is also useful in distinguishing that, while some female characters were benevolent, several were deceptive and even harmful. Choice *C* is incorrect because it lacks the comma after *However*.

63. D: Choice *D* is the best answer because it uses a comma between an independent clause and a dependent clause and gets rid of the word *himself*, eliminating wordiness. Choice *A* is incorrect because the comma between two independent clauses causes a comma splice. Additionally, the word *himself* is repetitive. Choice *B* is incorrect because the absence of a semicolon or period after *harder* creates a run-on sentence.

64. C: We would say *By the time Odysseus reaches* home to denote that one event occurs before the other. The other answer choices don't make this distinction.

65. A: Choice *A* is correct because it is in active voice rather than passive voice. Choice *B* is incorrect because *he had to be concealed himself* is passive voice and also creates wordiness with *himself*. Choice *C* makes the sentence grammatically incorrect. Choice *D* is incorrect because *concealing* does not go with the helping verb *had*. *Had concealing* is not a proper verb phrase.

66. B: Choice *B* is the best answer. Choice *A* is incorrect because it is a run-on sentence. Choice *C* is incorrect because the comma between two independent clauses creates a comma splice. Choice *D* is incorrect; semicolons should have independent clauses on either side of them, and the first phrase is not a complete sentence.

67. B: Choice *B, conceals,* is the best option because Odysseus does in fact hide (or conceal) his true identity behind a false name. Choice *A* is incorrect; *relinquishes* means to give up or to voluntarily cease control of something. This is not something Odysseus does because he does not surrender his true name—he just hides it. He does not *withhold* (Choice *C*) his true identity but offers an alternative. Choice *D, surrenders,* is synonymous with *relinquishes*.

68. A: Reading through the sentence, one can see that it flows and uses proper punctuation and grammar, which means that no change is necessary; Choice *A* is the correct answer. Choice *B* lacks the necessary comma after *Clearly*. Choice *C* utilizes an unnecessary semicolon. Choice *D* makes the sentence awkward by placing *clearly* in the middle of the sentence.

69. C: Choice *C* is the best answer choice. Choice *A* is incorrect because the author of the passage uses present tense when speaking about the text in question, so the verb should be *describes*. Choice *B* is incorrect because *passages* should be *passage*, singular. Choice *D* is incorrect because the word *These* should be *This*, describing a singular passage.

70. B: Choice *B* is the best answer because it avoids the wordiness of the original phrase *also like*, which makes Choice *A* incorrect. Choice *C* is compelling, but it lacks the necessary information that the original sentence has: we need to have Polyphemus still in the sentence. Choice *D* is a decent option, but much of it is unnecessary and already addressed in the remainder of the sentence that isn't underlined.

71. B: The issue with this word is that it lacks proper punctuation. *One* is referring to an individual, and it needs to show possession of *identity*. Therefore, *ones* must have an apostrophe to show ownership and to be correct. Thus, Choice *B, One's*, is the correct answer.

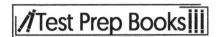

72. C: The current phrase repeats itself, so we can eliminate Choice *A*. Choices *B* and *D* are compelling but are somewhat specific. What must be communicated is that all men who reach the island, in whatever fashion, risk being seduced by Circe. Choice *C* is the most practical revision and is more direct, while allowing for other circumstances in which men come to Circe's island.

73. B: The best answer is Choice *B, ensure*, which means to make certain. Odysseus is trying to make certain that he and the crew will be safe by beating Circe at her own game. Choice *A, assure*, means to speak to someone in a way that eliminates doubt. This indirectly relates to what Odysseus wants to do, but to *assure* specifically refers to speaking to someone. Choices *C* and *D* are totally irrelevant. *Vindicate* means to free from blame, while *prevent* means to stop from happening.

74. B: The best verb to use here is *returns*. When talking about text we use present tense verbs.

75. A: Choice *A* is the best answer. Choice *B* is incorrect because it is missing a comma after the introductory clause, *As the text progresses*. Choice *C* is incorrect; Odysseus is the subject of the sentence and must be outside of any phrases—Choice *C* has the subject *Odysseus* inside a prepositional phrase starting with the word *with*, so this is incorrect. Choice *D* is incorrect because again, our subject is inside a clause and therefore does not pair with the verb *encounters*.

Math

1. D: This problem can be solved using basic arithmetic. Xavier starts with 20 apples, then gives his sister half, so 20 divided by 2.

$$\frac{20}{2} = 10$$

He then gives his neighbor 6, so 6 is subtracted from 10.

$$10 - 6 = 4$$

Lastly, he uses $\frac{3}{4}$ of his apples to make an apple pie, so to find remaining apples, the first step is to subtract $\frac{3}{4}$ from one and then multiply the difference by 4.

$$\left(1 - \frac{3}{4}\right) \times 4 = ?$$

$$\left(\frac{4}{4} - \frac{3}{4}\right) \times 4 = ?$$

$$\left(\frac{1}{4}\right) \times 4 = 1$$

2. C: The product of two irrational numbers can be rational or irrational. Sometimes, the irrational parts of the two numbers cancel each other out, leaving a rational number. For example, $\sqrt{2} \times \sqrt{2} = 2$ because the roots cancel each other out. Technically, the product of two irrational numbers can be complex because complex numbers can have either the real or imaginary part (in this case, the imaginary part) equal zero and still be considered a complex number. However, Choice *D* is incorrect because the product of two irrational numbers is not an imaginary number so saying the product is complex *and* imaginary is incorrect.

3. B: The car is traveling at a speed of five meters per second. On the interval from one to three seconds, the position changes by ten meters. By making this change in position over time into a rate, the speed becomes ten meters in two seconds, or five meters in one second.

4. C: The number negative four is classified as a real number because it exists and is not imaginary. It is rational because it does not have a decimal that never ends. It is an integer because it does not have a fractional component. The next classification would be whole numbers, for which negative four does not qualify because it is negative.

5. B: Since $850 is the price *after* a 20% discount, $850 represents 80% of the original price. To determine the original price, set up a proportion with the ratio of the sale price (850) to original price (unknown) equal to the ratio of the sale percentage (where x represents the unknown original price):

$$\frac{850}{x} = \frac{80}{100}$$

To solve a proportion, cross multiply and set the products equal to each other:

$$(850)(100) = (80)(x)$$

Multiplying each side results in the equation:

$$85{,}000 = 80x$$

To solve for x, divide both sides by 80:

$$\frac{85{,}000}{80} = \frac{80x}{80}$$

$$x = 1062.5$$

Remember that x represents the original price. Subtracting the sale price from the original price ($1062.50 - $850) indicates that Frank saved $212.50.

6. D: $0.45

List the givens.

$$\text{Store coffee} = \$1.23/\text{lb}$$

$$\text{Local roaster coffee} = \$1.98/1.5 \text{ lb}$$

Calculate the cost for 5 pounds of store brand.

$$\frac{\$1.23}{1 \text{ lb}} \times 5 \text{ lb} = \$6.15$$

Calculate the cost for 5 pounds of the local roaster.

$$\frac{\$1.98}{1.5 \text{ lb}} \times 5 \text{ lb} = \$6.60$$

Subtract to find the difference in price for 5 pounds.

$$\begin{array}{r} \$6.60 \\ -\$6.15 \\ \hline \$0.45 \end{array}$$

7. C: The first step in solving this problem is expressing the result in fraction form. Multiplication and division are typically performed in order from left to right but they can be performed in any order. For this problem, let's start by solving the division operation of the last two fractions. When dividing one fraction by another, invert or flip the second fraction and then multiply the numerator and denominator.

$$\frac{7}{10} \times \frac{2}{1} = \frac{14}{10}$$

Next, multiply the first fraction with this value:

$$\frac{3}{5} \times \frac{14}{10} = \frac{42}{50}$$

In this instance, you can find the decimal form by converting the fraction into $\frac{x}{100}$, where x is the number from which the final decimal is found. Multiply both the numerator and denominator by 2 to get the fraction as an expression of $\frac{x}{100}$.

$$\frac{42}{50} \times \frac{2}{2} = \frac{84}{100}$$

In decimal form, this would be expressed as 0.84.

8. E: To find the average of a set of values, add the values together and then divide by the total number of values. In this case, include the unknown value of what Dwayne needs to score on his next test, in order to solve it.

$$\frac{78 + 92 + 83 + 97 + x}{5} = 90$$

Add the unknown value to the new average total, which is 5. Then multiply each side by 5 to simplify the equation, resulting in:

$$78 + 92 + 83 + 97 + x = 450$$

$$350 + x = 450$$

$$x = 100$$

Dwayne would need to get a perfect score of 100 in order to get an average of at least 90.

Test this answer by substituting back into the original formula:

$$\frac{78 + 92 + 83 + 97 + 100}{5} = 90$$

494

9. D: 1, 2, 3, 4, 6, 12. A given number divides evenly by each of its factors to produce an integer (no decimals). To find the factors of 12, determine what integers multiply to 12. $1 \times 12, 2 \times 6$, and 3×4 are all the ways to multiply to 12 using integers, so the factors of 12 are: 1, 2, 3, 4, 6, 12.

10. E: The augmented matrix that represents the system of equations has dimensions 4×3 because there are three equations with three unknowns. The coefficients of the variables make up the first three columns, and the last column is made up of the numbers to the right of the equals sign. This system can be solved by reducing the matrix to row-echelon form, where the last column gives the solution for the unknown variables.

11. B: There are two zeros for the function: $x = 0, -2$.

The zeros can be found several ways, but this particular equation can be factored into:

$$f(x) = x(x^2 + 4x + 4) = x(x + 2)(x + 2)$$

By setting each factor equal to zero and solving for x, there are two solutions: $x = 0$ and $x = -2$. On a graph these zeros can be seen where the line crosses the x-axis.

12. D: This problem involves a composition function, where one function is plugged into the other function. In this case, the $f(x)$ function is plugged into the $g(x)$ function for each x-value. The composition equation becomes:

$$g\big(f(x)\big) = (2)^3 - 3(2)^2 - 2(2) + 6$$

Simplifying the equation gives the answer:

$$g\big(f(x)\big) = 8 - 3(4) - 2(2) + 6 = 8 - 12 - 4 + 6 = -2$$

13. D: This system of equations involves one quadratic function and one linear function, as seen from the degree of each equation. One way to solve this is through substitution. Solving for y in the second equation yields $y = x + 2$. Plugging this equation in for the y of the quadratic equation yields:

$$x^2 - 2x + x + 2 = 8$$

Simplifying the equation, it becomes:

$$x^2 - x + 2 = 8$$

Setting this equal to zero and factoring, it becomes:

$$x^2 - x - 6 = 0 = (x - 3)(x + 2)$$

Solving these two factors for x gives the zeros $x = 3, -2$. To find the y-value for the point, each number can be plugged in to either original equation. Solving each one for y yields the points $(3, 5)$ and $(-2, 0)$.

14. D: The expression is simplified by collecting like terms. Terms with the same variable and exponent are like terms, and their coefficients can be added.

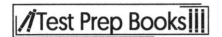

15. A: Finding the product means distributing one polynomial onto the other. Each term in the first must be multiplied by each term in the second. Then, like terms can be collected. Multiplying the factors yields the expression:

$$20x^3 + 4x^2 + 24x - 40x^2 - 8x - 48$$

Collecting like terms means adding the x^2 terms and adding the x-terms. The final answer after simplifying the expression is:

$$20x^3 - 36x^2 + 16x - 48$$

16. E: Finding the zeros for a function by factoring is done by setting the equation equal to zero, then completely factoring. Since there is a common x for each term in the provided equation, that should be factored out first. Then the quadratic that is left can be factored into two binomials, which are $(x + 1)(x - 4)$. Setting each factor equal to zero and solving for x yields three zeros.

17. A: 13 nurses

Using the given information of 1 nurse to 25 patients and 325 patients, set up an equation to solve for number of nurses (N):

$$\frac{N}{325} = \frac{1}{25}$$

Multiply both sides by 325 to get N by itself on one side.

$$\frac{N}{1} = \frac{325}{25} = 13 \; nurses$$

18. E: The equation can be solved by factoring the numerator into $(x + 6)(x - 5)$.

Since that same factor exists on top and bottom, that factor $(x - 5)$ cancels.

This leaves the equation $x + 6 = 11$.

Solving the equation gives the answer $x = 5$. When this value is plugged into the equation, it yields a zero in the denominator of the fraction. Since this is undefined, there is no solution.

19. D: This problem can be solved by using unit conversion. The initial units are miles per minute. The final units need to be feet per second. Converting miles to feet uses the equivalence statement 1 mi = 5,280 ft. Converting minutes to seconds uses the equivalence statement 1 min = 60 s. Setting up the ratios to convert the units is shown in the following equation:

$$\frac{72 \; mi}{90 \; min} \times \frac{1 \; min}{60 \; s} \times \frac{5,280 \; ft}{1 \; mi} = 70.4 \frac{ft}{s}$$

The initial units cancel out, and the new units are left.

20. B: The formula can be manipulated by dividing both the length, l, and the width, w, on both sides. The length and width will cancel on the right, leaving height by itself.

21. B: The domain is all possible input values, or x-values. For this equation, the domain is every number greater than or equal to zero. There are no negative numbers in the domain because taking the square root of a negative number results in an imaginary number.

22. D: This problem can be solved by setting up a proportion involving the given information and the unknown value. The proportion is:

$$\frac{21 \text{ pages}}{4 \text{ nights}} = \frac{140 \text{ pages}}{x \text{ nights}}$$

Solving the proportion by cross-multiplying, the equation becomes $21x = 4 \times 140$, where $x = 26.67$. Since it is not an exact number of nights, the answer is rounded up to 27 nights. Twenty-six nights would not give Sarah enough time.

23. D: The slope from this equation is 50, and it is interpreted as the cost per gigabyte used. Since the g-value represents number of gigabytes and the equation is set equal to the cost in dollars, the slope relates these two values. For every gigabyte used on the phone, the bill goes up 50 dollars.

24. C: Graphing the function $y = \cos(x)$ shows that the curve starts at $(0, 1)$, has an amplitude of 2, and a period of 2π. This same curve can be constructed using the sine graph, by shifting the graph to the left $\frac{\pi}{2}$ units. This equation is in the form:

$$y = \sin\left(x + \frac{\pi}{2}\right)$$

25. B: Start by squaring both sides to get $1 + x = 16$. Then subtract 1 from both sides to get $x = 15$.

26. A: This inverse of a function is found by switching the x and y in the equation and solving for y. In the given equation, solving for y is done by adding 5 to both sides, then dividing both sides by 3. This answer can be checked on the graph by verifying the lines are reflected over $y = x$.

27. B: The zeros of this function can be found by using the quadratic formula:

$$x = \frac{-b \pm \sqrt{b^2 - 4ac}}{2a}$$

Identifying a, b, and c can also be done from the equation because it is in standard form. The formula becomes:

$$x = \frac{0 \pm \sqrt{0^2 - 4(1)(4)}}{2(1)} = \frac{\sqrt{-16}}{2}$$

Since there is a negative underneath the radical, the answer is a complex number:

$$x = \pm 2i$$

28. E: Setting up a proportion is the easiest way to represent this situation. The proportion becomes $\frac{20}{x} = \frac{40}{100}$, where cross-multiplication can be used to solve for x. The answer can also be found by

497

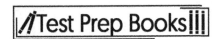

observing the two fractions as equivalent, knowing that twenty is half of forty, and fifty is half of one-hundred.

29. C: Division with scientific notation can be solved by grouping the first terms together and grouping the tens together. The first terms can be divided, and the tens terms can be simplified using the rules for exponents. The initial expression becomes 0.4×10^4. This is not in scientific notation because the first number is not between 1 and 10. Shifting the decimal and subtracting one from the exponent yields 4.0×10^3.

30. A: The relative error can be found by finding the absolute error and making it a percent of the true value. The absolute error is $36 - 35.75 = 0.25$. This error is then divided by 36 — the true value — to find 0.7%.

31. B: The y-intercept of an equation is found where the x-value is zero. Plugging zero into the equation for x allows the first two terms to cancel out, leaving -4.

32. A: The equation is *even* because:

$$f(-x) = f(x)$$

Plugging in a negative value will result in the same answer as when plugging in the positive of that same value. So, the function:

$$f(-2) = \frac{1}{2}(-2)^4 + 2(-2)^2 - 6 = 8 + 8 - 6 = 10$$

This yields the same value as:

$$f(2) = \frac{1}{2}(2)^4 + 2(2)^2 - 6 = 8 + 8 - 6 = 10$$

33. C: The equation $x = 3$ is not a function because it does not pass the vertical line test. This test is made from the definition of a function, where each x-value must be mapped to one, and only one, y-value. This equation is a vertical line, so the x-value of 3 is mapped with an infinite number of y-values.

34. A: The function can be factored to identify the zeros. First, the term $3x$ is factored out to the front because each term contains $3x$. Then, the quadratic is factored into $(x + 3)(x - 2)$.

35. C: A die has an equal chance for each outcome. Since it has six sides, each outcome has a probability of $\frac{1}{6}$. The chance of a 1 or a 2 is therefore $\frac{1}{6} + \frac{1}{6} = \frac{1}{3}$.

36. A: The slope is given by:

$$m = \frac{y_2 - y_1}{x_2 - x_1} = \frac{0 - 4}{0 - (-3)} = -\frac{4}{3}$$

37. B: The table shows values that are increasing exponentially. The differences between the inputs are the same, while the differences in the outputs are changing by a factor of 2. The values in the table can be modeled by the equation $f(x) = 2^x$.

38. C: The formula for continually compounded interest is:

$$A = Pe^{rt}$$

Plugging in the given values to find the total amount in the account yields the equation:

$$A = 2000e^{0.05 \times 8} = 2983.65$$

Choice A is incorrect because it uses annually compounded interest instead of continuous,

$$A = 2000 \times 1.05^8 = 2954.91$$

Choice B is incorrect because it fails to apply the formula for continuously compounded interest. Choice D is incorrect because it simply adds 40% (or eight times 5%) to the original investment rather than compounding annually.

39. E: The sample space is made up of:
$$8 + 7 + 6 + 5 = 26 \text{ balls}$$

The probability of pulling each individual ball is $^1/_{26}$. Since there are 7 yellow balls, the probability of pulling a yellow ball is $\frac{7}{26}$.

40. B: For the first card drawn, the probability of a king being pulled is $\frac{4}{52}$. Since this card isn't replaced, if a king is drawn first, the probability of a king being drawn second is $\frac{3}{51}$. The probability of a king being drawn in both the first and second draw is the product of the two probabilities:

$$\frac{4}{52} \times \frac{3}{51} = \frac{12}{2,652}$$

This fraction, when divided by $\frac{12}{12}$, equals $\frac{1}{221}$.

41. E: The addition rule is necessary to determine the probability because a 6 can be rolled on either roll of the die but not both. The rule used is:

$$P(A \text{ or } B) = P(A) + P(B) - P(A \text{ and } B)$$

The probability of a 6 being individually rolled is $\frac{1}{6}$ and the probability of a 6 being rolled twice is:

$$\frac{1}{6} \times \frac{1}{6} = \frac{1}{36}$$

Therefore, the probability that a 6 is rolled at least once is:

$$\frac{1}{6} + \frac{1}{6} - \frac{1}{36} = \frac{11}{36}$$

42. A: $(A \cap B)$ is equal to the intersection of the two sets A and B, which is $\{1, 2, 3, 4, 5\}$. $A - (A \cap B)$ is equal to the elements of A that are *not* included in the set $(A \cap B)$. Therefore:

$$A - (A \cap B) = \{6, 7, 8, 9, 10\}$$

499

43. B: An equilateral triangle has three sides of equal length, so if the total perimeter is 18 feet, each side must be 6 feet long. A square with sides of 6 feet will have an area of $6^2 = 36$ square feet.

44. A: If each man gains 10 pounds, every original data point will increase by 10 pounds. Therefore, the man with the original median will still have the median value, but that value will increase by 10.

The smallest value and largest value will also increase by 10 and, therefore, the difference between the two won't change. The range does not change in value and, thus, remains the same.

45. C: Because the triangles are similar, the lengths of the corresponding sides are proportional. Therefore:

$$\frac{30 + x}{30} = \frac{22}{14} = \frac{y + 15}{y}$$

This results in the equation:

$$14(30 + x) = 22 \times 30$$

When solved, this gives:

$$x = 17.1$$

The proportion also results in the equation:

$$14(y + 15) = 22y$$

When solved, this gives:

$$y = 26.3$$

46. A: Robert accomplished his task on Tuesday in $\frac{3}{4}$ the time compared to Monday. He must have worked 4/3 as fast.

47. B: To simplify this inequality, subtract 3 from both sides to get $-\frac{1}{2}x \geq -1$. Then, multiply both sides by -2 (remembering this flips the direction of the inequality) to get $x \leq 2$.

48. E: Each value can be substituted into each equation. Choice *A* can be eliminated, since:

$$4^2 + 16 = 32$$

Choice *B* can be eliminated, since:

$$4^2 + 4 \times 4 - 4 = 28$$

Choice *C* can be eliminated, since:

$$4^2 - 2 \times 4 - 2 = 6$$

But, plugging in either value into $x^2 - 16$ gives:

$$(\pm 4)^2 - 16 = 16 - 16 = 0$$

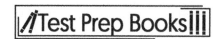

49. B: The technique of completing the square must be used to change the equation below into the standard equation of a circle:

$$4x^2 + 4y^2 - 16x - 24y + 51 = 0$$

First, the constant must be moved to the right-hand side of the equals sign and each term must be divided by the coefficient of the x^2-term (which is 4). The x- and y- terms must be grouped together to obtain:

$$x^2 - 4x + y^2 - 6y = -\frac{51}{4}$$

Then, the process of completing the square must be completed for each variable. This gives:

$$(x^2 - 4x + 4) + (y^2 - 6y + 9) = -\frac{51}{4} + 4 + 9$$

The equation can be written as:

$$(x - 2)^2 + (y - 3)^2 = \frac{1}{4}$$

Therefore, the center of the circle is $(2, 3)$ and the radius is:

$$\sqrt{\frac{1}{4}} = \frac{1}{2}$$

50. D: When an ordered pair is reflected over an axis, the sign of at least one of the coordinates must change. When it's reflected over the x-axis, the sign of the y-coordinate must change. The x-value remains the same. Therefore, the new ordered pair is $(-3, 4)$.

51. A: Because the volume of the given sphere is 288π cubic meters, this gives:

$$\frac{4}{3}\pi r^3 = 288\pi$$

This equation is solved for r to obtain a radius of 6 meters. The formula for surface area is $4\pi r^2$, so:

$$SA = 4\pi 6^2 = 144\pi \text{ square meters}$$

52. E: SOHCAHTOA is used to find the missing side length. Because the angle and adjacent side are known, $\tan 60 = \frac{x}{13}$. Making sure to evaluate tangent with an argument in degrees, this equation gives:

$$x = 13 \tan 60 = 13 \times \sqrt{3} = 22.52$$

53. A: Let the unknown score be x. The average will be:

$$\frac{5 \times 50 + 4 \times 70 + x}{10} = \frac{530 + x}{10} = 55$$

Multiply both sides by 10 to get $530 + x = 550$, or $x = 20$.

501

54. A: First, the sample mean must be calculated:

$$\bar{x} = \frac{1}{4}(1 + 3 + 5 + 7) = 4$$

The standard deviation of the data set is $s = \sqrt{\frac{\sum(x-\bar{x})^2}{n-1}}$, and $n = 4$ represents the number of data points. Therefore:

$$s = \sqrt{\frac{1}{3}[(1-4)^2 + (3-4)^2 + (5-4)^2 + (7-4)^2]}$$

$$\sqrt{\frac{1}{3}(9 + 1 + 1 + 9)} = 2.58$$

55. D: For manufacturing costs, there is a linear relationship between the cost to the company and the number produced, with a y-intercept given by the base cost of acquiring the means of production and a slope given by the cost to produce one unit. In this case, that base cost is $50,000, while the cost per unit is $40. So, $y = 40x + 50,000$.

56. C: To find the expected value, take the product of each individual sum and the probability of rolling the sum, then add together the products for each sum. There are 36 possible rolls.

The probability of rolling a 2 is $\frac{1}{36}$.

The probability of rolling a 3 is $\frac{2}{36}$.

The probability of rolling a 4 is $\frac{3}{36}$.

The probability of rolling a 5 is $\frac{4}{36}$.

The probability of rolling a 6 is $\frac{5}{36}$.

The probability of rolling a 7 is $\frac{6}{36}$.

The probability of rolling an 8 is $\frac{5}{36}$.

The probability of rolling a 9 is $\frac{4}{36}$.

The probability of rolling a 10 is $\frac{3}{36}$.

The probability of rolling an 11 is $\frac{2}{36}$.

Finally, the probability of rolling a 12 is $\frac{1}{36}$.

Each possible outcome is multiplied by the probability of it occurring. Like this:

$$2 \times \frac{1}{36} = a$$

$$3 \times \frac{2}{36} = b$$

$$4 \times \frac{3}{36} = c$$

And so forth.

Then, all of those results are added together:

$$a + b + c \ldots = expected\ value$$

In this case, it equals 7.

57. B: From the slope-intercept form, $y = mx + b$, it is known that b is the y-intercept, which is 1. Compute the slope as $\frac{2-1}{1-0} = 1$, so the equation is $y = x + 1$.

58. A: This has the form $t^2 - y^2$, with $t = x^2$ and $y = 4$.

It's also known that:

$$t^2 - y^2 = (t + y)(t - y)$$

Substituting the values for t and y into the right-hand side gives $(x^2 - 4)(x^2 + 4)$.

59. A: Simplify this to:

$$(4x^2y^4)^{\frac{3}{2}} = 4^{\frac{3}{2}}(x^2)^{\frac{3}{2}}(y^4)^{\frac{3}{2}}$$

Now:

$$4^{\frac{3}{2}} = (\sqrt{4})^3 = 2^3 = 8$$

For the other, recall that the exponents must be multiplied, so this yields:

$$8x^{2 \cdot \frac{3}{2}}y^{4 \cdot \frac{3}{2}} = 8x^3y^6$$

60. B: The independent variable's coordinate at the vertex of a parabola (which is the highest point when the coefficient of the squared independent variable is negative) is given by $x = -\frac{b}{2a}$. Substitute and solve for x to get:

$$x = -\frac{4}{2(-16)} = \frac{1}{8}$$

Using this value of x, the maximum height of the ball (y), can be calculated.

Substituting $\frac{1}{8}$ into the equation for x yields:

$$h(t) = -16\left(\frac{1}{8}\right)^2 + 4\frac{1}{8} + 6 = 6.25$$

Reading

Fiction

1. B: Strong dislike. This vocabulary question can be answered using context clues. Based on the rest of the conversation, the reader can gather that Albert isn't looking forward to his marriage. As the Count notes that "you don't appear to me to be very enthusiastic on the subject of this marriage," and also remarks on Albert's "objection to a young lady who is both rich and beautiful," readers can guess Albert's feelings. The answer choice that most closely matches "objection" and "not . . . very enthusiastic" is *B, strong dislike.*

2. C: Their name is more respected than the Danglars'. This inference question can be answered by eliminating incorrect answers. Choice *A* is tempting, considering that Albert mentions money as a concern in his marriage. However, although he may not be as rich as his fiancée, his father still has a stable income of 50,000 francs a year. Choice *B* isn't mentioned at all in the passage, so it's impossible to make an inference. Finally, Choice *D* is clearly false because Albert's father arranged his marriage, but his mother doesn't approve of it. Evidence for Choice *C* can be found in the Count's comparison of Albert and Eugénie: "she will enrich you, and you will ennoble her." In other words, the Danglars are wealthier but the Morcerf family has a more noble background.

3. D: Apprehensive. There are many clues in the passage that indicate Albert's attitude towards his marriage—far from enthusiastic, he has many reservations. This question requires test takers to understand the vocabulary in the answer choices. *Pragmatic* is closest in meaning to *realistic*, and *indifferent* means *uninterested*. The only word related to feeling worried, uncertain, or unfavorable about the future is *apprehensive.*

4. B: He is like a wise uncle, giving practical advice to Albert. Choice *A* is incorrect because the Count's tone is friendly and conversational. Choice *C* is also incorrect because the Count questions why Albert doesn't want to marry a young, beautiful, and rich girl. While the Count asks many questions, he isn't particularly *probing* or *suspicious*—instead, he's asking to find out more about Albert's situation and then give him advice about marriage.

5. A: She belongs to a noble family. Though Albert's mother doesn't appear in the scene, there's more than enough information to answer this question. More than once is his family's noble background mentioned (not to mention that Albert's mother is the Comtesse de Morcerf, a noble title). The other answer choices can be eliminated—she is deeply concerned about her son's future; money isn't her highest priority because otherwise she would favor a marriage with the wealthy Danglars; and Albert describes her "clear and penetrating judgment," meaning she makes good decisions.

6. C: The richest people in society were also the most respected. The Danglars family is wealthier but the Morcerf family has a more aristocratic name, which gives them a higher social standing. Evidence for the other answer choices can be found throughout the passage: Albert mentioned receiving money from his father's fortune after his marriage; Albert's father has arranged this marriage for him; and the Count speculates that Albert's mother disapproves of this marriage because Eugénie isn't from a noble

background like the Morcerf family, implying that she would prefer a match with a girl from aristocratic society.

7. A: He seems reluctant to marry Eugénie, despite her wealth and beauty. This is a reading comprehension question, and the answer can be found in the following lines: "'I confess," observed Monte Cristo, "that I have some difficulty in comprehending your objection to a young lady who is both rich and beautiful."' Choice *B* is the opposite (Albert's father is the one who insists on the marriage), Choice *C* incorrectly represents Albert's eagerness to marry, and Choice *D* describes a more positive attitude than Albert actually feels (*repugnance*).

8. B: The passage is mostly made up of dialogue. We can see this in the way the two characters communicate with each other, in this case through the use of quotations marks, or dialogue. Narration is when the narrator (not the characters) is explaining things that are happening in the story. Description is when the narrator describes a specific setting and its images. Explanation is when the author is analyzing or defining something for the reader's benefit.

9. D: The meaning of the word *ennoble* in the middle of the paragraph means to give someone a noble rank or title. In the passage, we can infer that Albert is noble but not rich, and Mademoiselle Eugénie is rich but not noble.

10. C: Because he finally understands Albert's point of view but still doesn't agree with it. The other choices aren't mentioned anywhere in the passage. Remember, although this passage is part of a larger text, the test taker should only pay attention to what's in the passage itself in order to find the correct answer.

Social Science

11. C: In lines 6 and 7, it is stated that avarice can prevent a man from being necessitously poor, but it also makes him too timorous, or fearful, to be wealthy. Choice *A* is incorrect because avarice prevents a man from being poor. Choice *B* is incorrect because the passage states that oppression, not avarice, is the consequence of wealth. Choice *D* is incorrect because the passage does not state that avarice drives a person's desire to be wealthy.

12. D: Paine believes that the distinction that is beyond a natural or religious reason is between king and subjects. Choice *A* is incorrect because he states that the distinction between good and bad is made in heaven. Choice *B* is incorrect because he states that the distinction between male and female is natural. Choice *C* is incorrect because he does not mention anything about the distinction between humans and animals.

13. A: The passage states that the Heathens were the first to introduce government by kings into the world. Choice *B* is incorrect because the quiet lives of patriarchs came before the Heathens introduced this type of government and Paine puts it in opposition to government by kings. Choice *C* is incorrect because it was Christians, not Heathens, who paid divine honors to living kings. Heathens honored deceased kings. Choice *D* is incorrect because, while equal rights of nature are mentioned in the paragraph, they are not mentioned in relation to the Heathens.

14. B: Paine asserts that a monarchy is against the equal rights of nature and cites several parts of scripture that also denounce it. He doesn't say it is against the laws of nature. Because he uses scripture to further his argument, it is not despite scripture that he denounces the monarchy. Paine addresses the law by saying the courts also do not support a monarchical government.

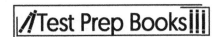

15. A: To be *idolatrous* is to worship someone or something other than God, in this case, kings. Choice *B* is incorrect because it is not defined as being deceitful. Choice *C* is incorrect because, while idolatry is considered a sin, it is an example of a sin, not a synonym for it. Choice *D* is incorrect because, while idolatry may have been considered illegal in some cultures, it is not a definition for the term.

16. A: The essential meaning of the passage is that the Almighty, God, disapproves of this type of government. Choice *B* is incorrect because, while heaven is mentioned, it is done so to suggest that the monarchical government is irreverent, not that heaven isn't promised. Choice *C* is incorrect because God's disapproval is mentioned, not his punishment. Choice *D* is incorrect because the passage refers to the Jewish monarchy, which required both belief in God and kings, and the tendency of monarchies to gloss over the anti-monarchical passages of scripture to support their form of government.

17. A: The word *timorous* means being full of fear. The author concludes that extreme greed (avarice) makes people too afraid to be prosperous.

18. B: The author's attitude is closest to Choice *B, impassioned and critical.* Choice *A* is incorrect; the author is not *indifferent or fatigued*—on the contrary, there is a lot of energy and some underlying passion in the writing. Choice *C* is incorrect; the word *enchanted* means delighted, and the author is more critical and concerned of a monarchial government than enchanted with it. Choice *D* is not the best answer; although the author is passionate and critical of a monarchy, there is more logic than anger coming from the words.

19. B: To explain how monarchs came into existence and how Christians adapted to this way of government. Choice *A* is incorrect; the author does not agree that heathens were more advanced than Christians in this paragraph, it only explains the catalyst of the monarchial systems. Choice *C* is incorrect; the author would in fact disagree with the divination of the English monarchs. Choice *D* is incorrect; the paragraph *does* believe that monarchs cause damage, but the paragraph does not act as a counterargument to the one preceding it.

20. D: The author implies that the recorded history of creation is a collection, collage, or pattern taken from various accounts of cultures. Choice *A* is incorrect; there is no talk of cells or biology in the paragraph. Since "mosaic" modifies the word "account," we know that it is the account of creation that is mosaic, not creation itself, which makes Choice *B* incorrect. Choice *C* is also incorrect; the paragraph does not mention kings developing a system of recording accounts of creation.

Humanities

21. B: But in fact, there is not much substance to such speculation, and most anti-Stratfordian arguments can be refuted with a little background about Shakespeare's time and upbringing. The thesis is a statement that contains the author's topic and main idea. The main purpose of this article is to use historical evidence to provide counterarguments to anti-Stratfordians. Choice *A* is simply a definition; Choice *C* is a supporting detail, not a main idea; and Choice *D* represents an idea of anti-Stratfordians, not the author's opinion.

22. C: Rhetorical question. This requires readers to be familiar with different types of rhetorical devices. A rhetorical question is a question that is asked not to obtain an answer but to encourage readers to consider an issue more deeply.

23. B: By explaining grade school curriculum in Shakespeare's time. This question asks readers to refer to the organizational structure of the article and demonstrate understanding of how the author provides

506

details to support the argument. This particular detail can be found in the second paragraph: "even though he did not attend university, grade school education in Shakespeare's time was actually quite rigorous."

24. A: Busy. This is a vocabulary question that can be answered using context clues. Other sentences in the paragraph describe London as "the most populous city in England" filled with "crowds of people," giving an image of a busy city full of people. Choice *B* is incorrect because London was in Shakespeare's home country, not a foreign one. Choice *C* is not mentioned in the passage. Choice *D* is not a good answer choice because the passage describes how London was a popular and important city, probably not an undeveloped one.

25. B: This sentence is an example of a metaphor. Metaphors make a comparison between two things, usually saying that one thing *is* another thing. Here, the author is saying that Shakespeare *is* "the great magician." Choice *A, personification*, is when an inanimate object is given human characteristics, so this is incorrect. Choice *C, simile*, is making a comparison between two things using *like* or *as*, so this is incorrect. Choice *D, allusion*, is an indirect reference to a place, person, or event that happened in the past, so this is also incorrect.

26. D: Remember from the first passage that anti-Stratfordians are those who believe that Shakespeare *did not* write the plays, so Stratfordians are people who believe that Shakespeare *did* write the plays. The author of Passage 2 is disbelieving and critical of the Stratfordian point of view. We see this especially in the second paragraph, where the author states it is a supposition "so wild that it can only be entertained by those who are prepared to accept it as a miracle." All of the other answer choices are incorrect.

27. D: Sentence 2 is a contrast to the idea in Sentence 1. In the first sentence, the author states that they, at one time, believed that Shakespeare was the author of his plays. The second sentence is a contrast to that statement by saying the author no longer believes that the author of the plays is Shakespeare. The other answer choices are incorrect.

28. B: This writing style is best described as persuasive. The author is trying to persuade the audience, with evidence, that Shakespeare actually wrote his own dramas. Choice *A*, expository writing, means to inform or explain. Expository writing usually does not set out to persuade the audience of something, only to inform them, so this choice is incorrect. Choice *C*, narrative writing, is used to tell a story, so this is incorrect. Choice *D*, descriptive writing, uses all five senses to paint a picture for the reader, so this choice is also incorrect.

29. C: Topography is the shape and features of the Earth. The author is implying here that whoever wrote Shakespeare's plays studied the physical features of foreign cities. Choices *A, B,* and *D* are incorrect. Choice *A* is simply known as climate. Choice *B* would just be considered the "agriculture of a particular area." Choice *D*, aspects of humans within society, would be known as *anthropology.*

30. A: The author of Passage 2 believes that Shakespeare the actor did not write the plays. We see this at the end of the first paragraph where the author contends that the "'Stratford rustic' is not the true Shakespeare." The author does believe that Shakespeare was an actor, as the author calls this Shakespeare a "Player" throughout the text, so Choices *B* and *D* are incorrect. Choice *C* is incorrect, as the author does not believe that Shakespeare wrote the plays.

Natural Science

31. C: *Extraneous* most nearly means *superfluous*, or *trivial*. Choice *A, indispensable,* is incorrect because it means the opposite of *extraneous*. Choice *B, bewildering,* means *confusing* and is not relevant to the context of the sentence. Finally, Choice *D* is incorrect because although the prefix of the word is the same, *ex-*, the word *exuberant* means *elated* or *enthusiastic*, and is irrelevant to the context of the sentence.

32. A: The author's purpose is to bring to light an alternative view on human perception by examining the role of technology in human understanding. This is a challenging question because the author's purpose is somewhat open-ended. The author concludes by stating that the questions regarding human perception and observation can be approached from many angles. Thus, the author does not seem to be attempting to prove one thing or another. Choice *B* is incorrect because we cannot know for certain whether the electron experiment is the latest discovery in astroparticle physics because no date is given. Choice *C* is a broad generalization that does not reflect accurately on the writer's views. While the author does appear to reflect on opposing views of human understanding (Choice *D*), the best answer is Choice *A*.

33. C: It presents a problem, explains the details of that problem, and then ends with more inquiry. The beginning of this paragraph literally "presents a conundrum," explains the problem of partial understanding, and then ends with more questions, or inquiry. There is no solution offered in this paragraph, making Choices *A* and *B* incorrect. Choice *D* is incorrect because the paragraph does not begin with a definition.

34. D: Looking back in the text, the author describes that classical philosophy holds that understanding can be reached by careful observation. This will not work if they are overly invested or biased in their pursuit. Choices *A, B,* and *C* are in no way related and are completely unnecessary. A specific theory is not necessary to understanding, according to classical philosophy mentioned by the author.

35. B: The electrons passed through both holes and then onto the plate. Choices *A* and *C* are incorrect because such movement is not mentioned at all in the text. In the passage, the author says that electrons that were physically observed appeared to pass through one hole or another. Remember, the electrons that were observed doing this were described as acting like particles. Therefore, Choice *D* is incorrect. Recall that the plate actually recorded electrons passing through both holes simultaneously and hitting the plate. This behavior, the electron activity that wasn't seen by humans, was characteristic of waves. Thus, Choice *B* is the correct answer.

36. C: The author mentions "gravity" to demonstrate an example of natural phenomena humans discovered and understood without the use of tools or machines. Choice *A* mirrors the language in the beginning of the paragraph but is incorrect in its intent. Choice *B* is incorrect; the paragraph mentions nothing of "not knowing the true nature of gravity." Choice *D* is incorrect as well. There is no mention of an "alternative solution" in this paragraph.

37. A: The important thing to keep in mind is that we must choose a scenario that best parallels, or is most similar to, the discovery of the experiment mentioned in the passage. The important aspects of the experiment can be summed up like so: humans directly observed one behavior of electrons and then through analyzing a tool (the plate that recorded electron hits), discovered that there was another electron behavior that could not be physically seen by human eyes. This summary best parallels the scenario in Choice *A*. Like Feynman, the colorblind person can observe one aspect of the world but

508

through the special goggles (a tool), he is able to see a natural phenomenon that he could not physically see on his own. While Choice *D* is compelling, the x-ray helps humans see the broken bone, but it does not necessarily reveal that the bone is broken in the first place. The other choices do not parallel the scenario in question. Therefore, Choice *A* is the best choice.

38. B: The author would not agree that technology renders human observation irrelevant. Choice *A* is incorrect because much of the passage discusses how technology helps humans observe what cannot be seen with the naked eye; therefore, the author would agree with this statement. This line of reasoning is also why the author would agree with Choice *D,* making it incorrect as well. As indicated in the second paragraph, the author seems to think that humans create inventions and tools with the goal of studying phenomena more precisely. This indicates increased understanding as people recognize limitations and develop items to help bypass the limitations and learn. Therefore, Choice *C* is incorrect as well. Again, the author doesn't attempt to disprove or dismiss classical philosophy.

39. B: The word *conundrum* most nearly means *enigma,* which is a mystery or riddle. *Platitude* means a banal or overused saying. *Solution* is incorrect here; and *hypothesis* implies a theory or assumption, so this is also incorrect.

40. A: To prove to the audience the thesis of the passage by providing evidence suggesting that electrons behave differently when observed by the human eye. The thesis' best evidence is found in this paragraph because of the experiment depicting how electrons behave in a dual nature. Choice *B* is incorrect; the paragraph mentions nothing about the experiment being unethical. Choice *C* is incorrect; this is characteristic of the first paragraph. Choice *D* is incorrect; this is more characteristic of the second paragraph.

Science

1. C: There is a 99% probability of PCR testing identifying *Histoplasma.* GM assay was more specific for identifying *Aspergillus,* 95% to 85%. True positive is defined by sensitivity. The sensitivity of GM assay testing is less than 70%.

2. D: *Histoplasma* is detectable 90 days from exposure. PCR testing is able to detect *Histoplasma* 91 days from exposure—one day after sufficient organisms exist for detection. *Candida* is detectable 45 days from exposure. PCR testing is able to detect *Candida* 72 days from exposure—27 days after a sufficient number of organisms exist for detection. *Aspergillus* is detectable 118 days from exposure. ELISA testing is able to detect *Aspergillus* 134 days from exposure—16 days after a sufficient number of organisms exist for detection. *Candida* is detectable 45 days from exposure. GM assay testing is able to detect *Candida* 56 days from exposure—11 days after a sufficient number of organisms exist for detection.

3. B: The probability that the GM assay will identify *Candida* is 69%. Therefore, there's a 31% probability that it won't be identified. ELISA sensitivity and specificity for *Histoplasma* are both greater than 80%. False-negative probabilities are represented by the specificity of a given testing method. The sensitivity and specificity for GM assay testing for Aspergillus is 59% and 96% respectively. All testing methods had greater than 90% specificity for the organisms.

4. C: The sensitivity of PCR testing for *Histoplasma* is 99%, and the test can identify the organism one day after it reaches a detectable colony size. The sensitivity for GM assay testing for *Histoplasma* is 65%. If physicians rely on GM assay testing, they may determine that the individual doesn't have the *Histoplasma* infection. Treatment will depend on the presence or absence of the infection as indicated

509

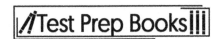
by testing. Waiting for PCR testing is based on the sensitivity of the test, not the individual's current symptoms. The subclinical phase of *Histoplasma* is 28 days.

5. A: ELISA testing detects *Candida* three days after the organism is present in sufficient numbers to be recognized. PCR detects the organism more than three weeks after it is first detectable. ELISA testing sensitivity for *Candida* is 87% and PCR testing is 92%. However, the ability to identify the presence of the organism earlier in the process of infection (allowing early intervention) outweighs the differences in the probability of identifying the presence of the organism. There's a 92% probability that PCR testing will identify the presence of *Candida*. PCR testing is more sensitive than ELISA: 92% versus 87%.

6. D: The main difference in the scientists' opinions is related to the cause of mad cow disease. The existence of species-specific proteins was used by Scientist 2 to support viral infection as the cause of the disease. Transmission rates of the disease and the conversion of normal proteins to prions were not debated in the passage.

7. A: Scientist 2 proposed that viruses were the cause of mad cow disease because chemicals inactivated the viruses. The remaining choices are correct.

8. B: According to Scientist 1, abnormal prions are capable of "refolding" normal proteins into harmful prions. Abnormal proteins accumulate to produce the damaging conglomerations. Scientist 2 didn't find species-specific DNA and used this fact to support viruses as the cause of mad cow disease. According to Scientist 1, prions are located in the central nervous system, not the peripheral nervous system.

9. D: Mad cow disease can be spread between animal species and from animals to humans through consumption of diseased animal products. The resulting damage to the central nervous system is irreversible and will eventually cause the death of the animal. Scientist 2 would not agree that the infecting agent contained amino acids, as they form proteins, and Scientist 2 believes that a virus causes the disease. Scientist 2 demonstrated that the infected tissue of animals that were infected by a different species didn't contain species-specific DNA, which would have been the expected outcome if the infecting agent were a protein.

10. B: The accumulated masses of abnormal prions eventually form sponge-like holes in the brain and spinal cord that result in death. The passage doesn't mention the effects of the synapses, nerves, or blood supply.

11. D: The absence of disease resulting from the inactivated viral particles best supports the views of Scientist 2. There were no species-specific DNA sequences found in the infected particles. Scientist 2 didn't support the existence of prions as the cause of mad cow disease.

12. C: The actual process of "refolding" the normal protein into the abnormal protein isn't clear from this passage. Scientist 1 claims that prions cause the disease. Prions are an abnormal protein, not a virus. Scientist 1 claims that mad cow disease is caused by abnormal proteins.

13. A: The main hypothesis for this study involved the influence of 2-AG levels combined with sleep deprivation on eating behaviors. The combination of the two conditions, not each one separately, constitutes the main hypothesis. The passage didn't discuss a placebo effect in the normal saline injection group.

14. D: The study results support the hypothesis because the participants who received 1-AG injections and were sleep deprived gained more weight than participants who received sterile normal saline injections. The remaining choices do not support the hypothesis.

15. A: Participant H gained more than 1 pound (450 g) per day. There was little fluctuation in the day-to-day weight gain for each participant. Participant H in trial 2 gained more weight than participant D in trial 1.

16. B: Sleep deprivation increases the levels and duration of action of 2-AG, an endogenous cannabinoid, especially in the late afternoon. The stress effect increases with the degree of sleep deprivation. The passage doesn't discuss a relationship between sleep deprivation and the hunger response. Eating behaviors are increased in late afternoon as a result of the extended duration of 2-AG action.

17. A: Circadian fluctuations increase the levels of 2-AG during the afternoon and evening. This increase is believed to stimulate food intake beyond the point of satiety. Endogenous cannabinoids decrease gastric motility. 2-AG may have a calming effect on mood, but food intake is still increased in the presence of afternoon and evening levels of 2-AG. Endogenous cannabinoids work with the opioid system to mediate the pain response, not food-seeking behaviors.

18. A: In trial 3, the plants grown with the combined-wavelength LED's reached 150 millimeters by day 21. The plants grown with white light reached 160 millimeters by day 35. Therefore, the LED plants will be packaged 14 days sooner than the white light plants.

19. C: In trial 3, with LED lighting that included green and yellow wavelengths, plant growth was greater than trial 1 or trial 2 with either blue or red wavelengths. However, from the available information, it can only be said that green and yellow wavelengths *contributed to* plant growth in trial 3, but not that green and yellow wavelengths *alone* were responsible for plant growth in trial 3. There was plant growth in all lighting conditions.

20. B: In trial 1, from day 28 to day 35, white light growth increased by 71 millimeters, and red light increased by 78 millimeters. In trial 2, from day 28 to day 35, white light growth increased by 71 millimeters, and blue light increased by 78 millimeters.

21. C: The average daily growth with LED lighting was not twice the white light average daily growth. LED systems did result in better growth rates and they do require less water and electricity. However, the question is based on recorded average daily growth, and that rate was not double the white light rate.

22. D: The passage says that green and yellow wavelengths are reflected by the plant. Therefore, it's expected that those wavelengths would result in slower growth than the blue or red wavelengths, which are absorbed.

23. B: *Anacardiaceae Mangifera* is the family and genus name for the mango. The *Colletotrichum* fungus causes the spoilage. The remaining choices are correct.

24. C: According to Table 1, at 20 days, the fungal level at 7.5 °C was the same as the fungal level at 5 °C. Because the 7.5 °C temperature is less expensive than the 5 °C temperature, the 7.5 °C model is best. The 10 °C model is less expensive than the 7.5 °C, but fungal levels are greater. Only the 7.5 °C and 5 °C models had acceptable fungal levels at 20 days.

25. B: The hot water wash pre-treatment fungal level increased by 15 millimeters from day 26 to day 28 at 10 °C. It was the single largest one-day increase across the trials. Air cooling at 10 °C increased by 5 millimeters from day 14 to day 16. Air cooling at 7.5 °C increased by 7 millimeters from day 26 to day 28. Hot water wash at 7.5 °C increased 11 millimeters from day 26 to day 28.

26. C: The hot water wash fungal level at 10 °C reached 35 millimeters on day 20. The maximum fungal level for air cooling at 5 °C was 19 millimeters, and at 10 °C, 35 millimeters on day 26. The maximum fungal level for hot water at 7.5 °C was 39 millimeters on day 28.

27. C: The fungal levels were acceptable with air cooling at 7.5 °C, and the 7.5 °C temperature is less expensive to maintain. Air cooling and hot water wash pre-treatment at 5 °C resulted in acceptable fungal levels, but the 5 °C temperature is costlier. Fungal levels were not acceptable at 28 days at 10 °C.

28. B: Shipping mangoes at 5 °C is costly, but for the 28-day trip, the fungal levels were only acceptable in the 5 °C model. Air cooling fungal rates at 5 °C were lower than the hot water wash rates, but each was acceptable. Fungal rates at 7.5 °C and 10 °C were unacceptable.

29. A: The correlation was positive, because when one variable increased, the other increased, and when one variable decreased, the other decreased. There are two forms for a curvilinear relationship. In one curvilinear relationship, when variable 1 increases, a second variable increases as well, but only to a certain point, and then variable 2 decreases as variable 1 continues to increase. In the other form, variable 1 increases while variable 2 decreases to a certain point, after which both variables increase. In a negative relationship, high values for one variable are associated with low values for the second variable.

30. D: Mitochondrial activity is suppressed by elevated blood glucose levels. Mitochondria use sugar to produce cellular energy, and the presence of large numbers of mitochondria in BAT gives BAT a brownish color. Mitochondria contain DNA and can reproduce additional mitochondria when additional energy is required. In the body, mature red blood cells are the only cells that don't contain mitochondria.

31. D: Blood sugars for all groups identified in Figure 5 were highest at 2 p.m.

32. B: Circadian rhythms control sleep by stimulating the release of melatonin from the pineal gland. Ganglia are nerve cells, not hormones, that affect sleep. BAT doesn't release sugar; it utilizes sugar for heat production. Shivering on cold mornings is a desirable form of thermogenesis but isn't associated with sleep.

33. D: The average blood sugar for participant 6 was 115. Participant 1 was 105, participant 3 was 112, and participant 4 was 82.

34. B: The daytime blood glucose levels in Figure 1 decreased as the day progressed. The blood glucose levels in Figure 5 peaked for the day at 2 p.m. Night blood glucose levels didn't reach 100. Group I's levels are irrelevant to the question.

35. A: Based only on Figure 2, the researchers' hypothesis wasn't confirmed. Subsequent trials confirmed the hypothesis.

36. A: Increased algae levels can block sunlight, limiting growth of species inhabiting lower zones. The passage doesn't identify the effects of rainfall or cold temperatures on phytoplankton growth, so

Choices *B* and *D* are incorrect. The passage identifies the effect of phosphorus and nitrogen residue on algae growth, but not as a food source for cyanobacteria.

37. D: The passage identifies freshwater contamination by phosphorus and nitrogen as the most common cause of algae overgrowth. Population density would be more common in Florida than Kansas.

38. B: As algae levels increase above normal, organisms in the aphotic level plants don't receive adequate light for normal growth and oxygen levels are decreased, resulting in the death of oxygen-dependent species.

39. C: Algae block the sunlight, which limits growth.

40. A: Algae growth was greater in July, which limited the amount of light reaching the lower zones of the lake, decreasing the levels of cyanobacteria. Cyanobacteria existed in less-than-normal concentrations at 20 meters, but there were measurable levels of the organisms. Algae growth at 3 meters wasn't measured. The passage states that cyanobacteria growth is associated with algae growth, not independent of algae growth.

Dear ACT Test Taker,

We would like to start by thanking you for purchasing this study guide for your ACT exam. We hope that we exceeded your expectations.

Our goal in creating this study guide was to cover all of the topics that you will see on the test. We also strove to make our practice questions as similar as possible to what you will encounter on test day. With that being said, if you found something that you feel was not up to your standards, please send us an email and let us know.

We would also like to let you know about other books in our catalog that may interest you.

SAT

This can be found on Amazon: amazon.com/dp/1628456868

ACCUPLACER

amazon.com/dp/1637750250

TSI

amazon.com/dp/1628457341

AP Biology

amazon.com/dp/1628456221

We have study guides in a wide variety of fields. If the one you are looking for isn't listed above, then try searching for it on Amazon or send us an email.

Thanks Again and Happy Testing!
Product Development Team
info@studyguideteam.com

FREE Test Taking Tips Video/DVD Offer

To better serve you, we created videos covering test taking tips that we want to give you for FREE. **These videos cover world-class tips that will help you succeed on your test.**

We just ask that you send us feedback about this product. Please let us know what you thought about it—whether good, bad, or indifferent.

To get your **FREE videos**, you can use the QR code below or email freevideos@studyguideteam.com with "Free Videos" in the subject line and the following information in the body of the email:

  a. The title of your product

  b. Your product rating on a scale of 1-5, with 5 being the highest

  c. Your feedback about the product

If you have any questions or concerns, please don't hesitate to contact us at info@studyguideteam.com.

Thank you!

Made in United States
Orlando, FL
29 March 2023